THE BOEING XF8B-1 FIGHTER: LAST OF THE LINE

JARED A. ZICHEK

Schiffer Military History
Atglen, PA

Cover Illustration: What might have been: a group of production Boeing F8B-1s escort fellow B-29s over the Pacific on a mission to bomb the Japanese home islands sometime in 1946. This was one of the key missions the carrier-based XF8B-1 fighter was designed for when conceived in 1943. However, the fall of Iwo Jima in March 1945 led to the establishment of an AAF base for both the B-29 and land-based North American P-51 Mustangs, reducing the need for long range carrier-based fighter escort. As the reader will discover, this was but one of several factors that led to the cancellation of Boeing's final piston engine fighter.

Book design by Jared Zichek.

Library of Congress Control Number: 2006929193

Printed in China.
ISBN: 0-7643-2587-6

Published by Schiffer Publishing Ltd.
4880 Lower Valley Road
Atglen, PA 19310
Phone: (610) 593-1777
FAX: (610) 593-2002
E-mail: Info@schifferbooks.com.
Visit our web site at: www.schifferbooks.com
Please write for a free catalog.
This book may be purchased from the publisher.
Please include $3.95 postage.
Try your bookstore first.

In Europe, Schiffer books are distributed by:
Bushwood Books
6 Marksbury Avenue
Kew Gardens
Surrey TW9 4JF, England
Phone: 44 (0) 20 8392-8585
FAX: 44 (0) 20 8392-9876
E-mail: Info@bushwoodbooks.co.uk.
Visit our website at: www.bushwoodbooks.co.uk
Free postage in the UK. Europe: air mail at cost.
Try your bookstore first.

CONTENTS

Introduction & Acknowledgements

The Boeing XF8B-1 is one of the many experimental aircraft built during World War II that never reached mass production. Only three examples of this large and impressive naval fighter were built, all of which ended up in the scrapyard within a few years thereafter. For this reason, it has largely been forgotten. The author has attempted to rescue the XF8B-1 from this obscurity, uncovering a short but interesting history of an aircraft that possessed several advanced features for its time, foremost being its massive 3,000 hp Pratt & Whitney "Wasp Major" radial engine. This engine drove a large Aeroproducts counter-rotating propeller that utilized the power of the Wasp Major to the fullest while simultaneously neutralizing torque. The XF8B-1's most unusual feature was its internal bomb bay, the only US fighter of the period to have one. Even more ordnance could be hung from the aircraft's large, robust wing. These features, combined with its long range, considerable internal fuel volume, and formidable armament, made the XF8B-1 stand out from its contemporaries.

Unfortunately, many of the characteristics that made the XF8B-1 unique also contributed to its failure. It was built to a requirement that was flawed from inception, resulting in an oversized aircraft with largely inferior performance to types already in service. Its advanced engine and counter-rotating propeller suffered numerous teething problems, causing serious delays and cost overruns. Poor management and organization at Boeing also unnecessarily slowed development of the aircraft. By the time of its first flight on November 27, 1944, the XF8B-1 had already been eclipsed by other propeller-driven fighters and the advent of early jet fighters. It could have been modified into a useful attack platform, but Boeing failed to vigorously pursue this option, compelling the Navy to stick with Douglas and Martin for its attack aircraft requirement.

Thus, this is the story of a failure, one that resulted in Boeing being shut out of the fighter business for over three decades. However, this failure is an interesting one, providing insights into the frequently contentious relations between the military and defense contractors during WW II as well as how rapidly aircraft, engine, and armament technology evolved in this period, resulting in an aircraft that was state-of-the art when conceived in early 1943 but ended up being virtually obsolete by the end of 1944. This book is by no means the last word on the XF8B-1, but it provides the most comprehensive overview thus far published of Boeing's failed "five-in-one" fighter, a classic jack-of-all-trades and master of none.

This book could not have been written without the generous help of Bob Lamson, former Boeing test pilot; Tom Lubbesmeyer and Mike Lombardy of the Boeing Historical Archives; Barry Zerby of the National Archives; and Robert Dorr. Special thanks to my wife Yvanne for her patience and understanding during the long process of putting this book together.

Jared A. Zichek
San Diego, California
March, 2006

Photo: Bob Lamson Collection

Evocative shot of XF8B-1 no. 57984 undergoing inflight landing gear tests near Mr. Rainier in 1946; test pilot Bob Lamson was at the controls. By this time, the contract for the fighter had been cancelled and its fate all but sealed.

1943
Design and Development
1

In the opening months of the Pacific War, the effectiveness of the US Navy's offensive strategy was handicapped by the short range of its carrier aircraft and the requirement that its carriers remain beyond the reach of land-based Japanese aircraft. This problem affected fighters especially, which were crucial to providing air cover for attack aircraft and the fleet. This situation prompted the Navy to investigate the development of a fighter aircraft with exceptional range and performance that could equal the best of Japanese fighters.

Boeing was interested in the requirement and eager to get a contract from the Navy. Its last naval aircraft had been the XF7B-1 of 1933, an advanced all-metal cantilever monoplane with retractable gear that was rejected for production because of its high approach speed and poor vision. From 1940 to 1942, Boeing submitted several unsuccessful fighter proposals to the Bureau of Aeronautics (BuAer), the configurations of which ranged from the relatively ordinary to the outright bizarre. These proposals will be covered by the author in a separate book.

In 1943, Boeing finally succeeded in getting the go-ahead with their Model 400, designated by BuAer as the XF8B-1. Boeing's negotiation team was headed by R. H. Jewett. The "Specification and Data for Class VF Single Engine Monoplane" was executed by the Chief of BuAer and Wellwood E. Beall, Boeing's VP of Engineering, on April 10, 1943 under contract NOa(s) 742. This specification, later designated SD-349, required the XF8B-1 to attain a maximum speed of 342 mph, a minimum speed of not more than 79 mph, a ceiling of at least 30,000 ft., a take off in a 25 knot wind at 262 ft., and a rate of climb at sea level of 3,760 ft. per minute.

In the letter that accompanied the specification, Boeing stated its desire to build an experimental VF design around the newly developed Pratt & Whitney R-4360. Boeing requested that it be made solely responsible for the design of the product, in order to design, construct, test and complete the development of the this type of aircraft as expeditiously as possible. Boeing claimed that this procedure also had an additional advantage in that it would allow greater originality in the development to be put into the design. Therefore, it was proposed that the airplane be described by a brief objective specification, that no approval of design or release for manufacture would be required and that Navy specifications be used as guides but their provisions not be mandatory. Boeing also pointed out that under the terms of the proposed form of contract, it was obligated to make in the design all changes that the Trial Board requested.

Boeing asserted that its experience in the development, design and construction of aircraft merited special consideration of its proposal, which covered a quantity of three flight airplanes, a static test article, spare parts, and engineering information to be furnished under a cost-plus-fixed-fee form of contract. Given the prevailing conditions of uncertainty as to labor, material and other factors, the company found it extremely difficult to accurately estimate the cost or delivery schedule for the aircraft. It proposed a figure of $3,621,587.00, which included a 4% fixed fee.

Boeing asked the Navy to put the project on a high priority and make every effort possible to assist it with obtaining the materials and supplies required. The design, principal construction and testing, including flight testing, of the project was to be conducted at or near Boeing's plants in Seattle and Renton, Washington. Boeing hoped that the design of the XF8B-1 would render itself to rapid quantity production at plants located outside of Seattle, and the engineering information would be such that if quantity production were desired there would be a minimum of additional engineering work required. The design not only contemplated construction of component assemblies in complete form, but also the complete installation of all operating parts in these component assemblies in such a manner as to permit a wide distribution of assembly and installation effort, thereby making fast and economical production possible in large quantities. The three aircraft were given BuAer serial numbers 57984, 57985 and 57986; Boeing's numbers for the airframes were 8484, 8485, and 8486, respectively.

On April 14, BuAer produced a table comparing the performance of the proposed Boeing Model 400 to the Grumman XF7F-1 and Vought F4U-1:

Performance Comparison	Boeing Model 400	Grumman XF7F-1	Vought F4U-1
T.O. Condition			
Gross Wt. – lbs.	19,000	20,080	12,734
Fuel – gals.	663	660	359
Max Speed – mph	420.8	398	384.5
Airplane Critical Altitude – ft.	25,200	25,200	25,400
Rate of Climb @ Sea Level – ft./min.	2,780	2,390	2,670
Rate of Climb @ 22,000 ft.	2,050	1,660	1,670
Stalling Speed – mph	87.5	91	86.2
T.O. Distance – 25 knots	365	356	325
At Combat Radius			
Gross Wt. – lbs.	17,100	17,870	11,990
Fuel – gals.	400	360	235
Max Speed – mph	422.3	417	387
Airplane Critical Altitude – ft.	25,200	25,200	25,400
Rate of Climb @ Sea Level – ft./min.	3,200	2,830	2,905
Rate of Climb @ 22,000 ft.	2,440	2,080	1,865
True Combat Radius – nautical mi.	450	?	300

On paper, the Model 400 appeared to offer superior performance over the XF7F-1 and F4U-1, though its takeoff distance was longer and its stalling speed slightly higher. It was also remarkably heavy for a single engine fighter, weighing almost as much as the twin engine XF7F-1.

Notes in BuAer files indicate that its analysts were initially very enthusiastic about the design. A Captain Pearson remarked:

> *"This is an exceptionally attractive design with far reaching possibilities. The specifications are now being prepared as dictated by Boeing. They give Boeing complete control. This is unsatisfactory but Boeing will not play under other rules. I think they are in good faith, however, and will listen to reasonable recommendations. [I] think it['s] better to accept this compromise than to lose their engineering capacity to the Army."* A Mr. Stevens concurred: *"The design has already been crystallized into the sort of characteristics the Navy considers a good compromise, with full cooperation from Boeing, and a reasonably satisfactory arrangement has been reached for further cooperation. I believe the government is relinquishing only legal rights to making final decisions on matters that may arise in [the] future, [and] that those rights are seldom if ever exercised in practice. We have set up the machinery for keeping us informed, which is really about all we need to make our necessary points."*

An internal BuAer memorandum from Captain H.R. Oster, Head of Engineering, to the Director of Planning dated April 24 further outlined the unique arrangement under which the XF8B-1 was procured. Boeing had secured the power of making final decisions on all points of non-agreement between it and the Navy with the exception of the mock-up's cockpit. Boeing made no guarantees – it merely stated that it would make every effort to meet the estimated performance and produce a satisfactory Navy fighter. Boeing also agreed to go over Navy specifications and notify BuAer of deviations as soon as they were determined.

Oster believed that Boeing was in good faith in its effort to produce a superior product and would take all reasonable advice. He recommended that the arrangement be accepted, both for the purpose of obtaining a promising airplane from a company not producing for the Navy and to determine the result of placing such responsibility on Boeing. The Engineering Branch would keep close touch with the project and if at any time it appeared that the airplane would be an unsatisfactory fighter, appropriate recommendations would be made. In the final analysis, Oster felt the contract could be cancelled but it would entail the loss of what was expected to be a very important addition to Fleet aircraft and such an action would be considered a last resort.

Oster called attention to the very favorable reception of the F6F-3 airplane by the Fleet. It was the result of BuAer exercising control but giving Grumman enough latitude to prevent delays. The feature of the F6F-3 that contributed most to its success, namely vision from the cockpit, was obtained only after BuAer forced Grumman to change its design. If entire control of the design had been in Grumman's hands, it would have refused to make the change.

Oster believed that Boeing would go to extremes to make the XF8B-1 a successful airplane and to remedy any deficiencies that appeared. Most of BuAer's requirements had already been accepted and he believed that the design was generally sound. However, the engineering arrangements of the particular contract were not necessarily applicable or acceptable for other contracts, and the widespread efforts of all contractors to further free themselves of government control, which could result from this case, were not to be handled by BuAer with this as an unrestricted precedent.

By June, Boeing was constructing the XF8B-1 mock-up. Boeing was uncertain about which method of wing folding to use, electing to mock up two configurations involving the Grumman type folding and the straight vertical type folding. Boeing also contacted Douglas in El Segundo, California for information concerning their double slotted flap. Boeing was already simultaneously conducting wind tunnel and layout work for several flap configurations.

On June 23, Lt. E.J. Bataille, Inspector of Naval Aircraft at Boeing, responded to a report by the Los Angeles General Inspector of Naval Aircraft (GINA) which asserted that progress on the XF8B-1 contract had been unsatisfactory. Bataille disagreed with the GINA's assessment, supporting Boeing's contention that it had assigned and would continue to assign the most qualified personnel at its disposal and in the maximum practicable quantity to the project. However, Boeing refused to freeze the design and to expedite construction before adequate consideration of features that could be critical in arriving at an optimum basic configuration. Bataille agreed with this policy in theory, though he noticed that Boeing had a tendency to overrate the importance of this consideration to the extent of retarding the progress of the aircraft. Bataille promised to continue urging upon Boeing

Photo: National Archives, RG 72

Photograph of the completed XF8B-1 mock-up dated September 29, 1943. Note the canopy bracing and mid-war Navy tricolor scheme, neither of which were carried over to the prototype as built. More photos of the mock-up can be found in Appendix 4.

the utmost importance of expediting the construction and delivery of the XF8B-1.

At the time, the status of the fighter was as follows:

a) The general arrangement of the wing including fuel tank space, location of guns, and method of folding had been fairly well determined. The particular wing flap arrangement to be used had yet to be determined by wind tunnel testing.
b) General landing gear arrangement had been decided upon.
c) Engine installation with air-ducting was rapidly approaching a solution.

d) Several sample tail assemblies had been tried out on the drawing board and would be tested in the wind tunnel, decision depending upon results of the wind tunnel tests.

Boeing suggested that BuAer assist it in obtaining scheduled wind tunnel test time at the University of Washington and California Institute of Technology (CIT) prior to the earliest scheduled date of August 16 at the University of Washington and August 30 at CIT.

Delays in delivering and perfecting the XF8B-1's engine and counter-rotating propellers plagued the project from its inception. On July 18, Boeing procured four Hamilton Standard counter-rotating propellers (three to be installed plus one spare) for use on the XF8B-1. It also prepared a cost proposal to provide one Aeroproducts Division of General Motors propeller and one Curtiss-Wright Corporation propeller for comparative performance tests. This procedure involved minimal risk and minimized delays in flight testing through the failure of the propeller development program to proceed as contemplated. It also offered an opportunity to make a direct comparison of the effect of these different propellers, including the weight, on airplane performance. There was a spread of approximately 300 lbs. in weight between the three propellers, with the Hamilton Standard being the lightest but probably least developed of the three.

From early on, Boeing sought the advice of NACA in the development of the XF8B-1. On August 12, NACA sent Boeing preliminary data on "Wind Tunnel Tests of a 1/3 Scale Model of the North American P-51B Airplane." On November 6, Boeing requested from NACA a copy of the report on the tail section test of the one-fifth scale model Republic XP-69 aircraft tested in their high speed 8 ft. wind tunnel. The report was subsequently forwarded on November 11, 1943. Several other reports regarding NACA tests on other aircraft were also forwarded.

On August 14, a progress report was sent to BuAer regarding the status of the XF8B-1 contract. At the time, the aircraft was in the preliminary design stage. About 55 engineers were employed on the project, with about 10 more scheduled to be added in the next 30 days. The status of the various component parts was as follows:

Photo: National Archives, RG 72

Photograph dated September 18, 1944 showing a set of counter-rotating propellers provided by Aeroproducts to Boeing for use on the XF8B-1. The large counter-rotating props generally worked well, but delays in their delivery slowed progress on the overall contract.

Power Plant Group. This group was working out a method of arranging the power plant area to enable maximum utilization of available space, minimize engine change time, etc. The main problems then under consideration were the cowling and exhaust system. However, the entire design was in a state of flux and no definite decisions concerning arrangements had yet been made. Determination of mating (or interfering) members had been made for mock-up purposes and would be incorporated in the complete airplane mock-up. A detail power plant mock-up would be made after completion of the airplane mock-up.

Armament Group. The location and supports for guns on the

mock-up had been determined. The method of ammunition feed for the 20 mm. guns was under study. It was expected that few changes would be made between the mock-up and experimental airplane.

Landing Gear Group. The method of folding landing gear had been determined. Detail design of structures involved was under way. Mock-up parts were under construction.

Wing Group. Boeing had decided on the vertical type folding wing used on the TBD-1, as it was 100 lbs. lighter than the Grumman type fold and resulted in a cleaner wing. The wing would be of the single spar type. The location and size of the main spar had been determined. The locations and sizes of the wing ribs had been fairly well determined but changes were anticipated if detail calculations, wind tunnel testing, or the mock-up indicated need for them. Wing mock-up, including flaps and aileron, had been completed.

Fuselage Group. The fuselage lines previously submitted to BuAer had been changed as the result of engineering studies made by the group. Additional changes were to be expected as the result of wind tunnel testing and mock-up experience.

Tail Group. Little design work was being done on this section as the tail arrangement was to be determined by the wind tunnel tests of spin characteristics, wing wash-off, etc. Mock-up drawings had been released and the mock-up was underway.

Engineering had determined a tentative component breakdown. Consultations with the production department were in process to determine the final fix. Wind tunnel testing of the complete model was started on August 13. Wind tunnel tests of a wing of infinite aspect ratio with flaps and aileron were completed. It was expected that the mock-up would be ready for the Mock-up Board on approximately September 15. Determination of completion date was to be made August 16.

Under the terms of the contract, Boeing was able to send at government expense one representative for a period not to exceed 6 months to a theatre of war to observe naval and military aircraft combat operations. Boeing selected Richard ("Dick") L. Stith for this role, as he possessed considerable engineering experience and was already assigned as a Boeing Field Service Representative to the U.S. Army in the South Pacific. Boeing had already discussed the plan of having Stith released by the Army Air Service Command, which was willing to release him for the project. The company wanted Stith released at Brisbane, Australia and designated a Naval Officer at the U.S. Naval Headquarters there. After this was accomplished, Boeing asked the Navy to permit Stith to observe the operation of shipboard fighters from an aircraft carrier in a war zone for a period of three weeks to two months. The Navy complied with Boeing's request.

Before Stith departed, he separated 55 men from Boeing's preliminary design to begin the XF8B-1 project group. Stith selected B-17 designer Ed Wells as head engineer and Lyle A. Wood as the assistant engineer. Wells subsequently left the project and Wood took over the head engineer position. His team was primarily made up of veterans. Fourteen members of the team had a combined 203 years of aircraft engineering experience. In house, the XF8B-1 contract was nicknamed the "Boeing Engineer's Pension Project."

The design of the XF8B-1 was basically finalized on October 7, 1943. It utilized a landing gear retraction system that Boeing had designed in the early Thirties which was licensed to Curtiss-Wright in 1934. Curtiss-Wright employed it in their Hawk fighter series. The XF8B-1 was the only Boeing aircraft to use this outdated type of landing gear, in which the gear folded straight back while pivoting 90° to lie flat in the wing.

The XF8B-1 was designed with many safety features in mind. It featured a control surface lock that automatically unlocked the controls when the throttle was advanced. It also was equipped with oleo locks, a firing safety switch, and a flap pressure switch that auto-retracted the flaps at 150 mph, which was included to prevent damage to the flaps during a carrier wave-off.

The Navy Mock-up Board inspected the XF8B-1 mock-up in early October. The mock-up as a whole was considered good, but lacking in detail

Photo: National Archives, RG 72-AC

The main gear of the XF8B-1 partially retracted. This installation resulted in a drag-inducing protruberance on the lower surface of the wing and was widely considered to be anachronistic at the time the XF8B-1 was being designed.

except for the cockpit. At the time of the inspection, the engine was not mocked-up except superficially and comment on the power plant items was withheld until a complete power plant mock-up was completed. The guns and ammunition were not mocked-up completely and an armament mock-up was held at a later date.

The Board strongly and unanimously recommended removal of the bomb bay which was conceived by Boeing to hold either bombs or a 288 gal. droppable leak proof fuel tank. This recommendation was based on:

a) The fact that the 450 nautical mile radius of action could not be achieved with the fixed protected tankage provided but required the partial and uneconomical use of the bomb bay tank, thereby invalidating the droppable feature inasmuch as it couldn't be dropped at the beginning of combat.
b) The unnecessary complexity of a bomb bay in a fighter airplane.
c) The economic inadvisability of providing special expendable tanks containing highly critical rubber.
d) The logistical difficulty of supplying and storing such tanks.
e) The weight and aerodynamic penalties involved.
f) The undesirable fuel system complications and increased fire hazard. Boeing agreed to conduct further studies to ascertain the possibility of achieving the 450 nautical mile radius of action with approximately 375 gals. fixed

Photo: National Archives, RG 72

The bomb bay of the XF8B-1 as photographed during door retraction tests on May 2, 1945. An unusual feature for a fighter, the bomb bay would prove to be a source of controversy in BuAer and an overall liability for the aircraft.

> internal protected fuel plus droppable fuel carried in standard Navy tanks.

Boeing was nonetheless able to convince BuAer to retain the bomb bay despite the Navy Mock-up Board's critique, resulting in a fighter that was bigger and of lower performance than necessary. During subsequent tests of the actual aircraft, the bomb bay would prove to be a focal point of criticism and a contributing factor to the big fighter's cancellation.

Photo: National Archives, RG 72

Photograph of the XF8B-1 port wing section as tested at Naval Air Station (NAS) Patuxent River, Maryland on June 23, 1945. The wing was designed to accommodate both 20 mm. cannon and 50 cal. gun installations. More photos from these tests, which largely validated the soundness of Boeing's armament design, can be found in Appendix 7.

The problem of the XF8B-1's armament provision was also the subject of considerable discussion. It was agreed that the battery of six 20 mm. cannon should be designed with mounts capable of substituting .50 caliber (cal.) guns. Boeing stated that the additional structure to provide for this interchangeability was in the neighborhood of 20 lbs. Use of the front barrel jacket mounts designed by Chance-Vought for the XF5U-1 eliminated this 20 lb. penalty. Drawings of this mount were procured from Chance-Vought and forwarded to Boeing. The battery of six .50 cal. guns with 400 rounds each was to be fitted initially. The weight penalty paid for the possible use of a battery of six 20 mm. guns (in addition to the weight of the guns and ammunition) was in the neighborhood of 65 lbs. Who would of thought that Vought's bizarre "Flying Flapjack" influenced, in an admittedly minor way, the design of the Boeing XF8B-1?

Allied with the problem of the bomb bay was that of structural design strength due to the increased weight of the installations required. Boeing agreed to a structural redesign based on the specification weight of 15,861 lbs. plus the weight necessary to provide armor protection against .50 cal. gunfire, space and weight for 20 mm. guns and ammunition, and fixed protected fuel necessary to fight, return 450 nautical miles and land aboard an aircraft carrier. With these three weight increasing items included, the structure was redesigned for a strength of 7.5 g with six .50 cal. guns and 2,400 rounds of ammunition carried. The redesign weight was expected to approximate 16,500 lbs.

2

1944

Construction, Early Flight Tests, and Stirrings of Discontent

On January 7, 1944, Boeing's Chief Aerodynamicist, George S. Schairer, sent drawings, templates, technical data and other material to Lt. J.F. Sutherland at BuAer in order to construct a scale model of the XF8B-1 to be employed by NACA at Langley Field for spin model tests.

On January 11, the Bureau of Aeronautics Representative (BAR) in Seattle sent a telegram to Captain Pearson at BuAer regarding an upcoming visit by representatives of the British Ministry of Aircraft Production (MAP) accompanied by a representative of the British Air Commission and Lt. G.V. Schliestett of the US Navy to discuss the XF8B-1; both BuAer and the Army cleared the visit of the foreign guests. The author has thus far been unable to find documents recording the British visitors' opinion of the XF8B-1.

Continuing with the British theme, Boeing wrote BuAer on February 11, regarding the possibility of installing the British Mark II GGS gyro gun sight in the XF8B-1. W.E. Beall of Boeing had obtained drawings and photographs of the gun sight during a visit to England. This material had been furnished through the courtesy of Colonel Thomas Hitchcock, Acting Military Air Attache at the American Embassy, London. Boeing was impressed by the British design and proposed installing it in the XF8B-1, undertaking the construction of a mock-up sight from the drawings. Colonel Hitchcock offered to procure a sight if such was desired. Boeing requested that BuAer contact Hitchcock and request the sight and ancillary voltage regulator for installation in one of the XF8B-1 prototypes.

BuAer responded on February 12, noting that it had initiated action to procure a limited quantity of British Mark 18 turret gun sights modified as required for fixed gun sights. These modified Mk 18 sights were an improved model of the Mark II GGS. One of these modified Mk 18 sights was to have been shipped to the BAR in Seattle for installation in the XF8B-1. Therefore, BuAer did not consider it necessary or desirable to make an installation of the Mk II GGS in view of the above and due to the fact that the Mk 11 GGS was designed for .303 cal. guns. However, the mock-up gun sight made by Boeing from the drawings and photographs of the Mk II GGS could be used for mock-up purposes of the modified Mark 18 inasmuch as the two gun sights were externally similar.

In early February, Boeing attempted to secure early shipment of the R-4360-10 engine from Pratt & Whitney to permit an early check of engine and related installations in the XF8B-1 mock-up. Unfortunately, the engine could not be shipped prior to April 15, though Pratt & Whitney stated that it could loan Boeing an earlier version of the engine, a R-4360-4, by March 1. Boeing requested BuAer permit the engine manufacturer to ship the loaned R-4360-4 for a check installation to avoid a serious delay in the completion of the XF8B-1. BuAer contacted Pratt & Whitney in Baltimore and managed to get a promise for an XR-4360-8A to be shipped on or about

Photo: National Archives, RG 72-AC

Pratt & Whitney's powerful R-4360 Wasp Major 28-cylinder air-cooled radial engine. At the time of the XF8B-1's development, the design of this engine was not fully mature and it was not available in significant quantity, causing delays in the fighter's first flight. The R-4360 would eventually produce 3,500 hp and become the engine of choice for the USAF's postwar propeller-driven bomber and transport aircraft.

March 1 along with a dummy auxiliary stage. The engine was to be later flown in another aircraft and BuAer advised that Boeing handle it with care. Unfortunately, shipment of these items would be pushed well back into late March. Boeing subsequently requested that shipment of the XR-4360-8A be cancelled in favor of the XR-4360-10, which was scheduled for shipment on April 28. Pratt & Whitney would be consistently late in shipping subsequent versions of the R-4360 to Boeing throughout the remainder of the program, substantially slowing progress on the XF8B-1 contract.

On March 1, Boeing's L.A. Wood wrote BuAer regarding the possibility of NACA testing the ditching characteristics of the XF8B-1. During various conferences on the aircraft, the ditching characteristics had come into question. BuAer personnel had indicated that these characteristics were not of primary design importance but should be considered, if possible. The arrangement of the XF8B-1 with a large scoop beneath the engine near the leading edge of the wing was considered questionable by some parties interested in good ditching characteristics. Available literature was of little utility, indicating that model ditching tests on the airplane were desirable. NACA already had several other aircraft under test for ditching characteristics, and Wood requested that he be authorized to build and test a ditching model of the XF8B 1.

The BuAer replied on March 24, rejecting Wood's request. Ditching conditions were not included in the BuAer's current design requirements for class VF aircraft; such tests were considered of insufficient importance at that time to justify their performance. Pending a demonstration that practicable full-scale modifications could be obtained from model ditching tests already underway for other aircraft, BuAer preferred to employ engineering effort and the facilities of the NACA Seaplane Tank on projects of greater immediate importance.

G.S. Schairer wrote Captain W.S. Diehl of BuAer on March 6 requesting that the XF8B-1's airfoil section be tested at NACA's two-dimensional high speed wind tunnel with adjustable walls at Langley Field, the only wind tunnel in the country capable of testing airfoil characteristics at high Mach numbers where blocking effects could be controlled. Boeing's wind tunnel was incapable of providing accurate results at Mach numbers above .75. The request was subsequently granted

On March 24, BAR E.J. Bataille reviewed Boeing's report entitled "Gunfire Test of XF8B-1 Outer Wing Panels: Spotwelded and Riveted." The report made it clear that 20 mm. H.E. shells caused extensive damage to stiffeners spotwelded to wing skin, the method of wing construction favored by Boeing. Nonetheless, Bataille was of the opinion that the employment of spotwelding would be satisfactory in the XF8B-1 prototypes. Boeing advised Bataille that further tests on a full-length wing were planned prior to employment of spotwelding on production airplanes. If tests on the full-length wing indicated the same lack of resistance to 20 mm. H.E. shells, riveting would be used on the production models. Studies would be made to determine a method of spotwelding that was as resistant to all types of gunfire as riveting. Furthermore, Bataille considered the use of spotwelding desirable in view of the high speed of the XF8B-1 and the consequent necessity for smooth surfaces.

The armament portion of the XF8B-1 mock-up was still incomplete as of March 25. Wood stated that Boeing was proceeding to complete the mock-up to such a state as to demonstrate the installational features of both

Photo: National Archives, RG 72-AC

Gunfire tests were conducted with XF8B-1 outer wing panels on February 16, 1944, revealing the vulnerability of spotwelding to 20 mm. H.E. shells. Nonetheless, BuAer elected to stick with this method of construction for the prototypes, as it created less drag than traditional riveting.

the M2 20 mm. guns, ammunition tracks and boxes and of the .50 cal. guns' tracks and boxes; he estimated that the work would be completed by April 20, 1944. The BuAer rejected installation of the M2 20 mm. guns, as they were nearing obsolescence; it preferred the improved lightweight T-31 20 mm. gun, one of which was in the hands of the BAR in Seattle.

The same day, L.A. Wood wrote the BAR requesting 20 mm. and .60 cal. guns, complete with necessary adapters, feed mechanisms, and ammunition, be delivered to Boeing on or before April 15, 1944. He also requested 1000 rounds of both 20 mm. and .60 cal. ammunition of the Ball or AP variety. Boeing planned to test one complete 20 mm. wing installation from the XF8B-1 and one remote controlled tail turret with one 20 mm. and two .50 cal. guns from the B-29 airplane.

On March 25, L.A. Wood wrote BuAer regarding the XF8B-1 cockpit mock-up. It had been satisfactorily revised according to the recommendations made previously by the Navy Mock-up Board, but there was some confusion regarding the aircraft's windshield. It was originally planned to build two types of windshield, both with improved vision and with a minimum of structural members. The first of these was to incorporate the bullet proof panel to the rear of the windshield, and the second was to incorporate the bullet proof glass as the front pane of the windshield. Subsequent developments made it more desirable to construct only the second type of windshield with panels to either side of the bullet proof glass consisting of single curvature non-shatterable glass. The enclosure to the rear of the windshield consisted of a controlled blown canopy of Plexiglas. BuAer's response to Wood's inquiry has not been located

Boeing's W.E. Beall took a personal interest in the development of the XF8B-1 and set up a special organization within the company to build it. He only put engineering and assembly personnel on the project, excluding such critical people as purchasers and tooling crews, supervisors of which put the XF8B-1 on a low priority due to the more pressing demands of B-17 and B-29 production. This would have adverse effects on the progress of the XF8B-1 contract.

The engineering crew worked on the floor near the XF8B-1 prototype, drafting parts as they were needed. Tooling makers were not directly assigned to the project and worked in another Boeing plant several miles away, and they often rejected sketches of urgently needed parts that were deemed incomplete. This slowed construction of parts and assembly of the prototype considerably. Parts were not numbered on the drawings and separate drawings of individual parts were not made on the floor in order to accelerate construction of the aircraft. Boeing hope to be able to create the detailed drawings demanded by the Navy as the aircraft was being assembled, but it was slow in doing so, provoking complaints from BuAer. Boeing eventually put 117 engineers on the XF8B-1 contract, producing 3,300 drawings and 9,400 deviations; the engineering time involved totaled 636,000 hours.

The landing gear and wings of the XF8B-1 were manufactured at the Renton plant, the main work of which was construction of subassemblies for the B-17 and B-29. The XF8B-1 work was therefore accorded a low priority. Problems were experienced in forming the leading edge of the aircraft's wing, as their Farnham Roll machine could only produce sections six feet in width, necessitating extensive spotwelding. The wing was of the single spar type and was the smoothest constructed by Boeing up to that time.

On April 19, Commander Sheldon W. Brown, another BAR in Seattle, updated BuAer regarding the evolving armament situation. Deliveries had started on the T-31 20 mm. guns, only one of which had been received by Boeing, with deliveries being slow and erratic. One T-26 20 mm. gun, which generated reaction loads equal to those generated by the T-31 gun, had also been delivered to Boeing for use in the aircraft. No .60 cal. gun had yet been delivered to the Navy, nor could any estimated delivery date be ascertained. One 75 mm. gun had been shipped from NAS Patuxent River. A 40 mm. Vickers "S" gun was also ordered from England for the XF8B-1, but it was never installed.

On April 24, 1944, L.A. Wood once again wrote the BAR to seek assistance in expediting the delivery of the XF8B-1's engine and propellers. Delivery of the Pratt & Whitney R-4360-10 engine had been delayed for at least thirty days due to Pratt & Whitney's inability to procure certain parts, pushing the estimated delivery date to the end of April.

Hamilton Standard's delivery of the four propellers was scheduled as follows:

First unit – Late September 1944

Second Unit – October 1944
Third Unit – November 1944
Fourth Unit – January 1945

Aeroproducts Division of General Motors advised Boeing that the propeller that they were to supply would be delayed due to the design changes caused by vibration difficulties encountered on their type test. Their shipping date was given as June 1, 1944.

Curtiss-Wright Corporation, Propeller Division, advised Boeing of difficulties in securing satisfactory castings for the propeller they were to supply and extended their delivery date to approximately the end of April 1944.

BuAer's reaction to the delays in the delivery and first flight of the XF8B-1 was predictable. The Navy was not convinced by Boeing's contention that the delay to work under the XF8B-1 contract was, to any great extent, brought about by default of the Navy. Rather, it believed that the fault was Boeing's, for the reasons set forth in a letter from the BAR. A contributing factor was, undoubtedly, Boeing's initial underestimate of the engineering work involved and a reluctance to rectify this early mistake by a vigorous attack with adequate personnel. The matter was discussed with Lt. Commander Sweeney (representative of the BuAer Fighter Desk) and it was agreed that the BuAer would endeavor to have Boeing take the necessary and available steps to improve on its anticipated first flight date of September 29, 1944.

Boeing's President, P.G. Johnson, wrote the BAR on May 1, 1944, summarizing the many difficulties Boeing was experiencing with the XF8B-1 contract to that point and soliciting his assistance in addressing them. First, as a result of the low priority accorded the project, there had been delays in securing wind tunnel time for testing the XF8B-1 model at the University of Washington and the California Institute of Technology. This retarded selection of a final configuration for the airplane, and Boeing had not attempted to expedite completion of the XF8B-1 at the expense of serious compromises in aerodynamic design.

Second, Pratt & Whitney had consistently failed to provide Wasp Major engines in a timely manner. On May 12, 1943, Boeing was quoted a delivery of one engine in January, 1944. Boeing's purchase order for the necessary engines was issued June 28, 1943. The first engine on this order still had not been received and would not be received for some time, resulting in Boeing enlisting the Navy's assistance through the loan of the XR-4360-8A engine to permit an accurate check of the power plant installation. The Navy's help was appreciated, but the arrival of an R-4360-10 engine on or about March 1 would have helped expedite delivery of a finished aircraft. Delivery of propellers for the XF8B-1 was rapidly becoming even more critical to actual flight than the delayed delivery of the engine.

Boeing had also experienced considerable difficulty in securing a mock-up engine and in gaining accurate information concerning the subject engine. These matters were taken up with Pratt & Whitney Aircraft Company and their various local, Southern California, and Connecticut representatives.

Boeing felt that BuAer had also fallen short. There was still a shortage of seventeen items of Government Furnished Equipment (GFE) out of a total of fifty-three required for flight of the first airplane. In addition, information required to complete engineering design was lacking on certain items of GFE; all of this material had been requested for delivery by March 1, 1944. While it was obvious that the XF8B-1 was not yet ready for installation of this equipment, engineering work and the fabrication of parts and sub-assemblies would have been facilitated by its availability.

Finally, Selective Service activity had resulted in a shortage of personnel to work on the XF8B-1, slowing its development.

These factors caused delivery of the first prototype of the XF8B-1 to be pushed back to July 4, 1944, with the first flight not occurring until approximately September 29, 1944, well behind the schedule outlined in the original specification.

On May 4, BAR E.J. Bataille wrote BuAer regarding Boeing's complaints and excuses for delays in the XF8B-1 program. He concurred with Boeing's statements with respect to delays incident to obtaining the engines, propellers, GFE items, and installation information. Bataille also agreed that Selective Service had delayed work on the contract. However, Bataille contended that these factors were not primarily responsible for the delay in delivery of the XF8B-1. Instead, he felt that the following factors were far more significant:

a) The pronounced emphasis on the B-29 had severely militated against XF8B-1 requirements. Insufficient engineering man hours were assigned to the XF8B-1 contract to meet the required drawing release dates. In addition, wind tunnel personnel and time were assigned to B-29 work rather than the XF8B-1.
b) Bataille believed that Boeing did not fully realize the amount of work entailed in the design and construction of the XF8B-1.
c) Boeing's lack of a Navy Contract Administrator, or any individual vested with responsibilities and authority of that office, resulted in definite delays in transmission of information to the project and replies to correspondence of an urgent nature. Delays of a week between forwarding of data by the BAR and receipt by the XF8B-1 Project or other Boeing department had been noted. To obviate the delay, Bataille began sending one copy of all required information directly to the XF8B-1 Project.

Bataille promised to continue exerting every effort to expedite delivery of items required for the XF8B-1 contract. Forms which exempted critically needed employees from Selective Service called "42A Specials" were being forwarded to BuAer in support of Boeing's request for deferment of employees to materially ease the engineering manpower difficulty for the present and raise the morale of employees assigned to the project.

Bataille informed Boeing of his opinions and requested that the necessary actions be taken. Boeing responded by making the following changes:

a) It increased the staff of engineers on the project to the maximum efficient work force considered practicable.
b) It completed the Boeing Wind Tunnel, which would prevent delays in obtaining wind tunnel time and personnel for work under the XF8B-1 contract.
c) It appointed a Contract Coordinator to expedite action on all correspondence and contract matters.

Up till then, the majority of delays had been concerned with engineering and correspondence. Bataille also anticipated delays caused by Boeing's production and tooling departments:

a) Scheduled fabrication of XF8B-1 parts had been delayed to permit fabrication of B-29 parts.
b) Tooling for the XF8B-1 had not progressed as rapidly as Bataille believed necessary. There was a marked contrast between emphasis on B-29 and XF8B-1 tooling.
c) Bataille anticipated difficulty in obtaining the necessary qualified mechanics. Seattle had an acute labor shortage and Boeing's labor force was occupied in meeting the demands of B-17 and B-29 production.
d) Bataille perceived a question in the minds of many minor employees regarding the importance of the project. Many employees failed to realize the necessity for constant and unremitting attention towards expediting all work connected with the XF8B-1.

Bataille promised to eliminate the aforementioned conditions through consultation with Boeing's representatives. He ended his letter by noting the pronounced variation in magnitude between the B-29, B-17 and XF8B-1 contracts which, in his opinion, resulted in a perhaps unconscious lower priority in the minds of many employees engaged on the subject contract. This condition would continue as long as production contracts for the XF8B-1 remained a matter of conjecture.

BuAer wrote NACA on May 8 regarding spin tests on the 1/20-scale model of the XF8B-1 airplane. Construction of the model at the David Taylor Model Basin was nearly completed, and the model was to be shipped to Langley Field Laboratory on May 22, 1944 for the tests. The model did not arrive till July 18. The general design and construction of the model met with the approval of the laboratory. NACA was instructed to expedite the spin-tunnel tests of the XF8B-1 model since the airplane was nearly ready to fly; tests were expected to start August 9, 1944, but were delayed till the fall of 1945. The results of the tests revealed no serious problems with the XF8B-1's airfoil.

By the middle of May, engineers on the XF8B-1 were demanding organization changes, specifically the formation of special tool group assigned to the project. Parts being received under the existing arrangement were not uniform and difficult to assemble. It was obvious that building an experimental aircraft in a production environment with the organization established by Beall was slowing progress considerably.

Around this time at BuAer, the Deputy Director of Engineering (Experiments and Developments) sent a memo to the various branches of his organization requesting an evaluation of the XF8B-1 in order to help him decide whether the airplane was to be placed into production at that time. The responses turned out to be mostly negative.

The first of the memos came from the Engineering Branch on May 31; it outlined several reasons for not producing the airplane. Engineering items associated with this project which appeared questionable and mitigated against an immediate production commitment were as follows:

a) Development of a two stage R-4360 engine for production, particularly the supercharger drive.
b) Development of counter-rotating propellers for production use.
c) Control and handling qualities. These were predicted to be good but were unknown at the time of writing.
d) Modest performance for an airplane which would not be operational for two years. This was predominantly due to the size and gasoline capacity that had been built into the airplane to provide the possibility of long range.

Comparative performance figures were listed as follows:

	Boeing XF8B-1	Vought F2G-1	Vought F4U-4	Curtiss XF15C-1
Maximum Speed at Sea Level	342	393	372	440
Maximum Speed at Critical Altitude	421/25,000	425/16,000	436/25,000	478/25,000
R/C at Sea Level	3,000	3,975	3,120	5,240
Power used	3,000 (mil)	3,000 (mil)	2,325 (WI)	2,540 (WI)
Airplanes per 200 ft. of deck space on a CV9	18	35	35	20 (est.)
Combat radius	535 (with bomb bay tank) 890 (2 ext. tanks)	225 350*	355 (1 external tank)	352 (1 external tank)
* An additional internal tank was being developed which would give approximately this combat radius.				

It was noted that were the R-4360 engine pushed and a water injection (WI) power of approximately 3600 obtained (comparable to WI powers then being obtained from the R-2800 engine) the top speed of both the XF8B-1 and F2G-1 would have been increased approximately 20 mph. The possibility of obtaining such powers within the next two years depended upon the relative emphasis placed by Pratt & Whitney on the R-2800-E engine and on the R-4360.

The airplane was originally conceived as a long-range fighter. Although various alternate loads could be carried, without a complete study it was difficult to believe that the primary mission of the airplane could have been changed without serious compromise to the design.

From the above information it was believed that the major factor affecting future production commitments for additional XF8B-1 airplanes was whether the advantage of possible long range operation was sufficient to offset reduction in the number of airplanes that could be carried, and the reduction in performance during combat.

The Ships' Installations Branch of BuAer critiqued the carrier accommodation characteristics of the XF8B-1. The following numbers of each type of airplane under consideration could be spotted for a 400 ft. takeoff run on a flight deck of a CV-9 class carrier:

XF8B-1	41
F4U-1 or F6F-3	70
F7F-1	39
XBK-1	51
XBTM-1	45

Ships' Installations believed that the XF8B-1 would have been as easy to handle on the carrier deck as the XBK and XBTM for towing, spotting, etc. Because of the greater size, it would not have been, of course, as easily handled as the F4U and F6F-3. Although the catapulting arrangement and arresting hook location generally appeared satisfactory, insufficiently detailed data had been submitted to determine whether there were any inherent troubles to be anticipated. None that could not have been readily corrected were expected, however.

The Power Plant Design Branch of BuAer was more skeptical of Boeing's big fighter. They expressed considerable doubt as to the ability of the R-4360 engine to meet the production schedules as a satisfactory service engine. However, Power Plant Design Branch engineers did not believe that the engine lacked the potential to become in all respects a satisfactory engine or that the current state of development was unsatisfactory considering the time so far spent on development. This assessment applied to all R-4360 engines. In addition, although Pratt & Whitney had accumulated some running time on two-stage supercharged R-4360 engines, neither AEL nor Wright Field had run the two-stage engine.

Aside from the generally improved status of the engine as a whole, the hydraulic supercharger drive imposed a control problem that had not been satisfactorily solved. Lack of a satisfactory control system was not too serious a handicap for the single stage engine, but was of much greater significance in the two-stage system. It was therefore believed premature to make production commitments for early production two-stage R-4360 engines.

Development of the Hamilton Standard counter-rotating propeller hub, blade, and governor assemblies was still in progress. Boeing's delay had been caused mainly through difficulties encountered in their special blade development program and governing deficiencies at the high pump pressures required to give the propeller's high rate of pitch change. It was not believed that production propellers of this model would be made available for 18-24 months even if correction of the above difficulties was accomplished at an early date.

Boeing furnished the experimental propeller and was also planning to flight test an Aeroproducts counter-rotating propeller for comparison. It was possible that Aeroproducts production duals could be made available at an earlier date than initially indicated; they were to produce 50-70 counter-rotating propellers for the Army XP-72, with a rate of 25 per month by October 1944. (This of course did not occur, due to the cancellation of that aircraft).

The majority of the BuAer staff was in general agreement with delaying production of the XF8B-1. Lt. Commander J.F. Sutherland repeated several of the arguments above but had several positive things to say about the XF8B-1. For example, Sutherland believed the airplane's structure to be extraordinarily sound, generally conforming with BuAer's newer requirements. Maneuverability and control had been stressed from the beginning, the aim being to achieve a 150°/sec rate of roll at maximum speed. The wing had been designed for non-buckling up to 7g. The control surfaces appeared adequate for the maneuvers required of a Navy fighter. The wing loading was sufficiently low to give desirable turning radius. Sutherland predicted that the XF8B-1 would be a very maneuverable airplane in view of its size.

In terms of suitability, Sutherland felt that the best utilization of the XF8B-1 in its existing long-range fighter configuration was as an attack bomber, strafer, or rocket carrier. Carrying six 20 mm. cannon, one 1,600 lb. bomb and eight 4 in. rockets, the XF8B-1 could strike at over 600 nautical miles. Its API (dead reckoning tracer) made it ideal for long-range strikes over water, especially in conditions of limited visibility or at night. This use would have enabled a task force commander to neutralize enemy bases while still a day's steaming away and then convert to an escort fighter for the following day's strike. As a skip bomber for mopping up convoys from close range, the XF8B-1 would have been second-to-none due to its firepower on the run in (six 20 mm. cannon) and ability to carry four 500 lb. bombs internally which could be released electrically with the bomb doors closing again in ¾ of a second.

Additional misgivings regarding the XF8B-1 contract were voiced on June 1, when a Commander Simple wrote a damning memorandum to the Assistant Chief of BuAer regarding Boeing's big fighter. Simple noted that the Pratt & Whitney R-4360 was not considered ready for production by July of 1944 in any configuration. No ratings on the engine had been released for any produced prior to 1945. From a military standpoint, the R-4360 was second in priority to the Pratt & Whitney R-2800-E. At the time, eight Navy airplanes were being designed around or were using the R-2800 engine. In Simple's opinion, change to the R-2800-E represented a normal improvement which could not be forsaken.

The XF8B-1's propeller situation was little better. Production Hamilton Standard counter-rotating propellers were not expected to be available for 18 to 24 months. The Aeroproducts Company had a contract to produce a similar propeller for the Army at a rate of 20 per month beginning in late 1944. The company was essentially controlled by the Army. The Army had the Republic XP-72 with a counter-rotating propeller and a R-4360 two-stage engine; insufficient operating time prevented any evaluation of that combination.

A comparison of the XF8B-1 with contemporary Navy fighters that had been fighting for at least a year left much to be desired from a performance standpoint. The performance figures for the service fighters were from actual test data, those from the XF8B-1 were estimated:

Performance Comparison

	Boeing XF8B-1	Grumman F6F-5	Vought F4U-1
Maximum Speed - Sea Level (mph)	342	344	359
Maximum Speed - Critical Altitude (mph/ft.)	412/25,000	400/18,900	417/24,500
Time to climb to 20,000 ft. (min.)	8.1	8.0	7.7
Takeoff - 25 kt. Wind (ft.)	349	440	450
Stall Speed – No Fuel (mph)	76.8	80.8	81.8
Armament (no. guns/cal.)	6/50 cal. or 6/20 mm.	6/50 cal.	6/50 cal.
Fuel/Oil (gal./gal.)	618/35	400/19	361/20
Weight (lbs.)	18,559	13,455	12,836
Combat Radius (naut. miles)	535	395	350
Spot (no. airplanes for equivalent CV-9 deck length)	18	35	35

It was obvious that the XF8B-1, which was to be available in two years, would be inferior to the fighters of that day, since it was barely equal to those of mid-1944 which were at least three years old in design. Furthermore, the loss in numbers carried on the CV-9 aircraft carrier represented a critical loss in fighting power.

There was also considerable doubt as to the military need for a carrier-based fighter with the XF8B-1's range. The need for range in land-based-fighters was unquestioned, but they could accept the long takeoff. The carrier-based fighter had to sacrifice range for performance over the target. Navy Task Force Commanders did not make long-range strikes for the following reasons:

a) State of training of the Air Group.
b) Infrequency of successive strikes at a distance.
c) Loss of control of the group at greater distances than

150 miles.

d) Loss of maximum protection to the ship with the departure of the striking force beyond 150 miles.

The XF8B-1 would have been hopelessly outclassed over the target by contemporary land- or carrier-based fighters, due to either superior performance or superior numbers.

Commander Simple advised against the purchase of the XF8B-1 prior to completion of the demonstration flights due to the experimental nature of two of its major elements, i.e., the engine and the propeller. It was further advised that, prior to the letting of any contract for a production prototype, the following observations be considered:

a) The large size of the XF8B-1 caused critical loss of fighting power to the ship, due to the reduction of number that could be carried by 50%.
b) No mission requiring a combat radius greater than the capabilities of contemporary carrier fighters seemed likely to present itself to a carrier force.
c) At the time, the XF8B-1 was already outclassed in the target area, and would be more so by the probable date of its availability.

Due to the excellent takeoff and load carrying characteristics of the XF8B-1, Commander Simple argued that it would have great versatility as a carrier-based attack plane. It was capable of making rocket or masthead bombing attacks at high speed. Boeing had stated that it could carry two torpedoes externally to fulfill the torpedo bomber (VTB) role. At the time, the B-26 Marauder was carrying the "pickle barrel" torpedo externally in trial drops at Newport. The TBF was overloaded with many types of missions, about half of which the XF8B-1 could do better, namely a) masthead bombing; b) glide bombing; c) rocket attack; and d) strafing. Commander Simple therefore recommended that the XF8B-1 be evaluated as a carrier-based attack plane.

Later that June, the Deputy Director of BuAer assembled these responses and elaborated upon them in his memo to the BuAer Director of Engineering. At the beginning of the memo, the Deputy Director noted that the original concept of the XF8B-1 was that of a long range, carrier based fighter with good performance at is operational radius. The contract for the airplane was unique in that it permitted Boeing a great deal of freedom in design, with little BuAer control over detail design or requirements. The following items were pertinent to this phase of the design status:

a) At the time of the design proposal, Boeing insisted that a superior airplane could be produced in a much shorter period of time if it were allowed complete freedom of design, with BuAer stating on the broad, tactical requirements that should be met. At the time, it was impossible to prove this design procedure was unsound, although the time saving originally promised had not been realized. Contract guarantees of performance and delivery were not made, but statements that Boeing would exert his "best efforts" were made. The delivery date of 14 months from date of contract (May 4, 1943) was not realized, with the first flight then estimated for November 1944, and delivery not before the end of the year.
b) BuAer estimates of XF8B-1 performance were below those estimated by Boeing, though it expected to better these figures. Nonetheless, it was felt that any improvements would be minor in nature, with performance of the airplane being substantially unchanged from the original estimates. The combat radius increased from 450 to a maximum of 890 nautical miles, due to changes in fuel arrangements, and also to changes in the definition of "combat radius," while satisfactory takeoff was maintained. However, while the speed and climb of the XF8B-1 slightly decreased, contemporary carrier types increased markedly in these respects. For example, the change from the guaranteed maximum speed of the Vought F4U-1 with military power to the expected performance of the F4U-4 with war emergency

(water injection) power was 57 mph at 23,000 ft. Other airplanes had shown similar increases with engine changes and increased power ratings during the same period. As a result, the speed and climb performance of the XF8B-1 was considerably less attractive than just a year before, although future development of the R-4360 engine was expected to result in the availability of water injection ratings, which would have made the XF8B-1 approximately the same as the F4U-4 in speed, and somewhat superior in climb.

c) The power plant situation, especially in respect to production airplanes, was not clear. There was doubt that the R-4360 would meet current schedules as a satisfactory service engine, although the development of the engine had progressed about as well as could be expected. No two-stage engines had been delivered to date and trouble was being experienced in developing a satisfactory control system for the hydraulic supercharger drive. The latter problem was relatively serious in the two-stage engine, and mitigated against an immediate production commitment. The development of counter-rotating propellers had progressed more slowly than expected, and even though Boeing had three different types on order, it appeared doubtful that production quantities would have been available in less than 18 months. The counter-rotating propeller situation, however, was not unique to the XF8B-1, existing on the XTB2D-1 and the XBTC-2 as well.

d) Very little was known at the time on the adequacy of structural design conditions being used for the XF8B-1, but the contract required a complete demonstration to stand fighter requirements. Boeing's past performance in providing adequate strength had been good, although its recent experience had been on large airplanes. Previous BuAer experience on releasing airplanes for production prior to completion of static tests and demonstrations, even with rather complete design control, had been followed by imposing restrictions lower than desired operating limits.

e) The aerodynamic stability and handling qualities of the airplane were unknown at the time of writing. No wind tunnel test data were then available, although it was understood that Boeing had done considerable test work, and was attempting to provide better than average control. BurAer calculations indicated satisfactory stability within the existing c.g. positions.

f) The most unusual feature of the airplane for a fighter type was the incorporation of a bomb bay, which was undoubtedly due to the highly publicized advent of "skip bombing" at the time the design was started. There was no doubt that the bomb bay penalized the airplane for its primary mission, and because of this fact, BuAer recommended its deletion. Boeing disagreed with BuAer, believing the versatility of the resultant configuration offset the disadvantages. It appeared that deletion of the bomb baby could have resulted in a better fighter type with improvement in fuselage lines, reduction of folded span due to reduction of wing fuel tanks required, as well as the obvious weight saving and reduction in complexity.

g) The size of the XF8B-1 reduced its merit for carrier use. Using a 400 ft. takeoff (the minimum practicable due to landing space requirements) on the Essex Class carriers, the following number of airplanes could be spotted on the flight deck:

XF8B-1	41
F7F-1	39
F4U-1, F6F-3	70
XBK-1	51
XBTM-1	45

The general handling on the carrier would have been no worse than other large airplanes, but would have been definitely inferior to airplanes the size of the F4U.

If it was assumed that the XF8B-1 airplane performed as expected, the following comments were applicable:

a) The airplane was capable of operation at a combat radius great than current or project carrier types, and capable of operation at any given radius with a shorter takeoff distance than other types. The importance of extreme combat radius in carrier operations had recently been minimized, however, with contemporary thought being that other items of performance, which had been compromised in the XF8B-1, were paramount.
b) It was impossible to predict the exact nature of future enemy opposition to be encountered. The Deputy Engineer thought that it was probable that aircraft with performance approximating the original estimates on the Japanese "Tojo" (a larger engine was believed to have been installed) were to be met in the not too distant future. Against such an adversary, the XF8B-1 would have been at a disadvantage in climb and possessed a slight speed advantage with existing engine ratings. The performance advantage over the opposition would have certainly been less for the XF8B-1 than on other naval types that were to be operational at approximately the same time.
c) The spotting disparity between the XF8B-1 and smaller fighter types, such as the F4U, could be considered offset to some degree by its superior takeoff performance for normal combat radii. This particular comparison was obscured at the time by the poor calculated takeoff of the F4U with drop tanks installed, which was based on a single flight test check, but could not be justified by theory. If the existing calculations were substantiated, the F4U-4 would have theoretically required a 600 ft. spot (for a combat radius of 355 miles) as against a theoretical 300 ft. spot for the XF8B-1. Such landing space requirements dictated a minimum spot of approximately 400 ft., with 200 ft. of added spaced available to the XF8B-1, making the total number of airplanes on the flight aft of the spot 41 for the XF8B-1 and 40 for the F4U. The comparison with the F7F on equal radius (435 miles) and with the XF8B-1 spotted at 400 ft. (takeoff distance, 320 ft.) and the F7F at 450 ft., (its takeoff distance) showed 41 XF8B-1's and 35 F7F's. These calculations were rather theoretical, and in practice, the XF8B-1 would have probably shown a slight superiority over the F7F and definite inferiority to the F4U.

The XF8B-1, as configured, was adaptable to a great variety of missions. The large bomb bay enabled it to carry one 2,000 lb., two 1,000 lb., or four 500 lb. G.P. bombs; or two 1,600 lb. A.P. bombs with full factors for the bomb supporting structure. As an overload, at reduced factors, four 1,000 A.P. bombs could have been carried internally. In addition, two bomb racks were available on the wings to carry either drop tanks or bombs. The airplane would have been an excellent "skip" bomber or attack airplane with either six .50 cal. or six 20 mm. fixed guns in addition to its bomb load. The airplane was fitted with fast action bomb bay doors that enhanced its value in this respect.

From the above, it was believed that the existing policy of withholding immediate production commitments on the design was sound, but the airplane had sufficient promise to continue development. Changes in the military situation in the Pacific might have made development of a long-range fighter mandatory, and the development of a versatile ground and shipping attack airplane desirable.

On July 17, Boeing notified BuAer that the XF8B-1 was 806 lbs. overweight. Weight had been steadily escalating as the BuAer demanded more detail changes; the latest 50 lb. increase in GFE was due to redesign of the Hamilton Standard Propeller. The XF8B-1's excess weight continued to escalate in the following months, reaching 1,401 lbs. by the end of the contract.

On August 10, R. Selzenlichter, Boeing's Chief of Contract Administration, wrote the BAR at Boeing regarding the type of droppable fuel tank to be used on the XF8B-1. Originally, BuAer suggested that Boeing use the F4U, F6F, or P-38 type drop tanks. After studying the several suggested types of tanks, Boeing proceeded with the design of a tank installation using the P-38 tank, which was the same tank that had been previously used on the mock-up.

Boeing had made considerable progress in the engineering design of the P-38 type tank installation when the Navy asked it to discontinue work on that installation in favor of the 150 gallon Grumman type external droppable tanks, using sway bracing similar to that used on the 100 gallon droppable fuel tanks of the TBF-3 airplane. This change was requested inasmuch as the Grumman type tank was being adopted as standard for all Navy aircraft requiring 150 gallon droppable fuel tanks. This change not only increased costs but also slowed progress on getting the aircraft to flight test status.

A nearly complete XF8B-1 with 150 gallon Grumman type drop tanks as photographed on February 20, 1946. Boeing originally designed the fighter to carry P-38 type tanks, which were more aerodynamic, but BuAer elected to go with the Grumman alternative, as it was already in wide use with the F6F Hellcat.

In August of 1944, Pratt & Whitney tested a pre-production R-4360 in a Vought Corsair. These tests demonstrated that the engine's hottest cylinder was in the front and the coolest in the back at a power setting of 35" MP, 2,550 rpm at 8,000 ft. with cowl flaps open. Further test flights helped identify and correct such problems as engine surging, oil loss, and ignition difficulties above 20,000 ft. Pratt & Whitney passed data accumulated with these tests on to Boeing.

Boeing also received data regarding testing of the Republic XP-72, which was powered by the R-4360 driving an Aeroproducts counter-rotating propeller. Republic test pilot Ken Jernstedt experienced propeller overspeed problems when moving both the throttle and prop controls forward, the power setting leaping to 4,000 rpm in one test, far above the allowable limit. Aeroproducts recommended moving only one control at a time, but the problem reasserted itself and required further investigation.

On September 23, Boeing raised the subject of the .60 cal. machine gun with BuAer. Boeing did not have complete information on this weapon and was pressed for engineering time; it requested that BuAer review the need for the study of the .60 cal. gun in the XF8B-1.

BuAer responded by noting that the .60 cal. machine gun had been developed to the point where it was being considered for production in the near future. Since the performance of the gun was so outstanding, it was the desire of BuAer that all experimental airplanes be designed with space provisions for the gun, unless incorporation of such space provisions excessively penalized the design.

Nonetheless, it was satisfactory to BuAer that the .60 cal. gun study be deferred until the necessary engineering talent was available to complete it. It was anticipated that final information on the gun would be available in the near future at which time it would be forwarded to the Boeing. At that time, BuAer would be in a position to set the necessary priority on the installation study.

On September 25, BAR E.J. Bataille confronted Boeing with the thorny issue of the XF8B-1's rapidly rising costs. Final cost of the XF8B-1 contract was originally estimated to be $3,554,021.41, with a fixed fee of $102,869.06. As of August 31, 1944, the Navy had been billed for an amount of $3,525,079.00 and a fixed fee of $91,828.21. Everything was behind schedule: the first XF8B-1 had yet to be flown, construction of the static test article was only 30% complete and fabricated parts for the remaining two airplanes were about 50% complete.

It was obvious that the cost of the XF8B-1 contract would be greatly in excess of the estimated amount. It was requested that Boeing furnish Bataille with a comparison between the estimated costs outlined in the original contract, actual costs to date, and estimated costs for the completed contract. Bataille also wanted reasons for the increased costs. Costs in excess of the estimated amounts under the contract could not be reimbursed by the Navy Cost Inspector without additional authorization by BuAer.

Boeing subsequently fulfilled the request and additional funds were provided, but the cost overruns increased the Navy's dissatisfaction with the company and played a significant role in the XF8B-1 being passed over for production.

On October 16, N.D. Showalter, Chief of Flight Test at Boeing, wrote the BAR requesting approval of the test pilots to fly the XF8B-1. Approval was requested for Robert ("Bob") T. Lamson to act as the primary test pilot. Lamson had earned his Air Corps wings at Randolph field and had served as a primary and basic flight instructor. At the time, he had a total of approximately 2,050 hours flight time and had been employed by Boeing as an Engineering Flight Test Pilot since May 21, 1941. He had flown ten hours each or more in Army and Navy Pursuit and Fighter types including the P-51, P-38, F4F, FM2, F6F, and F4U.

Approval was also requested for Jack C. Jones to act as the alternate test pilot. At the time, Jones had a total of approximately 2,700 hours flight time and had been employed by Boeing since May of 1944 as an Engineering Test Pilot and was previously employed in the same capacity by Curtiss-Wright in Buffalo, NY. Mr. Jones' experience included engineering flight testing of the Curtiss P-40, XP-60, XP-62, and XF14C-2. He had also flown

Photo: Bob Lamson Collection

Test pilot Bob Lamson smiling in the cockpit of the XF8B-1 after its first test flight on December 27, 1944.

the SO3C, P-51, P-39, and P-47. Both pilots were subsequently approved by BuAer to test fly the XF8B-1.

When assembly of the first XF8B-1 was completed at Plant 1 in late October, it was towed to Plant 2 on Boeing Field to begin pre-flight tests. The engine of the big fighter was first brought to life on November 2; it lacked an operable second stage blower which restricted flights to 250 knots and 15,000 ft.; this was lifted to 400 knots a month later. On November 10, the aircraft was mounted on its main gear and tail jack in level attitude for 10 hours of propeller vibration tests. This was followed by taxi runs, which revealed weakness in the aircraft's brakes. The engine was difficult to start due to carburetor problems which were later fixed.

A.F. Logan, Assistant to the President at Boeing, wrote BuAer on November 4 regarding premium pay for test pilot Bob Lamson. It was planned to make the initial flights of the XF8B-1 in the very near future and Boeing proposed to pay Lamson a sum not to exceed $20,000 for performing the entire series of test flights, including initial flights, spins, dives, and preliminary and final Navy demonstrations. This sum was to be in addition to the regular salary which the pilot received in connection with his normal duties as test pilot. The actual amount paid was to be determined as the tests progressed dependent upon the nature of the problems that presented themselves as the actual flight characteristics of the airplane became known. The amount was pro-rated over the various types of tests in accord with the Vice President of Engineering and subject to agreement with the pilot. In the event these tests proved fatal to the test-pilot, it was also proposed to complete the payment of the amount then agreed upon for the complete series of tests to the estate of the deceased.

BuAer balked at Boeing's $20,000 figure and reduced it to $6,000, which Lamson accepted in a written agreement with Boeing on November 27, 1944. He was to receive $1,500 for the first 10 hours he flew or 10 landings he made in the XF8B-1. Thereafter, he was to receive $4,500 prorated against a series of flights covering stalls, spins, dives, and pullouts.

On November 17, C.L. Egtvedt, Chairman of Boeing, responded to the BAR regarding the spiraling costs of the XF8B-1 contract. The original contract was in the amount of $3,722,505.78 with a fixed fee of $109,608.43. Boeing revised its estimates for total costs for completion of the XF8B-1 program, exclusive of the estimated cost of change proposal then being prepared and estimated cost of future design changes, in the amount of $5,592,487.00, which required a $1,869,981.22 increase in the funds allotted.

Boeing required the funds for several purposes. Concerning design data and drawings, the original estimated cost was based on the use of streamlined engineering policies such as shortcut releases, informal part numbering, minimum use of master layout work and simplified design methods. As the design work progressed and information was released, it was found that production workers available for assignment to the XF8B-1 project were inexperienced and unable to work effectively only from production type engineering data. Consequently, design methods were revised and more detailed procedures were established. The lack of a satisfactory power plant mock-up and failure to receive the actual power plant from Pratt & Whitney on schedule caused a considerable amount of redesign, increasing overall costs.

With respect to tests and miscellaneous data, Boeing failed to obtain wind tunnel time as originally planned with resultant delay and difficulty in obtaining aerodynamic fixes, thereby causing considerable extra design work. Boeing needed a more extensive test program of both models and structural designs (in addition to the static test article) which the company found necessary to produce a satisfactory airplane. Boeing also had to use inexperienced workers due to the labor shortage. Finally, the company suffered an increase in the manufacturing overhead rate to approximately 110%, whereas the original proposal was made on the basis of an overage overhead rate of 90%. The increase in cost of engines and propellers was also not anticipated.

In sum, Boeing's original estimates were too low and it wanted $1,870,000.00 to complete the contract. Furthermore, it did not rule out further requests for funds to cover change proposals then in preparation and future proposals resulting from design changes.

The letter was generally endorsed by BAR Proctor and forwarded to BuAer on November 18. Proctor felt that in the event of a limited or extensive production of the XF8B-1, the expenditures outlined by Egtvedt would materially aid in expediting production drawing data and for improved tooling. He also noted that while certain inexperience on the part of the workers and possible lack of coordination may have been the basic cause of the cost overruns, the experience gained would assist in future production planning.

XF8B-1 no. 57984 finally took to the air for the first time on the afternoon of November 27 for just over an hour with Bob Lamson at the controls. The big fighter steadily accumulated more flight hours without major mishap until December 1, when the bomb bays doors accidentally sprung open in a tight turn. Boeing spent the rest of the month rerigging the XF8B-1, replacing the geared aileron balance tabs with spring loaded tabs to correct for excessively heavy aileron control. The aircraft's next flight did not occur until December 26 and featured Bud Zerega as flight engineer behind Lamson in the "piggy back" seat. Though the aircraft was designed as a single-place fighter, a second seat was provided for a flight engineer behind the pilot seat in late 1943. The role of the flight engineer was to aid the pilot during flight tests and accelerate development of the aircraft. The second seat was a temporary feature that had poor ergonomics, requiring Zerega to be hunched over during flights. The life of a flight engineer was not a glamorous one.

3
1945
Navy Evaluation & Accidents

On January 1, 1945, Boeing's R. Gelzenlichter wrote the BAR regarding a change in the propeller situation. Originally, BuAer requested that Boeing purchase four Hamilton Standard propellers, one Aeroproducts propeller, and one Curtiss propeller for the XF8B-1. The latter two propellers were to be used for test purposes to hedge against the possible failure of Hamilton Standard to produce a satisfactory propeller. Subsequent to this, Hamilton Standard requested a cancellation of Boeing's purchase order, and by correspondence with the BuAer it was established that Boeing would purchase four Aeroproducts propellers and one Curtiss propeller. Due to the priority of other testing on the XF8B-1, Boeing stated that it would be unable to conduct tests on the Curtiss propeller for several months.

BAR Proctor concurred in the desirability of deferring the Curtiss propeller tests until the completion of fundamental flight testing on the present airplane-engine-propeller combination was complete.

Boeing's W.E. Beall wrote Major General K.B. Wolfe of the Army Air Corps Air Technical Service Command on January 2 in an attempt to interest the Army in the XF8B-1. He emphasized the type's great range, low wing loading, unique internal bomb bay and the potential of the R-4360 to develop greater fuel efficiency and increased power. The letter and accompanying brochure sparked the interest of Wolfe, leading to the testing of the XF8B-1 both at Wright Field, Ohio and Eglin Field, Florida.

Colonel M.S. Ruth, Air Corps, Chief, Aircraft Projects, Service Engineering Section, Engineering Division wrote a letter on January 11 to his superior, Brigadier General F.O. Carroll, advising against the purchase of the XF8B-1. In the letter, Ruth noted the general inferiority of the XF8B-1 relative to the Republic XP-72 based on the following chart:

	Republic XP-72	Boeing XF8B-1
Weight empty (lbs.)	10,773	13,508
Gross weight (lbs.)	15,170	18,263
Engine	P & W R-4360	P & W R-4360
Horsepower	3,000	3,000
High speed 300 hp. (mph/ft.)	500 at 25,000	470 at 25,000
Rate of climb (ft. per min.)	4,360	2,600
Internal fuel (gal.)	320	302
Wing loading (per sq. ft.)	59.5	34
Wing area (sq. ft.)	300	489
Span (ft.)	41	54
Guns (no. x cal.)	6 x .50	6 x .50

The XP-72 appeared to be the better of the two airplanes thought its range was obviously much less. The maximum tactical radius of action was given as 1,290 with a total of 954 gallons of fuel, 570 of which was droppable. If 300 gallon external fuel tanks were hung on the XP-72, the total fuel carried would have been 950 gallons. The XP-72 would have probably achieved the same range in this condition due to its higher cruising speed. The weight of the XF8B-1 in its long-range condition was 21,810 lbs. Since the Army did not want the XP-72, Ruth felt there was no reason to become particularly interested in the Boeing fighter.

Ruth knew of no production commitment by the Navy to produce the XF8B-1. He felt that if the Army showed any interest in getting some of these airplanes, it could leave itself open to the Navy, using this as an excuse or an aid in getting into the Boeing plant with a production order.

On January 9, Lt. Commander J.F. Sutherland, USNR, made a preliminary evaluation flight of the XF8B-1. The airplane had accumulated approximately 15 hours of flight time and was restricted to 450 mph and 5 g. In his judgment, the configuration conformed basically to the design data previously forwarded to BuAer except that: a) the auxiliary blower was inoperative so that the engine operated as a single-stage powerplant; b) the control column was a temporary test configuration; c) the ailerons were fitted with geared balance tabs which were put on in place of the original spring balance tabs while Boeing was designing a new spring tab arrangement which was expected to be free of flutter; and d) the usual flight test equipment and controls were present.

The following information was noted during the flight with the XF8B-1 in the above configuration:

a) Ground handling characteristics were excellent for a conventional landing gear and were as good or better than the P-47. The brakes were a little oversensitive though pedal forces were light and pleasant.
b) Controls were well placed and easily operable.
c) Takeoff was effortless and required a surprisingly short run. There was no swinging tendency whatsoever. Initial climb away was quite good. The wheels retracted smoothly and produced a slight nose up change of trim.
d) The stability of the XF8B-1 was considered remarkable. Longitudinally the stability was positive in both the clean and dirty conditions and with or without power. Directional stability was positive in all conditions. Laterally the stability was weak positive to neutral and undoubtedly influenced by the temporary aileron geared tab installed. At low speeds near the stall, there was some evidence of an aileron force reversal.
e) The wave-off characteristics were superior. There was little rolling tendency and the nose-up change of trim was easily held with the stick. Rudder and aileron remained effective during the wave-off.
f) The stalling characteristics in both clean and dirty configurations were excellent. Very little rolling tendency was evident at the stall and the airplane was laterally controllable with aileron or rudder. As the stall approached the elevator force got desirably heavier. With elevator held full back the airplane could be held with aileron or rudder so that it sank straight ahead while buffeting heavily. When the control column was released in this condition the nose dropped rapidly until speed was regained when it returned toward the trimmed position with no divergence evident.
g) Level flight was easily maintained with very little attention to the controls, a highly desirable characteristic in an extreme range fighter.
h) Vision was good to the rear and over the nose. Downward it was obstructed by the wing as in the F6F and F8F. The view for low level flying was excellent for a single engine airplane because of the nose down attitude in flight. Vision for takeoff was comparable to the F6F.
i) Engine operation was satisfactory and inspired confidence. Starting was easy and no peculiar effects of the counter-rotating propeller were noted. An attempt was made to observe any stroboscopic effect in the propeller by swinging through all angles to the sun in the horizontal plane at several RPM settings but without results. The engine ran very cool throughout all power conditions with cowl flaps completely closed. Sutherland believed that the power plant was over cooled and that considerable loss in performance was being suffered due to excess cooling drag. The cowl flaps did not open on the ground without running the engine up which was considered unsatisfactory. Boeing subsequently designed a revised cowl flap mechanism and arrangement to address this.

On the basis of these very preliminary results Sutherland wrote the following:

a) The XF8B-1 should have excellent carrier handling, approach and landing characteristics.
b) The XF8B-1 appeared to be an excellent gun platform and consequently the dive bombing, skip bombing, strafing,

rocket firing, and low level bombing characteristics were assumed to be equal to existing service fighters.

c) The airplane should be able to stand considerable overloading and center of gravity abuse.

d) As a result of talks with Boeing, it appeared that the conversion of the XF8B-1 to an attack plane was practicable and could be made in a relatively short time if the power plant configuration was left unchanged. Boeing prepared a proposal for an attack version at the request of BuAer and submitted approximately a week later. As an attack airplane, space was available for the following armament in addition to that shown for the fighter version:

    1) 18 x 100 lb. bombs in bomb bay
    2) 7 x 1,600 lb. AP bombs (4 in bomb bay and 3 externally)
    3) 3 x Tiny Tim rockets externally
    4) 3 x 2,000 lb. GP bombs externally
    5) 16 x 5" HVAR externally
    6) 1 torpedo externally on the centerline

Sutherland believed that Boeing had done an excellent job of building an airplane with superior handling characteristics. Due to the simplicity of cockpit arrangement, good vision, ease of handling both on the ground and in the air, it was felt that this airplane would be extremely popular with service pilots. No comment was made on its military potentialities, though Sutherland felt them to be vast.

On January 31, the second XF8B-1, no. 57985, was rolled out. It was painted an overall glossy sea blue and was virtually finished except for the delivery of its R-4360 engine.

An accident with XF8B-1 no. 57984 occurred at approximately 4:30 p.m. on February 13. The accident resulted from the unexpected retraction of the landing gear during a high-speed taxi run. Pilot Bob Lamson was unaware of the retraction of the gear until it was too late to take corrective action. The airplane came to rest near the middle of the main runway,

Photo: National Archives, RG 72-AC

Results of the accident that occurred with XF8B-1 no. 57984 on February 13, 1945. Test pilot Bob Lamson was initially blamed for mistakenly retracting the landing gear during high speed taxi runs, but a subsequent investigation revealed the cause to be a faulty microswitch.

Boeing Field, after sliding approximately 1,000 ft. The fire department and other emergency crews arrived on the scene immediately but no fire occurred and no emergency measures were necessary. Reports of smoke and fire apparently resulted from the sparks and smoke caused by friction with the runway.

The XF8B-1 appeared to be in excellent condition, all things considered, and Boeing's Ground Operations Department, Plant Protection and a Mr. Harry Fisk were contacted to request that extreme care be exercised in the handling of the airplane to prevent further damage. The airplane was ultimately lifted by three cranes with the intention of placing it on a flat bed truck which was standing by. This would have made it unnecessary to disturb the landing gear prior to a detailed investigation. However, the cranes were unable to lift the airplane to a sufficient height and it was finally decided to

Front view of the first prototype with its gear collapsed, showing the extensive damage suffered to the costly Aeroproducts propellers; more photos of the mishap can be found in Appendix 7.

extend the landing gear manually in order to facilitate transportation of the airplane to prevent further damage to it. Extension of the landing gear was accomplished without difficulty and the airplane was towed to the hangar and placed under guard.

The subsequent crash investigation revealed that the malfunction was the cause of the unexpected retraction of the landing gear, the incident being reconstructed as follows: at some during the ground handling of the airplane prior to the taxi flight, pressure was applied in a backward direction to the landing gear control handle. This pressure was sufficient to snap the microswitch over to the gear-up position. However, the gear did not retract at the time because the safety switch on the landing gear oleo strut kept the circuit open. When the ship became airborne during the taxi test, the oleo extended, completing the circuit and resulting in the retraction of the gear.

This event was borne out by the testimony of numerous witnesses. One or more reliable witnesses indicated that the wheels began to retract and in fact assumed a "toed-in" position before the wheels actually left the ground. This was substantiated by wear on the edges of the diamond treads of the tires. The markings on the landing gear fairings and particularly on the tail gear door indicated quite conclusively that the landing gear was completely retracted at one time during the landing. However, at the time the airplane came to rest, the gear was extended somewhat. This could be explained by the fact that inertia forces or vibration affected the switch mechanism enough to cause the microswitch to return to its normal or gear-down position. When the extending gear reached the point at which it was blocked by the runway, the circuit breaker opened as described previously.

It took only 19 days for the XF8B-1 to be repaired; the P-23 engine was replaced by the P-31 and new bomb bay doors, induction scoop, gear doors, and propeller were installed. On March 10, Lamson and Douglas L. Edmonston flew the repaired aircraft from Seattle to Wichita on a cross country journey to NAS Patuxent River, where it would be tested by the Navy. During this leg of the journey, a crack in the canopy at high altitude caused the relief tube to burst, dousing both aviators with their own waste. After cleaning up from this unpleasant experience and enjoying a night's rest, they completed their journey on March 11. The flight covered 2,660 miles at an average indicated airspeed of 220 mph. Boeing support personnel George E. Grunewald, George E. McCloud and Earl L. Jensen traveled by commercial air. Boeing also requested priority for shipment of spare parts for the aircraft from NAS Sand Point in Seattle to Pax River.

On March 12, the aircraft was evaluated at Pax River by USN and USMC pilots. The first defect noticed by the pilots was the weakness of the XF8B-1's brakes, which could barely hold when full power for takeoff was applied. Seven measured takeoffs ultimately resulted in damage to the brakes. One pilot set the rudder tab .6 inches to the left to account for nonexistent torque, subsequently complaining of left wing heaviness. The pilot was reminded that the XF8B-1's counter-rotating propellers neutralized torque and the matter did not come up again. The aircraft was subsequently flown against the Grumman F7F Tigercat and Bell P-59 Airacomet on two occasions. Conservative piloting made the aircraft look disappointing in the first encounter, but with a more aggressive pilot it more than held its own in the second. The aircraft was often handled roughly, at one point being groundlooped 320° by an overzealous commander. Thirty-one pilots (including one from the Royal Navy) were checked out in 21 days, amassing 44:30 flight hours overall. Earl Jensen and his maintenance crew managed to have the aircraft ready for flight early each day with only two days of flying

Photo: Bob Dorr Collection

Side view of the first XF8B-1 at NATC, NAS Patuxent River on March 23, 1945 with an olive drab anti-glare panel applied to the nose. Other special markings included a long insignia blue stripe applied to the right side, as can be partially seen in the adjacent photo. Though not visible from this angle, new exhaust stacks identical to those used on the second and third prototypes were also installed. The aircraft received these modifications in wake of the accident that occurred on February 13, 1945.

missed.

During testing at NAS Patuxent River, the aircraft was almost lost when Major Marion Carl, USMC accidentally feathered the propeller while checking it for different stroboscopic effects. Carl pulled the prop control back against the low rpm stop while flying 130 mph at 7,000 ft. The prop rpm stabilized but then started to slowly drop, even after Carl advanced the throttle. The prop remained fully feathered even when he advanced the prop control to 2,700 rpm. In desperation, Carl dove the stricken XF8B-1 at a speed between 230 to 250 mph, regaining control of the prop at 4,000 ft. When informed of the incident, Aeroproducts attributed the near loss of the aircraft to bad piloting on the part of Carl.

The XF8B-1 was subsequently flown by Lamson and Jensen to Anacostia for further evaluation. BuAer sent out a memorandum to selected departments on March 28, 1945, advising that the aircraft would be available for inspection by interested personnel on April 5. Ten pilots checked out on

Photo: Bob Lamson Collection

Test Pilot Bob Lamson posing for the camera. This photo may have been taken after the XF8B-1 was evaluated by the Navy at NAS Patuxent River and Anacostia - note the weathering on the Insignia Blue stripe that ran along the right side of the fuselage

it April 6 and 7.

The XF8B-1 was returned to Seattle on April 9. The special organization set up to produce the XF8B-1 was broken up and new supervisors and employees were put on the contract. Veteran engineers were put on more promising projects, such as the B-47.

On March 16, Boeing advised the BAR that it had filed patent applications for the XF8B-1's ammunition storage and feed mechanism as well as its rudder pedal mechanism. It also advised that it was considering filing patent applications for other inventions made in the performance of the XF8B-1 contract, to which the BAR had no objection.

The issue of cost overruns came up again on April 21, when BAR Proctor wrote a letter to BuAer defending the "excessive" expenditure requests periodically submitted by the company for work done on the XF8B-1 contract. At the time, Boeing was drafting a request for an additional $2,500,000 to cover costs for XF8B-1 development, and Proctor sought to justify the request before it was sent. He noted that "...basically the Contractor's organization, as in the case of many other contractors, is geared to the high production of aircraft. In the transition from 'Small Business' to 'Big Business', the experimental shop and/or facilities for the prompt and inexpensive execution of minor changes has fallen by the wayside." Boeing's paperwork and procedures necessary to accomplishing a change on an experimental aircraft were similar to those required for changes in production aircraft, resulting in delays and complications. This in turn caused an increase in costs, and until such time that Boeing devised a special simplified provision for the handling of changes on the XF8B-1, Proctor felt that BuAer should expect rather "startling" figures, considering the nature of the work involved.

On April 24, Boeing sent its formal letter to the BAR requesting an additional $2,506,393.79 for a total of $7,950,027.15, exclusive of the estimated cost of change proposals then being prepared and the estimated cost of future design changes.

The additional funds were required for several reasons. The duration of the project had exceeded Boeing's expectations, and additional delays were anticipated that would cause the XF8B-1 contract to remain active for some time. The lack of engines prevented completion of the second and third prototypes, and it was impossible to get an accurate delivery date for the engines. The preliminary Navy flight tests then underway at NAS Patuxent River were not anticipated in any previous estimates and served to extend the duration of the flight test program. During flight testing at Boeing, unexpected difficulties with aileron flutter were encountered, necessitating additional work to correct the problem. Boeing held that as long as the XF8B-1 contract remained active and engineering problems remained to be solved, it was impossible to hold to original cost estimates. Continuing the project required the maintenance of both an engineering and production crew, which could not function efficiently due to delays and uncertainty as to future work to be accomplished as a result of desirable refinements in the airplanes. An increasing amount of engineering work resulted from BuAer's requests to perform complete and thorough stress analyses and extensive static testing. The thoroughness of these programs was to expedite possible future production.

Boeing was still holding out hope for a possible production contract and continued to investigate various alternate equipment for the XF8B-1. For example, the aircraft's landing gear knuckles were originally designed and released on the basis of available tools and materials; they were not the most efficient design from the standpoint of weight and aerodynamic drag. New knuckles were designed and procured, permitting a considerable reduction in the size of the fairing that extended below the rear star when the gear was retracted. Similar investigations were being carried out in connection with single disk brakes and other items. Flight tests had shown that aerodynamic refinements to the XF8B-1 materially benefited its performance; for instance, engine cooling drag had already been reduced and it was believed that additional refinements could be made when a satisfactory engine became available.

The company made a significant expenditure of engineering hours in connection with new proposals that, it was anticipated, would not be incorporated in the airplanes on the subject contract. These included the investigation of revised torpedo provisions as well as provisions for other external equipment. Also in this category were attack version studies of the XF8B-1, including two-seater arrangements.

Boeing wrote BuAer on April 24 to inform them that the completion of the second and third prototypes of the XF8B-1 was still being delayed by the non-availability of the engines; the company suggested installing the first production engine in the third article if it became available. Boeing also advised BuAer that the Aeroproducts propeller damaged in the belly landing of XF8B-1 no. 57984 had been returned to Aeroproducts for repair. The hub was repairable but the blades were a total loss. Boeing was uncertain as to whether a fifth Aeroproducts propeller should be procured, as the XF8B-1's future was in doubt.

BuAer responded on May 17 regarding the Aeroproducts propeller issue. Due to the cancellation of the Fisher P-75 program, the Army had a surplus of Aeroproducts AD7562-A1 counter-rotating propellers equipped with 12' 7" diameter blades. If required, one of these hubs could have been procured and allocated to Boeing for immediate installation. BuAer also authorized Boeing to procure a set of six additional 13' 0" diameter blades. These blades and a suitable hub procured from the Army would then be available for quick change, if required.

On May 30, the BAR sent BuAer a telegram with an update on the status of XF8B-1 flight tests. On May 29, two flights were made totaling 64 minutes. The total flight time to date was 105 hours and 4 minutes. A preliminary evaluation of a new aileron configuration with vibration instrumentation had been made at speeds up to 200 mph. The engine and associated equipment functioned satisfactorily, with additional flights taking place that day.

On June 4, the BAR sent a telegram to BuAer regarding ongoing problems with engine availability. BuAer had stated that R-4360 engine serial P-28 would be shipped by May 20, with a government furnished production engine following on June 1. However, Pratt & Whitney had advised Boeing that engine no. P-28 had failed on its final test and that it wouldn't be able to advise a new shipping date pending evaluation of the extent of damage and procurement of replacement parts. Boeing urgently desired to get the second XF8B-1 on flight status and asked BuAer to expedite delivery of a production engine to achieve this.

R.W. Schroeder of BuAer responded on June 7, advising the BAR that the first production R-4360-10 serial P-61 was assembled and would be shipped rail express when delivered. Engine serial P-28 was also to be shipped rail express when available. Pratt & Whitney was under continuous pressure to improve deliveries. BuAer suggested using an unmodernized serial P-30 engine, but as Boeing did not desire using an unmodernized engine, BuAer knew of no other action to improve engine availability.

On June 27, E.J. Gorman of the BuAer Costs and Changes Branch issued a detailed summary of the cost overruns occurring with the XF8B-1 contract. The original estimated cost of $3,482,295 and a fixed fee of $100,000 covered the design and manufacture of three XF8B-1 airplanes and one static test article. Engines and propellers were furnished by Boeing, and an item was included in the contract to furnish structural spare parts at a money value of approximately 20% of the value of the airplanes. Boeing later requested an additional $1,870,000 to complete the contract, which BuAer agreed to. Still struggling to hold down costs, Boeing subsequently estimated that the cost of the XF8B-1 contract would be $7,950,027.15, requiring BuAer to provide an additional amount of $2,506,393.79.

When the contract for the XF8B-1 was entered into in early 1943, very little information was available on just what engineering and manufacturing problems would be involved. Therefore, the only way of evaluating the proposed estimated cost was to compare the original estimate to the initial costs per pound for other experimental airplanes. No actual cost experience was available on other comparable experimental airplanes being manufactured under war time conditions, and as only a nominal fee was involved in the case of the XF8B-1 contract, the use of a cost per pound comparison as a basis for arriving at an estimated cost was considered to be reasonable under the circumstances. Based on a net structural weight of approximately 7,700 lbs. per airplane, Boeing's original estimated cost of approximately $3,018,610 for three airplanes and one static test article, less the cost of engines and propellers, amounted to $102.50 per pound. The cost per pound figure was less than the initial costs per pound established for other experimental airplanes, as the costs per pound for those ranged from $128.00 and $230.00 per pound.

Subsequent to negotiating the estimated cost for the subject contract, later information was obtained on the anticipated actual cost of some other experimental contracts, and in all cases the actual cost for such airplanes exceeded $250.00 per pound. In some cases the actual cost per pound was as much as $350.00 to $400.00 for combat airplanes. In the case of the XF8B-1 contract, the actual cost per pound was $241.00.

When consideration was given to the fact that many complications had arisen in the construction of these airplanes which were not foreseen at the time of entering into the contract, delaying completion of the project, Gorman believed that the overrun of cost was not unreasonable. Furthermore, the lack of experienced engineers and shop workers made it necessary to compile more complete engineering data and to manufacture more accurate tooling in order to insure proper fit and alignment of parts. Gorman considered that the expenditures were warranted, especially since only those costs which were considered by the BAR and the Cost Inspector to have been necessary for the performance of the contract were allowable under the contract. He also noted that if the anticipated actual cost under the contract had been established as the original estimated costs, Boeing would have received a fee of at least $110,000 more than was established under the contract on the basis of the original estimate. Gorman's report was persuasive, and BuAer ultimately released additional funds to cover the overrun.

On June 30, the Boeing raised the subject of flame damping with the BAR. Boeing noted that the exhaust system of the XF8B-1 consisted of fourteen exhaust headers, each of which received the exhaust gas from two cylinders so timed with respect to each other that the action within a single header was similar to that of a single stack. All of these headers were relatively long with the exception of two which were located on opposite sides of the aircraft.

In the event that a production version of the XF8B-1 was initiated, Boeing anticipated that development of flame damping would be preceded by observations of the visibility of the exhaust system under night flight conditions. It was believed that the existing system was basically good as a result of the relatively long stacks and because most of the existing outlet locations were such that the gas was expelled into the high velocity air stream. Boeing suggested rerouting the two shorter headers and conducting a study to realize the full advantage of the existing basic system and develop the best type of stack outlet shape, followed by actual installation and test of outlet sections. As far as is known, this study was never carried out.

On July 21, Boeing added two additional fuel tanks per aircraft after inspection of the mock-up by BuAer officials, increasing the wing span of the airplane to accommodate them. No photos or drawings of this proposed modification have thus far been located.

On August 8, Boeing Vice President J.P. Murray wrote the Aeronautical Board requesting a Release for Foreign Sale for the XF8B-1. He noted that Boeing had been informally advised by BuAer that the Navy was not interested in procuring a production quantity or even a service test quantity of the aircraft. Given the circumstances, Boeing felt it was justified in requesting the release of the XF8B-1 for foreign sale.

At the request of Boeing, this request was later canceled in a letter from the Aeronautical Board dated August 18. Perhaps the Navy had indicated that there was still the possibility of production, or Boeing felt that there wouldn't be sufficient foreign orders to warrant further investment in the program. The matter remains unclear.

On August 14, XF8B-1 no. 57984 was grounded due to a failure of the engine reduction gear. It remained grounded until BuAer released another R-4360 engine for flight operations.

Boeing wrote the BAR on August 31 regarding the general status of the XF8B-1 contract and costs incurred there under. Several engineering studies remained to be performed:

1) Installation of a Grizzly solid tire wheel on all three prototypes.
2) Study of a night fighter version.
3) Study of a .60 cal. gun installation.

The night fighter study was cancelled on October 2, while the .60 cal. gun study was cancelled shortly thereafter. The company also felt that some engineering changes were essential to the pilot and/or the airplane:

1) Redesign of cockpit enclosure. New enclosures were to be provided for all airplanes to improve opening and closing operation and jettisoning in flight. Actual manufacture had only recently started.
2) Construction and installation of dive flaps on all three prototypes. Although not proven necessary by actual flight tests, it was considered essential by Boeing that dive flaps be provided.

The final changes considered by Boeing to be the minimum commensurate with the delivery of an acceptable flying airplane:

1) Provision of proper spring tubes in the aileron spring tab system.
2) Provision of aileron tabs of contour in accordance with the configuration finally adopted.
3) Installation of a bus cable system to prevent aileron up-drift otherwise resulting from spring tab action.

Boeing re-examined the complete flight test program for the XF8B-1 with a view to the development of a minimum test program consistent with the then-current status of the prototypes and the lack of a requirement for a production version.

In September 1945, Boeing updated BuAer regarding the propeller situation. Boeing had 4 Aeroproducts propellers and 1 Curtiss propeller on order. Two Aeroproducts and 1 Curtiss propeller were in Seattle; 1 Aeroproducts was loaned for the XBTC-2 program and 1 reworked Aeroproducts was due for delivery in Seattle in the near future. Since 3 Aeroproducts propellers would soon be available in Seattle for the 3 XF8B-1 prototypes, Boeing felt that the Army surplus 12' 7" diameter Aeroproducts unit was not necessary for temporary installation.

On September 14, Boeing requested approval of pilots E.S. Osler and J.A. Fraser to test fly the XF8B-1. Each had significant experience as engineering test pilots and had already completed familiarization flights. BuAer subsequently authorized both to fly the aircraft.

On September 19, 1945 Boeing proposed procuring the Curtiss propeller but canceling its performance testing. Boeing was trying to deliver the XF8B-1 prototypes with the minimum expenditure of time at the earliest possible calendar date. Testing of the Curtiss propeller served a doubtful purpose, given that it would have delayed delivery of one of the prototypes and that there was no requirement for a production version of the aircraft. BuAer concurred with Boeing on October 12.

XF8B-1 no. 57984 was released for flight on October 22. Two flights of 53 minutes total time were accomplished, though difficulty with the electrical system was experienced, requiring investigation.

By October 31, Boeing had expended and/or obligated $7,190,000.00 against the $8,091,513.64 estimated contract cost. The allotted funds for the gun tests had already been exceeded, and Boeing suggested a reduction in the program. Boeing estimated that twenty to twenty-five thousand dollars would be required to cover tests of the .50 cal. M-3 gun demanded by the BuAer. Boeing wished to retain the remaining unexpended funds in full to cover anticipated costs in completing the contract, including the remaining gun firing tests.

In the last quarter of 1945, Boeing experienced a temporary stoppage of work due to a strike, considerably slowing progress on the XF8B-1 contract. To compound the company's misfortunes, BuAer requested that the BAR seek to immediately curtail the XF8B-1 contract in the most economical manner which would allow for the delivery of three airplanes useable for miscellaneous test purposes, a production contract being definitely unlikely. Partial termination was being considered on basis that work under contract would be limited to that necessary to demonstrate airplanes to suitable restricted limits and to that work necessary for delivery to the Navy of acceptable flying airplanes. BuAer requested that the BAR and a representative from Boeing come immediately to Washington, D.C. to assist in the termination procedure.

On December 26, test pilot Bob Lamson nearly lost his life in XF8B-1 no. 57985. Approximately 15 minutes after takeoff and some 30 miles north of Seattle at 3,500 ft. altitude, the aircraft experienced engine failure when the throttle was moved to full open. The failure was accompanied by emission of black smoke from the exhaust and a reduction of engine speed to slightly above normal idling RPM. Operation at idling speed appeared normal but the engine did not respond to increased throttle. Lamson checked the fuel, oil pressure and supercharger control position; he endeavored to secure normal engine operation by means of adjusting mixture control without success, whereupon a landing was made at Everett, Washington Municipal Airport. During the latter part of the landing, soft ground was encountered and the airplane nosed up, damaging the propeller and landing gear fairing. A possible cause of the engine failure was believed to be faulty carburetion or air inductions. Steps were taken to determine the exact cause of engine failure and return the damaged aircraft to the hangar at Boeing Field.

Subsequent investigation of the engine failure determined that a small screw had been sucked up through the induction system, becoming lodged under one of the intake valves and causing a backfire. Minor problems such as these paled in comparison to the larger problems the XF8B-1 contract was experiencing as a whole, with Boeing's big fighter now standing almost no chance of production.

4

1946
Army Evaluation & Navy Cancellation

In response to a request from the BAR, Boeing provided an update on February 15, 1946 regarding the remaining work schedule flight test program and anticipated delivery dates of the three XF8B-1 prototypes.

All remaining Boeing evaluation flight tests, as well as all final demonstrations to the BAR, would be accomplished with airplane no. 57986 and resulted in a delivery date sometime during the first half of July. Airplane nos. 57985 and 57984 would be delivered subsequent to the first of June and the first of May, respectively.

It was planned to have XF8B-1 no. 57986 completed by March 5, after which it would be placed on a flight test status with intent to perform the propeller vibration tests, remaining evaluation tests and final demonstrations. Airplane no. 57984 had been returned to the factory and was brought up to date in accordance to the latest standard. As this airplane had been on flight test status for over a year, there remained a considerable number of changes to be accomplished. Airplane no. 57985 was delivered on February 13, 1946 to the Army for evaluation tests by ATSC. This XF8B-1 was essentially complete except for items such as the new canopy, which were left incomplete in order to make the airplane available for Army tests at the earliest possible time. When this airplane was returned by the Army, it was necessary to complete several additional changes to bring it up to date.

On February 25, Boeing provided an outline to the BAR detailing the remaining work needed to complete each of the XF8B-1 prototypes:

Airplane no. 57984

1) New canopy, windshield and related work including removal of old windshield. This required removal of practically every installation in the cockpit.
2) Several items remained incomplete because of test requirements: the oxygen system, CO_2 system, heating system, landing gear uplock, and radio.
3) Installation of armament including alternate installation.
4) Installation of dive flaps, aileron buss system, wing folding mechanism, pin pulling mechanism, arresting hook, bomb door actuating system, gun camera, exhaust stack seals, landing gear fairings, Mach number indicators, and second stage coupling oil pressure gauges.
5) Revision of landing gear, landing gear doors, propeller controls, and aerodynamic tab nose contours. Re-alignment of right hand drag strut and examination of retracting mechanisms.
6) Complete checkout of electrical system to bring up-to-date after removal of instrumentation.

Photo: National Archives, RG 72-AC

XF8B-1 no. 57986 as it appeared on June 26, 1946. This was the third and final example of Boeing's big fighter. Note the Glossy Sea Blue color scheme, which had become standard for most Navy aircraft by this time.

7) Application of aerodynamic smoother, camouflage; installation of charts, chart boards, armor plate, relief tubes, cockpit finish.
8) Incorporation of about 500 deviations, most of which were included in work listed above; also included a number of minor installations.

Airplane no. 57985
1) New canopy, windshield and related work including removal of old windshield. This required removal of practically every installation in the cockpit.
2) Installation of wing folding and pin pulling mechanisms, gun camera, landing gear spherical collars, wing flap sliding connectors, reinstallation of landing gear uplock, reinstallation of cabin heating.
3) Approximately 100 deviations to be picked up.

Airplane no. 57986
This airplane was in the final stages of completion at the factory. The work remaining consisted of essentially of pick-up items, functional test and camouflage.

The BAR updated BuAer on March 6 regarding the state of the XF8B-1's exhaust system. Boeing made minor changes in the system which eliminated some of the trouble experienced during flight tests, but problems persisted, necessitating repair after 10 to 12 hours flight time. The condition was unsatisfactory and the exhaust system was considered not acceptable for final delivery to the Navy. Boeing was required to have a more acceptable exhaust system on the XF8B-1 prior to delivery.

On April 16, Boeing provided the BAR with a summary of the flight operations of XF8B-1 no. 57985 while under Army evaluation at Wright Field and while performing propeller vibration tests at Vandalia, Ohio. The airplane was delivered to the Army ferry pilot at Seattle on February 13 and delivery to Wright Field was accomplished in two flights without incident other than a slight oil leak, which was corrected at Ogden, Utah.

Between February 18 and March 5, 1946, the Army accomplished 15 pilot evaluation flights for a total of approximately 16 flight hours. These evaluation flights were accomplished on the airplane in a fighter gross weight condition, except for the addition of the empty internal bomb bay tank and the addition of the two external bomb racks and the two empty external fuel tanks. The only mechanical trouble reported during these flights was one minor crack in an exhaust stack and one instance wherein the wing flaps did not retract immediately upon operation of the wing flap switch. The latter difficulty was corrected by readjustment of the micro-positioner flap operation switch.

On February 28, March 7 and March 11, three attempts were made to accomplish long-range cruise flights with 954 gallons of fuel aboard. Each of these flights was terminated at 5.5 hours, 3.3 hours and 5.3 hours, respectively due to rough engine operation and excessive backfiring. This roughness developed toward the end of each flight after continuous operation in long-range cruise settings. The exact cause of the engine roughness had not been determined. However, as this condition did not apparently affect operation of the engine under higher powers, the long-range cruise attempts were discontinued and the Army proceeded to accomplish the remaining evaluation flights with external and bomb bay tanks removed.

Between March 11 and March 22, nine Army pilot evaluation flights for a total of approximately ten flight hours were accomplished on the airplane. For these flights the airplane was in the fighter configuration with bomb bay tank removed and with external bomb racks and tanks also removed. No malfunctions occurred on these flights.

Upon completion of the above tests, the Army delivered the airplane to Boeing representatives at Vandalia, Ohio in order to permit the company to conduct flight propeller vibration tests. By March 29, the installation of vibration test equipment in the airplane was completed. On March 30, one test was accomplished and on April 1 two further tests were successfully accomplished. These flights were without incident, other than difficulty with oscillation of the torquemeter indicator. Three flights were completed on April 2. Upon inspection after the last flight it was found that one exhaust stack was broken. During the first flight attempt on April 3 the engine lost power and an emergency landing was made at the Dayton Airport in Vandalia. Upon investigation it was found that the main engine impeller drive had sheared. Examination of the main engine screen revealed that some very small steel particles had passed through the accessory section oil screen. Upon removal of the accessory section oil screen some large portions of gear teeth were found. Further examination also revealed steel particles at the entrance to and in the oil coolers. As a result of this difficulty, Boeing and Pratt & Whitney recommended a complete engine change.

It was planned to have Pratt & Whitney ship XR-4360-10 engine serial no. P-30 by rail express to Vandalia on approximately April 12 for installation in the XF8B-1. Boeing representatives at Vandalia were to accomplish the engine change with the assistance of Aeroproducts facilities and return the damaged engine, serial no. P-23, to Pratt & Whitney, East Harford, Connecticut, for survey, repair and overhaul, if possible. Boeing estimated that the installation of the new engine required between two to three weeks; the XF8B-1 could not be returned to flight status prior to the second week of May.

The instrumented Aeroproducts propeller as well as the propeller vibration test equipment were removed from the airplane and shipped to Seattle, where Boeing planned on immediately completing the propeller vibration tests on airplane no. 57986, which had just been placed on flight status.

At the time, Boeing had not determined the action to be taken with respect to the XF8B-1 after completion of the engine installation. It was believed that if a propeller could be made available by Aeroproducts by the time the engine installation was completed, the airplane would be returned to the Army at Wright Field for completion of the previously scheduled evaluation of the airplane's offensive equipment at Eglin Field, Florida, which had been interrupted to allow Boeing to complete the propeller flight vibration survey.

On April 23, Boeing sent a letter to the BAR listing major design changes made to the XF8B-1 since preliminary evaluation at Pax River in March of 1945. A summary of these changes had been requested by Lt. Col. M.E. Carl, USMC while visiting the Boeing plant during the week of April 8, 1946.

Since the airplane returned from preliminary evaluation at NAS Patuxent River, Boeing had completed exhaustive flight tests with various control surface configurations in order to develop an airplane that equaled or exceeded the contract guaranteed performance. The configuration changes made greatly improved the flight characteristics and consisted basically of the following:

a) When the airplane was at Pax River, the ailerons were directly connected to the control stick and utilized a link tab for reduction in control forces. The previously designed spring tab aileron system was removed from the XF8B-1 because early test flights at Boeing had indicated the possibility of aileron flutter above 450 mph air speeds. Through redesign and the medium of mechanically induced vibration of the ailerons in flight, Boeing was able to completely eliminate any possibility of aileron flutter and equipped the ailerons with aerodynamically balanced spring tabs through which the ailerons were actuated. Replacement of the interim link tab aileron installed for the Pax River tests by the existing spring tab installation greatly improved the rate of roll. Roll rates in the neighborhood of 90° per second at 300 mph were obtained. It was believed that further improvement in aileron roll characteristics could be achieved either by refinements to the spring tab system by use of a power boost in conjunction with the existing arrangement. The operation of a boost mock-up suitable for use in this manner had shown very satisfactory control characteristics.

b) The elevators on the airplane tested at Pax River were of the conventional aerodynamically balanced type conforming to the basic stabilizer airfoil section. These elevators were replaced with aerodynamically balanced elevators having 1% bulbous contours and the elevator control tabs had been rerigged to provide an automatically variable boost ratio to provide the optimum pilot effort throughout the full elevator range. As a result, the heaviness of the elevators flown at Pax River was substantially reduced. Reduction in the landing forces was also achieved.

c) The rudder was lightened by use of more tab balance in order to provide better coordination with the lightened ailerons described above. Full rudder deflection was possible up to speeds of approximately 250 mph.
d) A cable buss system was installed to eliminate any undesirable affect from aileron up-drift which normally occurred at low speeds with ailerons operated through spring tabs.
e) The jet exhaust stack outlets were redesigned in order to increase the high speed of the airplane through reduction of internal engine cooling air drag, which reduction was made possible by the remarkably low cooling air requirements of the Wasp Major engine.
f) The leading edge contour of the engine airscoop was redesigned to increase its critical Mach number, thus improving performance.
g) The difficulties with the second stage section of the Wasp Major engine that had caused Pratt & Whitney to forbid its use when the airplane was at Pax River were corrected and operation of the engine in the second stage was satisfactory.

Boeing accomplished a number of revisions that enhanced the overall value of the XF8B-1, such as improved safety, improved functionality of airplane components, and generally improved reliability. Some of the major changes included:

a) A completely new canopy and windshield was designed and installed. This change raised the critical Mach number, reduced drag, improved the jettisoning characteristics of the canopy, increased the cockpit cabin pressure, improved visibility both fore and aft, and generally improved the overall appearance of the airplane.
b) The canopy jettison control was moved from the top of the windshield to a location in the cockpit floor between the pilot's feet. This relocation was made to cause the pilot to assume a crouched position in releasing the canopy and thus lessen the possibility of his being struck by the canopy as it left the airplane.
c) The Goodyear multi-disk brakes that were considered marginal at Pax River were replaced with Goodyear single-disk self-energizing brakes on airplane serial no. 57986.
d) A small dive flap was installed on the underside of each wing. This installation was made solely as a safety feature in the event of difficulty in dive recovery. If dive tests indicated the feature was unnecessary, they could have been eliminated from future procurement.
e) All changes required as a result of completion of static tests were accomplished and the airplane was structurally sounder than required by the contract.
f) The tail wheel lock control handle was lengthened to overcome objections noted by Pax River test pilots.
g) The development of the micro-position pre-selection wing flap control switch was completed and this switch replaced the inadequate up-down switch that was in the airplane at Pax River.
h) The wing flap and landing gear emergency manual retracting systems were redesigned to reduce the pilot effort required.
i) The propeller control was slightly revised to provide a more nearly linear relationship between governing and control handle movement.
j) The wing flap flexible drive control system was equipped with specially designed automatically adjustable connections to eliminate service and maintenance difficulties inherent in the original system.
k) The landing gear up-lock system was installed.
l) Changes were made in the design of some of the exhaust stacks to increase reliability.
m) The semi-automatic cowl flap system on the airplane at

Pax River proved sufficiently undesirable in service to make desirable a complete redesign of the cowl flap operation system. A new positive system was installed and was considered very satisfactory.

n) The airspeed indicator was replaced with a combination Mach number and airspeed indicator to increase safety by simplifying high speed placarding of the airplane.

Boeing completed the installation of certain design features required by specification but left them out of the airplane as tested at Pax River to facilitate developmental flight test work. Some of these items were:

a) Interchangeable .50 cal. and 20 mm. armament installations were completed.
b) All armor plate protection was installed.
c) All internal and external bombing provisions including the snap-action bomb door actuating system were completed.
d) All arrested landing provisions were completely installed.
e) The wing folding provisions were complete.
e) The installation of cockpit and windshield heating systems was completed and tested to satisfaction.

Commander J.P. Sager of BuAer wrote the BAR on May 2 regarding issues with the XF8B-1's engine and exhaust system. He noted that very little flight time had been accumulated on Navy airplanes employing the R-4360 engine. Reports had been received of failures on the F2G Super Corsair that occurred after a few hours, and failures of cylinder head exhaust inserts had occurred on both F2G and BTM type airplanes. Such failures indicated that neither of these two systems was entirely satisfactory. It was also believed that exhaust system operation on the R-4360 engine would be as severe as on the R-2800 or R-3350 engines.

BuAer considered that fifty hours of flight time at high power without failure should be accumulated on the XF8B-1 airplane exhaust system to assure satisfactory operation. If Boeing was unable to accumulate this flight time prior to delivery, part of it was to be conducted by the Navy; however, at least two sets of stacks were to be provided in order to prevent delay in tests in case of failures.

No drawings or photographs of satisfactory exhaust stacks for R-4360 engines were available at the time. It was considered that if the XF8B-1 airplane exhaust system were made identical to the BTM-1 exhaust system, a separate development program for the XF8B-1 airplane would not be necessary.

BuAer recommended that sufficient spare exhaust stacks be delivered with the airplanes to avoid delays in flight schedules due to stack failures. It was suggested that an alternate design of heavier gauge material be provided as a standby for tests at the Service Test Section of Pax River.

On May 15, the Army issued a report recording the results of pilot's

Photo: Bob Dorr Collection

Photographs of the second XF8B-1 prototype, BuAer No. 57985, have been difficult to find (or at least reliably identify). This photo may be of its first test flight, which occurred at Boeing on November 27, 1945. The aircraft would later be evaluated and rejected by the Army in May of 1946.

Photo: Bob Dorr Collection

Distant shot of the second XF8B-1, possibly during its first test flight. This is the only other photo the author has of no. 57985, which seems to be the least photographed of the three fighters. In any case, it differed little in external appearance from the third prototype.

observations conducted on XF8B-1 serial no. 57985 at Wright Field from February 15 to March 15, 1946. The airplane was flown by 18 pilots for a total of 35 hours, and their overall evaluation was not favorable.

Pilots found most of the controls, switches, and instruments in the cockpit to be conveniently located. They disliked the almost vertical position of the rudder pedal, which caused excessive leg fatigue. No parking brake was provided, also causing excessive fatigue. The flight indicator and rate of climb indicator were partially obscured by the gun sight. The cowl flaps required manual operation and frequent attention of the pilot. Pilots recommended that the mixture control be moved away from the throttle and propeller control. The control for the supercharger was very sensitive and the change from low to high stage was not accomplished satisfactorily. The location of the flap six position selector switch was such that it required a slight ducking of the pilot's head to select the desired position.

A manual tail wheel lock was controlled by a handle at the left side of the seat. The lack of torque reduced the necessity of a tail wheel lock. However, if the tail wheel was not straight, it would not retract properly when the wheels were retracted.

The canopy on the test airplane was poorly designed as to size and reduced the critical Mach number of the airplane. Boeing's engineers stated that future airplanes would be provided with a smaller canopy and re-designed windshield with a resulting increased critical Mach number. Fit of the canopy to the fuselage was also poor and even with it closed as completely as possible, cracks and gaps were present between the bubble and the windshield and around the lower edge of the canopy. Side vision was somewhat distorted by imperfections in the plastic bubble. The canopy was operated by a hand crank on the right side of the cockpit. The crank gear ratio was too high, causing slow canopy operation. The canopy latch consisted of a positive lock on the crank and was not very satisfactory. Emergency exit was accomplished by jettisoning the canopy. The release handle was located between the pilot's feet in the floor. This was considered a very good feature as it caused the pilot to bend over and lower his head before releasing the canopy. Access to the cockpit was difficult because of the height of the wing. A retractable step was recommended to provide easier access.

The brakes on the XF8B-1 were not considered adequate for the weight. All pilots reported heavy leg fatigue after just a few minutes of taxiing. The vertical surfaces of the tail were very large, the brakes were weak, making taxiing in a cross wind difficult. Locking the tail wheel helped offset this condition, but forward visibility was restricted, necessitating "S" turns for safe taxiing.

Takeoff was accomplished with a short ground roll of approximately 800 to 1,000 ft. The takeoff and landing roll was very satisfactory with no ground looping tendency or torque effect. The good directional stability during the takeoff run partially eliminated the necessity of having a locking tail wheel. A steerable tail wheel was recommended to improve takeoff, landing, and taxiing characteristics.

Control during initial climb was satisfactory due to the lack of torque and trimming of the airplane was easily accomplished. Vision was ample except for the normal straight ahead blind spot. Initial rate of climb was approximately 3,000 ft. per minute.

Control, trim and visibility during climb were satisfactory. Boeing stated that the best climbing indicated airspeed to be 163 mph; however, in the opinion of Fighter Section pilots, a figure of between 140 and 150 mph was more nearly correct. Due to the fact that no climb performance tests were run, this contention could not be substantiated.

The handling characteristics of the XF8B-1 were considered excellent at low speeds. Takeoff, landing, and "go-around" after an unsuccessful landing were accomplished with minimal effort. However, the controls tightened up considerably with increased speed. The rate of roll was about average at speeds 300 mph indicated airspeed (IAS). Above this speed the aileron forces were excessive. The radius of turn was excellent at all speeds.

Directional and lateral trim was easily accomplished with the controls provided. The airplane was well rigged for speeds from cruising (250 mph IAS) downward. Directional trim changed slightly at high speed but all control forces were easily trimmed out. Neutral lateral stability was evidenced.

Longitudinal stability of the airplane was acceptable. Short period longitudinal oscillations damped out in one-half to one cycle. However, if the XF8B-1 was not precisely trimmed before testing for this condition, a divergent long period oscillation was induced. Longitudinal trim was slightly difficult to accomplish because of this stability characteristic. This constituted an undesirable characteristic in a long-range airplane.

Stall warning was considered marginal, consisting of a slight buffeting and sinking sensation two or three mph before the actual stall. Indicated stall speeds for level flight, one "g" stall, power off, external wing tanks on, were observed to be: clean, 103 mph; wheels down, 105 mph; wheels and flaps down, 85 mph. With external tanks off, these speeds were reduced 3 mph. A severe break to the left was encountered in a stall in the landing configuration with external tanks installed and such a condition was considered quite dangerous if encountered during a carrier approach. All stalls without external tanks were clean and straight ahead. For the power on approach configuration, without external tanks, the indicated stall speed was 70 mph.

Maneuverability of the XF8B-1 was comparable to that of most conventional AAF Fighters. Control forces were reasonable in all maneuvers except that ailerons became increasingly stiff above 300 mph IAS. All aerobatics were easily accomplished. High speed dives required little change in directional trim and this condition enhanced the utility of the airplane as a dive bomber. Extension of either landing gear or flaps caused a slight nose heavy condition that was easily trimmed out.

The noise level of the XF8B-1 was slightly high and it was felt that a better fitting canopy would greatly reduce it. Vibration was moderate at cruising speeds or below. At high speeds, vibration became excessive. Engine and propeller vibration was low at all power settings.

The cockpit of the airplane was well arranged from the standpoint of minimizing effort on the part of the pilot. However, the relation of the seat position to the rudder pedal position was not suitable for comfortable seating. The control stick grip was a little high for pilot comfort. For long-range missions, it was recommended that some method be provided for the pilot to change his body position longitudinally as well as vertically.

Heat was provided by warm air taken from around the exhaust stacks. This was adequate for heating the cockpit but carried the possibility of carbon monoxide poisoning.

Vision in level flight was excellent. Vision while taxiing and in climbs was partially obscured by the nose but was fair. Vision in the approach was very good.

The normal approach speed was 120 to 130 mph IAS. Control was excellent at this speed. The airplane touched down on the landing at 85 mph IAS. There was no tendency to drop a wing or ground loop on the landing roll. "Go around" was accomplished very easily either with wheels and flaps down or by retracting them. Very little sink resulted from raising the flaps.

During normal, local flights the R-4360 was found to be a very satisfactory and smooth running engine, and no maintenance problems were encountered, with the exception of occasional slight oil leaks from the rocker boxes. Simulated long-range missions were attempted, but they had to be abandoned in each case after three to six hours at low powers, due to fouling of the spark plugs. Head temperatures varied from 130° to 220° C with fully closed cowl flaps. A rich mixture was possibly the cause of excessive cooling of the rear banks of cylinders. Sensitive and unsatisfactory supercharger operation also was noted in the one altitude flight that was made. Propeller operation was satisfactory and proper governing was attainable down to 1,300 to 1,400 rpm.

Landing gear retraction and extension were accomplished in a fairly short period. Flap extension was slightly slow. All engine accessories and cooling shutters operating electrically functioned normally.

The emergency system on the XF8B-1 was very poor, and the lowering of the landing gear or flaps was accomplished by placing a small hand crank in the proper hole on the right side wall of the cockpit and cranking them down. Two hundred and thirty turns were required to lower the landing gear; three hundred sixty for the flaps.

Performance flights with the XF8B-1 to obtain maximum range and endurance were not completed due to malfunctioning of the engine. Several attempts were made to obtain satisfactory results, but no flight lasted longer than 5.5 hours, which was less than half the time required to complete a mission. No accurate results could be shown using the limited amount of data obtained.

The general opinion of Army pilots was that an airplane as large as the XF8B-1 and designed to carry the load might also have the added safety of two engines. The advantages as a long-range fighter are greatly reduced by excessive fatigue of the pilot. High speed performance, maneuverability, and stability had been sacrificed for low speed stability and control. Observations were made according to standards as maintained for Army Fighter type aircraft.

On May 20, Boeing proposed to BuAer the design and construction of one complete production power plant quick-change engine unit at a price of $124,890.69, $52,975.12 more than initially estimated. The quick-change engine unit consisted of the entire power plant installation forward of the fuselage firewall. Despite the cost overrun, BuAer accepted the proposal.

The final demonstration of the XF8B-1 was accomplished in July of 1946 in the vicinity of Seattle, Washington before representatives of BuAer. Boeing felt that it had met most of the guarantees demanded in the original contract:

1) Each airplane as a fighter was satisfactory in all respects for naval service as a fighter airplane.
2) The XF8B-1 had not made a takeoff or landing on a carrier nor operated from a catapult, and thus could not be evaluated on these points.
3) The data of the final demonstration showed the airplane to be in correct flying balance, controllable and stable in the air about each of the three major axes with either free or fixed longitudinal, lateral and directional controls.
4) The data of the final demonstration showed the airplane to be controllable and stable on the ground.
5) The ability of the airplane to make satisfactory takeoffs and landings on an ordinary landing field was demonstrated to a representative of BuAer on each of the tests on the final demonstration.
6) BuAer held that Boeing was responsible the aircraft being 1,401 pounds overweight in empty condition.

The following chart represents a comparison of the actual performance with guaranteed performance:

Condition	Performance Comparison	
	Guarantee	Actual
(a) Maximum speed at engine military rated power (5 mins. max. duration) and at airplane critical altitude (external droppable fuel dropped)	not less than 429 mph	432 mph
(b) Maximum speed at engine normal rated power and airplane critical altitude	not less than 416 mph	420 mph
(c) Minimum speed without power at sea level	not more than 79 mph	79 mph
(d) Service ceiling, starting with normal load and using normal power	not less than 30,000 ft.	approx. 37,500 ft.
(e) Takeoff distance in a 25-knot wind (with all fuel required at start of problem)	not more than 300 ft.	330 ft.

(f) Initial rate of climb at sea level using military power	not less than 3,100 ft. per min.	3,110 ft. per min.

On July 18, BuAer wrote the BAR regarding acceptance and delivery instructions for the XF8B-1 prototypes. Each aircraft was to be accepted individually into the Navy inventory. Prior to the acceptance of each airplane, the BAR was to arrange for a ferry pilot with Naval Air Transport Service VRF-1 at Floyd Bennet Field, New York, New York. Airplane no. 57984 was to be delivered to the Naval Aircraft Factory, Philadelphia for use with project TED NAM 3259; airplane no. 57985 was to be delivered to Pax River, for use with project BIS 2170; and airplane no. 57986 was at Eglin Field, Florida being evaluated by the Army Air Force.

On October 15, Lt Frank J. Shaw accepted XF8B-1 serial no. 57984 from Boeing and flew it to Pax River via San Diego. XF8B-1 serial no. 57985 was accepted on November 5 by Lt. Cmdr. B. Hallett. It was assigned to Flight Test and used as a calibration plane at a "D" priority. Barner recommended that both XF8B-1 nos. 57984 and 57985 continue in their employment at Flight Test and Tactical Test.

Photo: Bob Lamson Collection

Engineer RIchard ("Dick") Stith and Bob Lamson sign over BuAer No. 57984 to Lt. Frank J. Shaw of the US Navy on October 15, 1946.

Photo: Bob Dorr Collection

Right front view of the third prototype under evaluation at the Army Air Forces Proving Ground Command at Eglin Field, Florida sometime during the latter half of 1946. This is one of the few photos showing the completed aircraft equipped with drop tanks. The Army found several faults with the aircraft and elected not to procure it in quantity.

On December 11, Boeing's Dick Stith issued a report pertaining to damage sustained by XF8B-1 airplane no. 57986 during gunnery evaluation tests by the Army Air Forces Proving Ground Command at Eglin Field, Florida on October 25, 1946.

During the morning of October 25, Captain Bert McDowell, Air Corps, was piloting the XF8B-1 on an air to ground gunnery strafing mission against an eighteen foot square target. The armament used was six .50 cal. guns firing standard ammunition. On one of the passes, which consisted of fairly shallow dives with a terminal velocity of 300 to 350 mph, the pilot was struck on the right side of the head by what was apparently a piece of the Plexiglass canopy. According to the pilot, he was momentarily rendered unconscious but had either started his pull-up at the moment of being struck or had instinctively pulled up. His first recollection following the incident was the blast of air from the fractured canopy. The mission was discontinued and the airplane was returned to the field without further incident.

Inspection of the airplane revealed several damaged areas:

a) The Plexiglas of the sliding canopy was broken on the right hand side.
b) The canopy frame was crushed and dented in the forward "hoop" portion at the location of a fracture in the Plexiglas.
c) Pieces of Plexiglas were strewn on the cockpit floor.
d) Small slivers of Plexiglas were imbedded in the right hand side of the pilot's head rest pad.
e) The leading edge of the right hand stabilizer was crushed just inboard of station 42, where slivers of Plexiglas were found in the fracture. The leading edge was also crushed just inboard of station 122.
f) The top of the fin was crushed at the leading edge. Particles of Plexiglas were found imbedded at this location.
g) The fin antenna was broken.
h) The top surface of the left hand stabilizer next to the fin was slightly marred.

Upon subsequent investigation of the terrain at the target range, a half dozen or more pieces of Plexiglas were found which matched Plexiglas portions found in the cockpit. All pieces found on the range were in a line to the target and located between 150 to 200 yards forward of the target (i.e. in the direction of the approach).

Based on the evidence, Stith made the following assumptions and conclusions:

a) That the damage was caused initially by ricochets from the ground of bullets fired from the XF8B-1. According to Army Ordnance Officers at the Eglin Proving Command, similar damage from ricochets had on occasion been experienced at Eglin before, particularly with fast airplanes such as the P-51 and P-80.
b) That the pilot misjudged his distance from the target and commenced firing considerably in excess of 300 yards. This assumption was based on location of Plexiglas on the ground and upon admitted overjudgments of distance on subsequent missions by the same pilot.
c) That the canopy was struck twice by ricochets.
d) That pilot was struck by Plexiglas.
e) That damage to fin and inboard end of the right hand stabilizer was caused by Plexiglas portions.
f) That the antenna was severed by Plexiglas.
g) That damage to the left hand stabilizer was caused by the broken antenna terminal and wire.

Photo: National Archives, RG 72-AC

The third XF8B-1 was damaged as a result of Army gunnery evaluation tests on October 25, 1946, during which the pilot misjudged the distance to the target and fired his .50 cal. guns too close to the ground, resulting in ricochets that twice struck the canopy. Additional photos from this accident can be seen in Appendix 7.

Repair of damage to the XF8B-1 consisted of the following:

a) Canopy – No attempt was made to repair the canopy at Eglin; a spare canopy was installed without difficulty.
b) The right hand stabilizer was repaired. After completion of the structural repairs the surface was smoothed with fairing compound, sanded, and finished with two coats of zinc chromate primer and one coat of Navy Sea Blue Semi-Gloss enamel.
c) The surface scratches on the left hand stabilizer were smoothed out, primed, and painted.
d) The major damage to the fin was in the removable nonstructural tip. This tip was removed and repaired in compliance with sound structural standards, smoothed with fairing compound, primed and painted.
e) A new antenna was installed

J.D. Barner, Commander of NAS Patuxent River, wrote BuAer on December 12 regarding future employment of the XF8B-1 aircraft assigned to Pax River upon completion of its use in connection with PTR BIS 2170. XF8B-1 serial no. 57984 assigned to Tactical Test continued to be profitably employed in the evaluation and comparison of tactical characteristics, potentialities, and relative combat efficiency of new and unusual aircraft. It was decided to transfer it to the Naval Air Material Command (NAMC), Philadelphia.

In late 1946, Richard Stith went to Washington, DC to try and convince BuAer to issue a production contract for the XF8B-1. The arrival of the jet age with the McDonnell FH-1 Phantom and the surplus of propeller-driven fighters in the Navy made production of the XF8B-1 as a fighter a nonstarter. Previous discussions with BuAer indicated that it was a good candidate for the attack role and could compete with the Douglas AD-1 Skyraider and Martin AM-1 Mauler. The officer in charge of the Torpedo Desk at BuAer agreed, but indicated that Boeing had demonstrated an unwillingness to build the XF8B-1 as an attack aircraft. The officer claimed that Boeing had been contacted by BuAer in the spring of 1946 with an order for 600 aircraft modified for the attack role with deliveries to start in December. W.E. Beall was out of the country, and the call was handled by the head of manufacturing, who placed priority with meeting production quotas for the B-17 and B-29. He felt that Boeing could not handle the production of a new type and promptly turned it down. Beall wasn't informed of this until Stith returned from Washington in December.

This account has been printed in several articles about the XF8B-1, but the author found no written evidence of it in BuAer files. Thus, it remains open to question.

Photo: Bob Dorr Collection

XF8B-1 BuAer No. 57984 on display at NATF Philadelphia, Pennsylvania sometime in the early postwar years.

5

1947 to 1950

Road to the Scrapyard

On January 13, 1947, Boeing advised BuAer regarding the status of the two remaining Aeroproducts propellers procured under the XF8B-1 contract. The first propeller was installed on the undelivered prototype no. 57986 and had been used during Boeing's dive tests, propeller vibration tests, Navy demonstration tests, and during the Army evaluation tests at Eglin Field. Due to the considerable number of dive pullouts accomplished during these periods, Boeing recommended that the propeller be limited to maneuvers not to exceed 4 g's. Boeing proposed delivering this airplane with the aforementioned propeller installed. The other remaining propeller was new; Boeing proposed assembling and balancing it before recrating it and delivering it to the Navy as a spare. Boeing believed that the spare propeller should not be installed on airplane no. 57986 but should be kept as a new propeller until need for installation on an airplane scheduled for high g performance flying.

BuAer agreed with Boeing's proposal. The first propeller installed on XF8B-1 serial no. 57986 was restricted to maneuvers of 4 g; Boeing was instructed to add a placard to the airplane regarding the limitation. The new propeller was assembled, balanced, crated and delivered to NAS Patuxent River along with complete installation instructions.

The BAR wrote BuAer on January 23 regarding the canopy damaged at Eglin Field. Only one undamaged canopy remained; the frame of the damaged canopy was in satisfactory condition and could be repaired by replacing the entire Plexiglas section at an estimated cost of $1,200.00. Given the imminent termination of the XF8B-1 contract, BuAer considered one spare canopy to be sufficient and declined to repair the damaged one.

On January 27, the Army issued a report summarizing the project to determine the functional reliability of the armament and bombing installation as well as the combat radius of action of the XF8B-1 as a fighter-bomber with maximum bomb load and full internal fuel supply (385 gals). For these

Photo: National Archives, RG 72-AC

After receiving an Aeroproducts propeller that had been previously used in dive tests, XF8B-1 no. 57986 was restricted to maneuvers of 4 g's or less in January of 1947.

tests, six fixed .50 cal. M2 machine guns were mounted in the wings.

From the tests, it was concluded that the .50 cal. M2 machine gun installation was functionally unreliable because of ammunition flow, feeding and inadequate gun cooling provisions; that the internal bomb installation was satisfactory for low level bombing only, because of bomb bay clearance limitations; that the XF8B-1 did not compare favorably with conventional fighter-bombers such as the P-47 and P-51; and that it only had a combat radius of action of 270 miles and a 45 minute reserve with a 4,000 lb. bomb load and 385 gallons of fuel at cruise power settings of 26.5" of manifold pressure and 1600 RPM. It was recommended that the aircraft be used only for low level bombing, the feed chutes be redesigned, the ammunition cans be made an integral part of the aircraft, and a more positive means of cooling the gun compartments be devised.

On March 4, Boeing wrote the commanding officer at Pax River regarding a crack that had formed in the aluminum alloy sheet of the propeller spinner installed on the remaining XF8B-1 at Boeing's factory. It was believed that the location of attaching bolt holes may have been a contributing cause. Boeing recommended that inspection of the spinners on the two XF8B-1s at Pax River be made; if the inspection revealed failures, it was requested that Boeing be advised immediately. Boeing negotiated with Aeroproducts relative to the repair of the spinner.

On March 14, the BAR updated BuAer regarding the status of XF8B-1 no. 57986. The airplane had received its final coat of paint including the new red stripe in the insignia. The airplane was at Boeing's hangar on Boeing Field. The blower section for the engine was shipped from Pratt & Whitney and had not been received. Upon receipt, it was immediately attached to the engine and the engine installed. Upon arrival of the engine blower, the BAR believed that flight tests would be completed and the airplane ready for delivery by approximately April 10.

On April 30, the Naval Aircraft Factory proposed installing .60 cal. guns in the XF8B-1 to test their effectiveness. Delivery of an XF8B-1 was expected on March 1, but all of the prototypes were grounded due to the discovery of malfunctions in another type of aircraft equipped with similar counter-rotating propellers.

BuAer made every effort to release the XF8B-1 from the grounding order and accelerate delivery, but to no avail. The authorization to manufacture, install, test and evaluate the .60 cal. gun installation and related smoke generating equipment at an estimated cost of $8,500.00 was cancelled on June 9. BuAer further directed that all component parts acquired for the project, with the exception of ammunition feed chutes and ejected ammunition link chutes, be disposed of as scrap.

By May 29, the engine nose section had been reinstalled on the XF8B-1 no. 57986 at Boeing in Seattle. A satisfactory engine run was conducted and the airplane was readied for pre-delivery flights. In view of possible strike action by Boeing employees, Boeing and the BAR recommended that the XF8B-1 be flown to NAS, Sand Point for temporary storage pending BuAer's delivery instructions. BuAer agreed to this proposal, and after temporary storage in Seattle, it was shipped to NAMC Philadelphia.

By July 2, all XF8B-1 aircraft had been permanently grounded; BuAer was not contemplating shipment of engines for purposes of ungrounding these aircraft. Airplane no. 57986 remained in storage status with the recommendation that the engine be preserved. The airplane was finally accepted by the Navy on August 1, 1947, which based it alternately between Seattle, San Diego, and Philadelphia. It was in the latter city that it was stricken from Navy inventory on March 16, 1950.

On July 16, BuAer authorized disposal of all parts peculiar to the XF8B-1, apart from the engines, landing gear struts, wheels and propellers, which were delivered to NAMC, Philadelphia for use in connection with the Barrier Development Program, Project TED NAM 34101. It was in this program that XF8B-1 no. 57984 was completely demolished during catapult and arresting tests; it was stricken from the Navy inventory on May 31, 1948. BuAer requested that the aircraft be salvaged for useful parts and the rest of it scrapped.

Boeing pilot Bob Lamson attempted to at one point to obtain one of the XF8B-1 prototypes from the Navy for racing in the National Air Races. He planned on clipping the wings and removing nonessential equipment to turn the aircraft into a racer. The Navy refused and the big fighters ended their days in the scrapyard.

Boeing executed the release under the XF8B-1 contract on February 14, 1950. The entire contract amounted to $8,053,545.93. Did the Navy get its eight million dollars worth? Unquestionably, it did not. However, while the contract did not result in a production fighter or attack aircraft, the Navy did get extensive experience testing the Pratt & Whitney R-4360 engine and counter-rotating propellers, though this wasn't of much value to it in the long run. The Air Force was the main operator of the R-4360 in the post war period, employing it in the B-50, B-36, C-74, and several other transports, so it may have benefited more from the engine performance data collected by BuAer, assuming it had access to it. The XF8B-1 also contributed in minor ways to tactical evaluation and catapult and arresting techniques in the postwar period. Finally, the Navy learned that fighters and internal bomb bays did not make a good combination.

BuAer faulted Boeing for the failure of the XF8B-1, and the company definitely deserved some of the blame. The initial management and organization set up by W.E. Beall to build the aircraft was flawed, and a higher priority was undeniably given to B-17 and B-29 production, slowing development of the XF8B-1. When the Navy indicated its preference to convert the XF8B-1 into a low level attacker, Boeing did not devote sufficient resources to pursuing this variant, resulting in a lost opportunity for a possible production contract.

On the other hand, one can argue that Boeing generally made a good faith effort to meet the requirements of a specification that was, in fact, unsound. In its final demonstration flight of July 1946, the XF8B-1 met or exceeded all requirements with respect to speed, service ceiling, and climb; it only failed to meet the 300 ft. takeoff distance requirement, exceeding it by 30 ft. Commander Simple's memo of June 1, 1944, as outlined in Chapter 2, provides a cogent critique of the XF8B-1 and the specification that produced it. Its engine and propeller combination was not mature; it was inferior to service types already in production; it would have been outclassed over the target area; and its large size caused a critical loss of fighting power for carriers, reducing the number of fighters carried by 50%. It took several months before his superiors in BuAer came around to Simple's view, but they eventually did, resulting in the cancellation of the contract.

The lack of a production contract for the XF8B-1 had little adverse effect on the Boeing; it went on to huge success in the design and production of bombers and commercial airliners, outlasting and purchasing several of the rivals who had consistently bested it in the fighter business, most notably McDonnell Douglas in 1997. It currently produces and supports the F-15, F/A-18, and F/A-22, the latter in a partnership with Lockheed Martin. It stumbled in the recent Joint Strike Fighter competition, with its ungainly X-32 losing to Lockheed Martin's X-35 for the biggest military aircraft procurement program in history. However, it is vigorously pursing development of the innovative X-45 unmanned combat air system, the success of which may ultimately reduce the number of JSF's procured. While it has taken the company decades to get back into the fighter industry after the cancellation of the XF8B-1, it is now producing the world's best fighters and may come to play a big role in the more promising field of unmanned aircraft systems.

Photo: Bob Dorr Collection

End of a brief career: the final XF8B-1 sits forlornly in the NAF Philadelphia scrapyard sometime during the early Fifties; note the red stripe on the insignia. The victim of a poorly conceived specification and rapidly technological progress, Boeing's big fighter never had the chance to prove itself in combat.

Appendix 1

Proposed Modifications and Variants

This appendix discusses the known proposals and studies derived from the basic XF8B-1 design. A fair number of such studies were generated, though most concentrated on the addition of various types of external ordnance and did not alter the basic design to a significant extent. General arrangement drawings of most of these studies are located in Appendix 2 and color artist impressions can be found in Appendix 10.

Night Fighter

On March 20, 1944, BuAer requested Boeing conduct a study relative to the installation of AN/APN-1 and AN/APX-2 radio equipment to adapt the XF8B-1 as a night fighter. This was to supplement a study showing the location of various units of the Model AN/APS-6 radio equipment requested by BuAer on November 22, 1943.

Boeing responded on April 14. No investigation was being conducted on the AN/APS-6 equipment and all available manpower was being expended on the early completion of the flight test articles of the XF8B-1. As a result, no investigations were in progress on the installation of any equipment to adapt the airplane as a night fighter and, for this reason, Boeing did not find it possible to make a study of the installation of the AN/APN-1 and AN/APX-2 radio equipment at that time.

The night fighter study was cancelled on October 2, 1945 when plans to produce the XF8B-1 in quantity were shelved.

The author has tracked down a three-view general arrangement drawing of what is believed to be a multirole two-place version of the XF8B-1, a tracing of which can be found in Appendix 2. Among the variety of stores this study featured was the AN/APS-4 transmitter-receiver on the outermost starboard hardpoint, giving it night-fighting capability. This was probably not the only XF8B-1 night fighter study drawn up, but it is the only one thus far located.

Rocket Installation

On June 15, 1944, BuAer requested that Boeing submit a design study and a proposal for installing the Mk. 5, Mod. 1 zero length rocket launcher and necessary electrical wiring in the XF8B-1. Provisions within the wing were to have been such that the launchers be readily installed or removed in service. The installation was to have been strong enough that rockets weighing 140 lbs. each could be carried under all flight and ground loading conditions consistent with the strength of the aircraft. An independent firing switch for rockets was to have been installed in an accessible position near the throttle. BuAer sent one complete installation kit for the Mk. 5, Mod. 1 aircraft rocket launcher to the BAR in Seattle to facilitate the study.

Notes accompanying this letter in BuAer files indicate that provisions for rockets were desired on the XF8B-1 to comply with the CNO's directive that all combat aircraft be so equipped. The Mk. 5 Mod. 1 launcher was specified, as it was the standard aircraft rocket launcher at the time.

From early on, Boeing had considered the idea of installing rockets on the outer wing panels but delayed submitting any drawings due to the desire to minimize interference with testing of the first flight article. In addition, the single pylon type launcher was expected to supercede the Mk. 5, Mod. 1. Subsequently, BuAer requested Boeing use the Rocket Selector Switch, Mk. 1 and to make a prototype installation in one of the XF8B-1 prototypes.

Boeing finally submitted its proposal on May 12, 1945. Rockets were supported by the Mk. 9, Mod. 1 launcher installed on the outboard wings. The electrical system incorporated the Mk. 1 rocket selector switch wired in series with the master armament switch, a bomb or rocket selector switch, and the bomb or rocket release switch operated by the button on the control stick. The aircraft was also equipped with a Mk. 23 computing sight. It was noted that the Mk. 23 or Mk. 8 sights were interchangeable on the third XF8B-1 prototype.

Boeing's basic study of the rocket installation was essentially complete prior to receipt of a revised request for a rocket installation prepared by BuAer on February 23, 1945. Thus, as submitted, it was not in agreement with the latest standards. Specifically, the release button used for bombs was also used for rockets, and no provision was made for firing rockets singly; Boeing questioned whether this method of release would require changes in the Mk. 1 rocket station selector and its wiring diagram.

Boeing decided to withhold incorporation of changes pending receipt of BuAer approval of the proposed rocket launcher provisions and authorization for their installation in the XF8B-1. This was prudent, as BuAer cancelled the rocket installation study on July 18, 1945. A note accompanying the decision stated that "since no production F8B-1 airplane (sic) are contemplated all requests for rocket installations are being cancelled." This is the first recorded evidence in the surviving contract correspondence that the XF8B-1 contract would definitely not go beyond the three prototypes. It was also one of many studies related to the aircraft that had been put on hold or cancelled in 1945, suggesting that the decision not to produce the aircraft was taken even earlier.

Two Seat Attack Airplane

On September 22, 1944, Commander R.E. Dixon of BuAer's Military Requirements section requested that the Navy Engineering Experiments and Developments section obtain from Boeing a study and proposal of converting the XF8B-1 to a low altitude, "scant" attack airplane. Dixon considered the XF8B-1 to have many features desirable in a replacement in the VTB class. The modified aircraft would have had the following changes to transform it into a long range scout, high performance attack airplane:

a) Modification of the fuselage to permit space for a second cockpit to provide for a radio/radar operator.
b) Replacement of the two stage R-4360 engine with a single stage two speed engine for weight saving.
c) Incorporation of provisions for as many different armament loads as possible within the existing bomb bay.
d) Torpedo provisions to carry a single Mk. 13 torpedo externally on the center line.
e) Provision of standard radio and radar equipment then scheduled for VTB class aircraft.

This request for proposal was in no way to affect the existing contract for the airplane. BuAer formally directed Boeing to prepare the study for the low altitude attack and scouting version of the XF8B-1 on October 24. The modifications necessary to accomplish the conversion were listed as follows:

a) Removal of the two-stage engine and substitution of an R-4360-4 single stage, variable speed, single rotation engine with a .425, no. 60 shaft.
b) Removal of the counter-rotating propeller and substitution of a suitable single rotation propeller for the aforementioned engine.
c) Modification of the control surfaces and empennage to provide for a single rotation propeller.
d) Relocation of the pilot's cockpit forward to provide 15° downward vision over the engine cowl.
e) Incorporation of a second seat behind the pilot for radar-radio operation, with sufficient armor protection against .50 cal. fire, from a 45° cone from the rear, oxygen equipment, radar controls and scope, seat and safety belt.
f) Provision for external mounting of a Mk. 13-3 aircraft torpedo with lug suspension either under a wing or on the centerline of the fuselage, whichever location involved lesser modification to the existing design.
g) Provision for carrying an APN/APS-4 detachable radar package under the right hand wing as far outboard as possible to obtain maximum radar vision ahead and above.
h) Provision for carrying the 11.75" "Tiny Tim" rocket projectile as well as an alternate load of four 5" HVAR rockets under each wing.
i) Provision for carrying one twin .50 cal. Douglas machine gun package, or one Mk. 1 single .50 cal. container, or

one Mk. 3 single .20 mm. cannon, under each wing.

j) Provision of installation for carrying one 150 gal. drop tank on each wing.

k) Items f), h), i) and j) were to have been interchangeable at one wing station if propeller clearance, lateral stability and flap or aileron clearance permitted.

l) Provision of various additional radar equipment at an additional weight of 563 lbs.

m) Recalculation of the XF8B-1's structural strength to establish the resulting design load factor. The minimum strength considered acceptable for this type of aircraft was 5 g at a gross load for a normal attack condition. This loading consisted of full internal protected fuel, two man crew, one 2,000 lb. bomb, six .20 mm. fixed cannon with 200 rounds per cannon, and all radio and radar equipment installed.

n) Determination of an approximate limit dive speed based on flutter analysis for the XF8B-1 as modified.

o) As an alternate engine installation, it was requested that a single stage counter-rotating R-4360 engine also be studied will all modifications from d) to n) included, if preliminary investigation showed an appreciable gain in performance by use of a counter-rotating propeller.

These design studies were to have contained estimates of all performance characteristics for the loading condition described in subparagraph m) above, three view drawings of the airplane configuration, and an internal general arrangement drawing. Boeing was advised that if certain modifications resulted in major interferences with other installations or seriously reduced the existing estimated performance of the XF8B-1 model, its comments and recommendations were expected. Boeing was authorized to proceed with the study in advance of a formal cost proposal. The work involved in the study was in no way to affect the existing contract for the XF8B-1 airplanes, and if interference developed the existing XF8B-1 program had priority in all respects.

Notes accompanying this letter in BuAer files indicate that the study was initiated to determine whether or not it would be better policy to start a new design for an attack airplane rather than attempt these extensive changes on the XF8B-1. The VTB section of BuAer was asked to prepare a second study proposal if this one appeared to be too extensive.

On December 26, 1944, a telephone conversation took place between Lt. Comdr. R.F. Farrington, Military Requirements Division, BuAer, and Ed Wells, Assistant Chief Engineer of Boeing regarding the proposed two-seat attack variant of the XF8B-1. Little had been accomplished since BuAer requested the study in September 1944, and Farrington reiterated the Navy's definite interest in the XF8B-1 as an attack airplane. He requested that Boeing submit their proposal(s) and an estimate of production facilities as soon as soon as possible. Farrington further stated that BuAer would endeavor to authorize the conversion of the third prototype to an attack configuration or possibly would be able to issue a letter of intent on two additional F8B airplanes with this attack configuration.

Wells stated that the company already had some layout plans for this attack configuration and that the company was interested in this new model. He promised to bring the matter up with other company officials and submit Boeing's proposals as soon as possible. Wells evinced considerable satisfaction at this show of interest in the airplane by the Navy.

On December 30, BuAer formally requested Boeing to expedite the study of converting the XF8B-1 to the two-seat, low altitude attack model. Boeing had indicated that certain items requested in this study were cause of concern due to the fact that their inclusion in the conversion plan adversely affected either performance or production. BuAer considered the items listed in the request to be necessary for the ideal attack configuration; Boeing's comments were requested if it considered certain of these installations as impractical of incorporation or of serious effect on performance. Since conversion of the XF8B-1 to an attack type appeared to be possible and could result in an effective combat weapon for carrier use, BuAer attached great importance to it.

BuAer requested that Boeing submit comments as to the possibility of converting the third XF8B-1 to the attack version, or in lieu of this program, an estimate as to the best completion date for two additional attack version flight articles. Final decision as to action to obtain this converted airplane depended on early receipt of the performance and configuration study, possible installations, and the most efficient method of obtaining an early flight test article.

Notes accompanying this letter indicate that it was written at the request of the Military Requirements section of BuAer to communicate the Navy's continued interest in the XF8B-1 and to permit Boeing latitude as to requirements and obtain comments as to its preferences in the event a flight article was delivered. Boeing was not taking much action on the original letter requesting conversion of the XF8B-1 to an attack version due to other commitments. Some personnel in BuAer considered the XF8B-1 to be the only plane that could satisfy VTB requirements and therefore pushed for the study to be accelerated.

As related at the end of Chapter 4, some authors assert that the officer in charge of the Torpedo Desk at BuAer contacted Boeing in the spring of 1946 with an order for 600 aircraft modified for the attack role with deliveries to start in December, but Boeing demonstrated an unwillingness to build the XF8B-1 as an attack aircraft. This appears unlikely given the documents in BuAer files, but cannot be entirely discounted, as not all documentation concerning the contract has been located.

As mentioned in the previous section, the drawing of the multipurpose two-place version of the XF8B-1 is located in Appendix 2. It appears to be an early study, as the design retains the early high drag canopy and R-4360 engine.

Torpedo Bomber (the "Boeing TFB")

On June 1, 1944, Lt. W.T. Estabrook wrote a memo on behalf of Commander W.W. Hollister, VTB Design Branch, to the Head of Experiments and Developments advising against adapting the XF8B-1 for Torpedo Attack. Although the airplane had a bomb bay, it could not accommodate a torpedo internally. The torpedo could be slung externally the same as on contemporary single seat dive bombers. Modification of the bomb bay to permit installation of a torpedo would have required major redesign and an extension of tail length. Carrying a torpedo in the bomb bay was not a necessity for torpedo attacks but it was a primary characteristic of a torpedo plane. If the torpedo was not carried internally, there was no reason to incorporate a bomb bay.

Photographs of the mock-up of the XF8B-1 showed clearance of the flaps over the deck which appeared to be in the neighborhood of a few inches. To obtain landing speed within carrier operating limits with a torpedo installed, these flaps would have been necessary. It was not believed that any reduction in flap area was possible and the flap clearance was unacceptable.

Comparative data with one torpedo:

	TBY-2	XTB2D-1	XF8B-1
Gross Weight – lbs.	17,430	28,060	20,787
Fuel – gals.	317	774	528
Maximum Speed at Sea Level – (mil) mph	268	304	308
Maximum Speed at Critical Altitude – (mil) mph	307	327	381
Stalling Speed, gross weight power off - mph	82.1	85.2	*
Takeoff – 25 knot – ft.	433	457	*
Source of Data	Boeing	BuAer	BuAer Estimate
* For XF8B-1: Flaps could not be lowered in torpedo condition, thus no stall or takeoff estimates were available.			

Lt. Estabrook noted that since the XF8B-1 was already stressed for dive bombing, it was felt that its primary mission should be either that of fighter or dive bomber with a secondary mission of torpedo attack.

Later that June, the Deputy Director remarked on the proposed XF8B-1 torpedo attack variant in his memo to the BuAer Director of Engineering summarized in Chapter 3, finding the airplane inadequate both as a dive bomber and torpedo airplane. No dive brakes were fitted, and none appeared possible without major redesign, though the airplane appeared fully as capable of dive bombing with wing bombs as the F6F or F4U. In comparison with the XBTM-1, the XF8B-1 had a longer takeoff and lower speed at sea level, with equivalent loadings. It was impossible to determine definitely whether the flaps could have been used if torpedoes were suspended from the wing racks, but the deck clearance was marginal and would have prohibited landing aboard with the torpedo installed. It was obvious that the XF8B-1 with its high altitude engine could not have been as effective a dive bomber or torpedo bomber as airplanes designed specifically for that purpose. No comparison with conventional torpedo bombers was considered proper or warranted, due to the widely variant design requirements of that type and the XF8B-1.

Despite these misgivings, Commander W.W. Hollister visited Boeing on September 20 for the purpose of inspecting the XF8B-1 and discussing the possibility of its use as a torpedo bomber. The first aircraft was approximately 75% complete and an investigation was made as to the possibility of converting the aircraft into a torpedo fighter bomber type; the following points were brought out during discussion with Boeing's engineers:

a) At the time, the XF8B-1 was not capable of carrying a torpedo either externally or in the bomb bay. External suspension under the wings was possible if torpedoes with center-line lugs were available.
b) The two stage supercharger was unnecessary for a VTB type.
c) Pilot visibility over the nose was only 7°. VTB requirements were 15°.
d) It was not believed that the aircraft's existing strength would be sufficient to result in a 5 g airplane with a torpedo loading.
e) There was a very small space aft of the pilot for possible incorporation of a second seat for a radar operator.
f) The specified radio was inadequate – no radar was to be installed.

All of the aforementioned changes were major and would have involved an almost complete redesign of the aircraft. The most critical point was that the type could not carry a torpedo as designed. Because of the above, extensive changes were mandatory before the airplane could be considered as a torpedo type, and because of the fact that another VTB airplane was already being built around the R-4360 engine, it was recommended that no further effort be expended toward converting the XF8B-1 to a VTB type.

Despite these recommendations, Boeing formally submitted its proposal to equip the XF8B-1 with a torpedo in December of 1944. A Mk 13 torpedo was to be slung under the fuselage centerline, supported by a Mk 51 Mod 9 Type "L" bomb shackle using a suspension beam designed by the Navy Bureau of Ordnance. The design of the sway braces was such that no difficulty was anticipated as a result of deflections of the support beam.

The angle between the centerline of the torpedo and the surface of the water with the airplane in level flight at 300 knots was 4.7° nose down. With the XF8B-1 in level flight at 200 knots, the angle was 3° nose down. The angles of unobstructed vision measured vertically downward from the line of flight over the nose of the airplane on the centerline were 9.4° and 7.7° at 300 knots and 200 knots, respectively. These angles were all computed for a launching weight of 19,000 lbs. No provisions were made for setting the torpedo depth index in flight, or dropping the torpedo in a dead condition. The use of the Mk 8 sight was contemplated for torpedo launching.

As a fighter in torpedo carrying condition, the XF8B-1 would have carried 384 gallons of fuel, 6 fixed guns, 2,400 rounds of ammunition, and a Mk 13 Mod 3 torpedo. The torpedo was to have been equipped with a drag ring assembly and a Mk 2 Mod 1 stabilizer assembly. Provisions were to be made for the support of a removable hoist to be used for hoisting the torpedo into position; this provision was to have been made on the third flight airplane only, no. 57986. Total increase in weight empty was only 22 lbs.

Boeing estimated the following figures relative to three variations of the torpedo installation on the XF8B-1:

Radius of action was based on the following time elements:

5 min. warm up
1 min. take off
X min. to target
20 min. over target at full military power
Y min. return

30 min. over carrier (landing)

On April 19, 1945, Commander Hollister wrote a memo to the Director of Military Requirements at BuAer supporting conversion of the XF8B-1 to a torpedo attack bomber configuration. This represented a complete reversal of policy from the negative assessment the VTB Branch had given the aircraft for the torpedo attack role on June 1, 1944. In the new memo, the VTB Branch had completed all preliminary investigations of the airplane's suitability for the role, received an engineering design study, and also received NAS Patuxent River's report on the preliminary evaluation of the model.

VTB had originally prepared a request for Boeing to submit design studies for modification of the existing configuration as follows:

a) Remove the two-stage R-4360-10 engine and substitute the two-speed R-4360-4 engine.
b) Change to a single rotation propeller.
c) Increase pilot's vision down and over the nose.
d) Incorporate a second seat for a radar operator.
e) Provide installation provisions for an aircraft torpedo.
f) Provide for radar and radio equipment for VTB Class.
g) Provide for "Tiny Tim" rockets.
h) Drop tank and package gun provisions.
i) Provide strength for 5 g load factor with normal torpedo loading.

Boeing's reply contained satisfactory designs for all but the following items:

a) Changing the two-stage engine and counter-rotating propellers to two-speed supercharger and single rotation was not practical since it involved almost complete redesign of the entire airplane.
b) Any change to the pilot's cockpit, or incorporation of a second seat for a radar operator, would have resulted in a major compromise of the existing estimated performance.

All other items requested could have been satisfactorily provided for on the existing design without major change in the airplane. The resulting configuration would have been essentially the same as designed, i.e. a two-stage R-4360 engine and six-bladed counter-rotating propeller, single seat torpedo attack model.

Since some doubt existed as to the flight characteristics of this model and since takeoff distances appeared excessive at torpedo load conditions, the first flight article was delivered to NAS, Patuxent River for preliminary evaluation. The report of these tests included the following data:

a) Takeoff distance in 25 knots at a gross weight of 20,000 lbs. was 380 ft.
b) Maximum speed at sea level, normal rated power was 320 mph, military power 342 mph.
c) "Lateral stability controls free" was unacceptable.
d) Control forces were unacceptable.

In general, the report was satisfactory and did not indicate that correction of deficiencies was impossible. Boeing had expressed its prior knowledge of control force difficulties and stability problems, and was considered fully capable of finding satisfactory solutions. The takeoff results as determined by Patuxent were very promising, even at the high gross weight value. The flight test report had been submitted by Patuxent and was being circulated in BuAer.

It was considered that the XF8B-1 performed very satisfactorily during its stay at NAS Patuxent River. Only very minor maintenance problems involving radio operation and brakes developed during these flights. In general, BuAer pilots were favorably impressed with the flight characteristics and performance of the airplane.

The VTB Branch felt that the XF8B-1 model had every possibility of being an excellent torpedo attack aircraft for carrier operation. The armament installation of six fixed 20 mm. cannons was being tested in a special wing section installation at Armament Test and appeared to be excellent. The bomb bay was capable of carrying a diversified bomb load up to a maximum weight of 4,000 lbs. The centerline external torpedo installation could have been satisfactorily incorporated. Total protected internal fuel was 384 gallons. The carrier spot of the XF8B-1 was 60 as compared to 88 in the same spot for the TBM. It was believed that this model could be developed into an efficient torpedo attack bomber fighter airplane.

The VTB Branch recommended that as few changes as possible be incorporated if the aircraft was put into production. The two-stage engine was to have been retained for fighter requirements since the airplane had excellent fighter characteristics. Only the single seat version was to have been considered, as the need for a radar-operator was vague and introduced major compromise in design and performance. It was felt that the existing design, with provisions for carrying a torpedo, was the configuration that would prove to be most efficient and effective.

It was recommended that the XF8B-1 as then designed be considered as a torpedo attack model to parallel the XTB3F design. It was recommended that steps be taken to start a production program as soon as possible and the designation of this model be changed to "TFB" or other suitable letters.

However, this was not the final word on the torpedo attack model. A BuAer memo entitled "Design Coordination Comment" drafted on April 28 advised against producing the XF8B-1 as a torpedo bomber. The memo started off by noting that a conference was held on February 6 reserving decision on a two place torpedo attack version of the aircraft pending Pax River evaluation of flying qualities and takeoff at high gross weights. Although the Pax River tests had been completed (PTR 1706), the author of the memo (whose name is illegible) felt that the tests were not conclusive since the gross weights tested were substantially lower than the expected operational weights. On the basis of actual weight data available, the airplane described in the basic memo grossed 22,893 lbs. with full main and bomb bay tanks, 1 torpedo, six 20 mm. guns and VTB radio and radar equipment. Pax River checked takeoffs at 20,000 lbs., and flying qualities at 17,000 lbs.

At the previous conference, the only apparent advantages of the XF8B-1 model over the BTM were its second man, high altitude performance, and possible greater versatility. The advantage of the second man had been eliminated because of the adverse effect on weight and center of gravity, leaving only advantages in high altitude performance and versatility to offset disadvantages of poor takeoff and spot.

The table on the following page lists the characteristics and performance of the XF8B-1, BTM, BT2D, BTK, and TB3F. From the data available, little justification could be found for considering the airplane as a VTB due to its inferiority to the other types as a load carrier. Its low altitude performance was approximately the same as the VTB models, but takeoff was inferior. The combat radii of 445 and 160 miles shown for the conditions with and without bomb bay fuel were no better than obtainable with the BTM and BT2D at substantially shorter takeoff distances. For land based operations, where takeoff distance could be considered less important, the XF8B-1 was capable of a longer radius than the others by the addition of external fuel.

Taking all factors into account, procurement of the XF8B-1 as a carrier-based VTB was not recommended. Although the airplane gave the promise of being an excellent flying machine, and capable of use in many roles, it appeared over-compromised and could not compete favorably with any of the carrier classes singly. The airplane was larger than necessary for a VF, because of the bomb bay and other features, yet the fighter provisions of high altitude performance and a propeller chosen primarily for high speed made it inferior to its bomber and torpedo counterparts. The facts had been evident since the inception of the design, and had been brought to the attention of interested parties at various stages in the past year. The conclusion had always been reached that unless the need existed for a long-range fighter, production commitments for the XF8B-1 were not justifiable.

On May 3, a BuAer engineer by the named of Spangenberg wrote a critique of the VTB Branch's evaluation of the XF8B-1 relative to the Martin BTM. VTB comments included a summary of the XBTM and XF8B-1 as tested at Pax River, which indicated that the latter was a superior load carrier. The reasoning by which this conclusion was reached was considered fallacious because of the following:

a) Concerning the weight comparison, although the XBTM at 18,600 lbs. included no bombs and 360 gals. of gas, it did include a "high degree of instrumentation," as noted in the PTR report. The XF8B-1 as tested at 18,600 lbs. included no bombs, but did include ballast. The 1,100 lb.

VTB Comparison						
Model	XF8B-1	XF8B-1	XBTM	XBT2D	XBTK	XTB3F-1
Gross Wt. (lbs.)	22,893	20,906	21,069	16,924	16,100	20,380
Torpedo	13-3	13-3	13-3	13-3	13-3	13-3
ASH Radar	ON	ON	ON	ON	ON	ON
Fuel - Total	645	375	500	515	375	520
Fuel - Fixed	375	375	500	365	275	370
Fuel – B.B.	270	0	0	0	0	0
Fuel – Drop	0	0	0	150	100	150
Fixed – Guns	6-20	6-20	4-20/800	2-20/400	2-20/400	2-20/400
Wing Loading	46.8	42.8	42.5	42.3	42.5	37.1
Power Loading – T.O.	7.6	7.0	7.0	6.8	7.7	-
Combat Radius B-1	445	160	285	450	295	350
T.O. Distance – 25 kts	649	466	343	371	462	420 (315*)
Max. Speed – NBHP – S.L.	289	290	291	271	262	243
Combat Cond. Torp. Ext. Tanks & ASH dropped						
Gross Wt.	20,585	18,598	18,782	13,500	13,005	16,940
Max Speed – MBHP – S.L.	338	339	340	337	330	285
Max Speed - Combat & Jet – S.L.	-	-	-	-	-	352
Max Speed – MBHP – 15,000	382	383	367	353	348	317
Max Speed – Combat & Jet – 15,000	-	-	-	-	-	370
Engine	R-4360-10	R-4360-10	R-4360-4	R-3350-24	R-2800-22	R-2800-34
Jet	-	-	-	-	-	19 XB
Prop Dia./No. Blades	13'-8"/6	13'-8"/6	14'8"/4	13'6"/4	13'7"/4	13'2"/4
Blade	2C15	2C15	830	V20P	2C15B	6557
Wing Area	489	489	496	400	380	549
Wing Span	54'	54'	50'	50'	48.7'	60'
Folded Span	29' 5"	29' 5"	23' 5"	24'	21'	24' 2"
Length	42' 10"	42' 10"	40' 8"	39' 8"	38' 8"	42' 1"
Spot – 200 ft. – CV-9	15	15	20	20	24	20

Notes:
1) XF8B-1 – single place, TB3F radio and radar, torpedo on centerline. Performance based on preliminary Patuxent data.
2) XBTM based on preliminary Patuxent data.
3) XBT2D-1 advance chart data subject to check.
4) XBTK-1 experimental chart of January 1, 1945
5) XTB3F advance chart data subject to check.

* with jet

figure quoted was determined by the subtraction of the normal fighter weight given in an August 1, 1944 chart from the flight test weight. The airplane under discussion was considerably heavier than the 17,508 lb. given in the chart. Based on Boeing weight data, the weight empty of the torpedo attack version of the XF8B-1 would have been 14,449, as compared to 14,097 for the XBTM. It appeared that the XBTM was at least equal to the XF8B-1 from a basic weight standpoint.

b) The takeoff distances quoted were not comparable, since the XBTM was tested with the 836 blade propeller, rather than the wide blade 830 propeller specified. The XF8B-1 takeoff distance at 18,600 lbs. was relatively lower than the other two points determined.

c) The speeds quoted were not comparable, since the XBTM speed of 348 mph was obtained at 5,000 ft. However, the XBTM was equipped with wing and centerline bomb racks, simulated guns, two yaw meters, and arresting gear, while the XF8B-1 was tested with none of these drag items.

The performance summary in the Design Coordination comments was based on actual weight data and Pax River flight tests where available. The performance, calculated by A&H, was based on the figures quoted by VTB, but reduced to comparable conditions.

It was believed that studies to date had proved the XBTM superior to the XF8B-1 for delivering a torpedo attack from an aircraft carrier. If the primary mission of the airplane was to be other than torpedo loading, more studies were indicated. In view of VTB's strong representations for the XF8B-1, Spangenberg suggested that they establish some typical loadings for the airplane, allowing for further comparisons.

On May 11, the BuAer Director of the Engineering Division wrote a memo to the Director of Military Requirements repeating several of the aforementioned arguments against procurement of the XF8B-1 as a torpedo attack airplane. It did contain several interesting and original observations though. For example, it was becoming increasingly apparent to the Director that the carrier based VBT and VTB class airplanes were tending to merge into a single type. All new dive bombers incorporated torpedo provisions, and were capable of delivering torpedo attacks equally as well as the so-called torpedo planes. The chief distinction of the VTB Class at the time was that, in general, VTB airplanes were multiplace with a bomb bay, and were more suitable for carrying large numbers of small bombs, being compromised to some degree for the supposedly primary torpedo mission. The XF8B-1 was a cross between all carrier types with its high altitude engine, external torpedo installation, and a bomb bay. A comparison between the XF8B-1, BTM, BT2D, BTK and TB3F showed that for the torpedo mission, the XF8B-1 was not too attractive with a longer takeoff run for a given radius than competitive types without compensating advantages. On the other hand, the XF8B-1 was capable of performing a greater variety of missions than any of the other airplanes.

Engineering was unable to make a strong recommendation for the procurement of the XF8B-1 as a torpedo plane since this involved setting up production of an airplane that had no apparent advantages for this mission over other airplanes already under procurement, and had the disadvantages of inferior takeoff and greater size. However, it was considered that the airplane could be made into a useful attack weapon for operation from either carriers or shore bases. As had been brought out many times in the past, the airplane as a fighter had performance approximately equal to the F4U, at equivalent engine ratings, but was operable at a much greater radius with excellent takeoff characteristics. In comparison with projected striking airplanes (BTM, BT2D and TB3F) with heavy bomb loads, its radius and takeoff were not outstanding but these characteristics were approximately equal to the then current service models (SB2C and TBM) while speed and climb performance was far superior.

From the available evidence, it appears that the torpedo attack variant was ultimately killed by BuAer due to the relative superiority of existing types specialized for that role. The story of the BuAer Torpedo Desk officer offering Boeing an order for 600 aircraft in the spring of 1946 seems unlikely given the volume of documents criticizing the proposed type in BuAer files, but cannot be refuted entirely.

The author has located a blueprint of an early proposal for a centerline torpedo installation on a single-seat XF8B-1, which has been traced and included in Appendix 2. However, this drawing probably doesn't represent the finalized installation. The two-seat torpedo attack version is depicted in the plan mentioned in the previous sections on the night fighter and two-seat attack variants of the aircraft. Finally, Boeing's November 1, 1945 press release regarding the XF8B-1 claimed that it could carry two 2,000 lb. torpedoes; a provisional drawing of this configuration has also been created.

Model 490 Carrier-Based ASW Airplane

The Boeing Model 490 was a 1950 proposal closely related to the XF8B-1. A conventional four-place low-wing single-engine all-weather anti-submarine warfare aircraft designed for the Navy, the Model 490 utilized the wing of its unlucky precedessor, which gave the design the advantage of having a wing with proven flying qualities and one on which complete aerodynamic data was available. This was considered by Boeing to be an important factor contributing not only to superior performance and control, but also to minimum structural weight and maximum structural integrity. The horizontal and vertical tail areas were slightly increased in order to more adequately meet the takeoff, carrier approach, and landing requirements of a slightly heavier aircraft. Despite this, the Model 490's resemblance to the XF8B-1 was striking, though aesthetically it did not benefit from its role as an anti-submarine warfare platform.

In the Original Specification for a Class VA (ASW) Airplane issued by BuAer on January 20 1950, prospective contractors were urged to explore single and twin engine configurations, though the aircraft was to be conventional with emphasis on simplicity, ease of maintenance, and good flight characteristics. Boeing selected a single-engine design with the wing of the XF8B-1, as it offered the lightest possible airplane with ample margins for carrier catapulting and arresting. Powered by the reliable Pratt & Whitney R-2800-C9-2 engine, Boeing claimed that the Model 490 complied with or exceeded all specified requirements and appeared to provide the maximum possible future growth within the weight and dimensional limitations outlined by the Navy.

Producibility and maintainability were achieved in the basic design

Drawing: National Archives, RG 72

Contemporary artist's impression of the Model 490 ASW aircraft. As one can see, the design of the wing, tail surfaces, and chin scoop owed much to the XF8B-1. Boeing recycled these features of its cancelled fighter to save time and money in the development of the Model 490.

through the use of simple, rugged construction and ample provisions for accessibility. The propeller and power plant were both proven units that had been used in other Navy aircraft and their cost was relatively low. Crew comfort with all electronic equipment placed in positions for the maximum utility was carefully considered. Armament and electronic equipment was arranged considering accessibility and the corresponding ease of maintenance. The Model 490 was designed to operate from the CVE-105, CVL, CV-9, CV-34 and CVB class carriers. JATO provisions were made for deck takeoff if required. Maximum endurance was over six hours.

The crew was made up of a pilot, an assistant pilot in charge of ABSAP operation and navigation, a crew member in charge of radar tuning, directional and non-directional sonobuoys, and 1FF interrogation, and a crew member in charge of the countermeasure receiver, MAD remote indicator, and the MHR key. The pilot and assistant pilot were seated side-by-side, slightly staggered, with the other crew members located behind facing rearwards. The cockpit was located well forward on the Model 490, allowing for excellent vision for the pilot in the carrier approach attitude and the maximum practicable all-around downward vision for visual submarine contacts.

Provision was made for the bomb-bay installation of one Mark 41-1 torpedo. Neither bullet resistant windshield glass nor armor plate was considered necessary for the Model 490, given its role. Strength and installation provisions were made for the installation of six 5 in. HPAG or HVAR rockets to be hung under the wing on Aero 14A launchers. Provision was also made for an illuminated MK2O Mod 1 or 2 gun sight at the pilot's station for installation when the rockets were carried. A cartridge dispenser for target illumination purposes to be fired by the assistant pilot was also included. The cartridges were free falling and produced a high illumination for approximately 3 seconds.

Overall, it was a competent and promising ASW design that benefited from Boeing's previous experience with the XF8B-1. In many ways, it was much simpler than its predecessor, substituting a less sophisticated engine and limiting itself to one specialized role, in contrast to Boeing's original "five-in-one" fighter. However, it never left the drawing board. This was

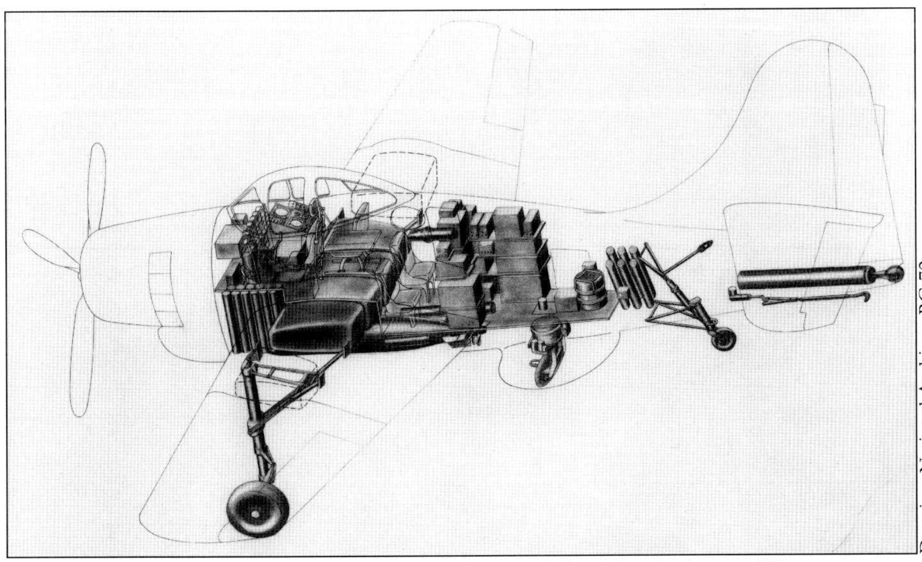

Drawing: National Archives, RG 72

Perspective interior arrangement of the Model 490. As is readily apparent, the design of the fuselage was changed substantially from that of the XF8B-1 to optimize it for the ASW role.

probably the final nail in the coffin for the XF8B-1 and its derivatives.

Appendix 2

General Arrangement Drawings

The following pages present several contemporary general arrangement drawings of the Boeing XF8B-1 at different stages in its development. Additional contemporary drawings are shown in the maintenance and pilot's manuals found in Appendices 8 and 9, respectively.

The drawings here are followed by a series of general arrangement drawings I have done that illustrate the three prototypes as well as the known projected variants. These are based on factory drawings, the aforementioned manuals, photos and promotional materials. Some speculation was required in depicting details of the projected variants, and I have noted this where appropriate. Accuracy is in the eye of the beholder - the reference drawings seldom agreed with each other, as is often the case. Nonetheless, I believe these drawings are a great improvement over what has heretofore been publicly available.

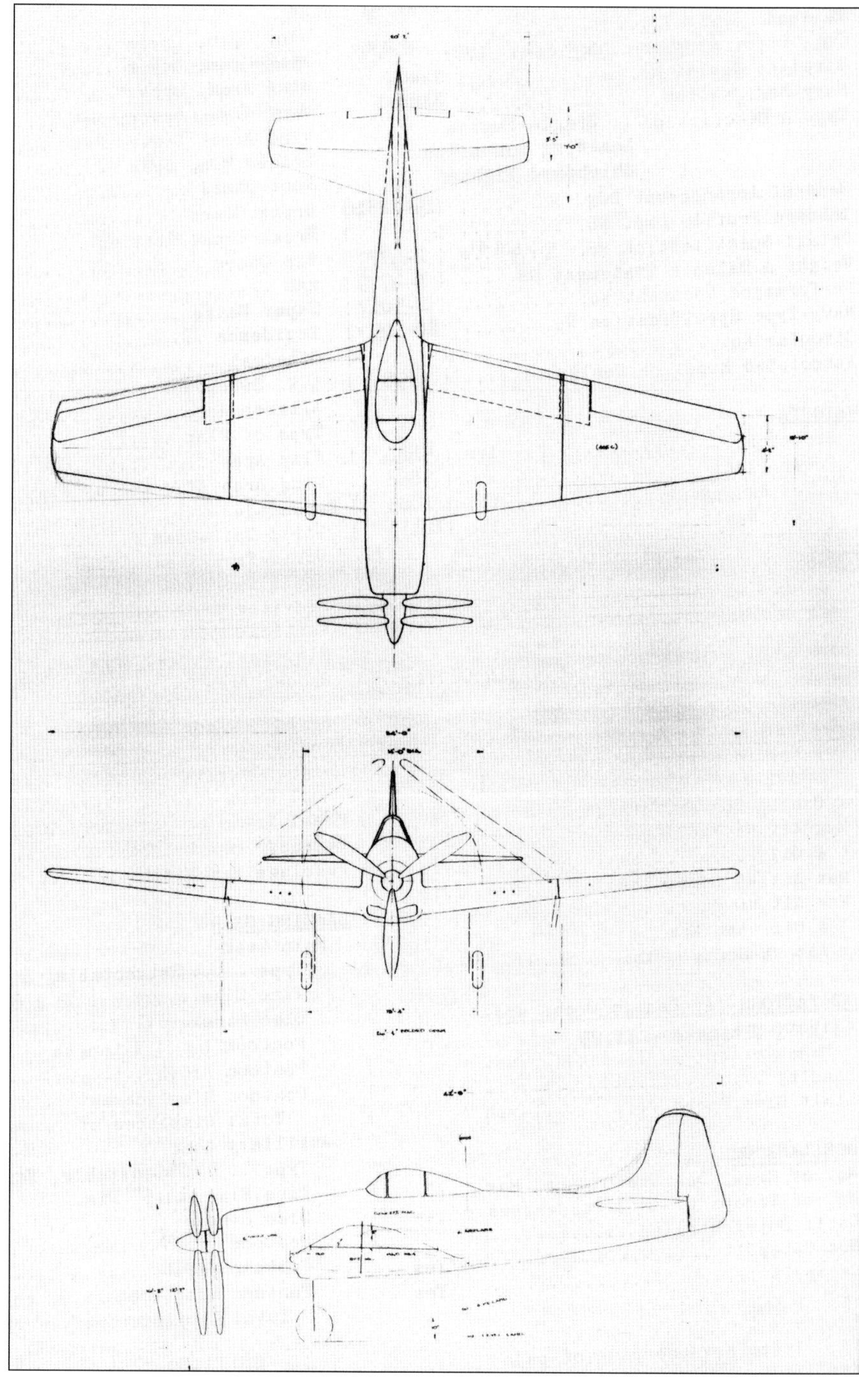

Drawing: Boeing Historical Archives

Right: **Perhaps the earliest known three-view of the Boeing Model 400, later known as the XF8B-1. The layout is close to what actually was adopted, though the wing and tail surfaces are more angular and smaller in area.**

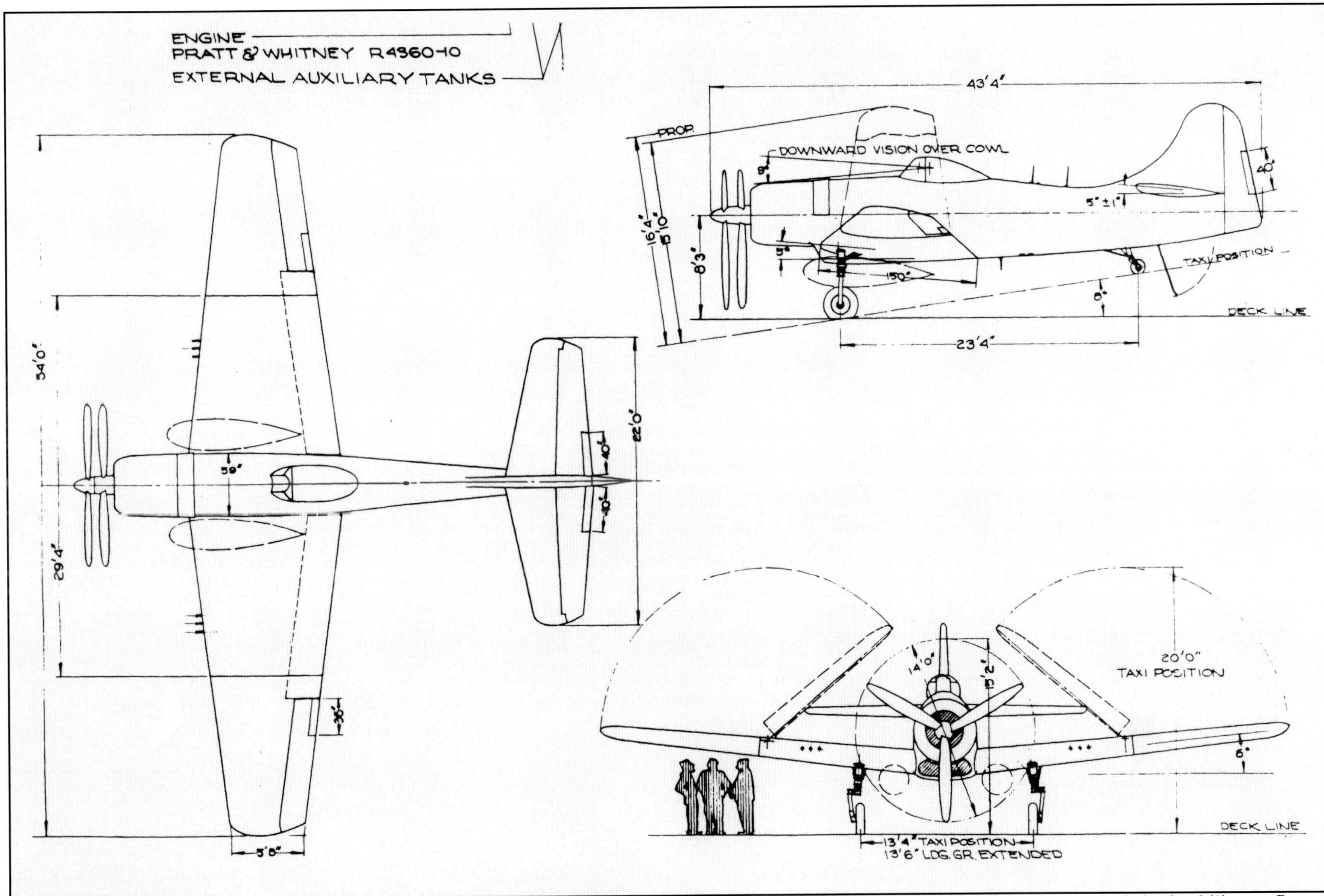

Drawing: Boeing Historical Archives

Above: Excellent general arrangement drawing of the first prototype of the XF8B-1 that is very close to what the aircraft looked like as flown. However, the drop tanks here differ slightly in shape and substantially in how they were mounted under the wing. These are mounted almost flush with the underside of wing, like slipper tanks. In addition, the guns/cannon did not project from the leading edge of the wing on the actual aircraft.

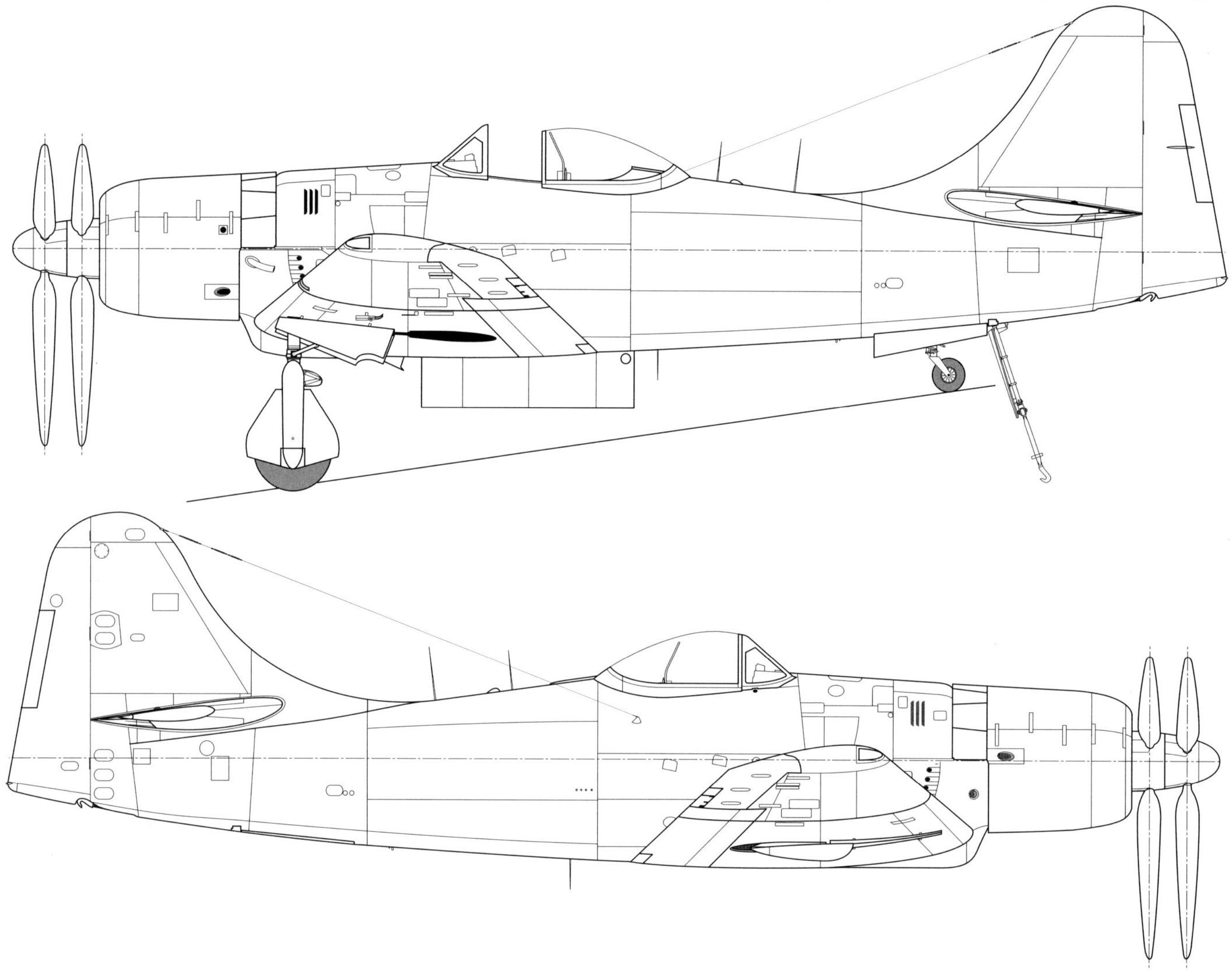

BOEING MODEL 400 (XF8B-1)
BuAer No. 57984
November 27,1944

0 1 2 3 4 5 6 feet
2 meters
SCALE BARS

Scale 1:72

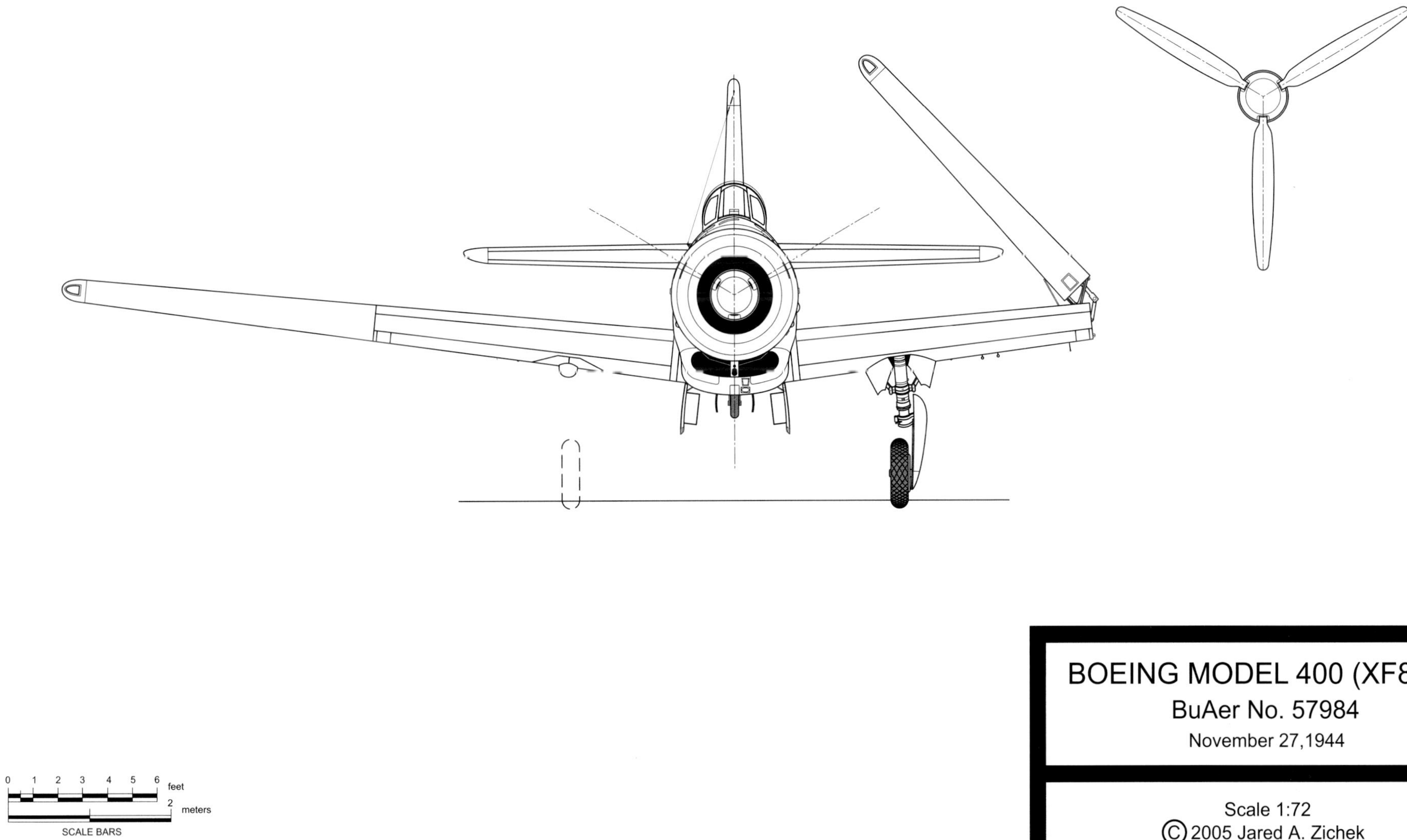

BOEING MODEL 400 (XF8B-1)

BuAer No. 57984

November 27,1944

Scale 1:72

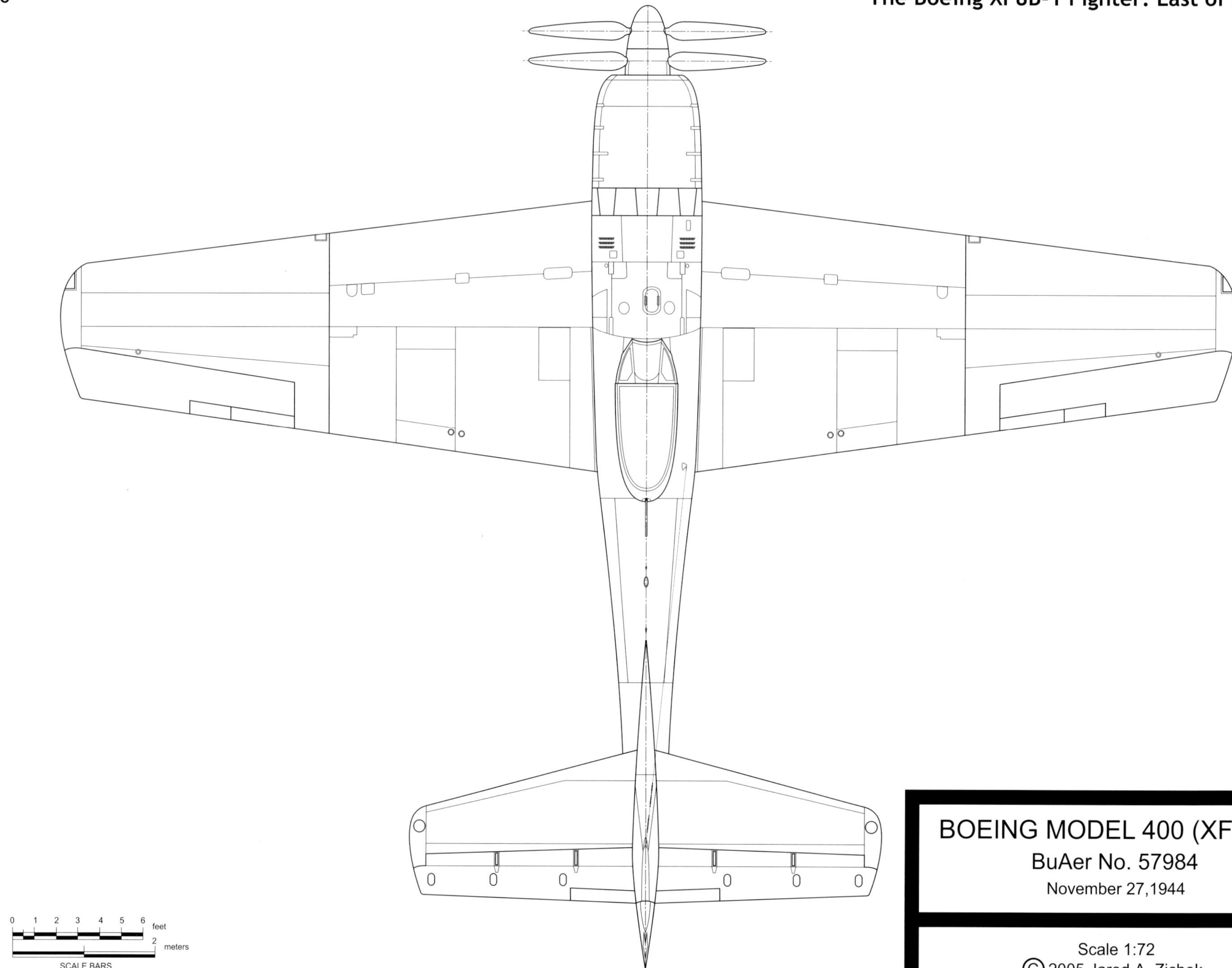

BOEING MODEL 400 (XF8B-1)

BuAer No. 57984

November 27,1944

Scale 1:72

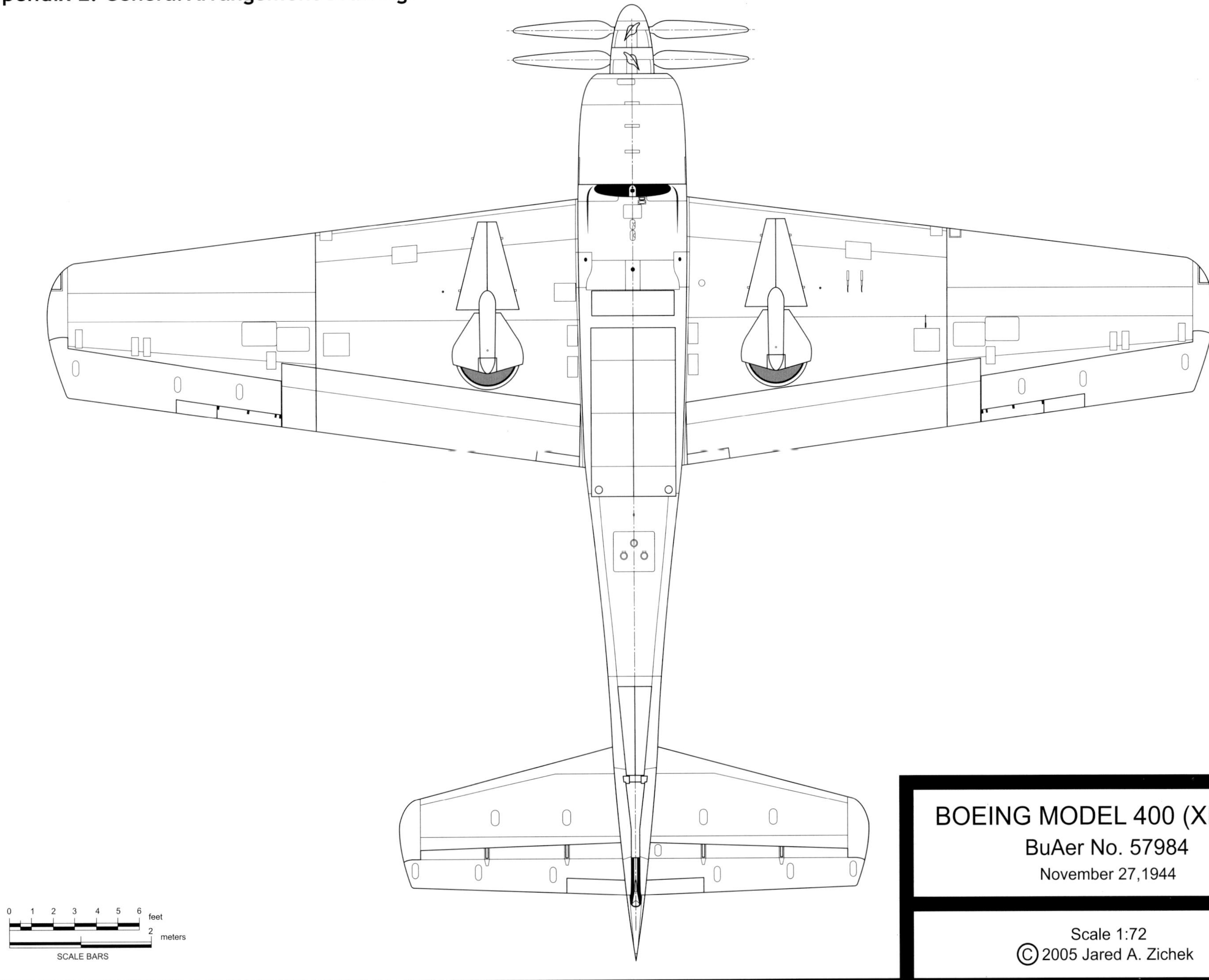

BOEING MODEL 400 (XF8B-1)
BuAer No. 57984
November 27,1944

Scale 1:72

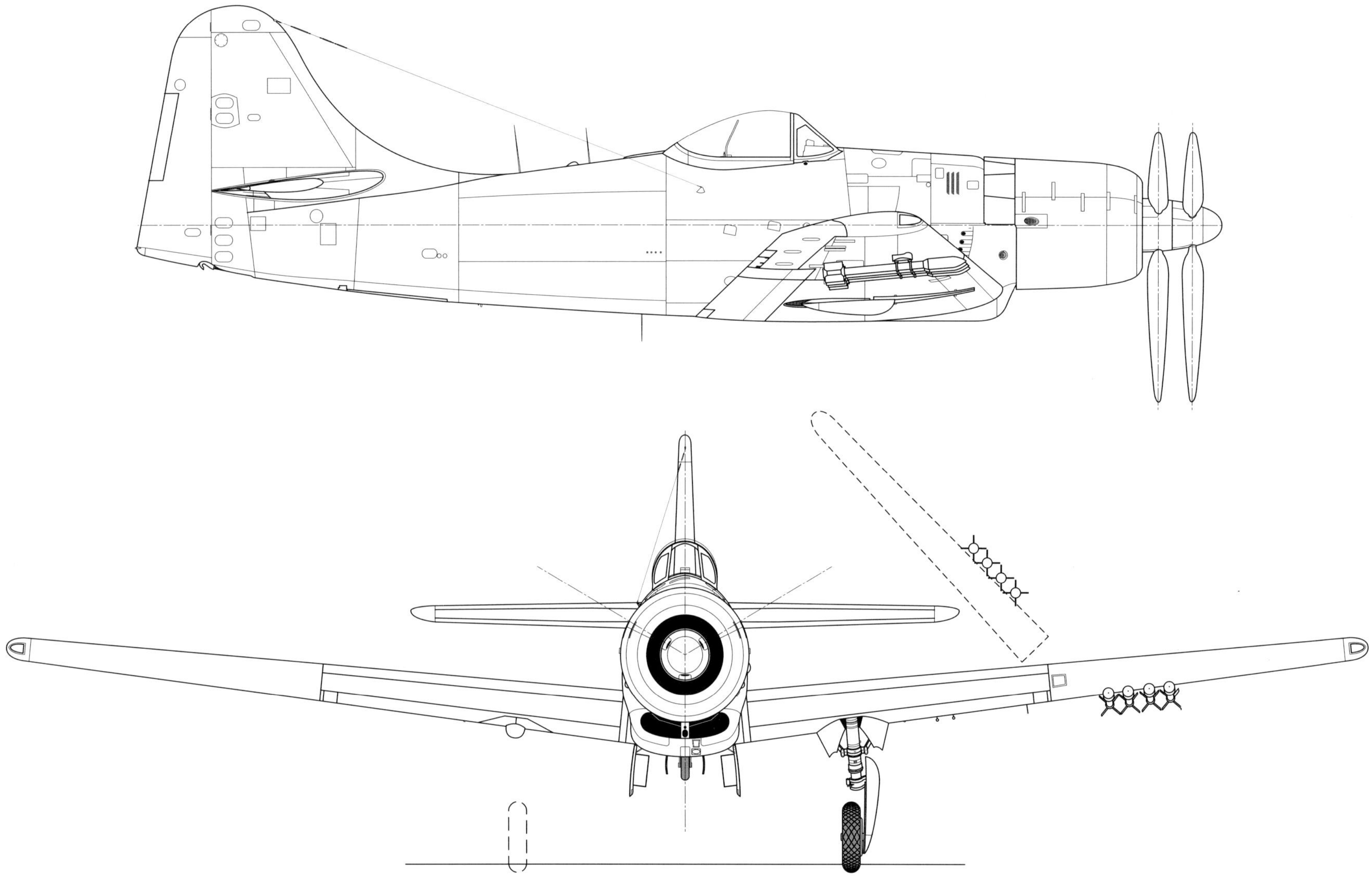

BOEING MODEL 400 (XF8B-1)

Proposed 4 Inch Rocket Installation

April 18, 1945

0 1 2 3 4 5 6 feet

2 meters

SCALE BARS

Scale 1:72

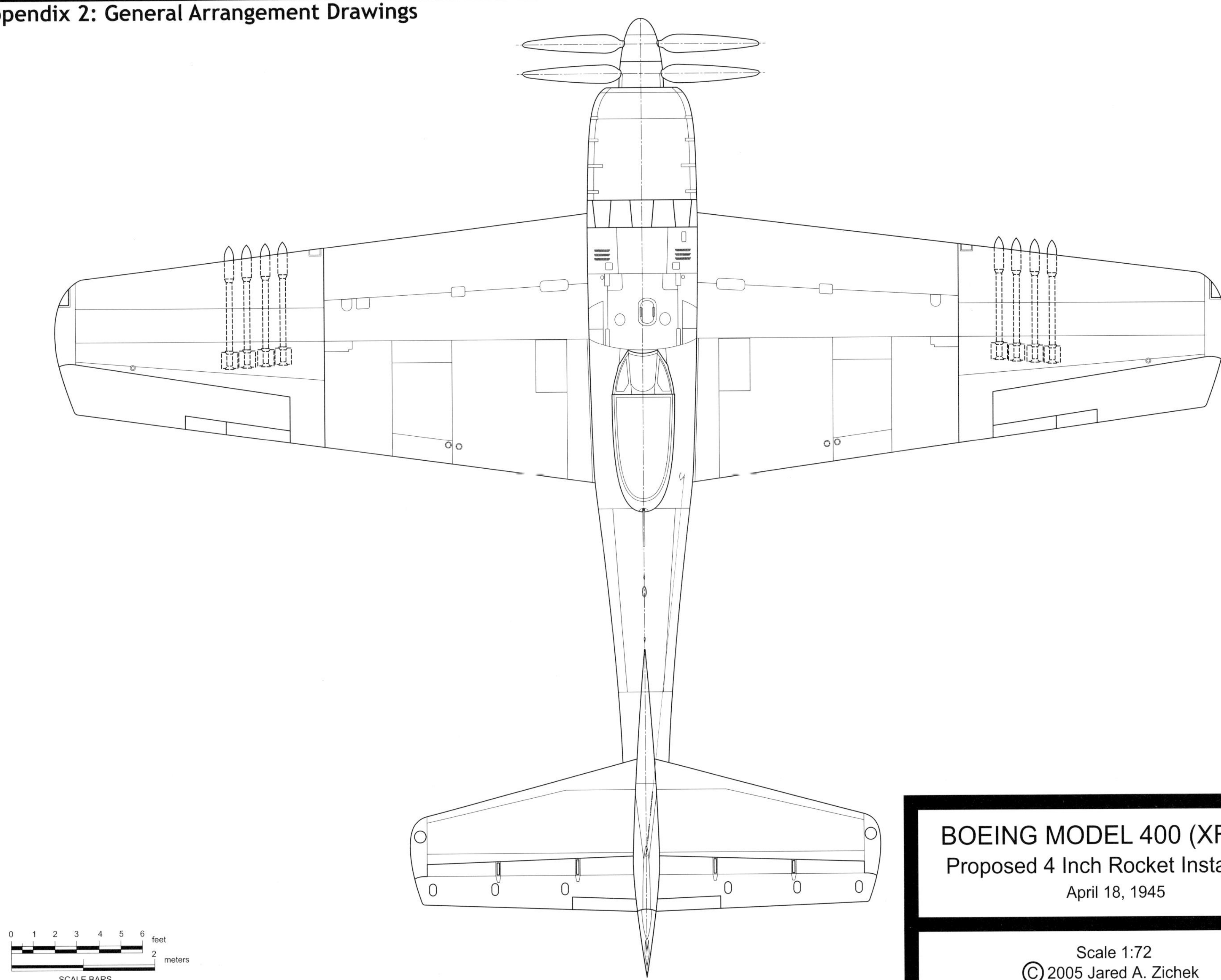

BOEING MODEL 400 (XF8B-1)
Proposed 4 Inch Rocket Installation
April 18, 1945

Scale 1:72

Scrap view of pitot fitted to port wing of 57986

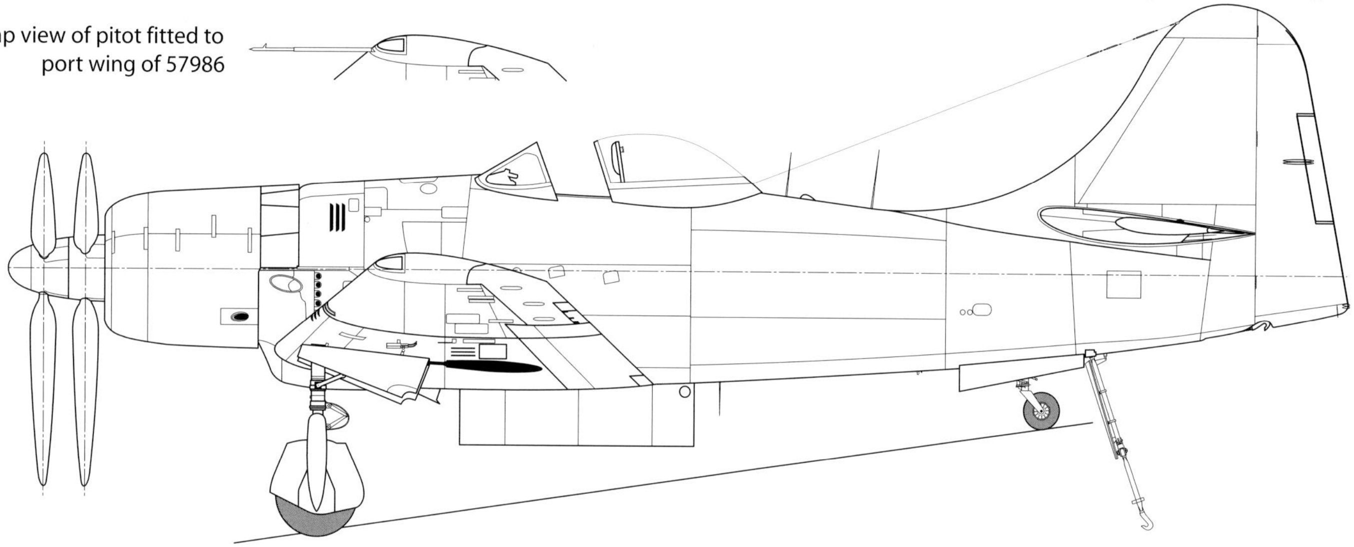

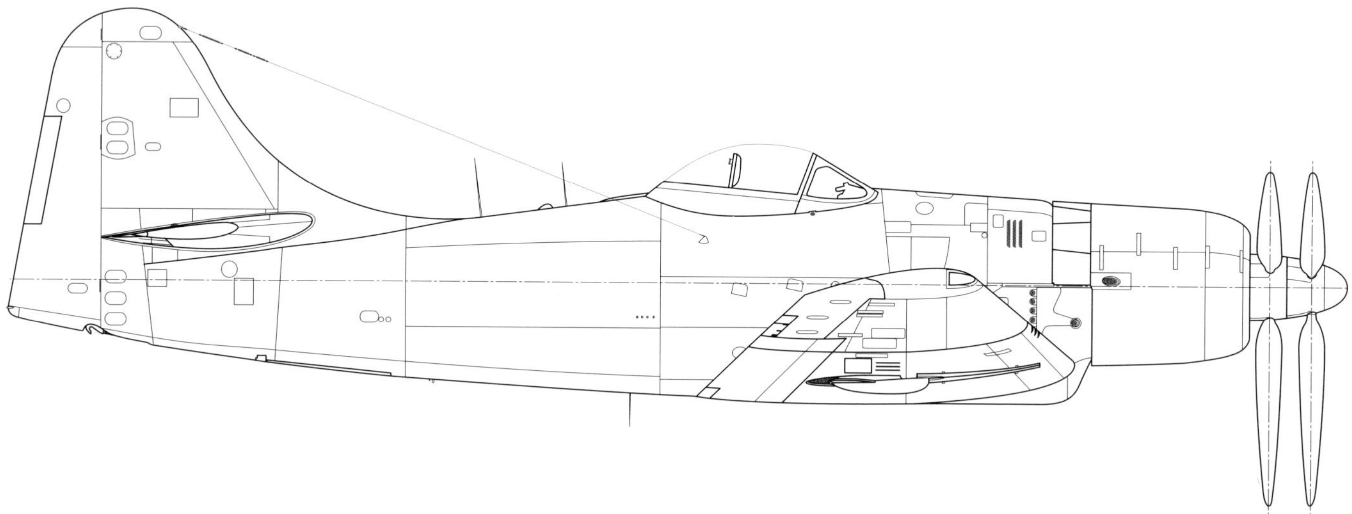

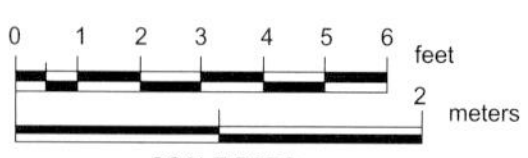

BOEING MODEL 400 (XF8B-1)

BuAer Nos. 57985 and 57986

1945 - 1947

Scale 1:72

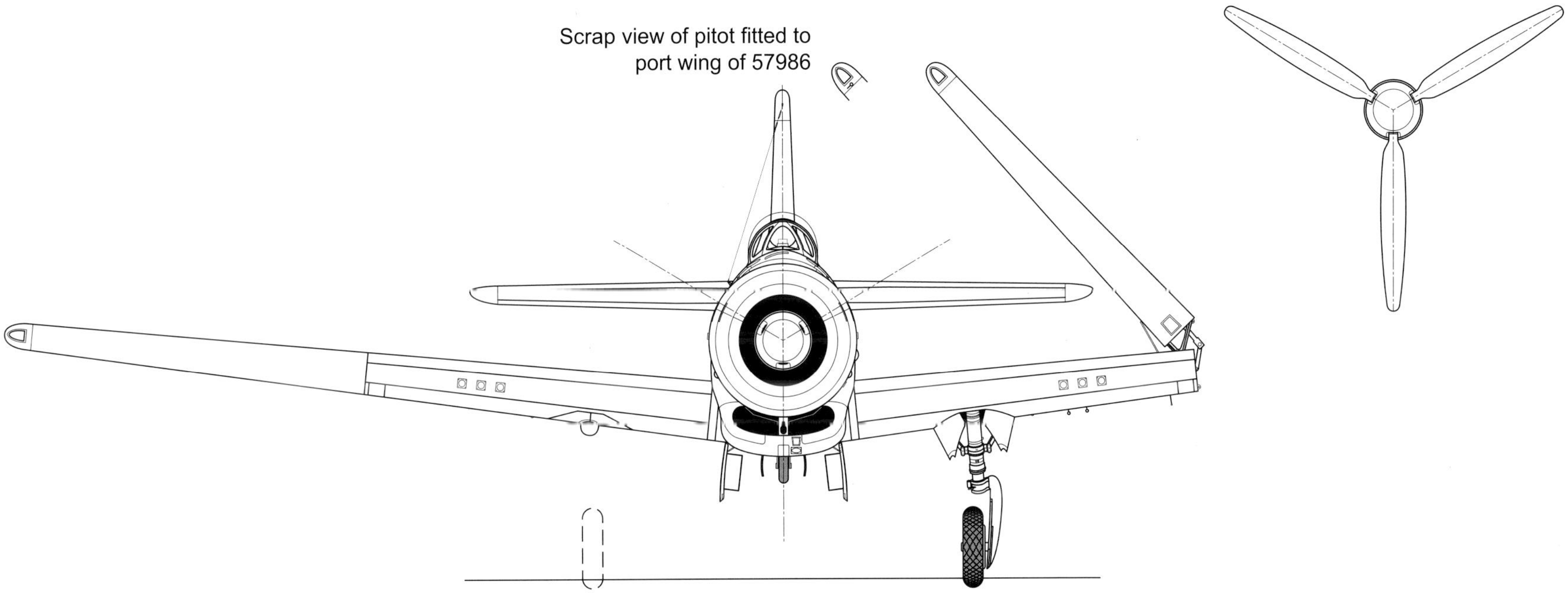

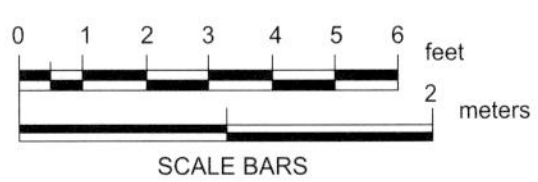

BOEING MODEL 400 (XF8B-1)

BuAer Nos. 57985 and 57986

1945 - 1947

Scale 1:72

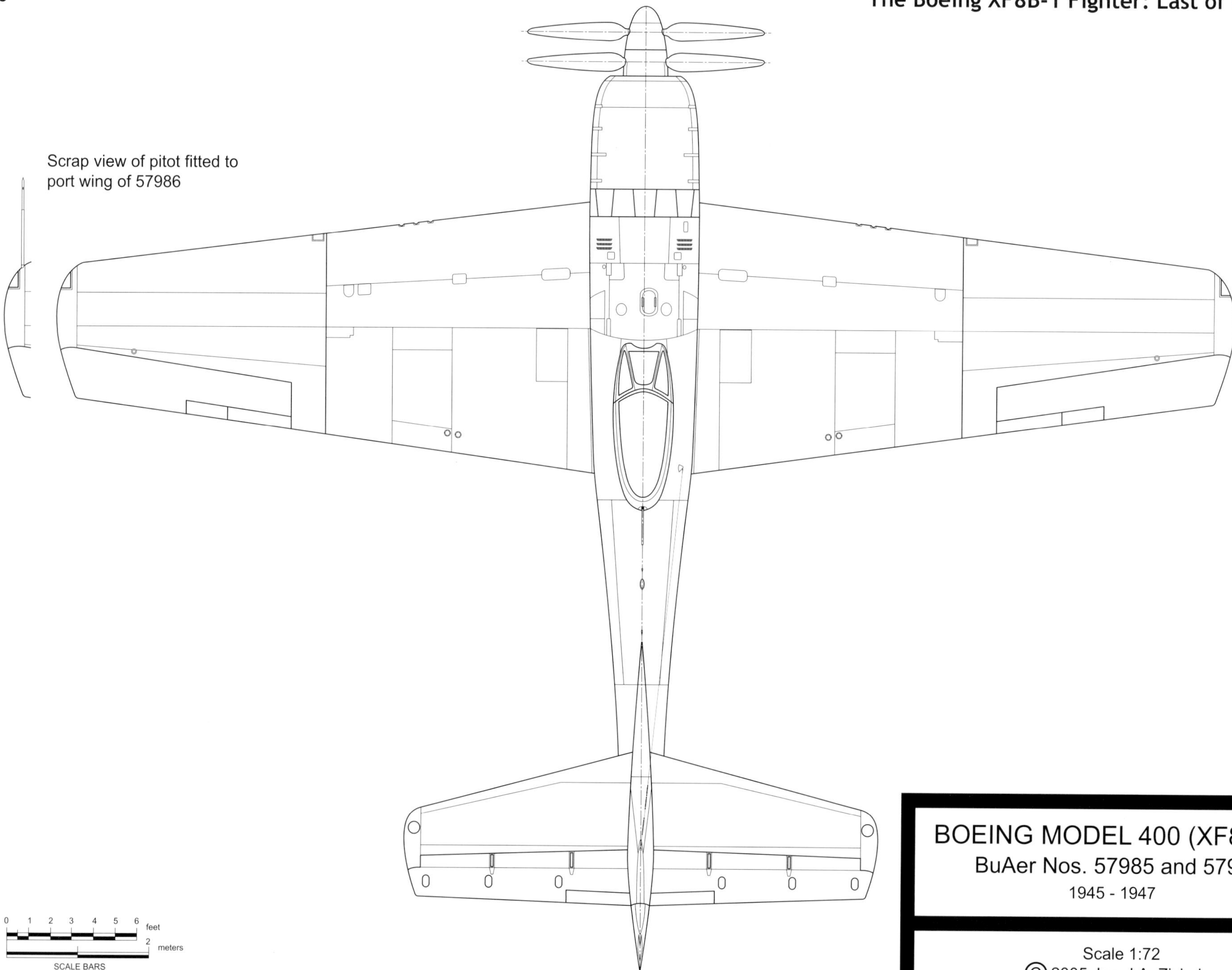

BOEING MODEL 400 (XF8B-1)
BuAer Nos. 57985 and 57986
1945 - 1947

Scale 1:72

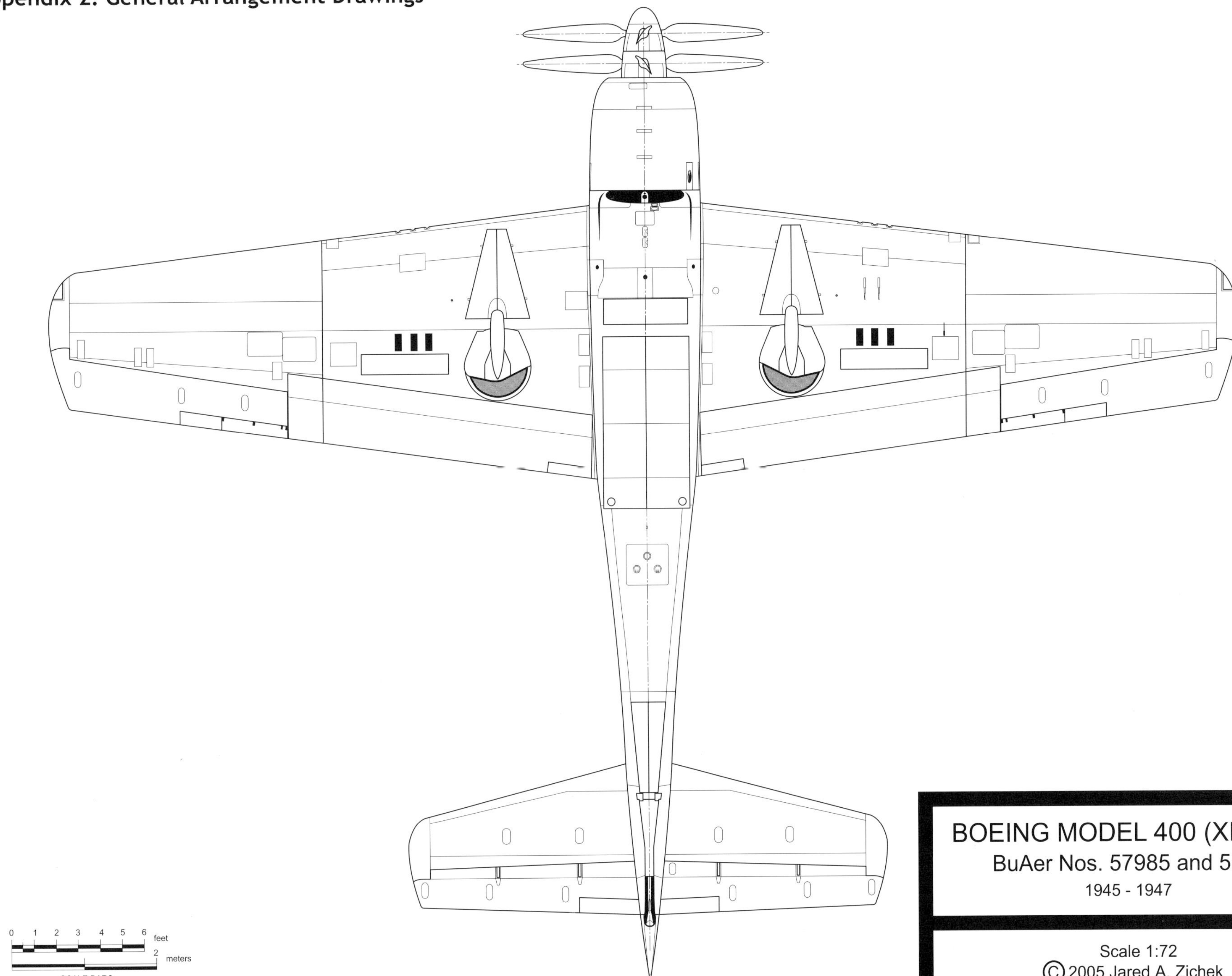

BOEING MODEL 400 (XF8B-1)
BuAer Nos. 57985 and 57986
1945 - 1947

Scale 1:72

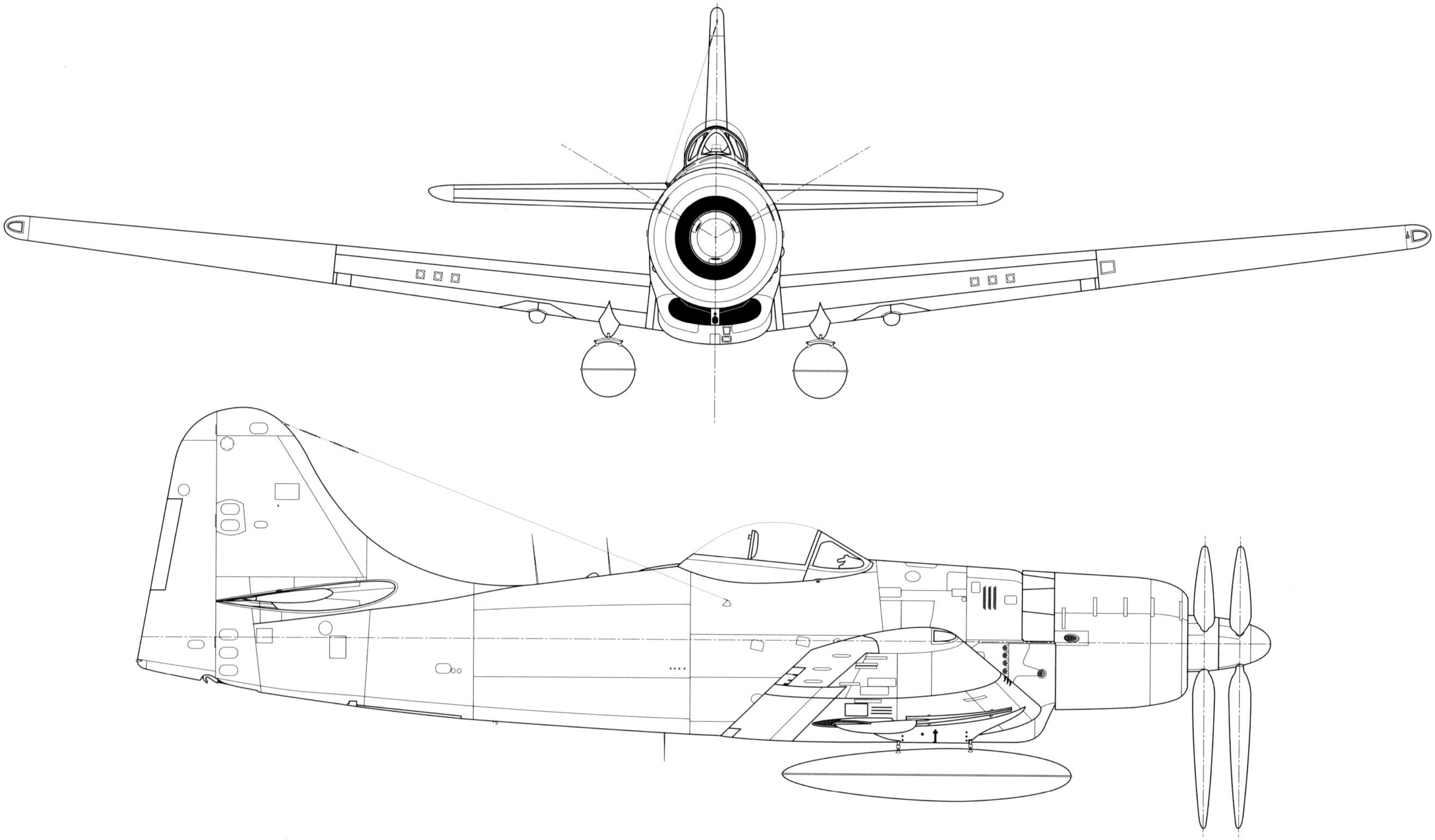

BOEING MODEL 400 (XF8B-1)
BuAer No. 57986
with 150 Gallon Drop Tanks

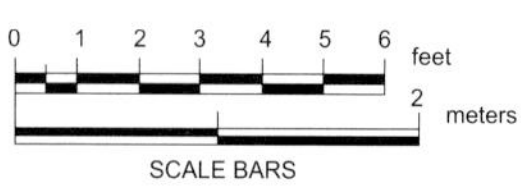

Scale 1:72

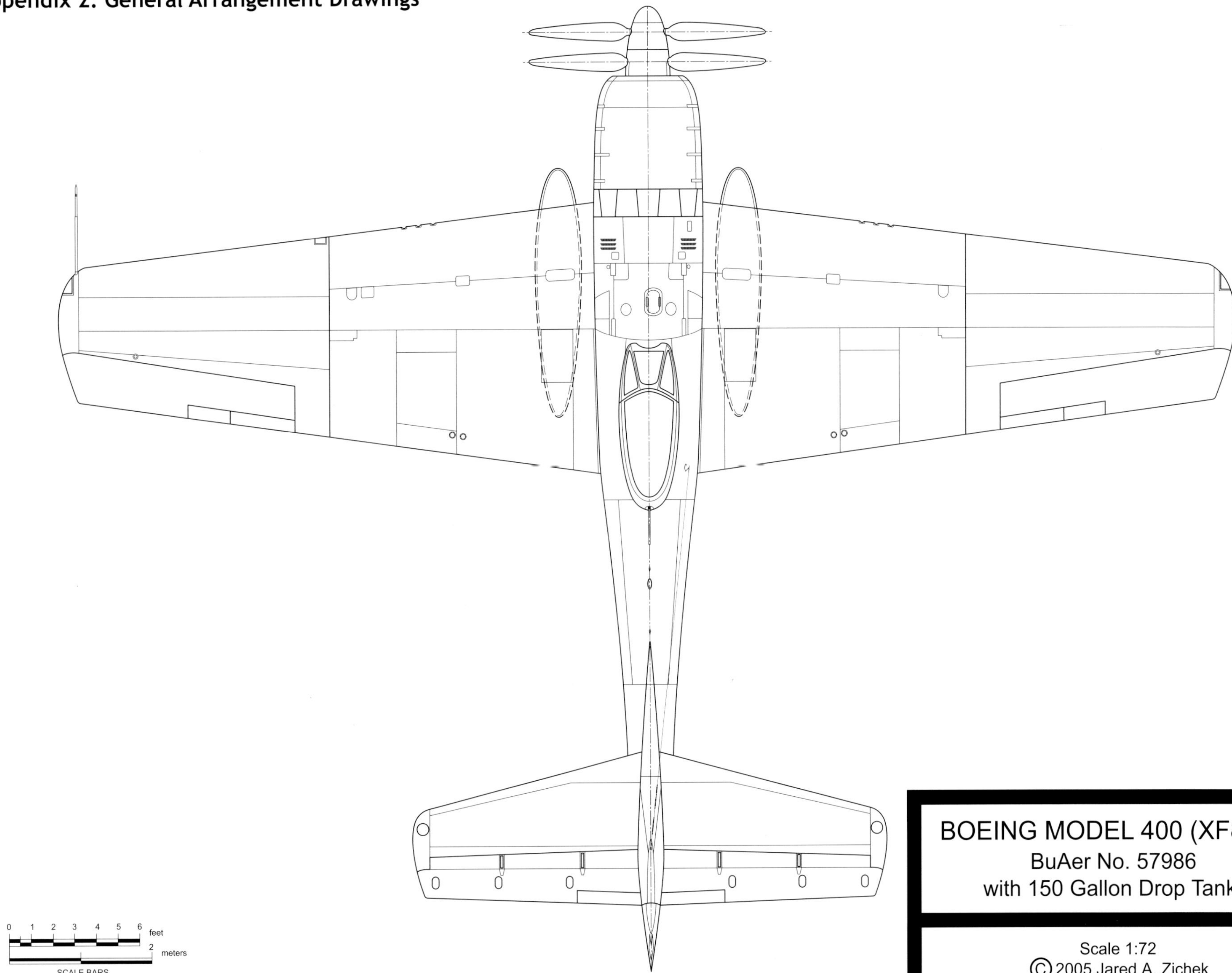

BOEING MODEL 400 (XF8B-1)
BuAer No. 57986
with 150 Gallon Drop Tanks

Scale 1:72

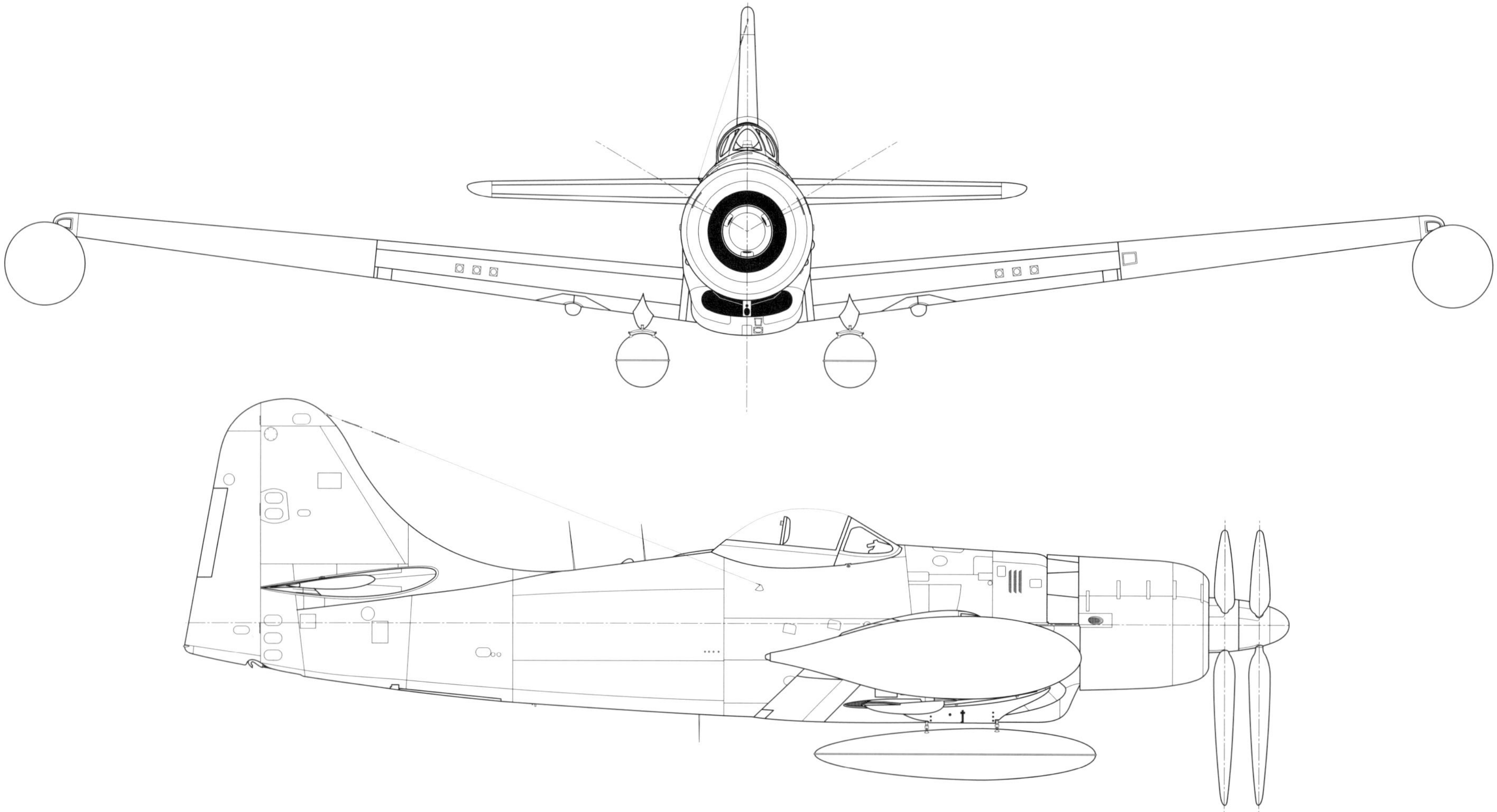

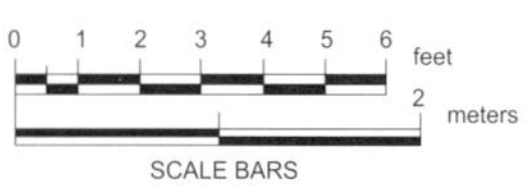

BOEING MODEL 400 (XF8B-1)

Proposed Long Range Variant
with 150 Gallon Drop Tanks on Inboard
Hardpoints and 300 Gallon Wingtip Drop Tanks

Scale 1:72

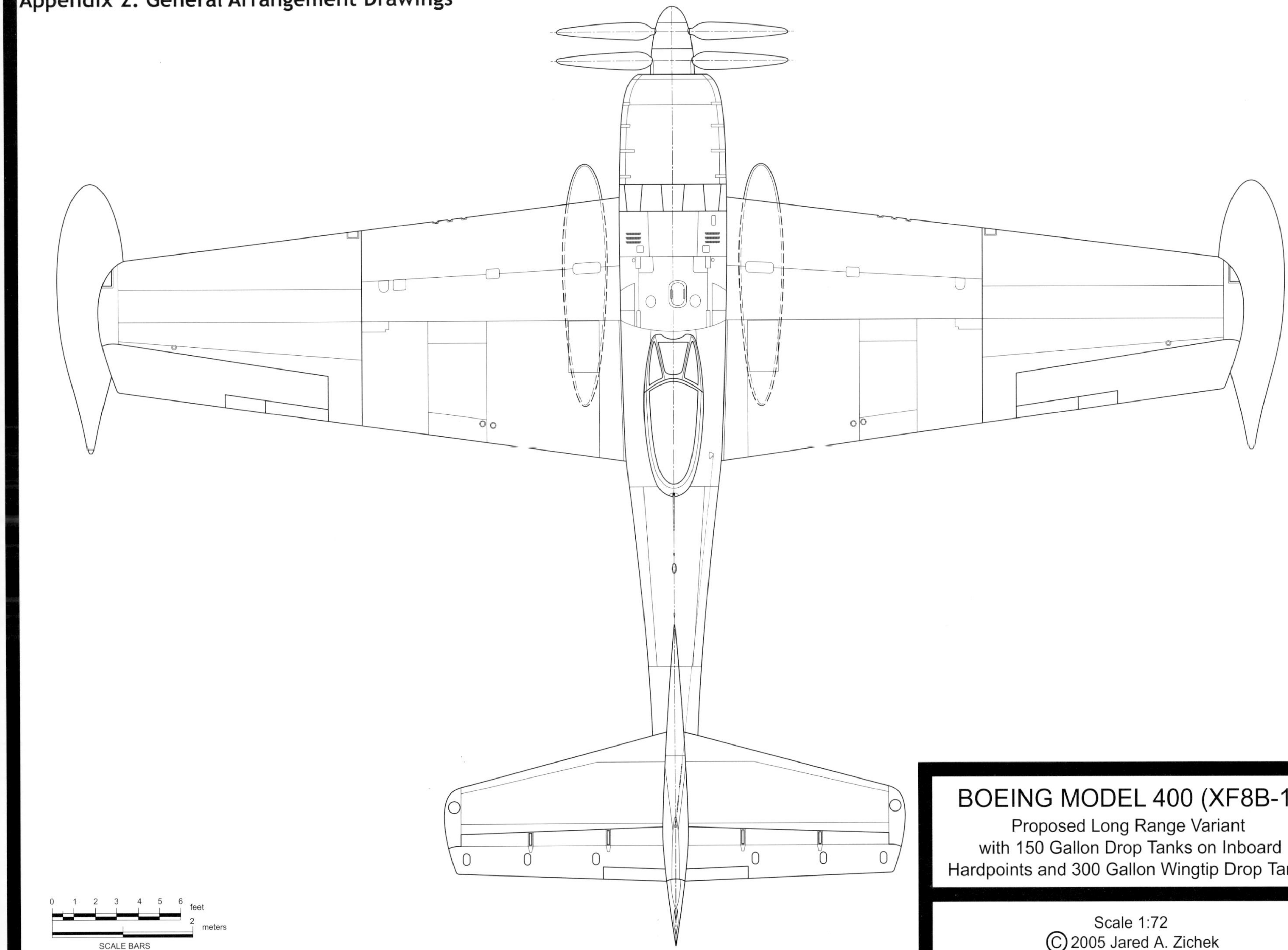

BOEING MODEL 400 (XF8B-1)
Proposed Long Range Variant with 150 Gallon Drop Tanks on Inboard Hardpoints and 300 Gallon Wingtip Drop Tanks

Scale 1:72

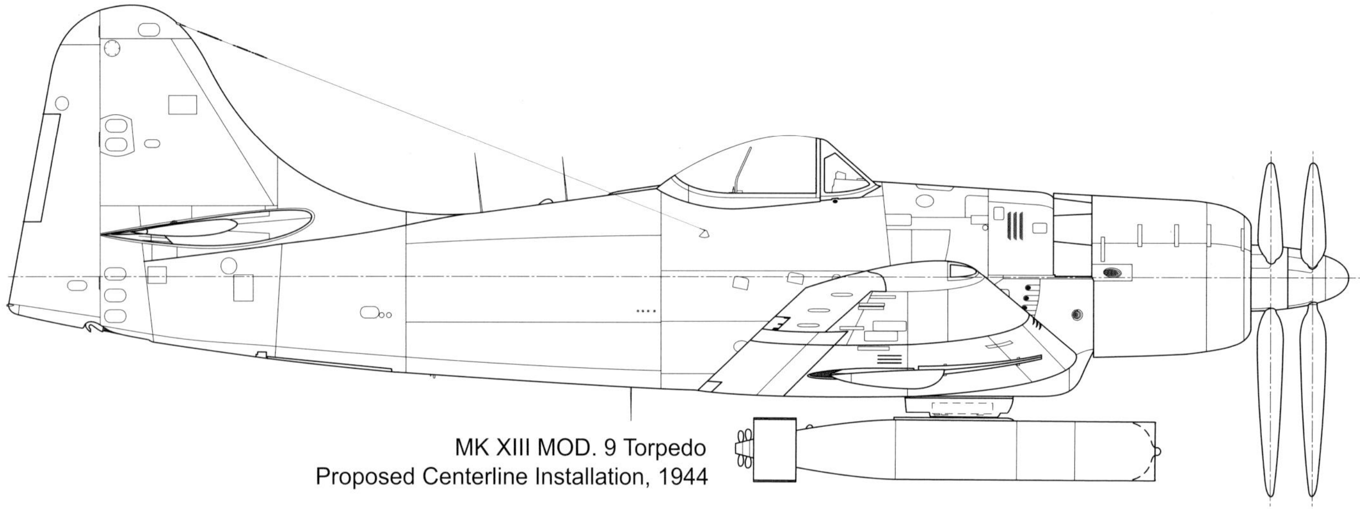

MK XIII MOD. 9 Torpedo
Proposed Centerline Installation, 1944

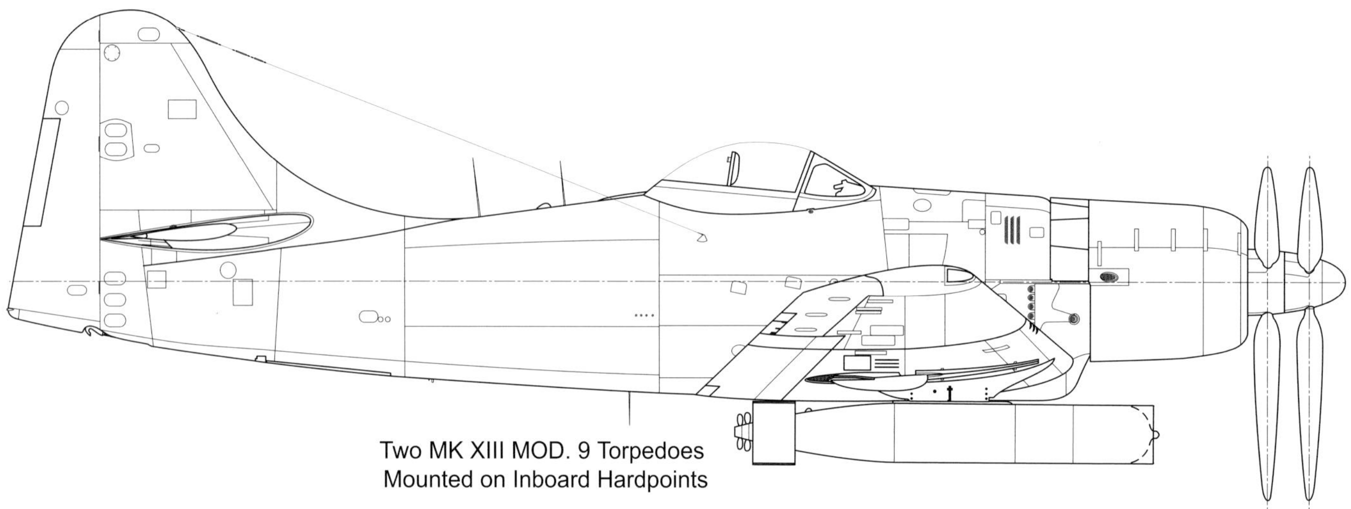

Two MK XIII MOD. 9 Torpedoes
Mounted on Inboard Hardpoints

BOEING MODEL 400 (XF8B-1)
Proposed Torpedo Configurations

Scale 1:72

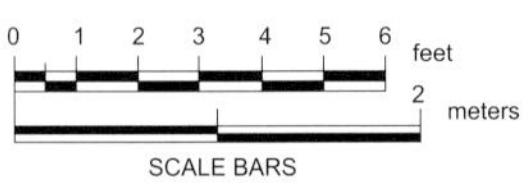

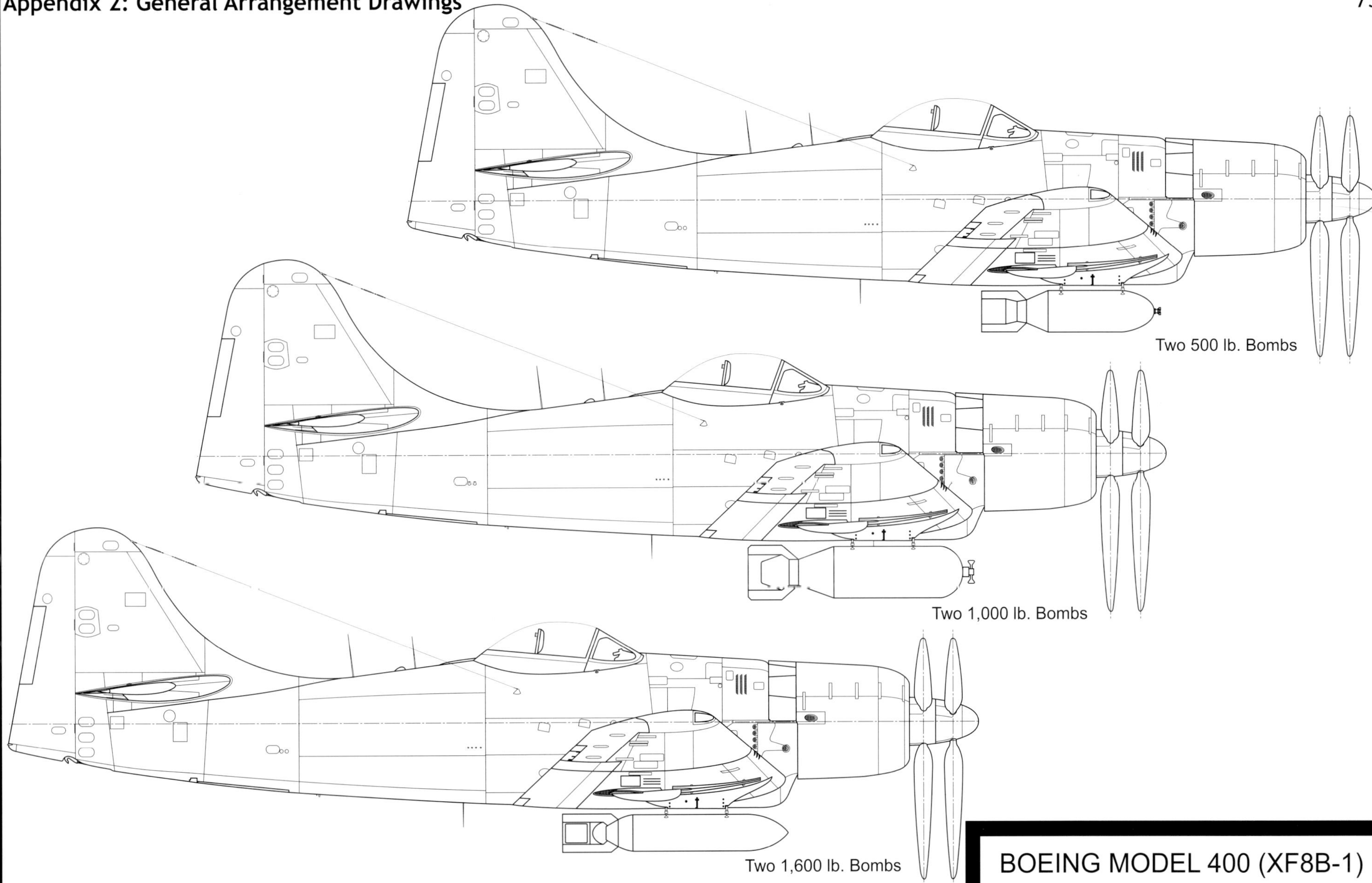

Note: Side profiles are based on a contemporary simplified front view drawing showing outlines of the bombs' external diameters. Mounting details are speculative and are based on that used for fuel tank. There is no evidence any of these configurations was ever tested.

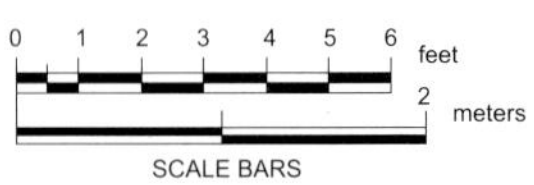

BOEING MODEL 400 (XF8B-1)

Proposed External Ordnance Configurations

Scale 1:72

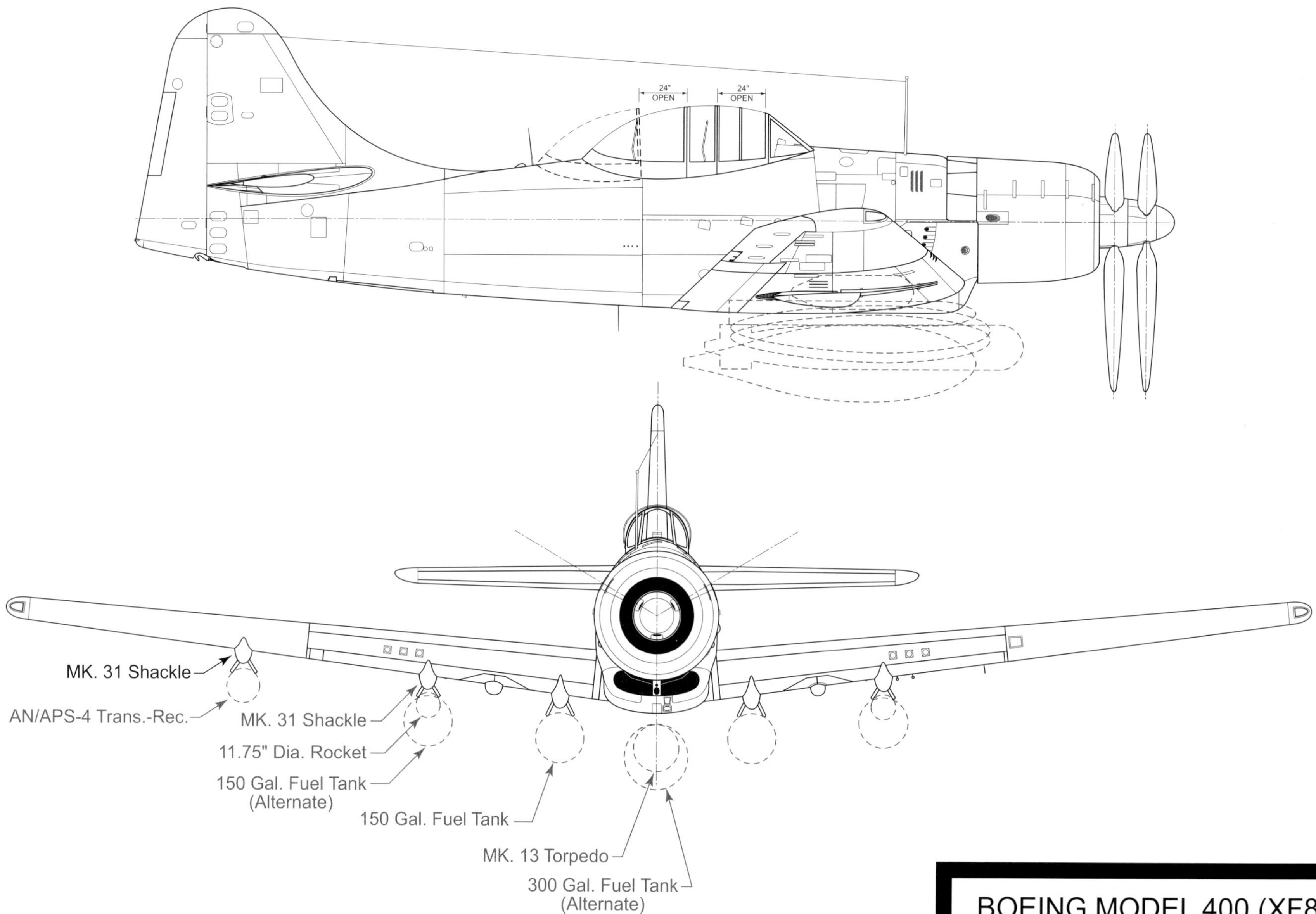

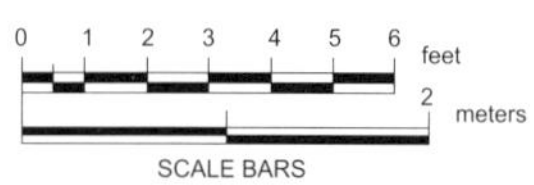

BOEING MODEL 400 (XF8B-1)

Early Two Seat Proposal

Scale 1:72

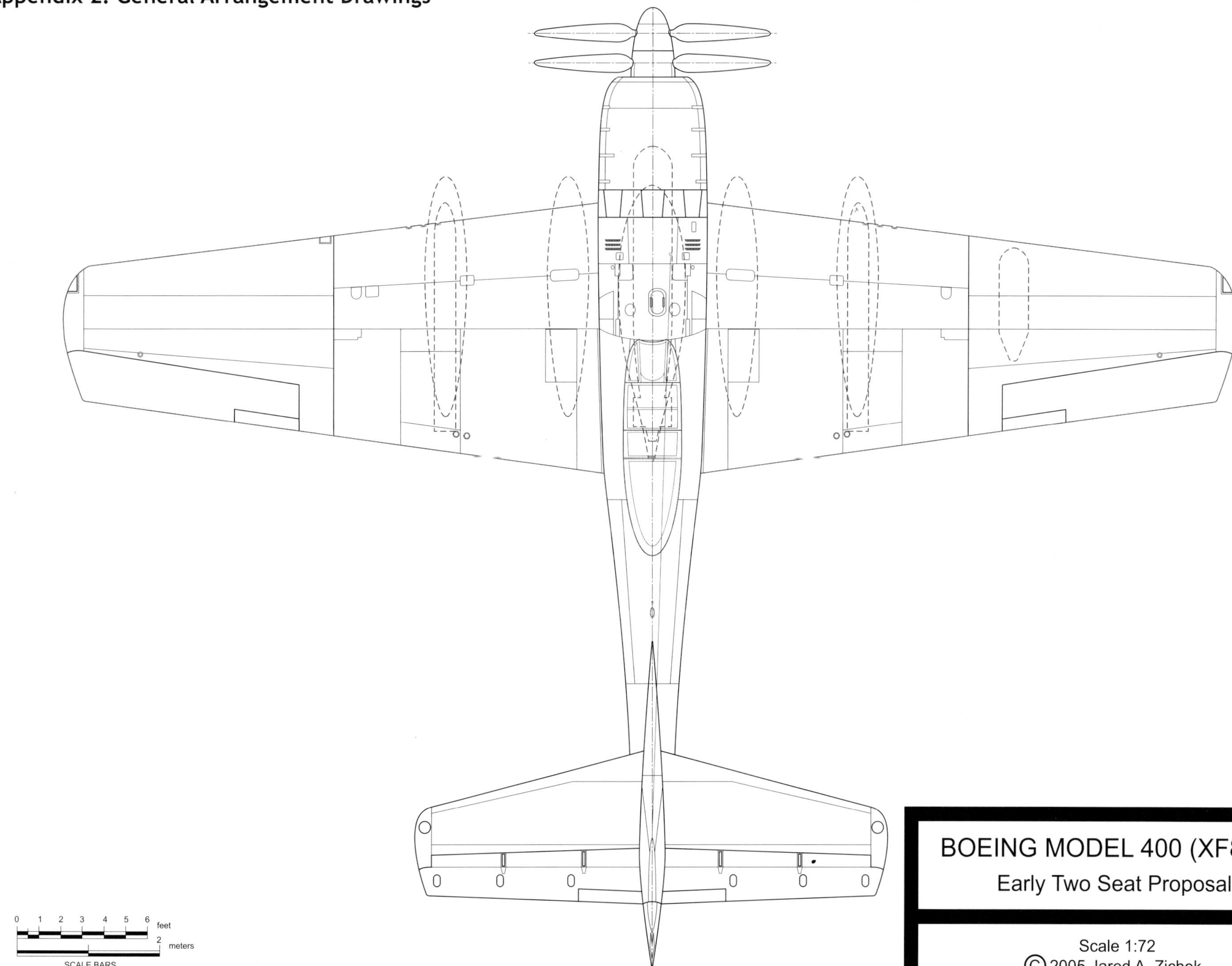

BOEING MODEL 400 (XF8B-1)
Early Two Seat Proposal

Scale 1:72

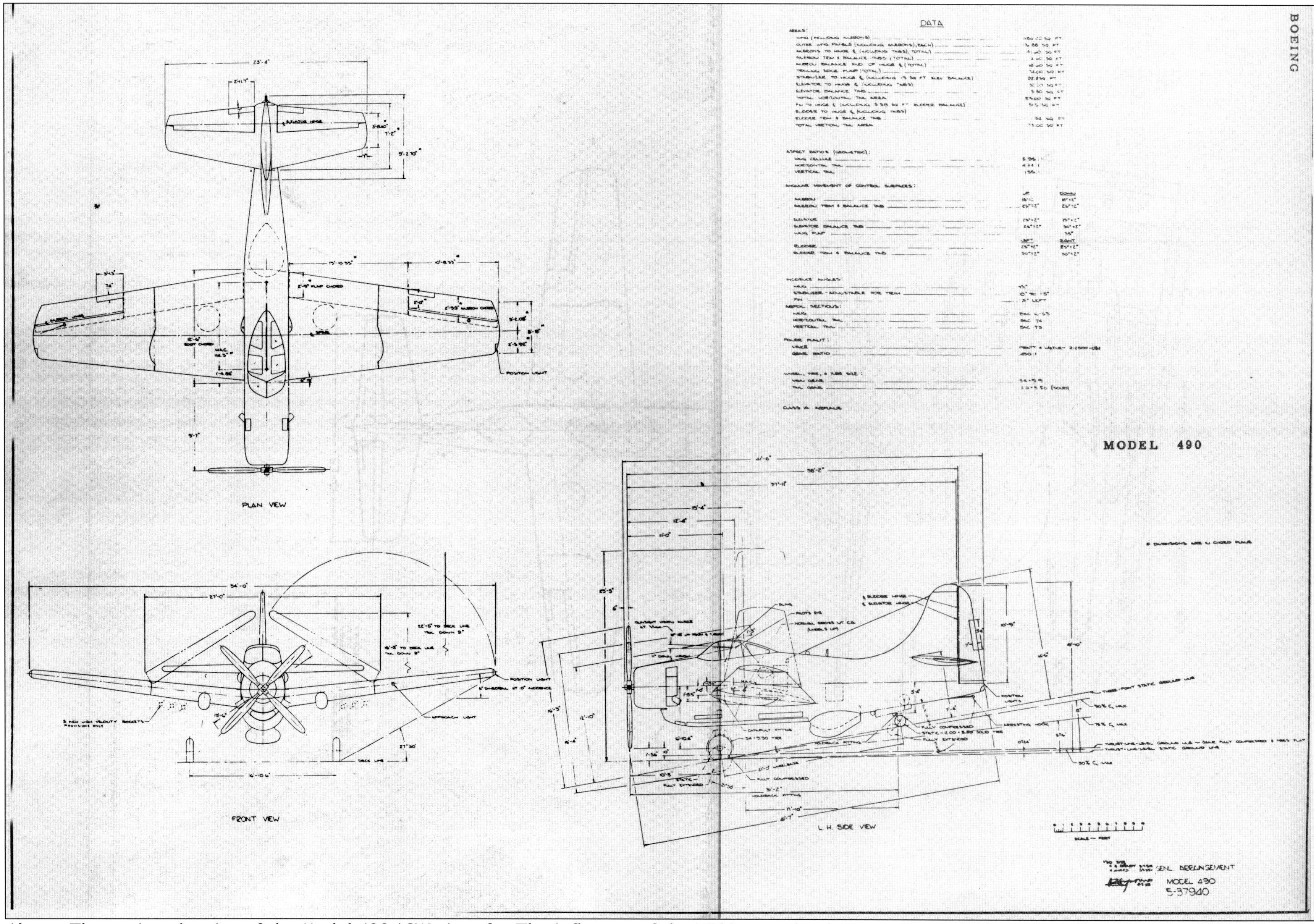

Drawing: National Archives, RG 72

Above: Three-view drawing of the Model 490 ASW aircraft. The influence of the XF8B-1 on the design of the flying surfaces is readily apparent.

Appendix 3

Wind Tunnel Reports, Photos, and Drawings

This appendix presents a large number of the wind tunnel reports and photos produced during the development of the XF8B-1. These were found in Navy Bureau of Aeronautics files in the National Archives, and it is remarkable that so many were preserved, considering the fact the type never reached quantity production. The photos that accompanied the wind tunnel reports are the main focus in this section, though summaries for particularly interesting reports are also provided. The remainder are quite technical and of little interest to the casual reader.

The quality of the photos is generally mediocre, as they were printed on inexpensive paper that often wrinkled during the printing process. Nonetheless, the photos provide a comprehensive record of the XF8B-1's evolution and the science of wind tunnel testing during the Forties. As one will see, the basic configuration of Boeing's big fighter was firmly established from early on, with subtle refinements being added as testing progressed.

Wind Tunnel Tests on the FR-46 .15 Scale Model of the XF8B-1 - April 19, 1944

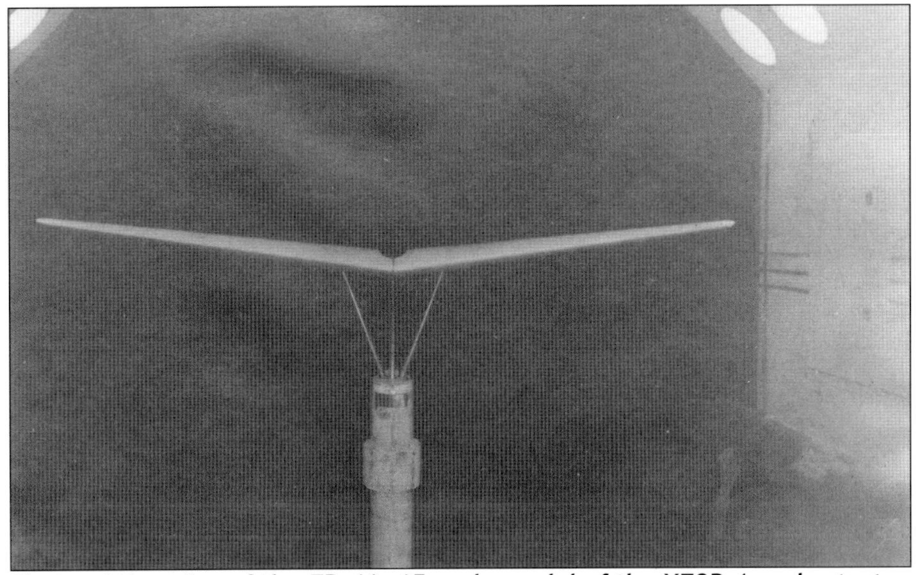

Photo: National Archives, RG 72

Photo of the wing of the FR-46 .15 scale model of the XF8B-1 under test.

Photo: National Archives, RG 72

Model with wing, body, and spinner.

Photo: National Archives, RG 72

Side view with the flaps deployed.

Photo: National Archives, RG 72

Aileron and transition strip.

Photo: National Archives, RG 72

Three-quarter view with the flaps deployed.

Photo: National Archives, RG 72

Aileron and transition strip.

Photo: National Archives, RG 72

Front view with counter-rotating propeller.

Photo: National Archives, RG 72

Ground plane installation.

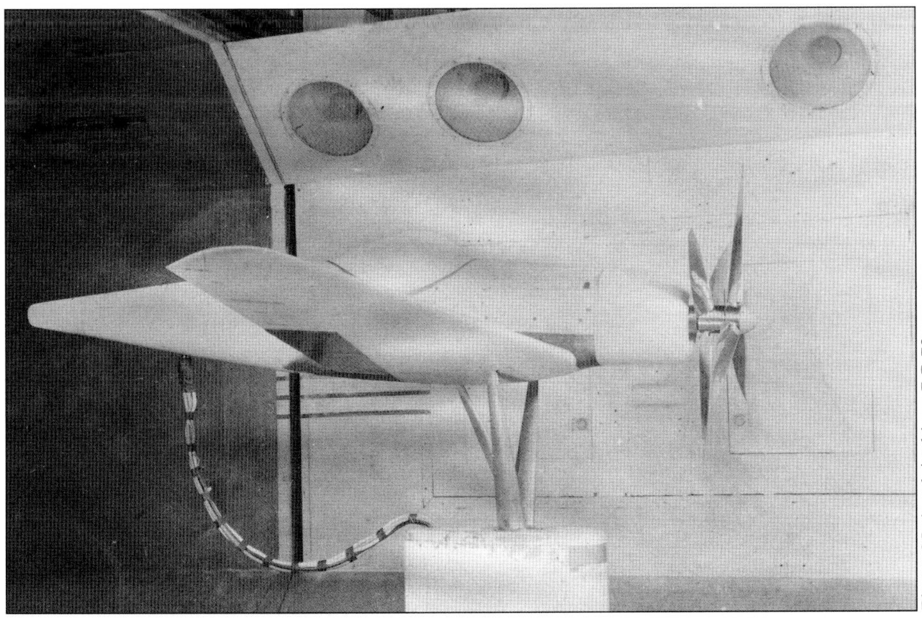

Photo: National Archives, RG 72

Side view with propeller showing power strut.

Photo: National Archives, RG 72

Top view of model with flaps down and ground plane installed.

Ground Cooling Investigation - July 11, 1944

Photo: National Archives, RG 72

Left hand side view of ground cooling pressure test setup.

Photo: National Archives, RG 72

Side view of cowl flaps and oil cooler flap.

Photo: National Archives, RG 72

Right hand side view of ground cooling pressure test setup.

Photo: National Archives, RG 72

Rear top view of cowl flaps and oil cooler flap.

Photo: National Archives, RG 72

Three-quarter front view of cowl flaps, oil cooler flap, and intercooler.

Photo: National Archives, RG 72

Side view of propeller and spinner.

Photo: National Archives, RG 72

Three-quarter rear view of cowl flaps.

Photo: National Archives, RG 72

Left hand side view of propeller and spinner.

Photo: National Archives, RG 72

Right hand side view of propeller and spinner.

Photo: National Archives, RG 72

Cowl flap hinge moment setup.

Photo: National Archives, RG 72

Front view of propeller and spinner.

Photo: National Archives, RG 72

Side view of cowl flaps.

Additional Wind Tunnel Tests - September 21, 1944

Photo: National Archives, RG 72

Front view of complete model with flaps at 35°, ground plane installed.

Photo: National Archives, RG 72

Rear view of model.

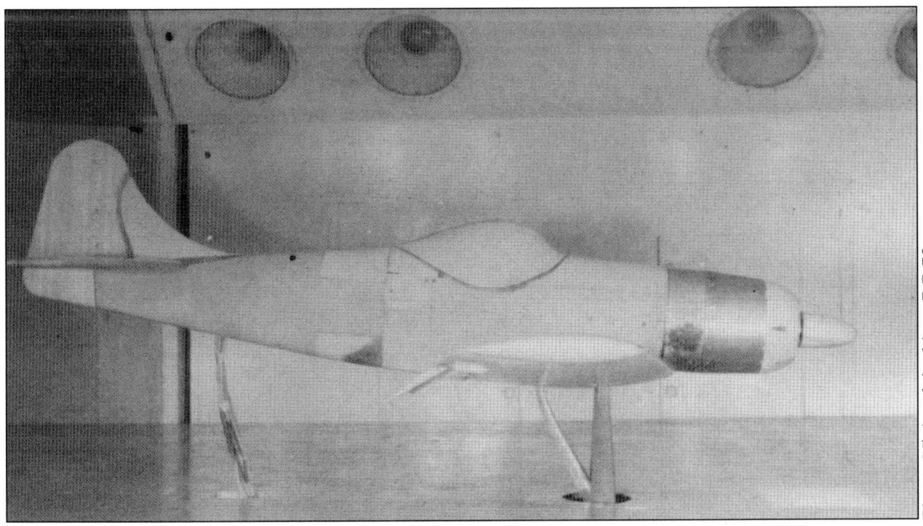
Photo: National Archives, RG 72

Side view of model.

Photo: National Archives, RG 72

Front view of model with landing gear down.

Photo: National Archives, RG 72

Side view of model with landing gear down.

Photo: National Archives, RG 72

Three-quarter front view of model with landing gear down.

Ground Cooling Investigation No. 2 - October 9, 1944

Photo: National Archives, RG 72

Ground cooling pressure test setup.

Photo: National Archives, RG 72

Same model with propellers slightly rotated.

Ground Cooling Investigation No. 3 - January 10, 1945

Photo: National Archives, RG 72

Three-quarter front view of spinner and propeller.

Photo: National Archives, RG 72

The propeller rotated to another position for measurements.

Photo: National Archives, RG 72

Photo of propeller rotated slightly to test effect on ground cooling.

Photo: National Archives, RG 72

Propeller adjusted again.

Photo: National Archives, RG 72

Front view of spinner and propeller.

Longitudinal Stability Investigation - April 13, 1945

Photo: National Archives, RG 72

Model (minus canopy & tail) with cowl flaps, gill, and oil cooler flaps.

Photo: National Archives, RG 72

Right hand side view of spinner and propeller.

Photo: National Archives, RG 72

Close-up view of sealed intercooler flap.

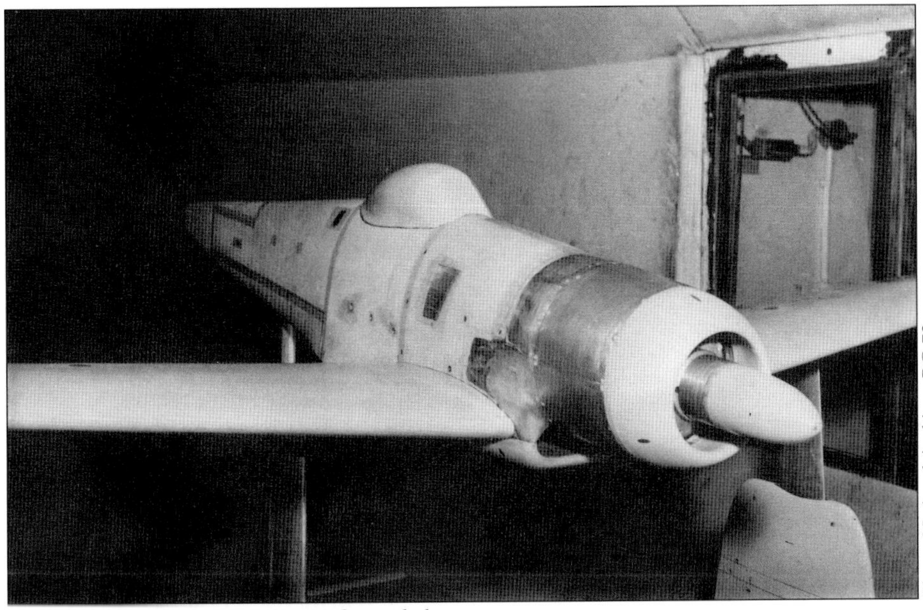

Photo: National Archives, RG 72

Three-quarter front view of model.

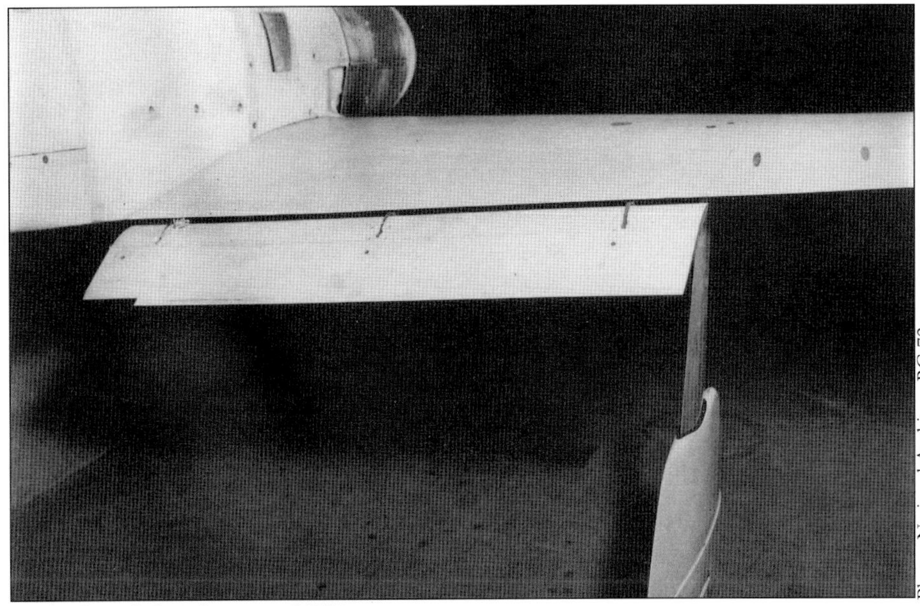

Photo: National Archives, RG 72

Right hand flap lowered 35°.

Photo: National Archives, RG 72

Landing gear oleo fairings.

Photo: National Archives, RG 72

Right hand flap lowered 15°.

Photo: National Archives, RG 72

Right hand flap lowered 25°.

Photo: National Archives, RG 72

Front view of both flaps lowered 35°.

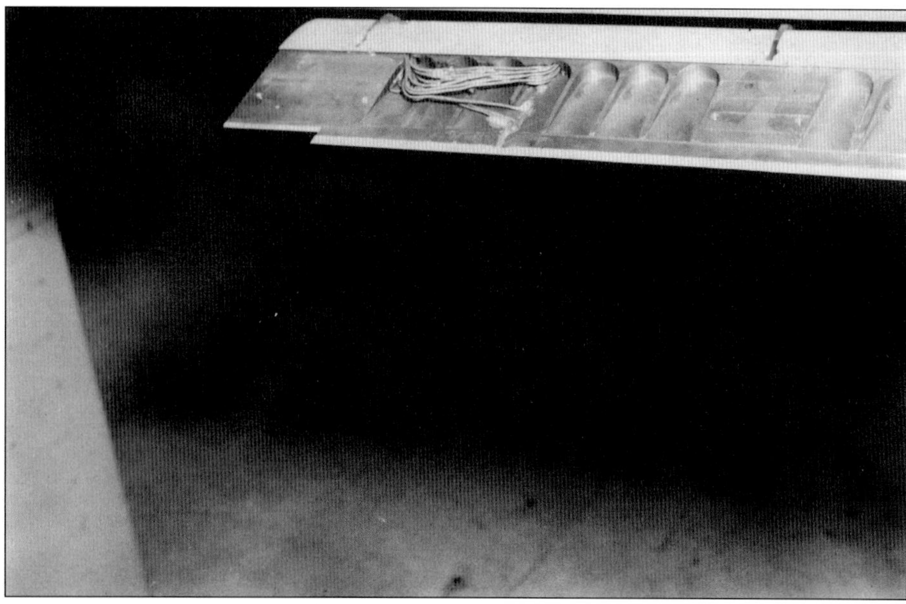

Photo: National Archives, RG 72

Right hand flap lowered 35°.

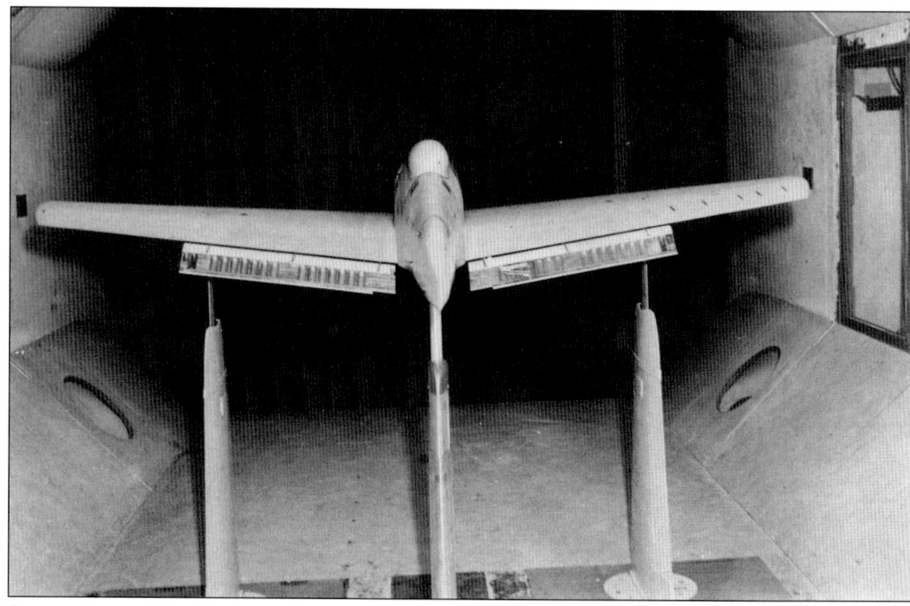

Photo: National Archives, RG 72

Rear view of both flaps lowered 35°.

Photo: National Archives, RG 72

Model with tail, landing gear down, and ground plane installed.

Photo: National Archives, RG 72

Model with tail, spinner, propeller, and landing gear attached.

Photo: National Archives, RG 72

Same model with dummy spinner.

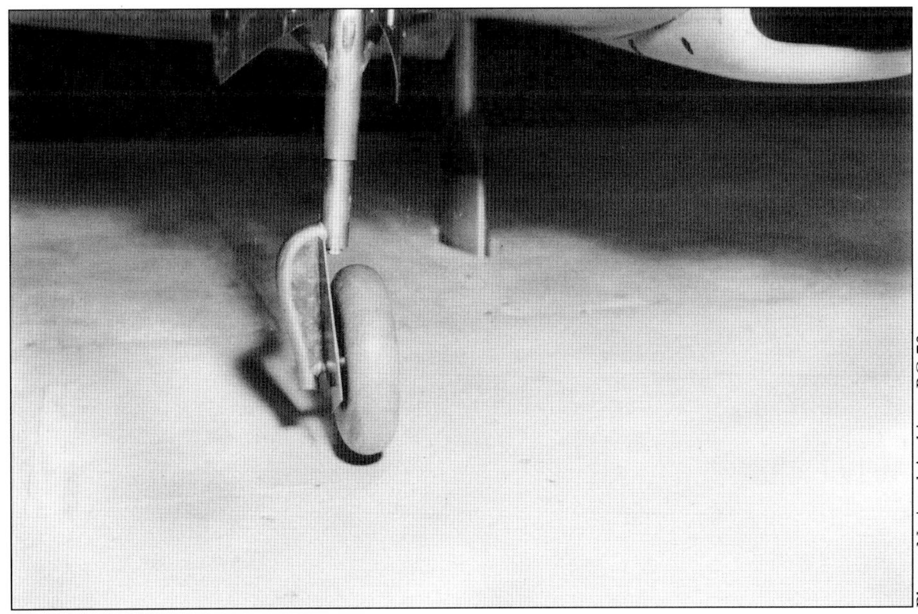

Photo: National Archives, RG 72

Close-up of landing gear.

Photo: National Archives, RG 72

Side view emphasizing elevator and horizontal tail.

Photo: National Archives, RG 72

Three-quarter front view of calibration set-up for directional rake.

Photo: National Archives, RG 72

Side view of horizontal tail.

Photo: National Archives, RG 72

Directional rake installed in place of horizontal tail.

Photo: National Archives, RG 72

Three-quarter front view of model with high-speed rear strut and fairing.

Photo: National Archives, RG 72

Top view of model with high-speed rear strut and fairing.

Photo: National Archives, RG 72

Side view of model with high-speed rear strut and fairing.

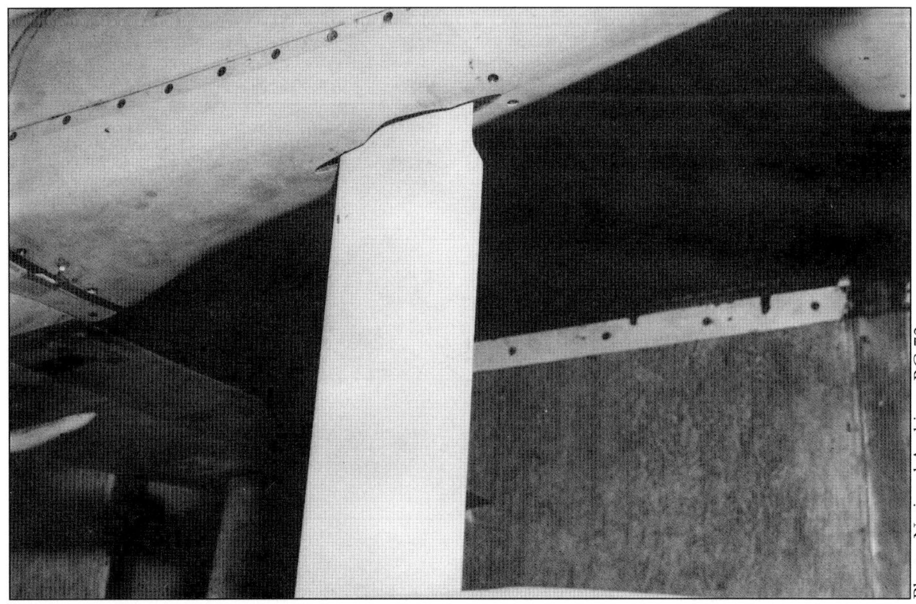

Photo: National Archives, RG 72

Three-quarter rear view of model with high-speed rear strut.

High-Speed Tests of XF8B-1 FR-49 Model with Two Different Elevators - June 6, 1945

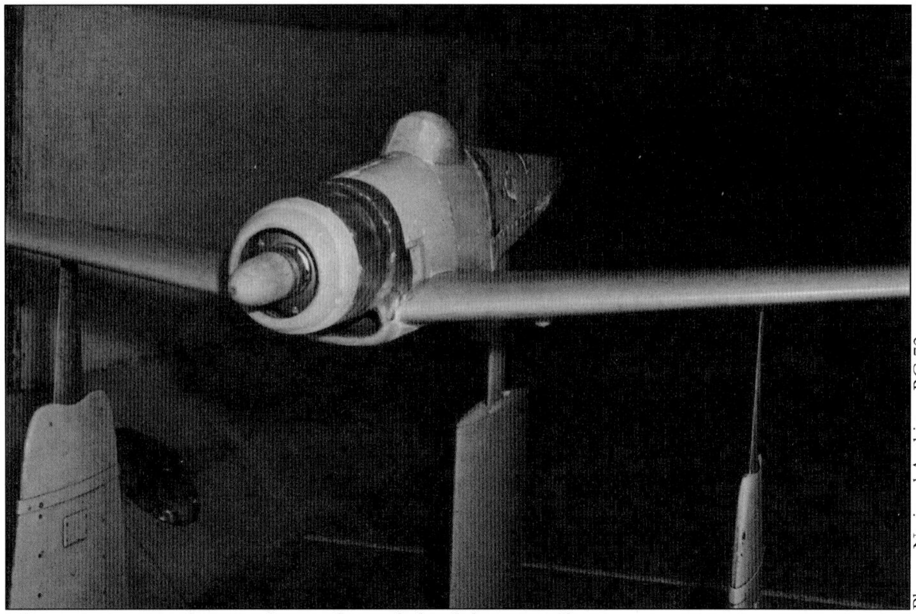

Photo: National Archives, RG 72

Three-quarter front view of model without tail.

Photo: National Archives, RG 72

Three-quarter front view of model with tail.

Photo: National Archives, RG 72

Three-quarter rear view of model without tail.

Photo: National Archives, RG 72

Three-quarter front view of fully sealed and faired gill.

Photo: National Archives, RG 72

Three-quarter front view of half sealed and faired gill.

Photo: National Archives, RG 72

Three-quarter front view of large, rear wing-body fillet.

Photo: National Archives, RG 72

Three-quarter front view of small, forward wing-body fillet.

Photo: National Archives, RG 72

Rear view of large, rear wing-body fillet.

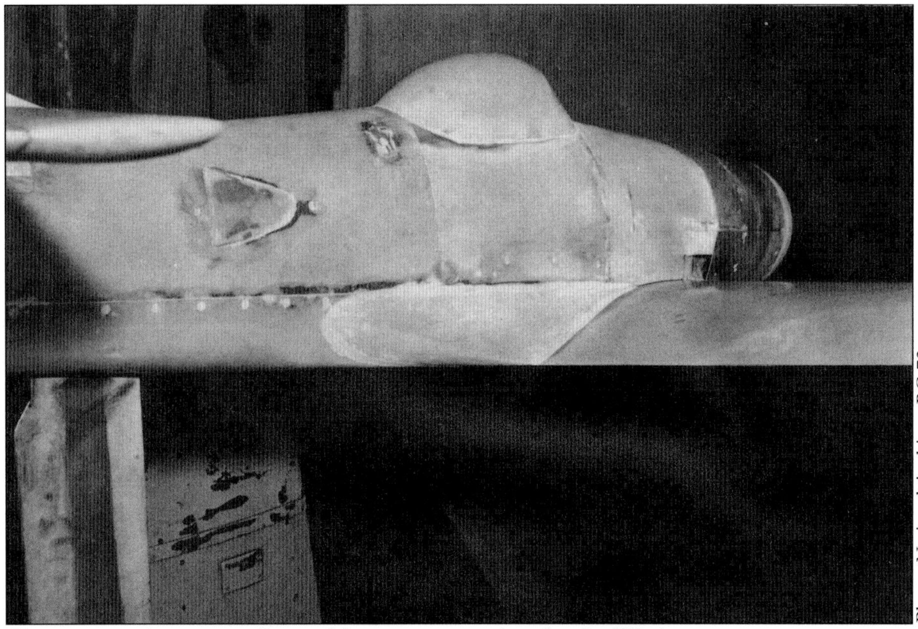
Photo: National Archives, RG 72

Three-quarter rear view of large, rear wing-body fillet.

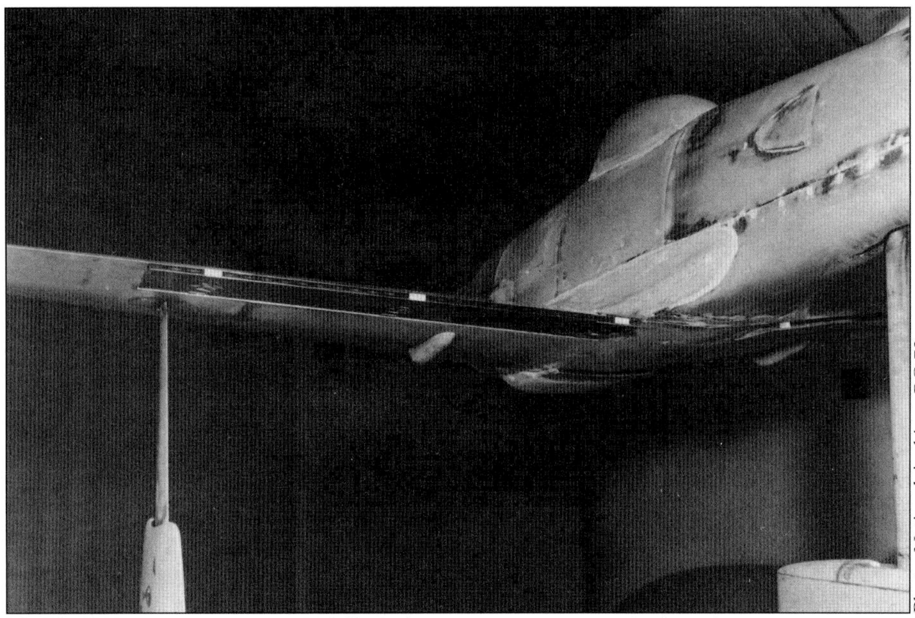
Photo: National Archives, RG 72

Three-quarter rear view of flap showing cerro-matrix brackets.

Effect of Cuffs & Spinner Island on the Cooling of the XF8B-1 Airplane with Aeroproducts, Curtiss, and Hamilton Standard Counter-Rotating Propellers - September 17, 1945

This was an analysis of the cooling data produced by a wind tunnel test of FR-51, a .15 scale powered model of the XF8B-1. The model was equipped for use with scale models of counter-rotating propellers of three manufacturers fitted with various propeller cuffs. The effect on engine cooling pressures at climb and high speed conditions of the cuff design variables (cuff airfoil section, duff angle, cuff-spinner gap, cuff-island gap, and island angle) was shown. Comparison was made on the basis of engine pressures only. A drag analysis could not be made because model power control was not sufficiently accurate. The following was a summary of results:

Design Variable	Effect on Engine Pressure
Cuffs	Improvement with increased fairing of shank of basic propeller.
Cuff Airfoil Section	Cuffs of cambered section showed no marked or certain gain over symmetrical sectioned cuffs.
Cuff Angle	Maximum cooling pressures obtained when zero lift line of cuff base is approximately 60° greater than the propeller blade angle at about ¾ propeller radius. (For climb the cuff base had to be approximately in its feathered position, at high speed about 10° beyond feathered).
Island Angle	Engine pressure drop increased up to 90° island angle. (Island angle was angle between centerline of island and plane of propeller).
Cuff-Spinner Gap	First .5" (full scale) gap caused greatest losses. From .5" to 2" gap caused negligible increase in loss over .5" gap.
Cuff-Island Gap	Small engine pressure drop losses because of small gap which could be maintained in full scale manufacture (.27 in.).
Spinner Afterbody	No worthwhile advantage was obtained from the use of spinners extending aft of the leading edge of the ring cowl on this airplane.

Data used in the report was from selected tests run between September 20 and October 7, 1944. Model FR-51, a .15 scale powered model of the XF8B-1 equipped with counter-rotating six blade propellers, was used in the test. Models of the propellers of three manufacturers (Aeroproducts, Curtiss and Hamilton Standard) were tested with various cuffs, with effort being made to isolate the relation of engine cooling pressures to the aforementioned cuff design variables. The effects of changes in spinner afterbody length were also investigated. Several tests were also made with four blade single rotation propellers.

Description of Model and Tests

Model FR-51 was equipped with a dummy engine, cowl, inner cowl, gill and adjustable cowl flaps. The dummy engine was a model of the Pratt & Whitney Wasp Major with cylinder head and base forward total pressure tubes in all rows and static pressure tubes aft of each cylinder of bank B. The spinner used with the Aeroproducts and Curtiss-Wright propellers corresponded to ordinates picked from early testing work. These ordinates were recommended to the respective propeller companies. Ordinates recommended to the Hamilton Standard Company did not provide sufficient clearance for the Hamilton Standard propeller hub. The large Hamilton Standard spinner, M32, was used with the Hamilton Standard propeller in this test.

To keep spinners interchangeable and in order that the same model propeller hub could be used for all configurations, the distances between the thrust nut and front and rear propellers were kept constant. The various configurations were run through a series of RPM's at two propeller blade angles, 42° for high speed and 28° for climb. The two propellers were connected to separate motors, but the motors were not controlled independently so constant RPM's could not be maintained on both propellers. No torquemeter was used so model power output could not be determined. The error in setting model powers was great enough to make drag data unreliable, so drags were not considered in the analysis; however, power control was sufficiently accurate to give consistent engine pressure results.

To get an approximate idea of XF8B-1 engine cooling conditions using a cuffed single rotation propeller, several runs were made using FR-51 equipped with four blade propeller and spinner configurations. The single rotation spinner-propeller combinations were from FR-57, a 1/8 scale model of the B-29 nacelle. The scales of FR-57 and FR-51 were such that the B-29 model propeller diameter corresponded to a full scale XF8B-1 propeller diameter of 13.75 feet as compared to 13.5 feet for the counter-rotating propellers.

In climb condition, cuffed single rotation propellers gave about the same engine pressure drop and forward total pressure variation as the uncuffed counter-rotating Aeroproducts propeller. It was probable that increased cuff angle of the single rotation propellers would have produced pressure drops near those of the counter-rotating propellers. Forward total pressure variation was about equal for single and counter-rotating propellers.

The drawings and photos that accompanied this report cover the next 3 pages.

Front view of Aeroproducts six blade counter-rotating propeller with cuffs mounted on the XF8B-1 fifteen percent scale model.

Photo: National Archives, RG 72

Photo: National Archives, RG 72

Close-up side view of Aeroproducts six blade counter-rotating propeller with cuffs.

Photo: National Archives, RG 72

Curtiss four blade propeller with cuffs and spinner islands.

Photo: National Archives, RG 72

Hamilton Standard four blade propeller with cuffs and spinner islands.

Photo: National Archives, RG 72

XF8B-1 model with Curtiss six blade counter-rotating propeller with cuffs.

Photo: National Archives, RG 72

Curtiss propeller with pitch adjusted for measurements.

Photo: National Archives, RG 72

Front view close-up of same.

Photo: National Archives, RG 72

Curtiss propeller with pitch further adjusted.

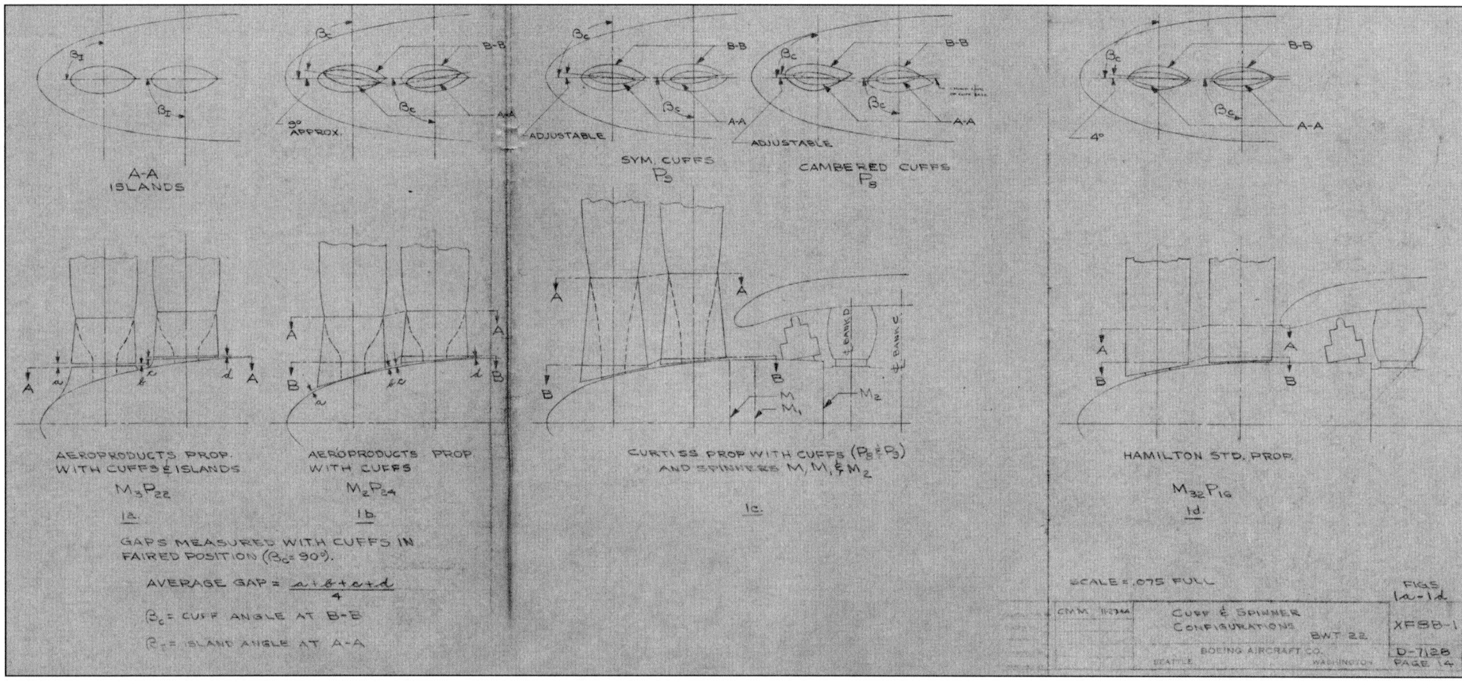

Drawing: National Archives, RG 72

Drawings of Aeroproducts, Curtiss, and Hamilton Standard counter-rotating propellers with various cuff and island arrangements...

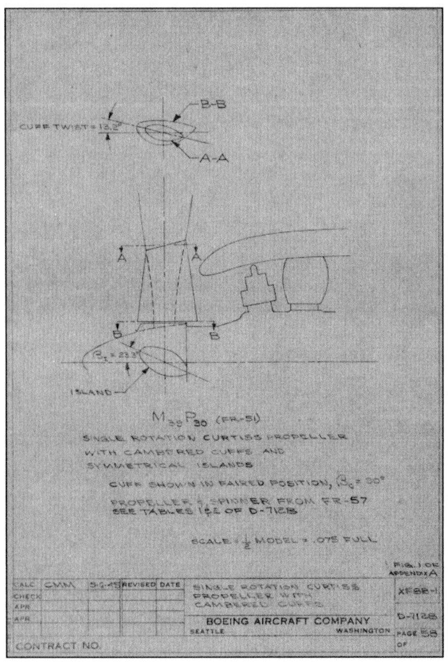

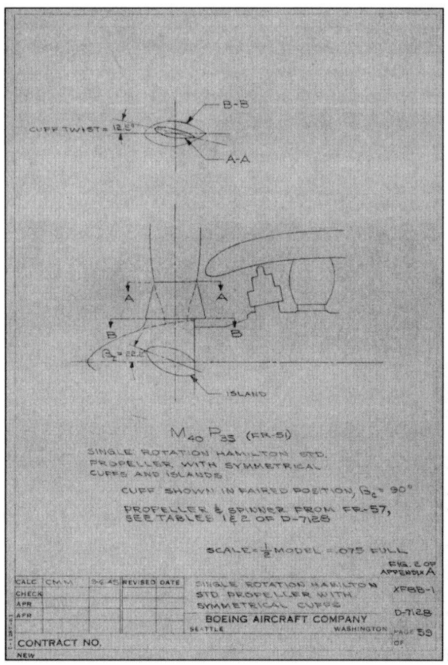

Drawing: National Archives, RG 72

...and the single rotation Hamilton Standard prope with symmetrical cuffs.

Elevator Investigation at Low Speed - September 28, 1945

This report described a series of low-speed experiments conducted on the .15 scale, FR-49 model for the purpose of investigating numerous elevator modifications on the XF8B-1. The testing was done in the 8' x 12' test section of the Boeing Wind Tunnel. Various horizontal tail configurations were obtained through elevator modifications consisting mainly of nose and hinge-line changes. The elevator was made up of a steel spar and detachable wooden noses and afterbodies. Provision was made for the utilization of ten different hinge lines and several different covers were also available for attachment to the rear of the stabilizer. The elevator control unit, located in the body aft of the rear motor, provided a means of setting various elevator angles from the tunnel control panel. The control unit also included an inductance-type strain gauge for measuring elevator hinge moments.

Photos from this report are presented on the adjacent page.

Photo: National Archives, RG 72

Aft view of model with complete tail.

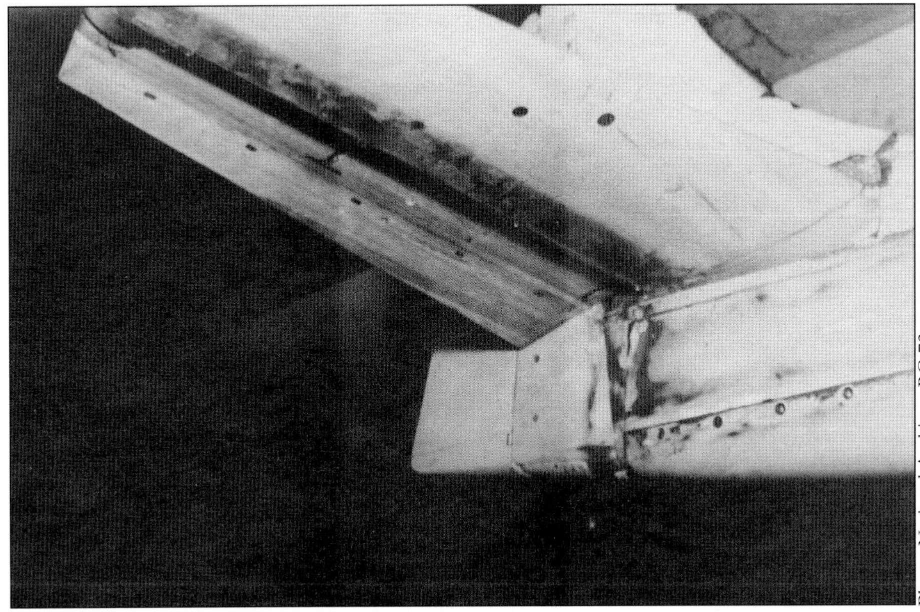

Photo: National Archives, RG 72

Close-up of tail with elevator deflected downward.

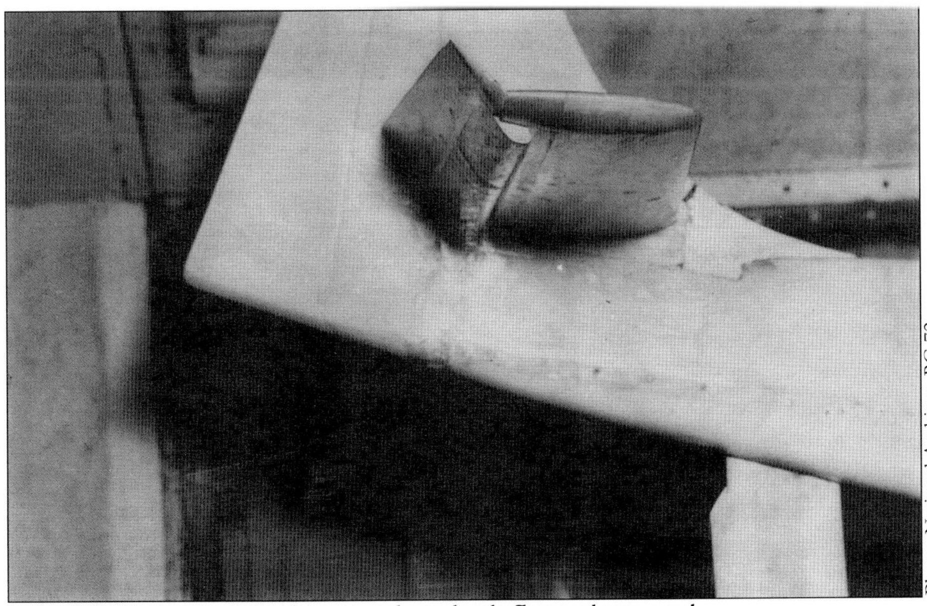

Photo: National Archives, RG 72

Side view of tail with elevator sharply deflected upward.

Photo: National Archives, RG 72

Close-up of tail with elevator deflected upward.

Low Speed Tests of Full Scale XF8B-1 Horizontal Tail - December 6, 1945

The tests summarized in this report were made for the purpose of investigating elevator hinge moments on 1/2 the span of a full size XF8B-1 horizontal tail surface. A further purpose was to also obtain chordwise pressure distributions and to coordinate force data with strain gauge readings for the purpose of stress analyses. It was intended that the tests be conducted for a large range of Mach numbers; however, early in the tests, the tail surface collapsed and was extensively damaged by the low pressures of the tunnel test section fillet door. It was therefore necessary to discontinue the experiments. The testing was done in the 8' x 12' test section of the Boeing Wind Tunnel from November 25 to December 16, 1944.

The full size Model XF8B-1 horizontal tail surface was constructed essentially for static test purposes. Additional elevators of one and two percent bulged afterbody were provided for further tests. In developing the bulged elevators, the percent bulge was defined as the maximum offset measured from a flat side afterbody to the bulge contour and referred to 30 percent of the tail chord.

Photo: National Archives, RG 72

Rear view of horizontal tail installation.

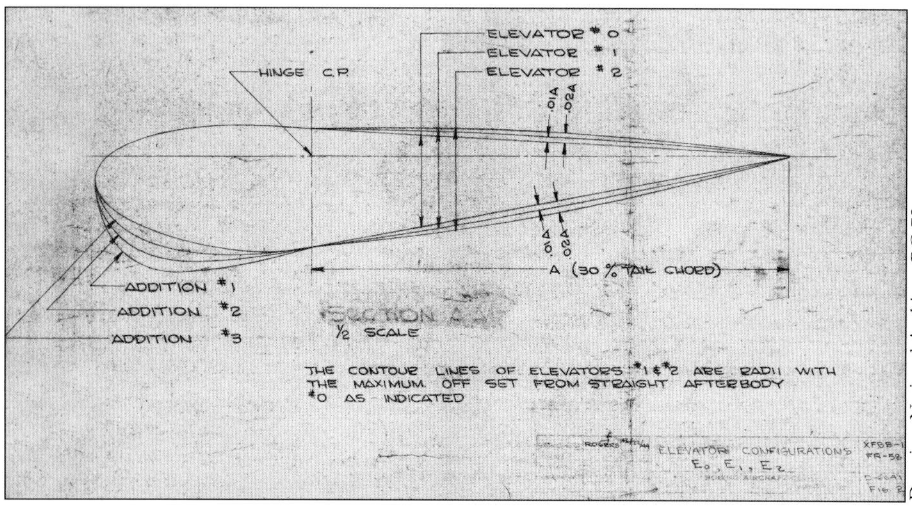

Drawing: National Archives, RG 72

Diagram of the elevator configurations tested in the wind tunnel.

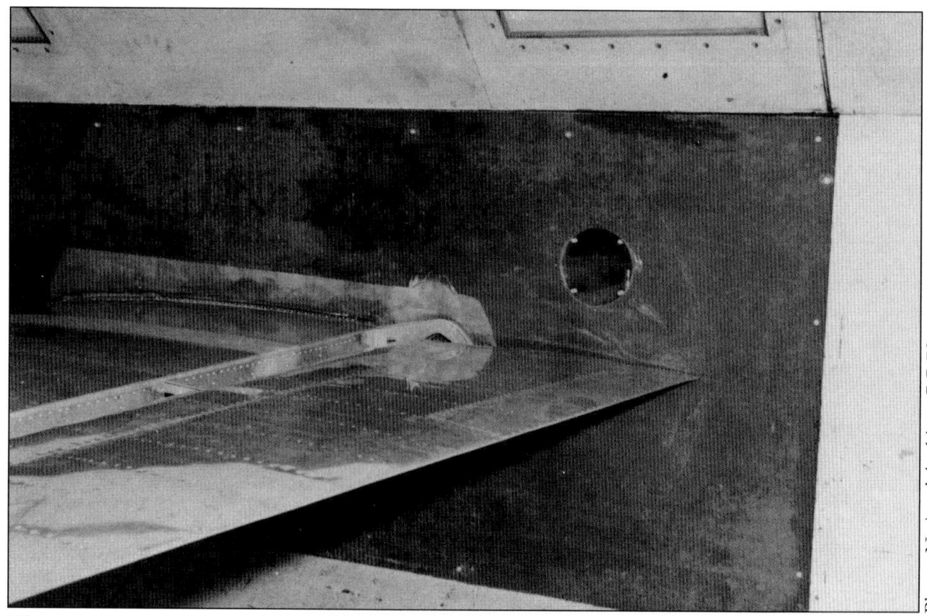

Photo: National Archives, RG 72

Three-quarter rear view of horizontal tail installation.

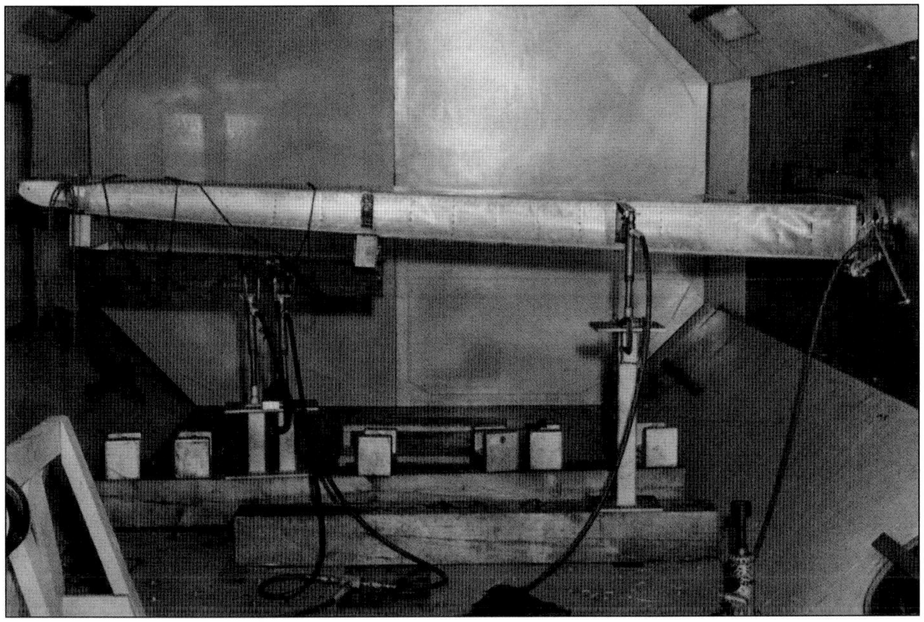

Photo: National Archives, RG 72

Rear view of hydraulic jack position for positive lift calibration.

Photo: National Archives, RG 72

Rear view of hydraulic jack position for positive pitch calibration.

Photo: National Archives, RG 72

Rear view of hydraulic jack position for negative lift calibration.

Photo: National Archives, RG 72

Rear view of hydraulic jack position for negative pitch calibration.

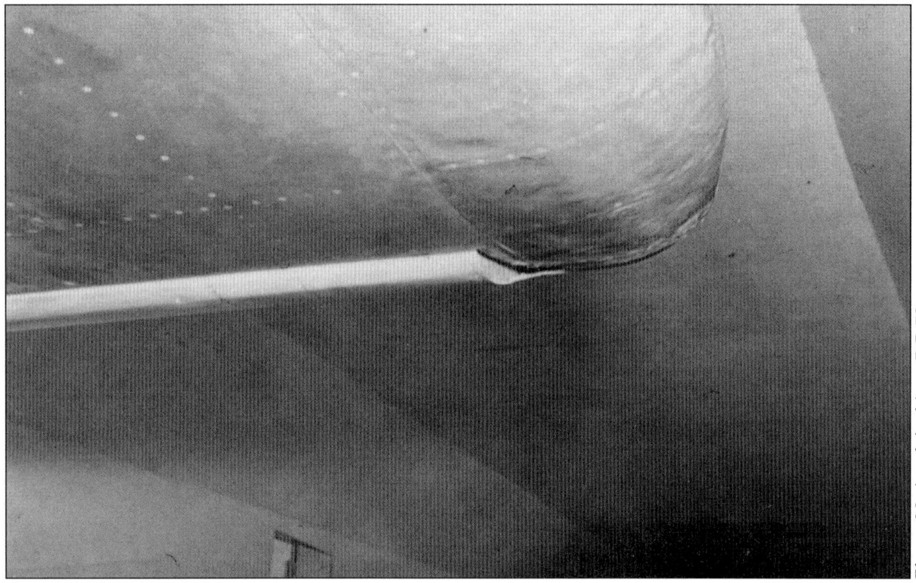
Photo: National Archives, RG 72

Three-quarter front view of elevator nose addition no. 1.

Photo: National Archives, RG 72

Three-quarter front view of elevator nose addition no. 3.

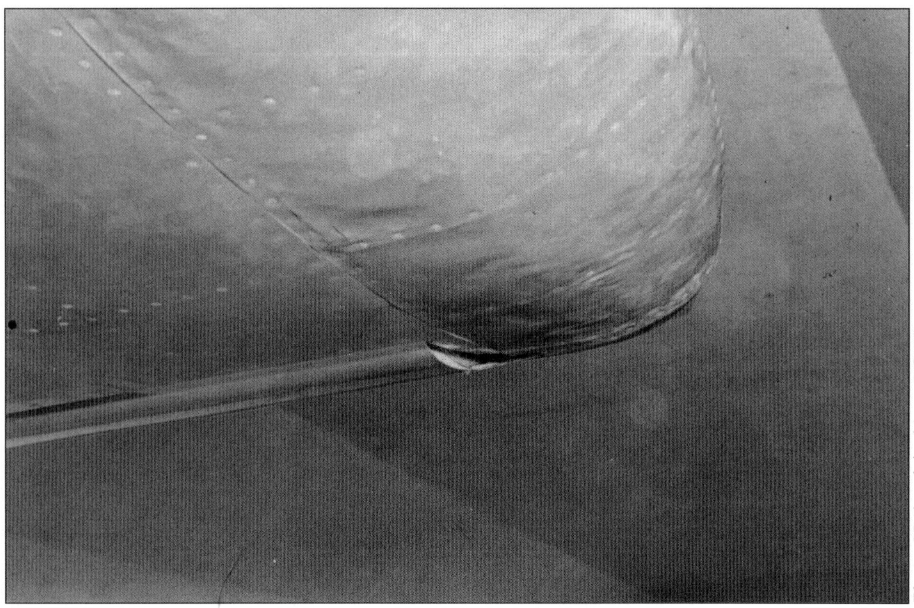
Photo: National Archives, RG 72

Three-quarter front view of elevator nose addition no. 2.

Photo: National Archives, RG 72

Three-quarter rear view of elevator nose addition no. 3.

Photo: National Archives, RG 72

Inboard side view of elevator pressure tubing installation.

Cooling Tests of .15 Scale XF8B-1 Model - November 8, 1945

Photo: National Archives, RG 72

Three-quarter front view of model installation.

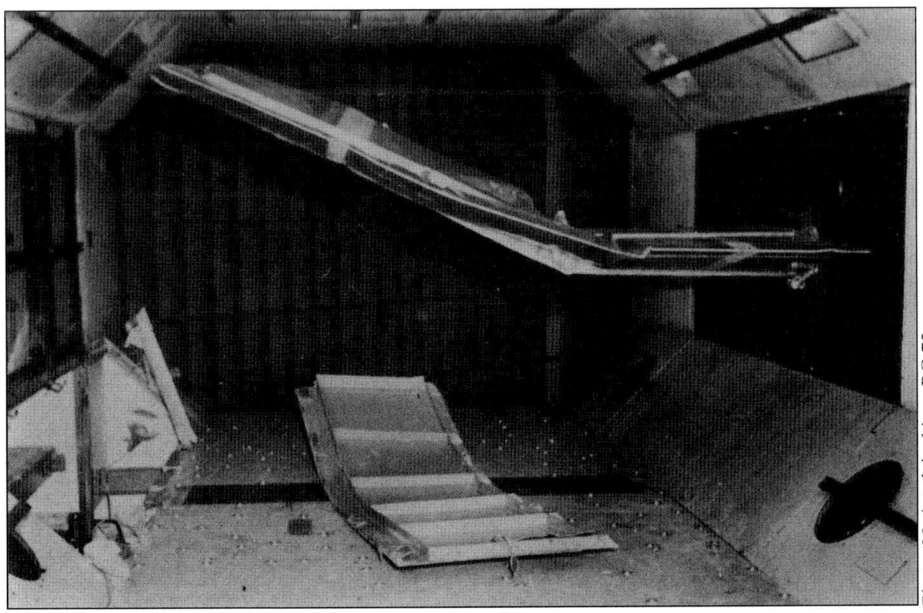

Photo: National Archives, RG 72

Damage resulting from collapse of fillet door.

Photo: National Archives, RG 72

Right hand side view of model installation.

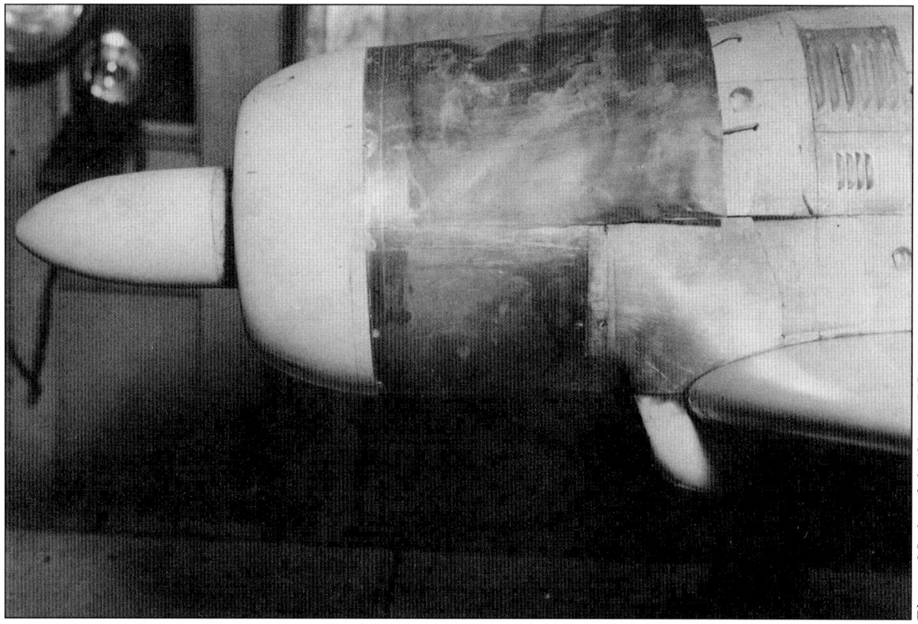
Photo: National Archives, RG 72

Left hand side view of wax cowl fairing.

Photo: National Archives, RG 72

Front view of Aeroproducts propeller and spinner, left hand side.

Photo: National Archives, RG 72

Three-quarter front view showing intercooler flap and spinner.

Photo: National Archives, RG 72

Front view of Aeroproducts propeller and spinner, right hand side.

Photo: National Archives, RG 72

Close-up view of Aeroproducts propeller and spinner

Photo: National Archives, RG 72

Front view of Curtiss propeller and spinner.

Photo: National Archives, RG 72

Close-up view of Aeroproducts propeller and spinner, left hand side.

Photo: National Archives, RG 72

Right hand side view of Curtiss propeller and spinner.

Photo: National Archives, RG 72

Front view of Curtiss propeller and spinner.

Photo: National Archives, RG 72

Close-up of Curtiss propeller and spinner.

Photo: National Archives, RG 72

Three-quarter front view of Curtiss propeller and spinner.

Photo: National Archives, RG 72

Front view of Curtiss propeller and spinner.

Photo: National Archives, RG 72

Three-quarter front view of single rotation Curtiss propeller and spinner.

Photo: National Archives, RG 72

Same model with single rotation Hamilton Standard propeller and spinner.

XF8B-1 Wing-Alone Tests - January 31, 1946

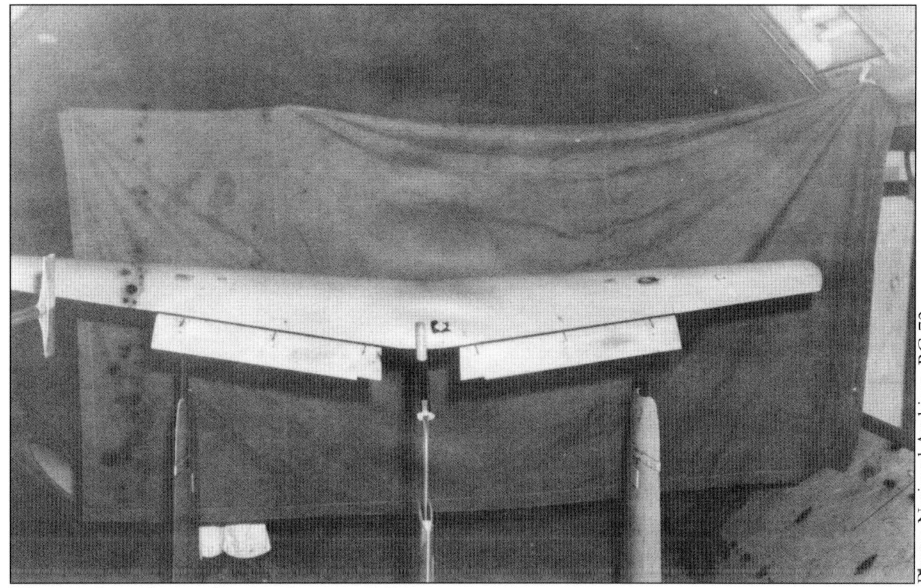
Photo: National Archives, RG 72

Photo showing wing, sting and flaps.

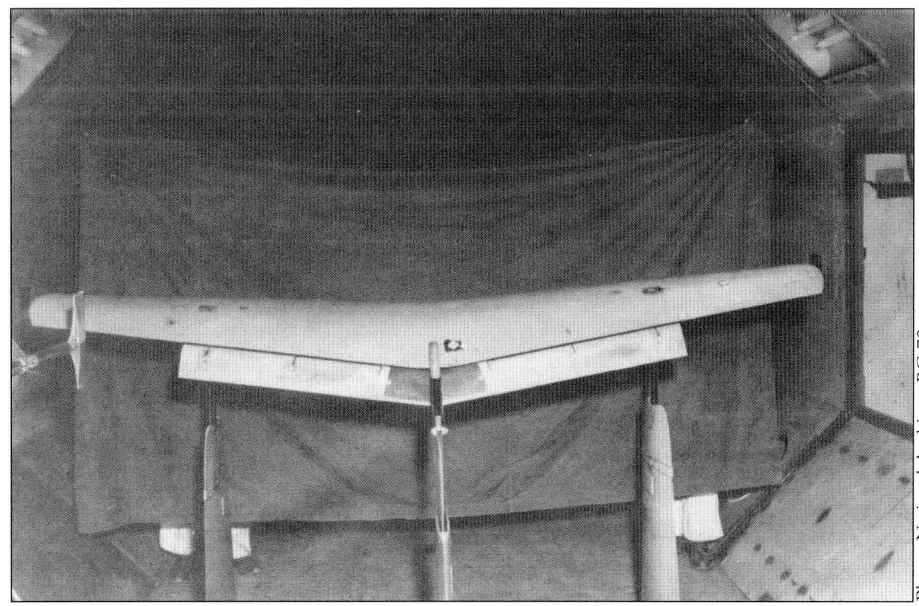
Photo: National Archives, RG 72

Flaps modified with extensions toward centerline.

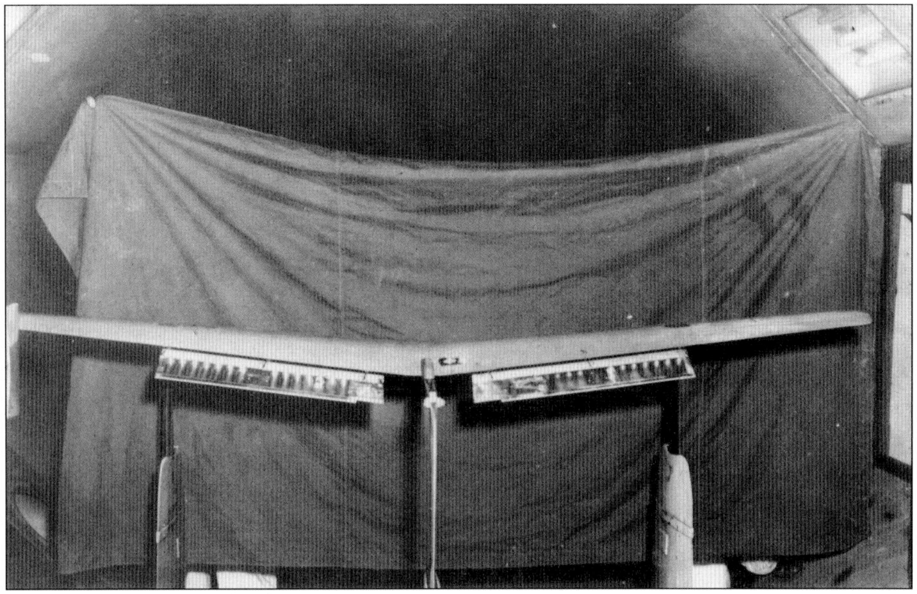

Photo: National Archives, RG 72

Flaps with exposed rib structure.

Photo: National Archives, RG 72

Photo of wing with full-span, 30% chord flaps.

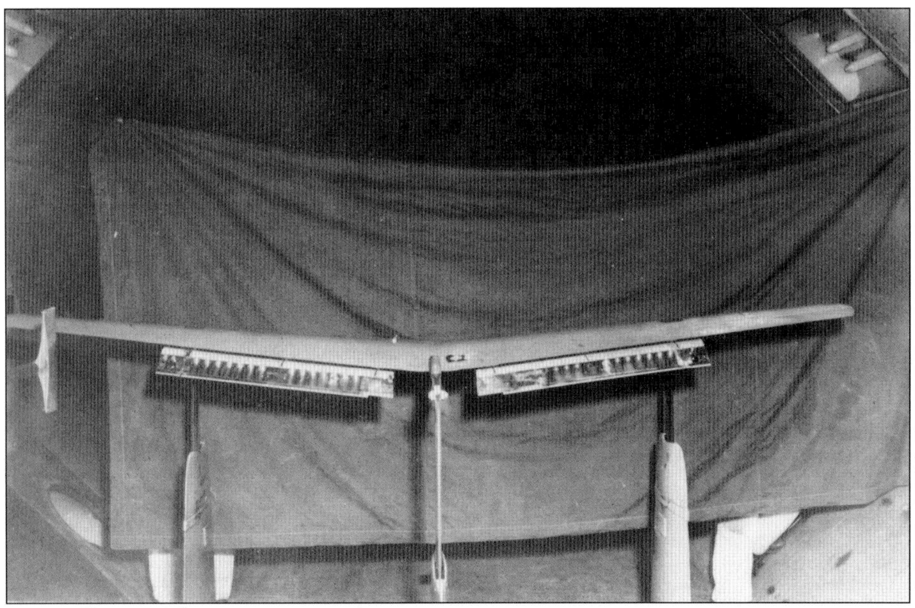

Photo: National Archives, RG 72

Same flaps with outer extensions.

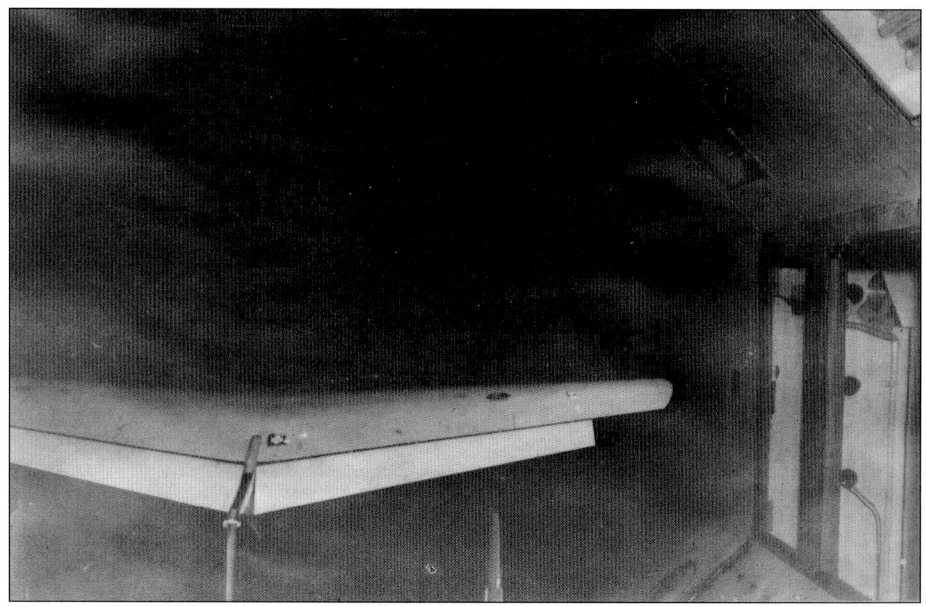

Photo: National Archives, RG 72

Flaps cut down slightly near wing tips.

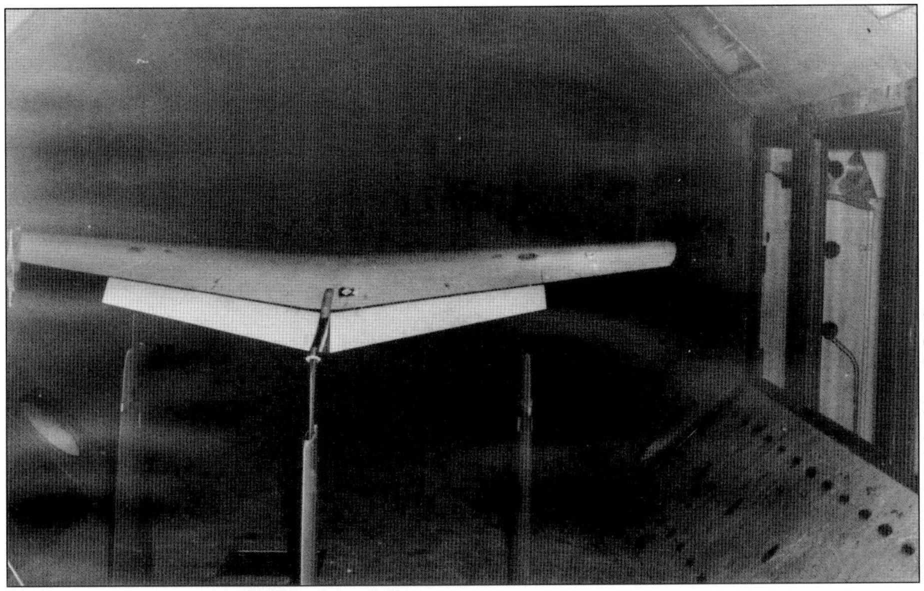

Sixty percent span, 30% chord flaps.

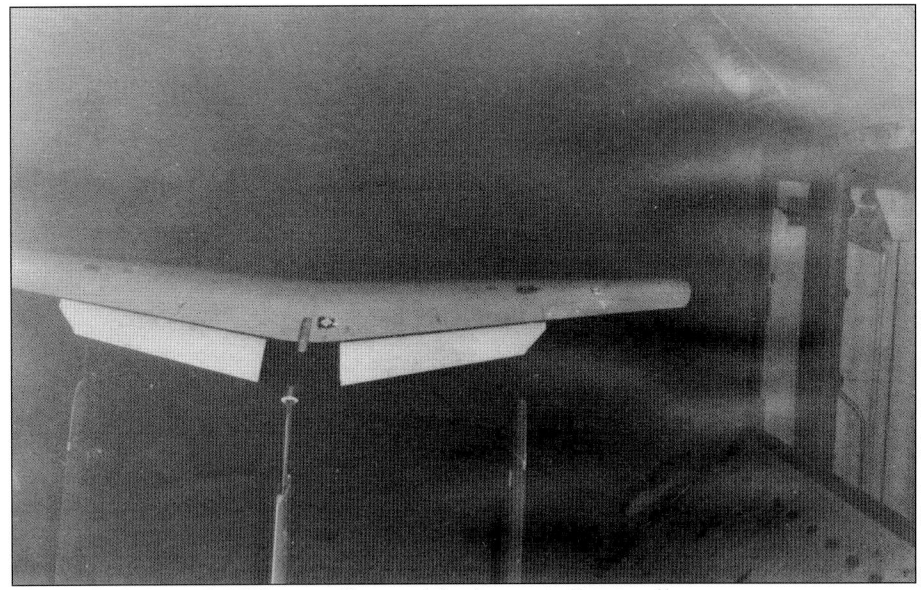

Slotted wing and 60% span flaps with tips cut diagonally.

Same flaps with inner part near centerline removed.

Flaps with smallest surface area tested.

Photo: National Archives, RG 72

Same flaps with surface area near centerline restored.

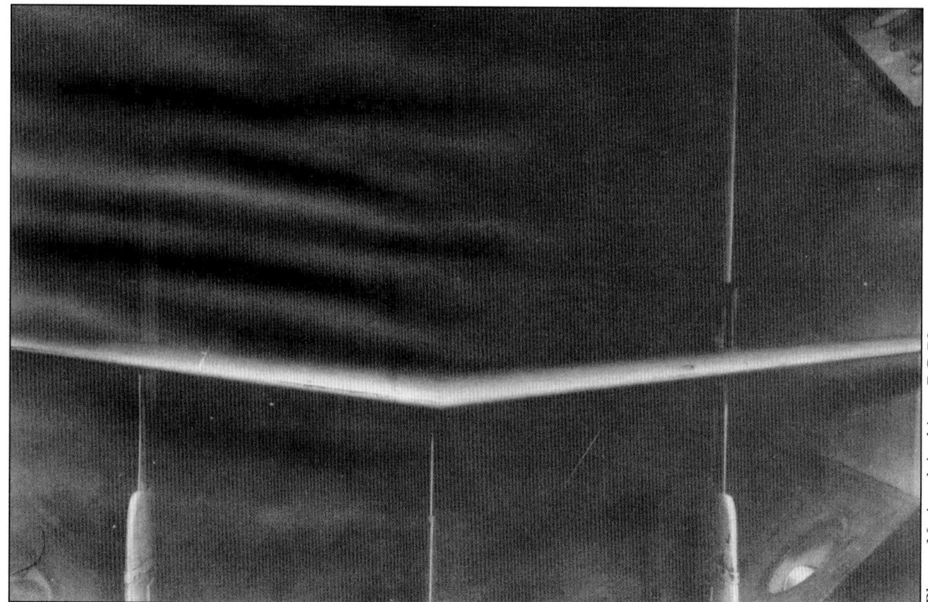

Photo: National Archives, RG 72

Rake and wing.

Photo: National Archives, RG 72

Photo of rake mounted on wing tip.

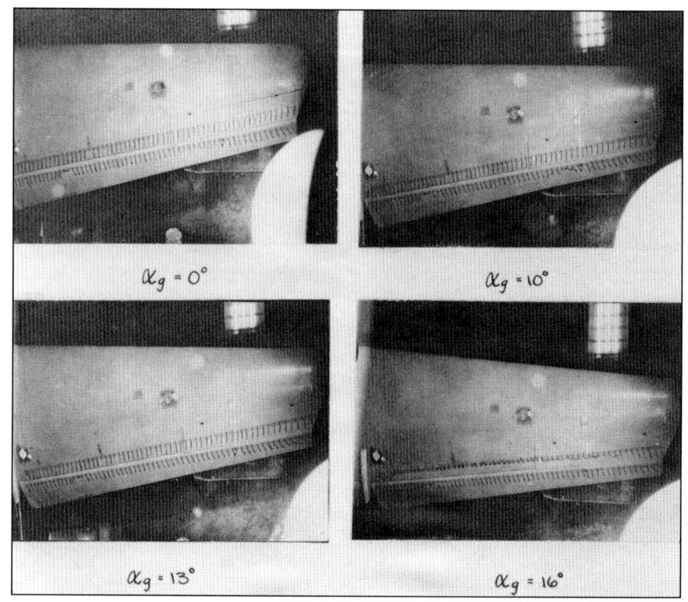

Photo: National Archives, RG 72

Photos of wool tuft testing on wing with full-span, 30% chord flaps.

Dive Flap and Canopy Tests - June 18, 1946

These tests were conducted from June 2 to June 5, 1945. The tests consisted of three dimensional high speed and low speed tests in the 8' x 12' test section of the Boeing Wind Tunnel. The purpose of the tests was to test methods of improving the longitudinal stability of the XF8B-1 at high Mach numbers as well as test various canopy configurations to improve the pressure distribution over the canopy and to increase its critical Mach number. The .15 scale wind tunnel model of the XF8B-1 was designated FR-49. It was made entirely of steel except for a wooden scoop, canopy, vertical tail and two landing gear oleo fairings.

Two Sawyer electric motors were mounted in the forward position of the body with a circular shell replacing the dummy engine. The shell had an annular orifice of 1.6 sq. in. for the passage of engine cooling air and had the same effective area as the dummy engine. Airflow through the orifice was regulated by cowl flap opening and exhaust gill opening. Throughout this test the cowl flaps were sealed and the exhaust gills were open and did not contain exhaust stacks.

The air intake scoop was in place although the oil cooler and intercooler restrictions and internal ducting were omitted. Oil cooler flaps were sealed to prevent the tail from being affected by oil cooler flow (as was noticed in previous tests), and the intercooler flap was opened 2.2" (full scale) to allow a flow through the intake scoop and thus minimize air flow reversal around the entrance to the intake duct.

The flat-sided elevators hinged at 30% chord were installed with fixed tab. The wing contained landing flaps and the right hand steel aileron. All control surfaces and the landing flaps were locked at zero deflection throughout the test.

The dive flaps tested were made of bent-up .040 steel sheet and attached to the under surfaces of the wing by means of csk.-head screws. The flaps were stiffened by chordwise wood ribs glued to the upper surface of the flap and extending to the lower surface of the wing.

A flap with 45" span, 8" chord and 30° deflection was considered the basic flap configuration and other flaps were made with one of the three above dimensions changed. These changes included spans of 36" and 60", chords of 4" and 16", and angles of 0°, 45° and 60°. The flap with zero deflection was made from .072 sheet steel to approximate the effects of a closed flap of 1/2" (full scale).

The six photos that accompanied this report start below and cover the next 2 pages.

Photo: National Archives, RG 72

Front view of model with dive flaps deployed.

Photo: National Archives, RG 72

Rear view of dive flaps.

Photo: National Archives, RG 72

Close-up of dive flaps retracted.

Photo: National Archives, RG 72

Three-quarter front view of dive flaps.

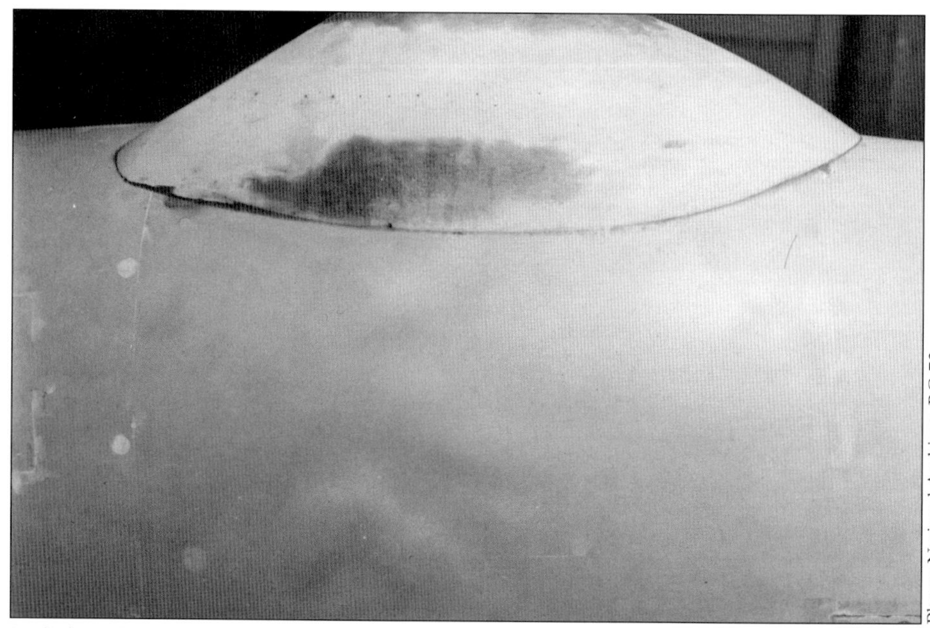

Photo: National Archives, RG 72

Left hand side view of canopy.

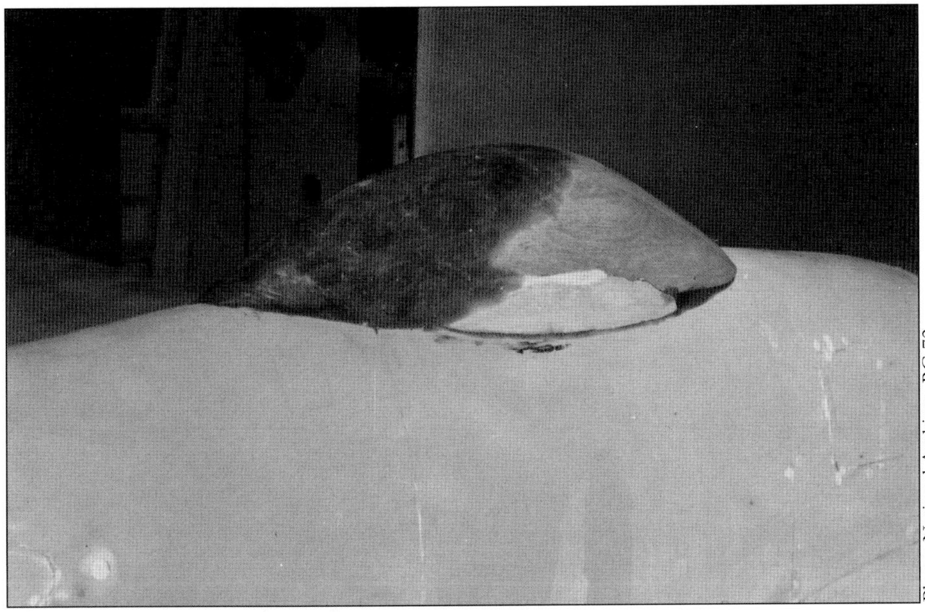

Photo: National Archives, RG 72

Three-quarter rear view of canopy.

Low-Speed Force Tests and Duct Pressure Investigation - June 19, 1946

From January 13 to 22, 1944, 4 three-dimensional wind tunnel tests were conducted in a 8' x 12' section on FR-51, a .15-scale cooling model of the XF8B-1 airplane. These tests consisted of force tests with and without power and pressure tests with power off. The purpose of the tests was to determine the effect of power on pitch characteristics with various horizontal tail configurations including change of airfoil section, vertical location and span; various wing-body fillets; and external modifications to scoop. The tests also were designed to investigate duct pressures with several duct modifications and different openings of intercooler and oil cooler air exits.

The FR-51 was a model of the XF8B-1 airplane built to .15 scale for low-speed testing. A complete cooling system was installed in connection with a dummy model of a Wasp Major engine. Cowl flaps over the top half of the cowl circumference and gills at the sides of the cowl controlled the flow of engine-cooling air. Air was also taken in through a scoop beneath the body at the wing leading edge and ducted to the intercooler oil coolers and carburetor. Intercooler air was expelled from an aperture produced by opening the intercooler flap situated on the lower surface of the duct under the wing. Oil cooler air exits were located on each side of the body aft of the lower cowl flaps and were controlled by oil cooler flaps. Carburetor air was exhausted through small louvers also located on each side of the body approximately midway between the lower cowl flaps and oil cooler flaps. Directly above the carburetor louvers were large louvers which emitted the boundary-layer air taken in between the body and the scoop proper.

The instrumentation for measuring pressures consisted of total-head tubes distributed as follows: 1 in the boundary layer duct between the body and scoop, 2 in the duct entrance, 6 in the forward face of the intercooler, 5 in the forward face of each oil cooler and 1 at the right hand oil cooler flap opening. Six shielded total-head tubes were mounted in the carburetor entrance, 4 aft of the intercooler and two aft of each oil cooler. One static-pressure tube was installed in the accessory compartment.

Model power was supplied by 2 Sawyer motors mounted in tandem in the body and driving a six-blade counter-rotating propeller by means of coaxial shafts.

Photo: National Archives, RG 72

Three-quarter rear view of XF8B-1 model with wing-body fillet.

Photo: National Archives, RG 72

Three-quarter front view of model with wing-body fillet.

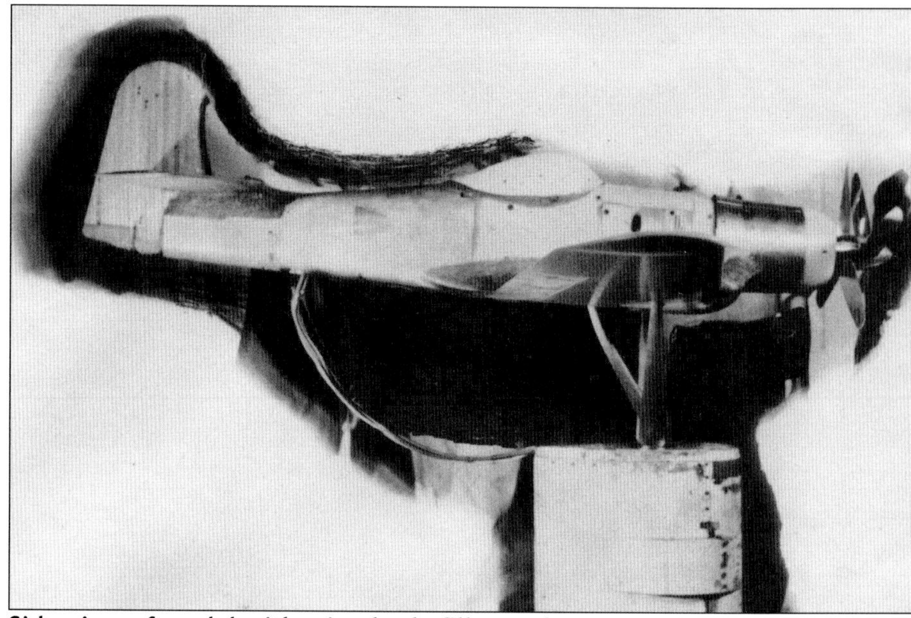

Photo: National Archives, RG 72

Side view of model with wing-body fillet and scoop.

Photo: National Archives, RG 72

Rear view of model with wing-body fillet.

Photo: National Archives, RG 72

Front view of model including scoop.

Photo: National Archives, RG 72

Side view of model with canopy and propeller removed.

Photo: National Archives, RG 72

Close-up of model with scoop and propeller removed.

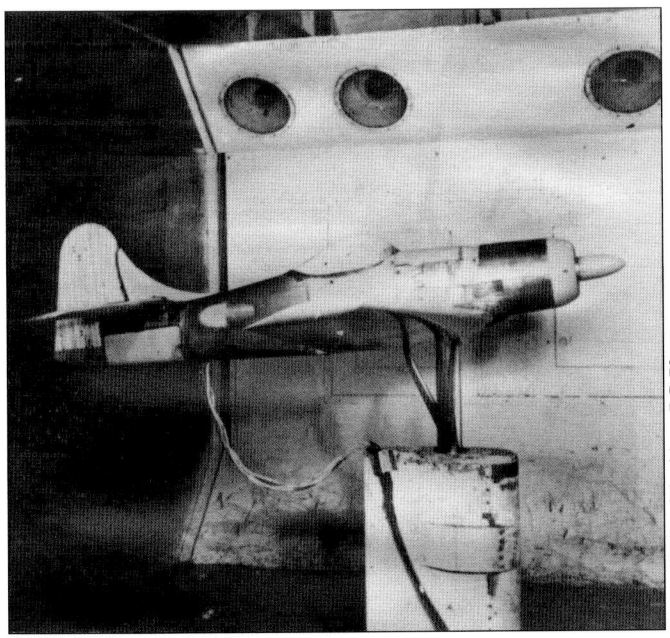

Photo: National Archives, RG 72

Propeller-off model with scoop removed and gills

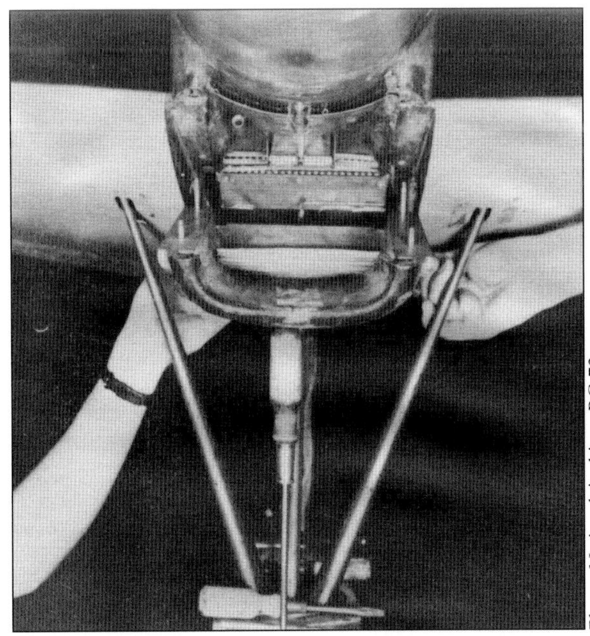

Photo: National Archives, RG 72

Scoop opened up to show vanes in duct

The Wind Tunnels

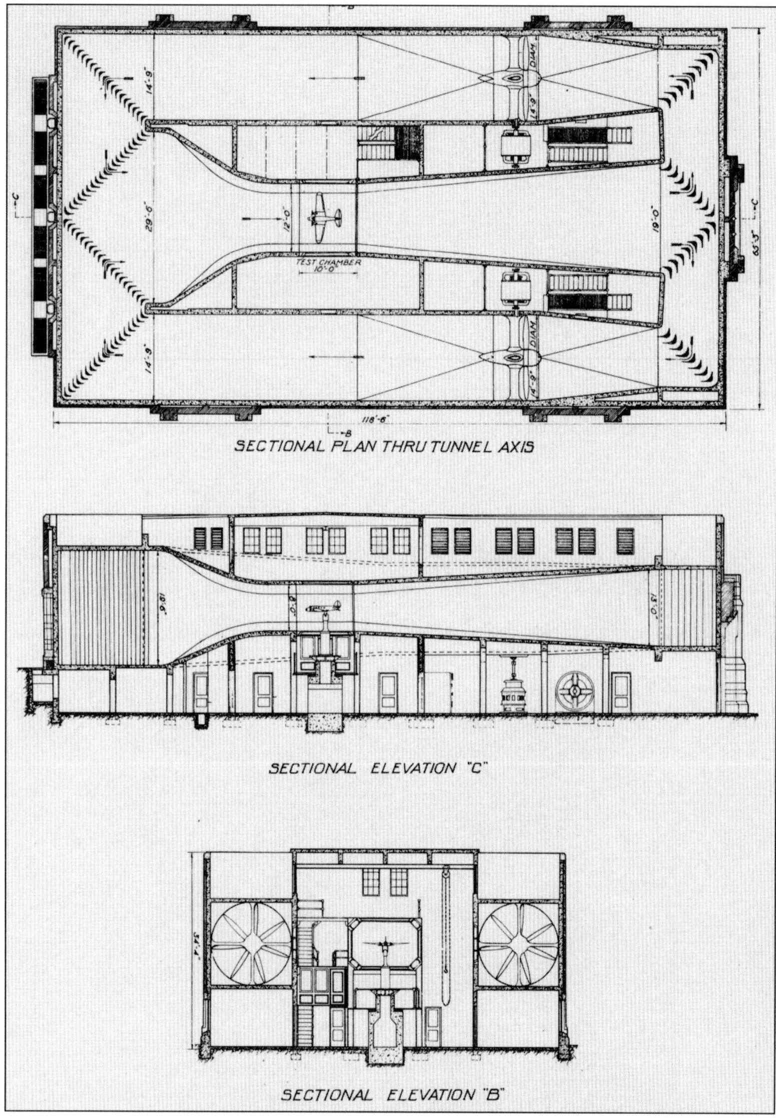

Drawing: National Archives, RG 72

Diagram of University of Washington Kirsten Wind Tunnel. Named after UW Aeronautics and Astronautics Professor Frederick K. Kirsten, the wind tunnel was funded jointly by Boeing, the state of Washington, and the federal government. Completed in 1938, it featured a rectangular cross section measuring eight by twelve feet, and it generated an airflow of 250 miles per hour. Low speed wind tunnel tests of the XF8B-1 were conducted in this facility throughout the development of the aircraft.

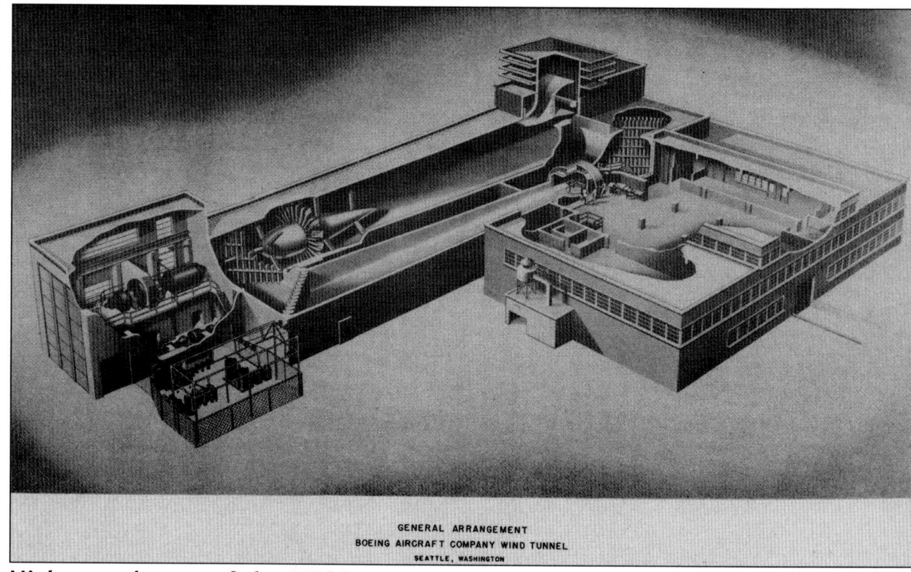

Drawing: National Archives, RG 72

High speed tests of the XF8B-1 were performed in the Boeing Wind Tunnel. Finished in 1944, the facility was dedicated to Eddie Allen, the famous test pilot who had been killed the year before while testing the B-29. At the time, it was the largest privately owned wind tunnel in the world.

Appendix 4

Mock-up Photos

As related in Chapter 1, the XF8B-1 mock-up was completed in September 1943 and inspected by the Navy Mock-up Board the following month. The photos presented in this appendix show that the mock-up was finished to a relatively high standard, though it lacked detail in the power plant and armament installations. More elaborate mock-ups of these areas were constructed and inspected at later dates; photos of them have yet to surface.

The differences between the mock-up and the aircraft as initially built were generally minor, the key ones being as follows:

1) The mock-up was finished in the mid-war Navy tricolor scheme of Non-Specular Sea Blue, Non-Specular Intermediate Blue, and Non Specular Insignia White with red surrounding the national insignia.
2) The canopy of the mock-up featured extensive bracing, which was revised when the technology matured enough to make cleanly blown Plexiglas canopies of sufficient strength.
3) The Grumman-type wing fold was used on the mock-up, but was later changed to the simpler inward folding arrangement to save weight and minimize complexity.
4) The propeller blades featured prominent cuffs at the base, variations of which were tested in the wind tunnel but not employed on the actual aircraft.
5) Lockheed P-38-style drop tanks with simple pylons were used on the mock-up, probably to save time and money. The actual aircraft featured Grumman-type drop tanks with pylons of a more aerodynamic shape.

These mock-up photos cover the next 5 pages and were captioned by Boeing before being sent to the Navy. Visible in the background of several shots is the mock-up of the XC-97 Stratofreighter, an aircraft which proved to be a far more successful and profitable design for Boeing than the XF8B-1.

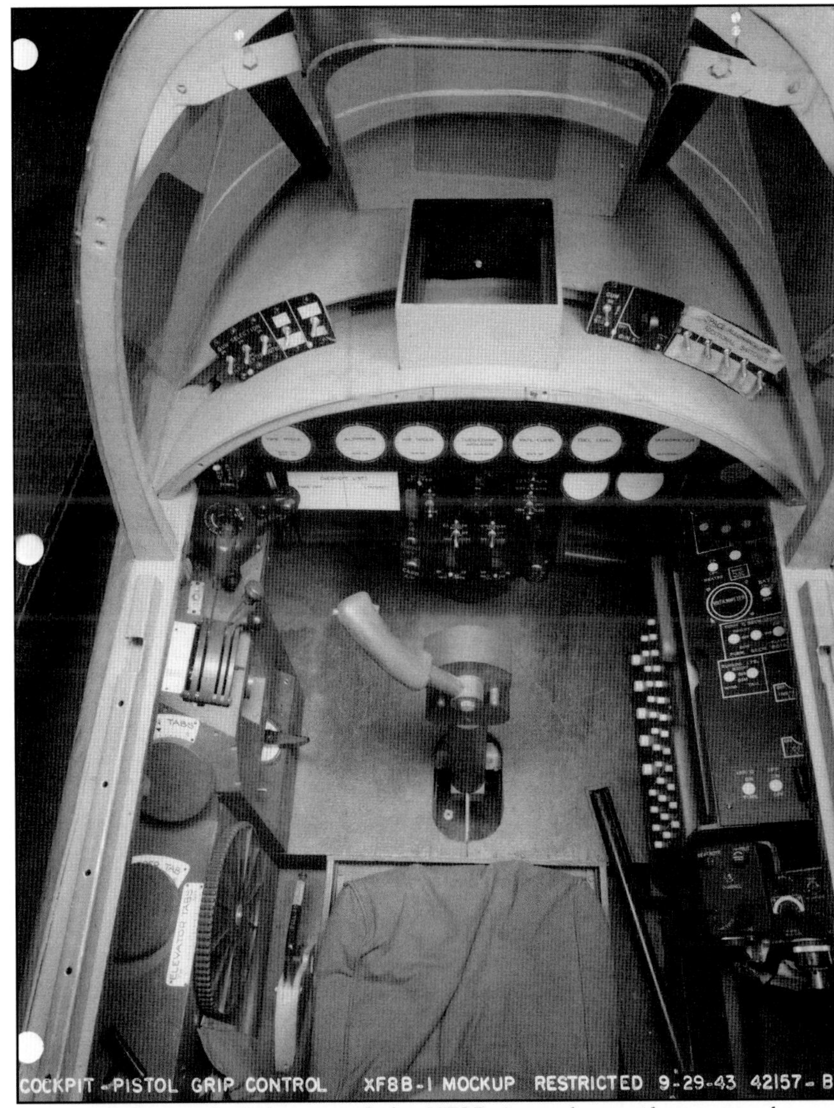

Photo: National Archives, RG 72

Close-up of the cockpit layout of the XF8B-1 mock-up, the general arrangement of which differed little from the aircraft as built.

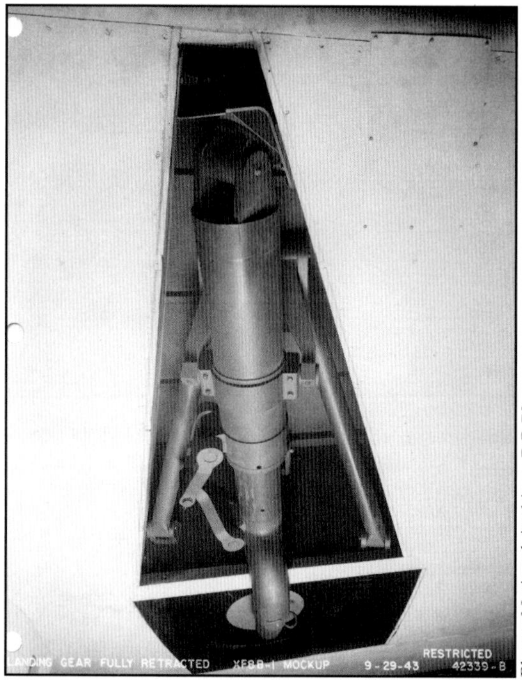

Photo: National Archives, RG 72

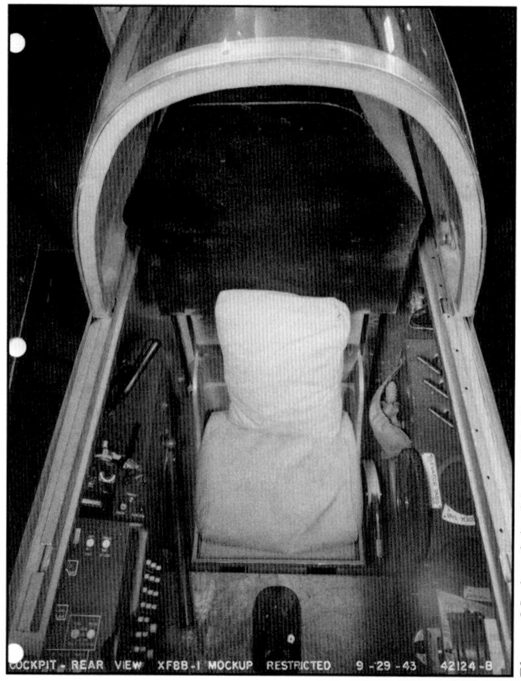

Photo: National Archives, RG 72

Photo: National Archives, RG 72

Photo: National Archives, RG 72

Photo: National Archives, RG 72

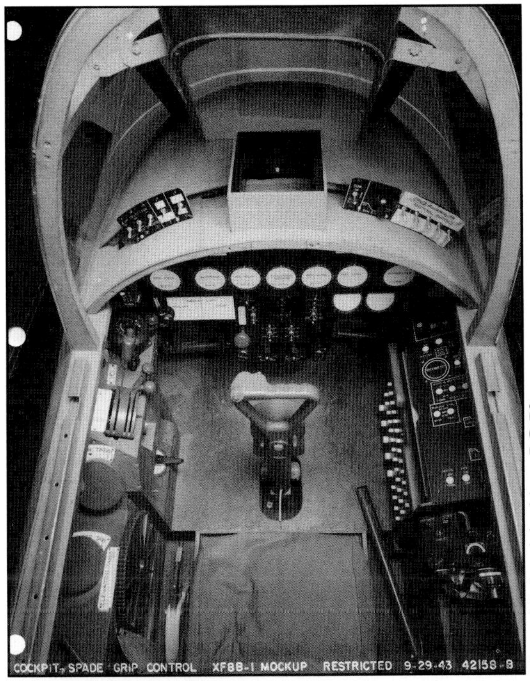

Photo: National Archives, RG 72

Photo: National Archives, RG 72

Photo: National Archives, RG 72

Photo: National Archives, RG 72

Photo: National Archives, RG 72

Photo: National Archives, RG 72

Photo: National Archives, RG 72

Photo: National Archives, RG 72

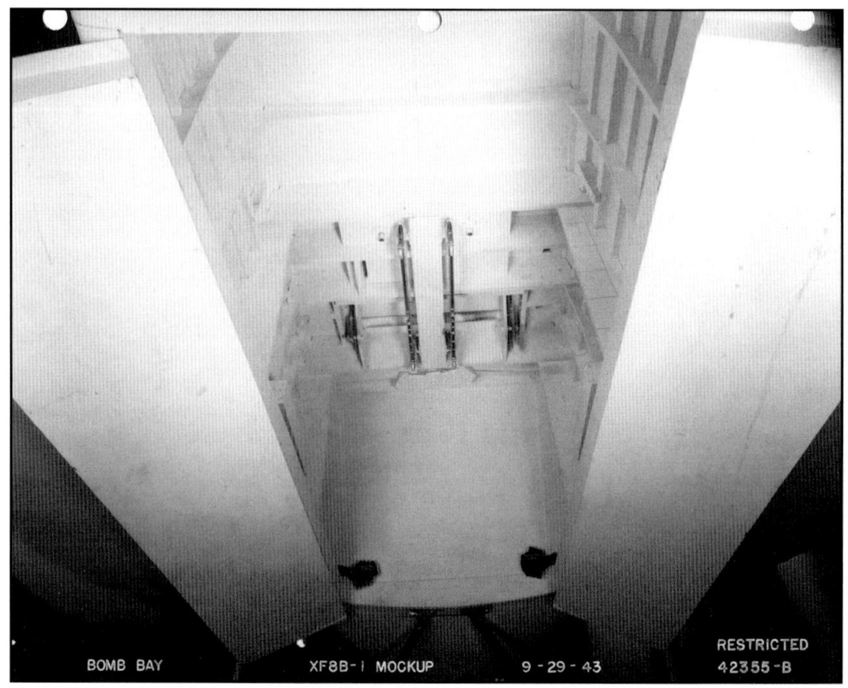

Photo: National Archives, RG 72

Photo: National Archives, RG 72

Photo: National Archives, RG 72

Photo: National Archives, RG 72

Photo: National Archives, RG 72

Appendix 5

Construction Photos

This appendix collects most of the known photos showing details of the construction and assembly of the Boeing XF8B-1. All photos originate from Boeing Report No. D-6839, *XF8B-1 Photographs*, dated April 7, 1945, which is held by the National Archives. The bulk of the photographs in this report depict details of the first prototype, no. 57984, though a few photos of the second and/or third prototypes may be interspersed throughout. I have only captioned a few of the pictures, as most were labelled by Boeing before being sent to the Navy. These photos provide a feast of detail for the modeler and engineering enthusiast.

Photo: National Archives, RG 72

Photo: National Archives, RG 72

Part A: Final Assembly

Photo: National Archives, RG 72-AC

Photo: National Archives, RG 72-AC

BREAKAWAY BOMB BAY & WING SEC. XF8B-1 2-19-45 87658-B

Photo: National Archives, RG 72-AC

ATTACHMENT AREA BOMB BAY TO WING SEC. XF8B-1 2-19-45 87662-B

Photo: National Archives, RG 72-AC

ATTACHMENT BOMB BAY TO WING SEC. XF8B-1 2-19-45 87659-B

Photo: National Archives, RG 72-AC

Part B: Armament

Photo: National Archives, RG 72-AC

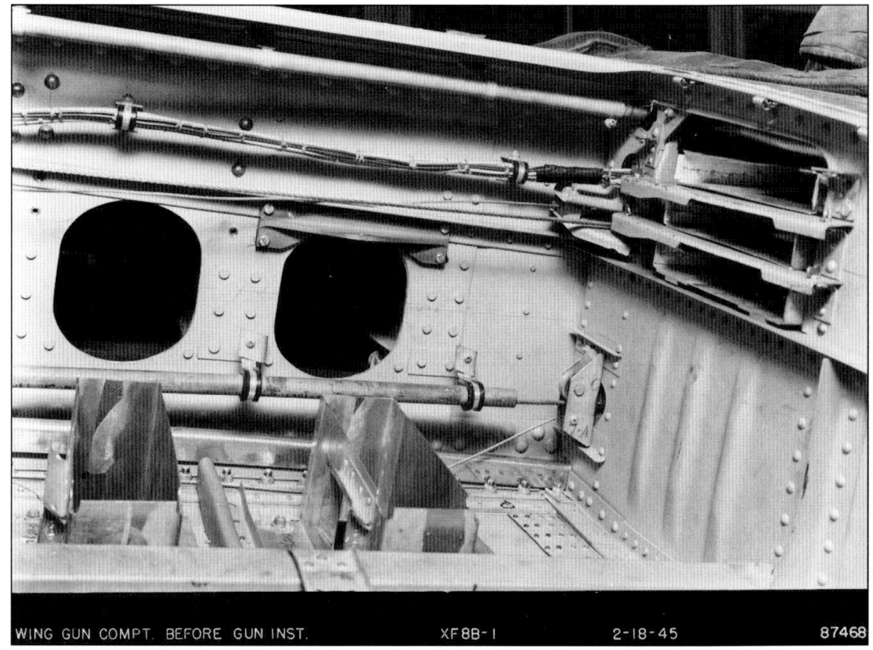

Photo: National Archives, RG 72-AC

Photo: National Archives, RG 72-AC

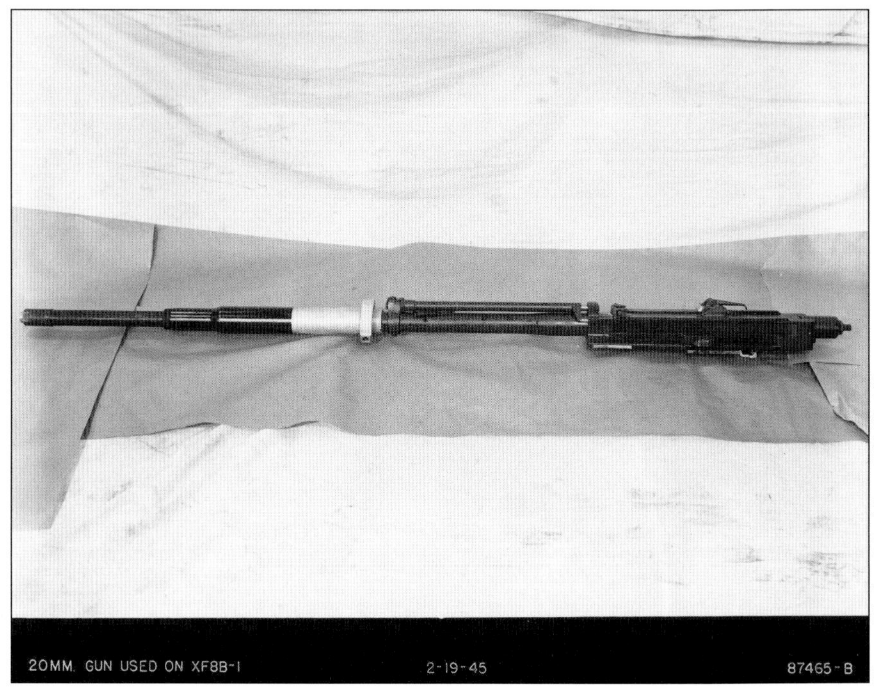

Photo: National Archives, RG 72-AC

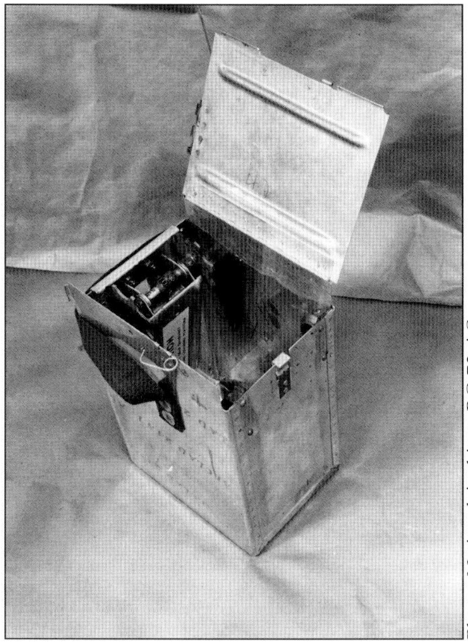

Photo: National Archives, RG 72-AC

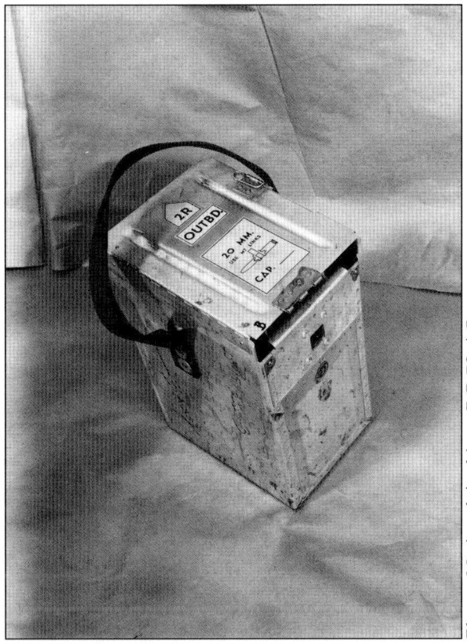

Photo: National Archives, RG 72-AC

87466-B/87467-B - 20 mm ammunition box with lid open and closed

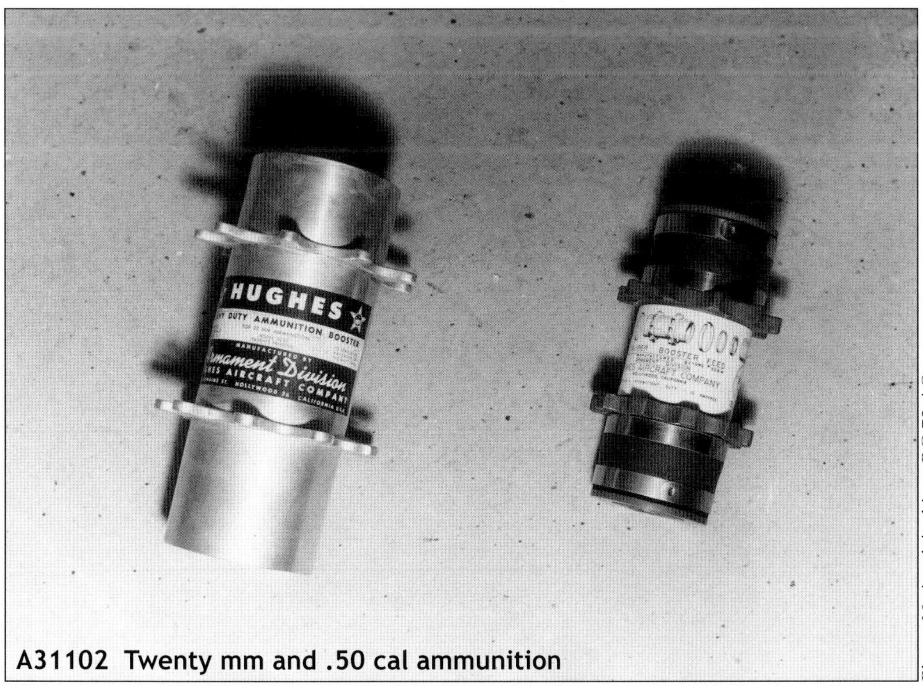

A31102 Twenty mm and .50 cal ammunition

Photo: National Archives, RG 72-AC

Part C: Wing

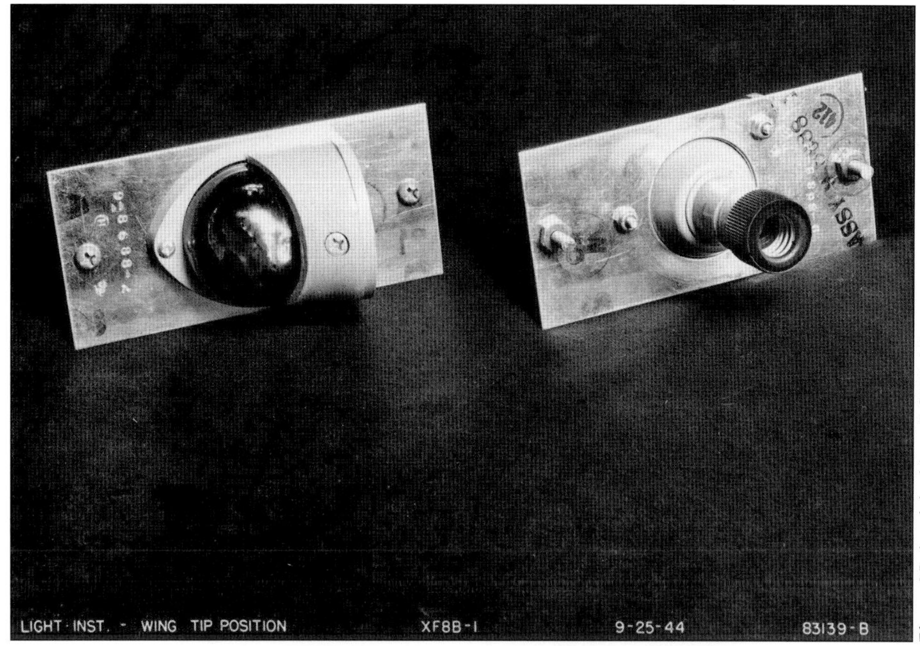

LIGHT INST. - WING TIP POSITION XF8B-1 9-25-44 83139-B

Photo: National Archives, RG 72-AC

SEC. 72 FRAMEWORK ATTACHMENT TO WING CENTER SECTION XF8B-1 80832-B

Photo: National Archives, RG 72-AC

Photo: National Archives, RG 72-AC

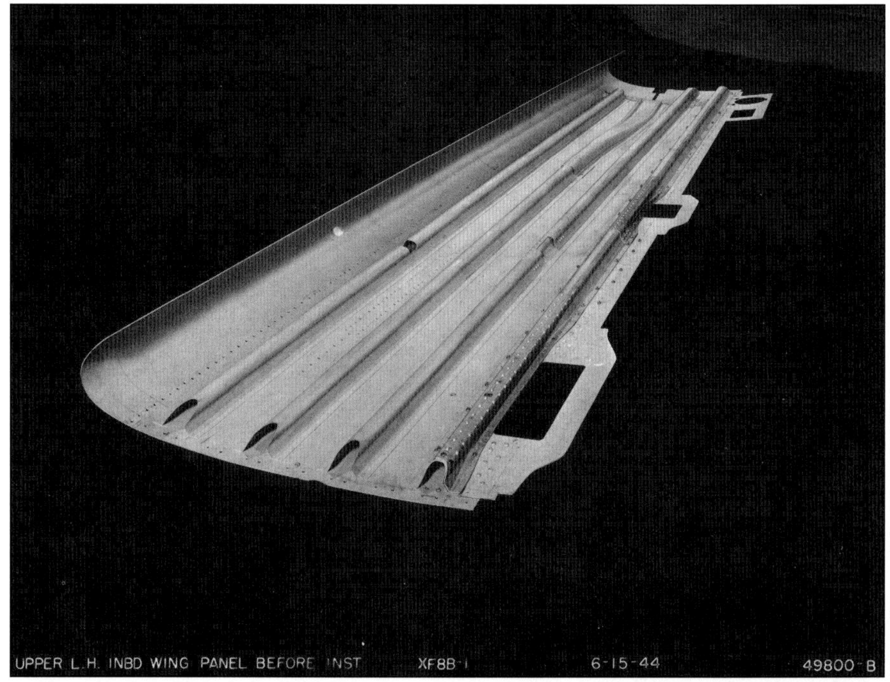

Photo: National Archives, RG 72-AC

Photo: National Archives, RG 72-AC

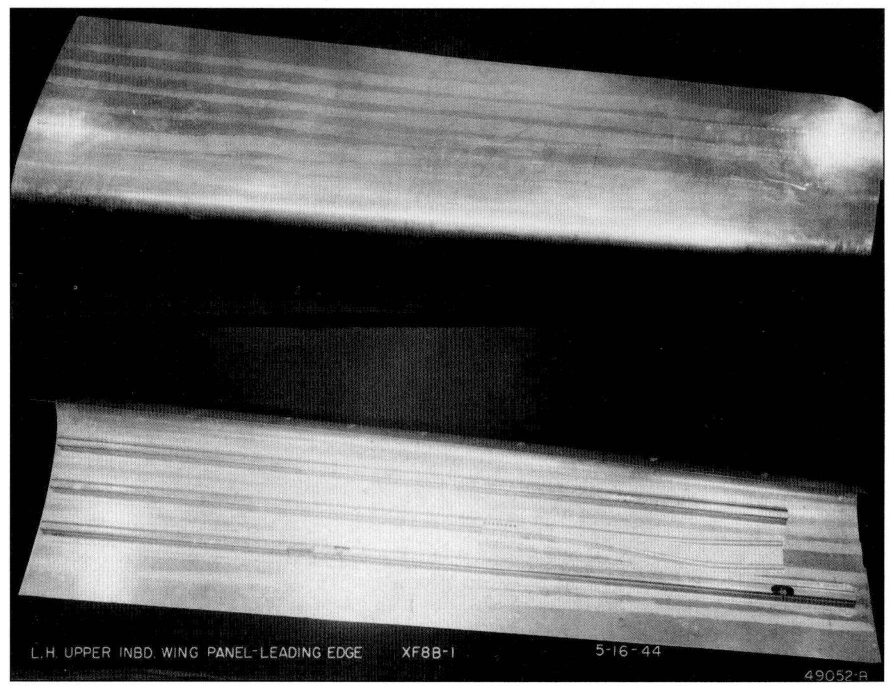

Photo: National Archives, RG 72-AC

Photo: National Archives, RG 72-AC

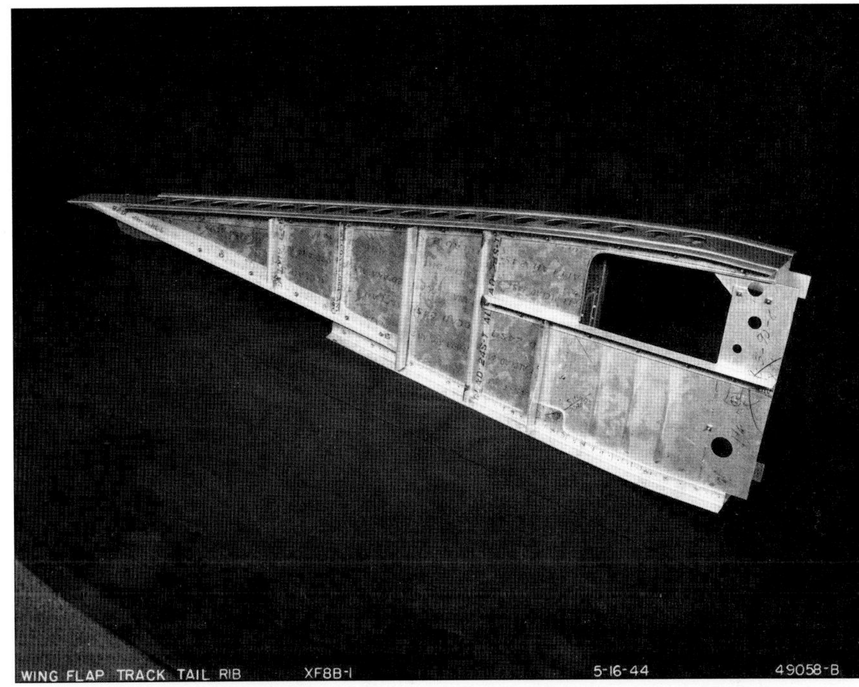

Photo: National Archives, RG 72-AC

Photo: National Archives, RG 72-AC

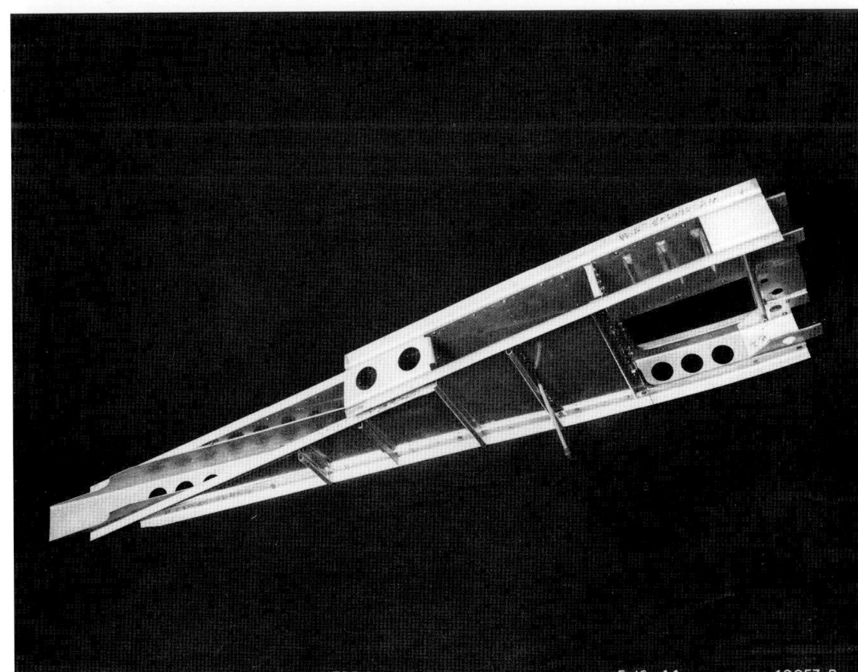

Photo: National Archives, RG 72-AC

L.H. OUTBD WING ASS'Y (OUTBD END) LOWER SURFACE UP XF8-1 8-7-44 81466-B

Photo: National Archives, RG 72-AC

STRINGER & SKIN FITTING L.H. OUTBD. WING/OUTBD. END XF8B-1 7-1-44 A8966

Photo: National Archives, RG 72-AC

OUTBD. END OF L.H. WING, TIP & AILERON REMOVED XF8B-1 9-5-44 82424-B

Photo: National Archives, RG 72-AC

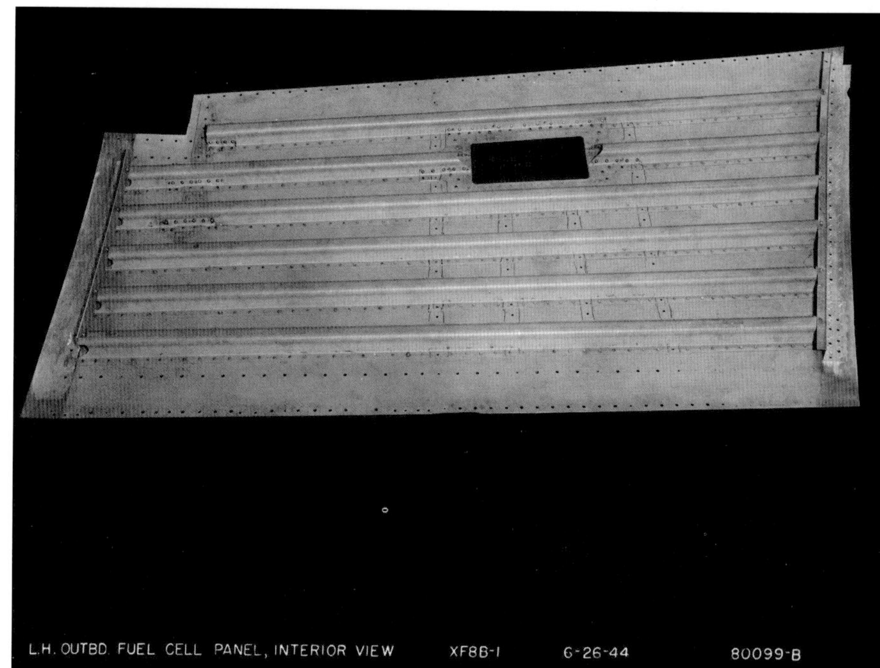

L.H. OUTBD. FUEL CELL PANEL, INTERIOR VIEW XF8B-1 6-26-44 80099-B

Photo: National Archives, RG 72-AC

Photo: National Archives, RG 72-AC

Photo: National Archives, RG 72-AC

Photo: National Archives, RG 72-AC

Photo: National Archives, RG 72-AC

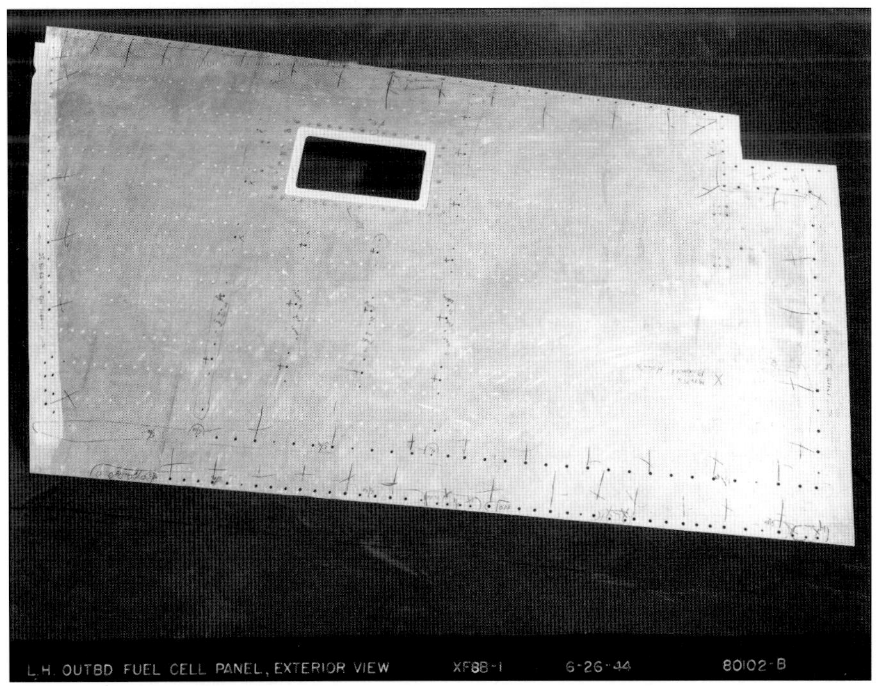

Photo: National Archives, RG 72-AC

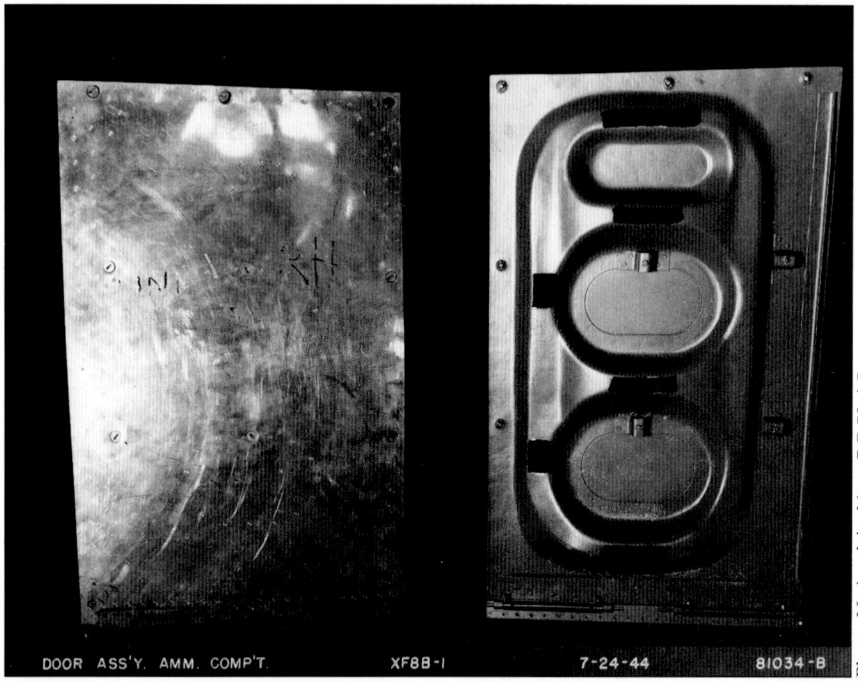

Photo: National Archives, RG 72-AC

Photo: National Archives, RG 72-AC

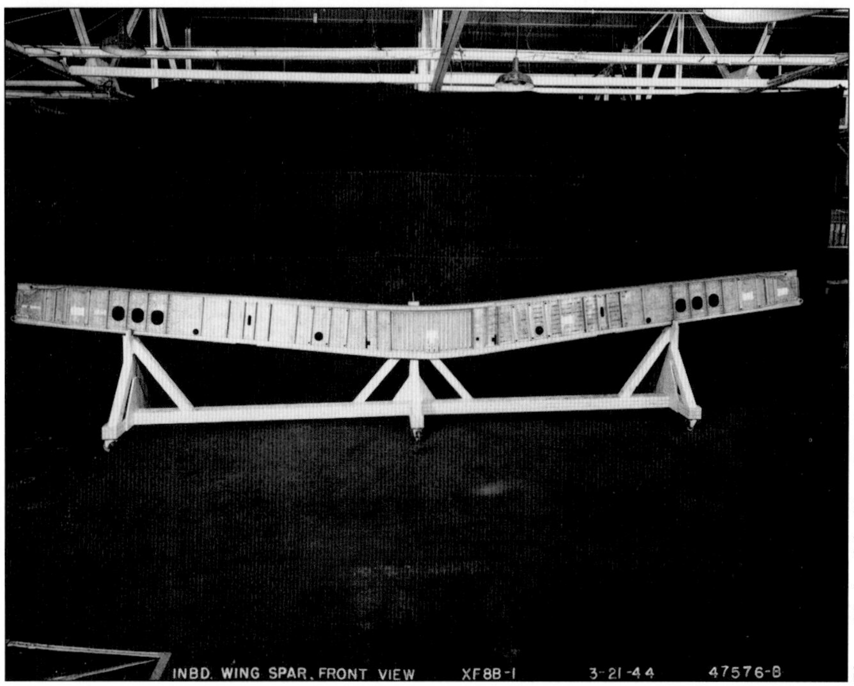

Photo: National Archives, RG 72-AC

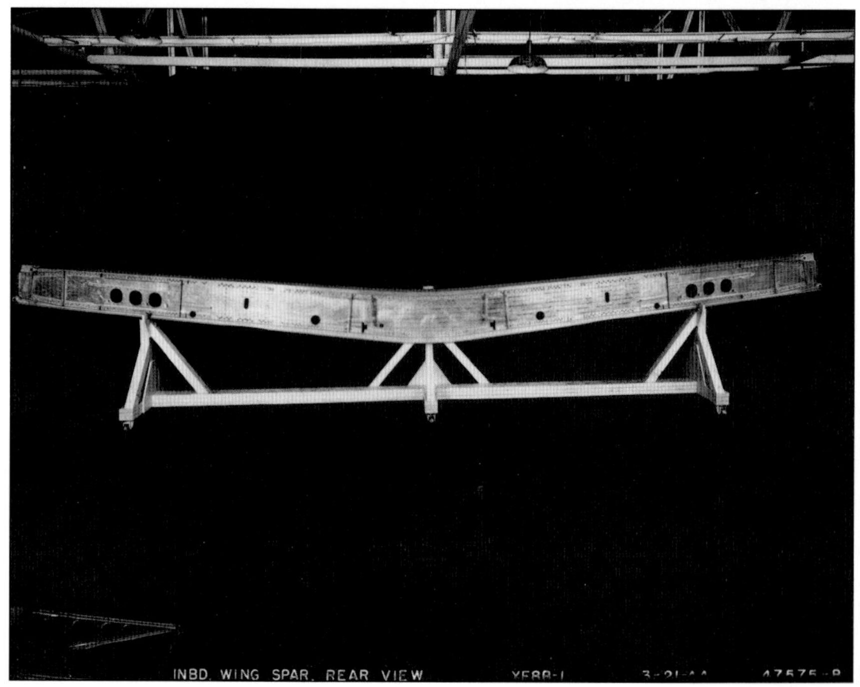

Photo: National Archives, RG 72-AC

Photo: National Archives, RG 72-AC

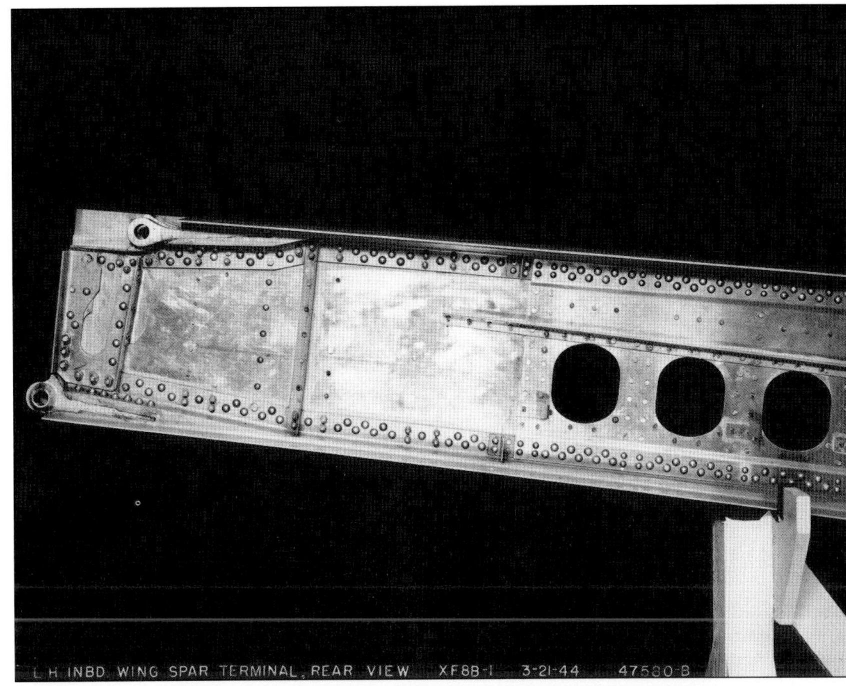

Photo: National Archives, RG 72-AC

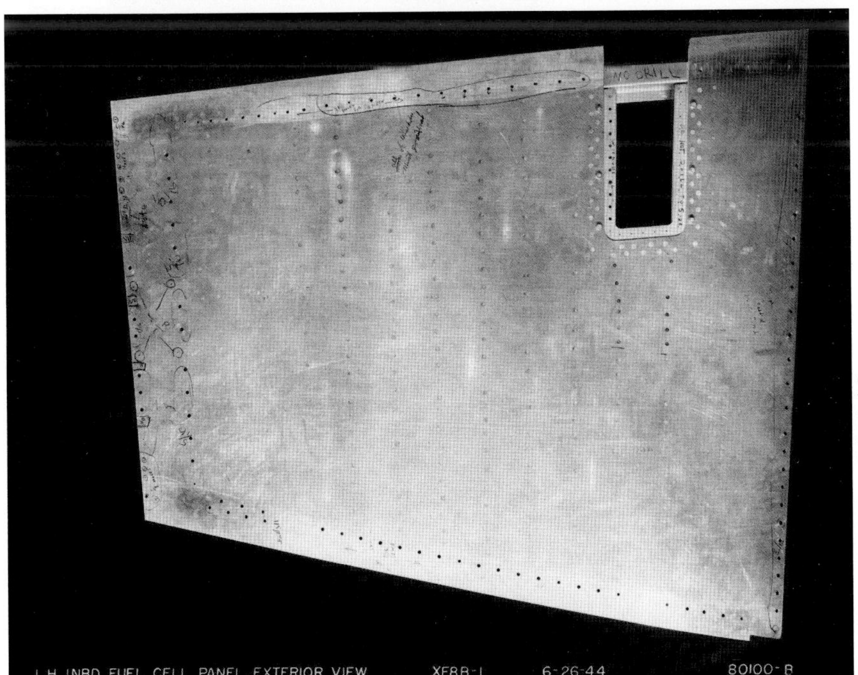

Photo: National Archives, RG 72-AC

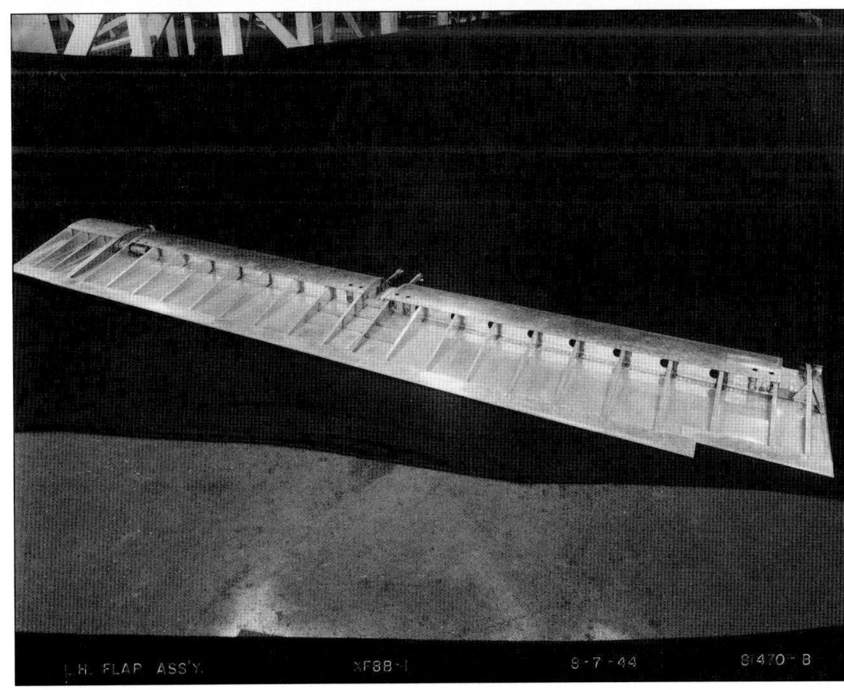

Photo: National Archives, RG 72-AC

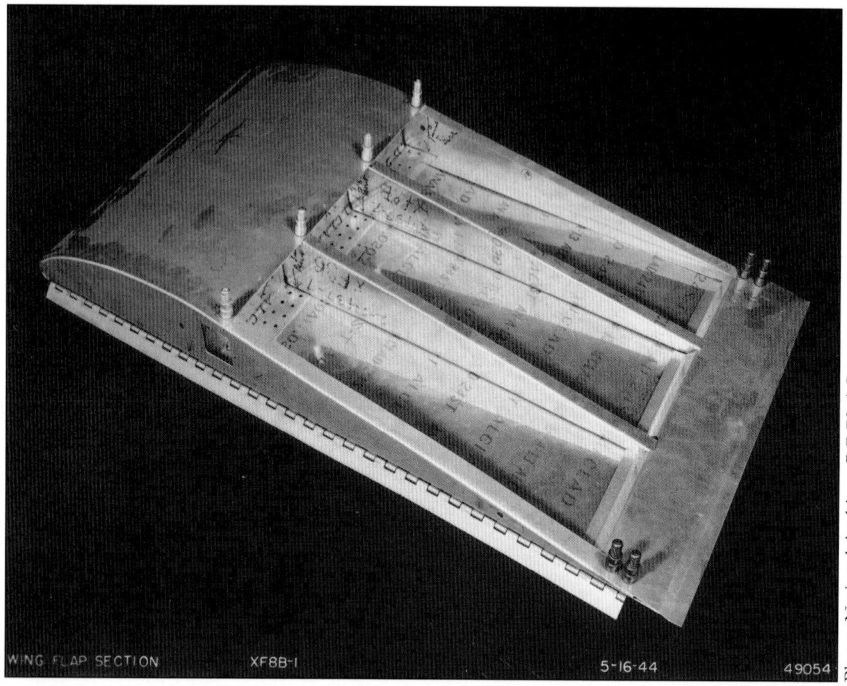

Photo: National Archives, RG 72-AC

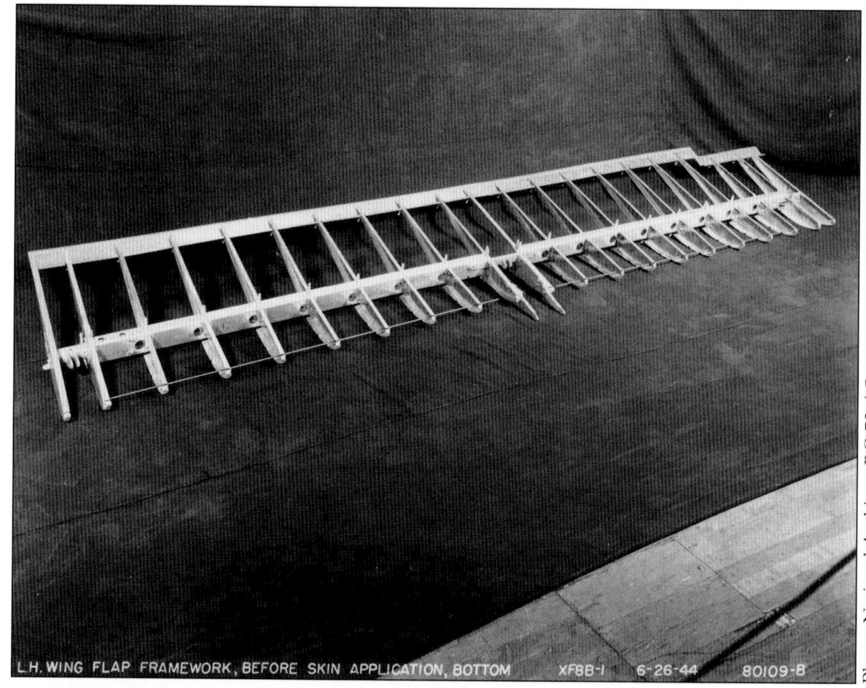

Photo: National Archives, RG 72-AC

Photo: National Archives, RG 72-AC

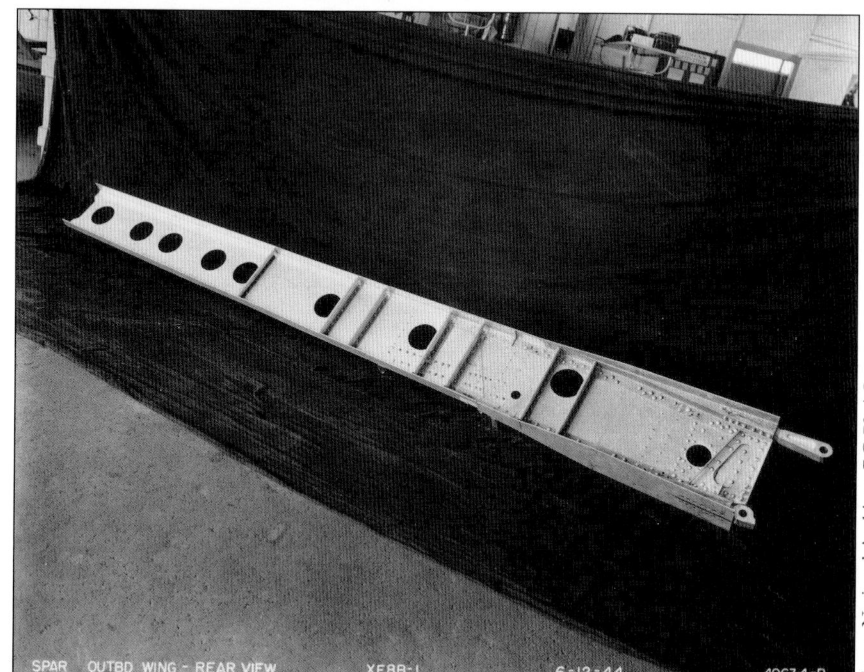

Photo: National Archives, RG 72-AC

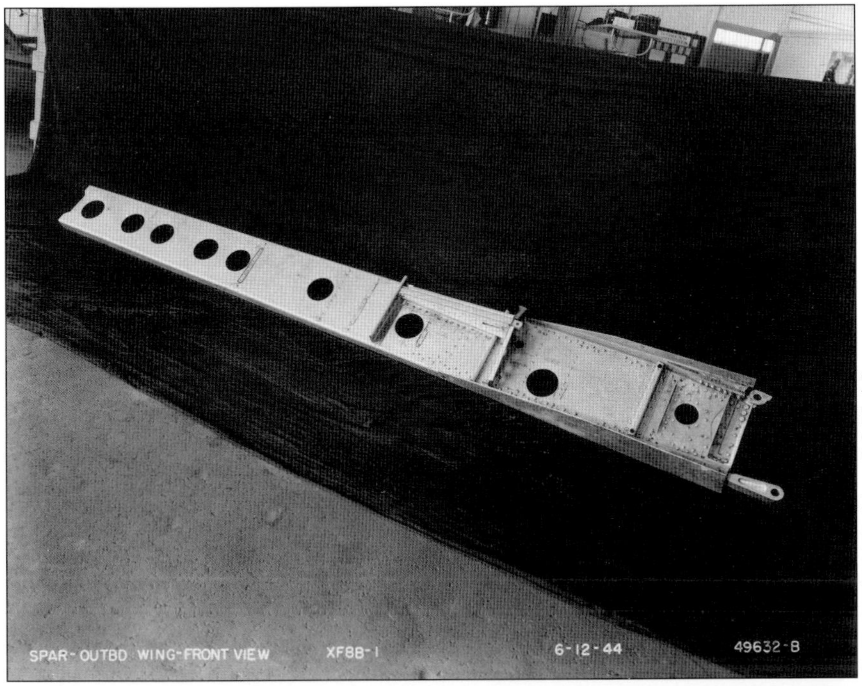

Photo: National Archives, RG 72-AC

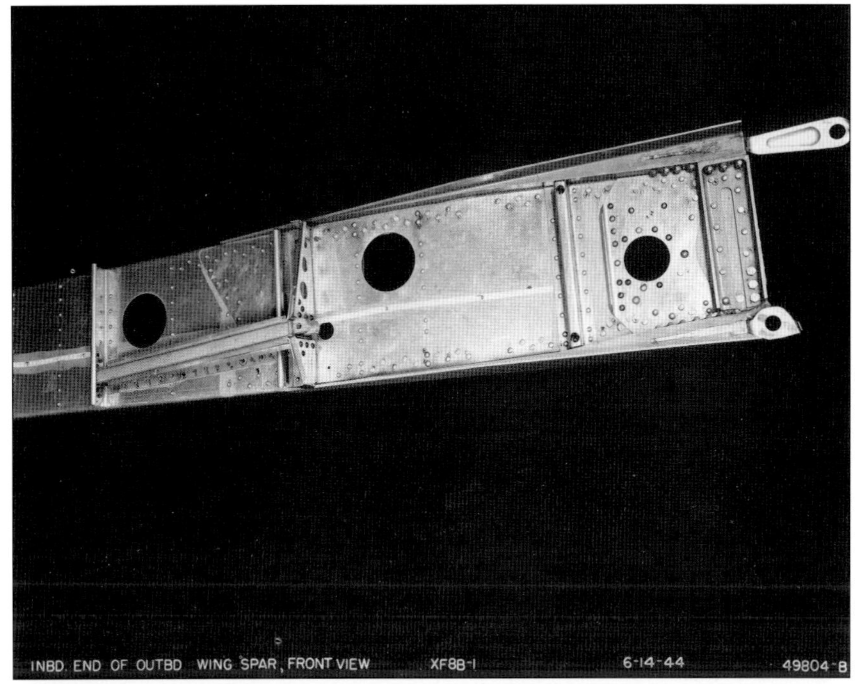

Photo: National Archives, RG 72-AC

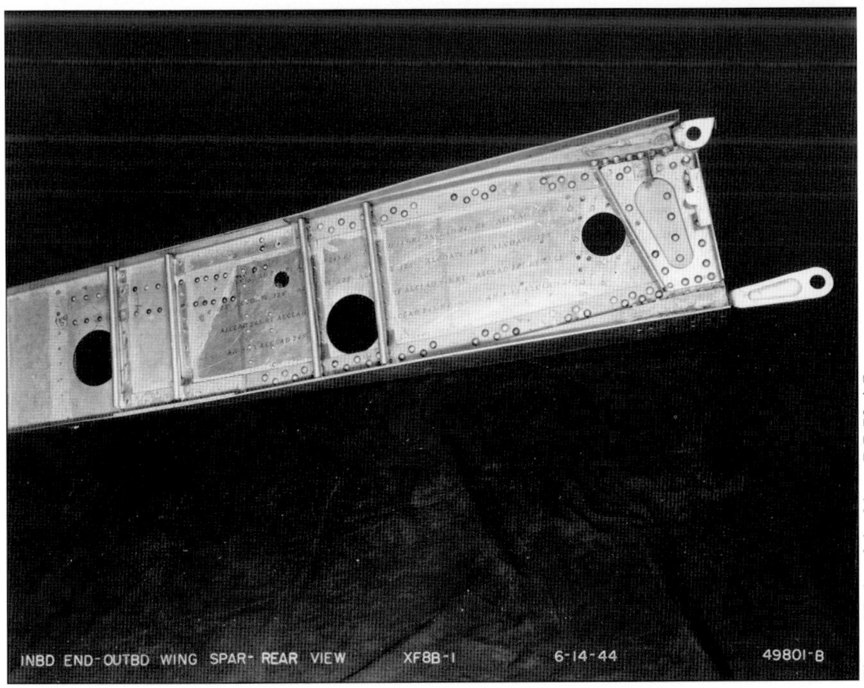

Photo: National Archives, RG 72-AC

Photo: National Archives, RG 72-AC

Photo: National Archives, RG 72-AC

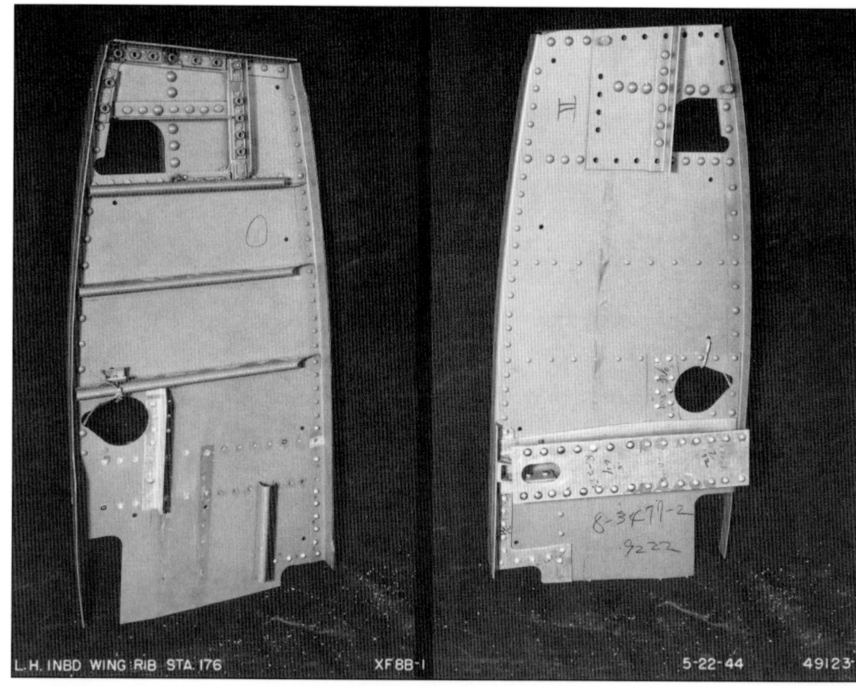

Photo: National Archives, RG 72-AC

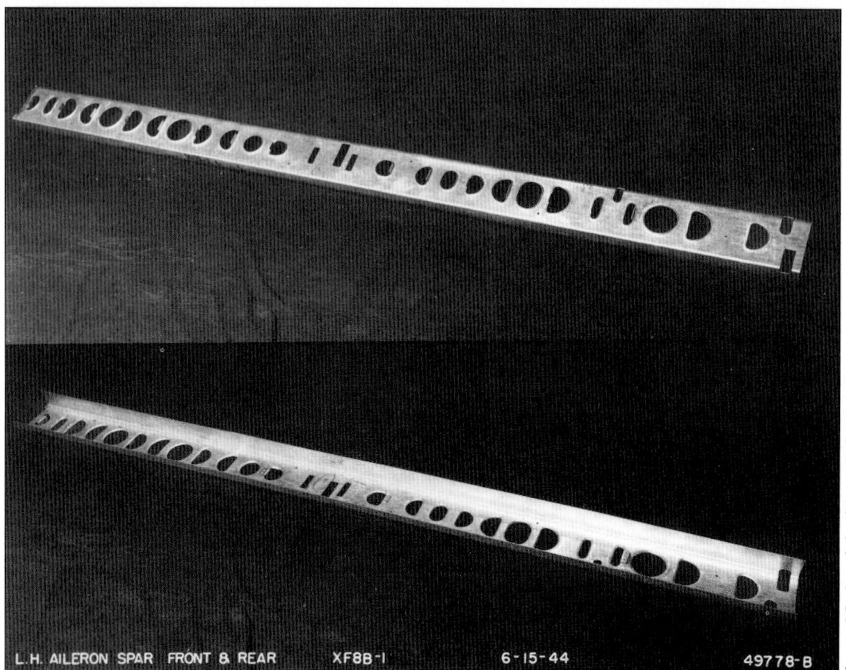

Photo: National Archives, RG 72-AC

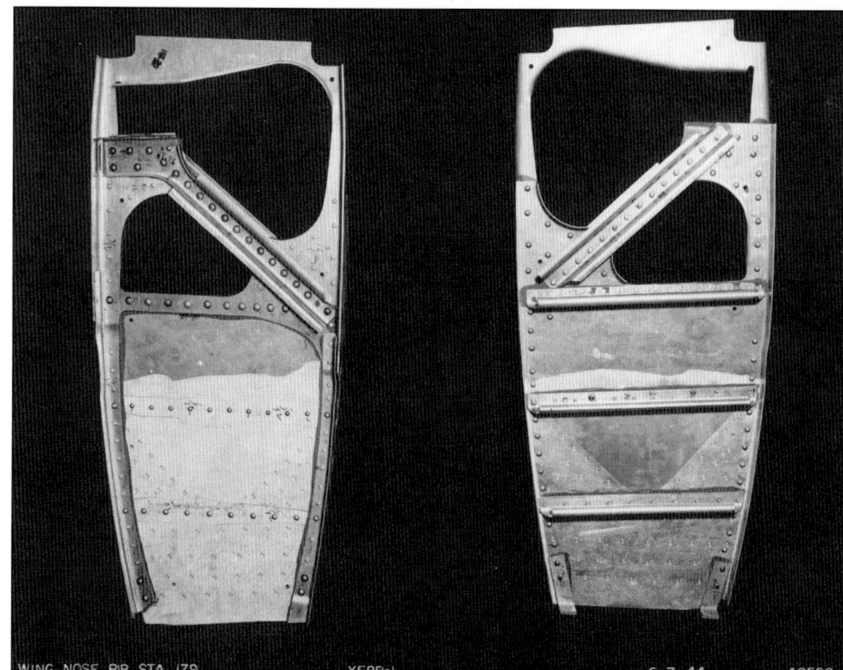

Photo: National Archives, RG 72-AC

Photc: National Archives, RG 72-AC

Photo: National Archives, RG 72-AC

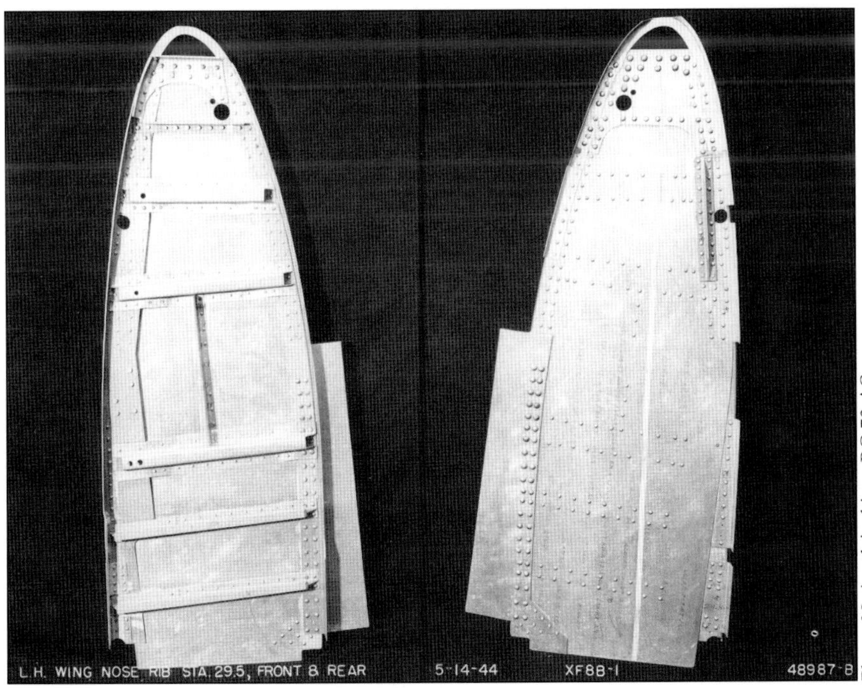

Photo: National Archives, RG 72-AC

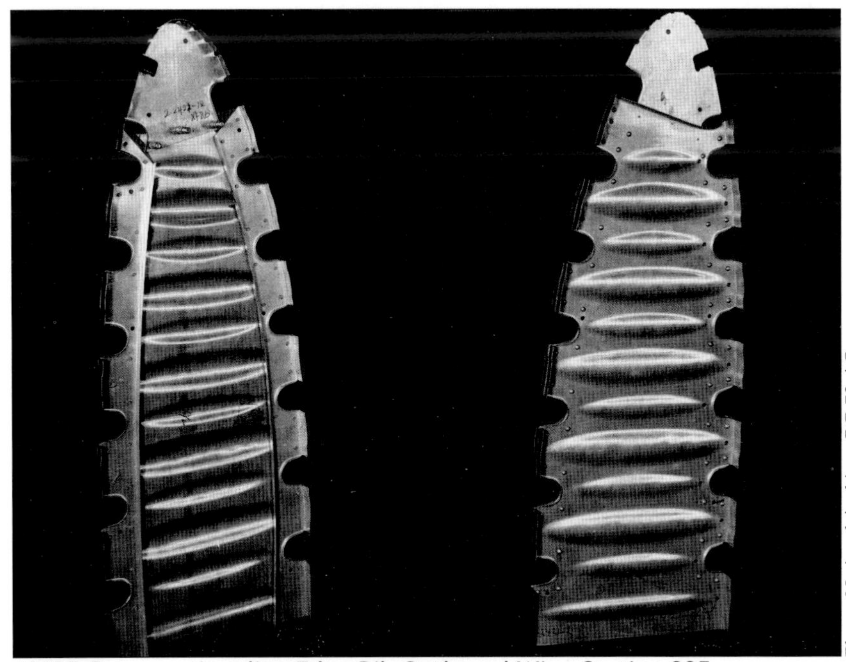

49125-B Leading Edge Rib Outboard Wing Station 235

Photo: National Archives, RG 72-AC

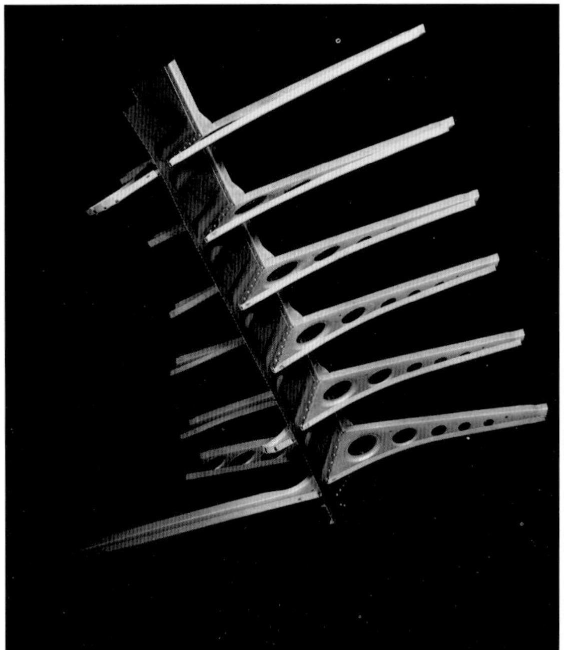
RIB ASSY TRAILING EDGE AFT OF WHEEL WELL XF8B-1 6-15-44 49803

Photo: National Archives, RG 72-AC

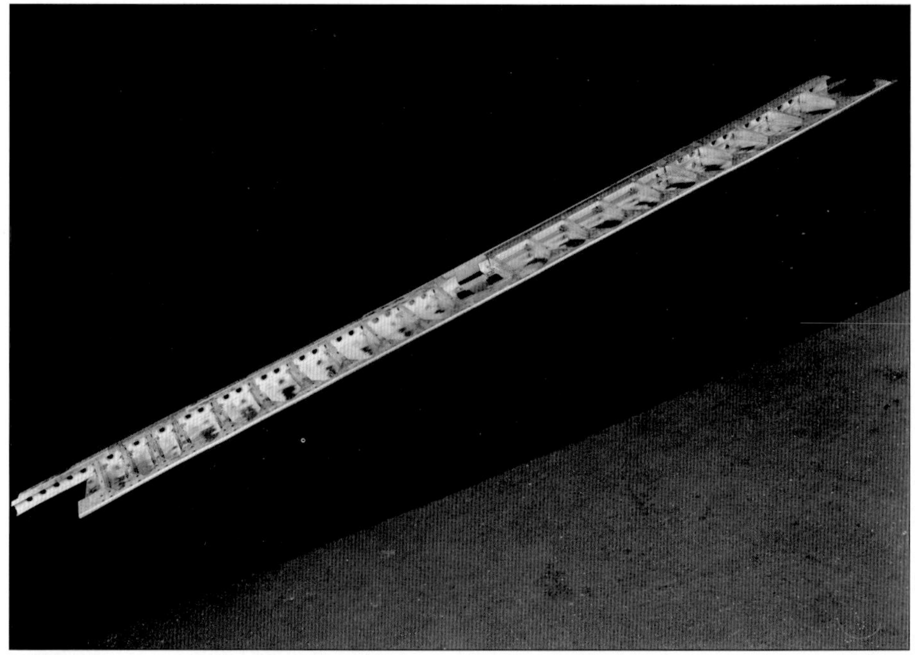
Photo: National Archives, RG 72-AC

86786-B Wing Trailing Edge

WING TAIL RIB STA. 61 XF8B-1 5-16-44 49061-B

Photo: National Archives, RG 72-AC

WING TAIL RIB STA 61 XF8B-1 5-16-44 49062-B

Photo: National Archives, RG 72-AC

Photo: National Archives, RG 72-AC

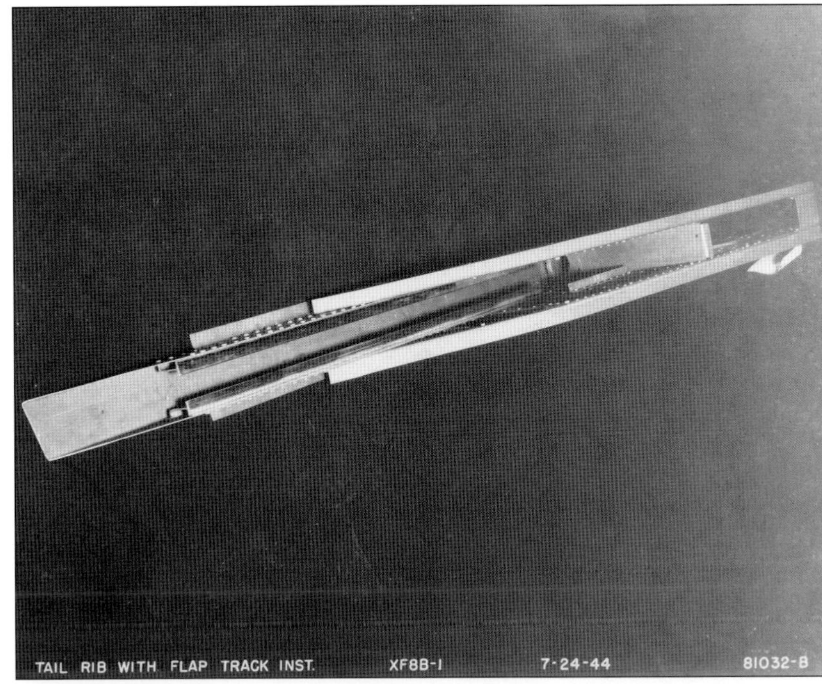

Photo: National Archives, RG 72-AC

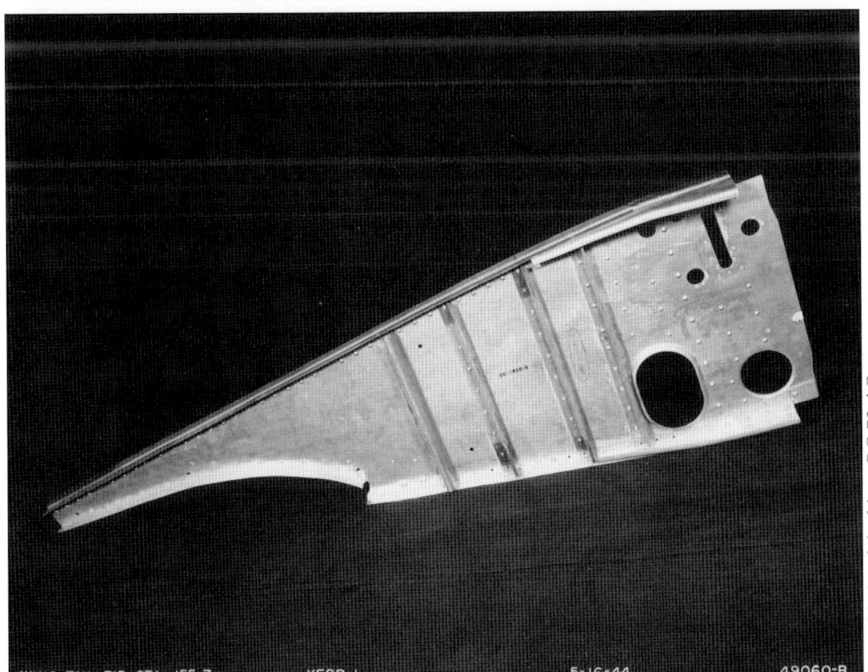

Photo: National Archives, RG 72-AC

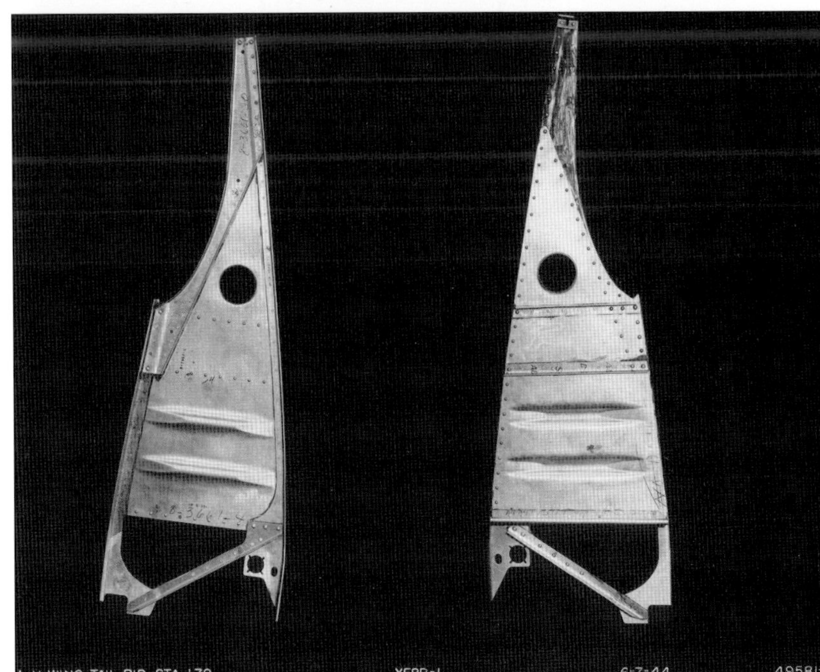

Photo: National Archives, RG 72-AC

Photo: National Archives, RG 72-AC

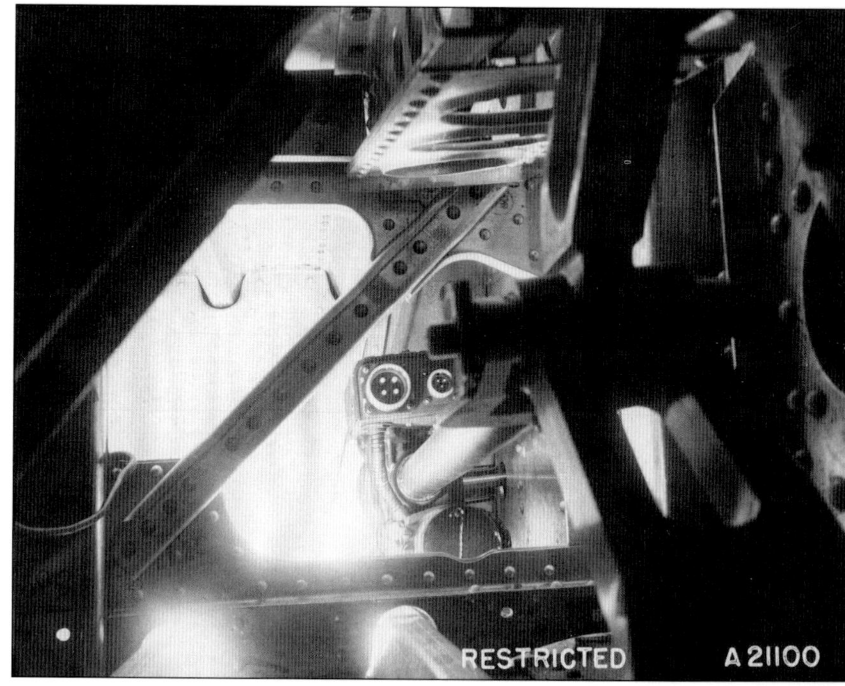

Photo: National Archives, RG 72-AC

Photo: National Archives, RG 72-AC

A21103 Wing Fold Actuator

Photo: National Archives, RG 72-AC

A21101 Wing Lock Assembly, Righthand Side View

Photo: National Archives, RG 72-AC

FA6762 Dive Flap, Lefthand Wing

Photo: National Archives, RG 72-AC

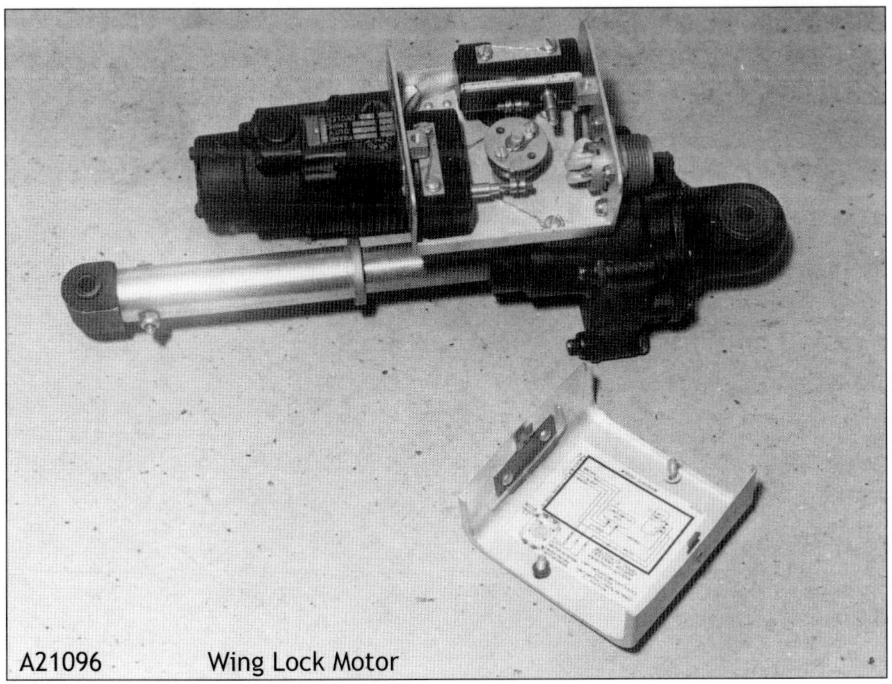

A21096 Wing Lock Motor

Photo: National Archives, RG 72-AC

A20131

TEMPORARY-JURY STRUT INST. XF8B-1 10-9-44 RESTRICTED

Photo: National Archives, RG 72-AC

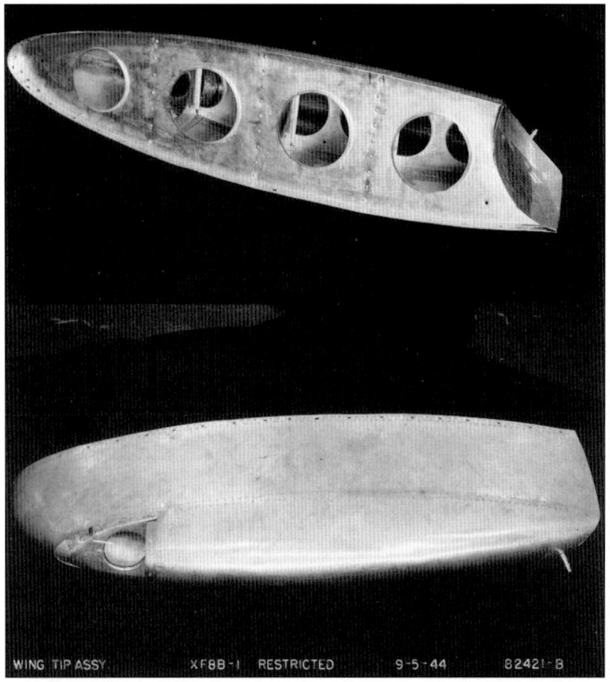

Photo: National Archives, RG 72-AC

Photo: National Archives, RG 72-AC

Photo: National Archives, RG 72-AC

Photo: National Archives, RG 72-AC

Photo: National Archives, RG 72-AC

Part D: Fuel Tank

Photo: National Archives, RG 72-AC

Photo: National Archives, RG 72-AC

Photo: National Archives, RG 72-AC

Photo: National Archives, RG 72-AC

Photo: National Archives, RG 72-AC

Photo: National Archives, RG 72-AC

Photo: National Archives, RG 72-AC

Photo: National Archives, RG 72-AC

Photo: National Archives, RG 72-AC

Photo: National Archives, RG 72-AC

Part E: Cockpit

Photo: National Archives, RG 72-AC

Photo: National Archives, RG 72-AC

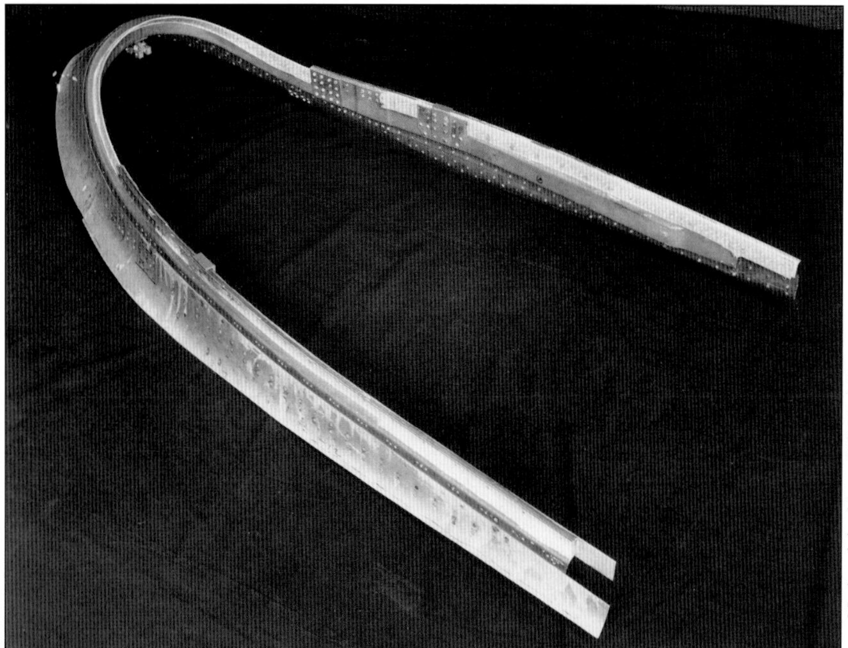
FRAME - PILOTS ENCLOSURE - 12-1640 XF8B-1 9-14-44 82811-B

Photo: National Archives, RG 72-AC

FLOOR SEC. PILOT'S COCKPIT, BOTTOM VIEW XF8B-1 5-14-44 49028-B

Photo: National Archives, RG 72-AC

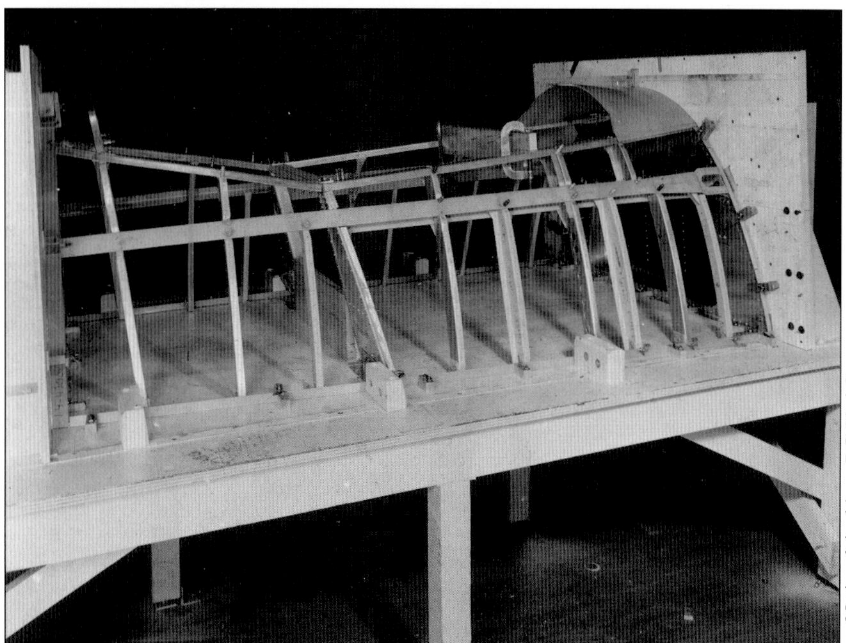
COCKPIT SEC. 41 FRAMEWORK IN JIG XF8B-1 6-7-44 49578-B

Photo: National Archives, RG 72-AC

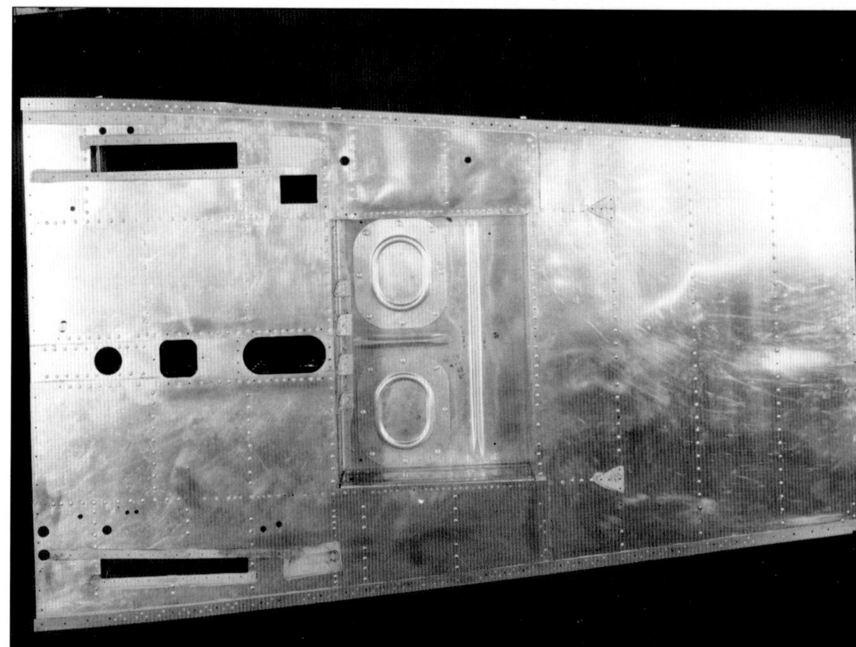
FLOOR SECTION PILOT'S COCKPIT TOP VIEW XF8B-1 5-14-44 49026-B

Photo: National Archives, RG 72-AC

Photo: National Archives, RG 72-AC

Photo: National Archives, RG 72-AC

Photo: National Archives, RG 72-AC

Photo: National Archives, RG 72-AC

Photo: National Archives, RG 72-AC

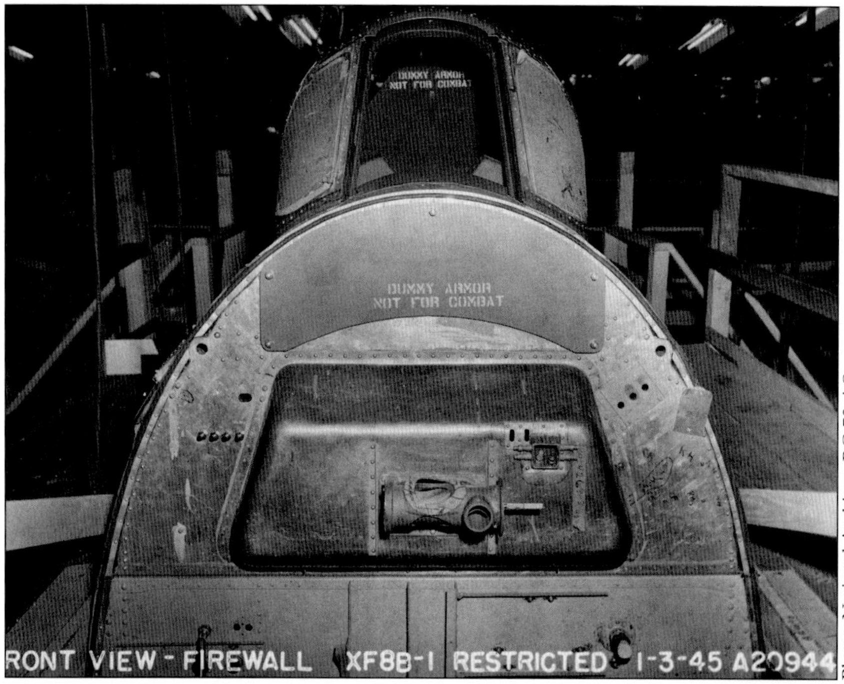

Photo: National Archives, RG 72-AC

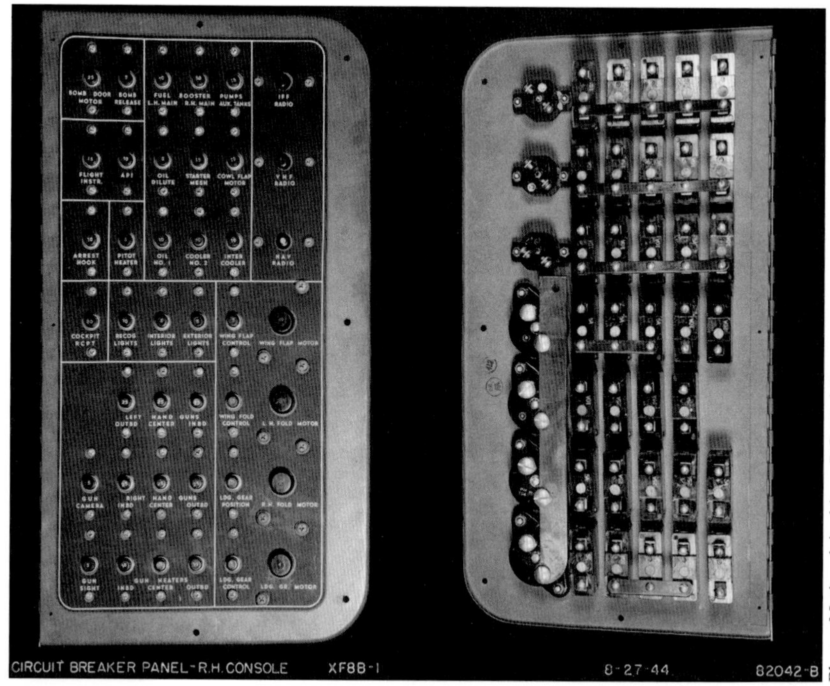

Photo: National Archives, RG 72-AC

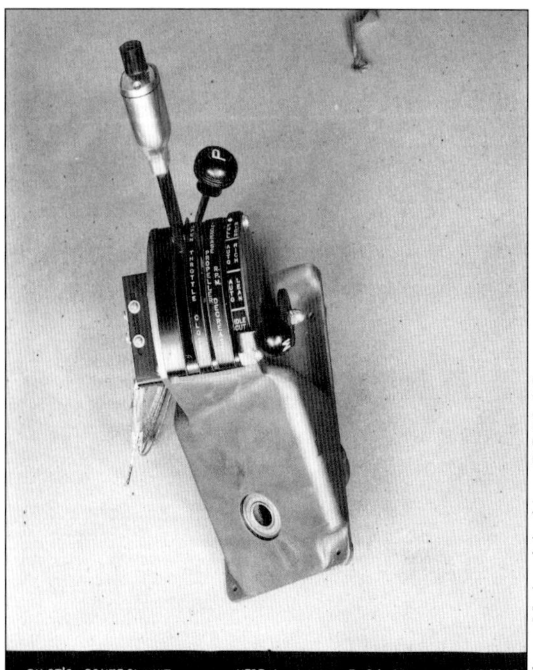

Photo: National Archives, RG 72-AC

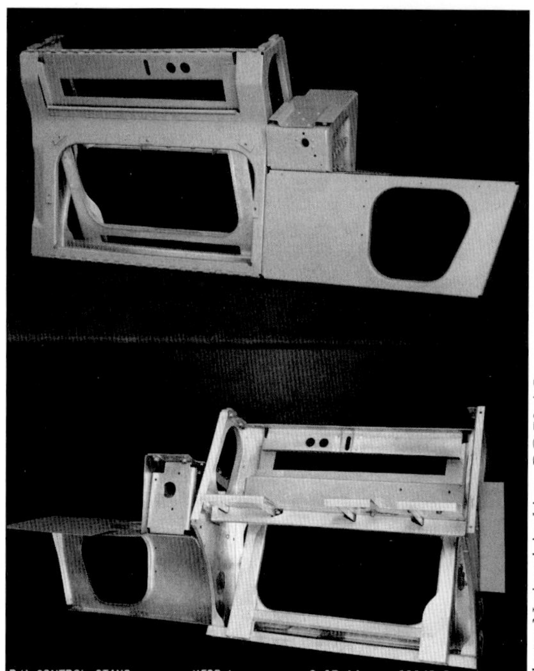

Photo: National Archives, RG 72-AC

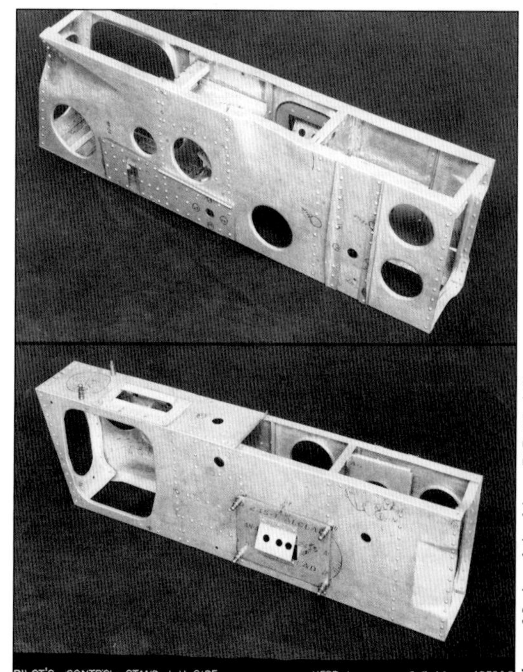

Photo: National Archives, RG 72-AC

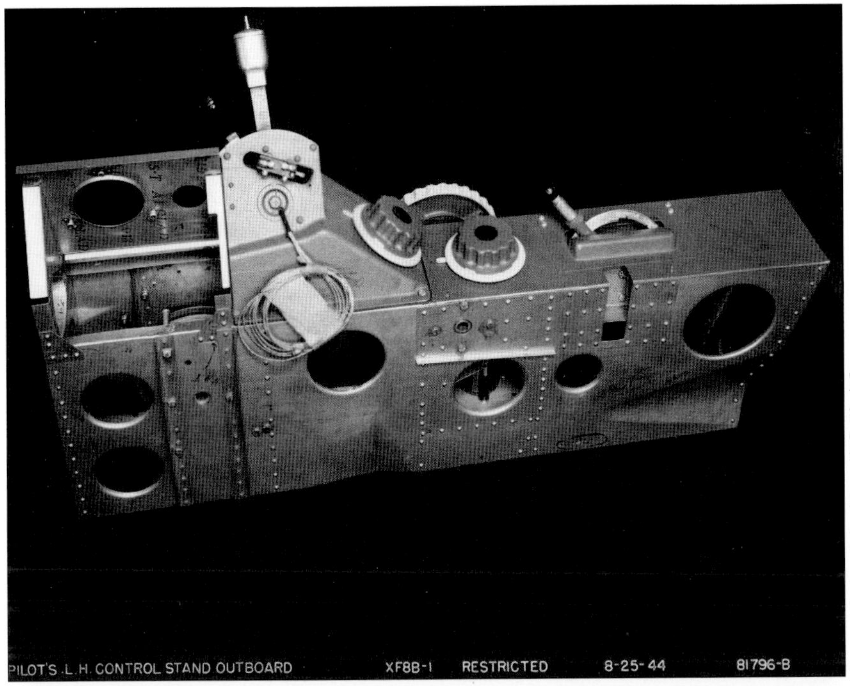

Photo: National Archives, RG 72-AC

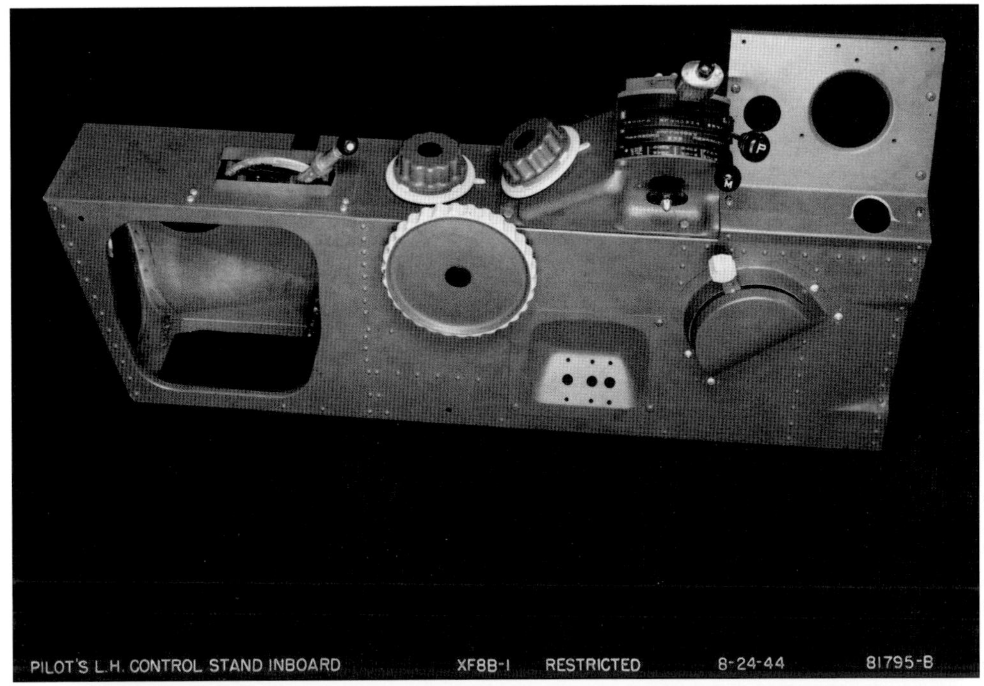

Photo: National Archives, RG 72-AC

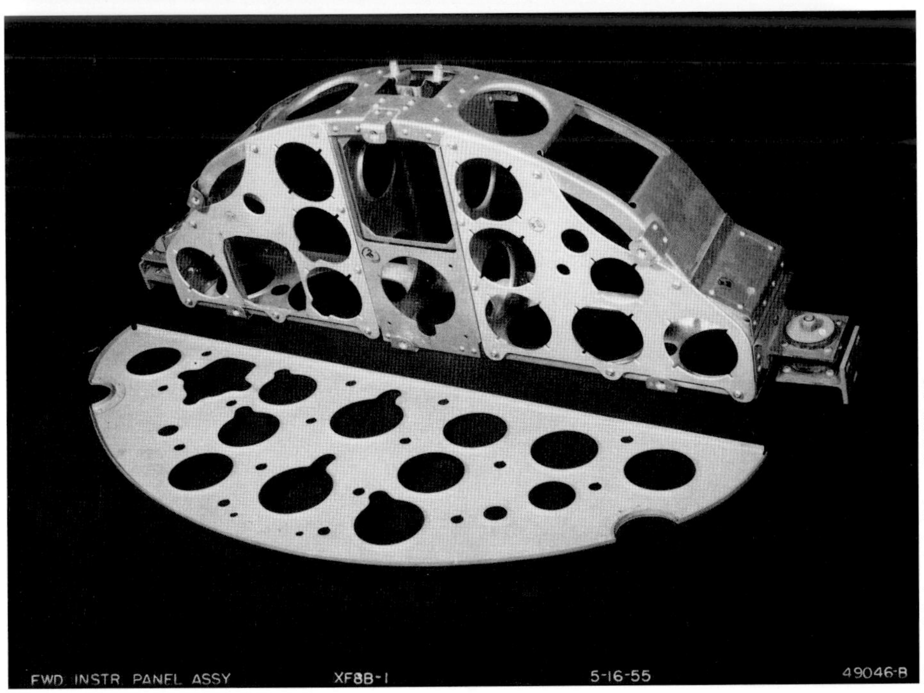

Photo: National Archives, RG 72-AC

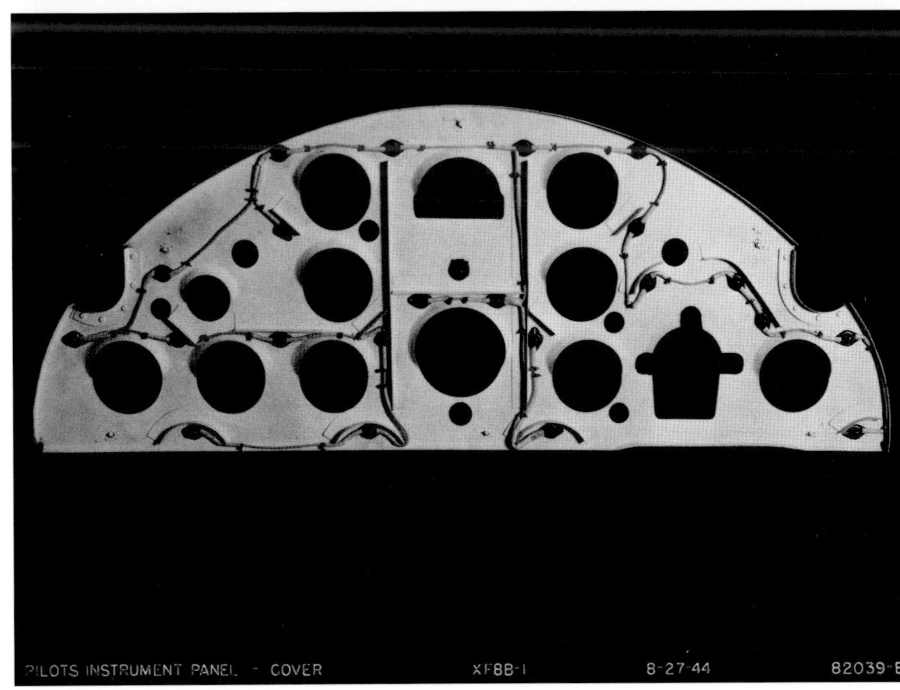

Photo: National Archives, RG 72-AC

Photo: National Archives, RG 72-AC

Photo: National Archives, RG 72-AC

Photo: National Archives, RG 72-AC

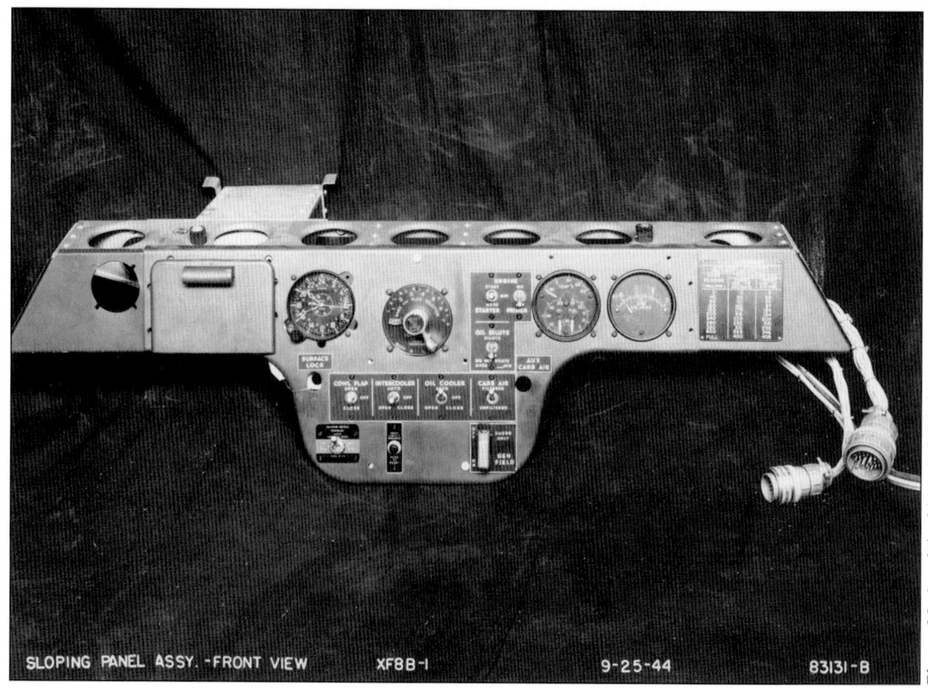

Photo: National Archives, RG 72-AC

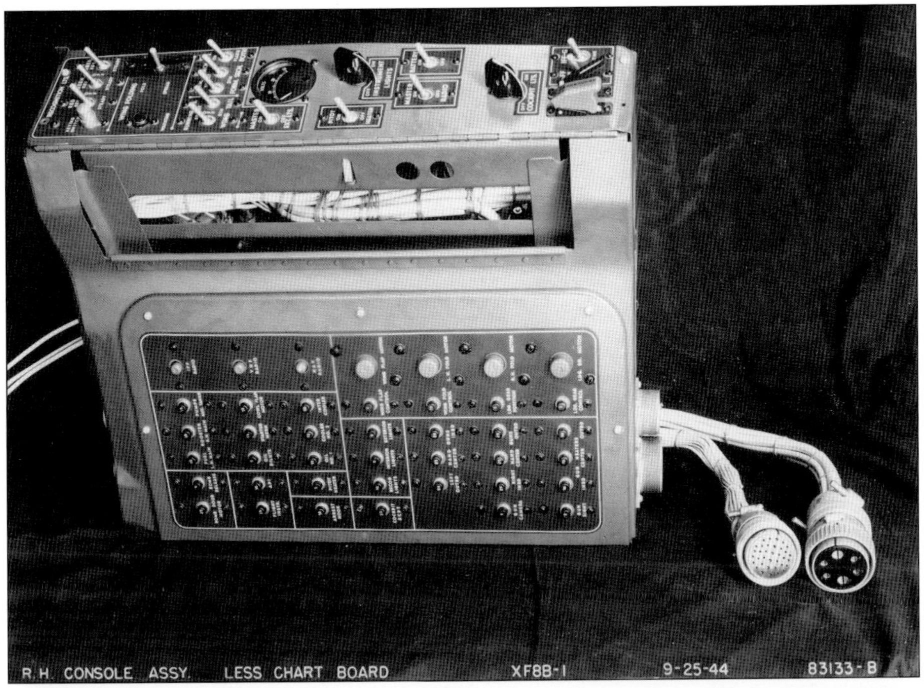

Photo: National Archives, RG 72-AC

Photo: National Archives, RG 72-AC

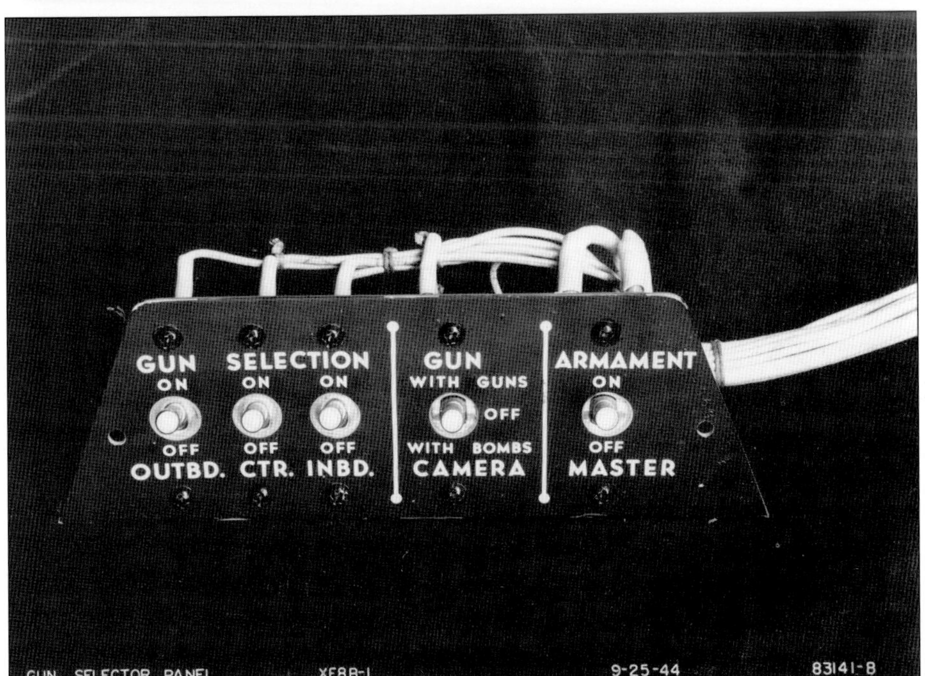

Photo: National Archives, RG 72-AC

Photo: National Archives, RG 72-AC

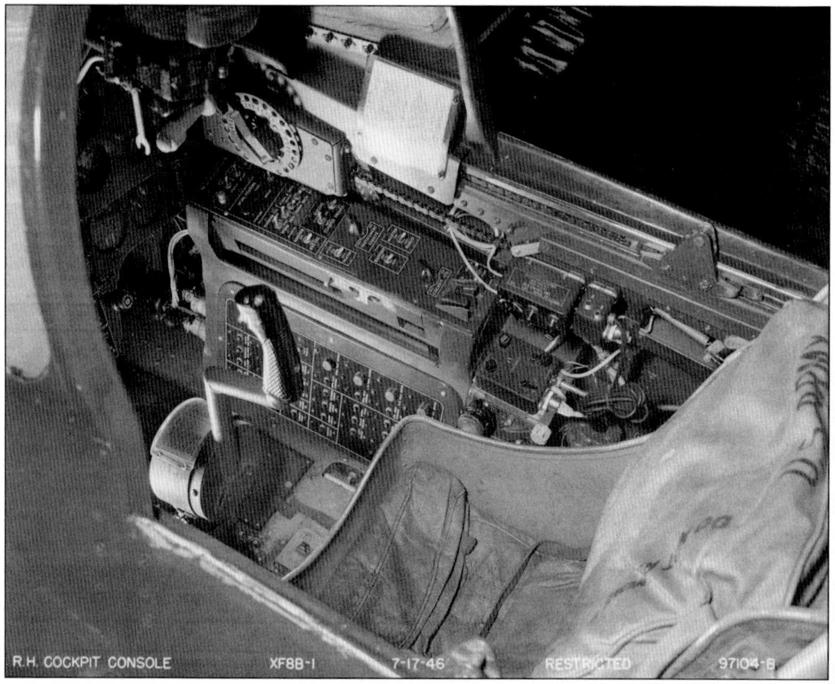

Photo: National Archives, RG 72-AC

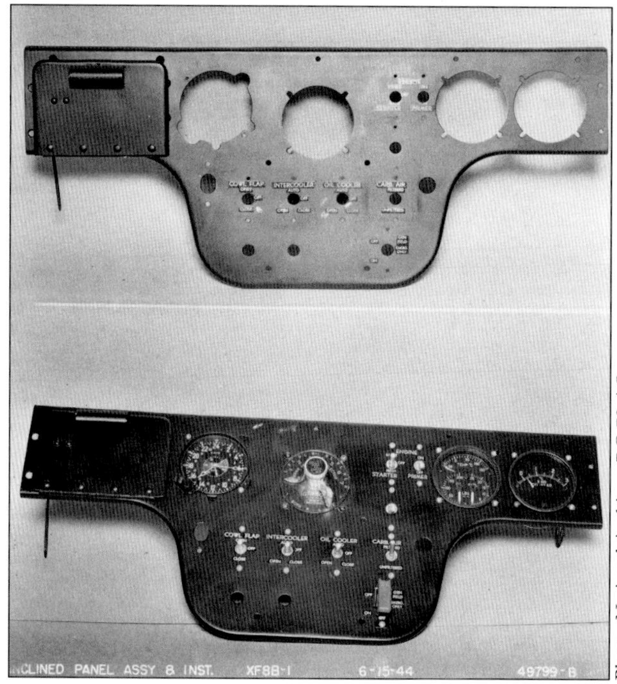

Photo: National Archives, RG 72-AC

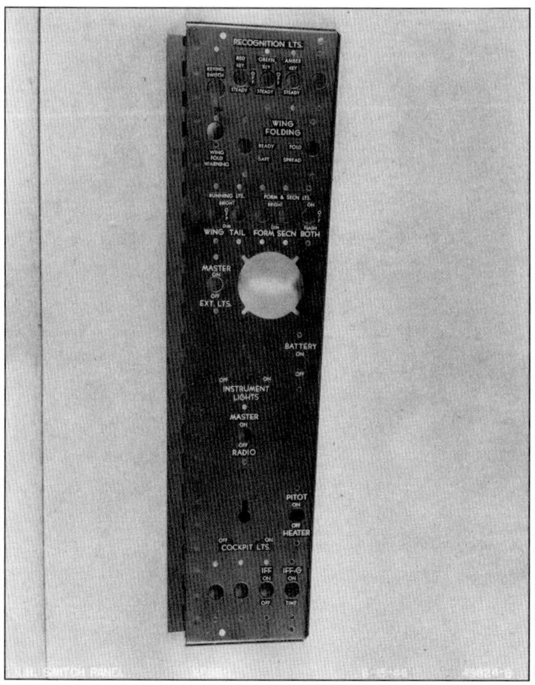

Photo: National Archives, RG 72-AC

Photo: National Archives, RG 72-AC

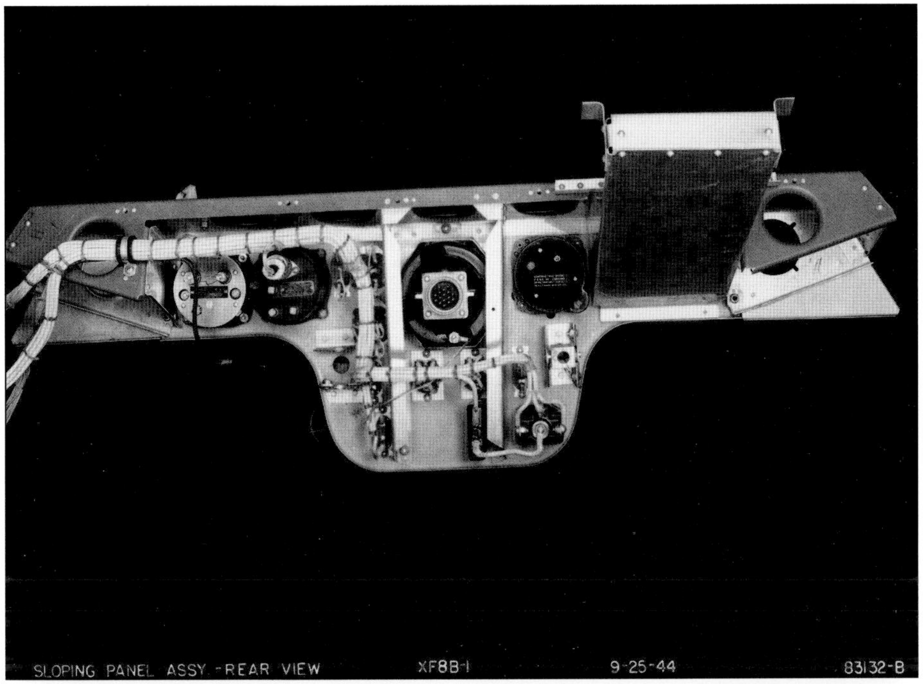

Photo: National Archives, RG 72-AC

Photo: National Archives, RG 72-AC

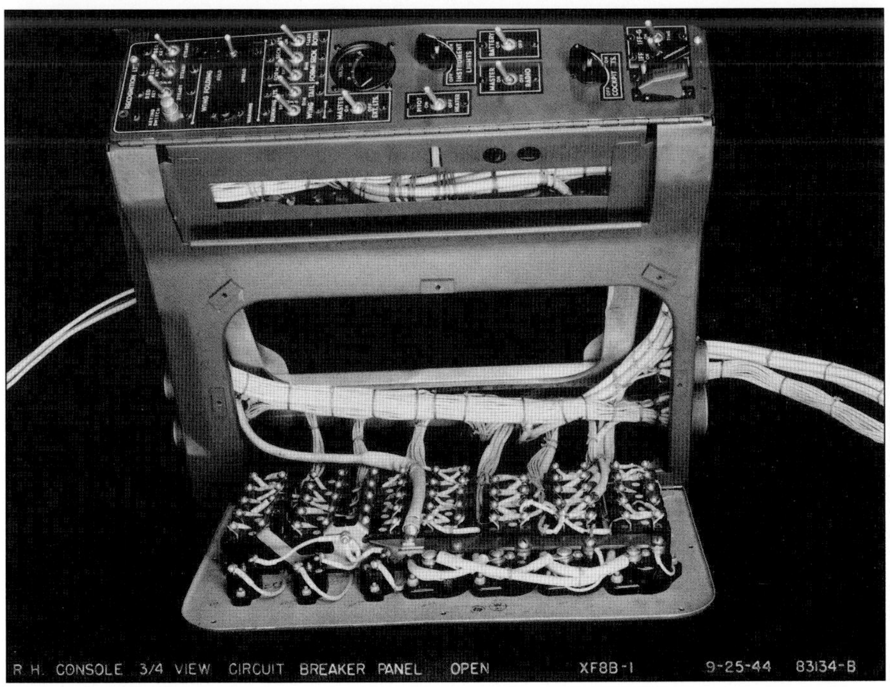

Photo: National Archives, RG 72-AC

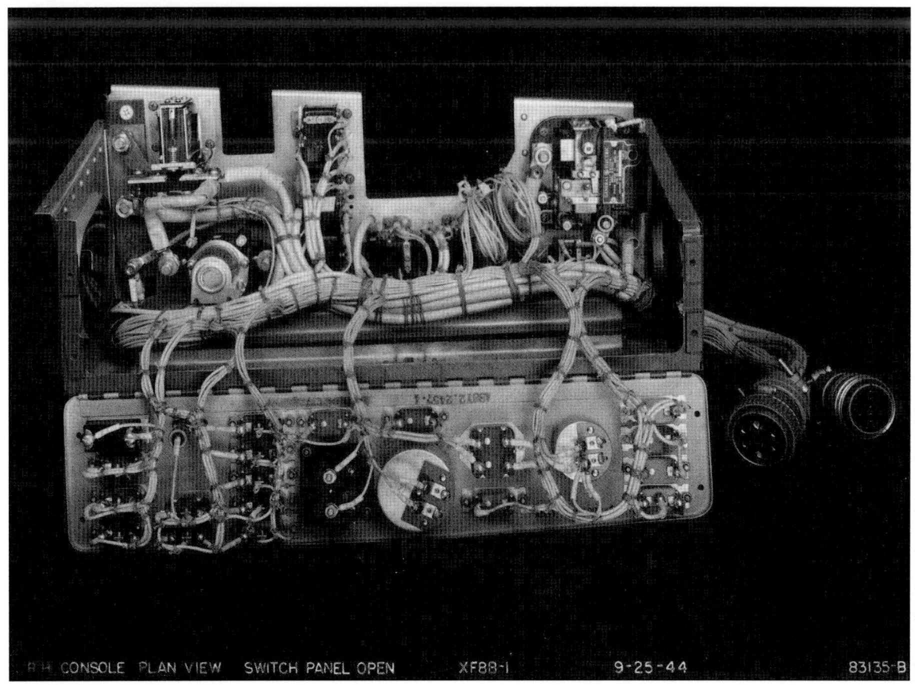

Photo: National Archives, RG 72-AC

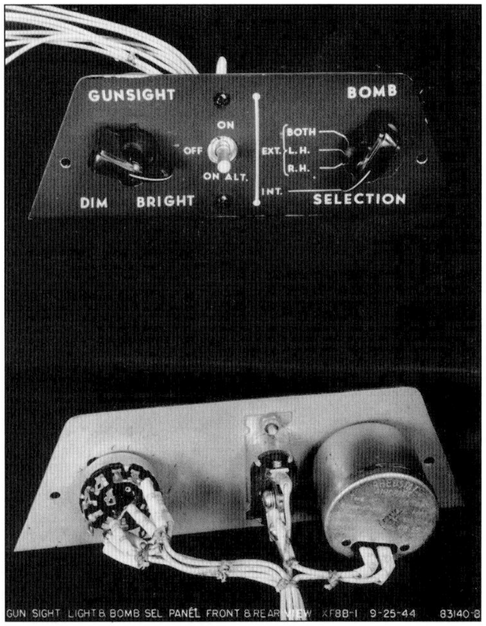

GUN SIGHT LIGHT & BOMB SEL. PANEL FRONT & REAR VIEW XF8B-1 9-25-44 83140-B

Photo: National Archives, RG 72-AC

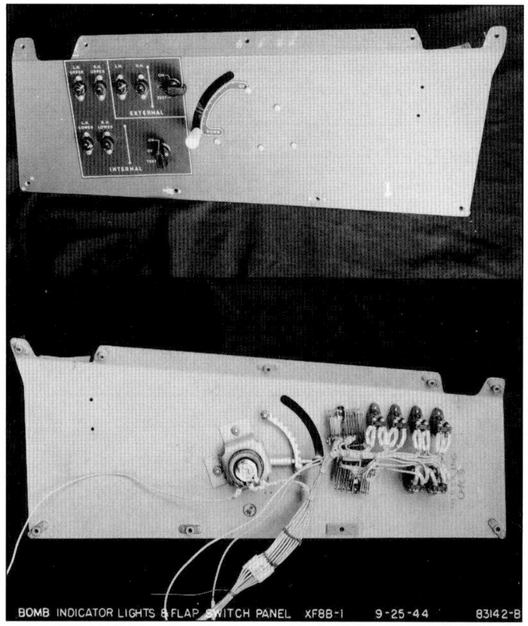

BOMB INDICATOR LIGHTS & FLAP SWITCH PANEL XF8B-1 9-25-44 83142-B

Photo: National Archives, RG 72-AC

RUDDER PEDAL ASS'Y. XF8B-1 7-6-44 80605-B

Photo: National Archives, RG 72-AC

COCKPIT SEC. RUDDER CONTROLS INSTALLED XF8B-1 7-17-44 80829-B

Photo: National Archives, RG 72-AC

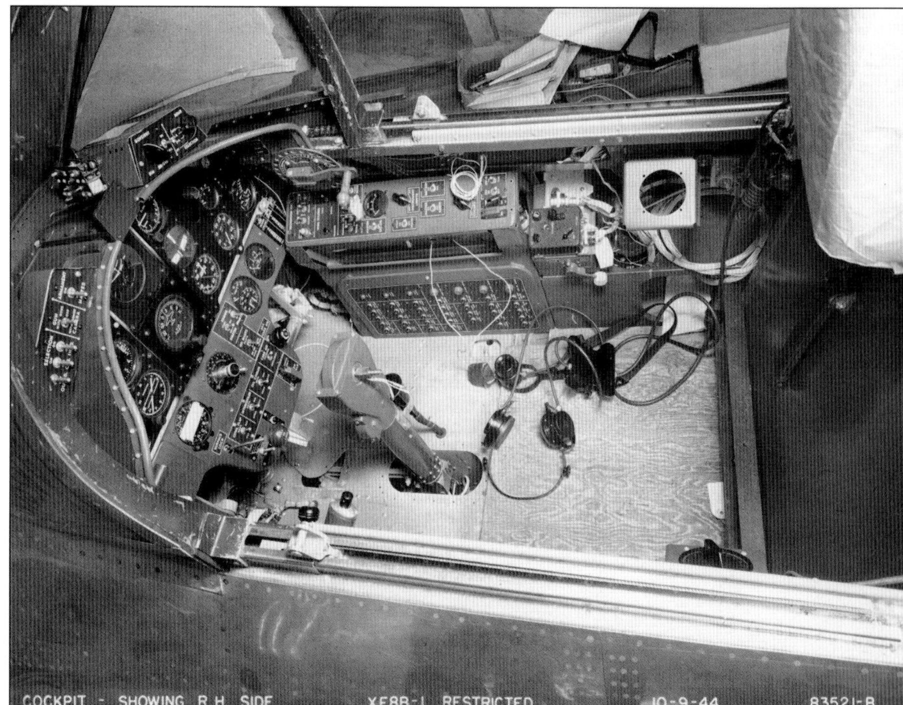
COCKPIT - SHOWING R.H. SIDE XF8B-1 RESTRICTED 10-9-44 83521-B

Photo: National Archives, RG 72-AC

Photo: National Archives, RG 72-AC

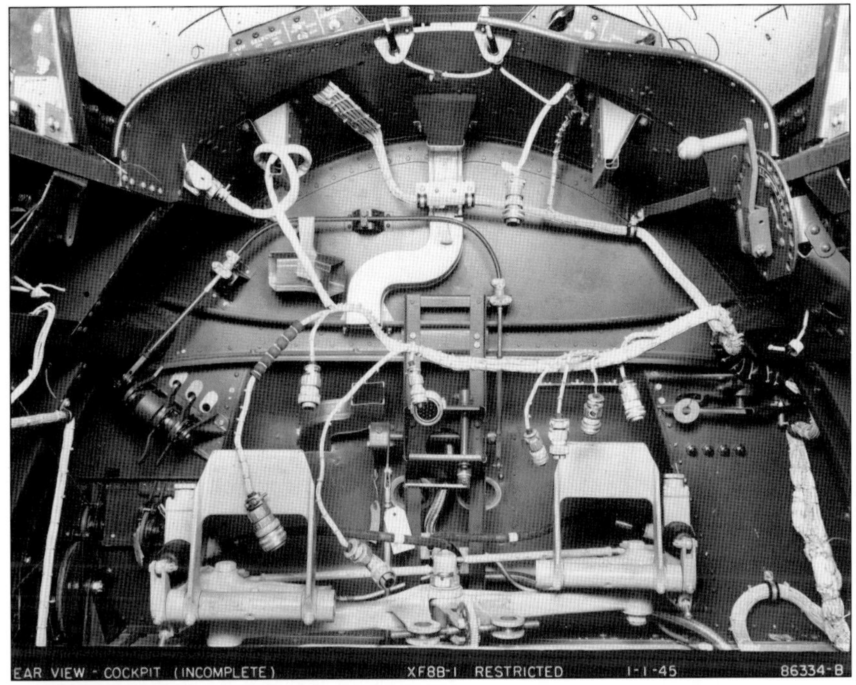

Photo: National Archives, RG 72-AC

Photo: National Archives, RG 72-AC

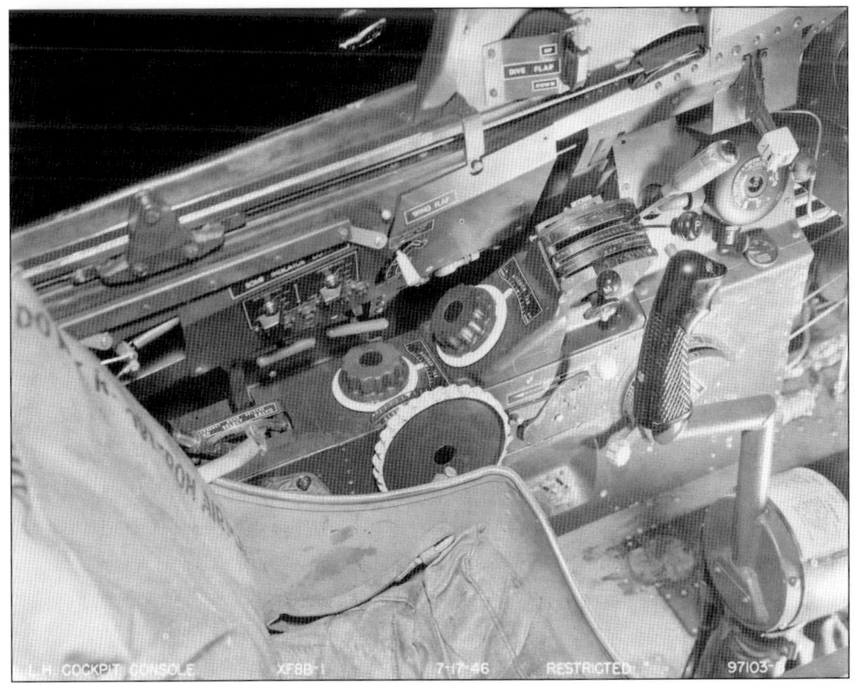

Photo: National Archives, RG 72-AC

Part F: Bomb Bay

Photo: National Archives, RG 72-AC

Photo: National Archives, RG 72-AC

Photo: National Archives, RG 72-AC

Photo: National Archives, RG 72-AC

Photo: National Archives, RG 72-AC

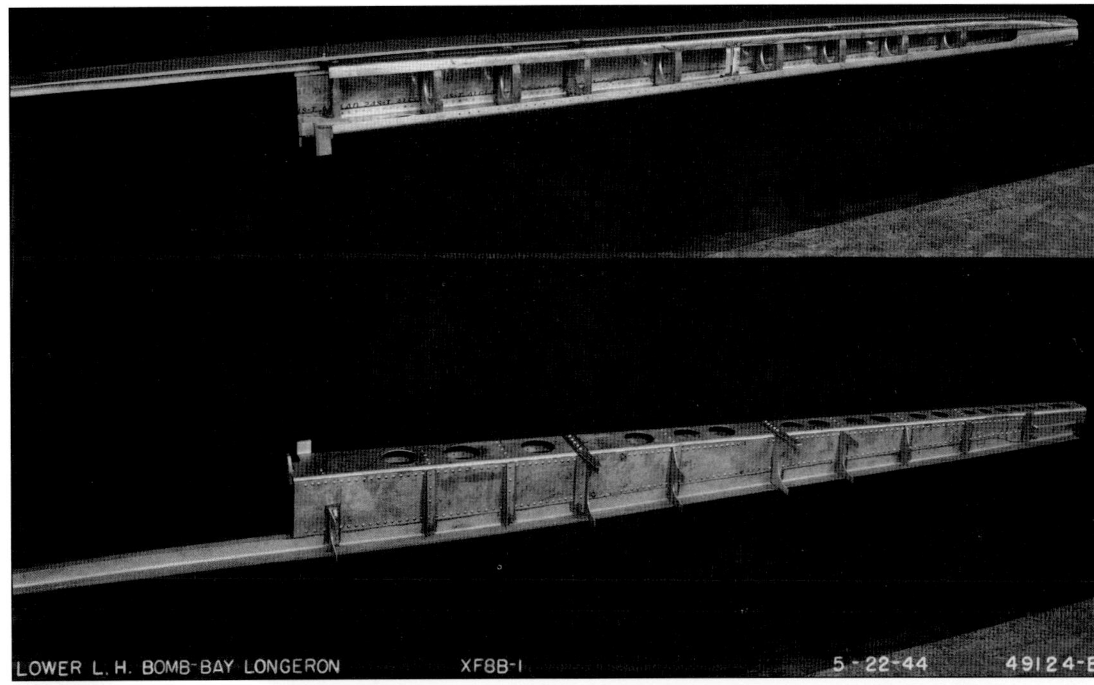

Photo: National Archives, RG 72-AC

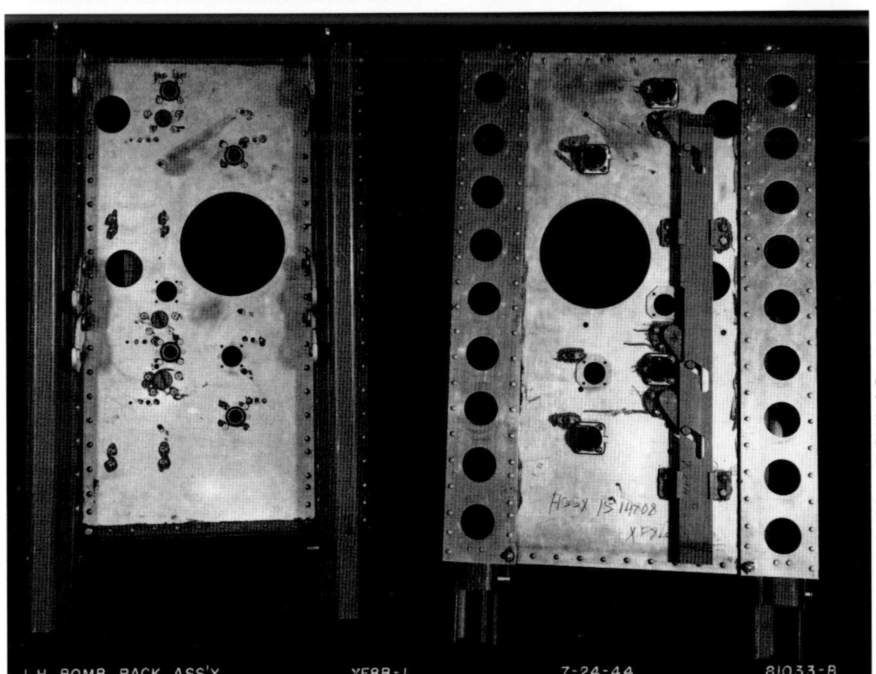

Photo: National Archives, RG 72-AC

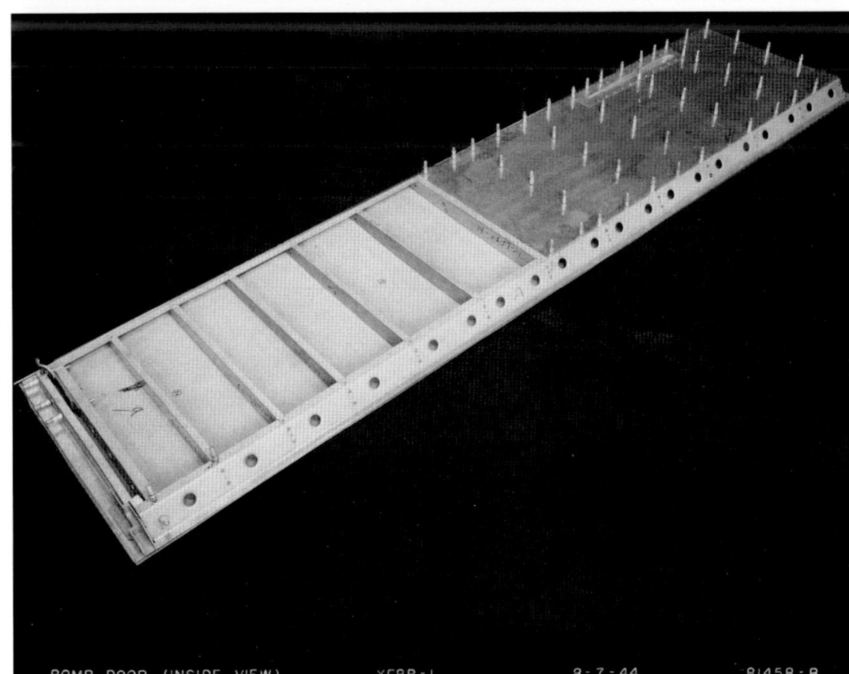

Photo: National Archives, RG 72-AC

Photo: National Archives, RG 72-AC

Photo: National Archives, RG 72-AC

Photo: National Archives, RG 72-AC

Photo: National Archives, RG 72-AC

Part G: Power Plant

Photo: National Archives, RG 72-AC

Photo: National Archives, RG 72-AC

Photo: National Archives, RG 72-AC

Photo: National Archives, RG 72-AC

Photo: National Archives, RG 72-AC

Photo: National Archives, RG 72-AC

Photo: National Archives, RG 72-AC

Photo: National Archives, RG 72-AC

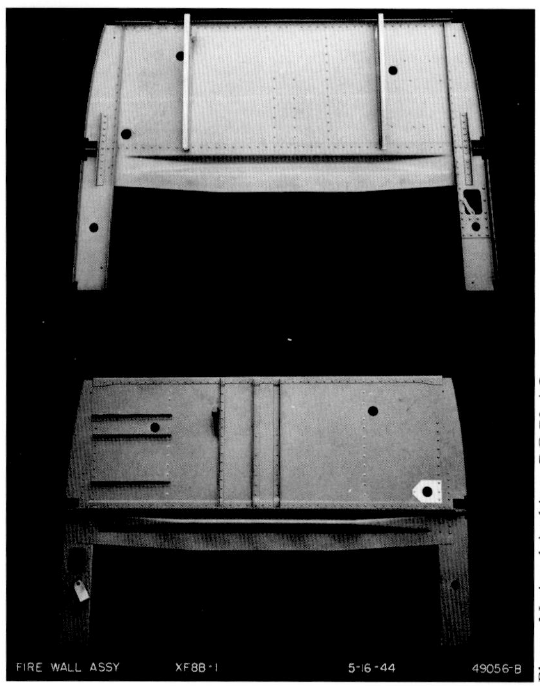

Photo: National Archives, RG 72-AC

Photo: National Archives, RG 72-AC

Photo: National Archives, RG 72-AC

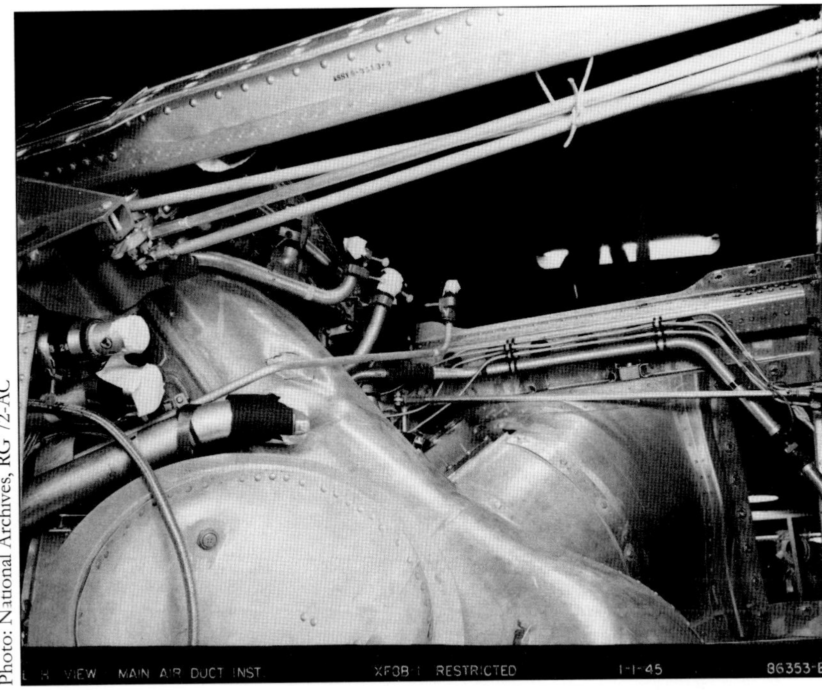

Photo: National Archives, RG 72-AC

Photo: National Archives, RG 72-AC

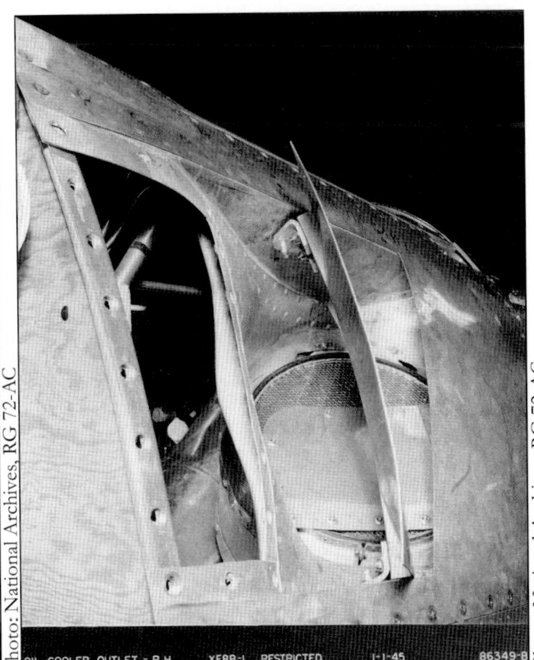

Photo: National Archives, RG 72-AC

Photo: National Archives, RG 72-AC

Photo: National Archives, RG 72-AC

Photo: National Archives, RG 72-AC

Photo: National Archives, RG 72-AC

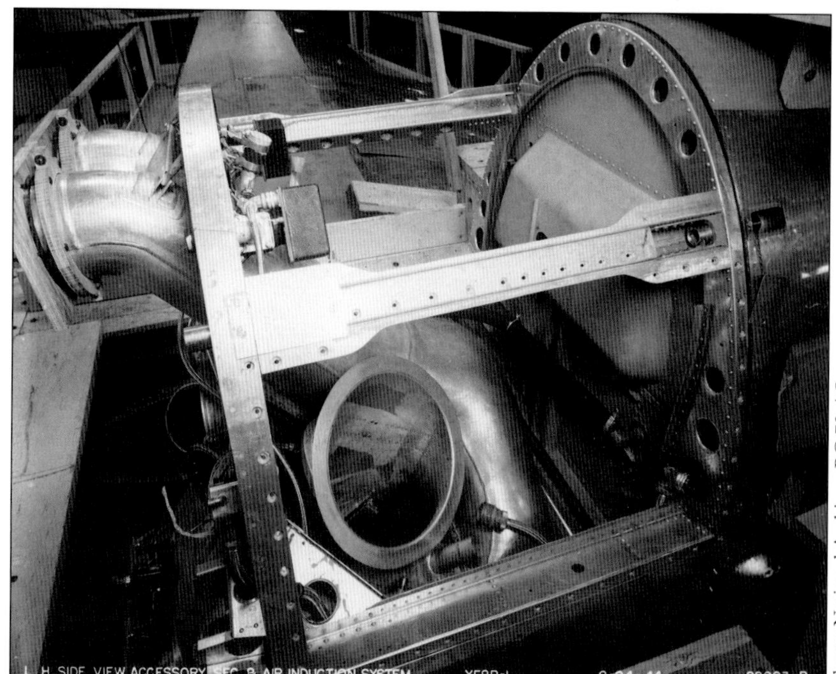

Photo: National Archives, RG 72-AC

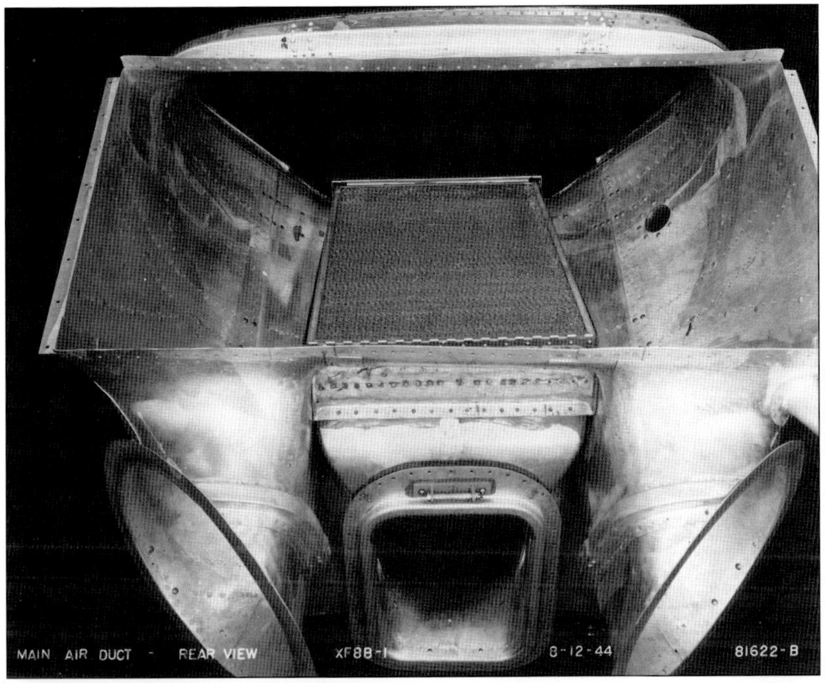

Photo: National Archives, RG 72-AC

Photo: National Archives, RG 72-AC

Photo: National Archives, RG 72-AC

Photo: National Archives, RG 72-AC

Photo: National Archives, RG 72-AC

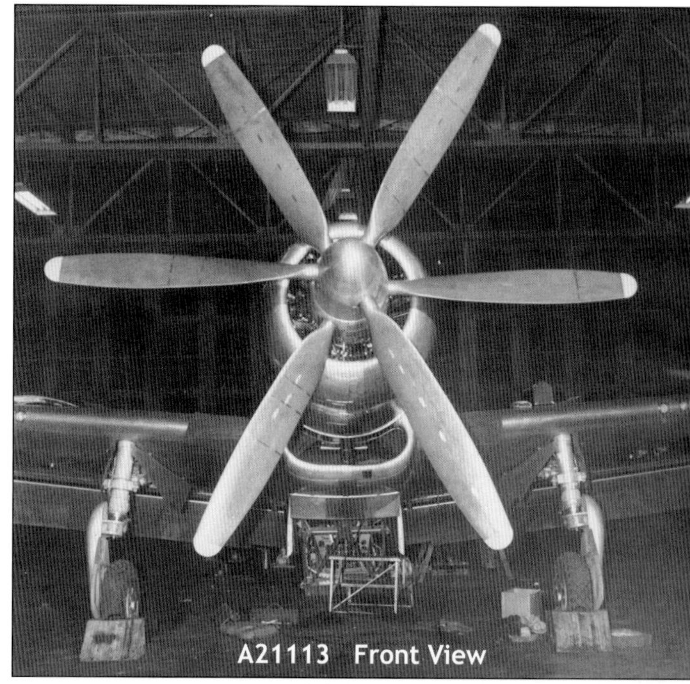
A21113 Front View

Photo: National Archives, RG 72-AC

Photo: National Archives, RG 72-AC

Photo: National Archives, RG 72-AC

Photo: National Archives, RG 72-AC

Photo: National Archives, RG 72-AC

Photo: National Archives, RG 72-AC

Photo: National Archives, RG 72-AC

Photo: National Archives, RG 72-AC

FA-6756 Aft view of cowling.

Photo: National Archives, RG 72-AC

Photo: National Archives, RG 72-AC

Photo: National Archives, RG 72-AC

Photo: National Archives, RG 72-AC

Photo: National Archives, RG 72-AC

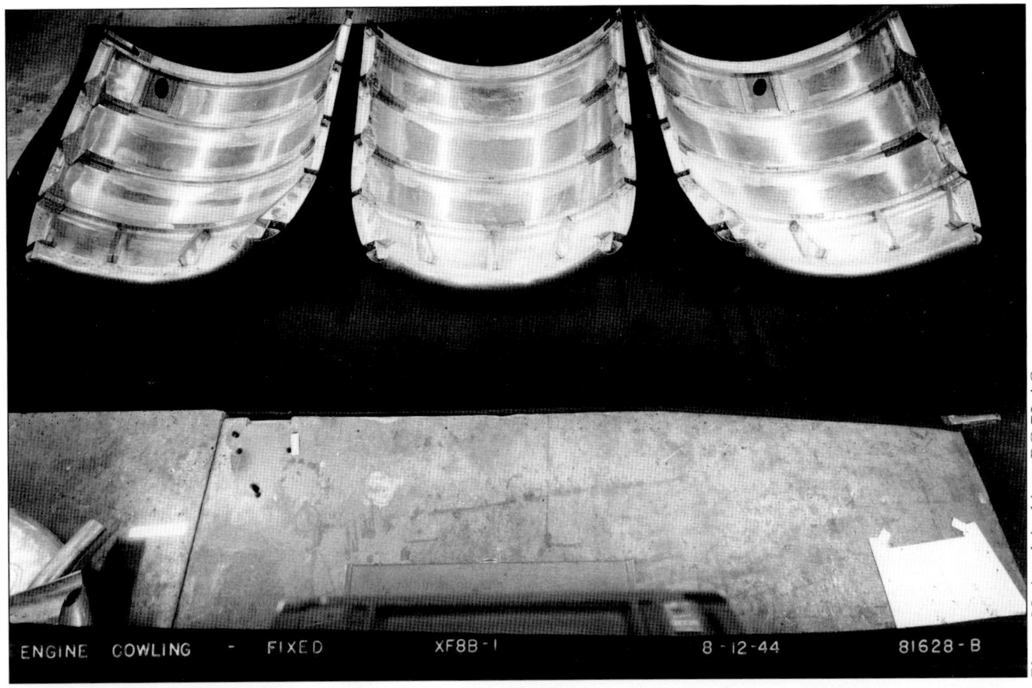

Photo: National Archives, RG 72-AC

Photo: National Archives, RG 72-AC

Photo: National Archives, RG 72-AC

Photo: National Archives, RG 72-AC

Photo: National Archives, RG 72-AC

Photo: National Archives, RG 72-AC

Part H: Landing Gear

R.H. LANDING GEAR WELL, ASSY XF8B-1 5-27-44 49238-B

Photo: National Archives, RG 72-AC

LANDING GEAR ASSY XF8B-1 6-14-44 9781-B

Photo: National Archives, RG 72-AC

R.H. LANDING GEAR EXTENDED XF8B-1 8-7-44 81464-B

Photo: National Archives, RG 72-AC

L.H. LANDING GEAR (PARTIAL RETRACTION) XF8B-1 8-7-44 81462-B

Photo: National Archives, RG 72-AC

TAIL GEAR ASSY. & ACTUATOR XF8B-1 8-24-44 82002-B

Photo: National Archives, RG 72-AC

Photo: National Archives, RG 72-AC

Photo: National Archives, RG 72-AC

Photo: National Archives, RG 72-AC

Photo: National Archives, RG 72-AC

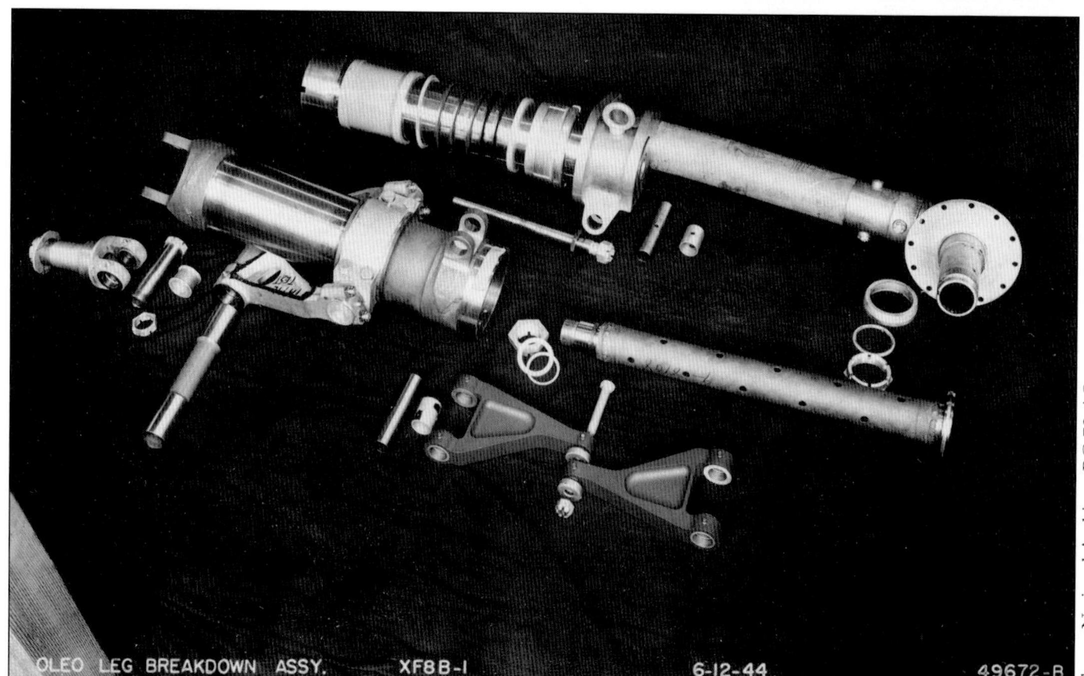

Photo: National Archives, RG 72-AC

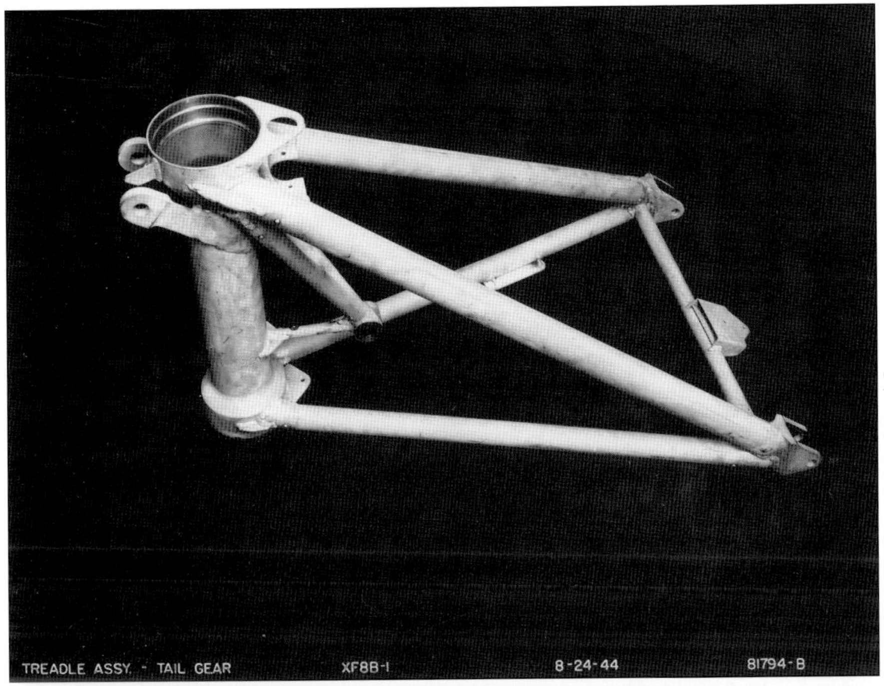

Photo: National Archives, RG 72-AC

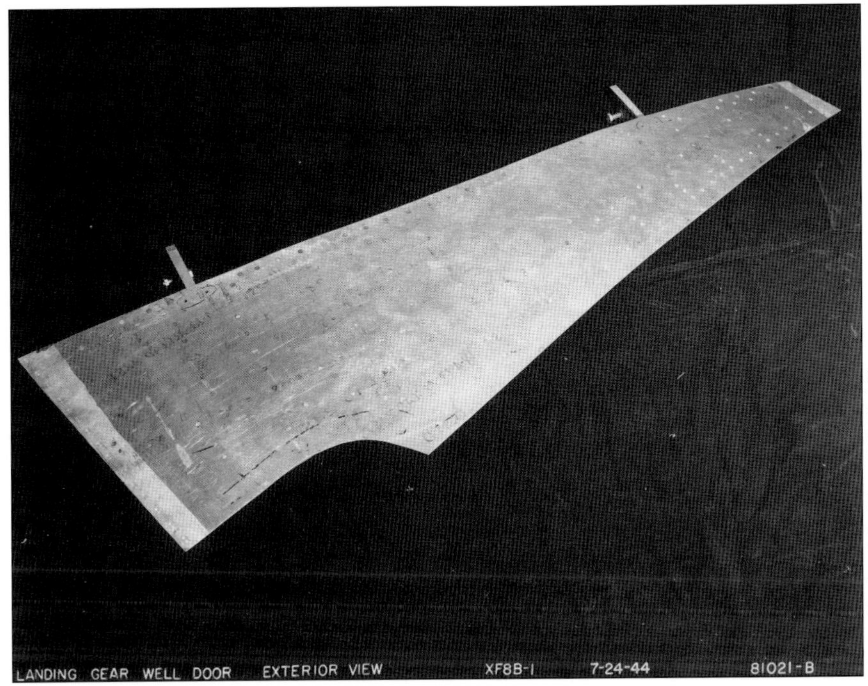

Photo: National Archives, RG 72-AC

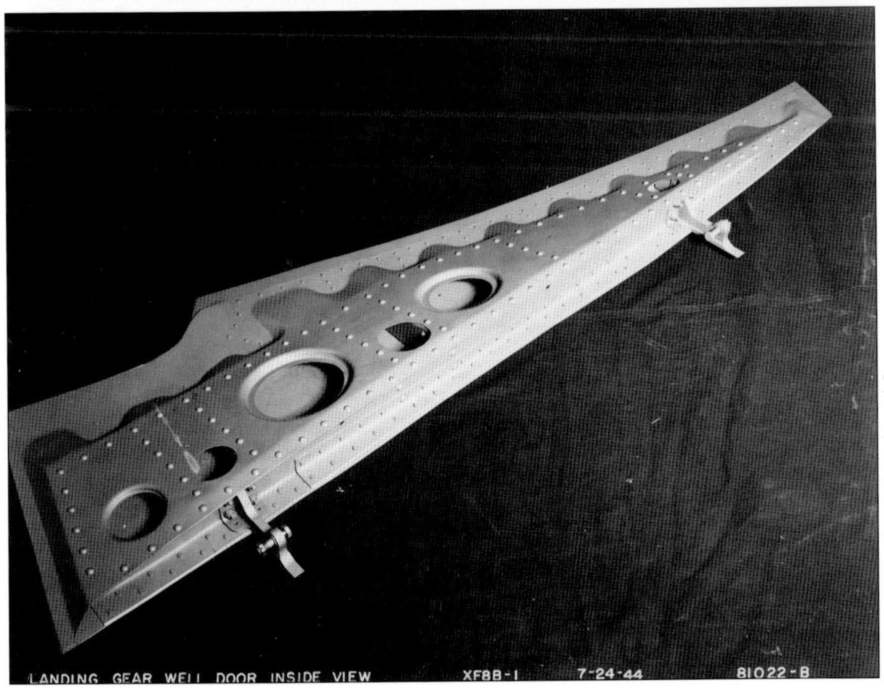

Photo: National Archives, RG 72-AC

Main gear with wheel removed.

Photo: National Archives, RG 72-AC

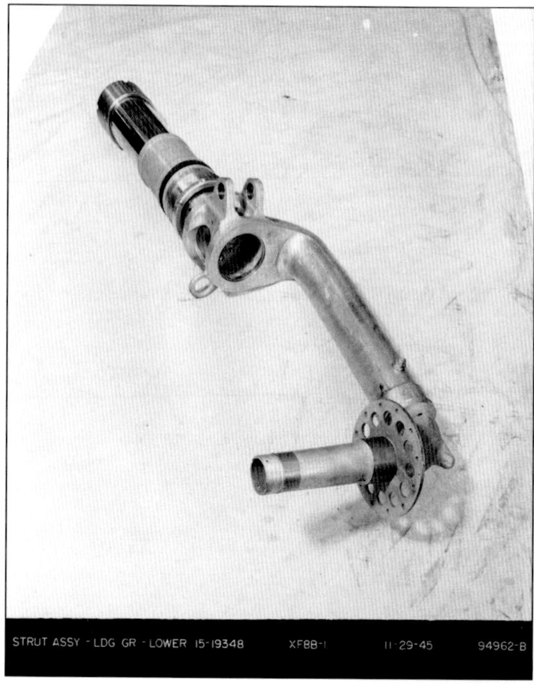

Photo: National Archives, RG 72-AC

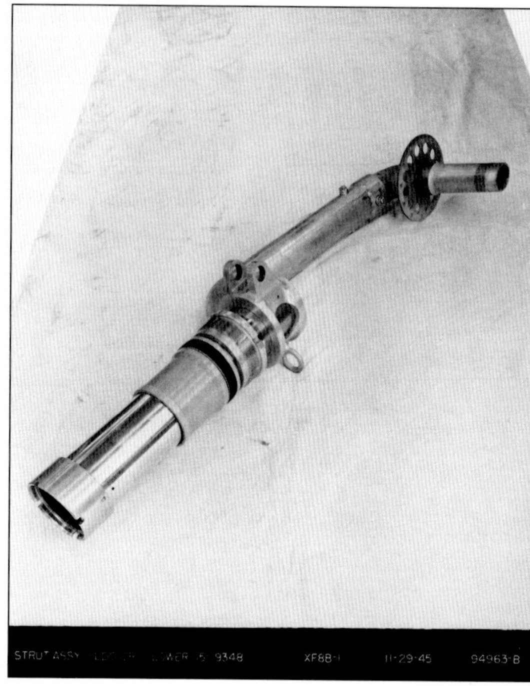

Photo: National Archives, RG 72-AC

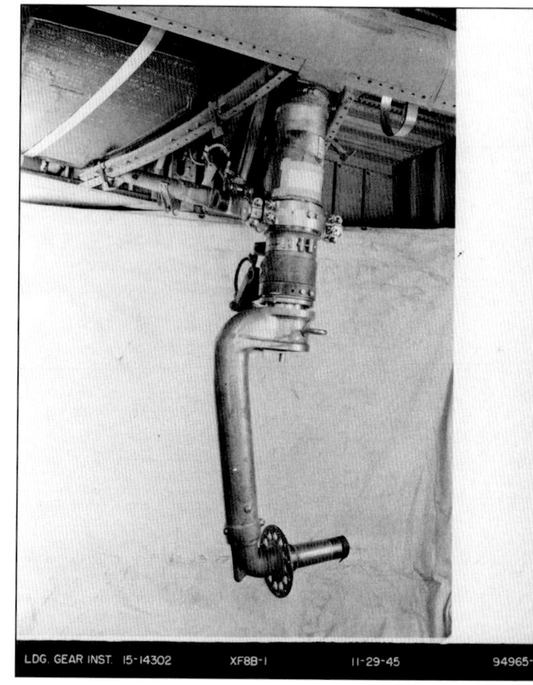

Photo: National Archives, RG 72-AC

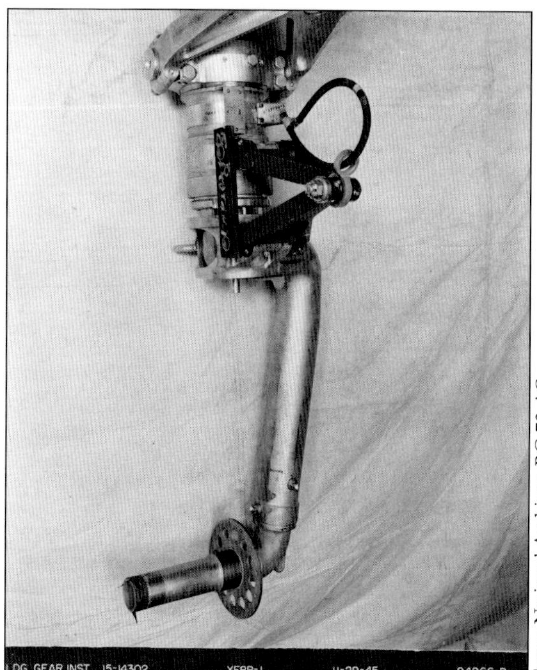

Photo: National Archives, RG 72-AC

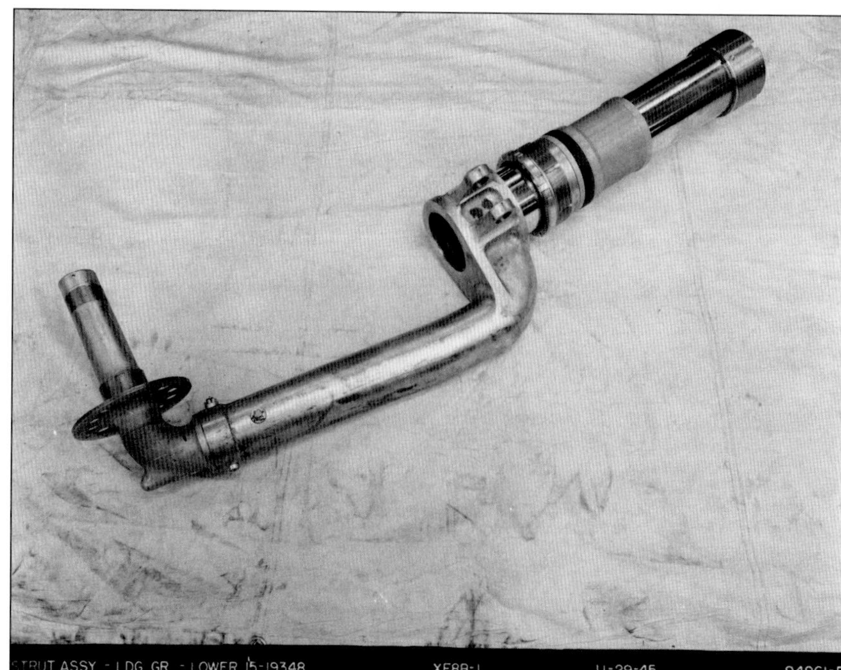

Photo: National Archives, RG 72-AC

Photo: National Archives, RG 72-AC

Photo: National Archives, RG 72-AC

Photo: National Archives, RG 72-AC

Photo: National Archives, RG 72-AC

Photo: National Archives, RG 72-AC

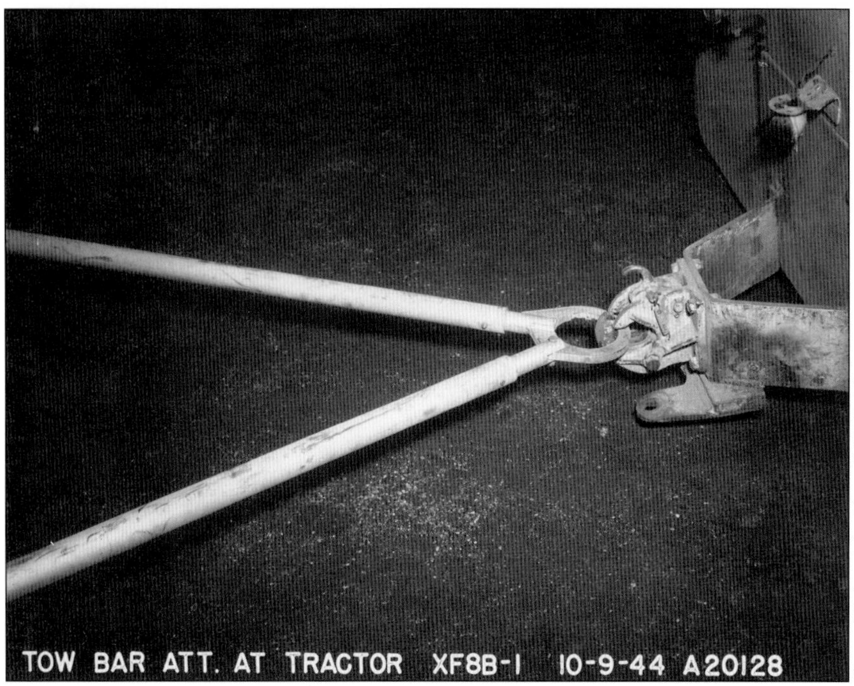

Photo: National Archives, RG 72-AC

Part I: Fuselage and Frame Assembly

Photo: National Archives, RG 72-AC

Photo: National Archives, RG 72-AC

Photo: National Archives, RG 72-AC

Photo: National Archives, RG 72-AC

Photo: National Archives, RG 72-AC

Photo: National Archives, RG 72-AC

Photo: National Archives, RG 72-AC

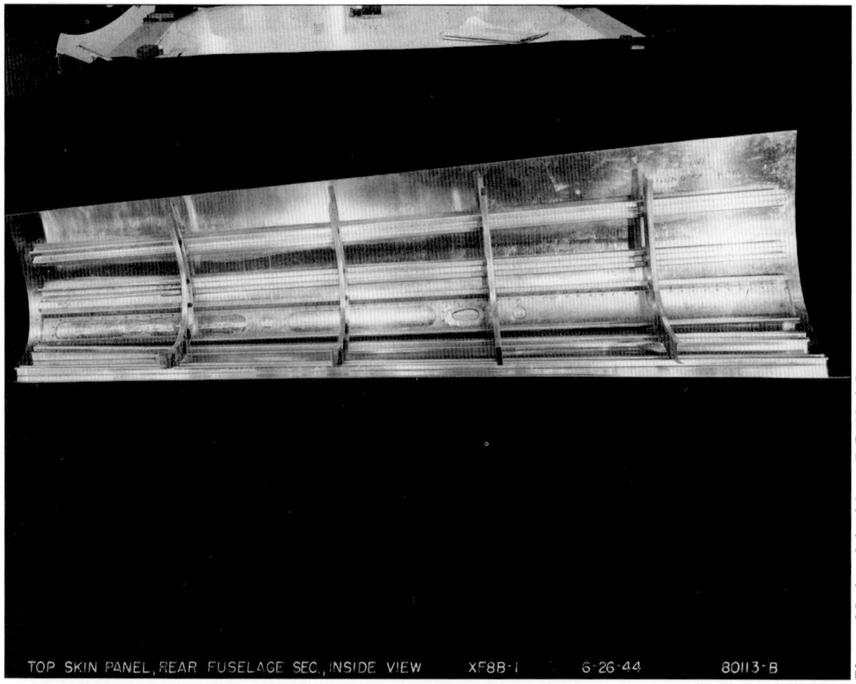

Photo: National Archives, RG 72-AC

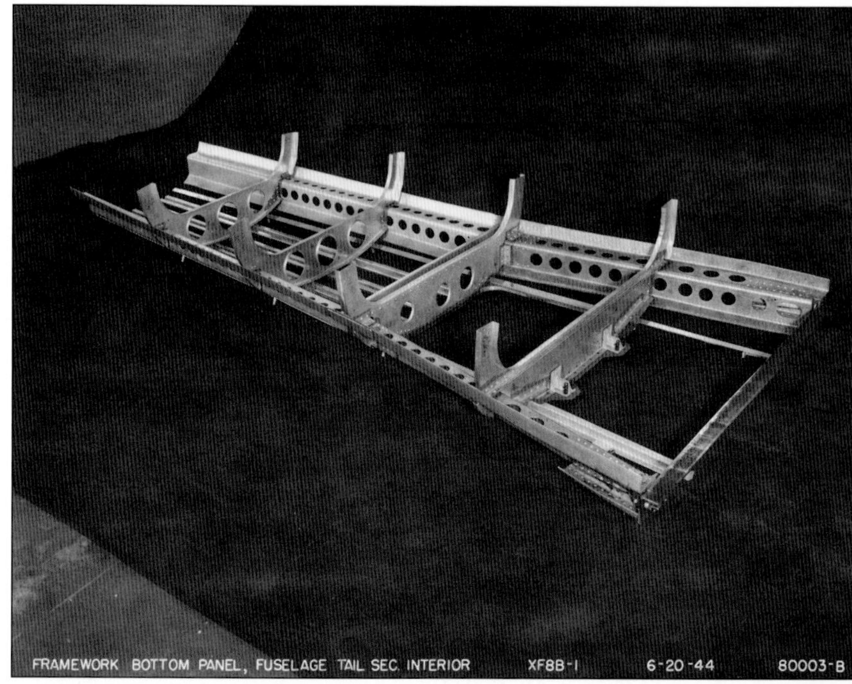

Photo: National Archives, RG 72-AC

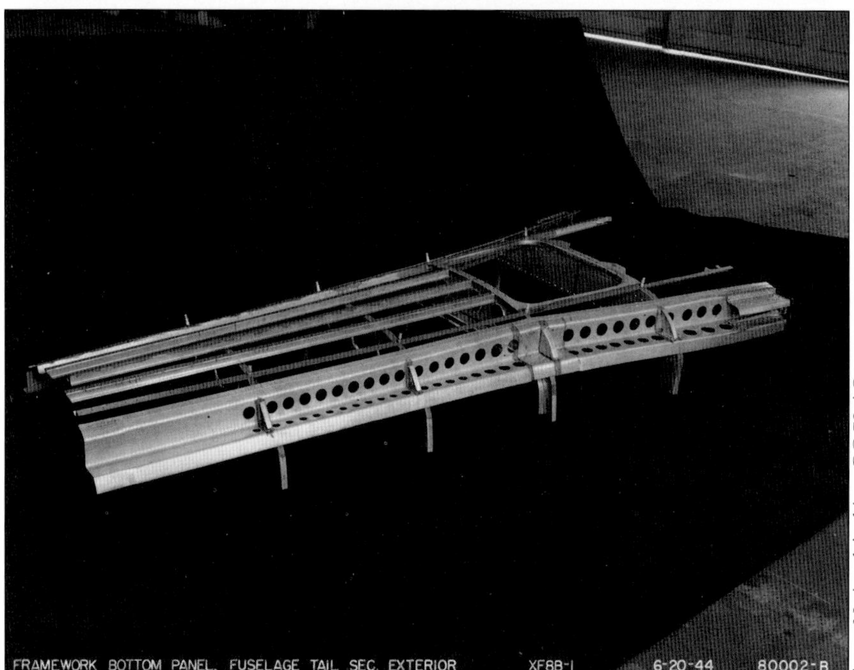

Photo: National Archives, RG 72-AC

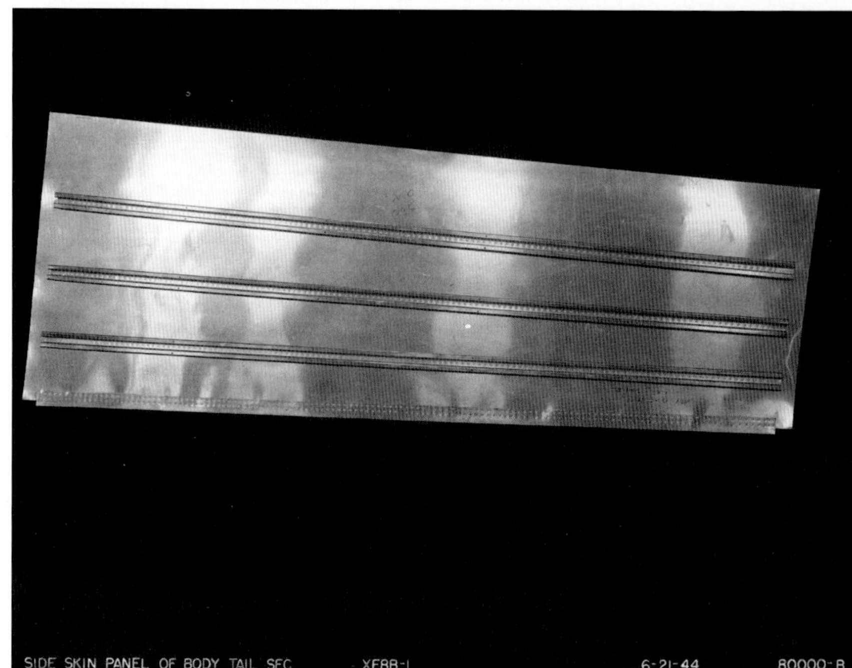

Photo: National Archives, RG 72-AC

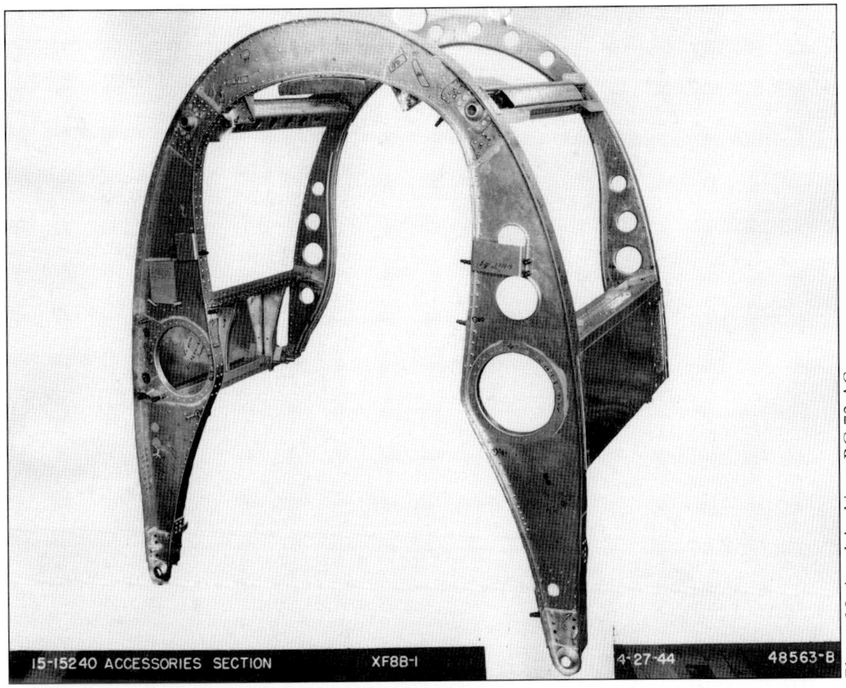

Photo: National Archives, RG 72-AC

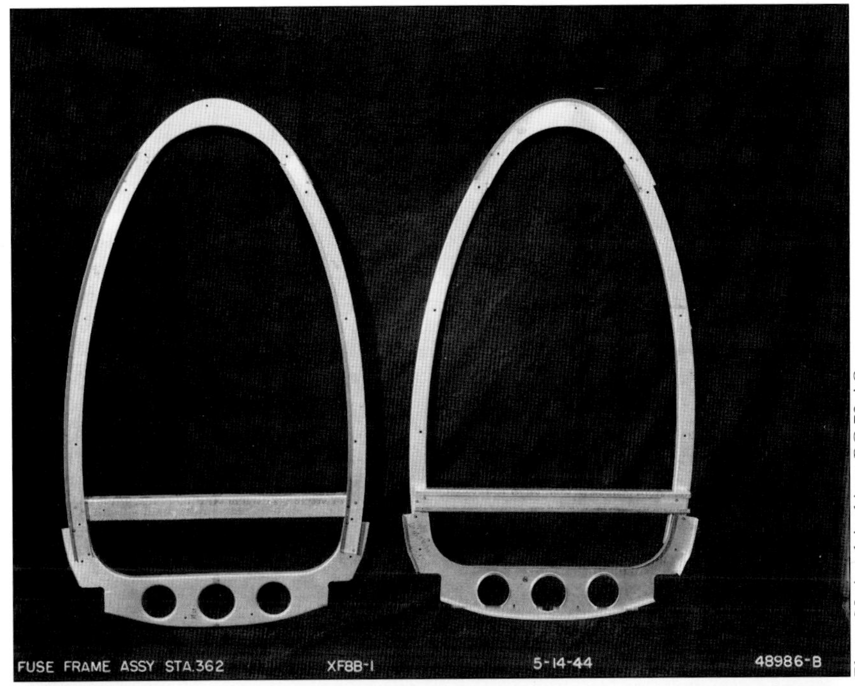

Photo: National Archives, RG 72-AC

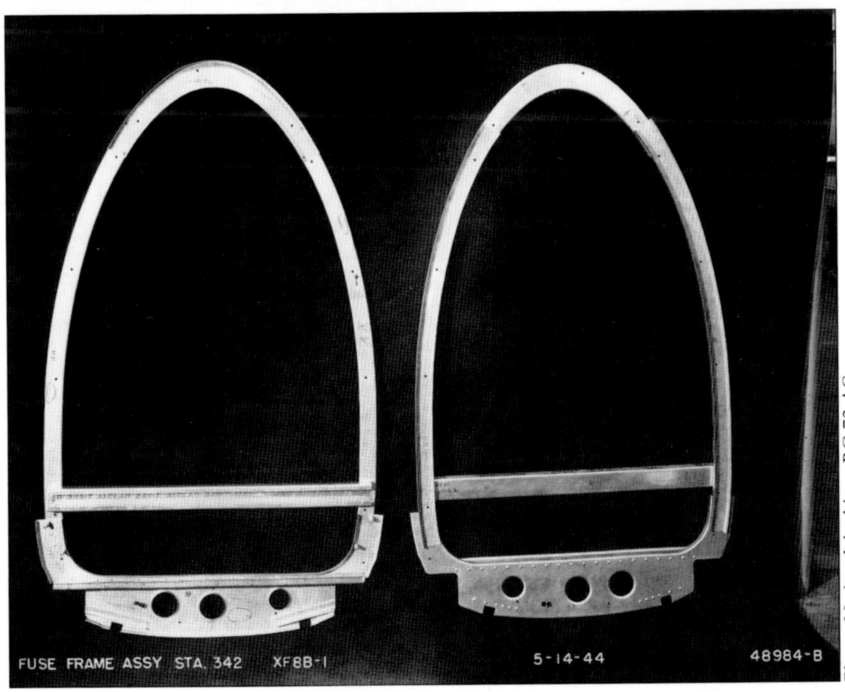

Photo: National Archives, RG 72-AC

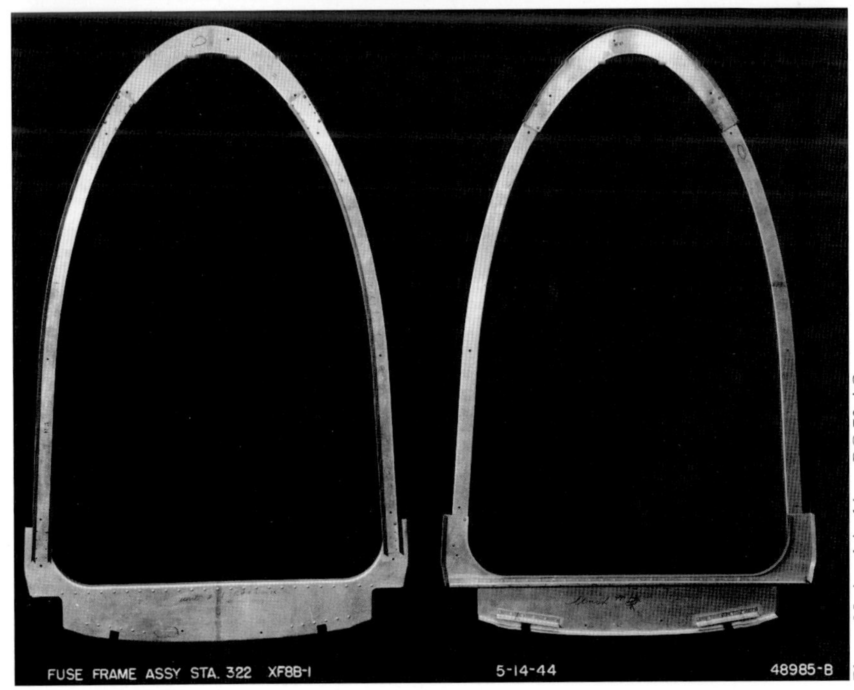

Photo: National Archives, RG 72-AC

Photo: National Archives, RG 72-AC

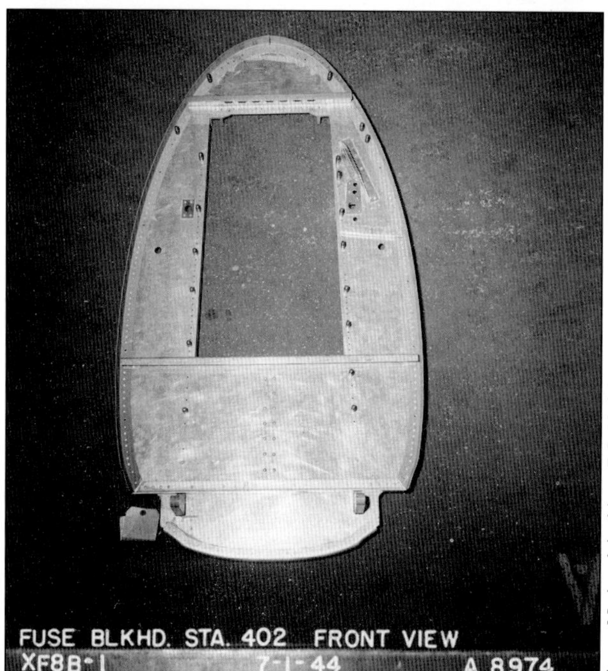

Photo: National Archives, RG 72-AC

Part J: Radio Compartment

Photo: National Archives, RG 72-AC

Photo: National Archives, RG 72-AC

RADIO COMPARTMENT - LOOKING THRU HATCH XF8B 10-4-44 83265-B

Photo: National Archives, RG 72-AC

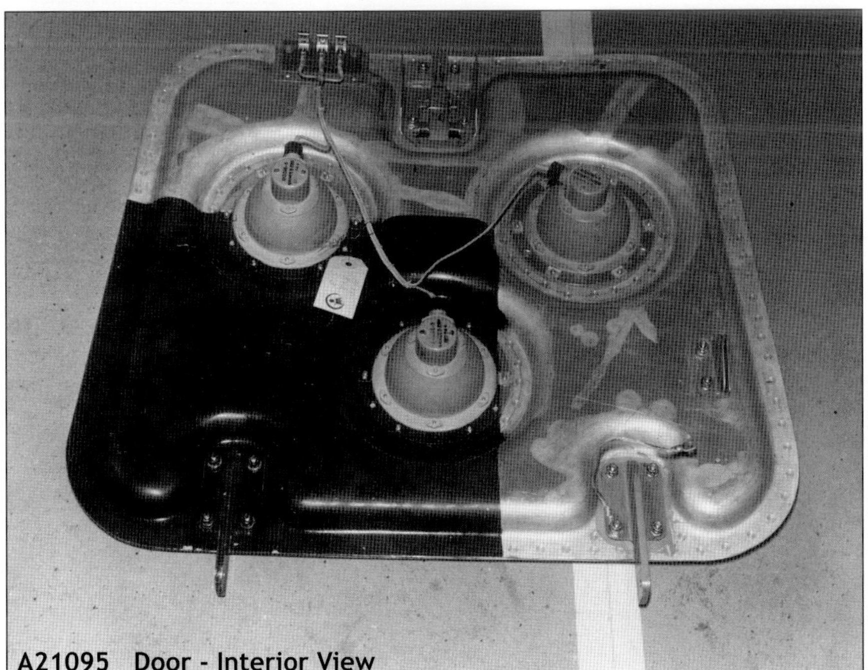
A21095 Door - Interior View

Photo: National Archives, RG 72-AC

Part K: Oil Tank and Cooler

OIL TANK ASS'Y. WITH FILLER NECK DETACHED XF8B-1 7-6-44 80608-B

Photo: National Archives, RG 72-AC

SEC. 72 PLAN VIEW OIL TANK REMOVED XF8B-1 9-14-44 82824-B

Photo: National Archives, RG 72-AC

Photo: National Archives, RG 72-AC

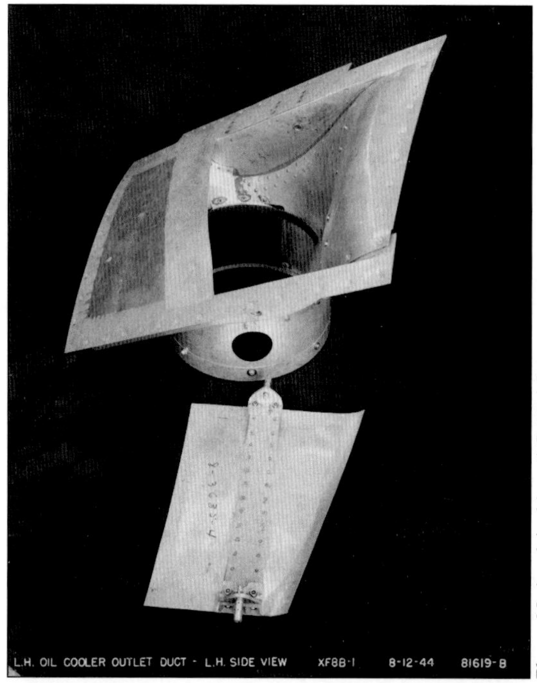

Photo: National Archives, RG 72-AC

Panel Assembly - Oil Cooler Outlet Duct

Photo: National Archives, RG 72-AC

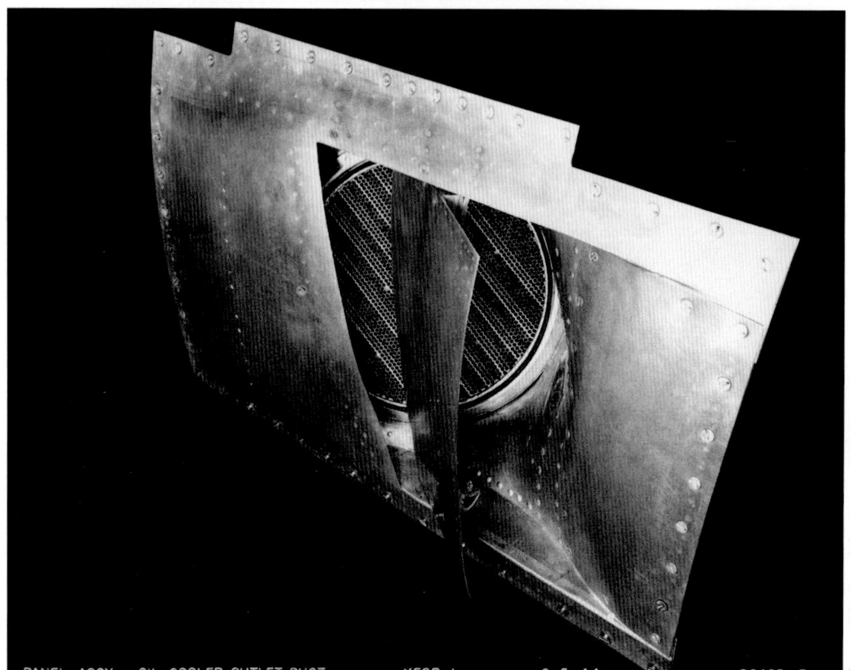

Photo: National Archives, RG 72-AC

Part L: Empennage

Photo: National Archives, RG 72-AC

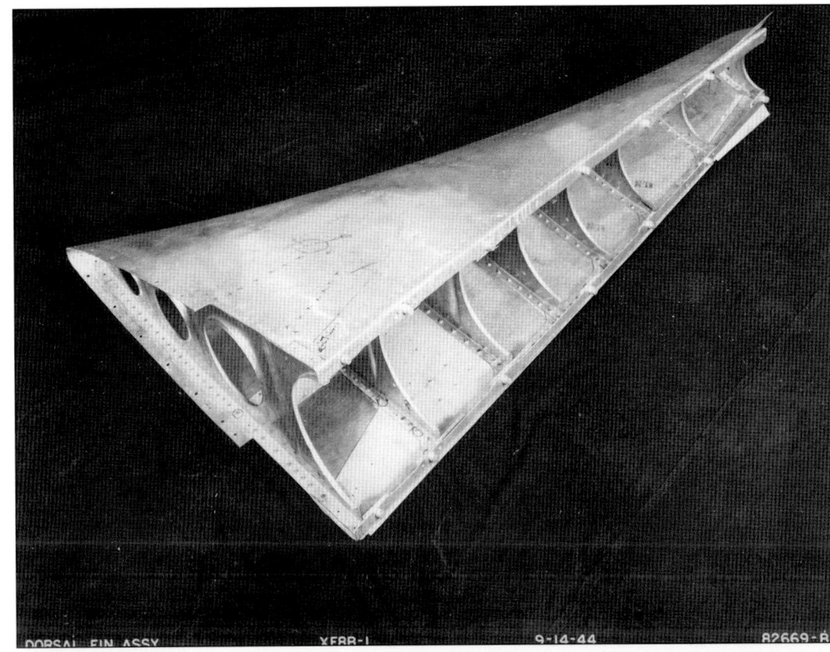

Photo: National Archives, RG 72-AC

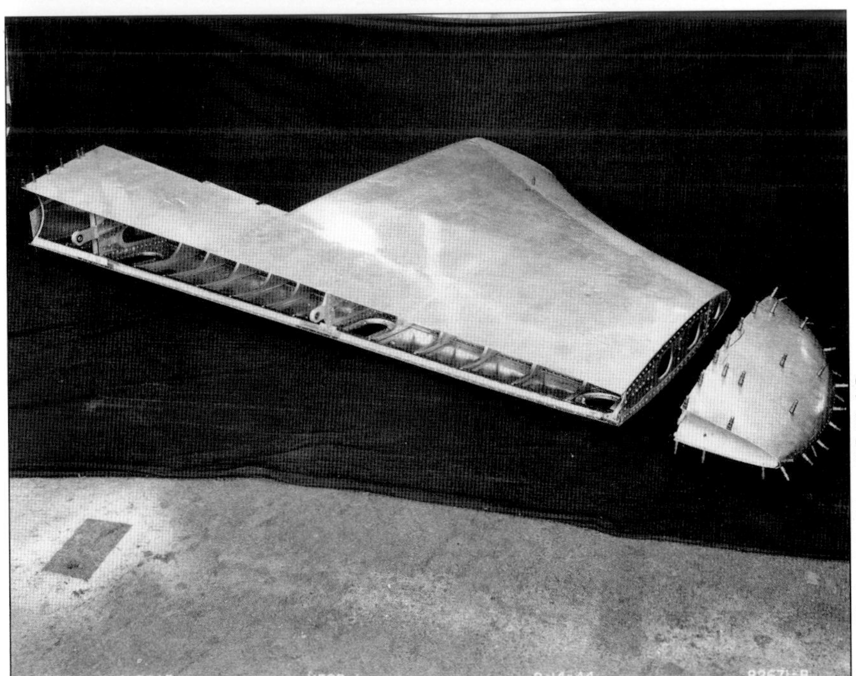

Photo: National Archives, RG 72-AC

Photo: National Archives, RG 72-AC

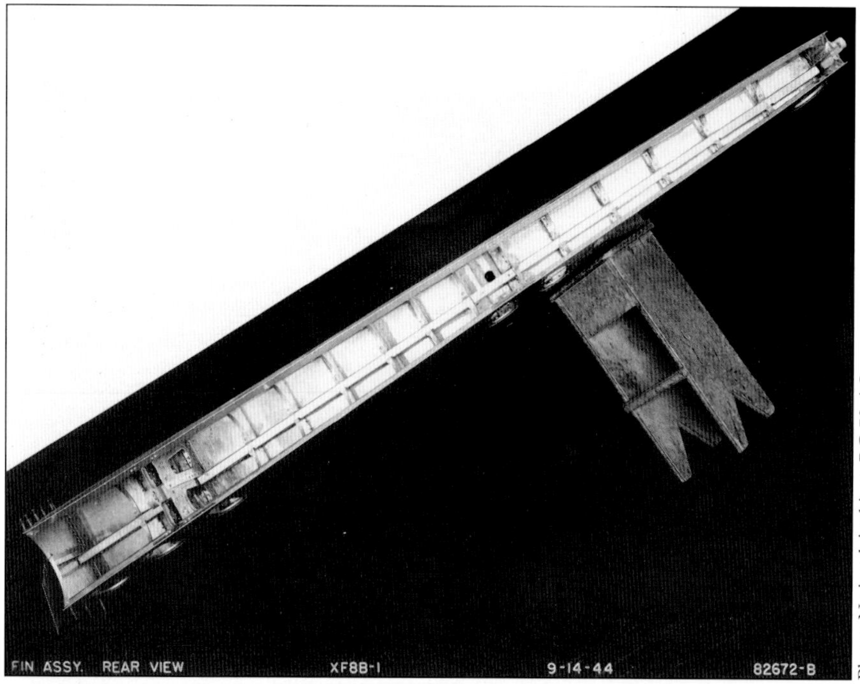

Photo: National Archives, RG 72-AC

Photo: National Archives, RG 72-AC

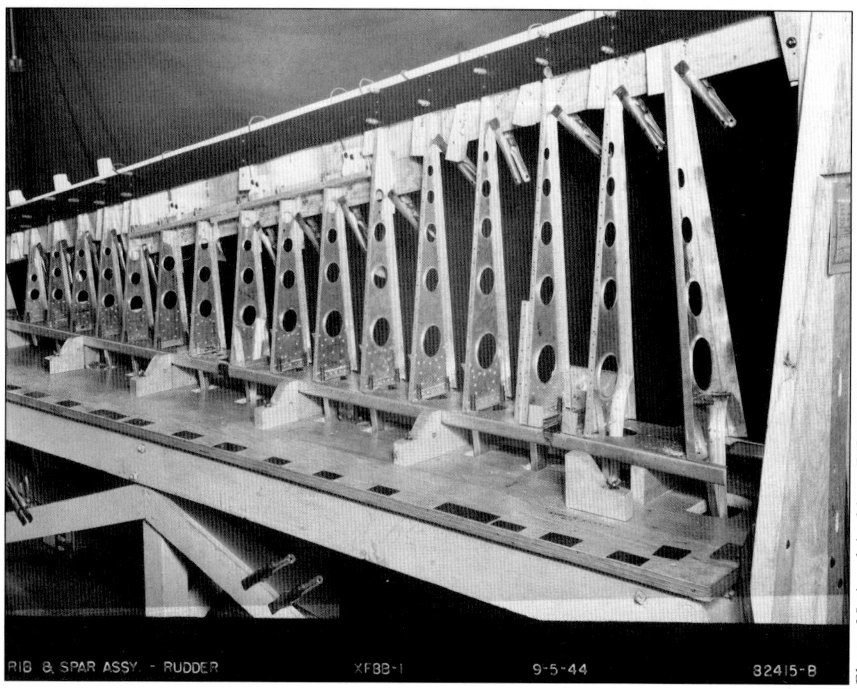

Photo: National Archives, RG 72-AC

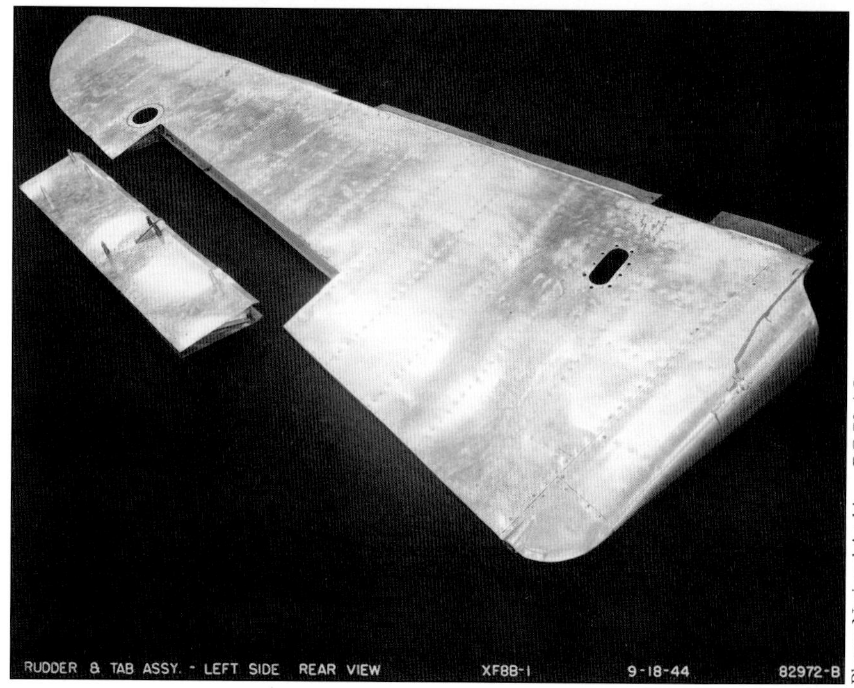

Photo: National Archives, RG 72-AC

Photo: National Archives, RG 72-AC

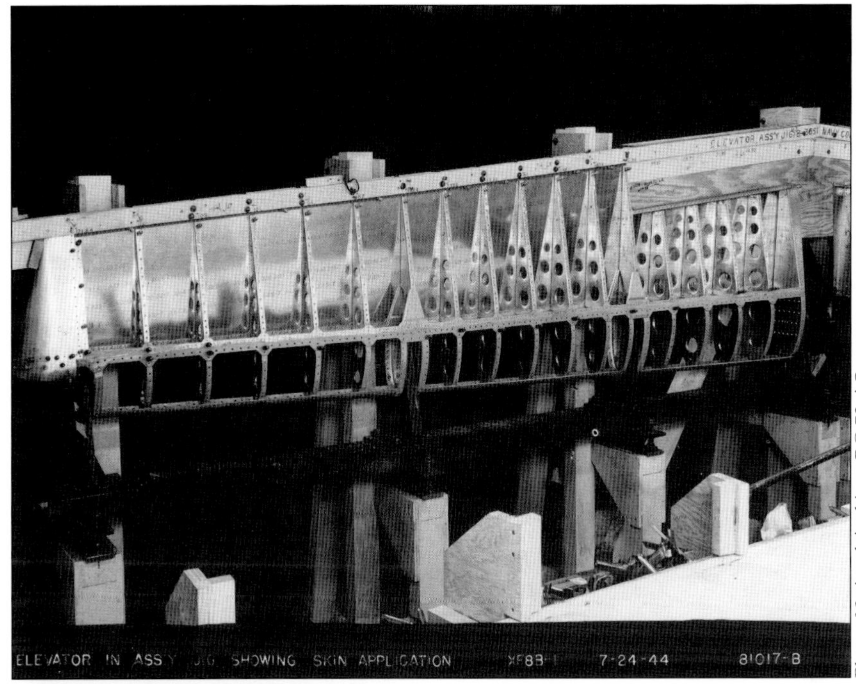

Photo: National Archives, RG 72-AC

Photo: National Archives, RG 72-AC

Photo: National Archives, RG 72-AC

Part M: Arresting Hook

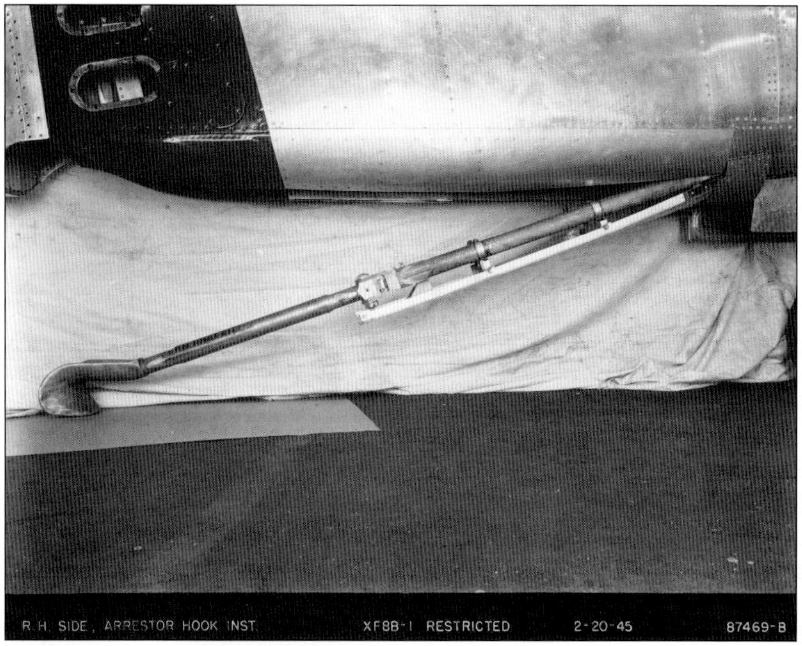

Photo: National Archives, RG 72-AC

Photo: National Archives, RG 72-AC

Photo: National Archives, RG 72-AC

Photo: National Archives, RG 72-AC

Photo: National Archives, RG 72-AC

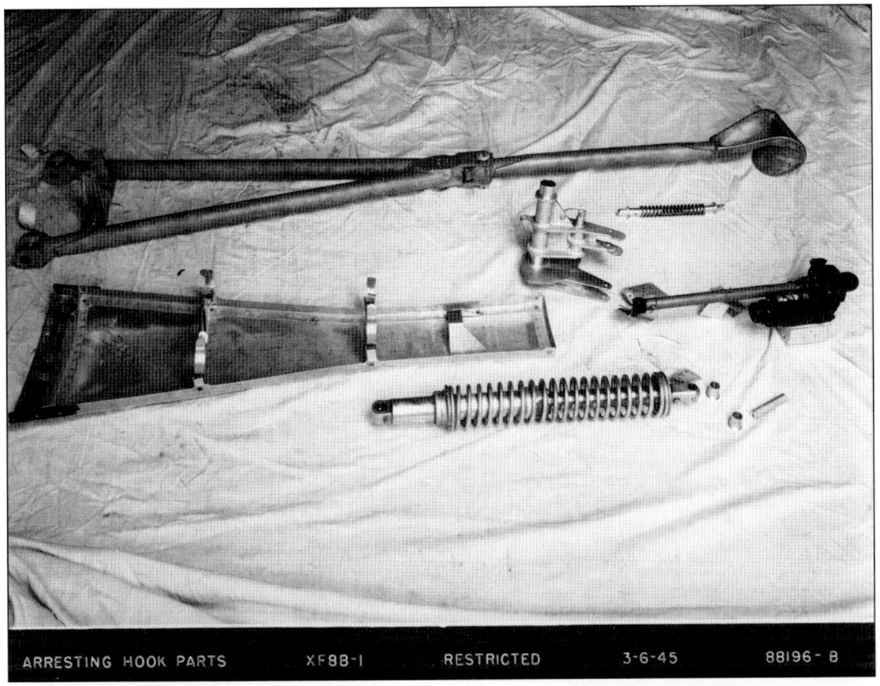

Photo: National Archives, RG 72-AC

Photo: National Archives, RG 72-AC

Appendix 6

General Photos

This appendix collects photos of the completed XF8B-1 prototypes on the ground and in the air. The number of surviving photos is remarkable, considering that only three airplanes were built. I am especially grateful to Bob Lamson for providing a large portion of the photos of the first prototype; the remainder originate from US Navy files held by the National Archives. Readers should ignore the "Restricted" and "Confidential" labels that occasionally appear - these photos were cleared by the Navy for release several decades ago.

Every effort has been made to correctly identify the aircraft and personalities pictured as well as place the shots in sequential order. However, photo numbers and captions were sometimes absent, making this task a challenge. Distant shots of the aircraft in the Glossy Sea Blue scheme were also difficult to categorize, as each prototype was finished in this scheme at some point in their brief careers and differences between them were subtle. Photos of XF8B-1 no. 57985 have proven to be the most elusive and are absent from this appendix; the only two confirmed photos of this prototype in the author's collection are shown in Chapter 4.

Part A: The First Prototype, No. 57984

Photo: National Archives, RG 72

Photo: National Archives, RG 72

The photos on this and the adjacent page record the move of the completed first prototype from the factory to the hangar at Boeing Field in Seattle, Washington on October 9, 1944. Except for the absence of the propeller, the aircraft looks complete and ready to fly, though it wouldn't take to the air until November 27, 1944.

Photo: National Archives, RG 72

Photo: National Archives, RG 72

Photo: National Archives, RG 72

Photo: National Archives, RG 72

Photo: National Archives, RG 72

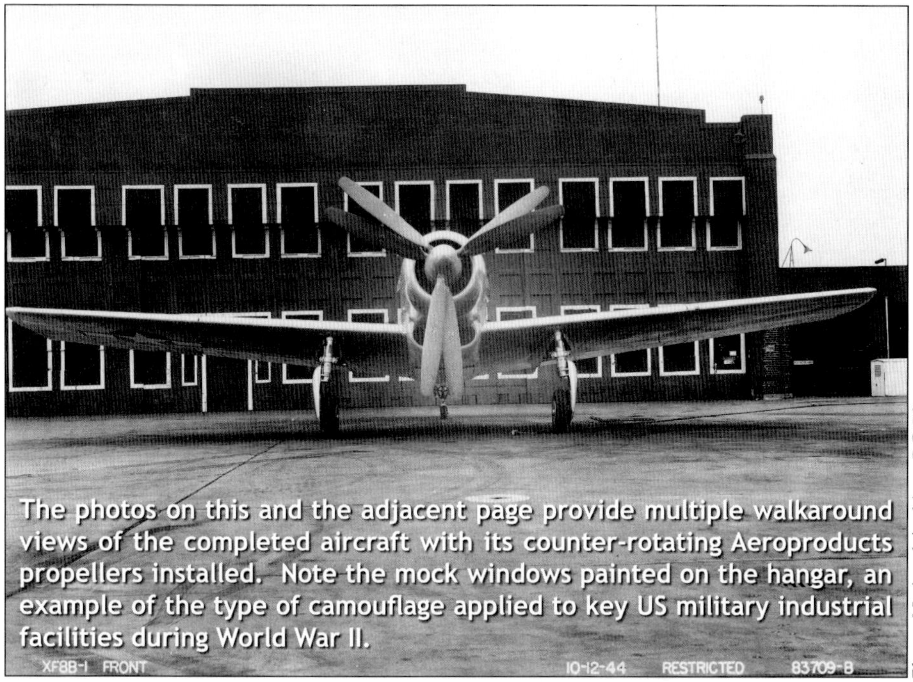

The photos on this and the adjacent page provide multiple walkaround views of the completed aircraft with its counter-rotating Aeroproducts propellers installed. Note the mock windows painted on the hangar, an example of the type of camouflage applied to key US military industrial facilities during World War II.

Photo: National Archives, RG 72

Photo: National Archives, RG 72

Photo: National Archives, RG 72

Photo: National Archives, RG 72

Photo: National Archives, RG 72

Photo: National Archives, RG 72

Photo: National Archives, RG 72

Photo: National Archives, RG 72

Test pilot Bob Lamson sits in the cockpit conversing with Boeing engineers standing alongside on the wings in preparation for high speed taxi tests on November 27, 1944. A flight engineer sat behind Lamson in a piggy-back seat during parts of the tests.

Photo: Bob Lamson Collection

High speed taxi tests were performed on November 27, 1944, as shown in this photo, the one below, and those on the next 2 pages.

Photo: Bob Lamson Collection

Close-up view of the Aeroproducts counter-rotating propeller and chin intake.

Photo: Bob Lamson Collection

Photo: Bob Lamson Collection

Photo: Bob Lamson Collection

Photo: Bob Lamson Collection

Photo: Bob Lamson Collection

Photo: Bob Lamson Collection

Photo: Bob Lamson Collection

Lamson in the cockpit of the XF8B-1 before its first flight on November 27, 1944; the photos here and on the following 3 pages cover this flight in detail. Lamson flew the aircraft for over an hour without major incident and was impressed by its flying qualities.

Photo: Bob Lamson Collection

Photo: Bob Lamson Collection

Photo: Bob Lamson Collection

Photo: Bob Lamson Collection

Photo: Bob Lamson Collection

Photo: Bob Lamson Collection

Photo: Bob Lamson Collection

Photo: Bob Lamson Collection

Photo: Bob Lamson Collection

Photo: Bob Lamson Collection

Photo: Bob Lamson Collection

Photo: Bob Lamson Collection

Photo: Bob Lamson Collection

Photo: Bob Lamson Collection

Lamson smiling after his first test flight in the XF8B-1.

Photo: Bob Lamson Collection

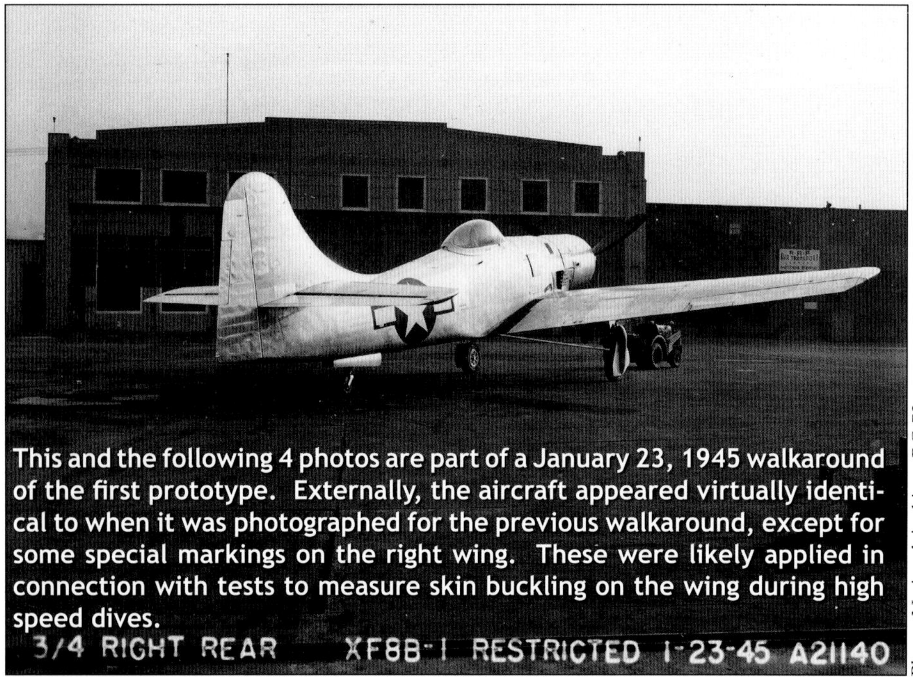

This and the following 4 photos are part of a January 23, 1945 walkaround of the first prototype. Externally, the aircraft appeared virtually identical to when it was photographed for the previous walkaround, except for some special markings on the right wing. These were likely applied in connection with tests to measure skin buckling on the wing during high speed dives.

Photo: National Archives, RG 72

Photo: National Archives, RG 72

Photo: National Archives, RG 72

Photo: National Archives, RG 72

Photo: National Archives, RG 72

Bob Lamson took the XF8B-1 into the air for another successful test flight on Janary 30, 1945, with flight engineer Bud Zerega crammed behind him in the piggy back seat. Eight additional photographs from this flight cover the following 2 pages.

Photo: National Archives, RG 72

Nice frontal view of the first XF8B-1 at Boeing Field circa 1944-45. Note the exhaust staining along the side of the fuselage.

Photo: National Archives, RG 72

Photo: National Archives, RG 72

Photo: National Archives, RG 72

Photo: Bob Lamson Collection

Photo: National Archives, RG 72

Photo: Bob Lamson Collection

Photo: Bob Lamson Collection

Photo: Bob Lamson Collection

Left and Below Left: Lamson posing on the wing of no. 57984 in a specially developed anti-blackout g-suit. An inflatable bladder on the abdomen reduced the amount of blood rushing to the lower extremities during high "g" maneuvers. With this suit, Lamson was able to put the XF8B-1 into dives and tests exceeding 7 g's. Additional photos of Lamson in the suit are on the following page.

Photo: Bob Lamson Collection

Photo: Bob Lamson Collection

Photo: Bob Lamson Collection

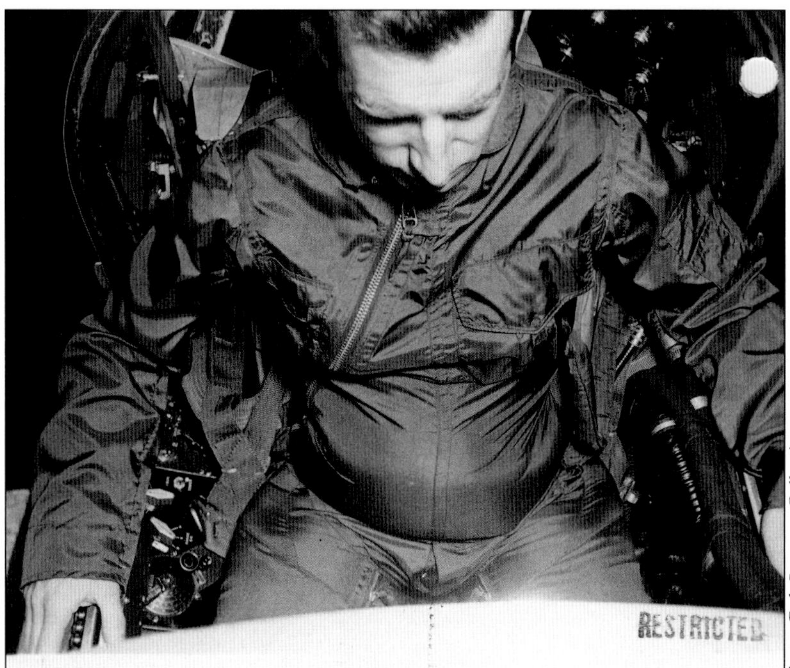

Photo: Bob Lamson Collection

Lamson posing in the cockpit of the XF8B-1 for Boeing photographers wearing his oxygen mask and full flight suit.

Photo: Bob Lamson Collection

Photo: Bob Lamson Collection

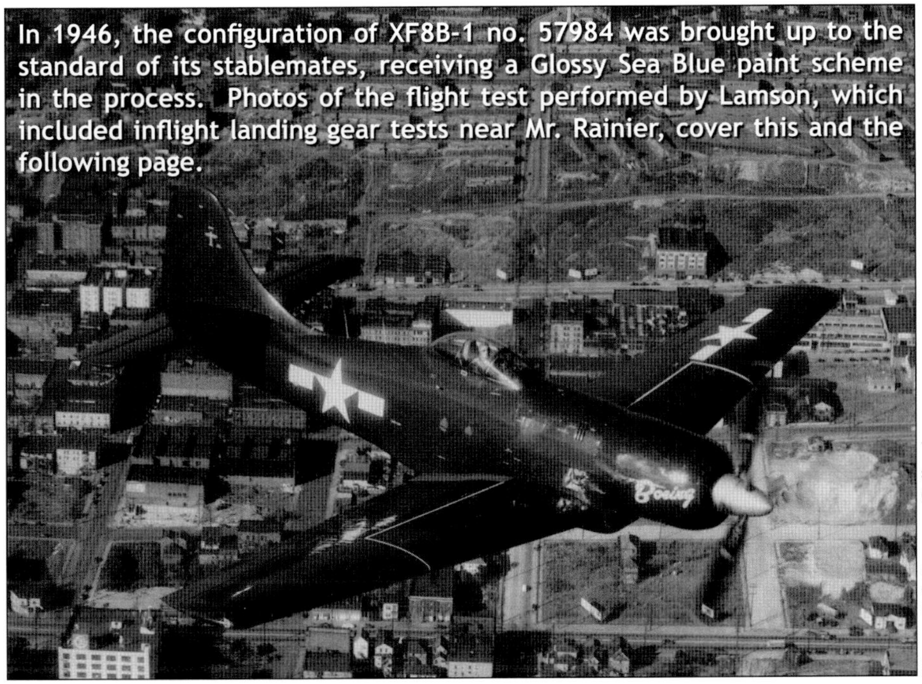

In 1946, the configuration of XF8B-1 no. 57984 was brought up to the standard of its stablemates, receiving a Glossy Sea Blue paint scheme in the process. Photos of the flight test performed by Lamson, which included inflight landing gear tests near Mr. Rainier, cover this and the following page.

Photo: 3ob Lamson Collection

Photo: Bob Lamson Collection

Photo: Bob Lamson Collection

Photo: Bob Lamson Collection

Photo: Bob Lamson Collection

Bob Lamson signs over XF8B-1 no. 57984 to Lt. Frank J. Shaw of the US Navy on October 15, 1946.

Photo: Bob Lamson Collection

Photo: Bob Lamson Collection

Dick Stith and Bob Lamson pose in front of the first prototype after signing over the aircraft to Lt. Shaw.

Photo: Bob Lamson Collection

Part B: The Third Prototype, No. 57986

A series of walkaround photos of the recently completed third XF8B-1 was taken on June 26, 1946. The walkaround covers this and the following 2 pages. The fighter was painted an overall Glossy Sea Blue with white Boeing logos on the cowling; the spinner was left unpainted.

Photo: National Archives, RG 72-AC

Photo: National Archives, RG 72-AC

Photo: National Archives, RG 72-AC

Photo: National Archives, RG 72-AC

Photo: National Archives, RG 72-AC

Photo: National Archives, RG 72-AC

Photo: National Archives, RG 72-AC

Photo: National Archives, RG 72-AC

Photo: National Archives, RG 72-AC

Photo: National Archives, RG 72-AC

Photo: National Archives, RG 72-AC

No. 57986 subsequently received a pitot tube on the left wingtip and had the Boeing logos removed from the cowling. The final page of this appendix features additional photos of the aircraft in this configuration.

Photo: National Archives, RG 72-AC

Photo: National Archives, RG 72-AC

Photo: National Archives, RG 72-AC

Photo: National Archives, RG 72-AC

The third prototype subsequently had its spinner painted Glossy Sea Blue prior to being delivered to the Navy in 1946.

Photo: National Archives, RG 72-AC

Appendix 7

Miscellanea

This appendix presents a miscellanea of reports, photos and drawings connected to the XF8B-1 contract. While several of the items covered are rather technical and of only passing interest to the casual reader, they offer important insights into the challenging and sometimes tedious work that went into creating a complex military aircraft during World War II.

Boeing Fighter XF8B-1 Brochure - 1944(?)

The author discovered this undated brochure in a slim Air Force file on the XF8B-1 in the National Archives. It was sent to Army Air Force Major General K.B. Wolfe by Boeing on January 2, 1945 in an attempt to interest the AAF in the aircraft; it was almost certainly originally prepared for the Navy. The brochure is illustrated entirely with sketches and charcoal drawings. The most notable illustration is a two page spread showing an attack on a Japanese airfield, complete with badly drawn caricatures of Japanese soldiers which the modern reader may find offensive but were common during World War II.

Excerpts from this brochure begin here and continue on the following 4 pages.

Image National Archives, RG 341

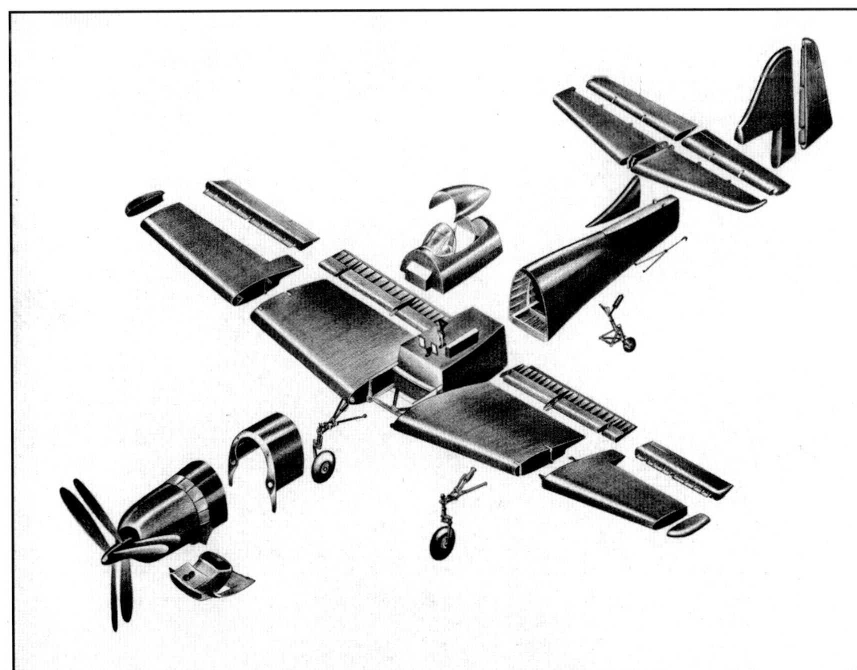

Image: National Archives, RG 341

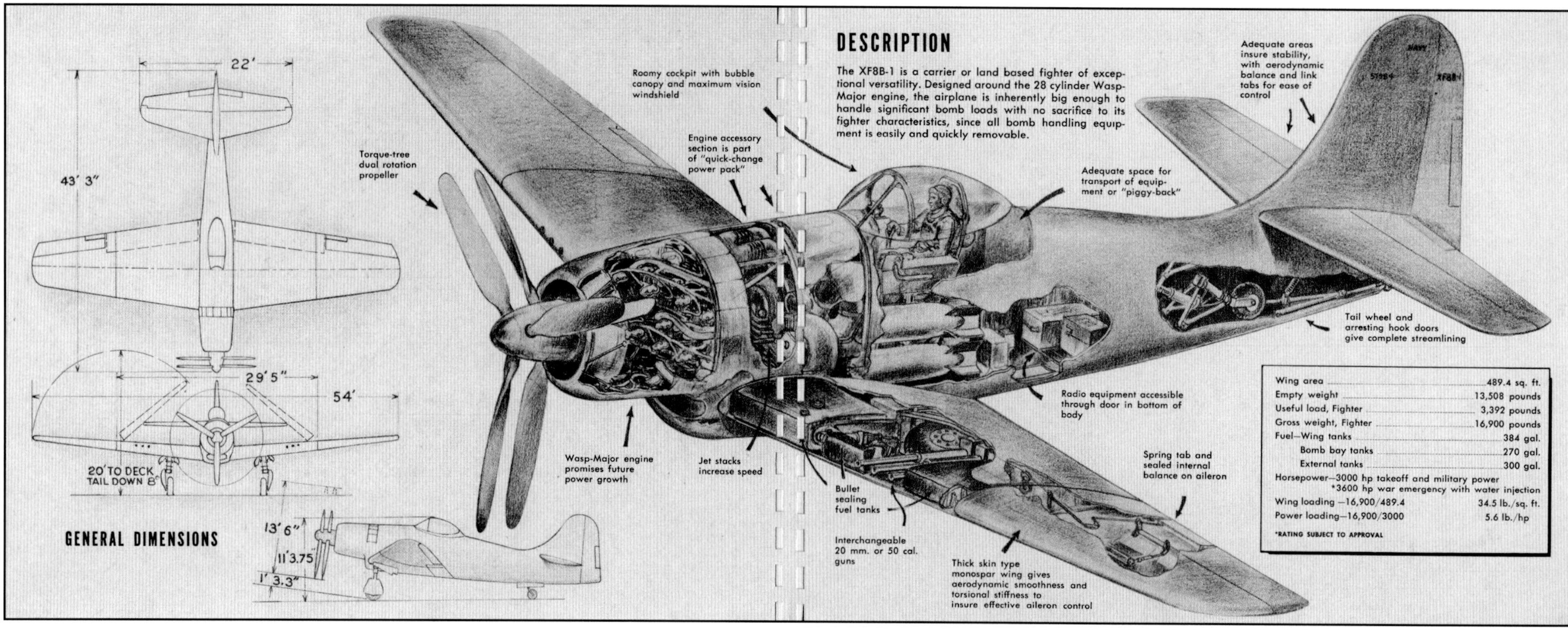

Image: National Archives, RG 341

V F

Conceived as a long range fighter, the achievement of fighter qualities has always been uppermost in the minds of Boeing designers.

The destructive firepower of six 20 mm. cannon or six .50 cal. machine guns to suit the anticipated target is available in a compact interchangeable gun mount design. Guns, feed chutes, ammunition boxes, boosters—all are easily accessible and quickly replaceable when changing gun types. 400 rounds per gun of .50 cal. or 200 rounds of 20 mm. ammunition are available. The MK 23 gun sight is installed with provision for the optional use of the old reliable MK 8. Lead angle over the engine cowl is 9° (250 mills) at 240 knots indicated airspeed, increasing at higher speeds.

Armor protection consists of 1½" head armor and ⅜" armor, ¼' dural at low angles of obliquity and ⅜" body armor protecting a 30° cone from the rear. 1½" armor glass combine to protect a 15° ;cone from the front, conforming to the latest changes in armor protecting thinking. The ease with which the pilot's seat may be removed plus the bomb bay access to the pilot's floor from below make possible many arrangements of under-seat armor plate for airplanes assigned to missions requiring this special protection.

Image: National Archives, RG 341

Image: National Archives, RG 341

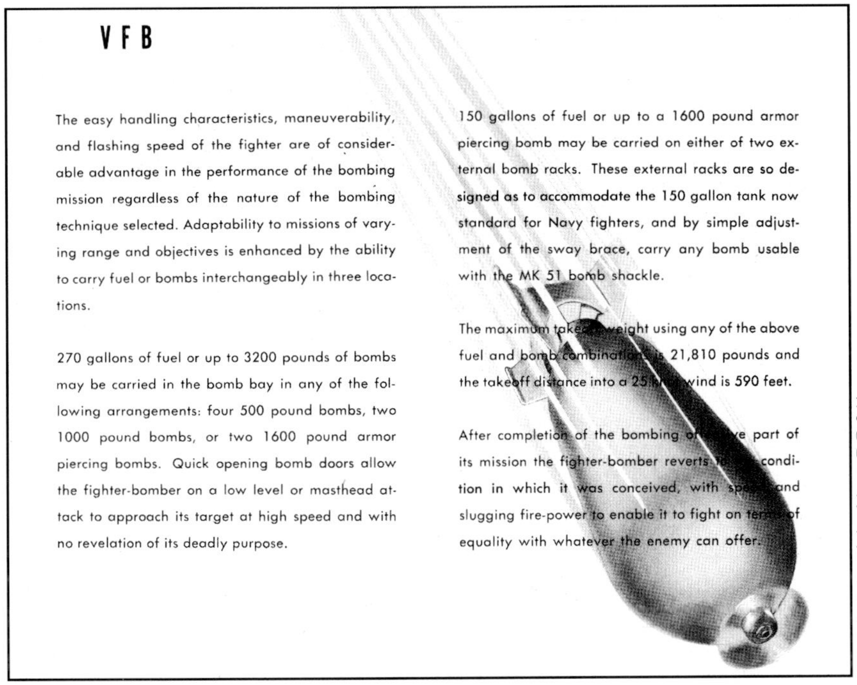

VFB

The easy handling characteristics, maneuverability, and flashing speed of the fighter are of considerable advantage in the performance of the bombing mission regardless of the nature of the bombing technique selected. Adaptability to missions of varying range and objectives is enhanced by the ability to carry fuel or bombs interchangeably in three locations.

270 gallons of fuel or up to 3200 pounds of bombs may be carried in the bomb bay in any of the following arrangements: four 500 pound bombs, two 1000 pound bombs, or two 1600 pound armor piercing bombs. Quick opening bomb doors allow the fighter-bomber on a low level or masthead attack to approach its target at high speed and with no revelation of its deadly purpose.

150 gallons of fuel or up to a 1600 pound armor piercing bomb may be carried on either of two external bomb racks. These external racks are so designed as to accommodate the 150 gallon tank now standard for Navy fighters, and by simple adjustment of the sway brace, carry any bomb usable with the MK 51 bomb shackle.

The maximum takeoff weight using any of the above fuel and bomb combinations is 21,810 pounds and the takeoff distance into a 25 knot wind is 590 feet.

After completion of the bombing objective part of its mission the fighter-bomber reverts to the condition in which it was conceived, with speed and slugging fire-power to enable it to fight on terms of equality with whatever the enemy can offer.

Image: National Archives, RG 341

VFT

The personality of the fighter is no less desirable on torpedo carrying missions than it is for bombing. The combination of an extremely fast torpedo airplane and the current improvements to the MK 13 aerial torpedo permits the use of launching ranges above 2,000 yards without requiring long water runs during which the target ship might avoid the torpedo's path.

Having accomplished its torpedo mission, the XF8B-1 becomes again a first class fighter requiring no special protective escort, but ready to team up with her sisters against any opposition.

Image: National Archives, RG 341

Image: National Archives, RG 341

Image: National Archives, RG 341

ATTACK

The XF8B-1 is an extremely effective destructive weapon against aircraft, surface vessels and ground installations. In addition to employing six 20 mm. cannons or .50 caliber machine guns it can carry several combinations of bomb loads and may be armed with eight rockets. Superior striking power, high speed and long range make the XF8B-1 an exceptional weapon for any type of attack mission.

Image: National Archives, RG 341

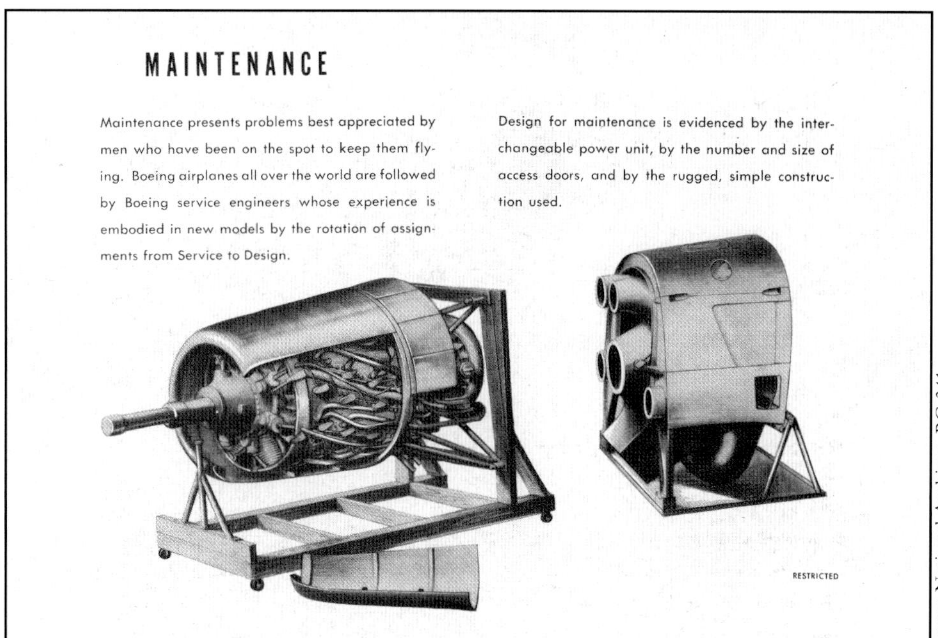

MAINTENANCE

Maintenance presents problems best appreciated by men who have been on the spot to keep them flying. Boeing airplanes all over the world are followed by Boeing service engineers whose experience is embodied in new models by the rotation of assignments from Service to Design.

Design for maintenance is evidenced by the interchangeable power unit, by the number and size of access doors, and by the rugged, simple construction used.

RESTRICTED

Image: National Archives, RG 341

Image: National Archives, RG 341

Image: National Archives, RG 341

Image: National Archives, RG 341

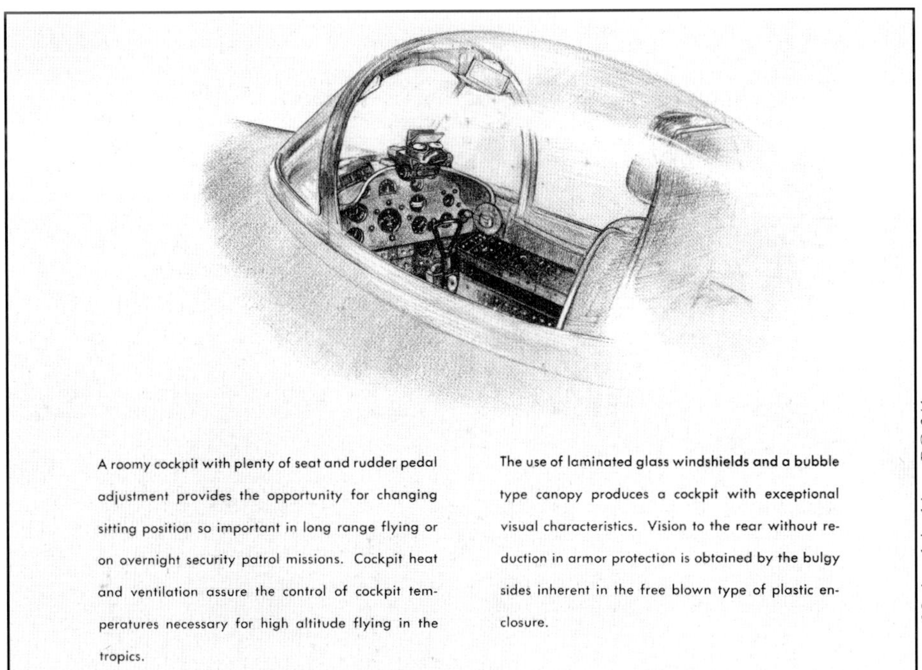

Image: National Archives, RG 341

Photos of the February 13, 1945 Crash Landing of the XF8B-1

Photo: National Archives, RG 72

Photo: National Archives, RG 72

On February 13, 1945, Bob Lamson and Bud Zerega were conducting high speed taxi runs with XF8B-1 no. 57984 when the landing gear retracted without warning, causing the aircraft to collide with the runway and slide approximately 1,000 ft. An investigation of the accident traced the involuntary gear retraction to a faulty microswitch; more details of the mishap can be found in Chapter 3. The photos on this page show the damage suffered by the propellers, which were a total loss. Cranes were required to raise the XF8B-1, lower the gear, and tow the aircraft off the tarmac. Additional photos of this unfortunate event cover the next 5 pages.

Photo: National Archives, RG 72

Photo: National Archives, RG 72

Photo: National Archives, RG 72

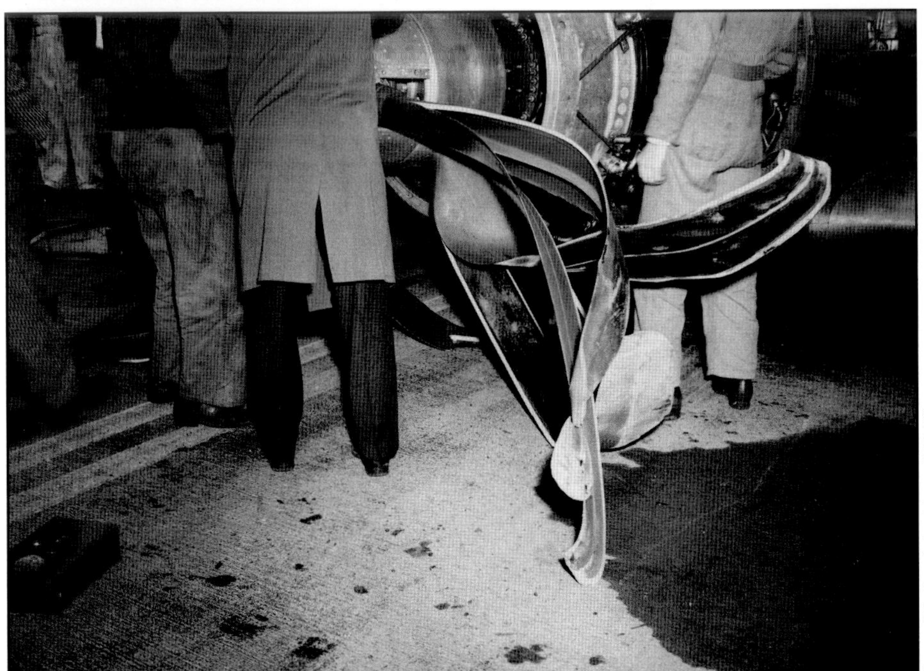

Photo: National Archives, RG 72

Photo: National Archives, RG 72

Photo: National Archives, RG 72

Photo: National Archives, RG 72

Photo: National Archives, RG 72

Photo: National Archives, RG 72

Photo: National Archives, RG 72

Left and Below Left: Close-up photos of the cockpit instrument panel after the accident.

Fuselage bottom and rudder looking aft.

Photo: National Archives, RG 72

Photo: National Archives, RG 72

Section forward of tail wheelwell and doors.

Photo: National Archives, RG 72

Righthand tire, showing wear on tread.

Photo: National Archives, RG 72

Tail wheel doors, lefthand side.

Photo: National Archives, RG 72

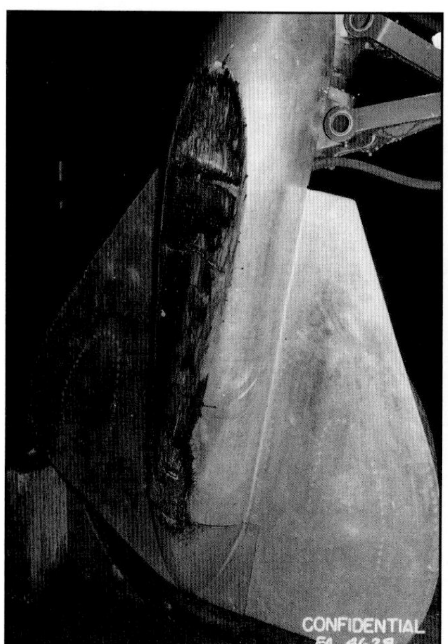

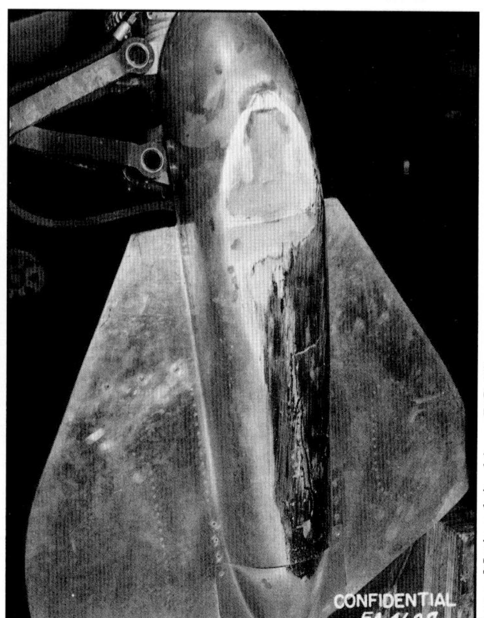

The damaged left- and righthand wheel fairings.

Photo: National Archives, RG 72

Tail wheel doors, righthand side.

Photo: National Archives, RG 72

Another cockpit shot

Photo: National Archives, RG 72

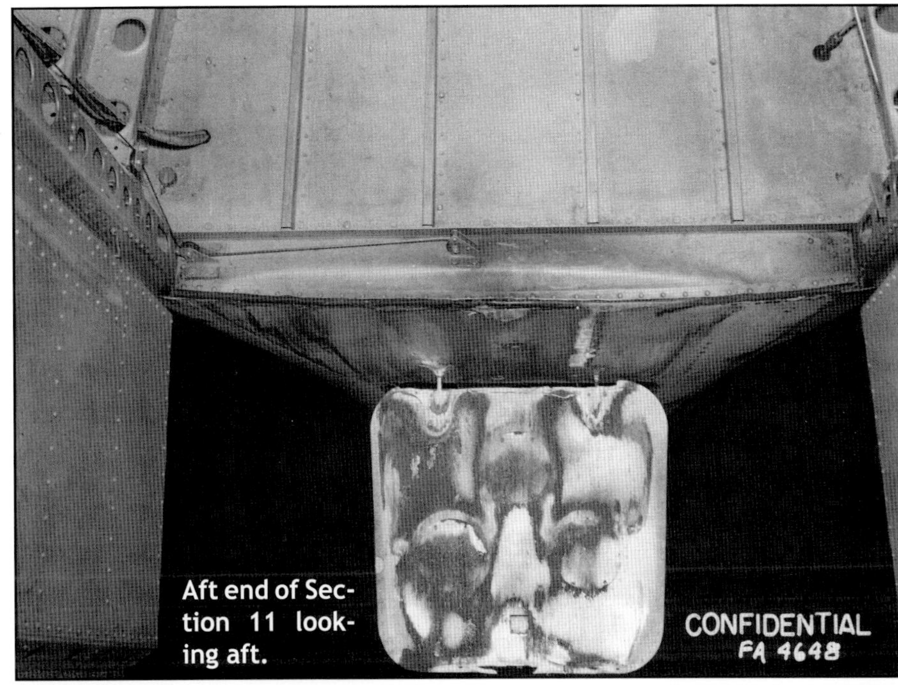

Aft end of Section 11 looking aft.

Photo: National Archives, RG 72

Tail wheel door showing abrasion.

Photo: National Archives, RG 72

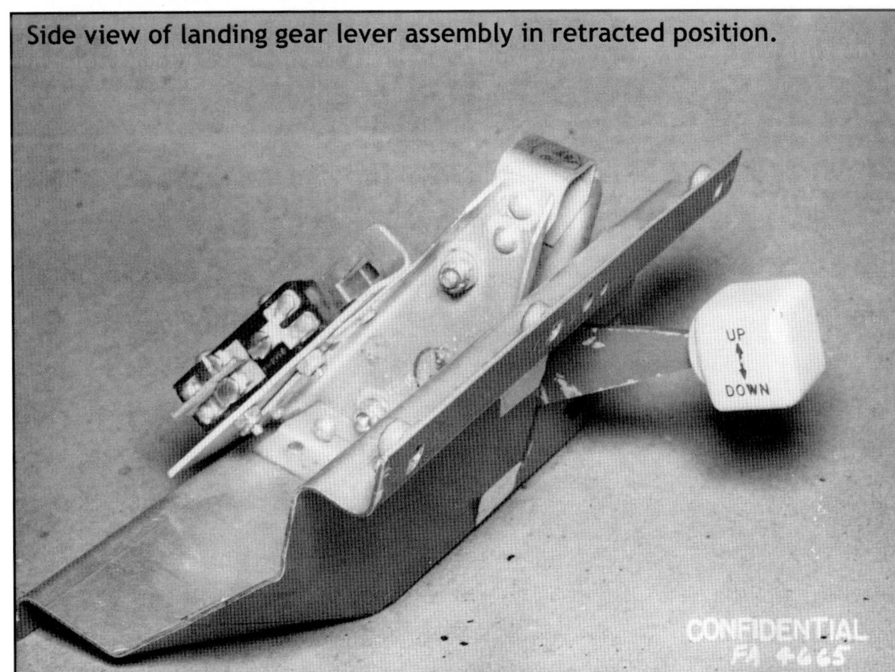

Side view of landing gear lever assembly in retracted position.

Photo: National Archives, RG 72

XF8B-1 Gun Installation and Ammunition System Test - March 9, 1945

The original gun requirements for the XF8B-1 called for six .50 cal. guns with an alternative of four .50 cal. guns and two 20 mm. M-2 cannons. In addition, an alternative of six 20 mm. M-2 cannons was designed. After installation, parts were made and a new design of 20 mm. cannon (M-3) was released that made the M-2 cannon obsolete. BuAer then requested that the first two XF8B-1 prototypes be completed according to the original requirements and that the third be designed to accommodate the new 20 mm. M-3 cannon. This request necessitated the design of an entirely new gun installation which was also made to be interchangeable with the .50 cal. gun installation and accommodate combinations thereof.

All gun installations were satisfactory. The M-3 version installations used on the third XF8B-1 presented considerable improvement over the original M-2 version installations used on the 1st and 2nd prototypes.

Upper and lower doors provided ample and convenient accessibility to the rear part of the guns for installing, loading, and bore sight adjusting. The lower forward door provided adequate access to the forward part of the guns for installing. The average capacity of the .50 cal. installation was 482 rounds per gun. This represented an increase of 80 rounds, 20% over the specified requirements. The average capacity of the 20 mm. installation was 212 per gun or 6% over the specified requirements. The anti-surge mechanisms prevented the surging and siphoning of the ammunition from one box to another, which caused the gun stoppages common to fighter aircraft of that period. Ammunition, assisted by boosters, fed satisfactorily through all chutes. Cases and links ejected freely.

No damage was caused by the muzzle blast of the guns. A maximum temperature of 1082° F was recorded on the surface of the blast tubes of the .50 cal. installation. However, the gun bay was well vented to carry off gases and maintain moderate temperatures during flight when guns were firing.

The inherent dispersion characteristics for all installations were exceptional and were attributed to the unusual sturdiness and unique design of the gun mounts.

Photos from the tests cover this and the following 4 1/2 pages.

AMM. SYSTEM TEST CAL. .50 - FRONT VIEW XF8B-1 7-7-44 RESTRICTED 80736-B

Photo: National Archives, RG 72

AMM. SYSTEM TEST CAL. .50 - 3/4 FRONT VIEW XF8B-1 7-7-44 RESTRICTED 80737-B

Photo: National Archives, RG 72

Photo: National Archives, RG 72

Photo: National Archives, RG 72

Photo: National Archives, RG 72

Photo: National Archives, RG 72

Photo: National Archives, RG 72

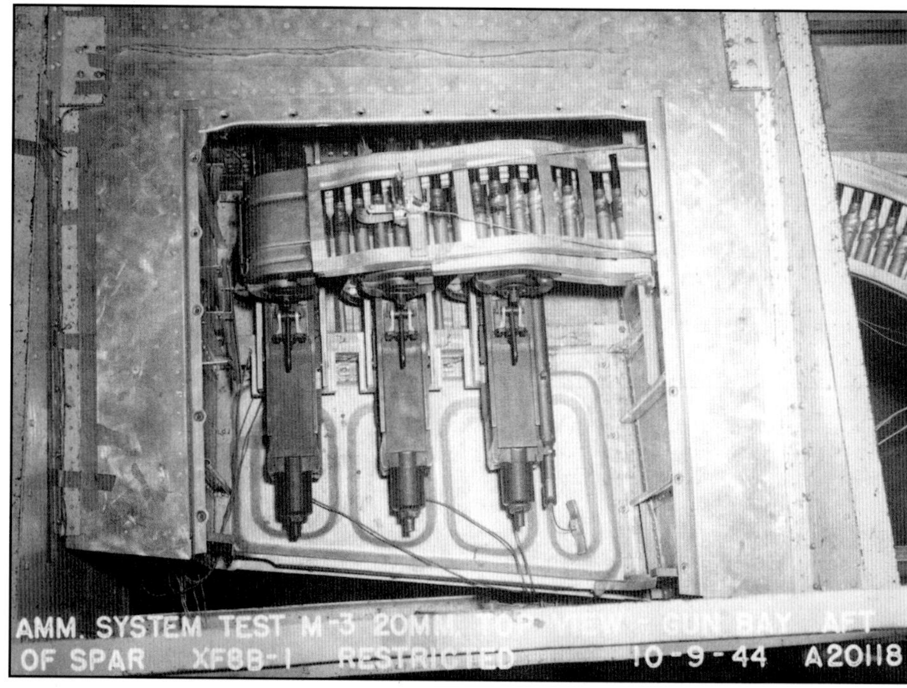

Photo: National Archives, RG 72

Photo: National Archives, RG 72

Photo: National Archives, RG 72

Photo: National Archives, RG 72

Photo: National Archives, RG 72

Photo: National Archives, RG 72

Photo: National Archives, RG 72

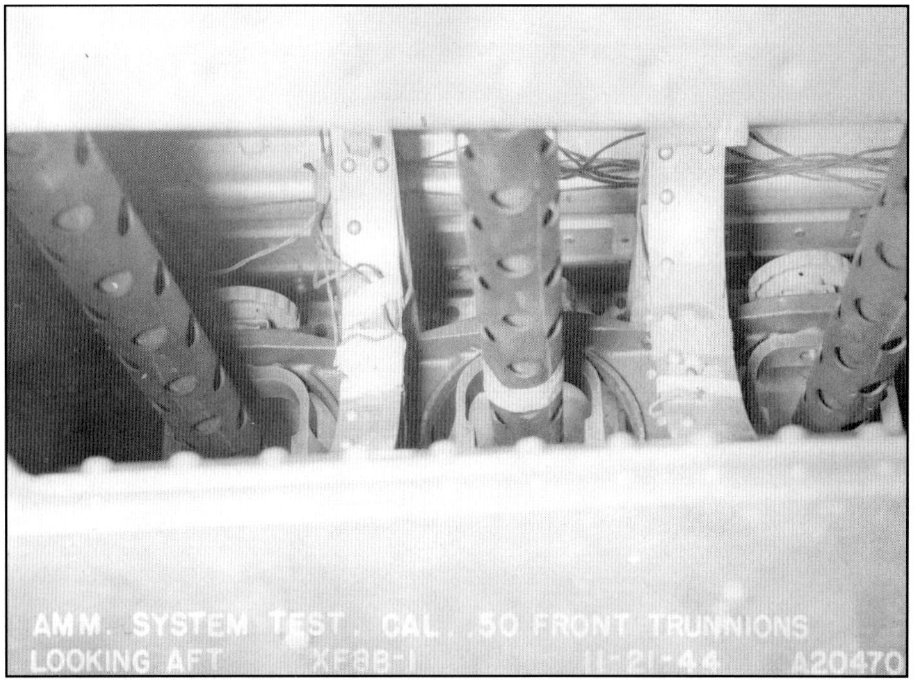

Photo: National Archives, RG 72

Photo: National Archives, RG 72

Photo: National Archives, RG 72

Photo: National Archives, RG 72

Photo: National Archives, RG 72

Photo: National Archives, RG 72

Fixed Gun Trial Tests of Armament Wing Section - June 23, 1945

The purpose of the firing tests of the XF8B-1 port wing section was to gain preliminary information concerning the suitability and adaptability of the wing gun armament in the production airplane. Tests were conducted with both 20 mm. and .50 cal. installations using a stand capable of rotation through 360° in June of 1945.

As a result of the tests, it was concluded that the installations were generally durable and serviceable, except for several problems. The major ones included the following:

1) The accessibility of the wing gun armament was good except for the fact that the lower wing gun access door to the forward gun mounts was secured by Phillips-head screws.
2) The front and rear gun mounts were satisfactorily rigid, though the light hexagonal locking nut holding spring on each forward mount loosened after firing a full load of ammunition; it was necessary to tighten the nuts after firing each load of 20 mm. ammunition. The same loosening of the securing nuts also occurred on the rear mounts.
3) It was found that the wing aperture provided for each blast tube restricted maximum use of the adjustability provided in the rear mount.
4) The manual gun charging at the guns without remote charging facilities for the pilot was considered unsatisfactory for both installations, as a majority of the stoppages, especially of the .50 cal. BAMG, could be cleared with a charging operation.
5) The ammunition cans constructed of 24 ST ALCLAD for both types of batteries showed excessive wear and were inadequately rigid in structure.
6) The combination link-case ejection chutes operated satisfactorily during tests, except for slight peeling of the wing skin at the forward edge of each aperture.

7) The blast tubes of both type batteries were too short for easy installation of the mid and inboard guns as the forward and rear mounts and the blast tube had to be aligned simultaneously. One strike occurred in a faulty tube which was warped at the weld in manufacture.
8) On the .50 cal. installation, the Burklin Quick-Release Hinge at the feed chute attachment to the gun did not provide sufficient rigidity for a smooth flow of ammunition in the feedway of the gun.
9) Provisions for adequate ventilation of the gun compartment for the .50 cal. installation were recommended to prevent ammunition from cooking off the feedway.
10) It was requested that the gun apertures in the leading edge of the wing be made of a non-corrosive metal.

Several other minor problems were noted, and Pax River personnel provided a list of recommendations to address each deficiency. None of the changes was particularly difficult and there is little doubt that the XF8B-1's armament installation could have been made more reliable had the contract not been cancelled.

Photo: National Archives, RG 72

Photo: National Archives, RG 72

Photo: National Archives, RG 72

Photo: National Archives, RG 72

Photo: National Archives, RG 72

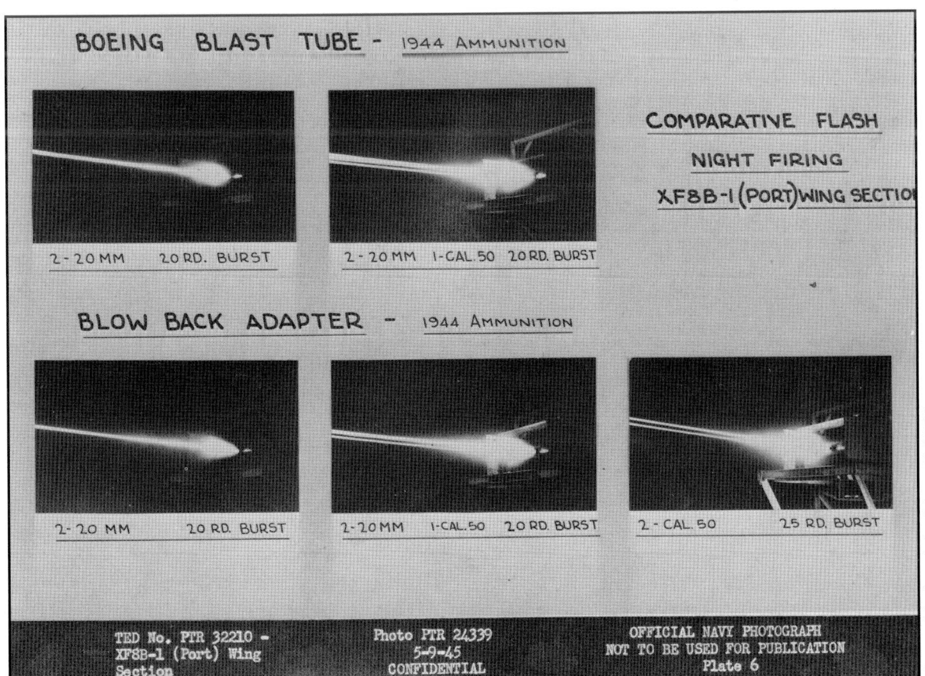

Photo: National Archives, RG 72

Photo: National Archives, RG 72

Photo: National Archives, RG 72

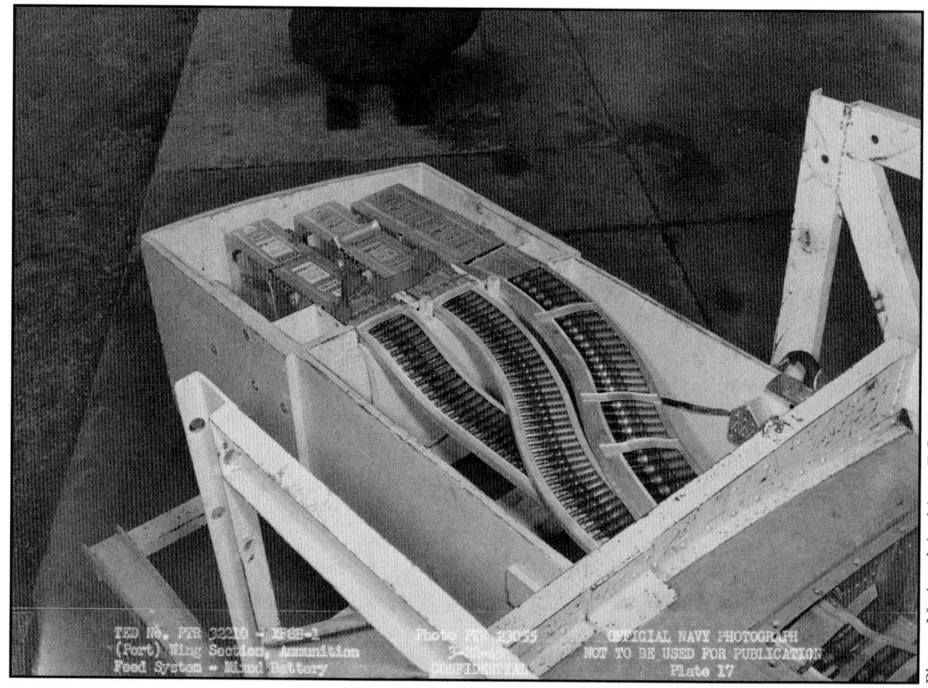

Photo: National Archives, RG 72

Photo: National Archives, RG 72

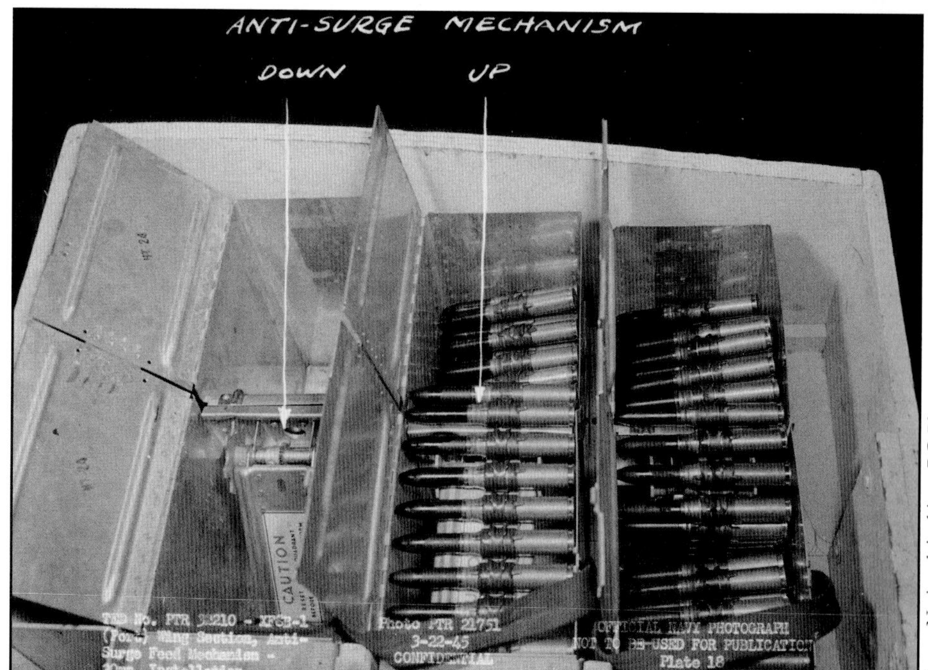

Photo: National Archives, RG 72

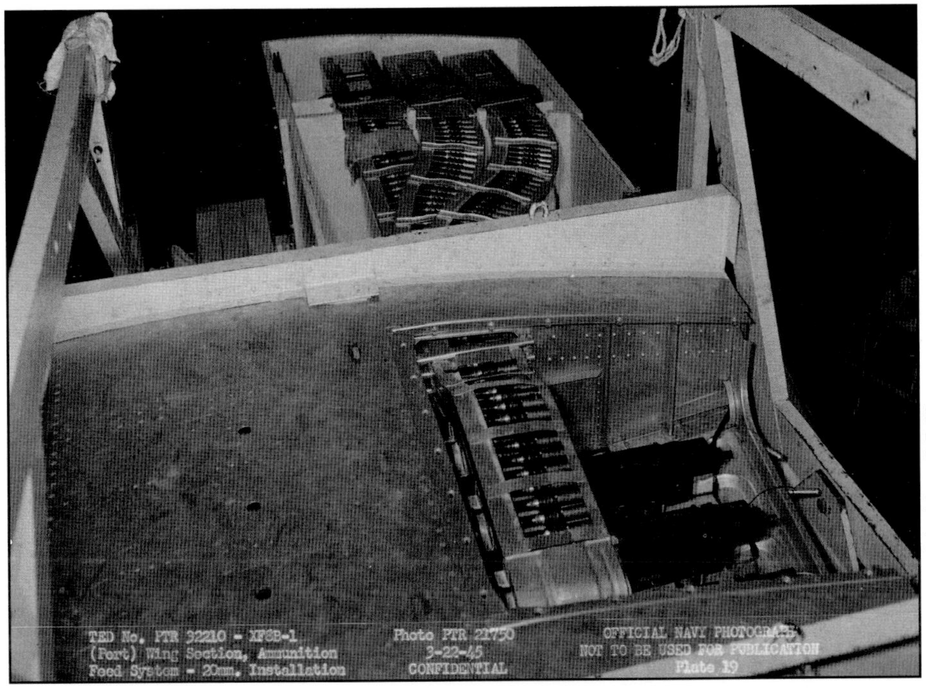

Photo: National Archives, RG 72

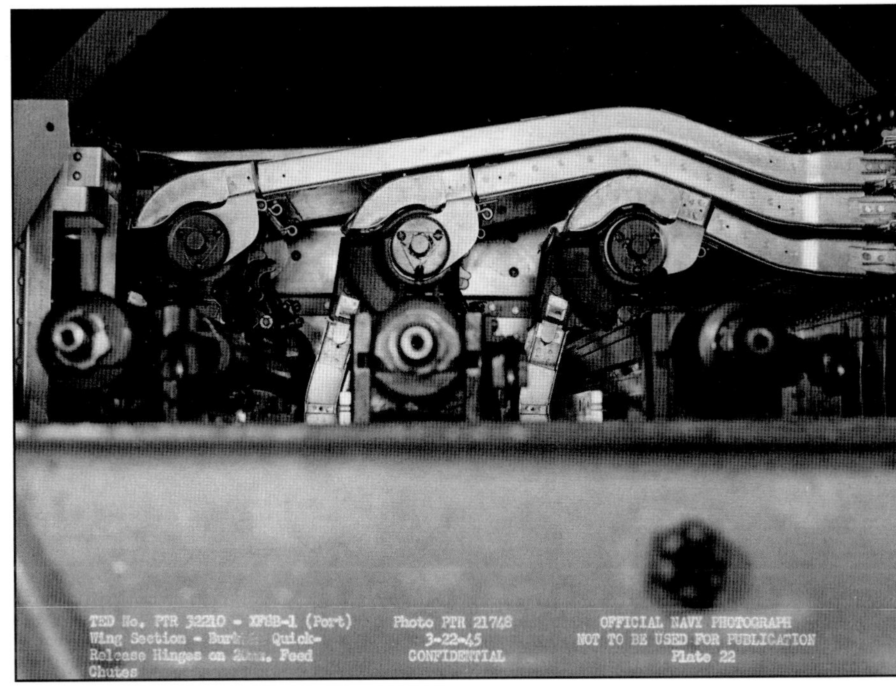

Photo: National Archives, RG 72

Photo: National Archives, RG 72

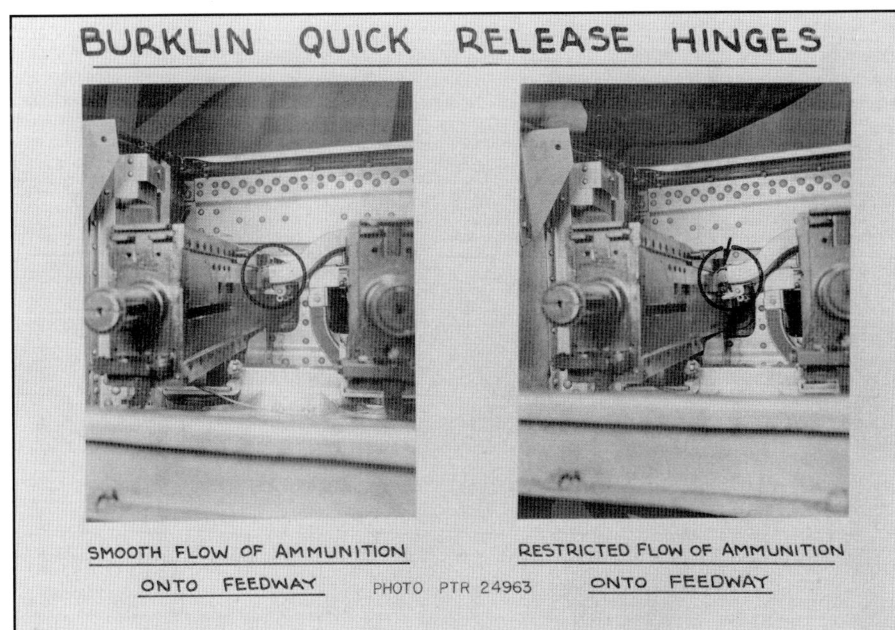

Photo: National Archives, RG 72

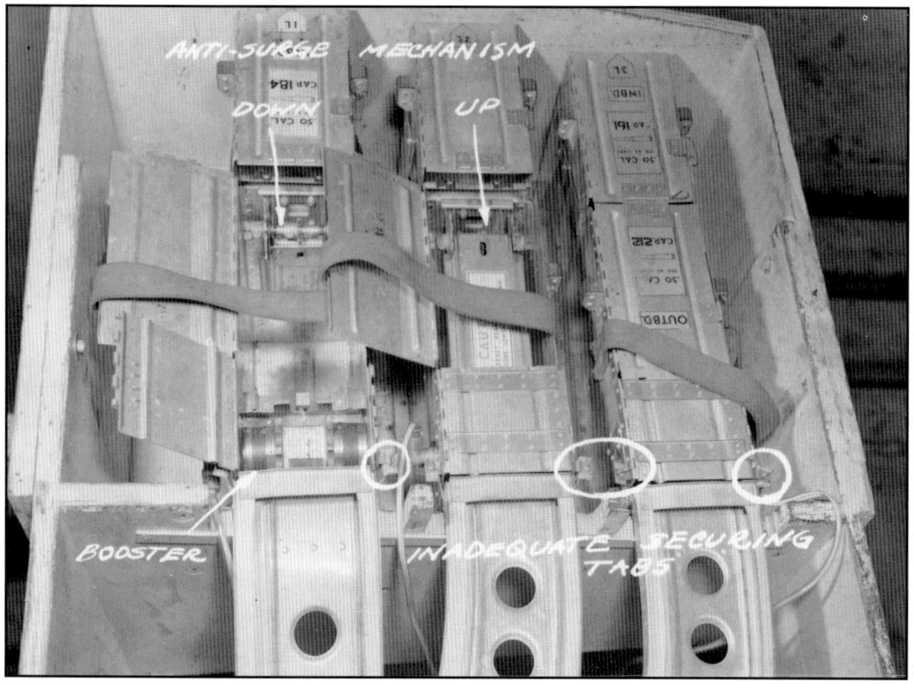

Photo: National Archives, RG 72

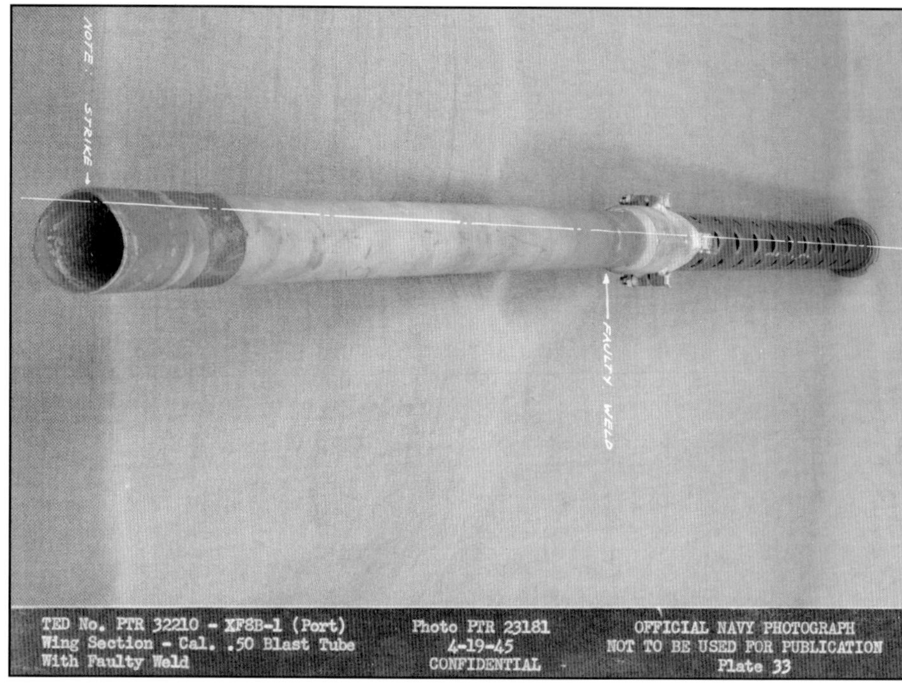

Photo: National Archives, RG 72

Photo: National Archives, RG 72

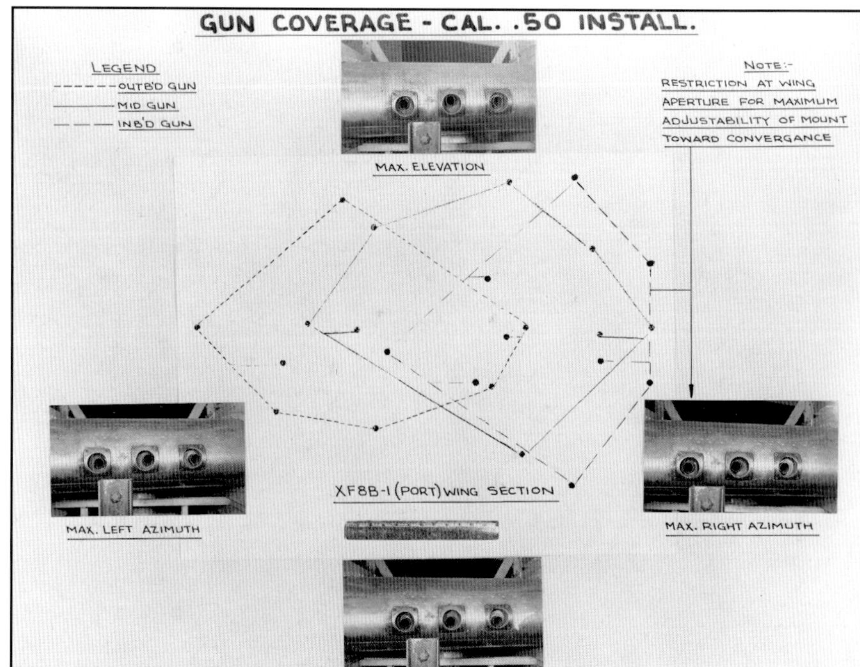

Photo: National Archives, RG 72

Photo: National Archives, RG 72

Photo: National Archives, RG 72

Photo: National Archives, RG 72

Photo: National Archives, RG 72

Photos of Damage Sustained by XF8B-1 No. 57986 during Gunnery Evaluation Tests by the Army Air Forces Proving Ground Command at Eglin Field, Florida - October 25, 1946

Photo: National Archives, RG 72

Photo: National Archives, RG 72

As related in Chapter 4, the third XF8B-1 was damaged during Army gunnery evaluation tests, in which the pilot misjudged the distance to the target and fired the .50 cal. guns too close to the ground, resulting in ricochets that twice struck the canopy. The resulting Plexiglas fragments struck the pilot and various parts of the aircraft, as can be seen in the photos on this and the following page.

Photo: National Archives, RG 72

Photo: National Archives, RG 72

Photo: National Archives, RG 72

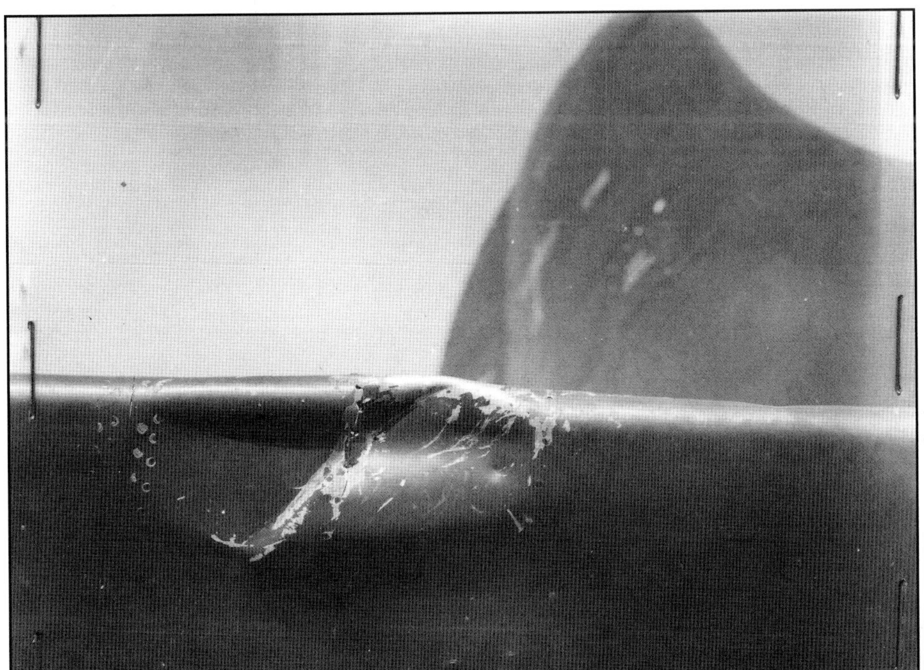

Photo: National Archives, RG 72

Photo: National Archives, RG 72

Appendix 8

Service and Maintenance Manual

This appendix presents selected content from the Boeing XF8B-1 Service and Maintenance Manual found in the National Archives. This massive document is a treasure trove of detail drawings, photos, and information for the aicraft enthusiast and modeler. Compared to other manuals for experimental Navy aircraft, the quality of the illustrations and overall presentation is quite high, a sign perhaps that at least a portion of it was produced when Boeing still had reasonable hope that the XF8B-1 would be produced in quantity. The fact that the vast majority of the illustrations and photos show the aircraft with the early, high drag canopy supports this theory. The manual also vividly shows how the XF8B-1's massive engine, counter-rotating propeller, and bomb bay would have made the aircraft one of the more complex piston engine Navy fighters of the era to maintain and operate.

A portion of the title page for the XF8B-1 Service and Maintenance Manual. The original document was remarkably well preserved and included a few pages printed in color, which are presented out of sequence at the end of the appendix, where the color section of this book begins.

Manual Scan: National Archives, RG 287

A poorly composited photo which appeared in the front of the manual showing XF8B-1 no. 57984 flying over Mr. Rainier.

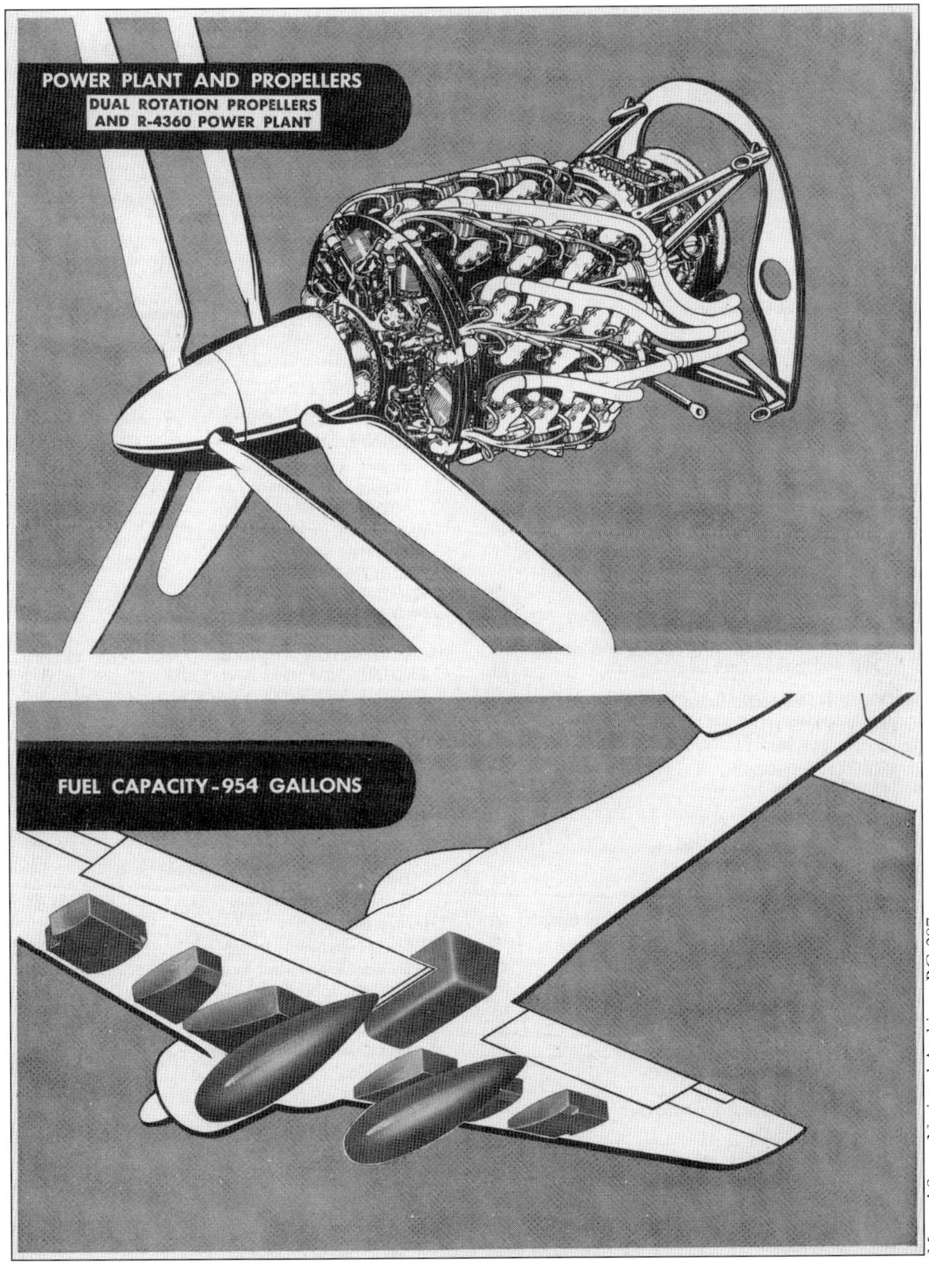
POWER PLANT AND PROPELLERS
DUAL ROTATION PROPELLERS
AND R-4360 POWER PLANT
FUEL CAPACITY-954 GALLONS

EASY ACCESS
AND
QUICK ENGINE CHANGE

SEC·I FAMILIARIZATION

FACTS AND FIGURES

The XF8B-1 is a single-place, low-wing fighter, armed with six .50-caliber machine guns or 20 MM cannon (or combination). It can also carry bombs. It is built around a Pratt and Whitney R-4360-10, 3000 HP engine with a dual rotation propeller. Its main identifying characteristics in the air are the single engine, the diamond-shaped wing, and the dorsal fin which sweeps up to the tall vertical tail. At close range the double propeller and the plexiglas bubble, over the cockpit, are also visible.

The airplane is designed for carrier use. Its wheels and arresting hook are electrically retractable, and the wings are electrically folded for spotting. The wing flaps are large and extend over the wing fold 20 inches. (The 20-inch sections at the outboard ends of the flaps are folded under by hand.)

Speed, maneuverability, and versatility are the design objectives of this medium altitude fighter. Flush riveting, 3000 HP, and aerodynamic smoothing on all major frontal surfaces to improve the laminar airflow, put the XF8B-1 in well over the 400 mile-an-hour class. The cross-section of the wing is designed so that the thickest part is further aft than in previous designs. With this shape, the wing cuts through the air instead of pushing into it, so a much greater speed can be attained before the "compressibility effect" limits the airplane's velocity. The horizontal tail or stabilizer is placed high to get it out of the propeller's slip stream and its airfoil has been inverted to reduce the angle of attack, and hence the drag. Both of these features increase speed of the airplane.

Because the control surfaces are large and metal covered, the airplane handles easily and safely at high speeds. Large control surfaces generally produce such heavy "wind loads" that the controls are stiff. This condition is overcome by the design of the trim tabs, which also act as balance and booster tabs. The large wing flaps increase the lift without proportional increase in drag, so that the airplane can take off in a short distance and land at steep glide angles with stall speeds around 75 MPH. These performance characteristics compare favorably with those of many smaller and lighter airplanes. Small dive flaps, electrically operated, are provided for emergency pull outs from high speed dives.

The fuel is carried in a main tank (three self-sealing cells in each wing), a droppable tank in the bomb bay, and a streamlined droppable tank under each wing. The top of the oil tank forms the top of the cowling forward of the windshield. The fuel and corresponding oil quantities are as follows:

FUEL TANKS	FUEL	OIL
Main	384	20
Bomb Bay and Main	654	32
External and Main	684	32
Main, Bomb Bay, and External	954	40

The XF8B-1 is quickly convertible into a fighter-bomber by hanging bombs instead of fuel tanks on the racks on the bomb-bay and under the wings. The racks are easily removed when not needed. The maximum bomb load is 4000 pounds. A tow target container is attached to the wing rack and a target can be trailed from a hook just forward of the tail wheel. It can be released before landing. The external racks with slight modification will carry smoke tanks.

The space behind the pilot's seat may be used for baggage.

The quick interchangeability of the power pack (engine and accessories, cowling, induction, and cooling systems) is of special interest to the maintenance man. If desired, the air scoop can be unfastened and dropped out of the way on its hinge and just the engine, accessories, and cowling removed.

The XF8B-1 is an "all-electric" airplane. The landing gear, wing flaps, wing folding mechanism, starter, bomb doors and racks, guns, instruments, fuel booster pumps, auxiliary fuel pump, cowl flaps, oil cooler doors, and intercooler door are electrically operated. The flight controls are cable-and-rod driven from the rudder pedals and control stick. The single disk hydraulic brake on each wheel is applied by the pressure on the corresponding pedal. The brake system has no accumulator or pump. The landing gear and wing flaps each have an emergency hand crank system. Miscellaneous short-run controls are cable or rod operated.

Figure 1—Comparison

RESTRICTED
D-5851

Section I
Facts and Figures

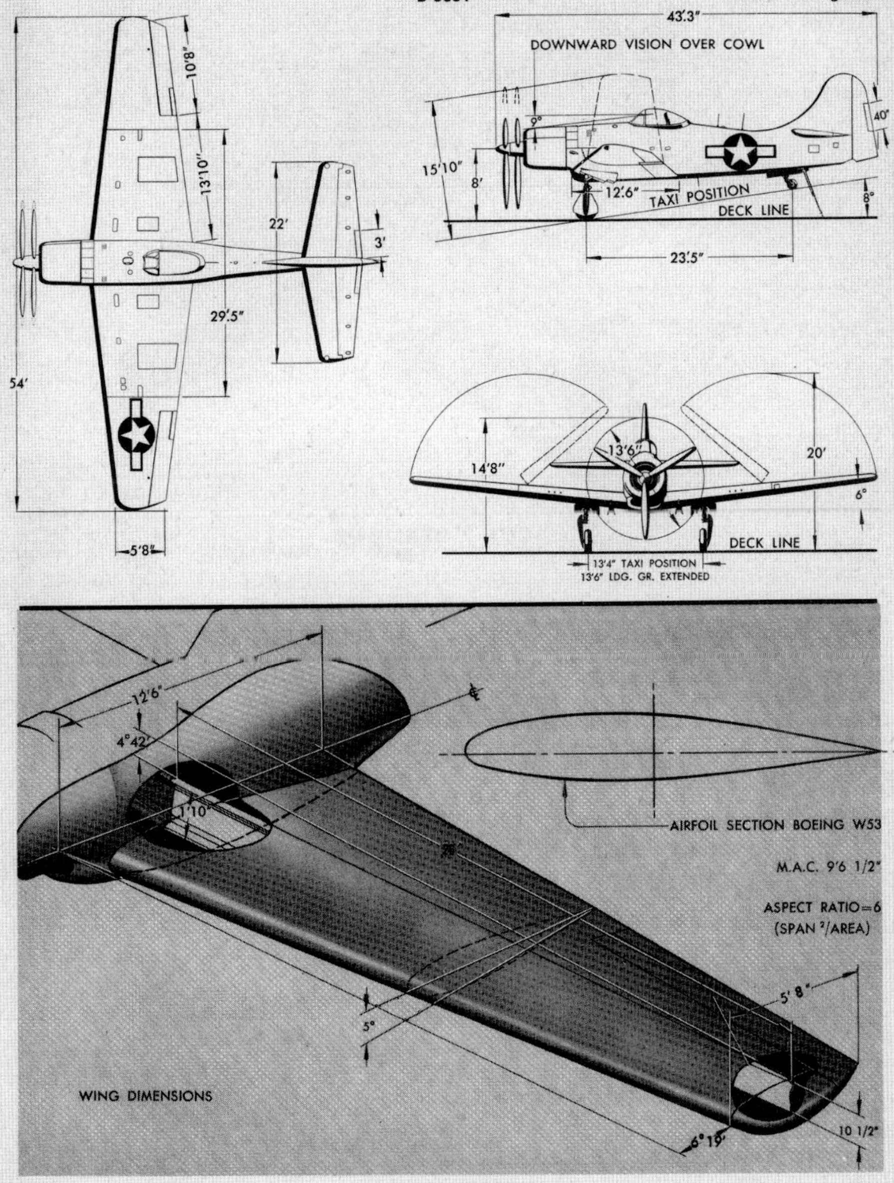

Figure 2—Dimensions

Section I
Facts and Figures

RESTRICTED
D-5851

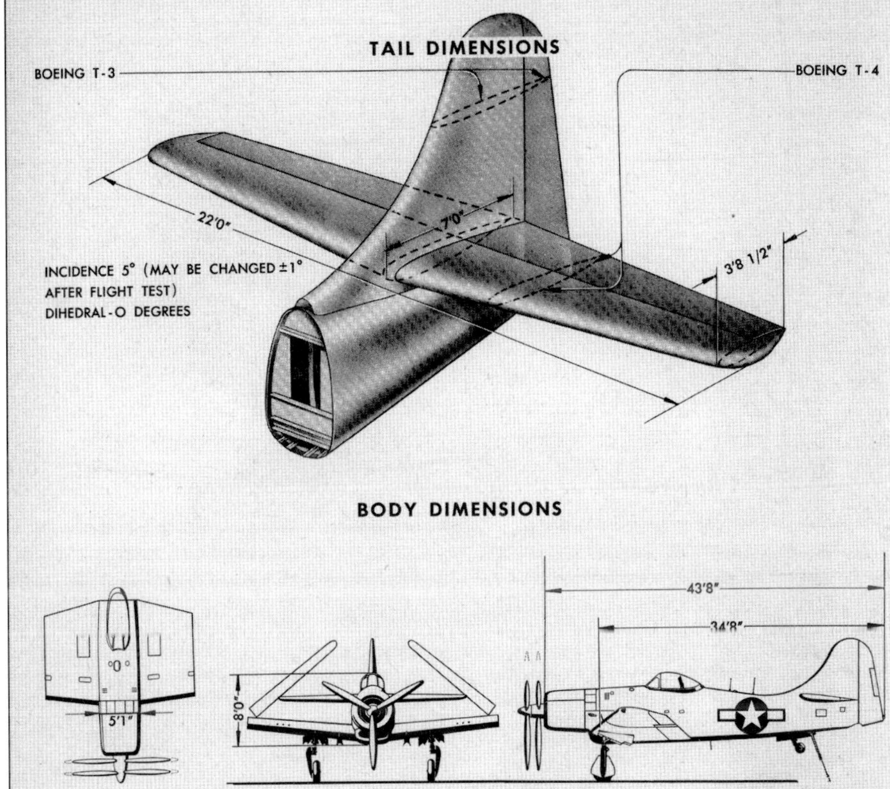

AREAS	
WINGS – TOTAL	489.4 SQ. FT.
OUTER WING PANELS – INCLUDING AILERONS	176.88 SQ. FT.
AILERONS	31.68 SQ. FT.
AILERON TABS	9.92 SQ. FT.
TRAILING EDGE FLAPS	74.0 SQ. FT.
STABILIZER	81.84 SQ. FT.
ELEVATOR	28.88 SQ. FT.
ELEVATOR TABS	3.30 SQ. FT.
FIN	39.68 SQ. FT.
RUDDER	17.26 SQ. FT.
RUDDER TABS	1.94 SQ. FT.

Figure 3—Dimensions

RESTRICTED
D-5851

Section I
Facts and Figures

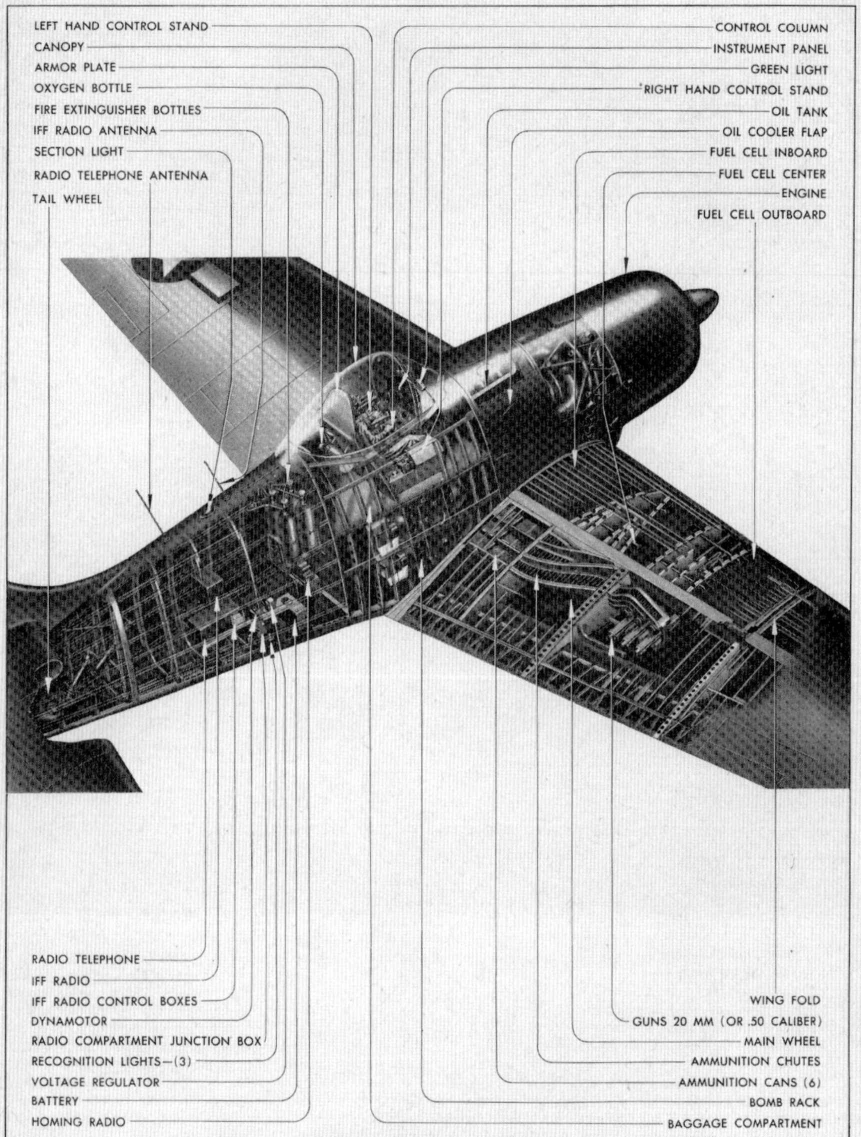

Figure 4—General Arrangement

Section I
Facts and Figures

RESTRICTED
D-5851

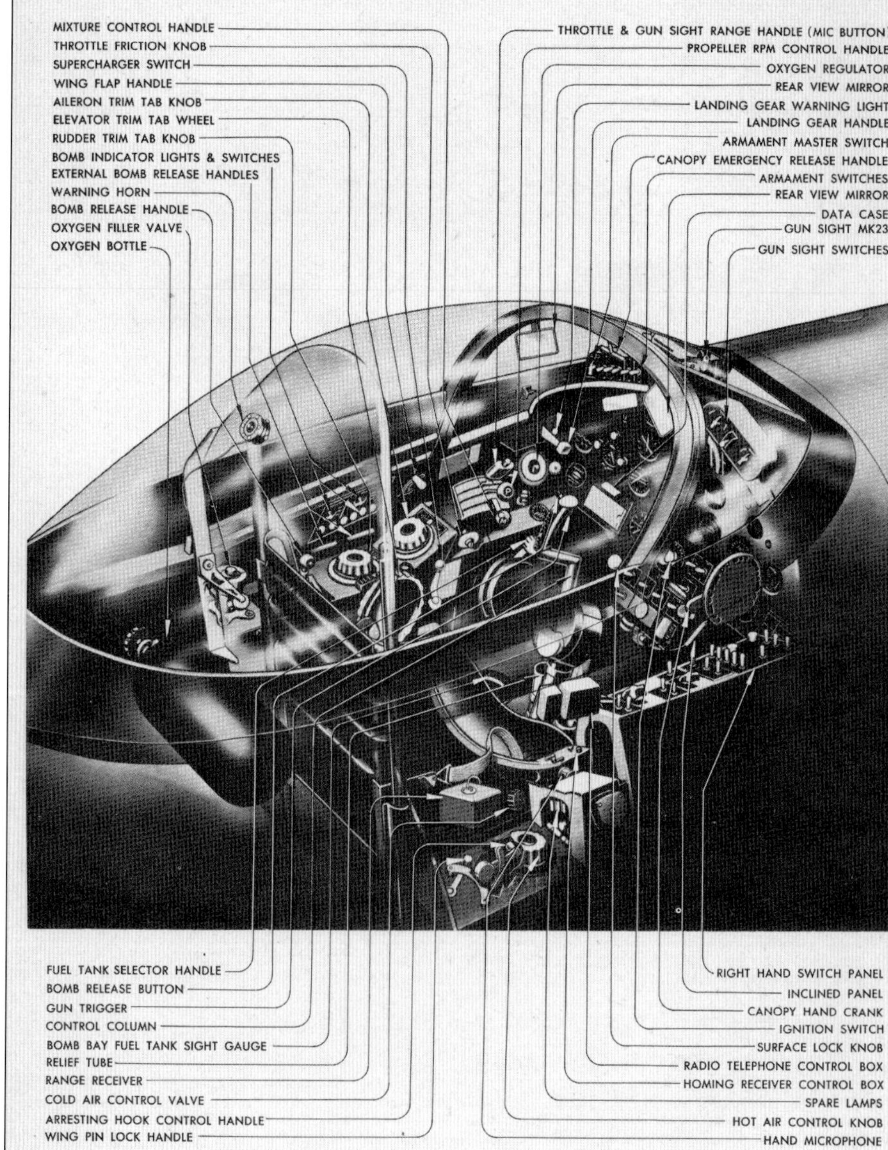

Figure 5—Cockpit Familiarization

PERFORMANCE, CONTROL LIMITS, LANDING GEAR

PERFORMANCE

ENGINE—PRATT AND WHITNEY R-4360-10
(SEE MANUFACTURER'S OPERATING INSTRUCTIONS FOR MORE DETAILED INFORMATION.)

TAKE-OFF—(SEA LEVEL)	3000 H P
MILITARY—(2500 FT)	3000 H P
MILITARY—(22,500 FT)	2500 H P
MAXIMUM CONTINUOUS AND CLIMB—(5500 FT)	2500 H P
MAXIMUM CRUISE—(9,500 FT)	1670 H P
MAXIMUM CRUISE—(24,000 FT)	1500 H P
MINIMUM FUEL CONSUMPTION—(SEA LEVEL)	57 GAL/HR AT 800 H P
MAXIMUM R P M OVERSPEED	3060 R P M FOR 30 SEC

AIRPLANE—ESTIMATED AT COMBAT WEIGHT

TRUE SPEED—SEA LEVEL AT MILITARY POWER	375 M P H
TRUE SPEED—14,500 FEET AT MILITARY POWER	412 M P H
TRUE SPEED—23,200 FEET AT MILITARY POWER	433 M P H
RATE OF CLIMB—SEA LEVEL AT 3000 H P	3660 F P M
TIME TO CLIMB TO 20,000 FT	5.9 MIN
CEILING	OVER 30,000 FT
TAKE-OFF DISTANCE—35 DEG FLAPS	550 FT
TAKE-OFF DISTANCE—25 KNOT WIND	261 FT

CONTROL SURFACE LIMITS OF TRAVEL

AILERONS—UP	18 (±2) DEG—7.5 IN
AILERONS—DOWN	18 (±2) DEG—7.5 IN
AILERON SPRING TAB—UP AND DOWN	25 (±2) DEG
AILERON BALANCE TAB (LEFT WING)—UP AND DOWN	14 (±2) DEG—1.72 IN
WING FLAPS (INCHES AT TRAILING EDGE)	35 DEG—32.1 IN
ELEVATORS—UP	27 ($\pm^{1}_{0}$) DEG—7.79 IN
ELEVATORS—DOWN	15 (±2) DEG—4.70 IN
ELEVATOR TABS—UP	22 (±2) DEG—2.55 IN
ELEVATOR TABS—DOWN	34 (±2) DEG—3.91 IN
RUDDER—LEFT AND RIGHT	25 (±2) DEG—14.54 IN
RUDDER TAB—LEFT AND RIGHT	30 (±2) DEG—3.63 IN

LANDING GEAR

MAIN—

TYPE	CONVENTIONAL—ELECTRICALLY RETRACTABLE
TREAD (INCHES CENTER-TO-CENTER)—COMPRESSED	159.80 IN
TREAD (INCHES CENTER-TO-CENTER)—TAXI	160.22 IN
TREAD (INCHES CENTER-TO-CENTER)—EXTENDED	161.94 IN
SHOCK STRUTS	
TYPE	COMBINATION AIR AND OIL
MAKE AND PART NUMBER	BOEING 15-14303
FLUID	HYDRAULIC FLUID SPECIFICATION NO. AN-VV-O-366
INFLATION—CENTER TO CENTER OF TORSION LINK	8.12 IN
AIR PRESSURE NEEDED TO INFLATE	800 P S I
WHEELS	
TYPE	WHEEL ASSEMBLY FOR SINGLE DISC BOOSTER BRAKE
MAKE AND ASSEMBLY NUMBER	GOODYEAR 530836

TAIL GEAR, ENGINE, PROPELLER

BRAKES	
TYPE	BRAKE ASSEMBLY—SINGLE DISC HYDRAULIC BOOSTER
MAKE AND ASSEMBLY NUMBER	GOODYEAR 540074
TIRES	
TYPE	RAYON STATIC CONDUCTOR, HIGH PRESSURE, NON-SKID 32 BY 8.8—10 PLY
MAKE AND SPECIFICATION NUMBER	GOODYEAR S-5
TIRE PRESSURE	110 P S I
TUBE	
MAKE AND TYPE	GOODYEAR 32 BY 8.8 REGULAR

TAIL GEAR—

TYPE	CONVENTIONAL—ELECTRICALLY RETRACTABLE
SHOCK STRUT	
TYPE	COMBINATION AIR AND OIL
MAKE AND PART NUMBER	BOEING 9-8613
FLUID	HYDRAULIC FLUID, SPECIFICATION NO. AN-VV-O-366
INFLATION—TOP OF OUTER ALUMINUM CYLINDER TO CENTER OF VALVE	4.07 IN
AIR PRESSURE NEEDED TO INFLATE	800 P S I
WHEEL	9-1/2 BY 4-3/4 SOLID GRIZZLY TYPE
TIRE	9-1/2 BY 4-3/4 SOLID GRIZZLY TYPE
WHEEL (ALTERNATE)	
TYPE	14-1/2 BY 5 HIGH PRESSURE
MAKE AND ASSEMBLY NUMBER	GOODYEAR 511493
TIRE (ALTERNATE)	
TYPE	RAYON STATIC CONDUCTOR, HIGH-PRESSURE RIB CHANNEL 14-1/2 BY 5—8 PLY
MAKE AND SPECIFICATION NUMBER	GOODYEAR S-5
TIRE PRESSURE	105 P S I
TUBE	
MAKE AND TYPE	GOODYEAR 14-1/2 BY 5 REGULAR

ENGINE

TYPE	RADIAL—28 CYLINDER, AIR COOLED, TWO STAGE ENGINE-DRIVEN SUPERCHARGER, DUAL ROTATION PROPELLER SHAFTS
MANUFACTURER AND DESIGNATION	PRATT AND WHITNEY R-4360-10
PROPELLER GEAR RATIO	.381:1
FUEL	GRADE 100/130 SPECIFICATION NO. AN-F-28
OIL	GRADE 1100 OR 1120 SPECIFICATION NO. AN-VV-O-446

PROPELLER

MANUFACTURER	AEROPRODUCTS
TYPE	6-BLADE, DUAL ROTATION, HYDRAULIC
MODEL	AD 7562-X8
DIAMETER	13 FT 5-11/16 IN
DISTANCE BETWEEN FRONT AND REAR BLADES	13.5 IN
BLADE SETTING—HIGH	32.5 DEG
BLADE SETTING—LOW	67.5 DEG

Section I
General Operating and Handling

RESTRICTED
D-5851

GENERAL OPERATING AND HANDLING

EXTERIOR OPERATIONS

This section is to acquaint you with some of the everyday operations performed by the maintenance man from the outside of the airplane.

Take care when walking on the wing to stay within twelve inches of the fuselage, or forward of the wing spar.

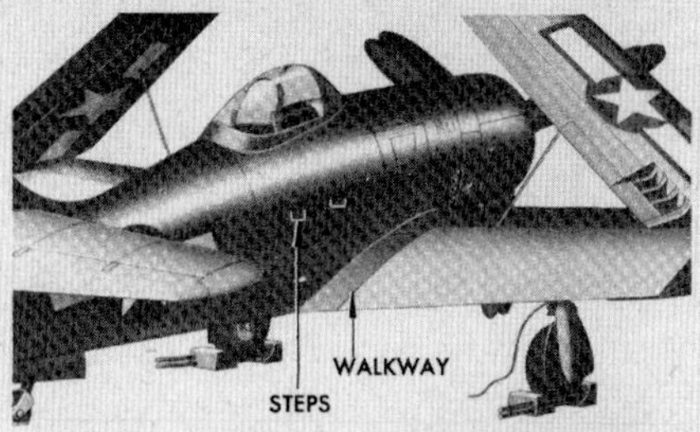

To open the canopy over the cockpit, press the round rubber spot just below the right side of the windshield, and slide the canopy back.

The oil quantity gage is in the filler well, forward of the windshield.

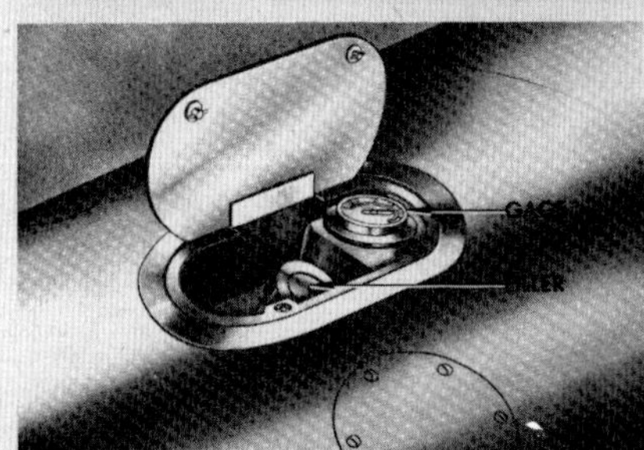

Connect the external power plug in the electrical receptacle above the right wing trailing edge. You will need a screw driver or a thin dime to open the hinged cover.

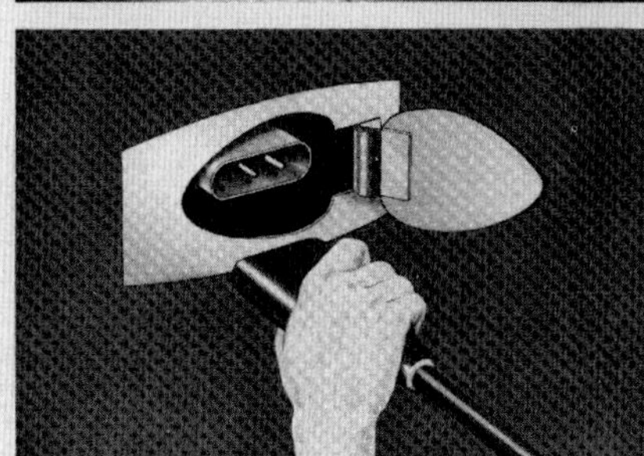

Manual Scan: National Archives, RG 287

RESTRICTED
D-5851

Section I
General Operating and Handling

Pull the prop through by hand before starting the engine if it has not been run within the last hour. No more than two men should pull for the first revolution. Watching out for a hydraulic lock, pull the prop through at least three revolutions.

The 34 ampere-hour battery will easily start the engine, but in case you have an extremely low battery or no battery and no external power, the engine can be started manually by the use of the hand starting equipment furnished with the airplane. Wind the crank up to about 96 RPM before meshing the starter with the meshing handle. In the case of the low battery, it might start easier if the "STARTER MESH" switch on the instrument panel is used to mesh, to gain ignition boost. There will be no ignition boost when using the meshing handle.

The guns have to be charged when the airplane is on the ground. The .50-caliber gun charging handle and the 20 MM gun charging rod are stowed in clips on the inside of the left wing gun bay just aft of the dive flap. Roll the wing flaps down and reach up into the wing ahead of the flap to get the gun charger. Insert it in the gun and pull back to charge. Running the dive flaps open may facilitate gun charging.

You can open the bomb doors from outside by pulling the handle in the radio compartment which trips the door latches and lets the doors fall open. If a bomb or a fuel tank is hung in the bomb bay, this is the only way the doors can be opened without dropping it. Close the doors by pushing them up until they both latch. A safety switch keeps anyone from closing the doors on you electrically when they have been opened by pulling the handle—BUT the safety switch has not operated if the doors were opened from the cockpit. If you don't *know* how they were opened, you had better trip the switch manually by pulling the handle in the radio compartment as mentioned above.

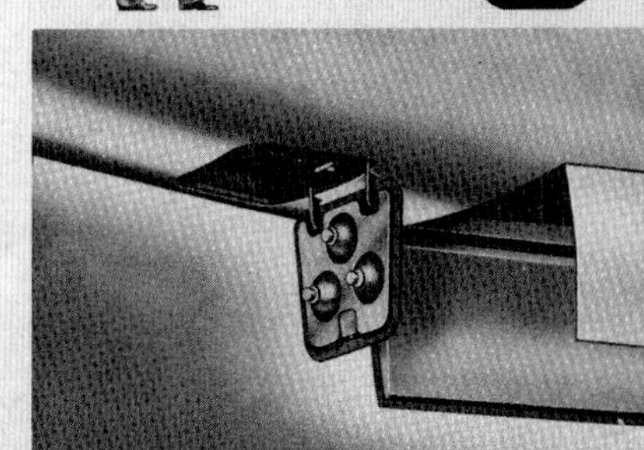

RESTRICTED

Manual Scan: National Archives, RG 287

Don't overlook the gun camera when servicing the airplane. It's in the bottom of the air scoop near the front and is accessible from below. It points forward through an optical glass window, which requires frequent cleaning.

The main tank defueling valve may be hard to find. It's up inside the intercooler opening on the bottom of the air scoop, and it's locked with the handle down by a spring catch. You can open the intercooler door by turning the battery switch "ON" and holding the "INTERCOOLER" switch on the instrument panel to "OPEN" until the door stops.

In winds above 30 knots (35 MPH) the wings should be braced with jury struts, which will brace the wings safely up to 60 knots (70 MPH). If a wind above 60 knots is expected unfold the wings and tie down the airplane.

CAUTION—*Actuation of the wing fold mechanism above 39 knots (45 MPH) is not safe.*

The stub of the wing flap that sticks out after the wing is folded has to be folded under by hand for close spotting. Push up on the flush button, which is on the under side of the stub about four inches from the fold. Swing the stub down and back up under the rest of the flap. To extend the stub, simply pull down on it, swing it out and up rather firmly to engage the locking pin. Check that the pin is fully engaged by trying to press up on the flush button. There should be no play.

If you want to raise or lower the wing flaps electrically when the wings are folded even a little, you'll have to depress a micro switch in the right wing fold with your finger, while a man in the cockpit operates the wing flap control handle. The decal shown is beside the switch in the right wing fold.

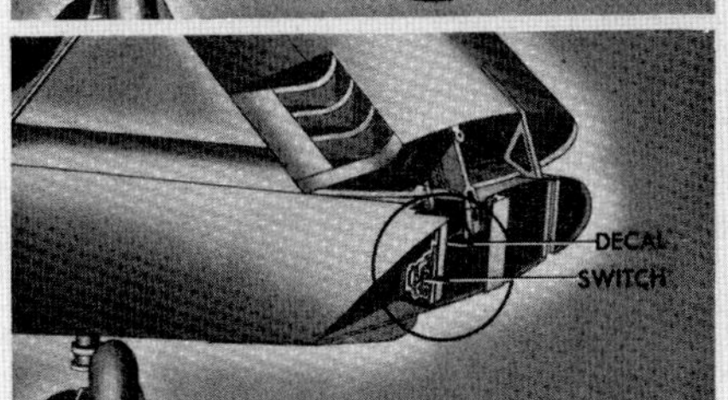

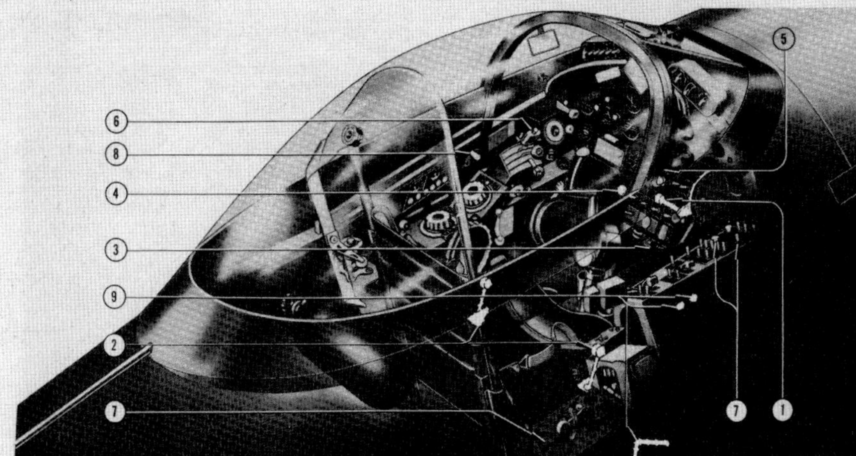

Figure 6—Cockpit Operations (sheet 1 of 2 sheets)

COCKPIT OPERATIONS

1. Open or close the canopy with the crank at the right of the windshield.

2. To raise or lower the seat, move the handle on the right side of the seat aft, lift your weight off the seat or bear down, and return the handle forward. The handle on the left side adjusts the shoulder straps.

3. If the rudder pedals are not properly adjusted for leg length, turn the small knurled wheel between the pedals (up to move them closer to you).

4. Always push in the "SURFACE LOCK" knob before you move the throttle or operate the control surfaces. Pull the knob out and neutralize the surface controls before you leave the cockpit. The knob must be turned to latch it out.

5. The ignition switch may be new to you. That knob marked "SELECT, PULL, AND CHECK L OR R" is used during ground test to check either half of any of the seven magnetos, along with the front (R) or rear (L) spark plugs on the four cylinders served by that half of that "mag."

6. If the wind is blowing more than 60 knots, don't fold the wings; and if it's blowing between 35 and 60 knots, brace them with the jury struts after they're folded. If the engine isn't running, you must have external power and the throttle must be closed. If the engine is running, the throttle must be opened to give at least 1000 RPM.

7. Fold the wings by pushing the "WING PIN LOCK" handle on the right control stand to "UNLOCK," then holding the "WING FOLDING" switch on "FOLD" until the wings stop folding. Spread the wings by holding the "WING FOLDING" switch on "SPREAD" until the wings stop; then returning the "WING PIN LOCK" handle to the "LOCK" position. Check the red cylinder out at the wing fold, and the red warning light. If the cylinder is sticking up, or if the light is on, the wing pin is not locked.

8. If the wings are spread, operate the wing flaps in setting the control handle on the left sidewall to the desired position. If the wings are folded, you'll have to have a man press the micro switch at the right wing fold while you operate the wing fold control handle. Before moving the control handle up or down, pull it away from the pivot point to unlatch it from the notched quadrant. External or generator power should be used for wing flap operation.

9. Use the hand crank, stowed in clips on the right control stand, to operate the wing flaps and landing gear if the engine is stopped and there is no external power. It takes 360 turns to lower the flaps and 230 turns to lower the landing gear. To keep you from getting hurt, a safety switch in each crank socket prevents electrical operation when the crank is inserted.

Manual Scan: National Archives, RG 287

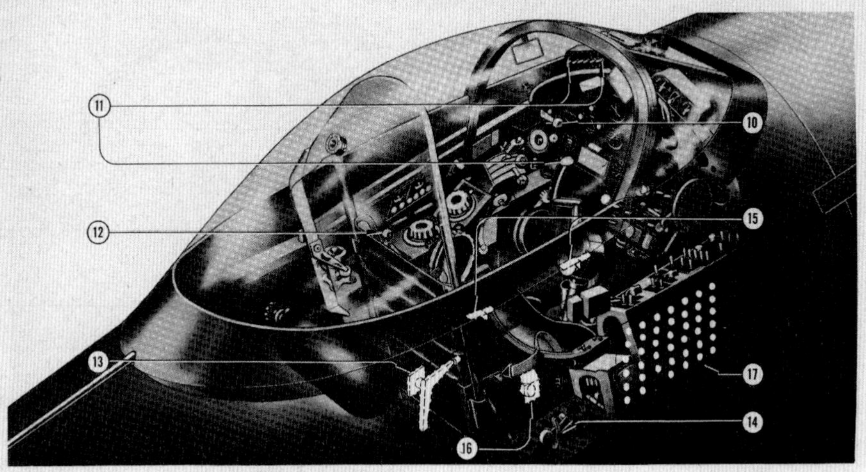

Figure 6—Cockpit Operations (sheet 2 of 2 sheets)

10. The landing gear control handle combines both the retracting motor control switch and an up-lock latch, which keeps the wheels from vibrating down when retracted. So, to crank the landing gear down by hand, put the crank in the socket, then move the control handle to "DOWN" before cranking.

11. You can open the bomb doors three different ways. If there is a fuel tank or bomb on the internal racks, you must get out of the airplane and pull the handle in the radio compartment. If there are no loaded racks, the simplest way to open the bomb doors is to push the bomb release handle on the left control stand from "LOCK" to "SALVO." If you want to check the doors electrically, set the bomb release handle on "SELECTIVE," turn the bomb selector switch on the instrument panel hood to "INTERNAL," turn on the "ARMAMENT MASTER" switch, and press the bomb release button on the control grip—but watch out! The doors will close again in 3 to 6 seconds.

12. To close the bomb doors from the cockpit, *make sure there is no one in between them,* turn on the "ARMAMENT MASTER" switch, set the bomb release handle on "SELECTIVE" for about 10 seconds, then return to "LOCK." (If the doors do not close, the safety switch is probably open. Close them by hand.)

13. Before towing or turning the airplane, unlock the tail wheel by raising the handle on the side of the left control stand.

14. Moving the arresting hook handle on the side of the right control stand to "NORM DOWN" turns on the retracting motor and runs the hook down in about 8 seconds. If you spring the handle inboard and move it past the stop lug to "EMERGENCY DOWN," it unlatches the hook so that it swings down freely, and the motor drives the retracting screw down to relatch with the hook and holds it down by the spring action. When you return the handle to "UP," the retracting motor brings the hook up in about 11 seconds.

15. The three red cockpit lights under the sill on the right side of the cockpit can be unsnapped from their mounts to replace burned-out bulbs, one can be used as short extension light to work around the control stand if you wish.

16. There are three receptacles where such portable equipment as drills, lights, and soldering irons can be plugged in: one in the bomb bay, one in the radio compartment, and one in the cockpit above the right control stand. The portable equipment must have connecting plug NAF1078-3 (AN3106-16-lip). The receptacles are "hot" all the time from the 24 volt direct current battery. Use the cap chain to the receptacle to cover them when not in use.

17. Circuit breakers protect nearly every piece of electrical equipment in the airplane, and all of the circuit breakers except three are on the panel on the right side of the cockpit. Of these three, one is on the radio junction shield in the radio compartment and one in each gun bay.

MAINTENANCE PRECAUTIONS

A safety switch on the right oleo serves two functions. It prevents retraction on the landing gear while the airplane is sitting on the ground, and folding of the wings while the airplane is in the air.

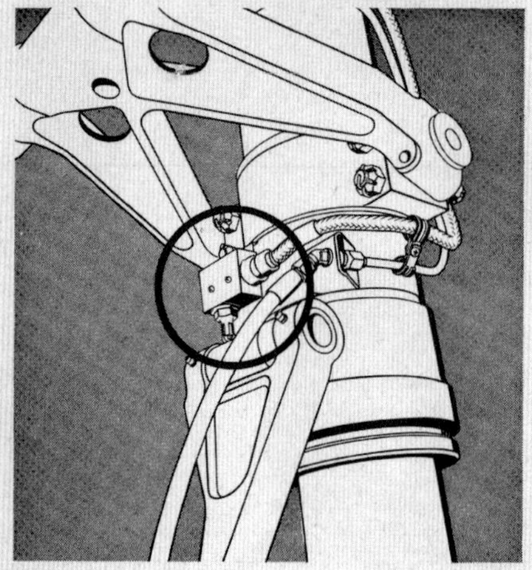

The tail wheel has an aluminum shear bolt, which will fail if you don't unlock the tail wheel before turning the airplane. If the bolt shears, replace it immediately with a new AN-5D-D-7 bolt and tighten it up with torque wrench to between 50 and 70 pound-inches.

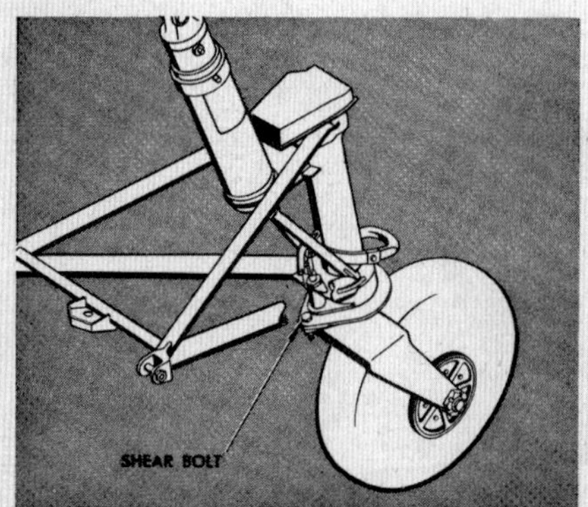

Don't turn on the fuel tank selector until you are ready to start the engine. The electric fuel booster pumps come on if the handle is set to "MAIN" and the auxiliary pump starts if the handle is set to any other tank. When the pumps start, a fuel bleed through the carburetor shoots fuel into the manifold blower and the engine will flood in a few seconds. The prop will then have to be pulled through by hand to clear the cylinders before the engine is started.

Finally, don't disconnect the wires of the ignition switch circuit at the inner cowl ring, the firewall, or the ignition switch unless the propeller has been removed. The engine might kick over and kill some one.

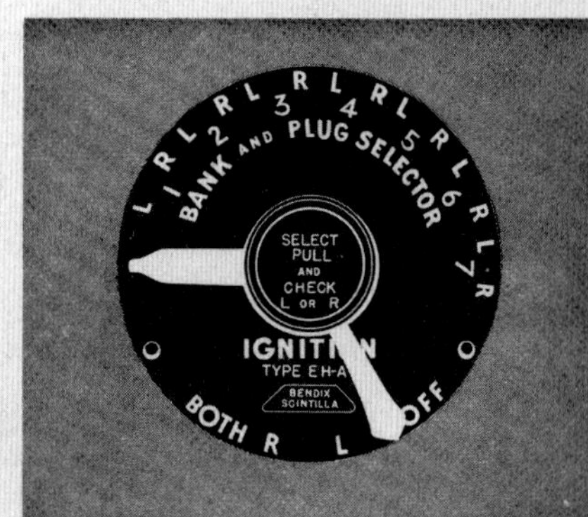

TAXIING

Only authorized personnel may taxi the airplane. See XF8B-1 Pilot's Manual and R 4360 Engine Operating Instructions.

Do not exceed 60 knots (70 MPH) with the jury strut installed when taxiing this airplane with the wings folded or 30 knots (35 MPH) without the jury strut.

TOWING

Tow bar assembly Boeing F-12000 (for towing or pushing from the front) is furnished with the airplane. The tow bar attaches to the lugs on the front of the main landing gear shock struts. Always have a man in the airplane unlock the tail wheel (to prevent shearing the bolt in the tail wheel treadle) and to operate the brakes when the airplane is being towed.

If overloaded, the tow-fitting connector bolts (1032, AN3-23A) will shear. This shearing prevents damage to the landing gear or tow bar; each bolt shears at 10,000 pounds, so the tow bar assembly can take a direct forward load of 20,000 pounds.

When dragging the tow bars to the airplane, swing them together, lock them with the locking clip on the caster carriage, and let them run on their casters.

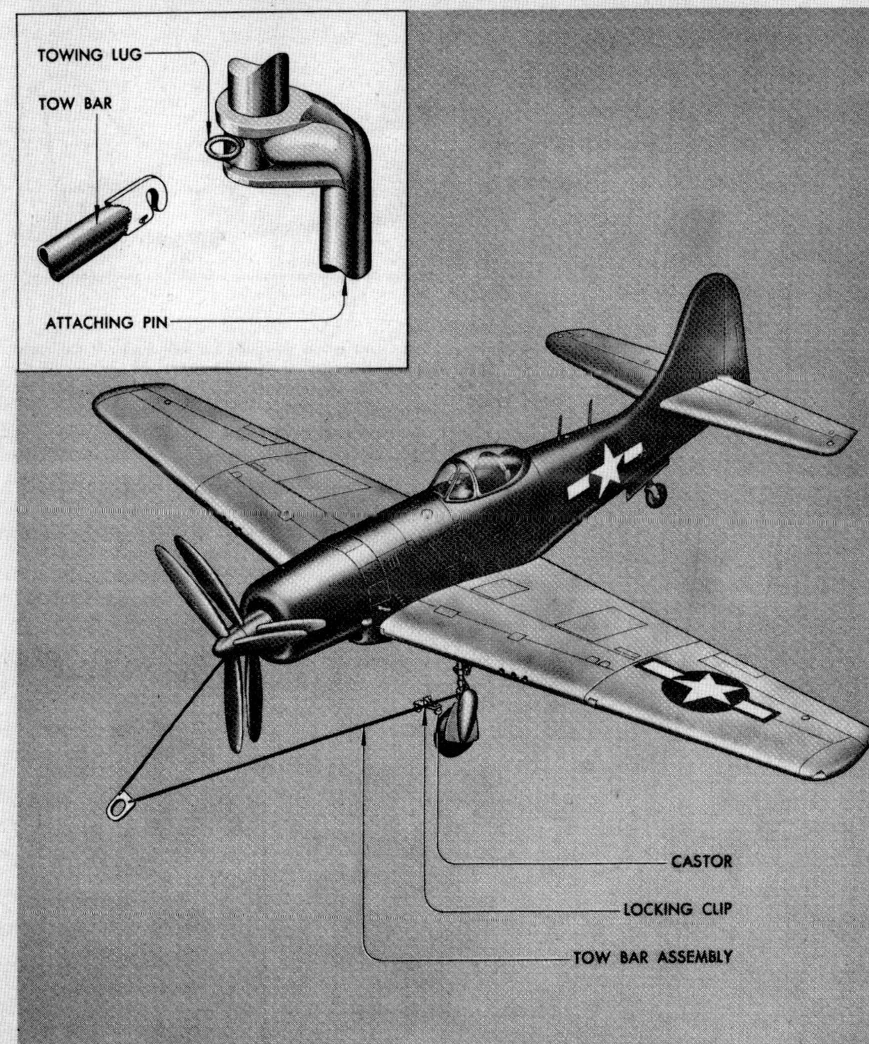

Figure 7—Towing Diagram

If the tow bar assembly is not available, use a cable. This cable must be 32 feet long. Each leg must be 16 feet long, and the towing point must be at least four feet in front of the propeller. Do not allow more than 7500 pounds pull on either leg, or more than 13,500 pounds total forward load. Do not turn the airplane by the cables only. As the tractor begins to turn, apply the brake in the direction of the turn to keep both cables taut.

To tow the airplane from the rear, use a standard

Navy tail-wheel tow bar attached through the tail wheel axle. If this tow bar is not available, use a cable. Attach the cable through the tail wheel axle or wrap it around the vertical spindle housing. Do not attach the cable to the catapult hold-back clevis; the clevis is not designed for side loads. If the cable is attached through the tail wheel axle, the maximum allowable load in any direction is 2500 pounds. If wrapped around the spindle, the load straight back must not exceed 10,000 pounds, and its side component must not exceed 2500 pounds.

CATAPULTING

This airplane has three catapult fittings (two towing hooks and a hold-back clevis). The towing hooks are bolted to the wing structure at its root. Remove the hooks if the airplane is not to be catapulted. To attach the hook, remove the access cover and bolt in place. See the catapult illustration for details.

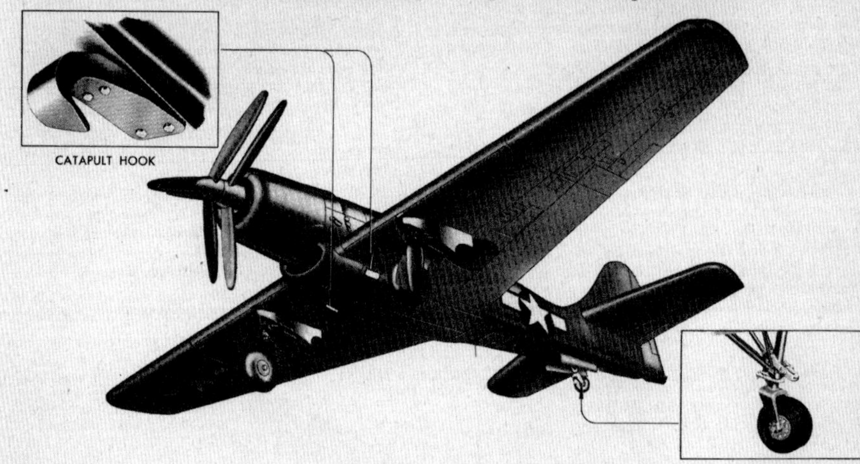

Figure 8—Catapult Fittings

TIE DOWN

There are five tie down points: one on each wing just inboard of the wing break (access to this is through the small door in the wing nose); the catapult hold-back clevis; and the towing lugs on the main landing gear. The landing gear wheel axles and struts can be used as additional tie down points.

Figure 9— Tie Down Fittings

JACKING

There are four fixed and three removable jacking cones. One fixed cone is in each wing inside of the access door, which covers the tie down rings, and one is on each main wheel axle. The removable cones are carried in the airplane tool kit. Two of them can be bolted to the catapult hook fitting brackets at the wing root, and the third to a bracket just forward of the tail-wheel well. Use the hoisting ring in the dorsal fin (under a cover) for raising the tail if the jacks don't give enough height.

In emergency jack along the wing spar to a point one foot beyond the wing break. If jacks are used along the spar, place the jacks carefully to prevent slipping. Remember, when using this method, the CG, with the power pack installed, is forward of the spar and so the third jacking point must be on the propeller shaft or some other point on the engine or mount. If the propeller shaft is used, protect it with felt, fibre, or other soft material and keep the bearing point as close to the thrust nut as possible.

Jacking Precautions—

1. Never support airplane at the wing leading edge cones unless all four main fuel tank cell access doors are installed with the attaching screws tight, and the fuel cell fitting access door (in the wing rib at station 175) is installed and secured.
2. Always jack the airplane on the catapult bracket cones before removing the inboard fuel cell access doors.
3. If the airplane is resting on the tail wheel or the tail jacking cone, or if the rear end is hanging by the body tail hook, the forward support must be at or aft of the main landing gear. Otherwise the space between supports will be too great.
4. When jacking along the wing spar, always use a protective pad or plank to prevent skin damage and slipping.

Figure 10—Jacking

Figure 11—Leveling

LEVELING

There are three plainly marked lugs in the aft end of the bomb bay for use in leveling the airplane.

HOISTING

Two slings are furnished with the airplane. The Boeing F12200 sling is used to hoist the whole airplane with outboard wing folded or extended. This includes the airplane complete with equipment as a fighter or fighter bomber, or in ferry condition. The Boeing F12221 sling is used to hoist the power pack only. This includes the engine and accessories unit minus propeller. (See illustrations "Hoisting" and "Hoisting Details").

Hoisting Whole Airplane—Attach sling Boeing F12200 as follows:

1. To attach sling to rear attachment points at body station 215.4, remove the sling attachment access door in the side of the airplane. (See illustrations, "Hoisting" and "Hoisting Details"). When the sling is about in position, push each tube into the body so as to engage the slotted end of the tube with the pin in the body. Turn the tube clockwise to lock.
2. To attach the sling at the forward attachment points (body station 172.5), remove the access door in the cowling and attach each cable terminal to its lug on the engine mount with the attached self locking pin.

Hoisting Power Pack — Attach sling (Boeing F12221) as follows:

1. To attach sling to rear attachment points at station 172.5, remove the two lower cowl panels forward of that station, and the upper ring cowl panel. Attach the sling cables to the lugs with the self-locking pins.
2. Attach the sling at its forward point, slide the hoisting sling ring over propeller shaft as far as it will go.

Manual Scan: National Archives, RG 287

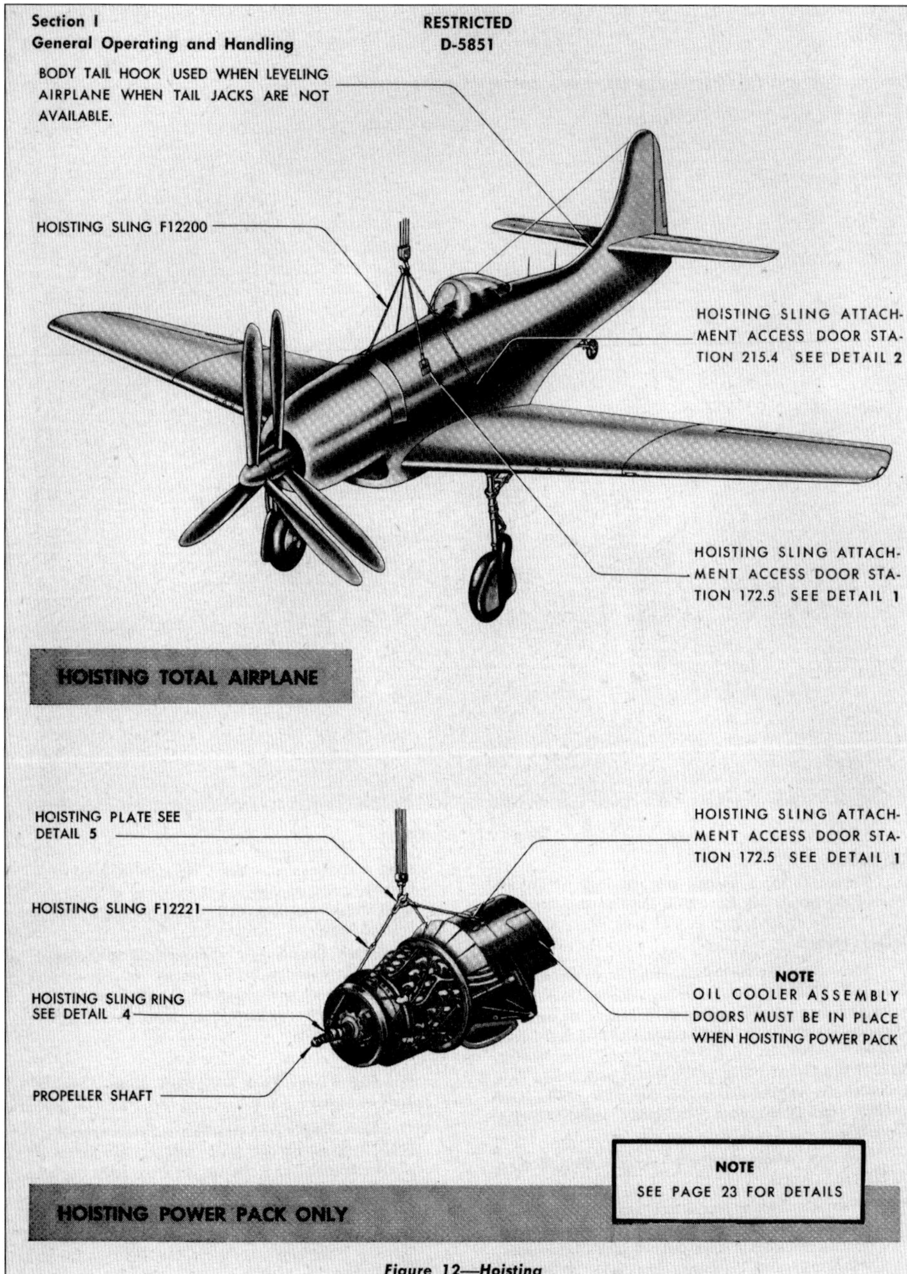

Figure 12—Hoisting

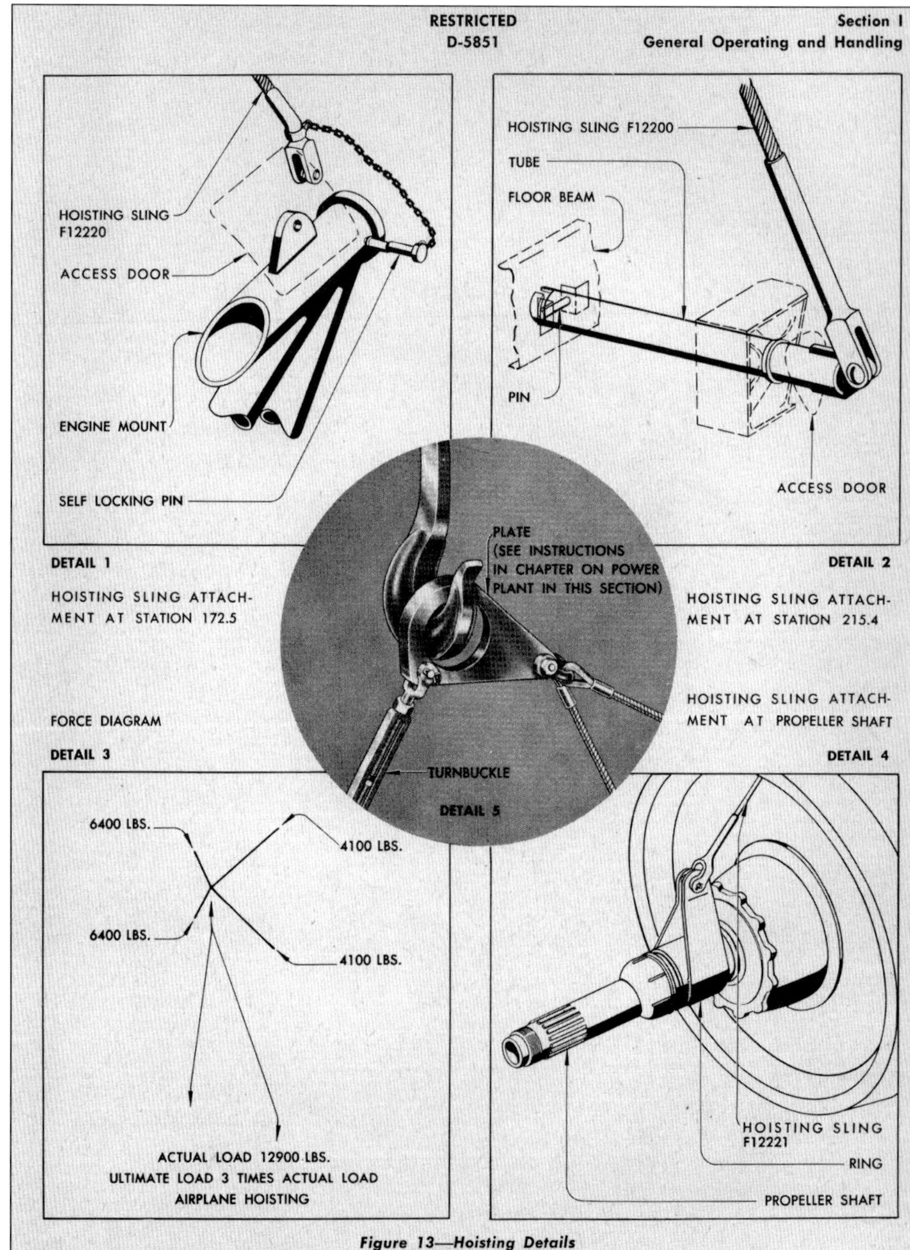

Figure 13—Hoisting Details

RESTRICTED
D-5851

Section II
Inspection Guide

RESTRICTED
D-5851

Section II
Replenishing

Figure 15—Replenishing

Section II
Lubrication

RESTRICTED
D-5851

LUBRICATION PERIODS			LUBRICATION INSTRUCTIONS
PARTS		LOCATION	
30 HOURS ○			1. DOOR HINGES AND LATCHES, CONTROL LOCK PINS, PIANO HINGES, ETC—LUBRICATE WITH AIRCRAFT INSTRUMENT OIL, SPEC. AN-O-6.
1	PIANO HINGES	ALL TRIM TABS AND OUTBOARD SECTION OF WING FLAP.	2. ZERK FITTINGS—USE SPEC. AN-G-3 LOW TEMPERATURE GREASE.
1	RUDDER, ELEVATOR AND AILERON LOCK PINS. (DO NOT LUBRICATE ENGAGING PINS)		3. RETRACTING SCREWS—USE SPEC. AN-G-10 LOW TEMPERATURE GREASE IN MAIN LANDING GEAR, COWL FLAPS AND SPEC. AN-G-3 IN ALL OTHER RETRACTING SCREWS.
1	WING LOCK PIN AND ENGAGING FITTINGS	WING BREAK	
1	LATCHES, SLIDING JOINTS, LINKAGES, ETC.		
3	RETRACTING SCREWS	MAIN LANDING GEAR AND WING FLAPS.	4. GEAR BOXES—USE SPEC AN-G-3, LOW TEMPERATURE GREASE, FLUSH AND FILL TO 1/3 CAPACITY. USE AN-G-10 GREASE IN COWL FLAP GEAR BOXES AND POWER UNIT.
240 HOURS △			
2	ZERK FITTINGS		5. WHEEL BEARINGS—USE SPEC. 3560 MEDIUM, HIGH MELTING POINT GREASE.
4	GEAR BOXES	SEE DIAGRAM	
5	WHEEL BEARINGS	MAIN AND TAIL GEAR	6. CONTROL CHAINS AND BRACKETS—USE LIGHT COAT SPEC. AN-G-3.
6	CONTROL CHAINS AND SPROCKETS.	CONTROL COLUMN AND ELEVATOR AND RUDDER TRIM TABS.	7. FLEXIBLE SHAFTING—USE A LIGHT COAT SPEC. AN-G-3, LOW TEMPERATURE GREASE.
480 HOURS □			8. ENCASED UNIVERSAL—USE AN-G-3, LOW TEMPERATURE GREASE. FILL TO 1/3 CAPACITY.
2	ZERK FITTINGS	OIL COOLER FLAP DOOR AND INTERCOOLER OUTLET DOOR ACTUATORS.	
3	RETRACTING SCREWS	RUDDER, ELEVATOR AND AILERON TAB SCREWS AND COWL FLAPS.	9. CONTROL CABLES—IF ON INSPECTION LUBRICATION APPEARS NECESSARY, APPLY A LIGHT COAT OF LOW TEMPERATURE GREASE SPEC. AN-G-3 AT THE FAIRLEADS, PULLEYS AND GROMMETS.
7	FLEXIBLE SHAFTING		
8	ENCASED UNIVERSALS		
9	CONTROL CABLES		

RESTRICTED
D-5851

Section II
Lubrication

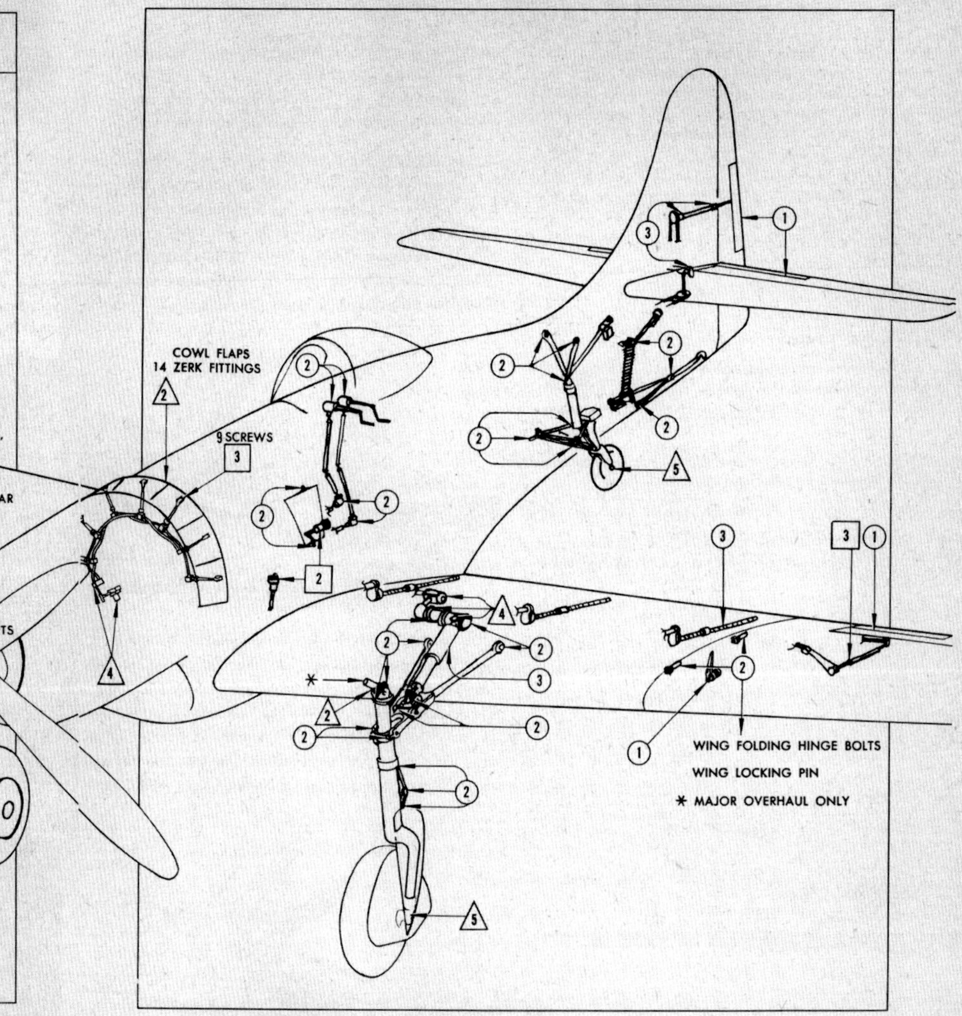

LUBRICATION CHART

CLEANING

Clean the airplane regularly to maintain airworthiness and responsiveness to controls, to eliminate fire hazard, to prevent corrosion, and to make inspection easier. Where extreme conditions exist, daily cleaning may be necessary; but washing just for looks is not advisable.

Precautions—

Before cleaning, take these following precautions to eliminate danger from fire and poisonous cleaning materials:

1. Have adequate fire fighting equipment handy.
2. Store inflammable solvents in small safety type containers, covered when not in use.
3. Do not allow smoking, open flames, or operation of any electrical equipment that may give off sparks, near the cleaning area; post conspicuous warning signs.
4. Ground the airplane thoroughly while cleaning it; to eliminate collection of static charges.
5. Avoid wearing shoes with exposed nailheads or iron cleats. These may cause sparks.
6. Dry all electrical parts thoroughly before they are used.
7. Use gloves or protective hand cream.
8. Avoid breathing the fumes from any cleaning agent. Keep to windward as much as possible.
9. Remove the battery from the airplane.

Body, Wing and Tail Surfaces—Use a mixture of one part aircraft cleaning compound, Specification No. 20015 and six parts cleaning solvent or kerosene. Spray it on at about 70 pounds pressure, using a pressure spray tank with petroleum resistant spray lines. Use a coarse spray. A fine spray is less effective, increases health hazards, and wastes the mixture. Ten minutes after spraying the airplane, hose it off with clear water. Water pressure of 80 to 120 pounds is desirable; an ordinary garden hose and nozzle can be used. For complete emulsification and removal of the dirt and grease, use plenty of water for "hosing down." Obstinate spots may require another application of the mixture, sprayed on after the surface has dried.

In freezing temperatures, where the airplane must be cleaned indoors, use a light duty cleaner (one part aircraft cleaning compound, Specification No. 20015 and twenty parts water) hosing it off with water after 5 or 10 minutes. This mixture is less effective than solvent, especially on engines, effectiveness being sacrificed in this case to prevent fire hazard.

Engine—The engine is ordinarily cleaned at 60-hour inspections. Between 60-hour inspection periods, clean it only if enough oil has accumulated to cause a fire hazard. Spray on one part aircraft cleaning compound, Specification No. 20015 with six parts of cleaning solvent or kerosene, allow the solution to soak ten or fifteen minutes, and wash the engine with water.

Propeller—Clean the propeller with soap and fresh water, or kerosene, using clean rags. After cleaning, coat the spinner and blades with corrosion preventive compound, Specification No. AN-C-52. If no compound is available, use engine oil.

Landing Gear—Use the same method as on the body and wings. *Do not use carbon tetrachloride.* Remove any obstinate deposits of grease with a rag moistened with aircraft cleaner mix. Clean cylinders with a rag moistened in hydraulic fluid, Specification No. AN-VV-O-366.

Winter Cleaning (—5°F and below)—To remove frost or ice from airplane surface, melt it off with a portable ground heater. Be careful not to overheat the surface, and melt only a small area at a time, wiping with a clean dry cloth. *Never* use hot water or alcohol.

Canopy—The sheet plastic material in the canopy is comparatively soft, and its transparency will be impaired by careless cleaning. Follow the cleaning procedure carefully to prevent any necessity for subsequent polishing. Once the original luster is lost as a result of buffing and polishing, it cannot be restored. For this reason, leave all minor scratches alone.

Before cleaning, flush the canopy thoroughly with fresh water to wash away any crystallized salt particles. If you do not do this, the salt particles may scratch the plastic.

After flushing, apply mild soap (Ivory or equivalent) and water to the plastic with bare hands. (A clean, grit-free cloth, chamois, or absorbent cotton may be used, but are generally less satisfactory.) Rinse with fresh water and dry with absorbent cotton or a damp chamois. Do not use a dry cloth, which may cause scratches and also builds a static charge that will attract dust particles.

Remove oily or greasy dirt from the canopy with kerosene, naptha, hexane, or, in the absence of these, with unleaded gasoline. *(Do not use aromatic fuel.)* Apply the cleaning agent with clean absorbent cotton. If there is considerable dirt and grease on the canopy, it may be necessary to follow this cleaning with a wash as described above. After cleaning, the application of a suitable wax is recommended to cover minor scratches, to give a good gloss to the surface and to help prevent further scratches. The following waxes have proved satisfactory:

3-M Automotive wax — Minnesota Mining and Manufacturing Company, St. Paul, Minnesota.

Simoniz wax (Not Kleener).

Wilco plastic polish—Wilco Company, Los Angeles, California.

Johnson's paste wax—S. C. Johnson and Sons, Incorporated, Racine, Wisconsin.

Any static charge caused by the waxing may be removed with a damp, clean chamois.

Do not use acetone, benezene, lacquer thinner, toluene, ethyl acetate, ordinary kitchen cleaners or commercial window cleaning sprays for cleaning the canopy. They will ruin the plastic and cause the surface to craze.

If there is ice on the canopy, melt it off. Brushing or scraping will ruin the plastic.

RESTRICTED
D-5851

Section III
Structure

STRUCTURE

The structure (airframe) of this airplane is of aluminum alloy construction with flush riveting and some spot welding on exterior skin surfaces. Its design provides for quick and efficient replacement of all major components.

For the purposes of this chapter, the structure is divided into three groups: Body Group, Wing Group, and Tail Group.

Special tools used in erecting the airframe are furnished in the airplane tool kit. Refer to the chapter on Miscellaneous Equipment for illustration and use of these tools.

All wing-folding information is given under Wing Group as the mechanism will be installed during erection of the wing.

Structure forward of station 212 bulkhead (firewall) is covered in the chapter on Quick Engine Change Unit.

The weights shown in the Airplane Breakdown illustration will aid the personnel in handling the component parts.

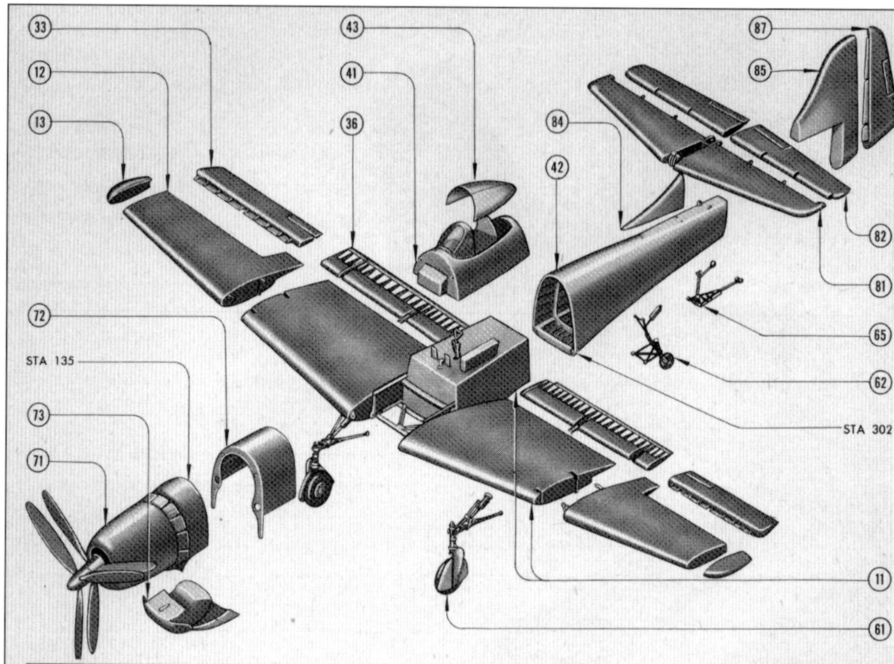

*SECTION	NAME	BOEING DRAWING	**WEIGHT
11	INBOARD WING & BOMB BAY	15-15914	3809 LB
12	OUTER WING SECTION	15-15915	365 LB
13	WING TIP	14-4450	(1) 8 LB
33	AILERON	8-3648	(1) 70 LB
36	FLAPS	8-3649	(2) 121 LB
41	COCKPIT SECTION	15-12288	636 LB
42	BODY TAIL SECTION	15-14292	560 LB
43	COCKPIT ENCLOSURE	15-15260	55 LB
61	MAIN LANDING GEAR	15-14302	(2) 910 LB
62	TAIL GEAR	15-15261	107 LB
65	ARRESTING HOOK	15-15917	63 LB
71	FORWARD POWER SECTION	15-14299	4584 LB
72	REAR ACCESSORY SECTION	15-15240	550 LB
73	SCOOP	12-1630	85.5 LB
81	HORIZONTAL STABILIZER	8-3650	246 LB
82	ELEVATORS	8-3651	(2) 97 LB
84	DORSAL FIN	12-1641	10 LB
85	VERTICAL FIN	8-3652	98 LB
87	RUDDER	8-3653	78 LB

* CORRESPONDS TO BOEING PRODUCTION CODE, NOT ORDER OF INSTALLATION.
** WITH ALL EQUIPMENT INSTALLED

Figure 17—Airplane Breakdown

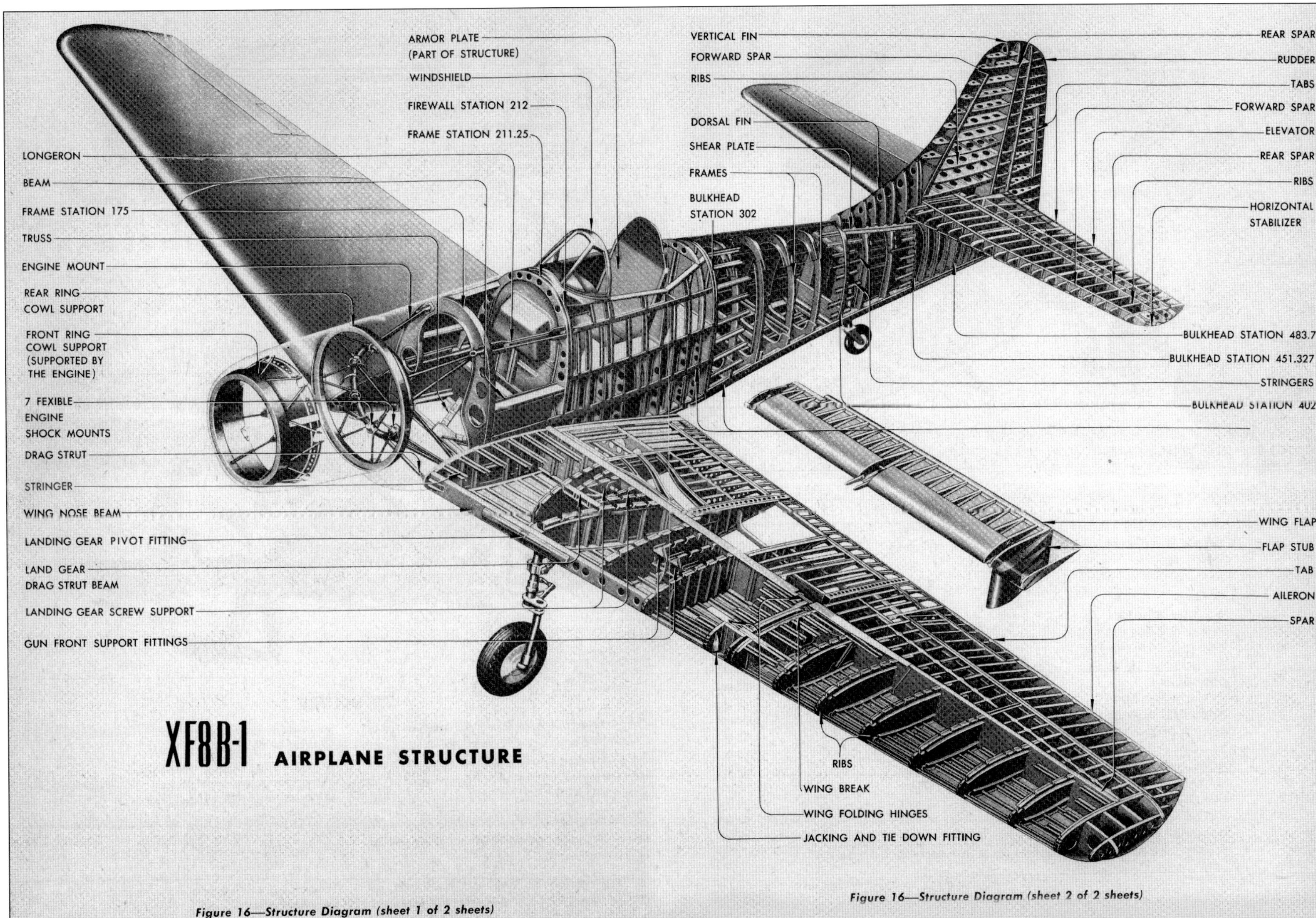

Figure 16—Structure Diagram (sheet 1 of 2 sheets)

Figure 16—Structure Diagram (sheet 2 of 2 sheets)

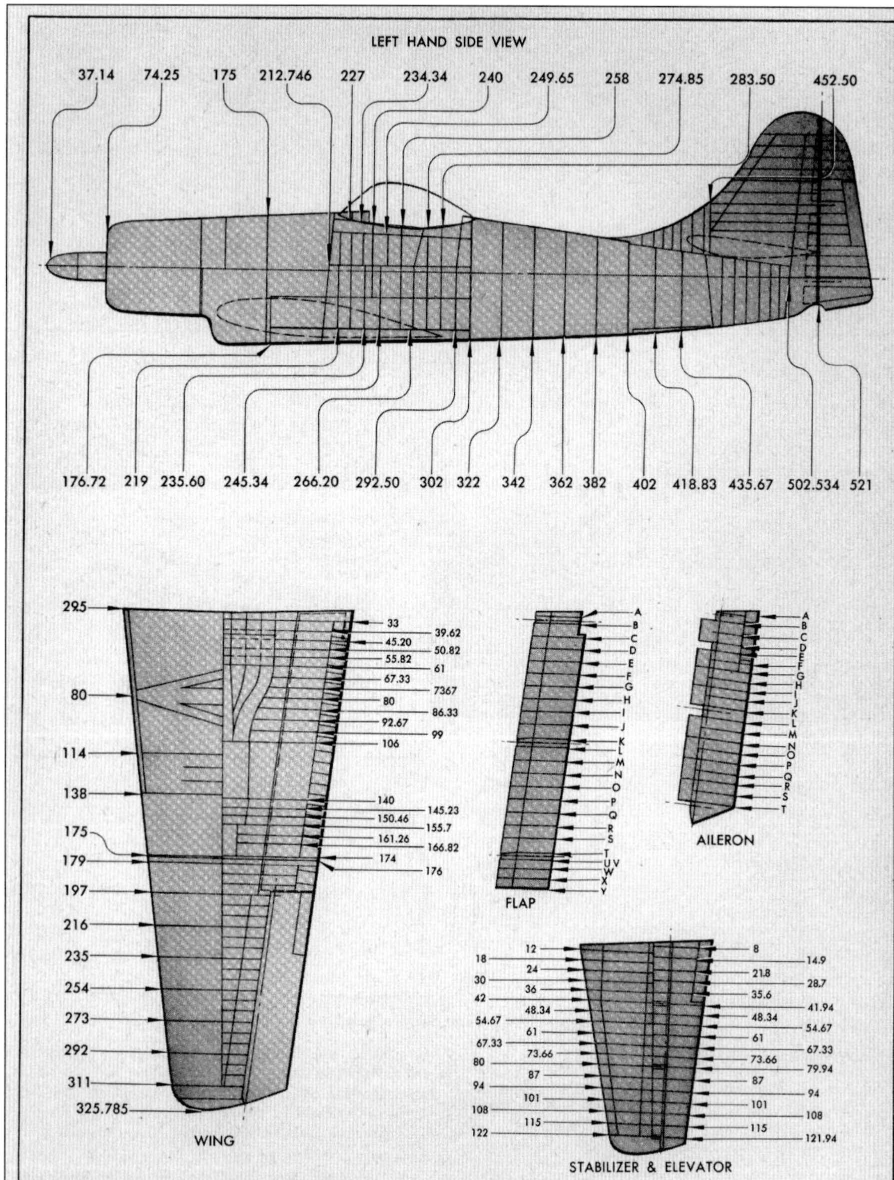

Figure 18—Station Diagram

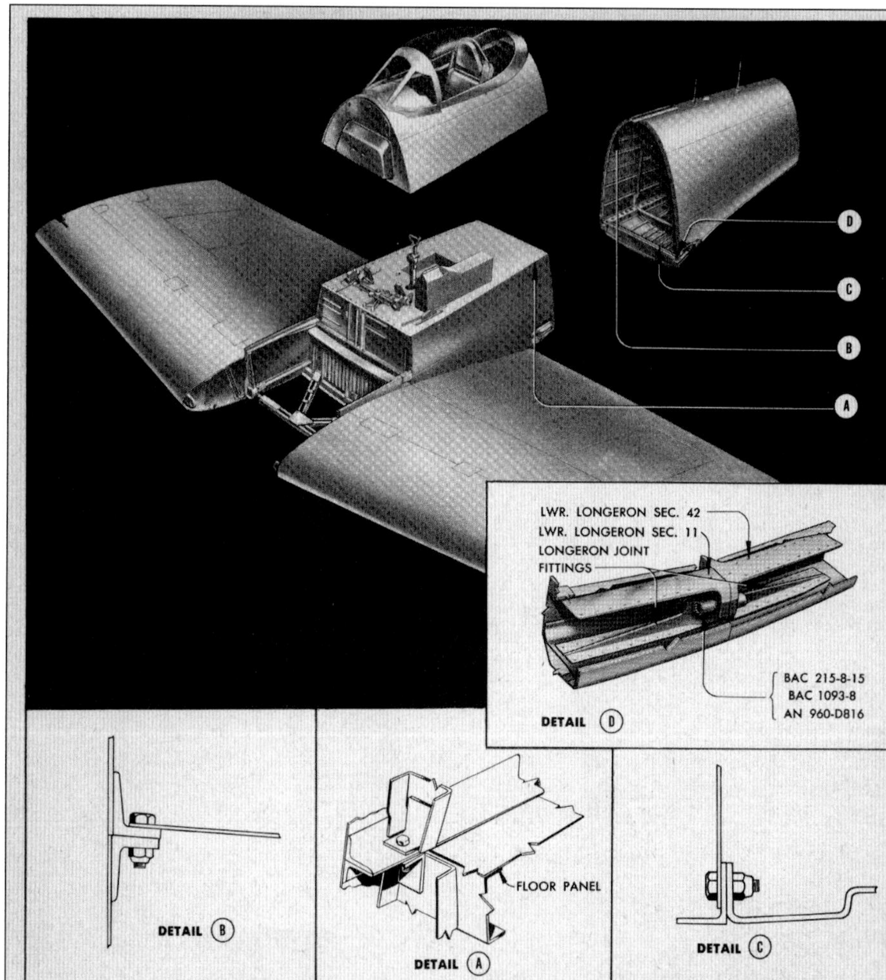

Figure 19—Cockpit Section Removed

BODY GROUP

The components of the body group are the cockpit (including canopy and windshield) and the body tail section. The bomb bay is considered part of the inboard wing section because the wing spar runs through the body and forms the lower part of the forward bomb bay bulkhead.

Major structural members of the body are the two longerons, the channel-type circumferential frames, the bulkheads, and stressed skin. The two longerons are extended along the bottom corners of the body from the firewall to the last body bulkhead. Hat-and-Z-section stringers stiffen the skin longitudinally.

The Body Group Connections illustration shows the way these body sections fit together, and gives the torque settings of the longeron bolts.

Control Stands and Panels— The left-and right-hand control stands, sidewall panels and the two instrument panels in the cockpit section have each been designed as removable units. All wiring, instruments, control levers, cables, push-rods and switches can be mounted in the metal frames of the stands and panels at the bench and each unit can then be placed in the cockpit as a compact installation.

Removal and installation of the two instrument panels are covered in the chapter on instruments in this section. Each control stand or sidewall panel can be removed as a unit or the individual controls on them can be taken out separately. There are no set procedures, but the following lists of steps will be useful.

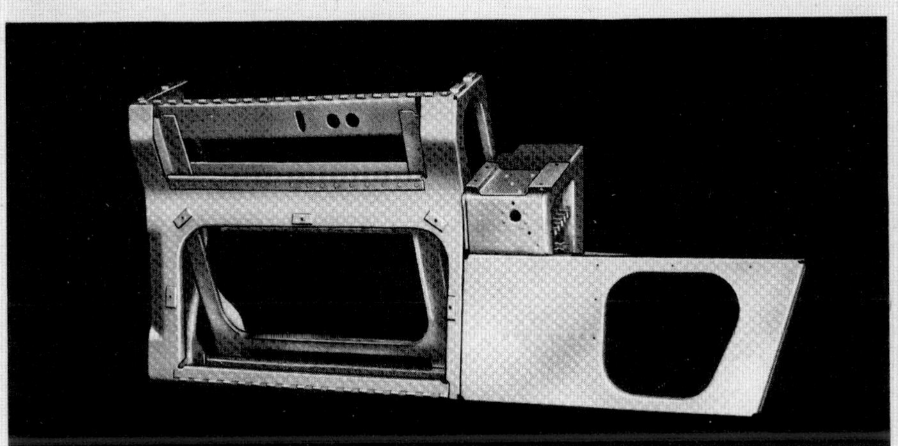

Figure 20—R.H. Control Stand Frame

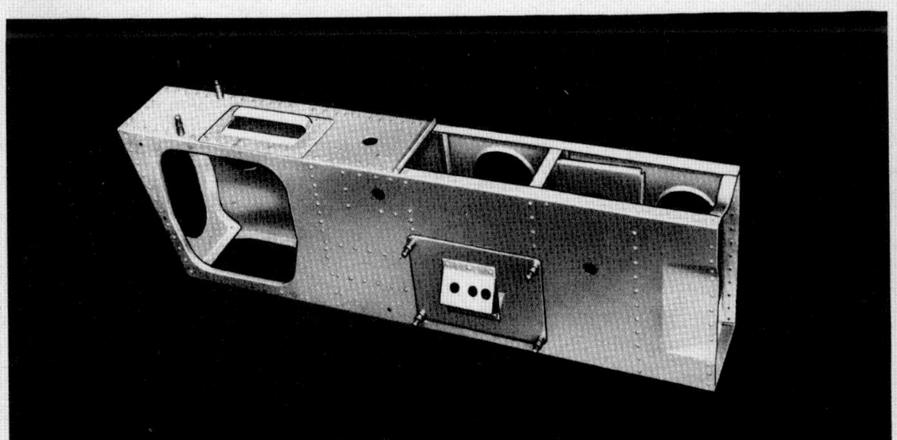

Figure 21—L.H. Control Stand Frame

1 SET LANDING GEAR CONTROL LEVER AT UP AND REMOVE CONTROL LEVER PANEL; DISCONNECT CABLE.
2 DISCONNECT ELECTRIC PLUG AT FORWARD END OF BOMB-INDICATOR-AND-WING-FLAP PANEL. REMOVE PANEL.
3 LOOSEN CABLE AT EXTERNAL TANK RACK, UNSCREW EXTERNAL TANK RELEASE BRACKET AND LIFT IT CLEAR OF STAND; THE PULL HANDLES PREVENT ITS COMPLETE REMOVAL.
4 DETACH OXYGEN LINE FROM DEMAND-AND-DILUTER VALVE. DISCONNECT TUBE FROM OXYGEN CYLINDER CHECK VALVE.

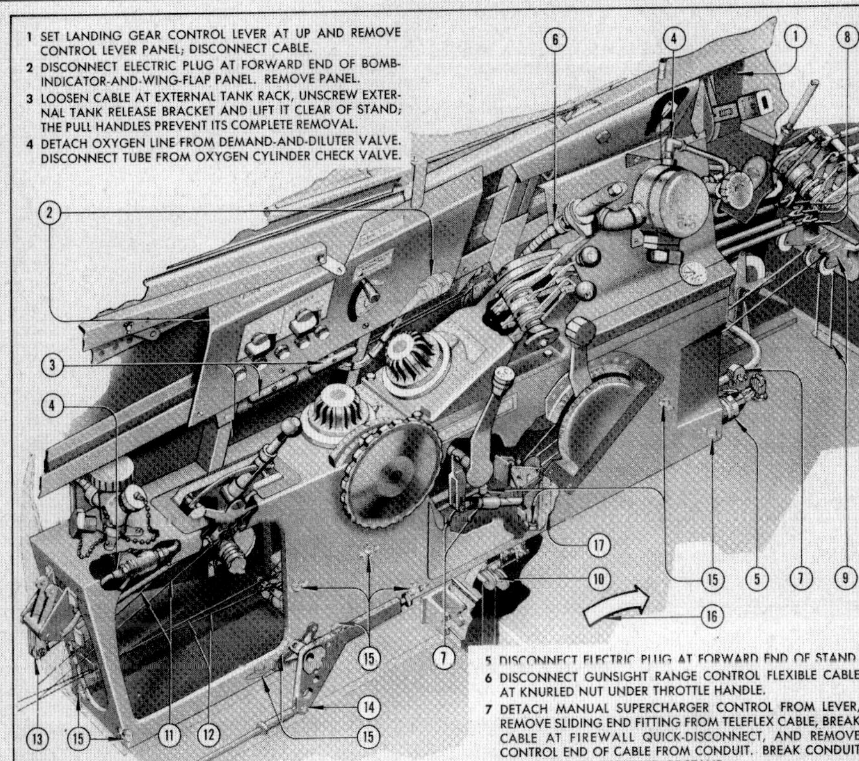

5 DISCONNECT ELECTRIC PLUG AT FORWARD END OF STAND.
6 DISCONNECT GUNSIGHT RANGE CONTROL FLEXIBLE CABLE AT KNURLED NUT UNDER THROTTLE HANDLE.
7 DETACH MANUAL SUPERCHARGER CONTROL FROM LEVER, REMOVE SLIDING END FITTING FROM TELEFLEX CABLE, BREAK CABLE AT FIREWALL QUICK-DISCONNECT, AND REMOVE CONTROL END OF CABLE FROM CONDUIT. BREAK CONDUIT AT CONNECTOR FORWARD OF STAND.
8 DISCONNECT ENGINE CONTROL RODS FROM BRACKET.
9 BIND AILERON TAB CABLES AT DRUM, DISCONNECT CABLES ABOVE DRUM, REMOVE PRESSURE SEALS FROM FLOOR, REMOVE PULLEYS; PULL CABLES INTO STAND.
10 DISCONNECT TANK SELECTOR CABLES AT TURNBUCKLES ON L. H. SIDE OF BOMB BAY AND REMOVE PULLEYS.
11 DETACH ELEVATOR TAB TURNBUCKLES IN RADIO COMPARTMENT, FAIR-LEAD IN RADIO COMPARTMENT FORWARD BULKHEAD, PULLEYS FORWARD OF FAIRLEAD, AND PRESSURE SEALS ABOVE FLOOR JUST AFT OF CONTROL STAND; PULL CABLES INTO STAND.
12 DETACH RUDDER TAB TURNBUCKLES IN RADIO COMPARTMENT, PULLEYS FORWARD OF TURNBUCKLES, AND PRESSURE SEALS ON BULKHEAD; PULL CABLES INTO STAND.
13 DISCONNECT SALVO AND BOMB DOOR RELEASE AT BRACKET AT AFT END OF STAND.
14 DISCONNECT TAIL WHEEL LOCK.
15 REMOVE CONTROL STAND ATTACHING SCREWS.
16 LIFT STAND SLIGHTLY FORWARD TO CLEAR SALVO AND BOMB RELEASE ROD WHEN IT IS DRAWN THROUGH SPLASH PLATE, WITH FORWARD END INBOARD FOR ACCESS TO TANK-SELECTOR-CABLE PRESSURE SEAL.
17 REMOVE PRESSURE SEALS AND TANK-SELECTOR CABLES UNDER CENTER OF STAND; PULL CABLES INTO STAND.
18 LIFT CONTROL STAND FROM COCKPIT.

Figure 23—L. H. Control Stand Removal

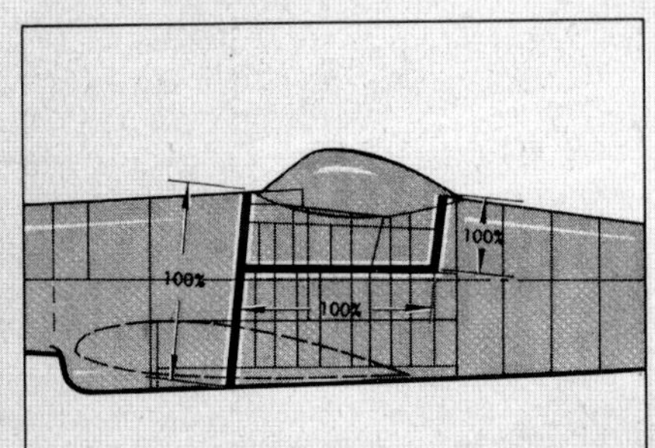

Figure 22—Cockpit Airtightness Diagram

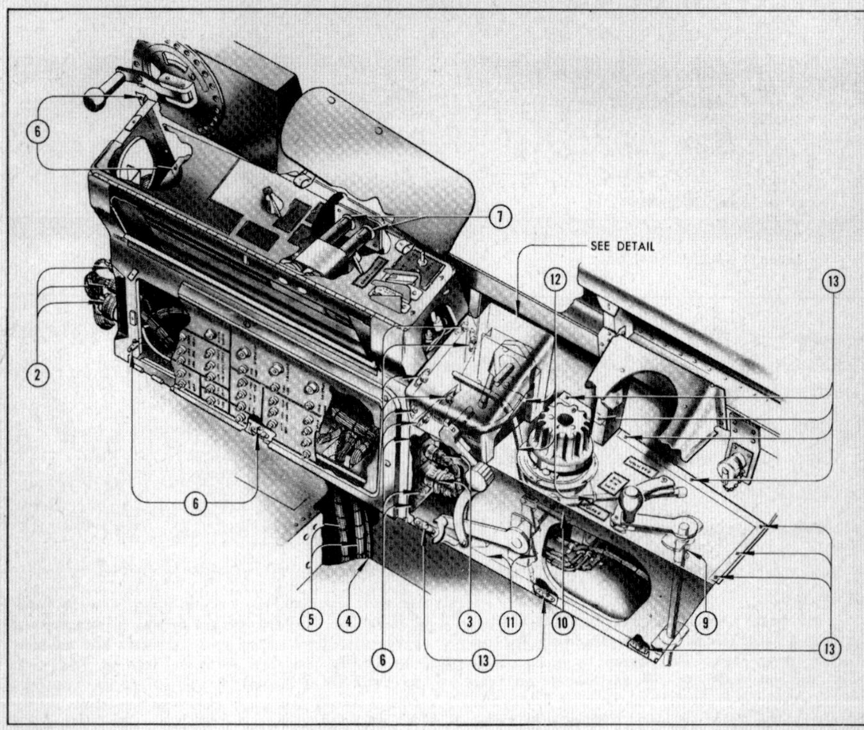

Figure 24—R. H. Control Stand Removal

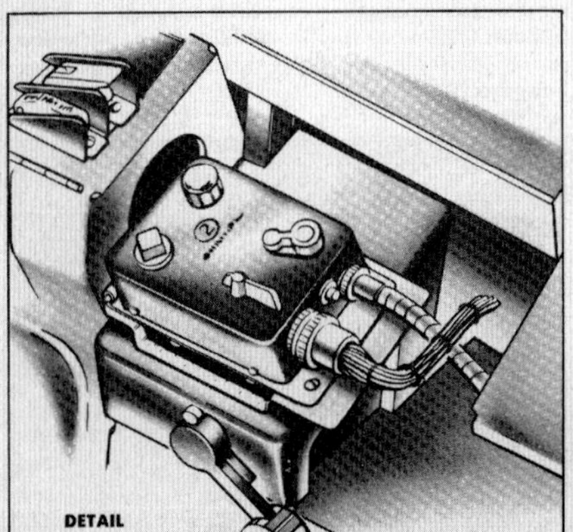

Figure 25—R. H. Control Stand Removal Detail

Removal of R. H. Control Stand (forward and rear sections)—

1. Remove the pilot's seat.
2. Disconnect electrical receptacles at front of stand.
3. Disconnect electrical receptacles at rear of front section of stand.
4. Disconnect electrical receptacle at bottom of control stand.
5. Disconnect electrical receptacles at R. H. bomb bay junction box and bracket.
6. Remove attaching screws.
7. Move stand inboard to clear emergency drives and lift from cockpit.
8. Detach radio control box.
9. Disconnect wing pin lock controls.
10. Remove cable from arresting hook control handle.
11. Disconnect wires from arresting hook actuator switches.
12. Disconnect cabin heat and vent (cold air) controls at entry nipples of teleflex units and remove teleflex cable. (See Heat and Vent System.)
13. Remove attaching screws and lift from cockpit.

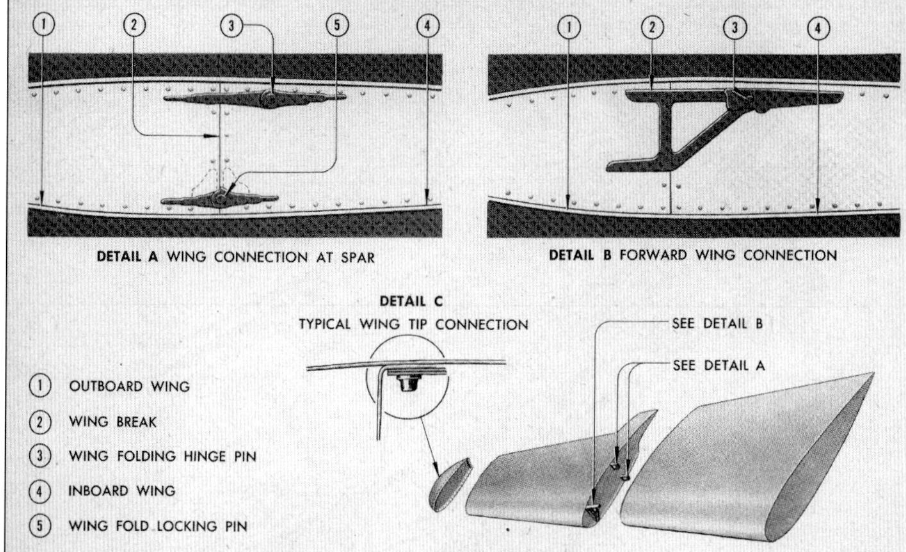

Figure 26—Wing Group

WING GROUP

The inboard wing section including the bomb bay, the two outboard sections, and the two wing tips comprise the wing group. The inboard wing houses the main fuel tank cells, guns, ammunition boxes, main landing gear when retracted and the wing flaps which, when retracted, form the lower trailing edge surface.

Structural members of the wing center section are: a single, continuous, web-type spar, the wing nose beam, ribs and skin. The heavy gage structural skin forward of the spar is reinforced by stringers. The rear wing hinge fitting is on the upper spar chord at the wing break and the locking fitting is on the lower chord. The forward hinge fitting is attached to a heavy channel stiffener in the nose. The heaviest ribs are the ones that form the landing gear well. Structure aft of the spar is light, since its main purpose is merely to support the wing flap tracks.

The outboard wing or folding panel is of similar but lighter construction. The folding hinges and lock are the only structural connections between the wing sections. The wing tip is of all-metal construction and is easily replaced, being attached by a series of bolts around the edge.

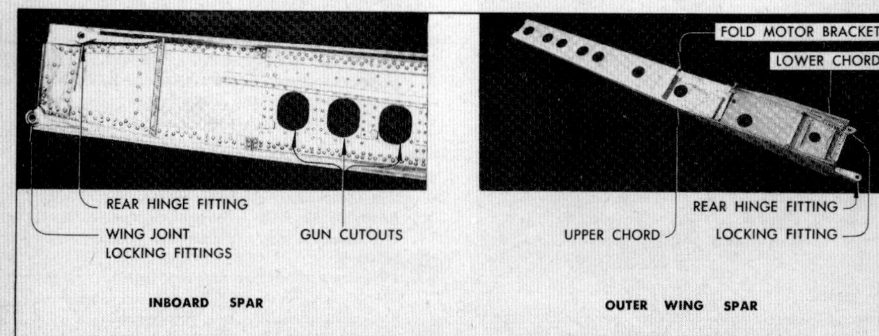

Figure 27—Wing Spar Details

Figure 28—Outboard Wing Panel Removal

Removal of Outer Wing Panel— Assuming that the wing is spread and locked and either there is no electrical power or the folding and locking motors are jammed, remove the outer wing panel as follows:

1. Open the access door in the lower surface of the wing just aft of the spar and outboard of the wing break.

2. Disconnect the electrical plugs just aft of the spar on the first rib of the outboard section (wing station 179).

3. Move the WING PIN LOCK lever in the cockpit to UNLOCK. Remove the bolt connecting the pin motor to the pin-puller arm; this allows the lock pin to be forced back, unlocking the wing joint.

4. Through the door mentioned in step 1 you can reach through a hole in the spar and take out the lockwired bolt connecting the wing-fold-motor yoke to the wing-fold lever arm assembly (the nut is held by a nut check plate). Four special steel washers will drop out when the bolt is removed.

5. Place surface controls in neutral and lock them. Disconnect the aileron control rod from the quadrant. The disconnection can be made either through the quadrant access door just inboard of the wing break in the wing's lower surface aft of the spar, or through the spring loaded hinge access door in the upper surface at the break. The latter door is latched when the wing is fully spread. To open the door, fold the wing just enough to release the latch, then hold the door open, lower the wing, and release the cable from the spring. Tape or wind the aileron trim tab cables (left wing only) on the drums in the bomb bay and outboard wing section to prevent unwinding; then disconnect these cables at the turnbuckles aft of the spar in the wheel well. Secure the inboard ends of the cables to the structure, remove the cable stop block in the wheel well and all cable guide pulleys. Pull the outboard cable ends out through the wing break.

6. Disconnect the aileron bus cables at the quadrant in the outboard wing section and remove the four cable pulleys in that section and pull the cables inboard, coil and tape them to the structure of the inboard section.

7. To reach the forward hinge bolt (pin), fold the wing manually and install the jury strut.

8. To reach the head of the forward hinge bolt, remove the door in rib station 175, just aft of the hinge (this door must not be removed if the airplane is resting on jacks at the leading edge cones). The self-locking nut is reached through the wing leading edge jacking cone access door. You will need 15/16-inch wrenches to remove this bolt.

9. Spread the wing and place cradle supports under the outboard section, then remove the rear hinge bolt through the hinge access door in the top surface. The head of the hinge bolt (on aft side of spar) is held by a check plate, which is fastened to the structure by two bolts. Remove this plate and use a 1 7/16-inch wrench to unscrew the bolt. The nut is held from moving or turning by a special nut check plate and as the bolt is unscrewed, it is forced aft. When the nut is free, the bolt can be pulled out to free the outer wing section. If proper equipment is available, the wing can be left folded and the outer panel supported with a hoist and straps. Remove the hinge bolts as described above and hoist outer section away after it is free. If this method is used, place straps in such a way as to protect trailing edge structure from damage (section weighs about 400 lbs.).

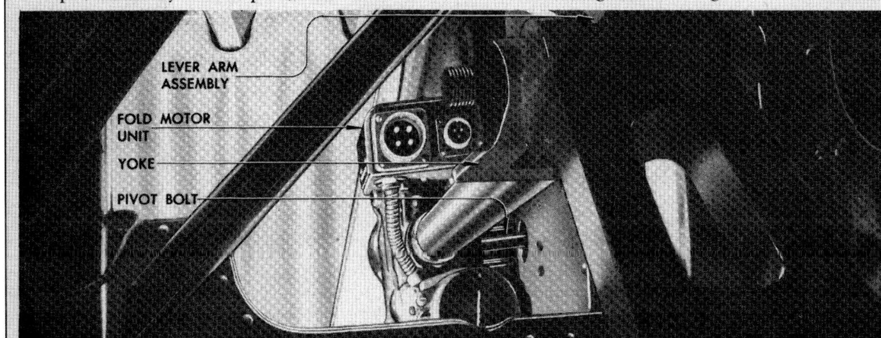

Figure 29—Wing Folding and Locking Mechanism—Looking Outboard

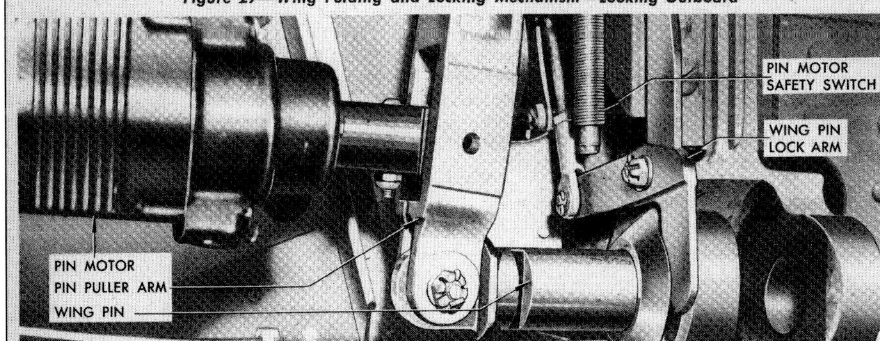

Figure 30—Wing Folding and Locking Mechanism—End View

Wing Folding and Locking Mechanism— The outboard wings fold, spread, and lock electrically. The folding and spreading mechanism is powered by a Lear Avia actuator unit, consisting of the wing-fold motor and jackscrew mounted to a bracket on the forward side of the spar in each outboard wing section. The inboard (yoke) end of the jackscrew is attached to a lever arm on the end of the inboard wing section. When the screw extends, it forces the outer wing section to swing upward about the wing hinge points; retraction of the jackscrew spreads the wings.

The wing is locked in the spread position by a lock pin inserted in the wing-joint lock fittings by another, smaller, Lear Avia actuator unit (consisting of the wing-pin motor and jackscrew), mounted aft of the lock fittings in each inboard wing section at the break. A little arm, cable controlled from the cockpit, locks the wing lock pin in the fittings.

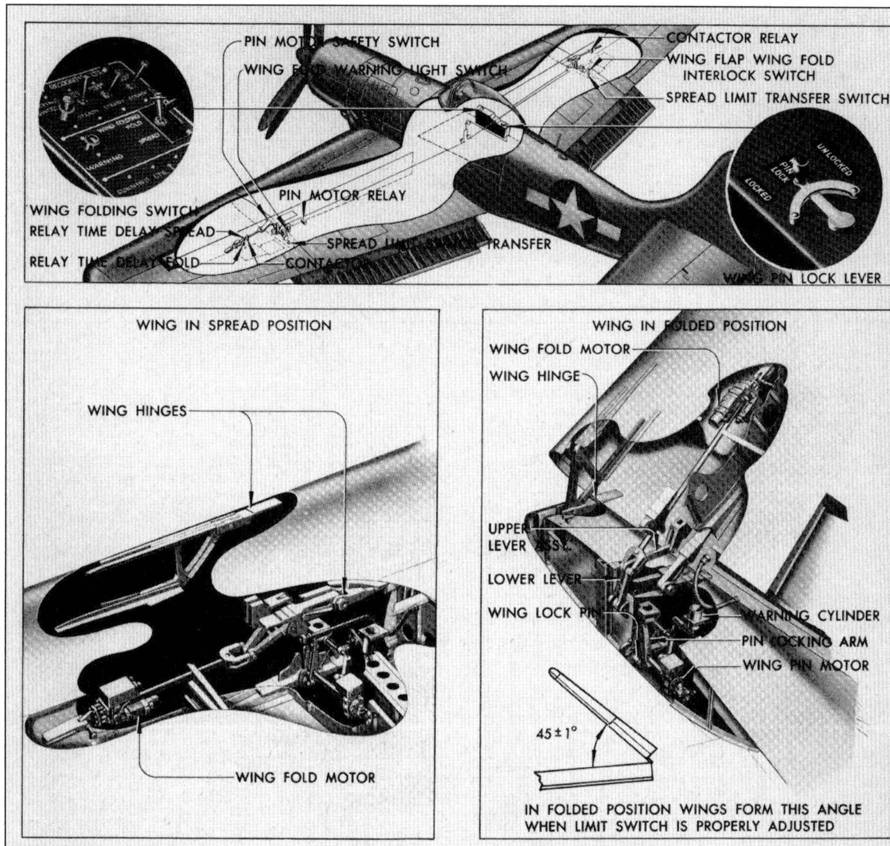

Figure 31—Wing Folding Diagram

Wing Folding and Locking Control System— This system is one of the most complicated in the airplane because of its safety features. Location of the following system units is shown on the Wing Folding and Locking Control System Diagram:

1. The WING FOLDING switch with the red warning light beside it.
2. The WING PIN LOCK lever.
3. Two wing-fold motor time-delay relays (one for folding and one for spreading).
4. Two wing-fold motor contactor relays.
5. Two wing spread limit-transfer switches.
6. A wing-pin relay and two switches (the wing fold warning-light switch and the pin-motor safety switch).
7. The wing lock-pin and motor.
8. The wing-fold motor.
9. The wing-fold and wing-flap interlock switch, which prevents the wing flap and wing fold motors from operating at the same time.

There is also a safety switch (squat switch) on the right-hand main gear shock strut, actuated by the torsion link, to prevent the wings from being folded or spread unless the weight of the airplane is on the landing gear.

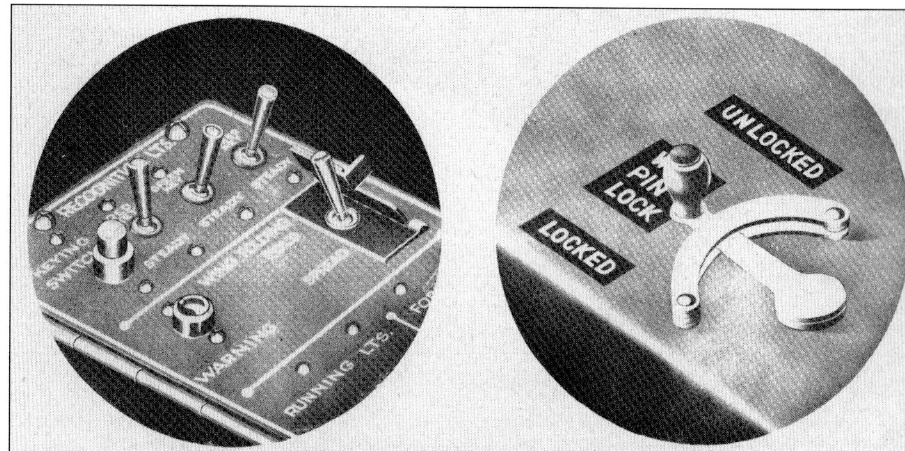

Figure 33A—Wing Folding Procedure Details

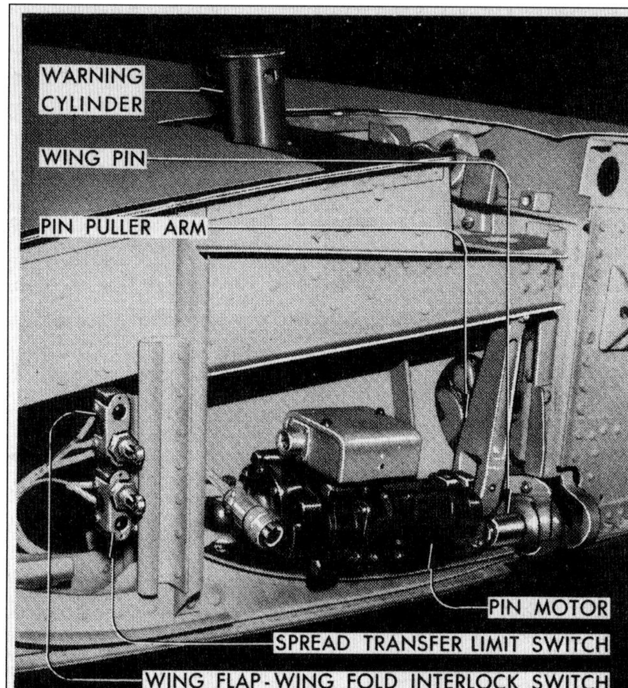

Figure 36—Wing Pin Motor

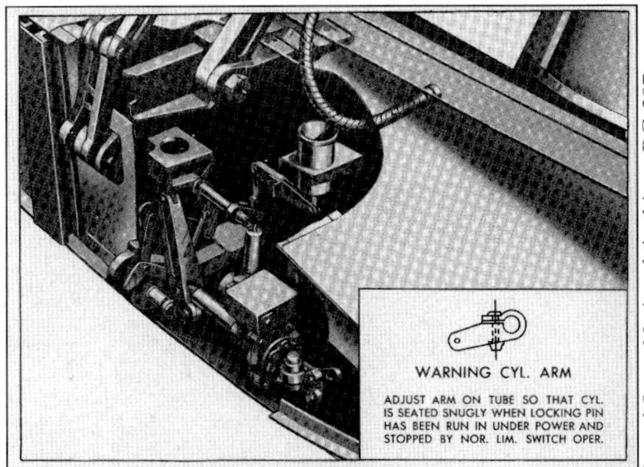

Figure 40—Lock Control Mechanism

Figure 41—Installation of Wing-Fold Switches at Right-Hand Wing Break

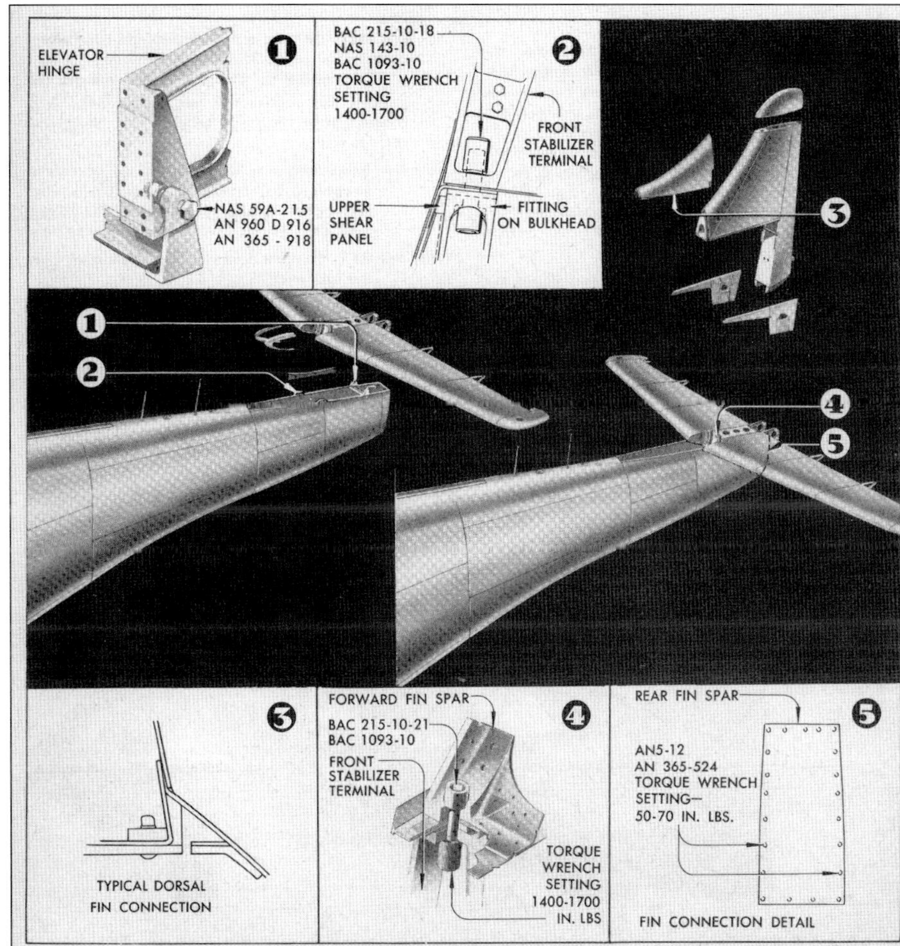

Figure 46—Tail Group Installation

FLIGHT CONTROLS AND SURFACES

SURFACE CONTROL SYSTEMS

The primary flight control surfaces are operated by the two conventional fighter type cockpit controls, rudder pedals and control column or stick. The surfaces, for ease of operation, are balanced statically by weights and aerodynamically by booster and balance tabs and air sealing strips. The ailerons each have two tabs, the outboard being link (or automatic balance) tabs, the inboard are spring (booster) tabs operated through the aileron control linkage. The left-hand link tab is also a trim tab operated from the cockpit. Elevator and rudder tabs are link (balance) tabs as well as trim tabs controlled from the cockpit.

Other flight controls discussed in this chapter are the electrically operated Fowler-type Wing Flaps, the electric Emergency-Dive Flaps, and the Control Surface and Throttle-Lock systems.

CONTROL COLUMN

The control column is located on the body center line in the cockpit. It consists of a tubular column and base assembly with a head assembly mounted on top. Fore and aft movement of the column is transmitted to the elevator torque tube, mounted below the pilot's floor, forward of the control column, by a link arm. The column itself has no side movement, but the head assembly has a lever arm which pivots from side to side for aileron control. Gears and a sprocket in the head transmit this movement through a chain and cable system to the ailerons. The aileron control lever has a standard fighter type pistol grip with bomb release button and gun trigger built in.

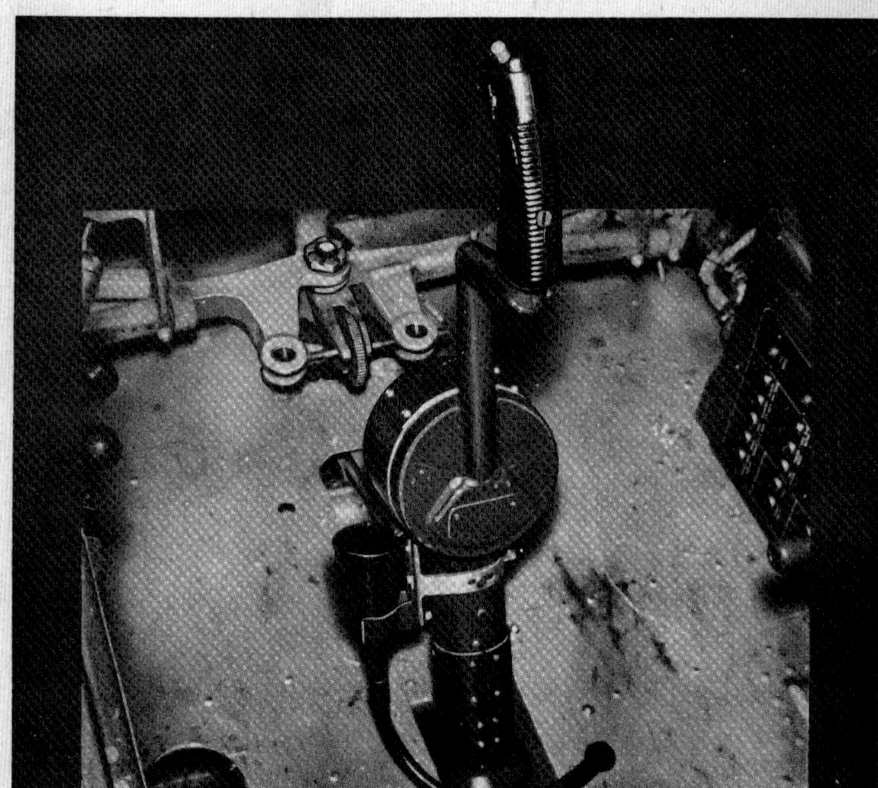

Figure 47—Control Column

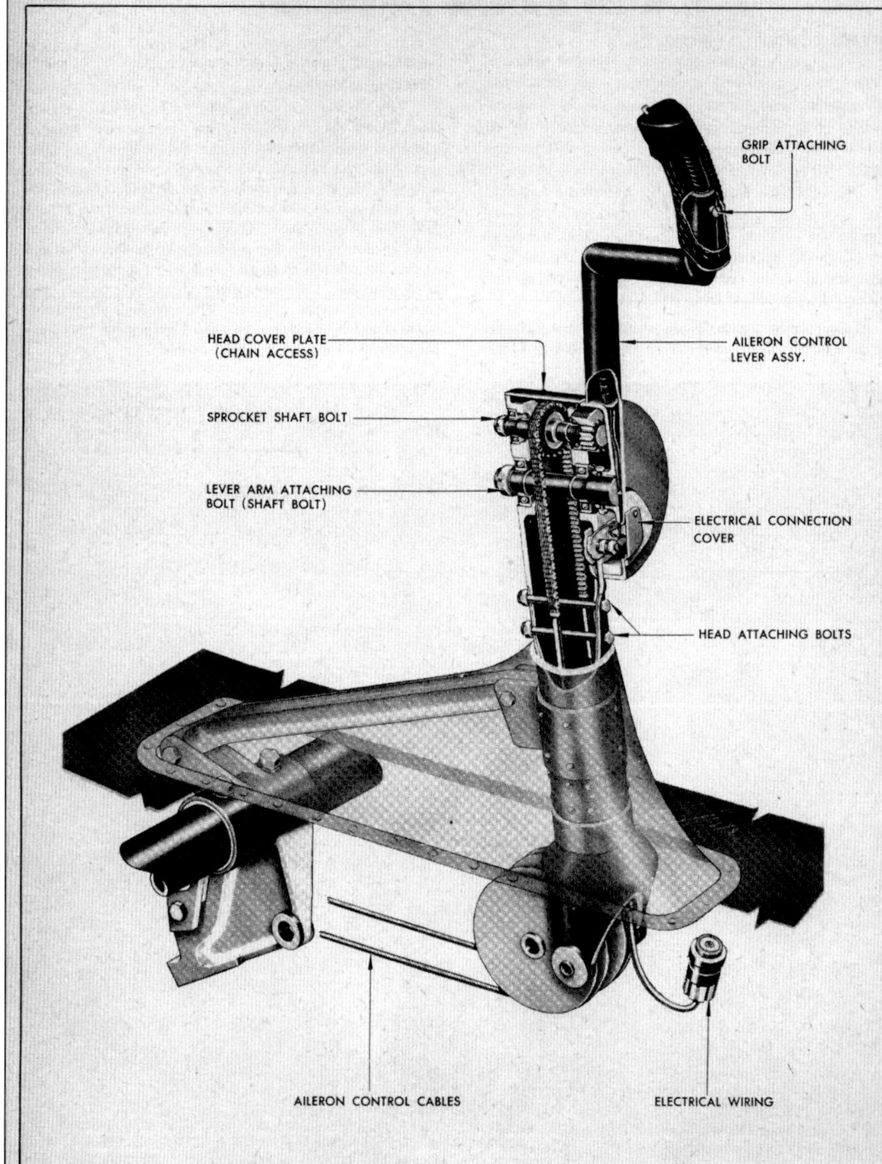

Figure 48—Control Column Details

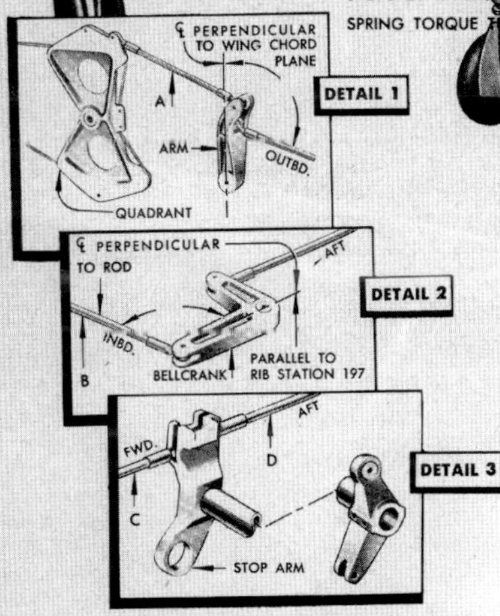

AILERON LINKAGE ADJUSTMENTS

1. QUADRANT SHOULD BE ADJUSTED SO THAT CABLE WRAP AT BOTH EXTREMES OF ITS MOVEMENT IS EQUAL. THIS SHOULD GIVE A NEUTRAL POSITION AS SHOWN IN (DETAIL 1) WHEN SYSTEM IS LOCKED IN NEUTRAL POSITION BY THE SURFACE CONTROL KNOB IN THE COCKPIT.
2. LOCK THE SYSTEM IN NEUTRAL AND ADJUST ROD A. (DETAIL 1) TO GIVE AN ARM POSITION AS SHOWN.
3. ADJUST ROD B. (DETAIL 2) TO GIVE BELL CRANK POSITION SHOWN.
4. AFTER ADJUSTMENTS OF DETAILS 1 AND 2 ARE MADE, CLAMP AILERON AND TAB. DISCONNECT ROD D (DETAIL 3) TO AILERON TAB AND ADJUST ROD C SO THE ATTACHING BOLT TO BELL CRANK (DETAIL 2) CAN BE INSERTED WITHOUT CHANGING ARM POSITION. ADJUST ROD D TO AILERON TAB FOR NO DOWN DROOP AND CONNECT. UNCLAMP AILERON AND TAB.

RIGGING LOAD

RIG CABLES TO OBTAIN 100 LBS ± 10 LBS TENSION

CABLE SIZES

DRUM TO QUADRANT . . . . 3/16, 7x19 STEEL
DRUM TO CONTROL COLUMN . . . 1/8, 7x19 STEEL

CABLE LENGTHS APPROX.

CONTROL COLUMN TO DRUM . . . . 107.5 INCHES
DRUM TO LEFT QUADRANT . . . . . . 188. INCHES
DRUM TO RIGHT QUADRANT . . . . . 148. INCHES
LENGTH OF LONGEST CABLE (CONTROL COLUMN TO LEFT QUADRANT) . . . . 295.5 INCHES

CONTROL MOVEMENTS

CABLE (NO LOAD TRAVEL) . . . . 5.27 INCHES
STICK . . . . 77 1/2° EACH SIDE OF VERTICAL
DRUM . . . . 46 1/2° EACH WAY FROM NEUTRAL
QUADRANT . . . . 27.5° (APPROX.) EACH WAY FROM NEUTRAL
AILERON . . . . 18° ± 2° UP, 18° ± 2° DOWN

SYMBOLS

CABLE GUARD (GUN BAY AND WHEELWELL)
CHAIN
TURNBUCKLE
PULLEY
MOVEMENT FOR RIGHT WING DOWN (RIGHT AILERON UP, LEFT DOWN)

CABLE	FUNCTION		COLOR CODE
AA	RIGHT AILERON LEFT AILERON	UP DOWN	WHITE-BLACK
AB	LEFT AILERON RIGHT AILERON	UP DOWN	WHITE

Figure 50—Aileron Control System

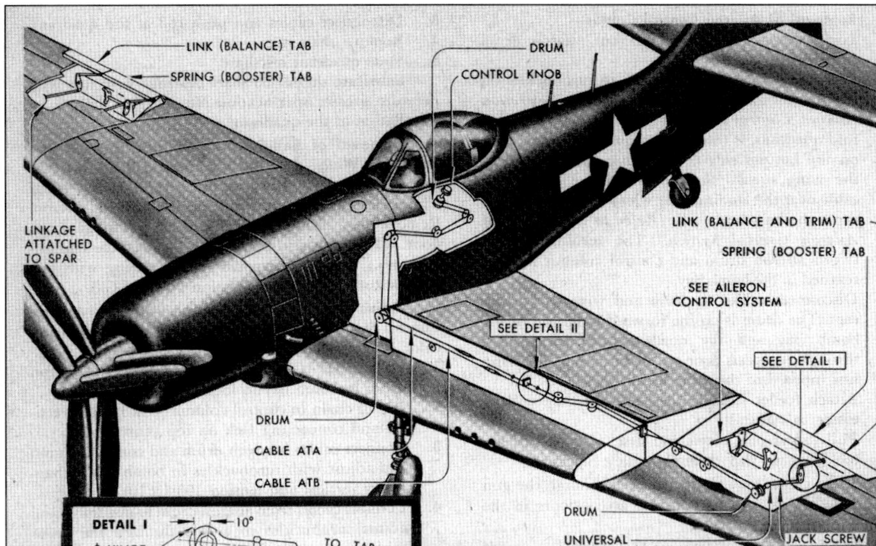

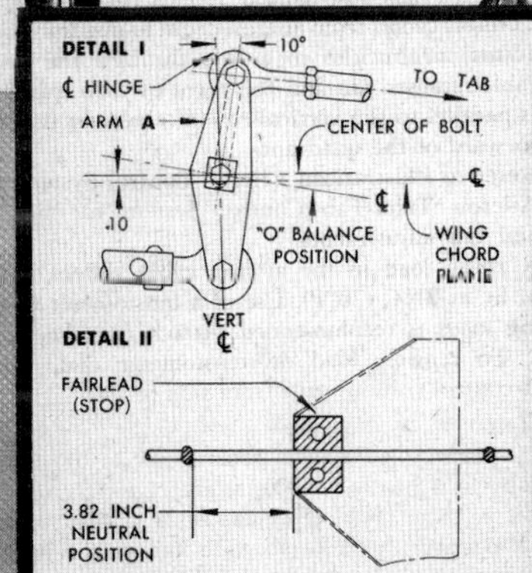

FINAL AILERON AND TAB ADJUSTMENTS

1. RIG AILERONS 3° **DOWN** FROM NEUTRAL BY LENGTHENING THE AILERON BUSS SYSTEM RODS (SEE AILERON BUSS SYSTEM). THIS SHOULD GIVE APPROXIMATELY 10° TO 15° **DOWN** TO THE SPRING (BOOSTER) TABS.

NOTE

SPRING (BOOSTER) TABS SHOULD HAVE NO DROP RIGGED INTO THEM WHEN IN NEUTRAL POSITION

2. RIG THE LINK (BALANCE) TABS 1/2 INCH **UP** AT THE TRAILING EDGE. THIS SHOULD BE DONE WITH ARM **A** IN THE BALANCE POSITION "O" AS SHOWN IN DETAIL I.

CABLE SIZE

3/32 7x7 STEEL

CABLE RIGGING

RIG CABLES FOR 30 LBS. ± 10 LBS. TENSION.

CABLE LENGTHS

(APPROX.)

CONTROL KNOB TO DRUM — 165 INCHES.
DRUM TO LINKAGE — 190 INCHES.

CONTROL MOVEMENTS

KNOB — 18 TURNS (EITHER WAY)
NO LOAD CABLE TRAVEL AT BOMB BAY DRUM — 23.12 INCHES
TAB — TO BE DETERMINED BY FLIGHT TESTS.

SYMBOLS

PULLEY
TURNBUCKLE
STOP AND FAIRLEAD
FAIRLEAD
TRAVEL FOR RIGHT WING DOWN (TAB UP)

CABLE	FUNCTION	COLOR CODE
ATA	TAB UP	WHITE
ATB	TAB DOWN	WHITE - BLACK

Figure 51—Aileron Tab Control System

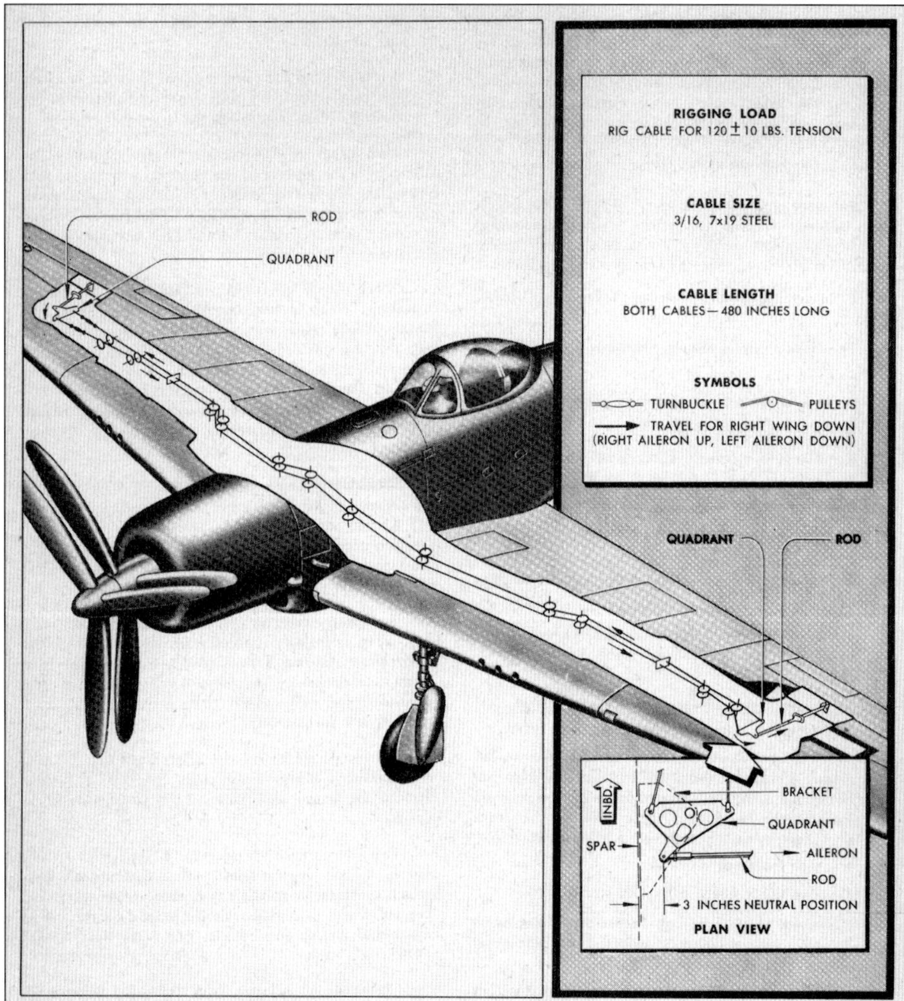

Figure 52—Aileron Bus System

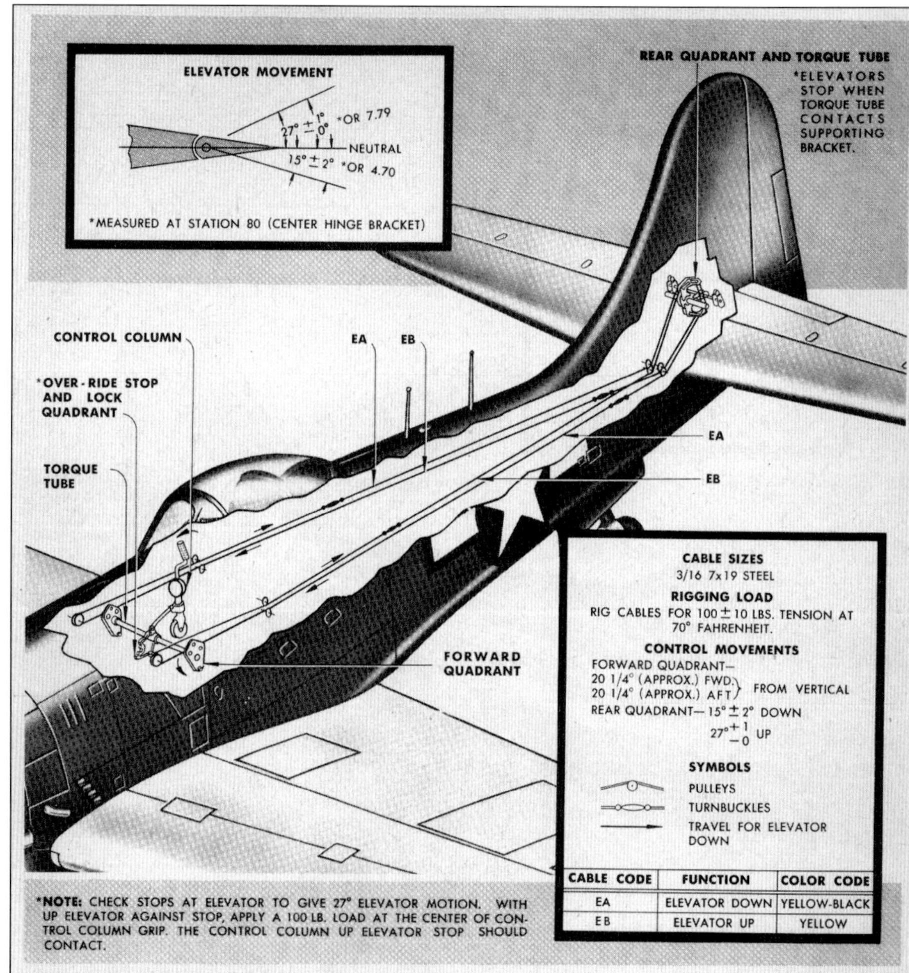

Figure 53—Elevator Control System

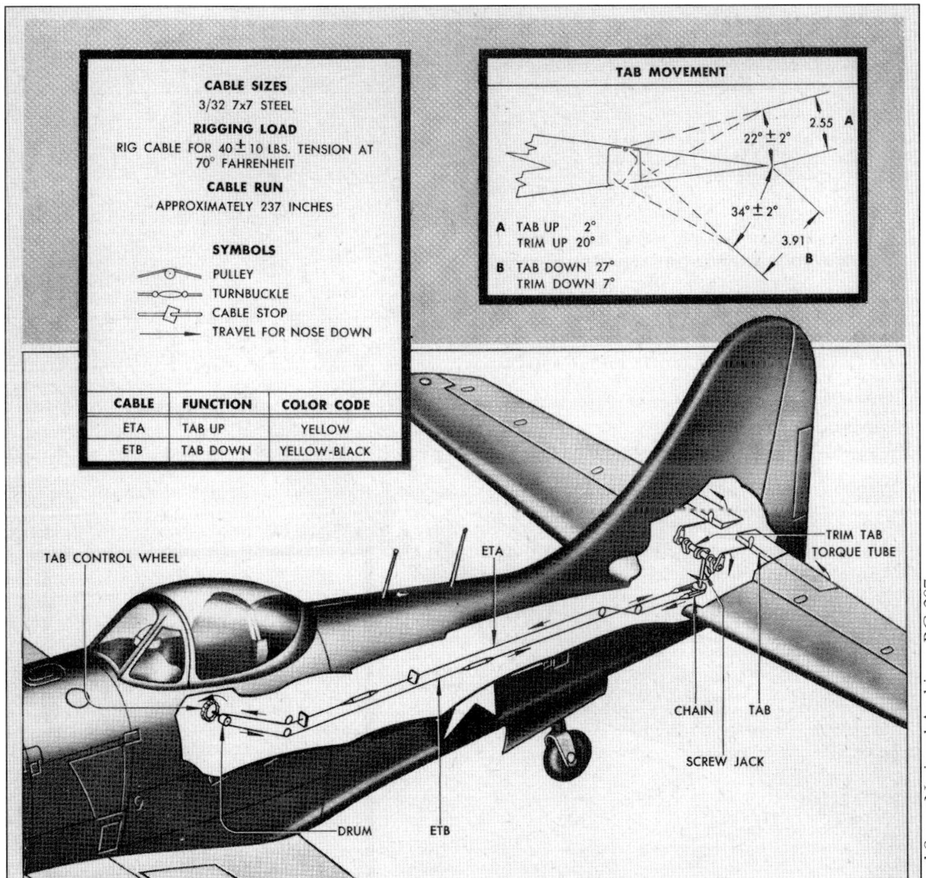

Figure 54—Elevator Trim Tab Control System

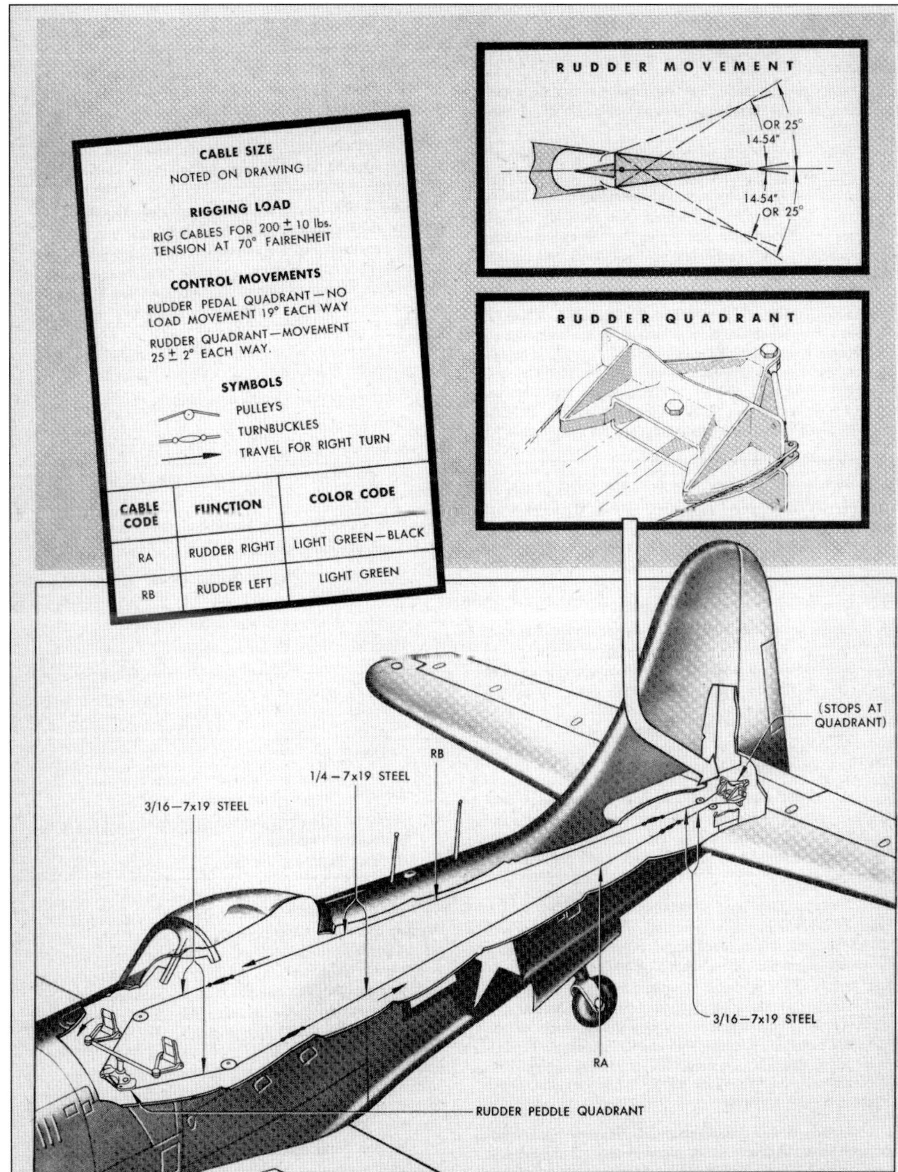

Figure 55—Rudder Control System

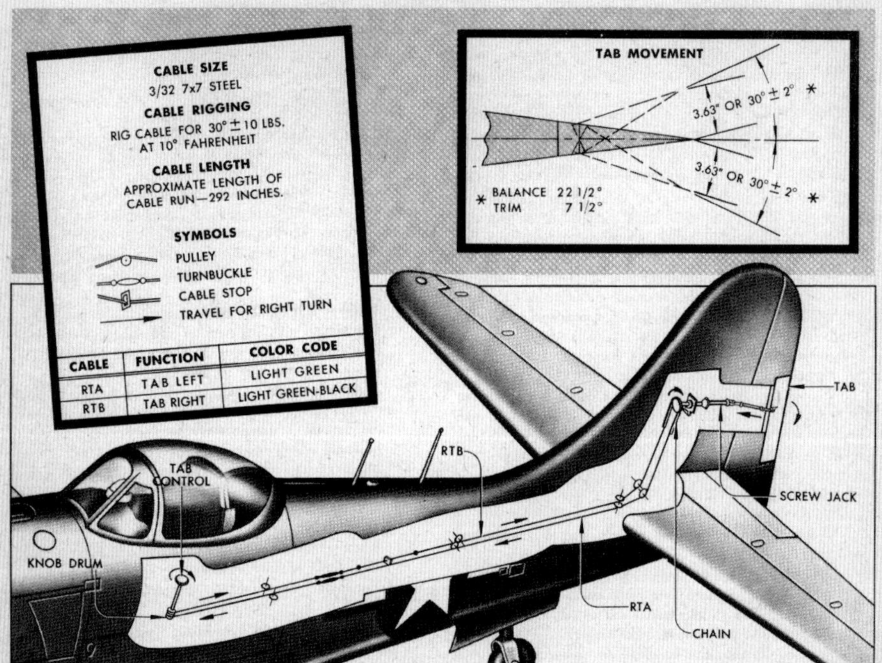

Figure 56—Rudder Trim Tab Control System

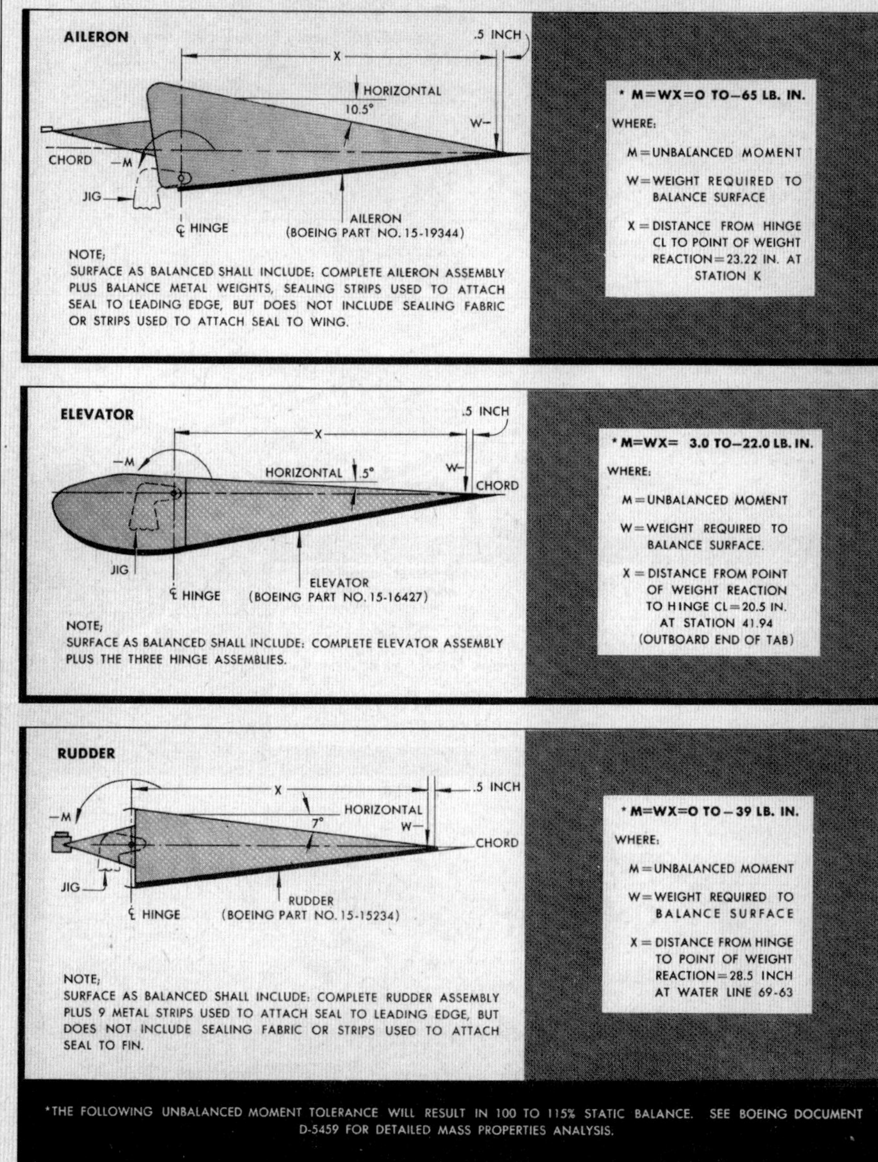

Figure 57—Control Surface Balance Data

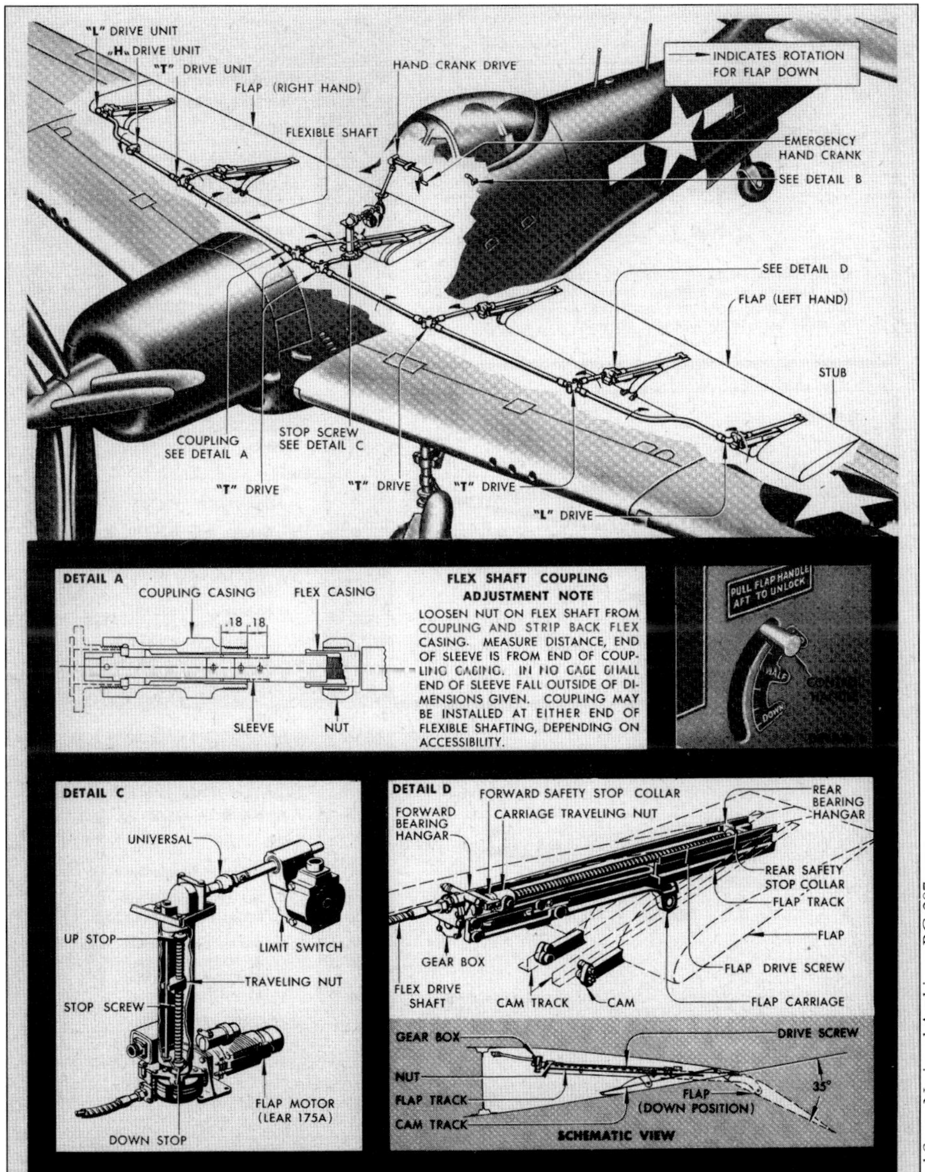

Figure 58—Wing Flap and Control

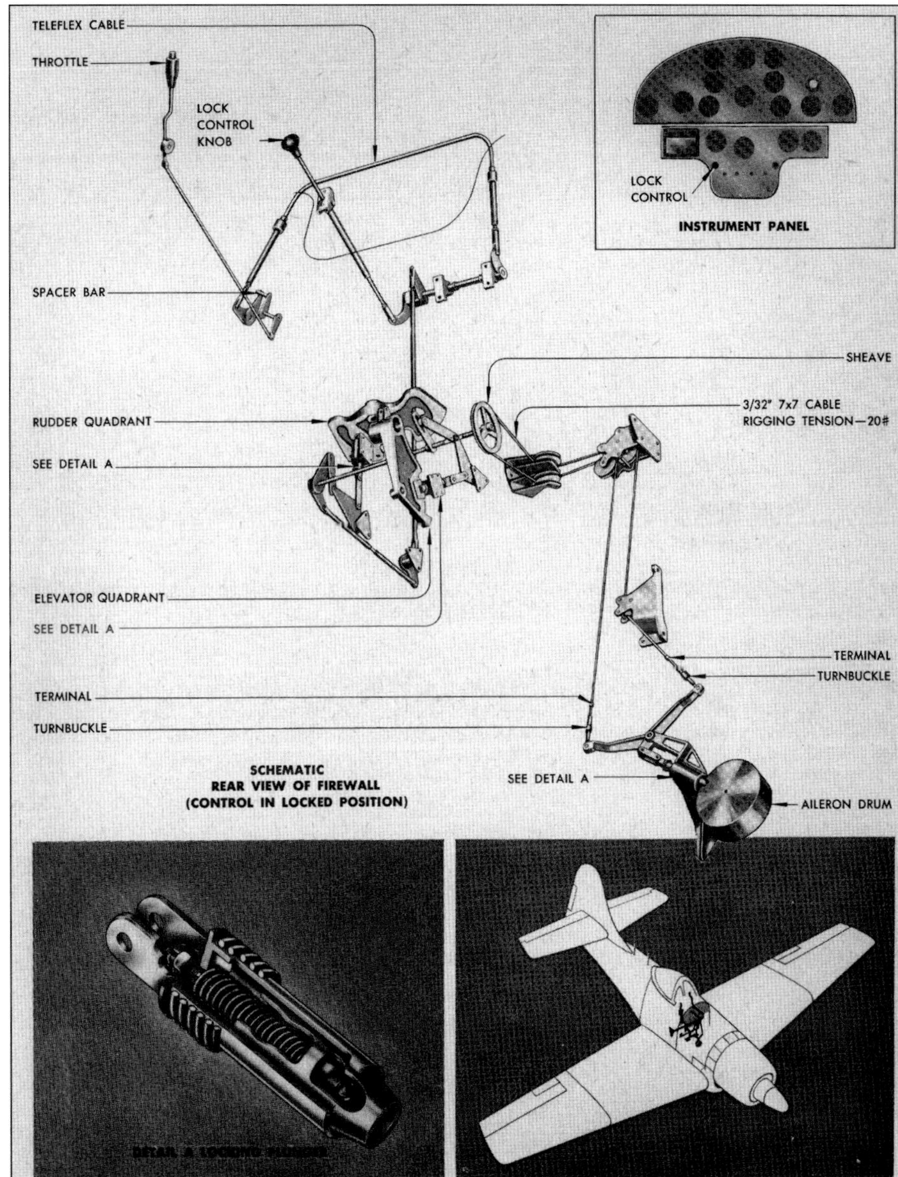

Figure 61—Surface Controls and Throttle Lock

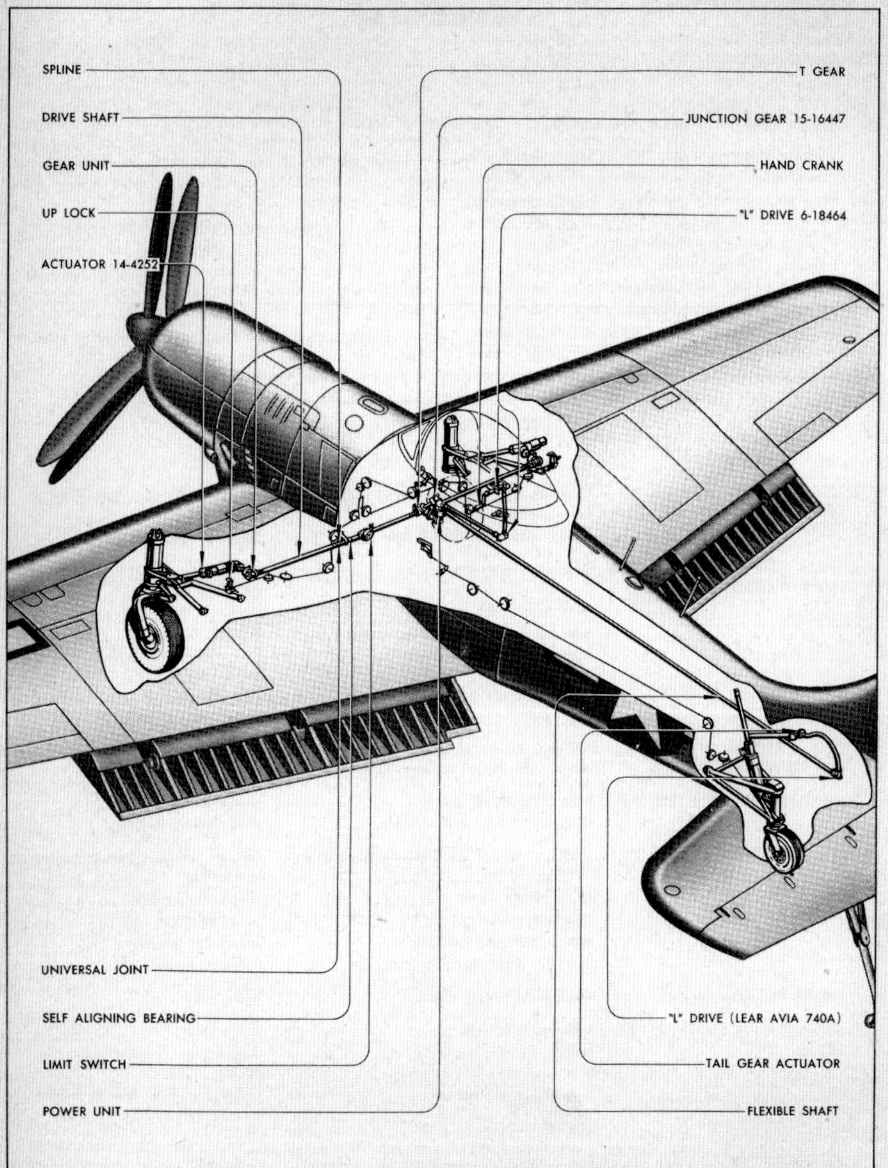

Figure 62—Landing Gear Diagram

LANDING GEAR

The X F 8 B-1 main and tail landing gear fold into door-covered wells. The doors are linked to the landing gear structure and are operated by movement of the gear. In the extended position the centers of the main gear wheels are 13 feet 4 inches apart.

A single motor and gear box in the forward end of the bomb bay retracts and extends all three wheels. The main gear operates through a system of torque tubes, spline joints, universal joints, and gear units; the tail gear through a flexible shaft, junction gear, and L-drive. Torque tubes, universal joints, and L-drives connect the handcrank fitting in the cockpit to the junction gear for emergency operation in case of power failure. There is a safety switch in the handcrank fitting in the cockpit to prevent injury from electrical operation while the handcrank is being used.

The position indicator and warning light are in the cockpit. The landing gear limit switch unit in the forward end of the bomb bay is actuated by the shaft to the left main gear. A safety (squat) switch on the right shock strut, actuated by torsion link, prevents retraction of the gear when the airplane is on the ground. Also a tail wheel centering switch on the tail wheel treadle prevents retraction of the landing gear unless the wheel is centered.

The two main wheels have Goodyear single disc hydraulic booster type brake. When toe pressure is exerted on the rudder pedals, the master cylinders force hydraulic fluid through the lines to the brakes. No parking brake is provided.

Maintenance of the landing gear requires a number of special tools. Refer to the Special Tool Table at the end of this section.

LANDING GEAR TROUBLE CHART

TROUBLE	PROBABLE CAUSE	REMEDY
1. LOSS OF HYDRAULIC FLUID OR AIR PRESSURE IN MAIN OR TAIL GEAR SHOCK STRUT	Valve body loose, valve core worn or valve body gasket compressed	Replace valve core or valve body gasket
	Leakage around shock strut packing	Tighten or replace packing
2. LANDING GEAR EXTENDS OR RETRACTS SLOWLY OR LANDING GEAR FROZEN	Excessive grease on actuator screw	Remove excess grease from lower end of screw housing
	Motor clutch slipping	Check clutch assembly
	Motor brushes worn causing motor to drag	Replace brushes
	Binding of actuator nut and screw	Check actuator nut and screw for freedom of movement
	Control mechanism binding	Check alignment of shafts and gear bosses
3. EXCESSIVE WHIPPING OF MAIN WHEELS, OR HAMMERING IN TORSION LINK	Ball thrust bearings at knuckle joint of torsion link worn or connecting bolt improperly tightened	Replace bearings if worn; check bolt for proper freedom of movement
4. BRAKES DRAGGING AND OVER-HEATING	Brake unit excessively dirty	Clean brake units
	Piston return springs weak or broken	Check piston return springs
5. BRAKES DO NOT HOLD PROPERLY	Insufficient hydraulic fluid in brake hydraulic system	Replenish hydraulic system with proper hydraulic fluid
	Air in hydraulic system	Bleed hydraulic system
	Brake lining pads worn too thin	Replace lining pads
	Master cylinder piston seal rings worn	Replace worn seal rings
	Main brake check valve malfunctioning	Replace check valve
6. EXCESSIVE TAIL GEAR VIBRATION	Centering springs weak or broken	Replace springs
7. TAIL WHEEL SPINDLE FAILS TO LOCK PROPERLY	Spring broken or weak	Replace spring
	Lock pin binding or dragging	Check lock pin for proper seating with lock plate
	Shear bolt partially severed	Replace shear bolt with an AN5DD-7 bolt with torque setting of 50-70 pound-inches
8. LANDING GEAR FAILS TO OPERATE	Failure of control or power circuit	Check circuits
	Burned out motor	Replace motor

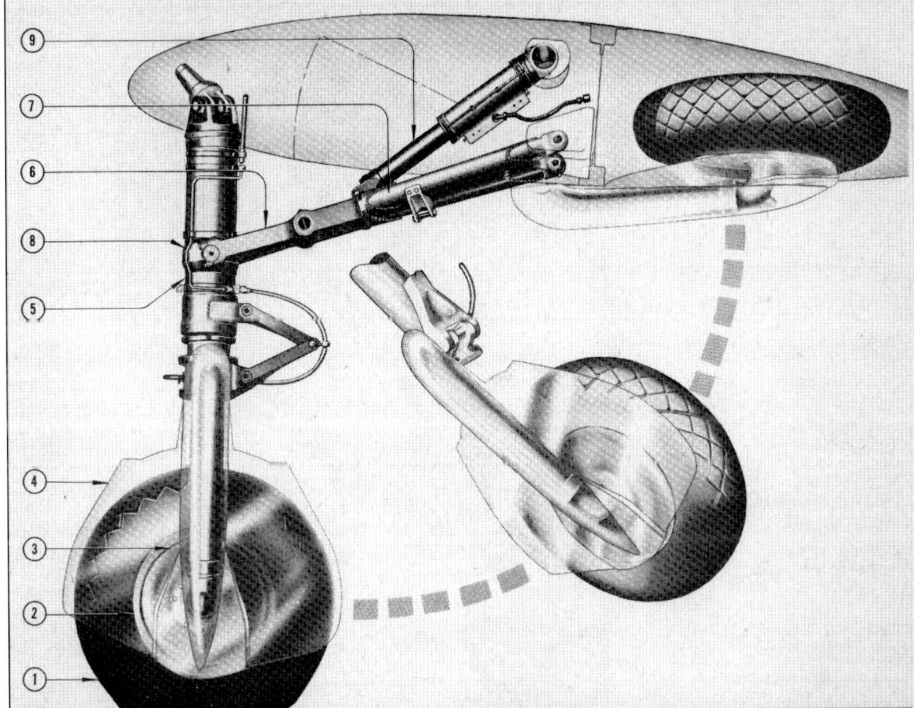

FIG. 63 - MAIN LANDING GEAR AND CONTROL MECHANISM

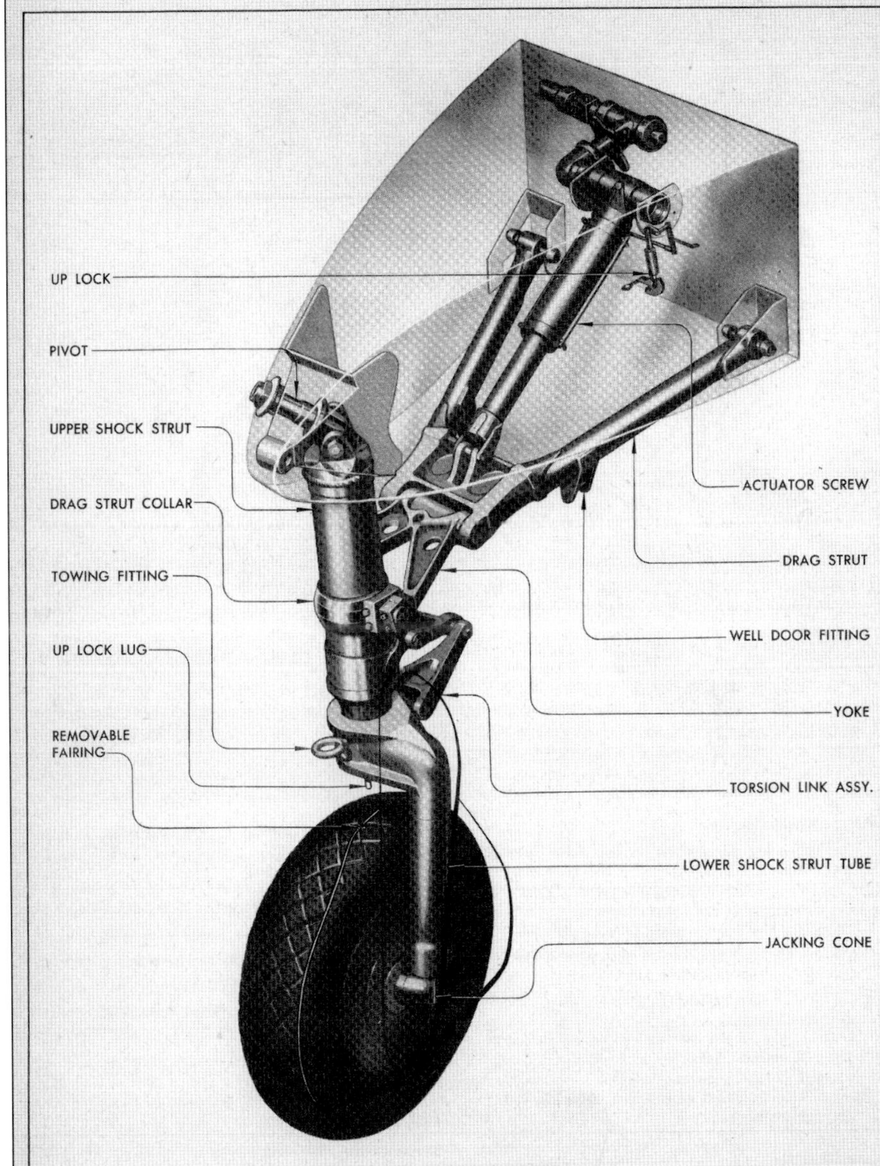

Figure 64—Main Landing Gear

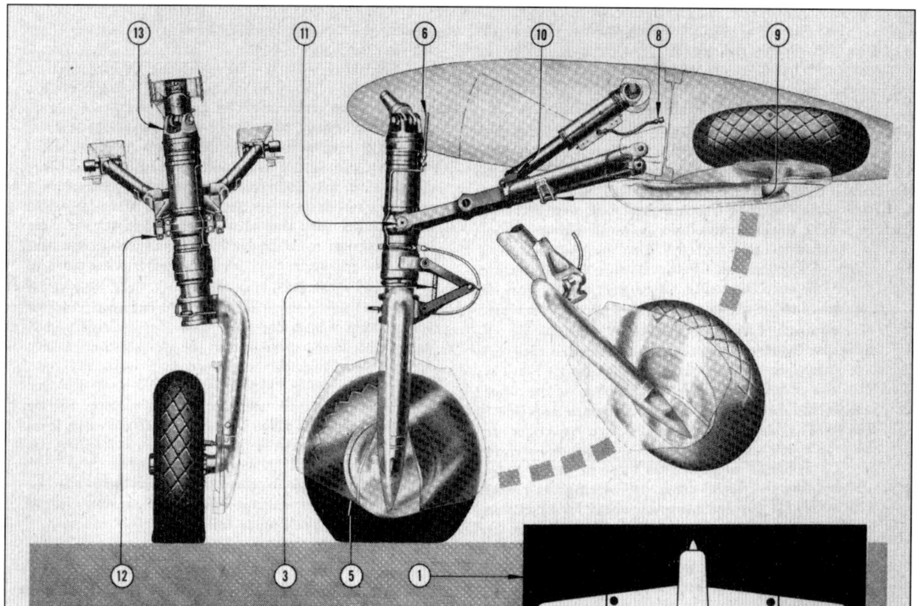

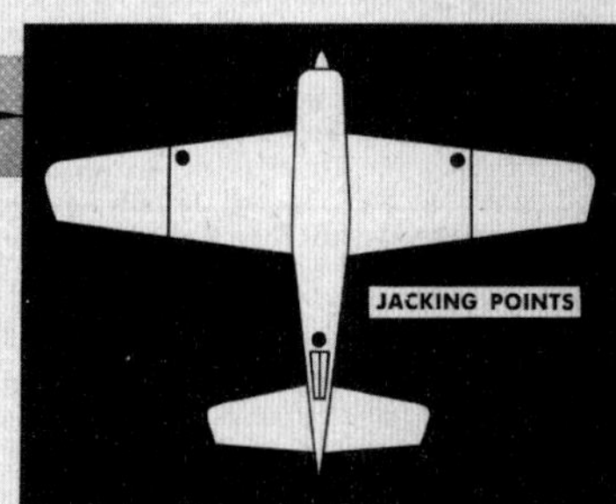

Figure 64A—Landing Gear Installation

Removal of Main Landing Gear—

1. Place jacks under the three jacking points (two in the wing leading edge and one forward of tail wheel well), and take up the weight of the airplane with them.
   CAUTION—All fuel cell doors (lower wing surface) and forward wing hinge pin access doors (wing ribs 175) must be installed before leading edge cones can support the airplane. Refer to Jacking in Section I of this book.
2. Release the air from the shock strut by depressing the air valve core. Wait until the air has stopped hissing and then remove the air valve body completely.
3. Attach a retaining link to the torsion link fitting to prevent the extension of the shock strut. (Special tool F12136).
4. Jack the airplane till the wheels clear the ground.
5. Remove the wheel fairing.
6. Disconnect the flexible hose brake line just above the shock strut terminal and seal the ends of the lines to prevent the loss of hydraulic fluid.
7. Retract the landing gear about one-third of the way.
8. Break the electrical connection at the actuating screw.
9. Disconnect the door linkage at the drag strut.
10. Remove the bolt at the lower end of the actuator screw and the outboard fitting at the upper end of the actuator screw. Let the actuator hang in a vertical position and slip it outboard till it is free of the inboard fitting. Turn the screw until it can be taken out of the airplane.
11. Remove the safety bolt and the shaft at the yoke-drag strut connection. Don't let the yoke or drag strut swing freely, they may be damaged. Identify the bolts so they can be returned to their former bolt holes. Remove the safety bolts and the internal wrenching bolts at the upper fittings of the drag strut and take it from the airplane.
12. Remove yoke from drag strut collar by taking off the yoke caps. Mark parts for reassembly.
13. The wheel, brake, lower and upper shock struts, torsion link, and drag strut collar can be removed as a unit by taking off the two nuts and withdrawing the shaft at the upper end of the shock strut. This unit weighs about 400 lb.

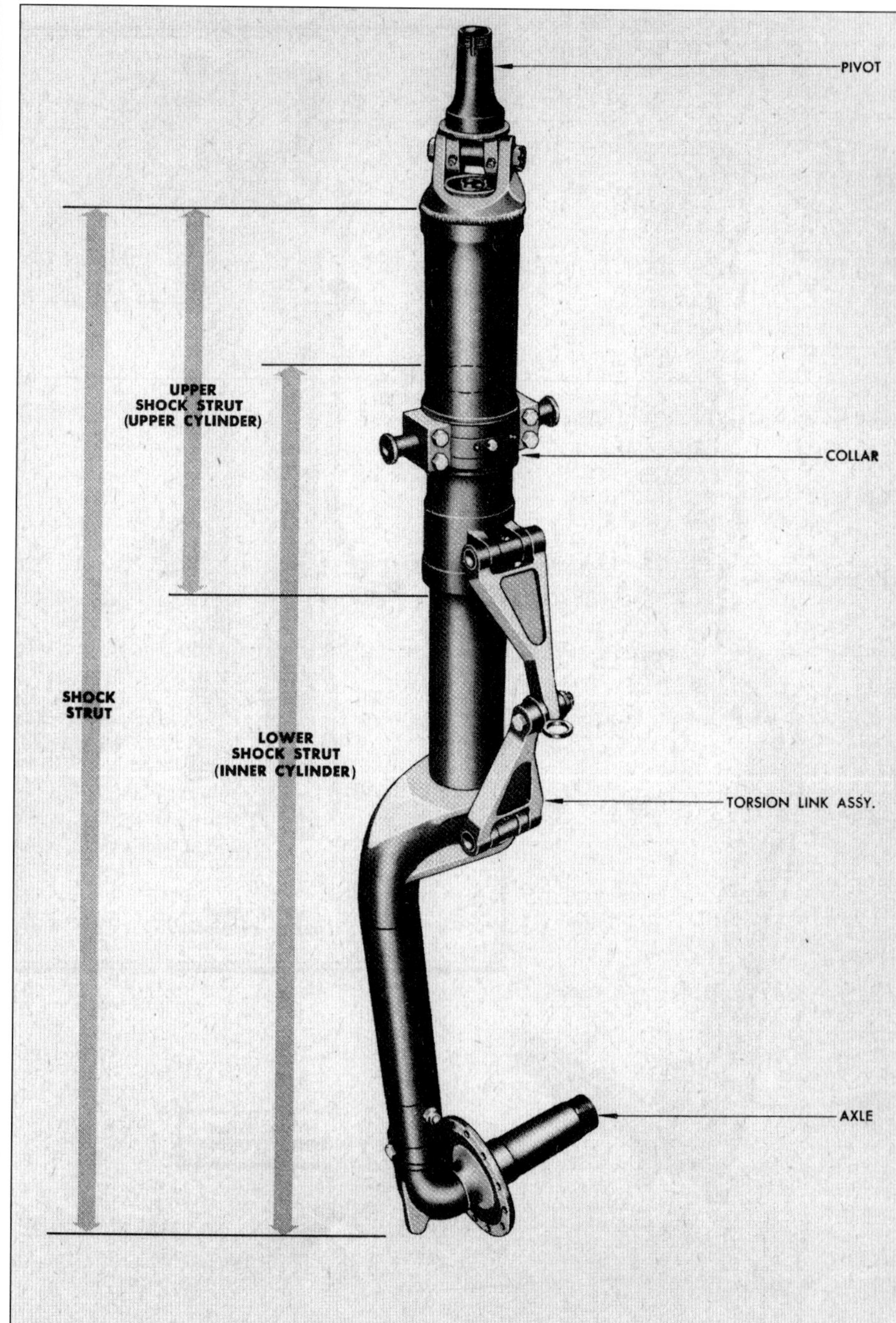

Manual Scan: National Archives, RG 287

Figure 68—Yoke and Drag Strut

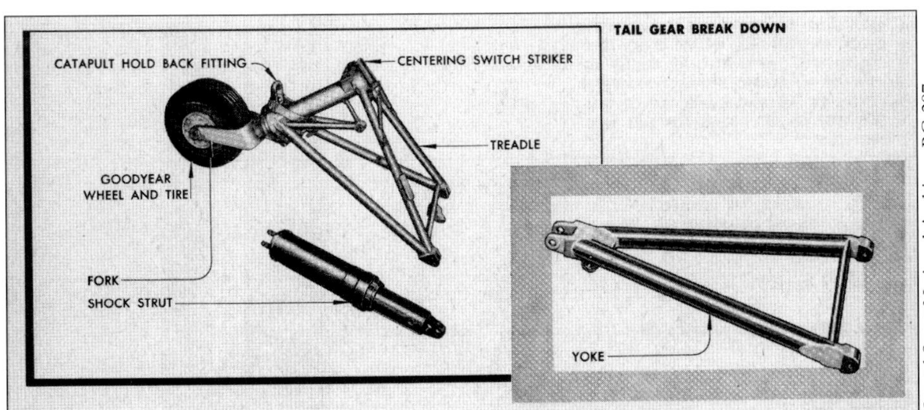

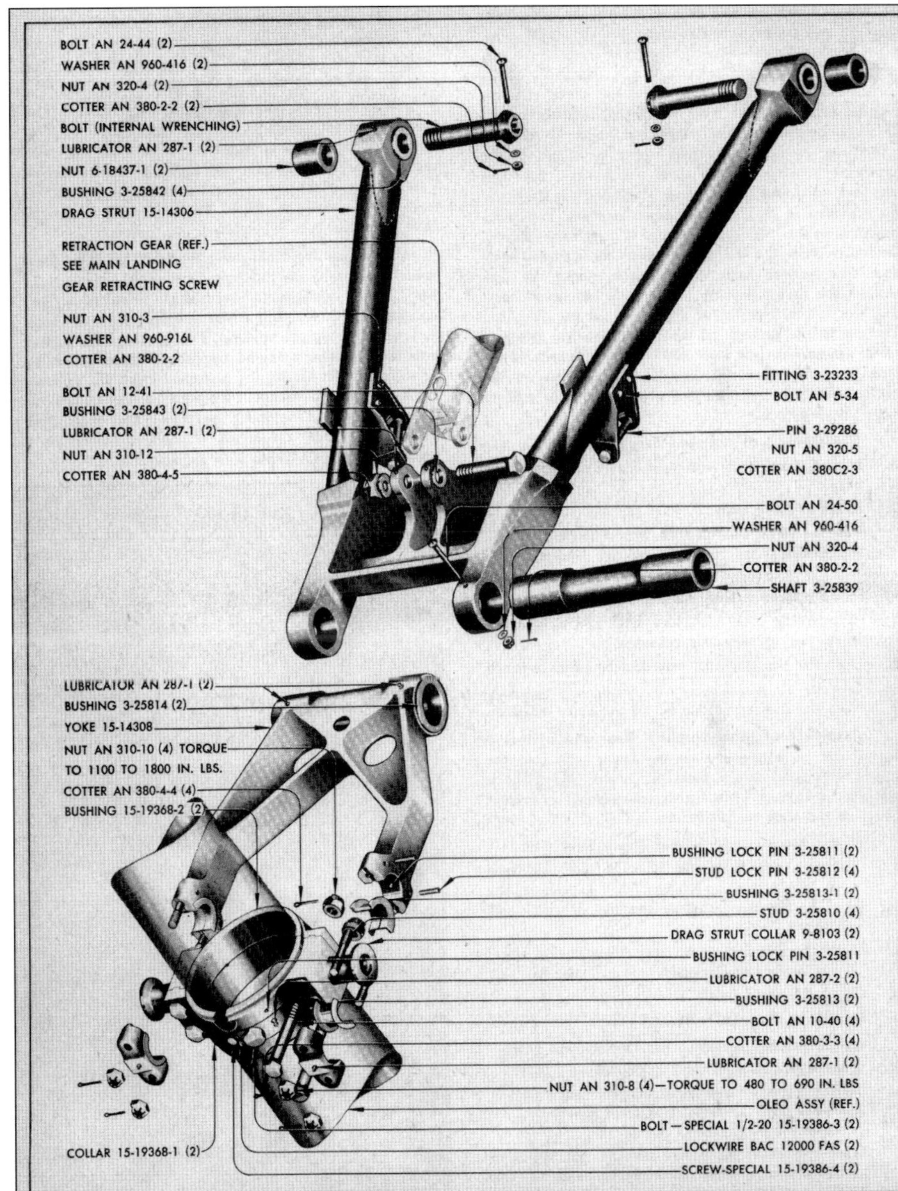

Figure 68—Main Landing Gear Yoke and Drag Strut

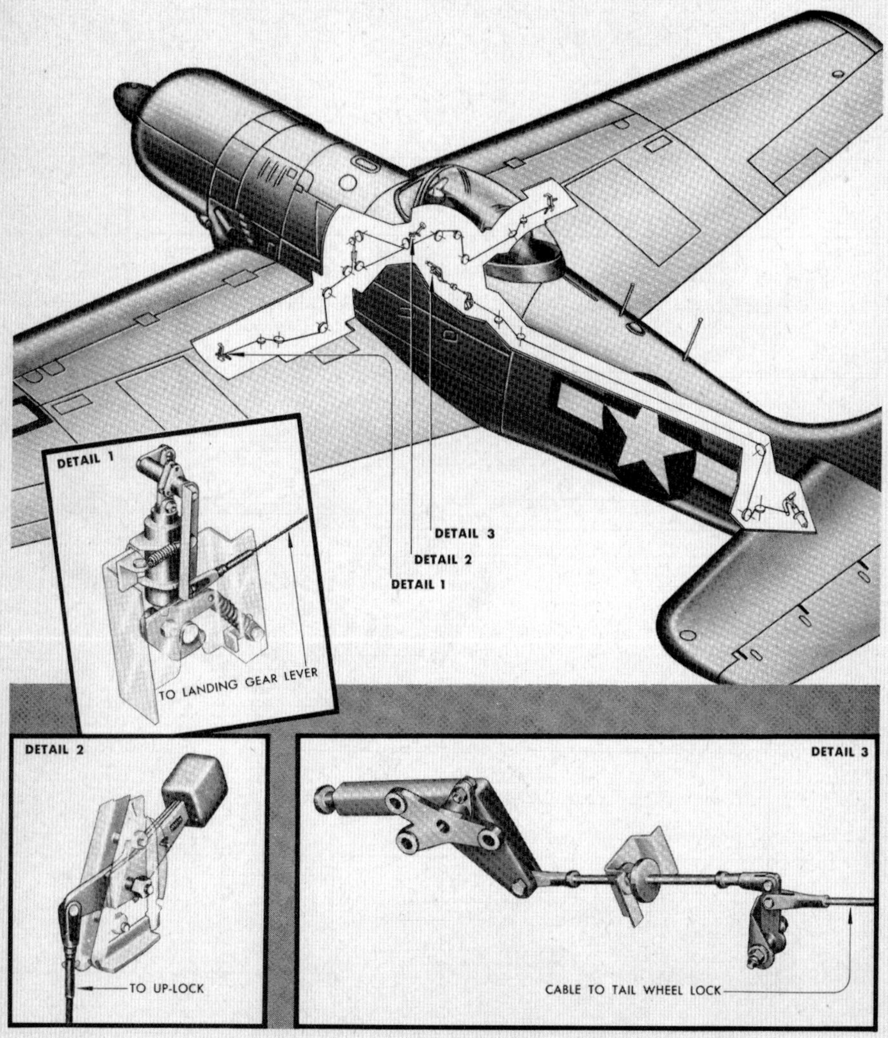

Figure 72—Landing Gear Up Lock and Tail Wheel Centering Control Systems

Manual Scan: National Archives, RG 287

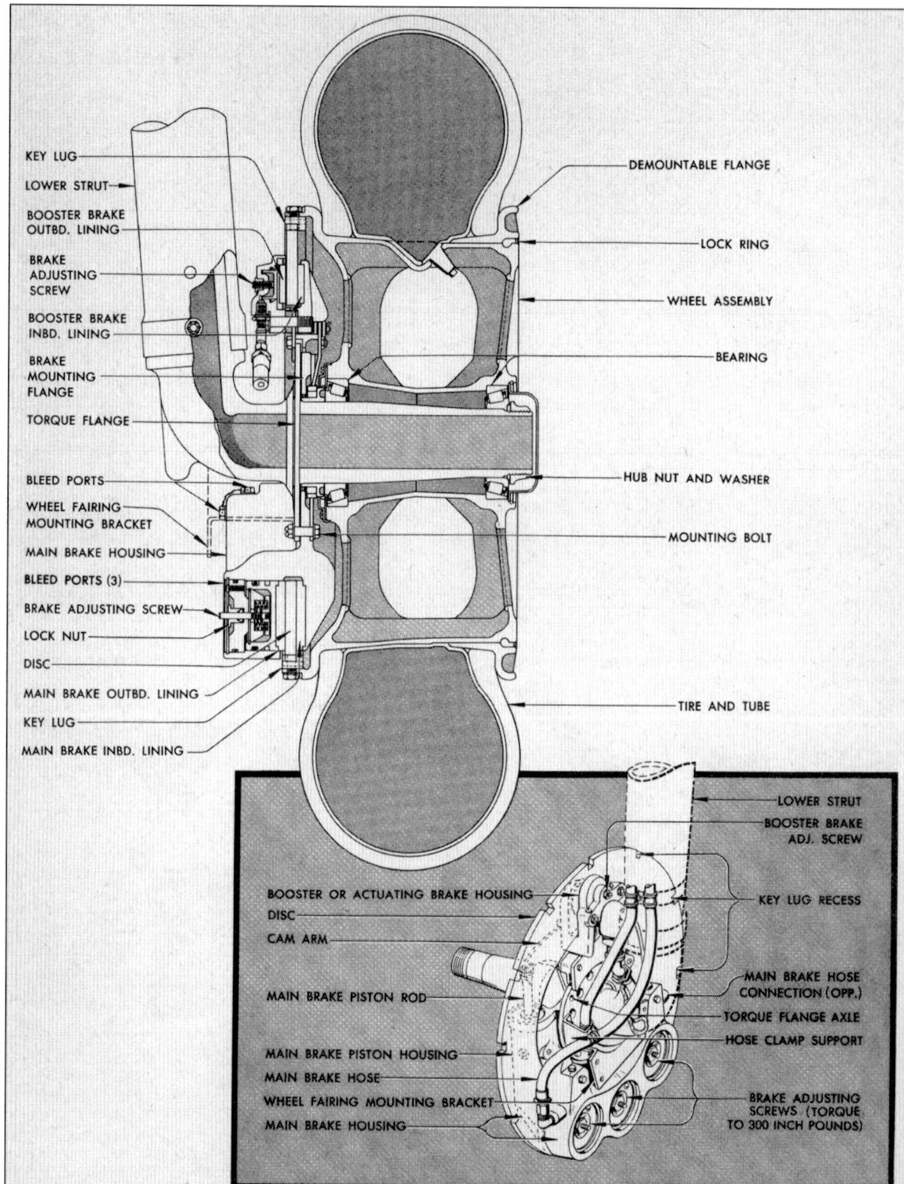

Figure 75—Main Landing Gear Wheel and Brake

Manual Scan: National Archives, RG 287

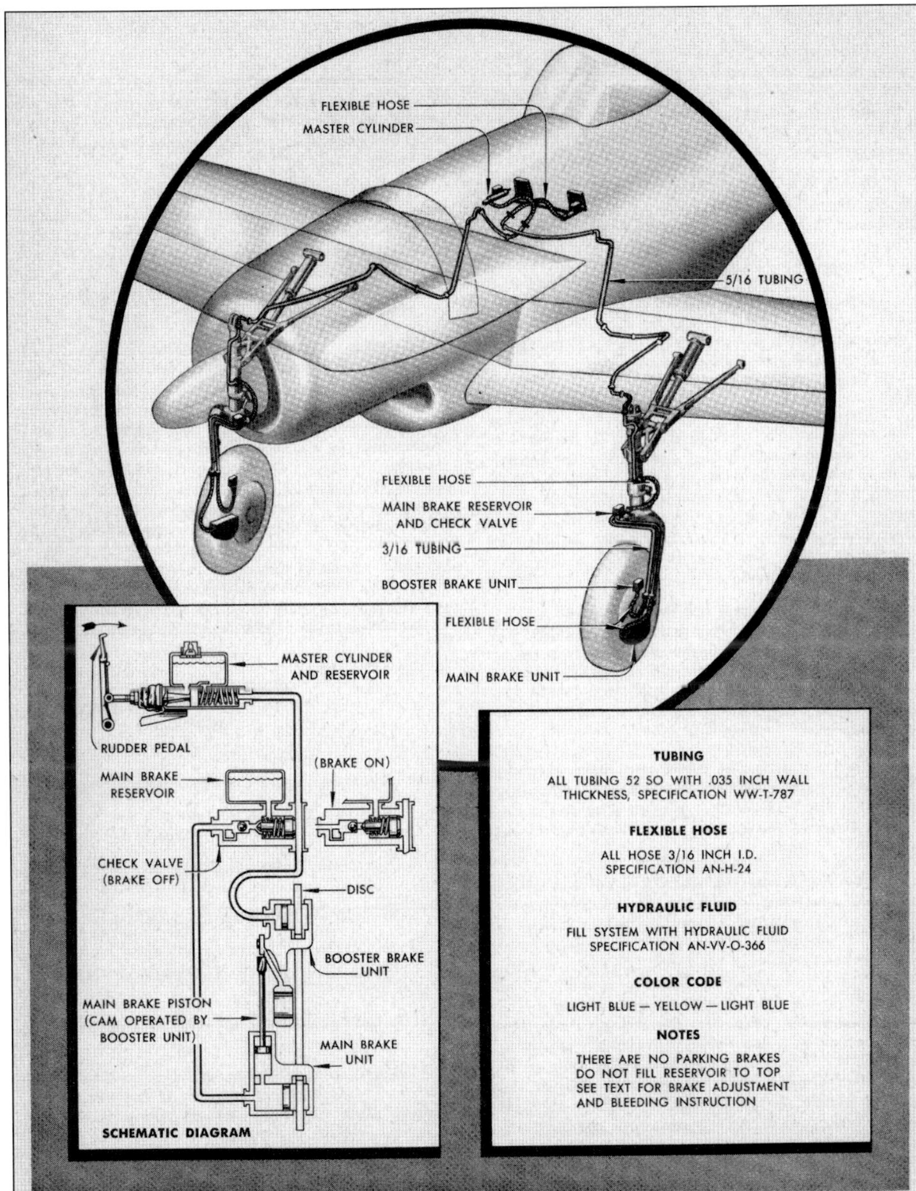

Figure 76—Brake Hydraulic System

TAIL GEAR

The tail gear consists of the wheel and tire, treadle and spindle assembly, centering springs, centering-switch unit, centering lock, shock strut, yoke, and actuator unit (retracting screw). Whether in the extended, taxi, or compressed position the wheel and spindle can turn through a full 360 degrees. The wheel must be centered within four degrees before the gear can be retracted. The centering lock is operated from the cockpit. A shear bolt protects the tail-gear structure from damage should the airplane be turned during taxiing and while the tail wheel is locked. A hold-back clevis is fastened to the spindle housing for use in catapult take-off (do not use for towing). The shock strut is of the air-oil type (pneumatic-hydraulic).

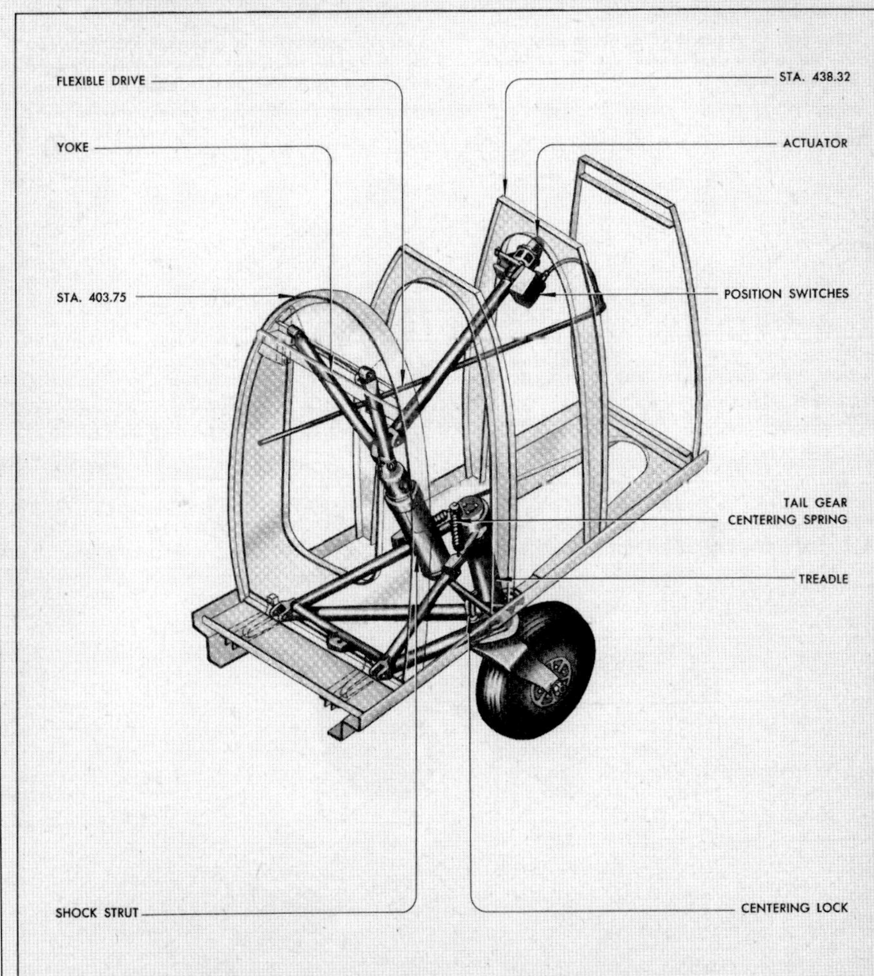

Figure 81—Tail Gear

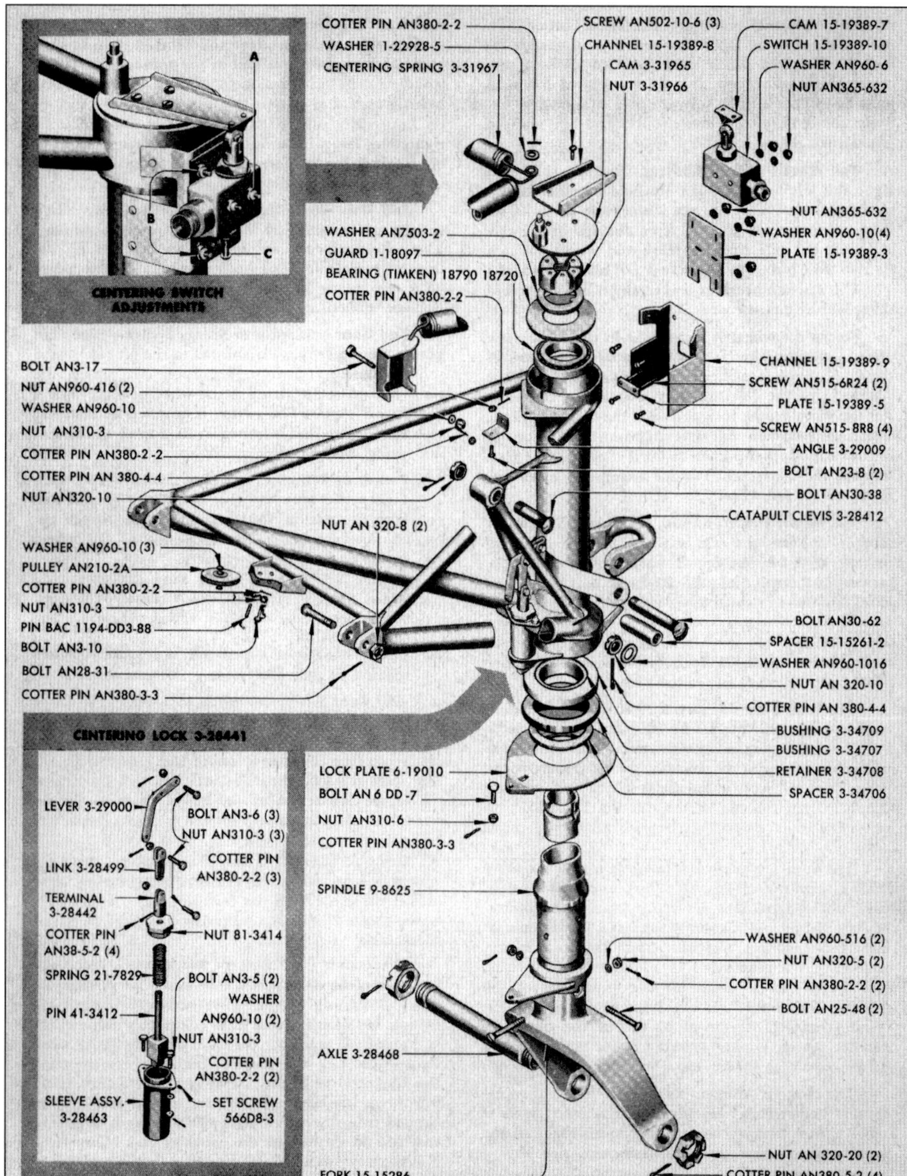

Figure 83—Tail Gear Treadle and Fork

ARRESTING HOOK

The arresting hook swings down to 20 degrees from the vertical. It extends about six feet below the tail. It is hinged for side play about three feet from the end and swings 15 degrees to either side when the airplane lands with a yaw. A cam and a spring return the hook to center. Another spring and a hydraulic shock strut prevent the hook from bouncing. The hook retracts into a well and the forward part of the hook (back to the side pivot) is covered by a fairing attached to the hook.

A handle on the right hand control stand in the cockpit controls the hook. When the handle is moved to NORMAL DOWN, it operates a lock and then a switch, which turns on the retracting motor. This motor runs the hook down in about eight seconds. It takes about eleven seconds to retract the hook.

If the hook fails to go down when the handle is moved to NORMAL DOWN, spring the handle inboard and move it past the stop lug to EMERGENCY DOWN. The hook, now unlatched from the retracting mechanism, swings down freely. If the electrical system has failed, the hook cannot be retracted, but if power again becomes available, the screw will follow the hook down and relatch to it. If the EMERGENCY DOWN position has been used, leave the handle down to prevent the hook from bouncing up and relatching.

CAUTION — *Never place control lever in EMERGENCY DOWN position when airplane tail is jacked up enough for the hook to swing to full down position, unless someone is at the hook to lower it. If it is allowed to swing down free, the impact may damage the bulkhead when the hook reaches the full down position.*

The arresting hook consists of the hook itself, the V-strut (hinged at the pointed end to the hook and at the open end to the airplane), the spring-hydraulic shock strut, an arm assembly which includes the latching mechanism, and the actuator, which includes the retracting motor, limit switches, gearing, and jack screw.

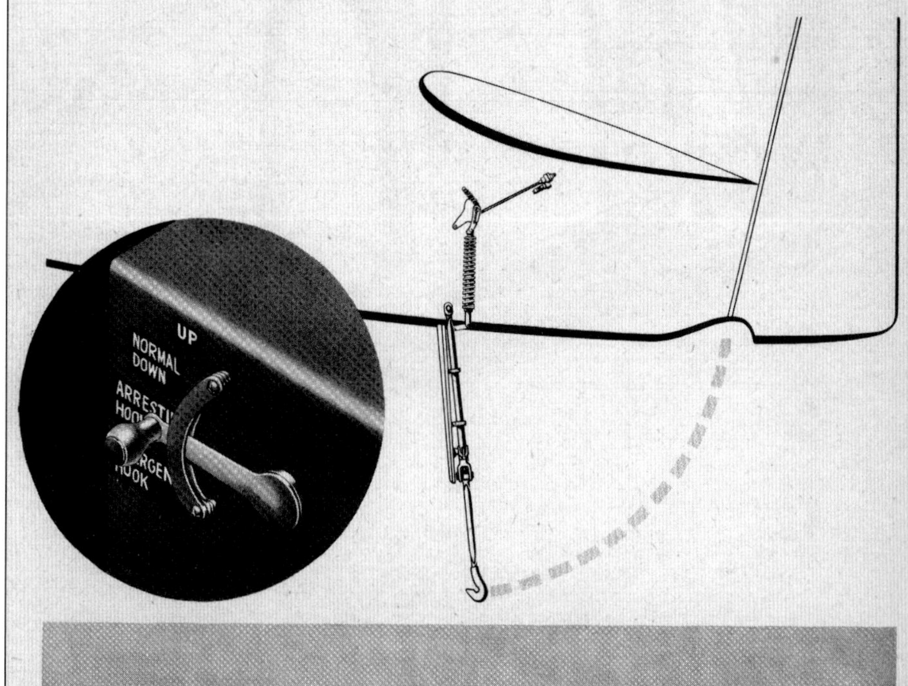

Figure 91—Arresting Hook and Cockpit Control Handle

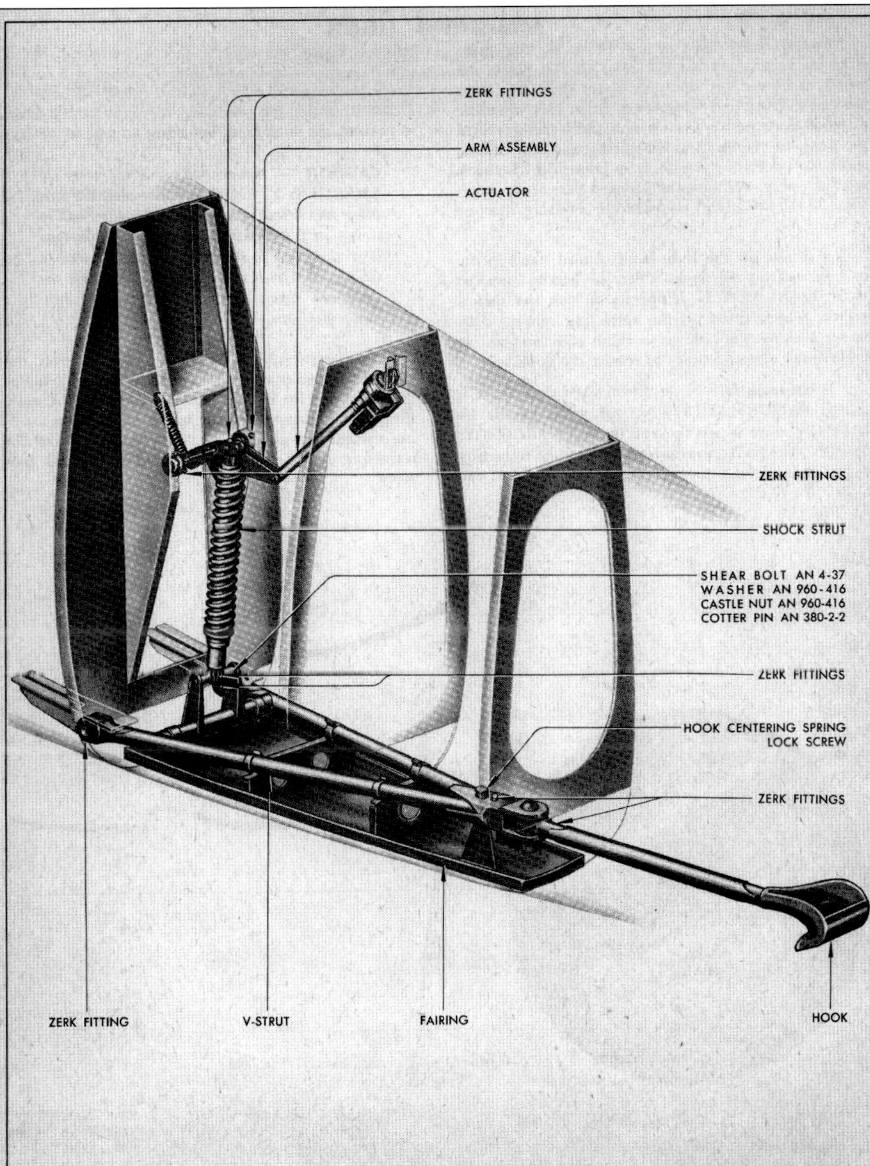

Figure 92—Arresting Hook Installation

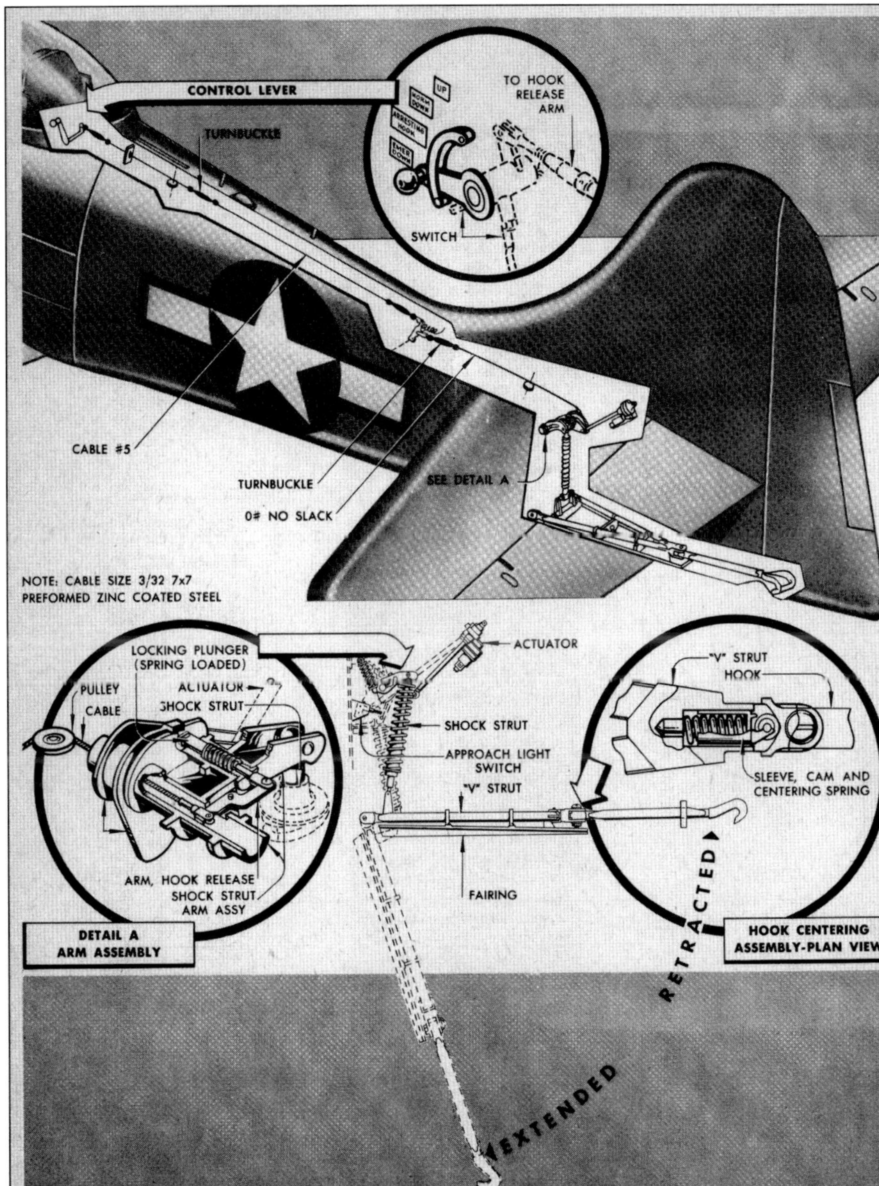

Figure 97—Arresting Hook Control

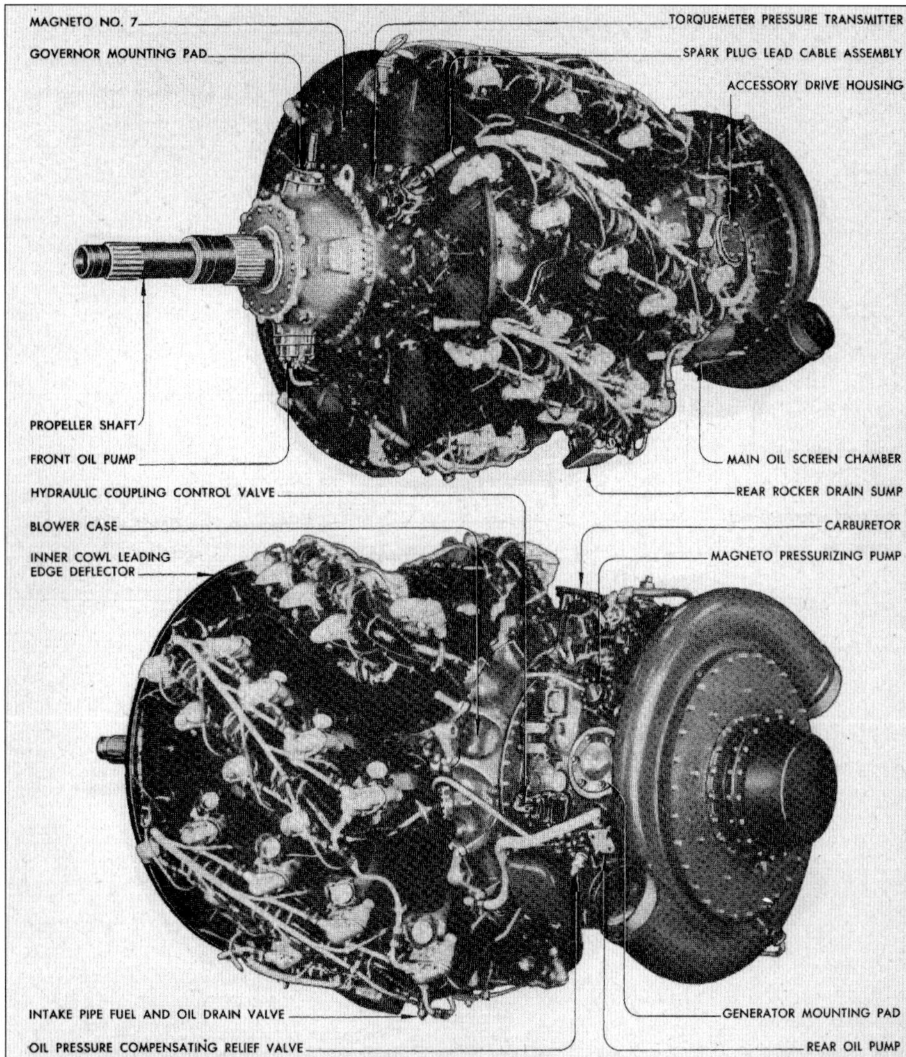

Figure 98—Engine—Left Hand View

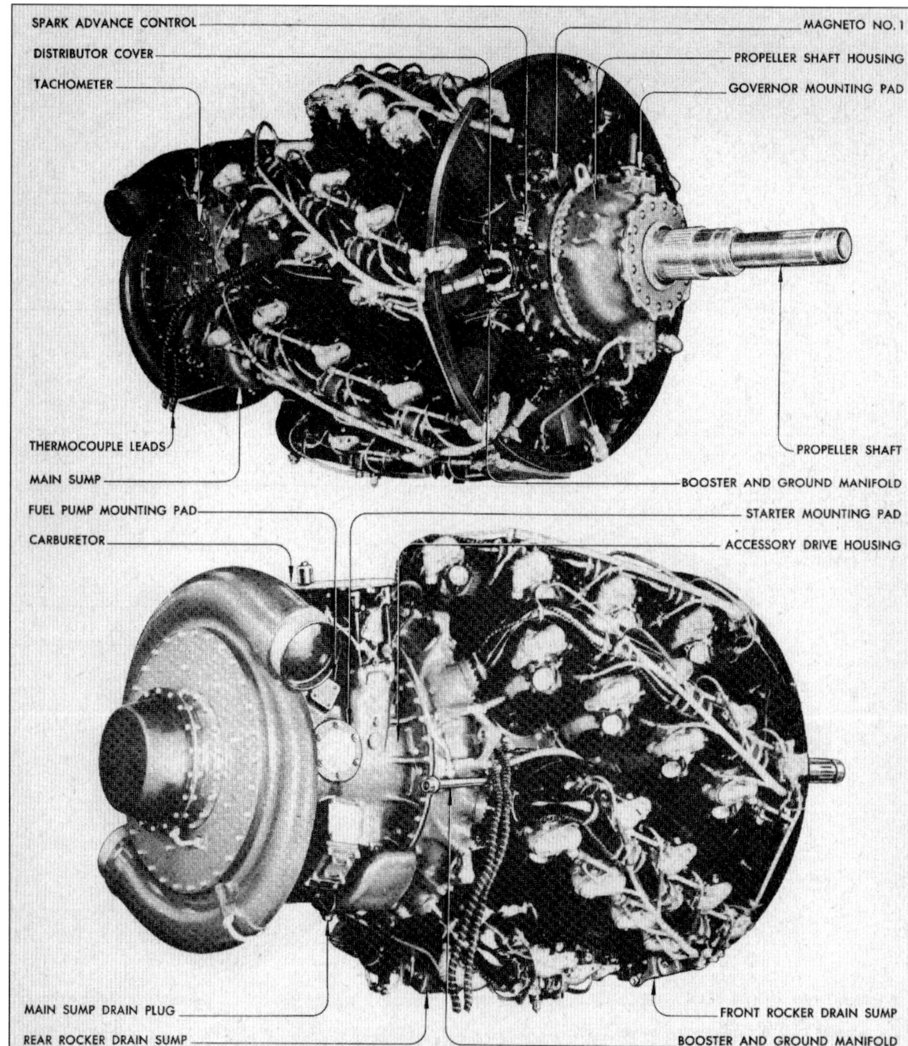

Figure 99—Engine—Right Hand View

ENGINE

The R-3260-10, Pratt & Whitney Wasp Major engine has 28 air-cooled cylinders arranged in four radial rows of seven cylinders each and has a two stage supercharging system. The main stage supercharger (regular manifold blower) is geared to the crank shaft and has a constant gear ratio; the second or auxiliary stage supercharger is a large, variable-speed blower in a housing on the rear of the engine-accessory drive section. It is driven through hydraulic couplings (fluid-drive units). A hydraulic valve on the accessory-drive section regulates the flow of oil to the fluid drives thereby varying the speed of the blower; the valve is operated by a flexible cable connected to a control lever in the cockpit.

The following equipment is delivered with the engine: magnetos, starter, fuel pump, oil pumps, ignition pressure pump, and the carburetor (in a separate box).

Engine firing order and master-rod location are shown on the Cylinder Arrangement illustration.

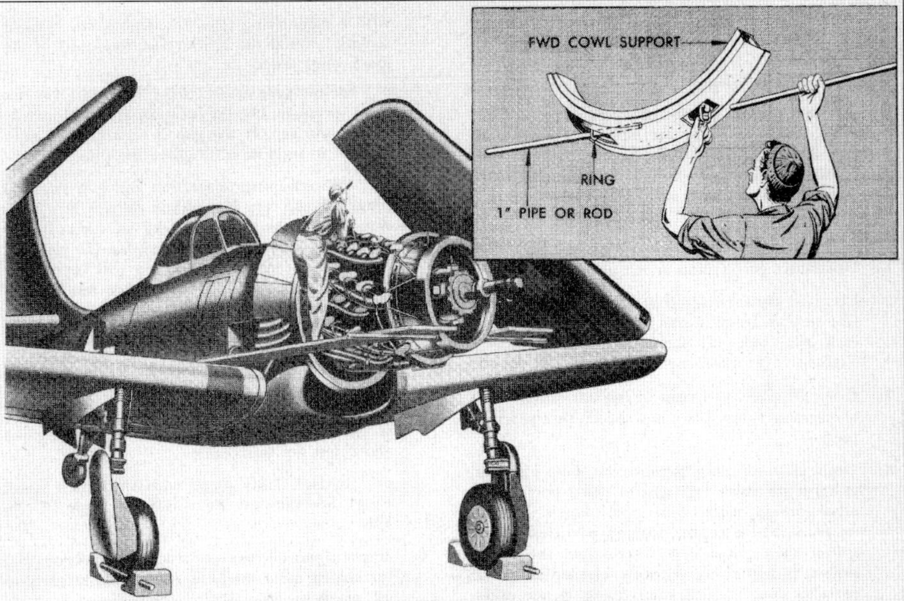

Figure 101—Emergency Service Platform

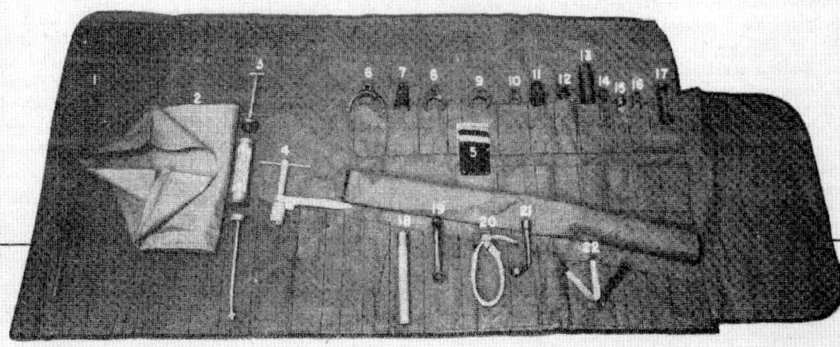

1. EXTENSION 16" x 3/8" SQ.
2. BAG – TOOL KIT
3. GUN – SPARK PLUG COMPOUND INJECTOR
4. WRENCH – VALVE ADJ. SCREW AND LOCK NUT
5. MIRROR 4 1/2" x 2 1/2"
6. WRENCH – INTAKE PIPE NUT
7. WRENCH – PUSH ROD NUT
8. WRENCH O.E. 1 1/4"
9. WRENCH 1 1/8" CROWFOOT
10. WRENCH – STARTER NUTS
11. DEPRESSER – ROCKER ARM.
12. WRENCH – ROCKER ARM NUTS
13. WRENCH – 7/8" SPARK PLUG
14. WRENCH – PAL NUT
15. WRENCH – ROCKER SHAFT HOLDING
16. WRENCH – GENERATOR NUTS
17. WRENCH – 3/4" SPARK PLUG ELBOW
18. DRIFT – FIBER
19. WRENCH – CYLINDER NUT SEMI-LONG
20. WRENCH – ADJUSTABLE STRAP
21. WRENCH – CYLINDER NUTS
22. GAGE – VALVE CLEARANCE

Figure 102—Engine Tool Kit

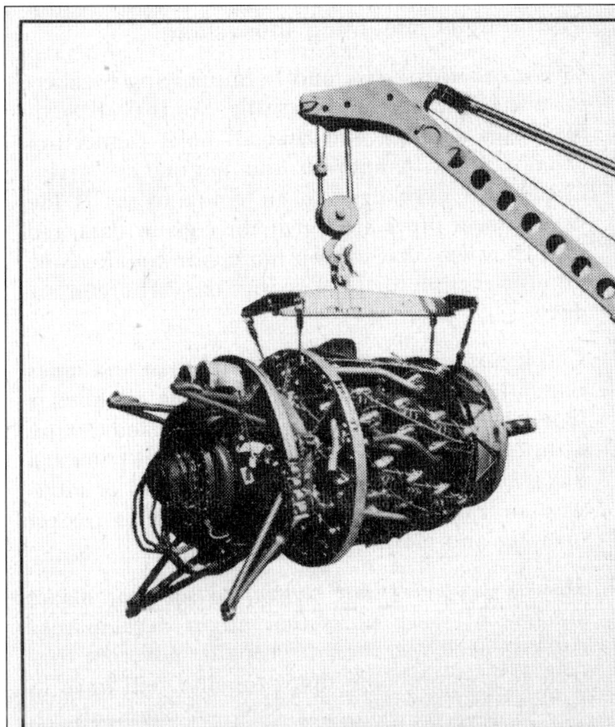

Figure 103—Engine Hoisting

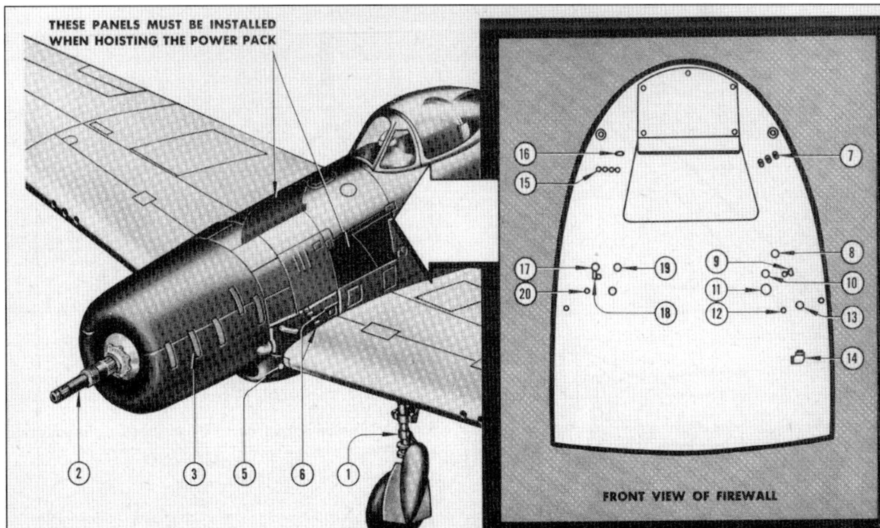

Figure 104—Power Pack Removal

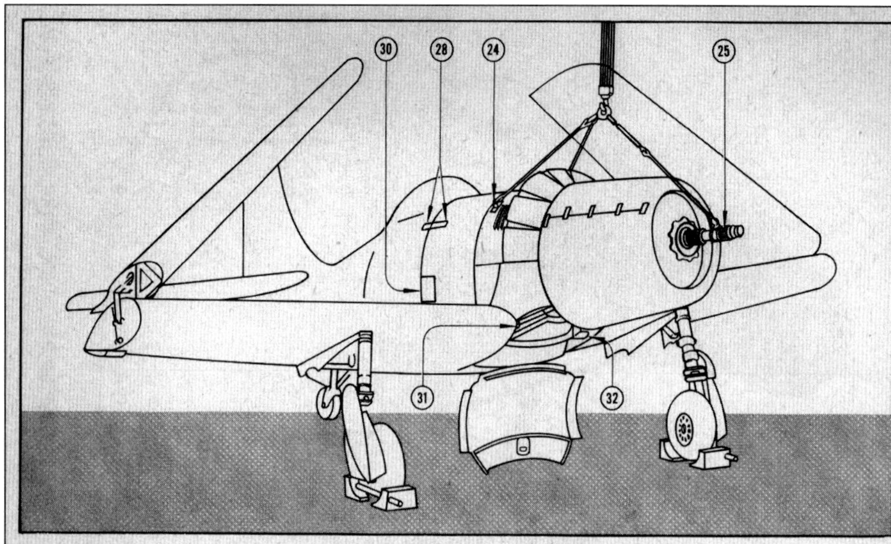

Figure 105—Power Pack Removal

Manual Scan: National Archives, RG 287

Figure 111—Spark Advance Controls

Manual Scan: National Archives, RG 287

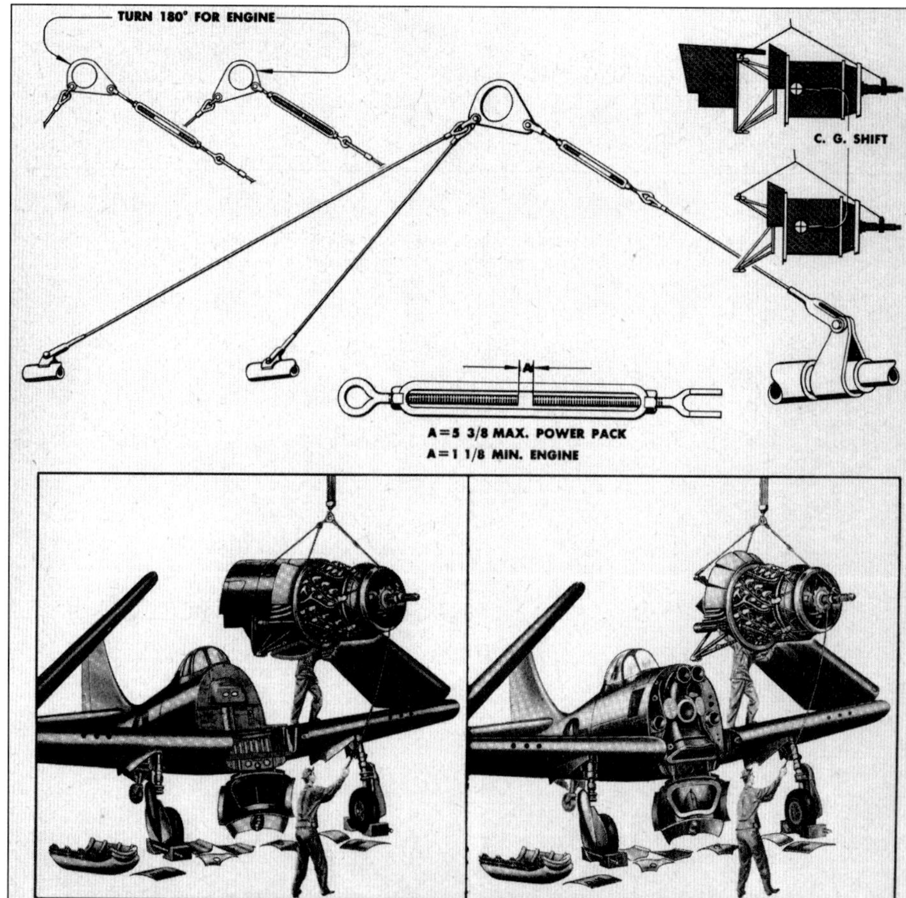

Figure 106—Power Pack Hoisting

Manual Scan: National Archives, RG 287

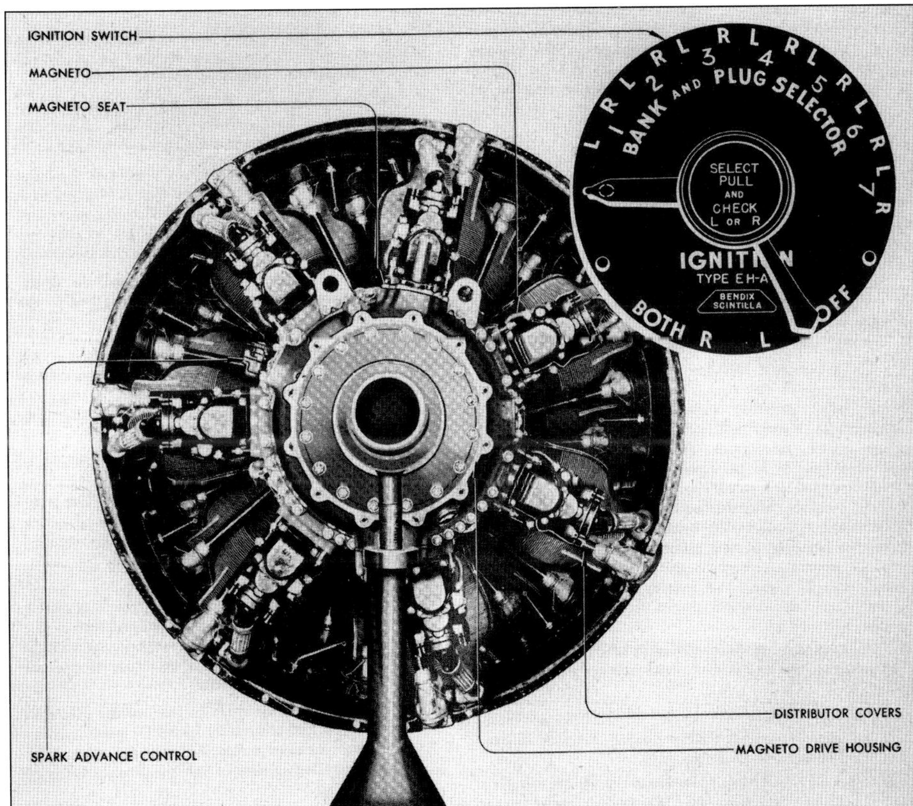

Figure 107—Ignition—Magneto and Switch

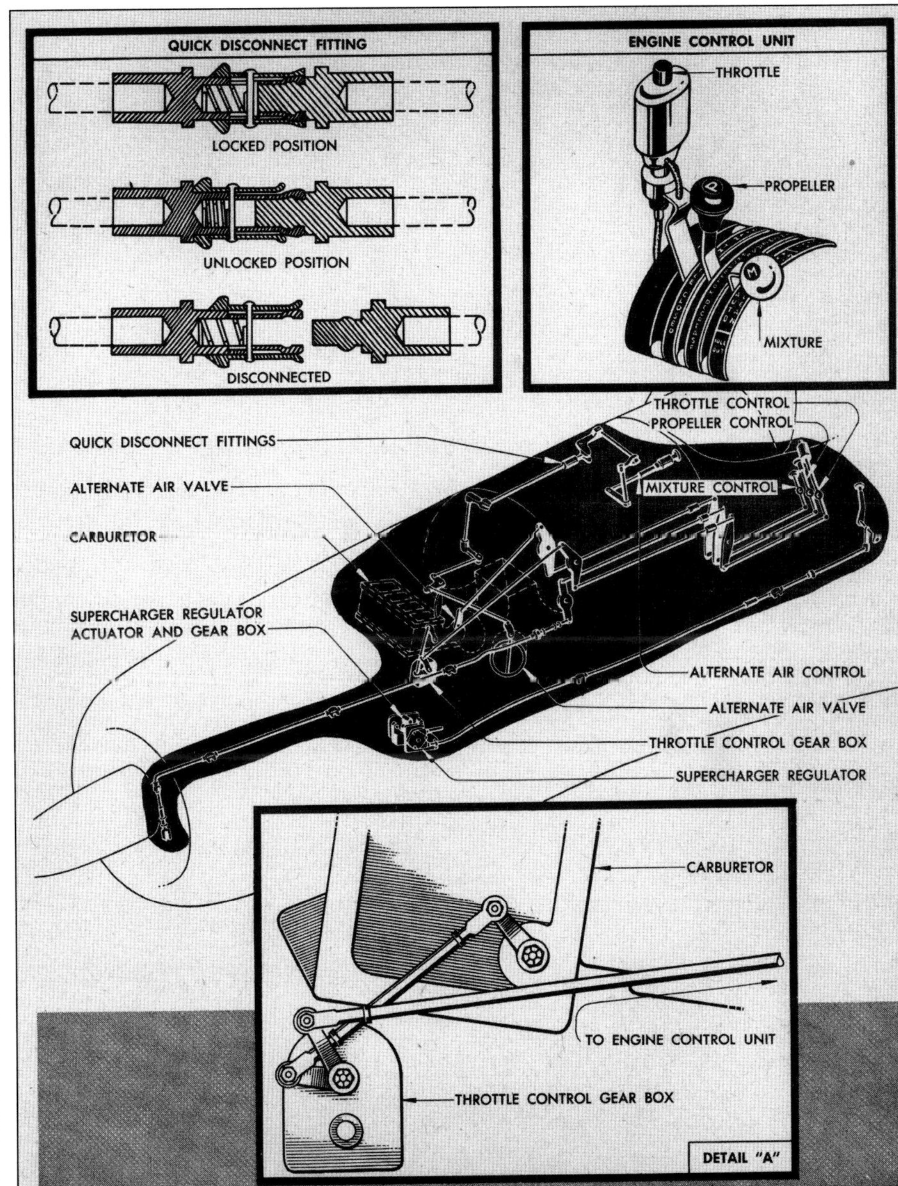

Figure 117—Engine Controls

PROPELLER

The AD7562-X8 propeller is made up of two propeller assemblies, each having a complete, self-contained hydraulic system for changing the pitch of its blades. The inboard assembly is controlled by a centrifugal governor. The speed of the governor is set by the cockpit control. (See Engine Controls.) The outboard assembly is controlled by coordinating or following mechanism so that its blade angle is correctly related to that of the inboard assembly at all times.

The propeller covered by this handbook is designed for 3345 HP at propeller speeds up to 1150 RPM (3018 engine RPM). Governor control covers a range from 610 to 1150 propeller RPM. The governor holds the propeller speed within 5 RPM of the setting under all normal conditions. This response is obtained with a rate of pitch change of 4.2° per second, which is adequate to maintain a constant engine speed.

GENERAL SPECIFICATIONS

Model Designation—AD7562-X8

Shaft Sizes—Outboard 50, Inboard 70

Number of Blades per Propeller Component—3, Total—6

Diameter—13′ 5-11/16″

Blade Angle Range—35°

Maximum Control Speed—1150 RPM (Propeller)

Engine Rating—3345 BHP at 2700 Engine RPM at take-off

Figure 118—Propeller

Figure 119—Propeller Installed

Figure 120—Propeller Installed (Without Front Spinner)

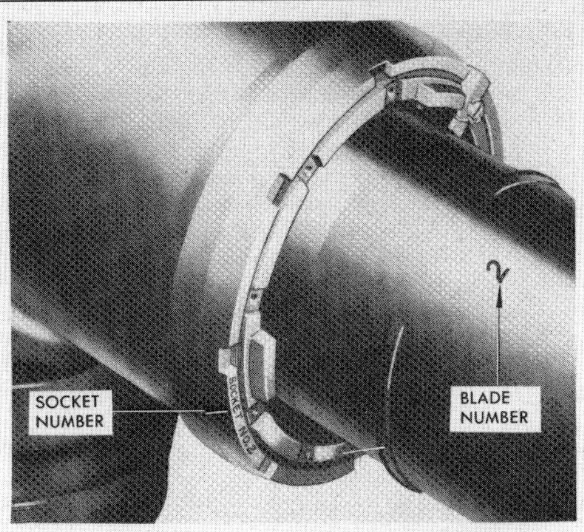

Figure 123—Checking Blade and Socket Numbers

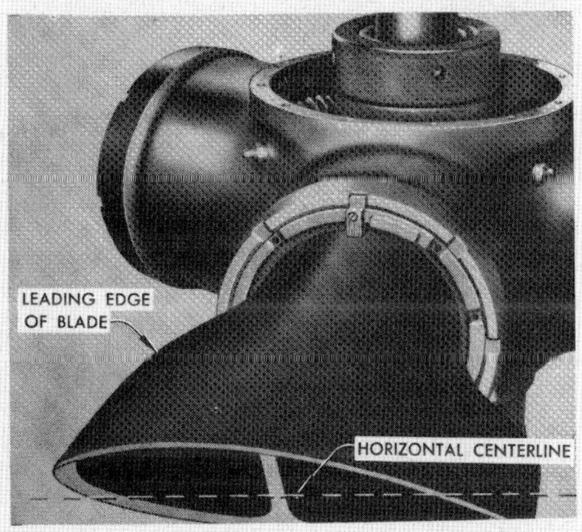

Figure 124—Checking Inboard Blade Installation

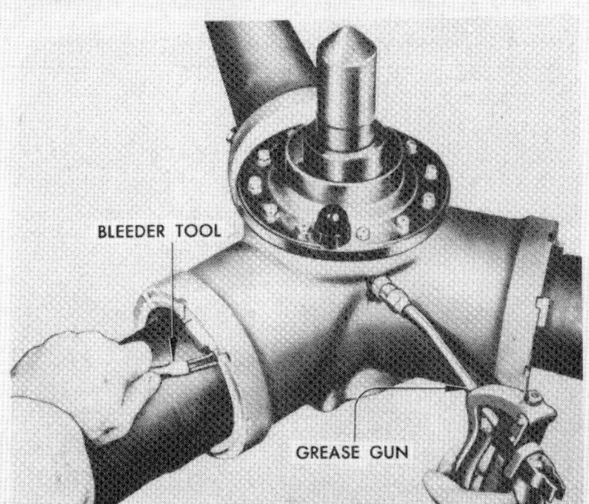

Figure 125—Greasing the Hub

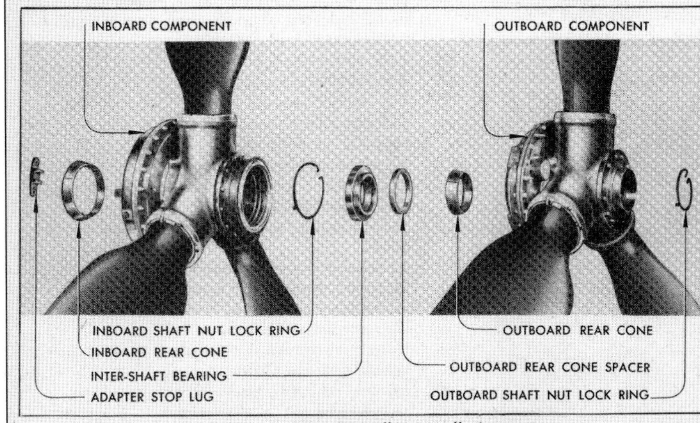

Figure 127—Propeller Installation

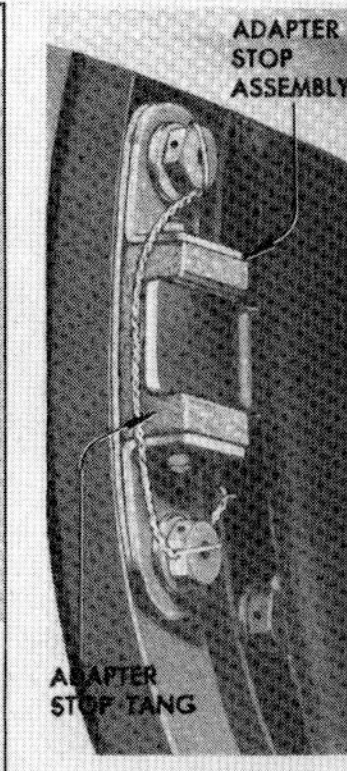

Figure 128—Aligning Adapter Plate with Stops

ENGINE COWLING AND COWL FLAPS

ENGINE COWLING

Engine cowling consists of a three-piece ring cowl, ring cowl supports, rings, ring-cowl inner panels, an inner cowl, an engine air seal, removable cowl panels and miscellaneous fixed cowling, cowl flaps (see Engine Cowling illustration) and the engine baffles (not shown in illustration). The use of spring cowl fasteners allows quick removal of cowl panels. Cowl flaps are operated by an electric-motor-driven-screw jack system.

Ring Cowls — The ring cowling is made up of three panels. They are locked together by latches and supported by the ring cowl front and rear supports.

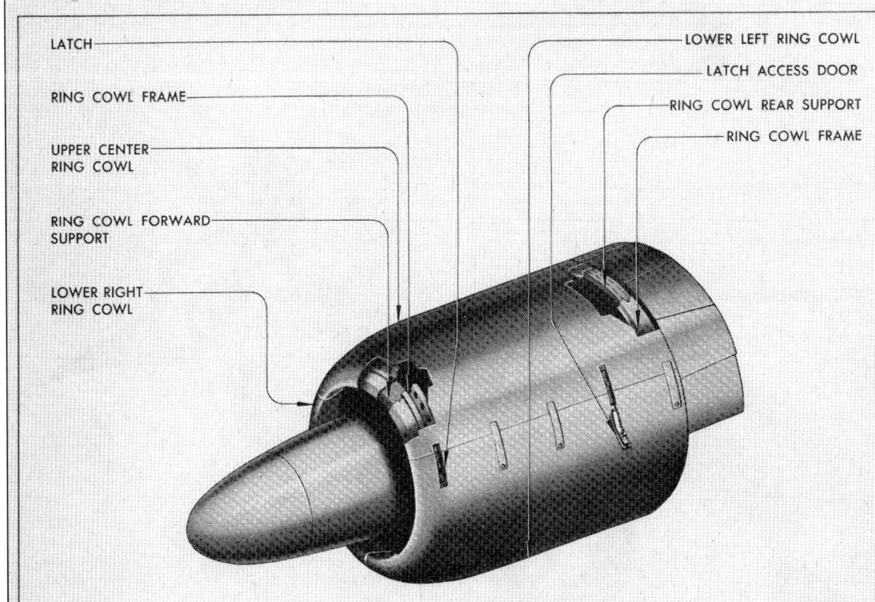

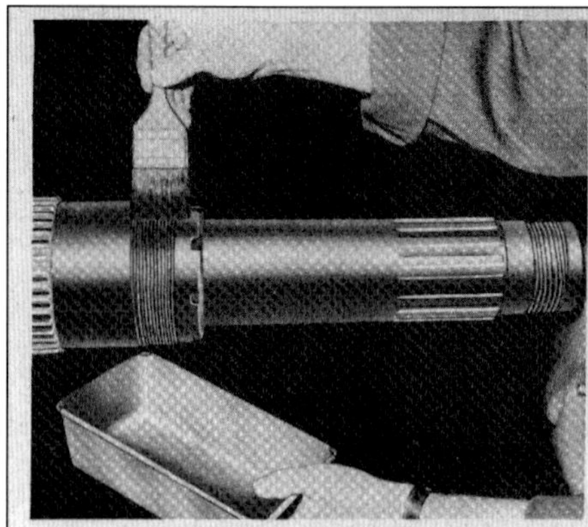

Figure 129—Cleaning Shafts

Installation of Inboard Propeller Components

1. Install the adapter stop lug assembly to the engine nose studs on the left hand side (on horizontal centerline facing engine) of the outermost bolt circle. Use the AN75-7 bolts provided with the propeller.
2. Remove the thread protectors from the propeller shafts.
3. Clean both shafts with gasoline or solvent.
4. Stone out any burrs on the threads and splines.
5. Any scratches on the threads and splines can be removed with crocus cloth.
6. Wipe both shafts clean and dry with a clean cloth.
7. Install the inboard rear cone. (The cone must be installed dry; there must be no oil on the shaft or cone when the cone is installed.)
8. Apply a light, even coat of oil to the inboard shaft splines only.

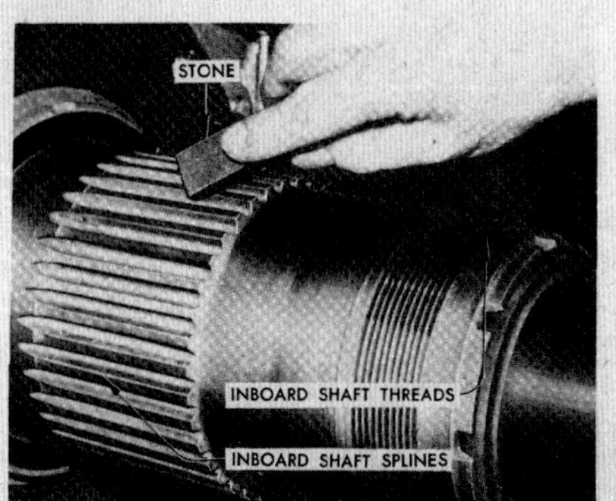

Figure 130—Removing Burrs

Figure 131—Removing Scratches

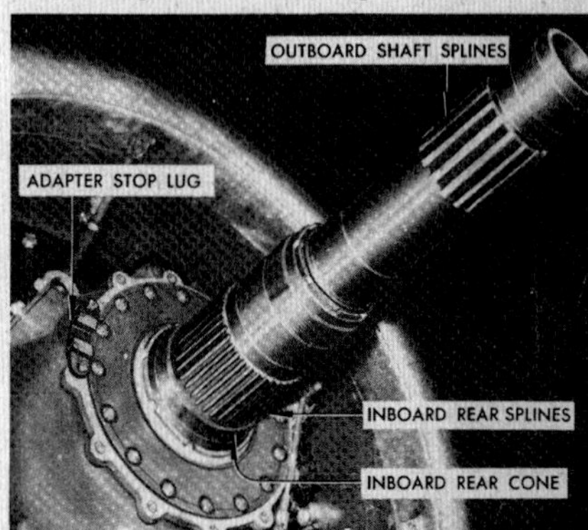

Figure 132—Shafts with Adapter Stop and Rear Cone Installed

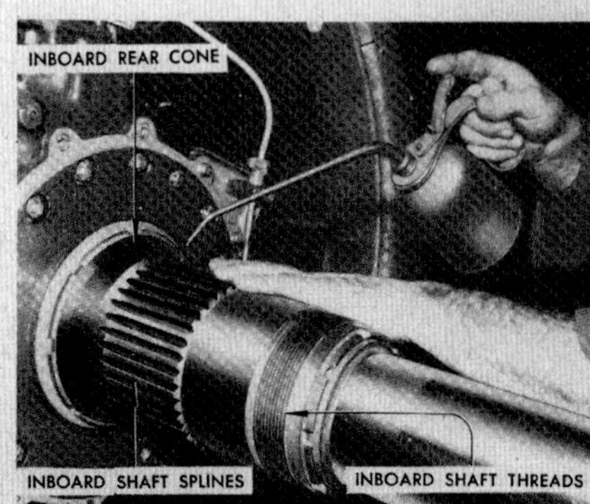

Figure 133—Oiling Splines

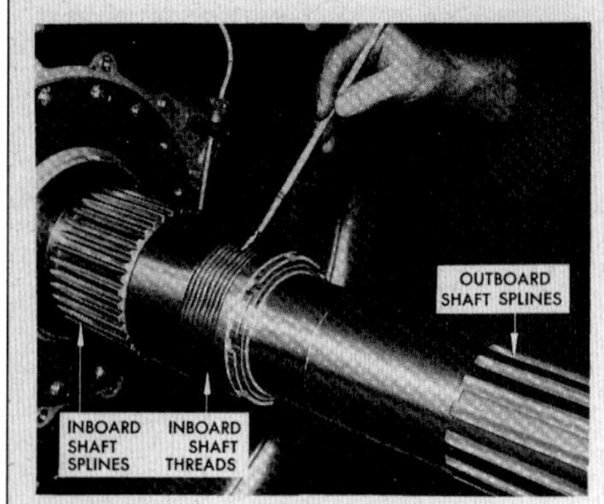

Figure 134—Brushing Anti-Seize Compound on Shaft Threads

Figure 135—Hoist Sling Attached with No. 1 Blade Down

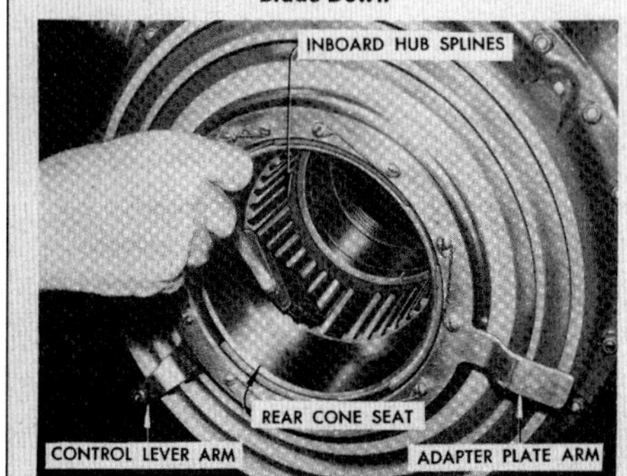

Figure 136—Cleaning Inboard Hub Splines and Rear Cone Seat

9. Apply a thin coat of anti-seize compound, Specification AN-C-53 to the inboard shaft threads.
10. Attach hoist slings to the two blades of the inboard component, opposite the wide spline valley in the hub. The number one blade will be down.
11. Hoist the inboard component and thoroughly clean the hub splines and rear cone seat with a brush and clean rag. (The cone seat must be dry when the propeller is installed.)
12. Align the propeller with the propeller shaft and guide it over the shaft. *Take care not to damage the cone seat, threads, or splines.*
13. Center the arm of the adapter plate in the slot in the adapter stop lug mounted on the gear box.

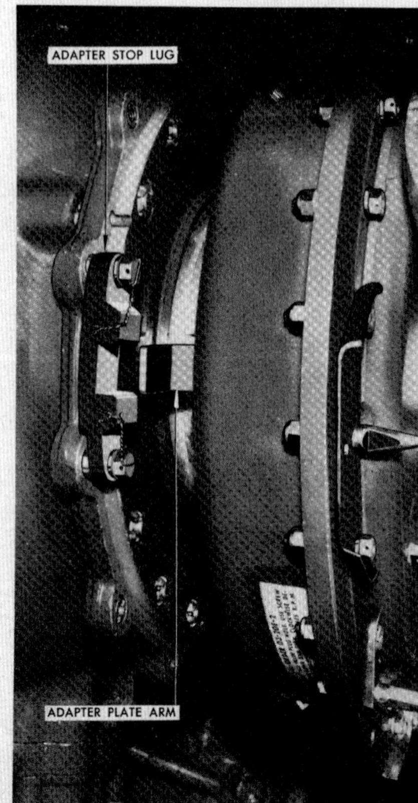

Figure 137—Aligning Adapter Arm and Adapter Stop Lug

Manual Scan: National Archives, RG 287

14. Insert the inboard shaft nut wrench adapter. Tighten the inboard component retaining nut to 1000 pound feet with the blade retaining nut wrench and a 4-foot bar.

15. Install the inboard component shaft nut lock ring. Be sure the slots are properly aligned.

16. Check to see that there is clearance behind the arm. This clearance is necessary to prevent the regulator from binding. If there is no clearance, the inboard component is improperly installed. *Never loosen shaft nut to align the slots; always tighten it.*

17. Connect the propeller control linkage to the control lever arm. See that the control lever is in the maximum RPM position and that there is at least 1/16 inch (maximum, 1/8 inch) spring-back at the control quadrant when the control is in the full "Increase RPM" position, to assure full travel of the propeller control lever.

18. Make certain that the inboard component is in full low blade angle as follows:

    Place the control quadrant in the full "Increase RPM" position.

    Turn the propeller so that the filler plug (filler hole) of the inboard component is above the horizontal center line. Remove the filler plug and install the hand adjustment pump in the filler hole.

    Remove the external filter and install the pump cap.

    Connect the hose to the pump. Turn the propeller until the hand pump is down.

    Operate pump until fluid flows through hose.

    Connect the hose to the pump cap.

Figure 138—Tightening Inboard Component Retaining Nut

    Operate the hand pump until a decided increase in resistance is felt. This indicates that the full low blade angle has been reached.

    Turn the propeller until the hand pump in the filler plug hole is horizontal. Remove the pump cap from the regulator well, then replace the external filter and safety.

19. Check the hydraulic fluid level in the inboard regulator as follows:

    With the hand pump installed in the regulator filler hole, turn the propeller so that the pump is in the horizontal position.

    Remove any hydraulic fluid above the horizontal position from the regulator with hand pump.

    If there is no excess fluid, remove pump and add fluid to the regulator until it appears at the regulator filler hole.

    Replace and safety the filler plug.

    Turn the propeller with number one blade down.

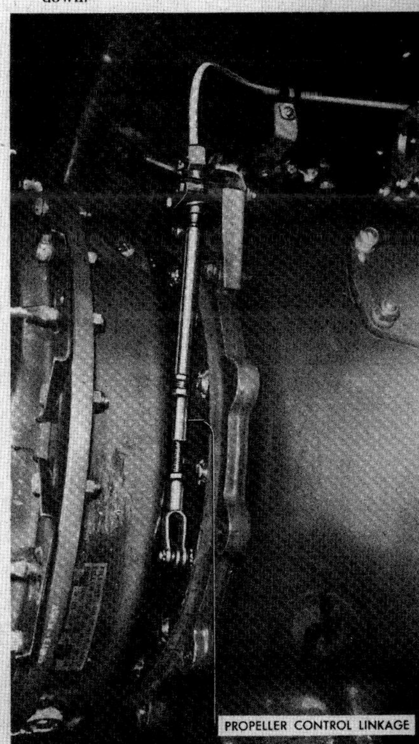

Figure 139—Propeller Control Linkage Connection

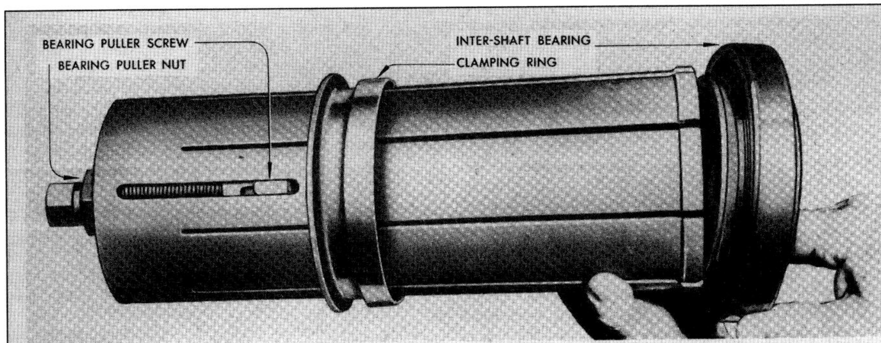

Figure 140—Installing Intershaft Bearing and Bearing Puller

20. Install the inboard spinner as follows:

    Slip the spinner over the shaft and hub.

    Align the spinner on spinner locating studs. The spinner may be aligned in any of three positions. (The chafing ring on the front of the spinner slips over the fixed gear drive plate.)

    Install the spinner attaching bolts through the blade cutouts. Install the cap screws from the rear side. The use of a ratchet with 1/4 or 3/8 inch drive will aid in installing the bolts.

Installation of Outboard Propeller Components

1. Apply a light coat of graphite base grease on the outer diameter and inner bore of the inter-shaft bearing. The inter-shaft bearing is packed with grease to last its entire life. *Do not wash this bearing in any solvent.*

2. Install the inter-shaft bearing in the bearing puller assembly (with the puller flange toward the puller). The puller flange has a shoulder. Pull the sliding collar up to the bearing.

3. Turn the bearing-puller screw clockwise to the end of its travel.

4. Install the bearing and puller assembly on the outboard component shaft. Carefully align the bearing on the shaft.

5. Apply anti-seize compound, Specification No. AN-C-53, to the threads of the bearing-puller screw.

6. Screw the bearing-puller nut completely onto the end of the outboard component shaft.

7. Turn the bearing-puller screw counter-clockwise until the bearing is forced entirely into the bore of the master gear retaining plate of the inboard component. Use a wrench with a 7/8-inch opening.

8. Slide collar back and remove puller from shaft.

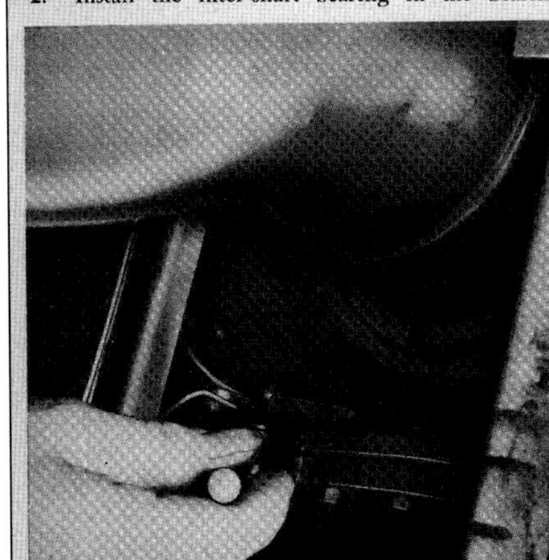

Figure 141—Tightening Spinner Attaching Bolts

Figure 142—Turning the Bearing Puller Screw

Manual Scan: National Archives, RG 287

Figure 143—Installing Outboard Shaft Nut Wrench Adapter

Figure 145—Installing Outboard Shaft Nut Lock Ring

9. Install the cone spacer on the outboard component shaft.
10. Install the outboard component rear cone. (The shaft and rear cone must be free from oil or grease. This cone is installed dry.)
11. Apply a light, even coat of engine oil to the outboard component splines.
12. Apply a light, even coat of anti-seize compound, Specification No. AN-C-53, to the outboard component shaft threads.
13. Thoroughly clean the internal splines and the rear cone seat of the outboard component hub. (The rear cone seat must be dry when the outboard component is installed.)
14. Install the outboard component on the shaft with the No. 1 blade down.
15. Install the outboard shaft nut wrench adapter.
16. Tighten the shaft nut to 1000 pound feet, with a 4-foot bar.
17. Install the outboard shaft-nut lock-ring. Be sure to align the notches in the nut with those of the transfer-gear retaining plate.

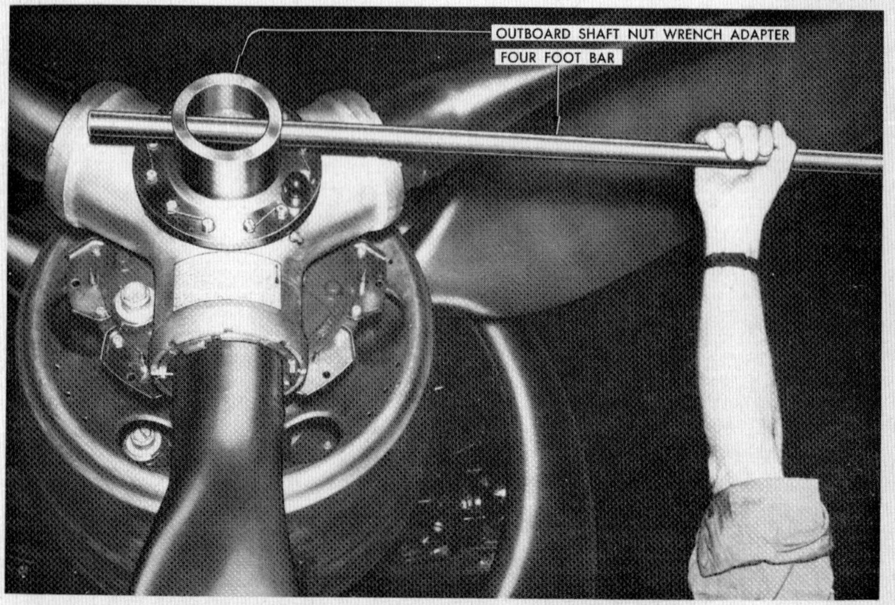

Figure 144—Tightening Outboard Component Retaining Nut

Figure 145A—Correct Alignment of Outboard Shaft Nut Lock Ring

18. Place the tangs of the coordinator assembly (outboard component) in the notches of the inner coupling of the inboard component (tangs and notches engage in only one position and an audible "click" can be heard when the correct position is found). The position can be found by slowly rotating the propeller by hand. After aligning the inner coupling notches and tangs, align the outer coupling tangs (inboard component) with the mating notches on the coordinator assembly of the outboard component. Turn the fixed gear in either direction until alignment is attained.
19. To adjust the coordinating mechanism between the two propellers proceed as follows (it is assumed that a blade template for the 42-inch radius and a protractor are available for making the adjustment):

Make sure inboard propeller blade angle setting indicates low pitch position, as described in step 18, under Installation of Inboard Propeller Component.

Remove external filter cap assembly between blade sockets on the face of the outboard regulator unit. Replace with cap 6500373. Then, with the outboard regulator filler hole 10 to 15 degrees above horizontal, fill the regulator with oil, Y-3587, until it reaches the level of the hole.

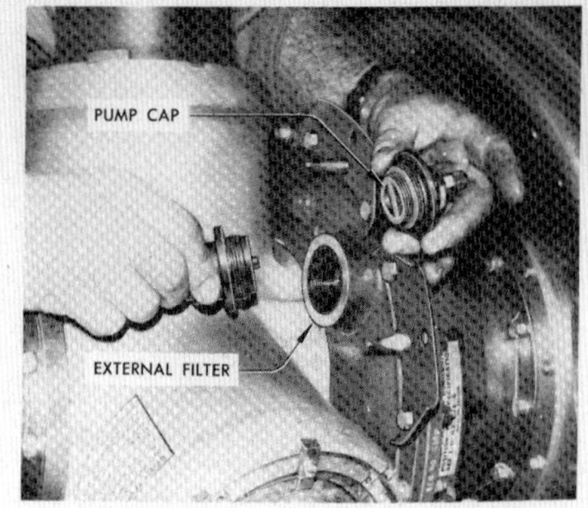

Figure 147—Removing External Filter Cap

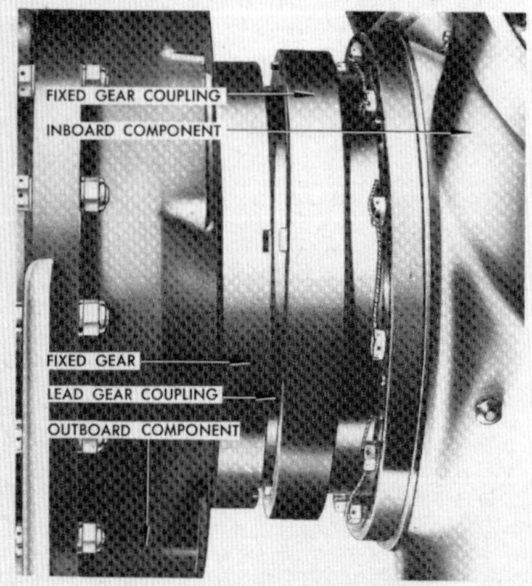

Figure 146—Engaging Coupling and Coordinator (Lead Gear not shown)

Figure 148—Engaging Fixed Gear Coupling (With Fixed Gear)

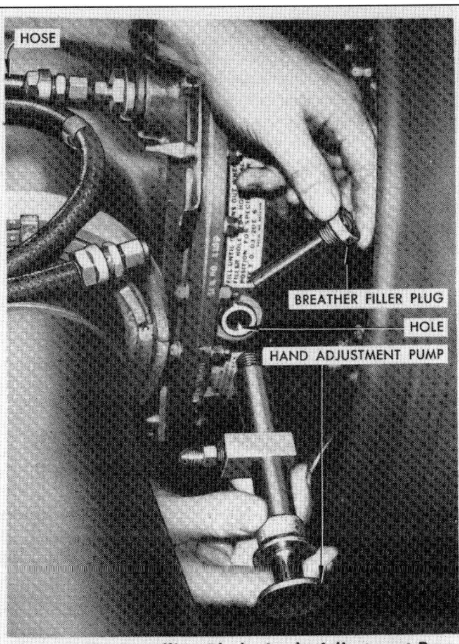

Figure 149—Installing Blade Angle Adjustment Pump

Figure 150—Blade Angle Adjustment Hose Assembly Connected

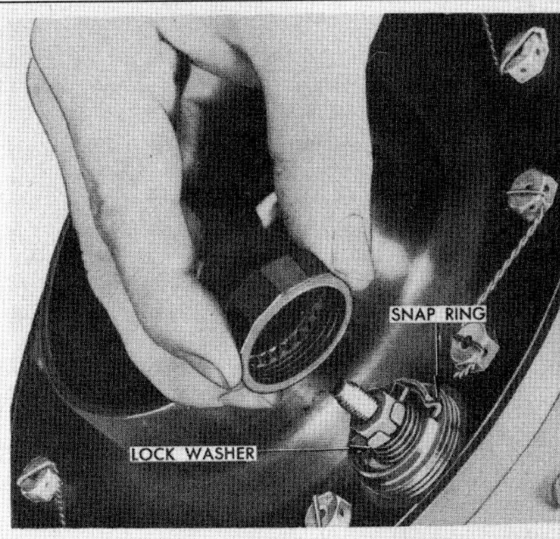

Figure 151—Removing Adjustment Shaft Cap

Screw the blade angle adjustment pump 6500372 into the regulator filler hole.

Connect the hose assembly 6500469 between the filler pad cap and the pump.

Remove black plastic cap.

Loosen the nut on the adjustment shaft to within .250 inch minimum of the shaft end.

Apply an inward pressure on the adjustment shaft and turn clockwise *slowly* until the shaft moves into an index hole. After shaft enters index hole, tighten the adjustment nut.

Rotate the propeller until the adjustment pump is several degrees below the level of the oil.

Pump until the neutral position of distributor valve is reached. This position is recognized by greatly increased force required to operate the pump.

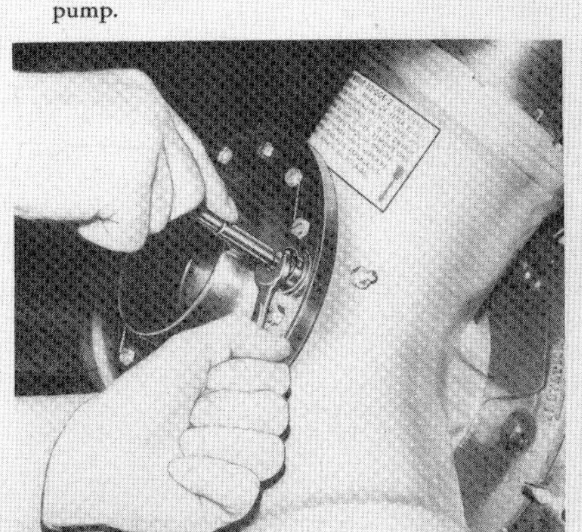

Figure 152—Loosening Blade Angle Adjustment Nut

Check the blade angles of both the inboard and outboard propellers at the 42-inch radius. Note any difference in blade angle between the inboard and outboard propellers.

If blade angles are the same, loosen adjustment nut two turns and rotate shaft through several clicks (increased-pitch direction) until blade angle increases when pump is operated. Make sure the adjustment shaft nut is tightened and shaft is turned toward increased-pitch direction before the hand pump is operated. After blade moves away from low pitch stop, each click of adjustment will give approximately .50 degree angle change. Increase blade angle until the outboard angle is 1.±.3 degree greater than the blade angle of the inboard propeller.

20. If a 42-inch radius blade template and protractor are not available, an alternate adjustment method is offered as follows:

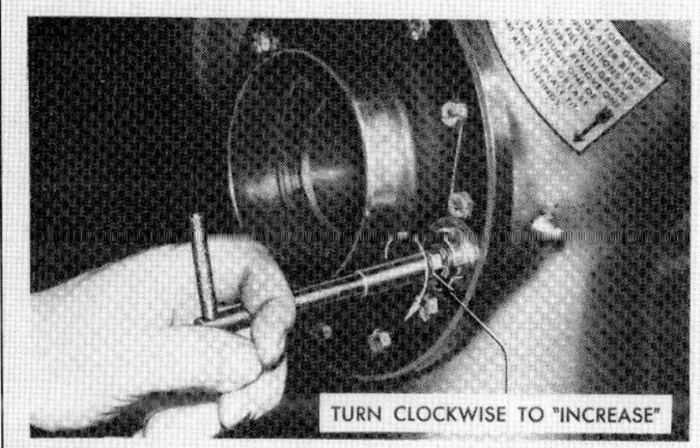

Figure 153—Blade Angle Adjustment

Follow instructions in step 19 above up to the point where the blade angles are to be checked.

Scribe a reference line, with a pencil, on the blade shank opposite the "0" on the graduated blade angle indicator. Each graduation of the indicator represents 1.5 degrees.

If blade angles are the same, loosen adjustment nut two turns and rotate shaft through several clicks (increased-pitch direction) until blade angle increases when pump is operated. Make sure the adjustment shaft nut is tightened and shaft is turned toward increased-pitch direction before the hand pump is operated. After the blade moves away from the low pitch stop, each click of adjustment will give approximately .5 degree angle change.

Check the position of the scribed pencil mark made on the shank of the blade. The mark should now be aligned at a point on the graduated blade angle indicator about 2/3 of the distance from "0" to the first graduation as shown in the illustration.

If the pencil line is not positioned as specified, turn the transfer shaft the number of notches necessary in the direction required to properly align the scribed pencil mark on the blade shank with the indicator.

21. Safety the lock nut on the transfer shaft by bending one tang of the lock washer.

22. Make certain the snap ring is in place. Replace the cap.

23. Turn the propeller until the hand pump in the filler plug hole is horizontal.

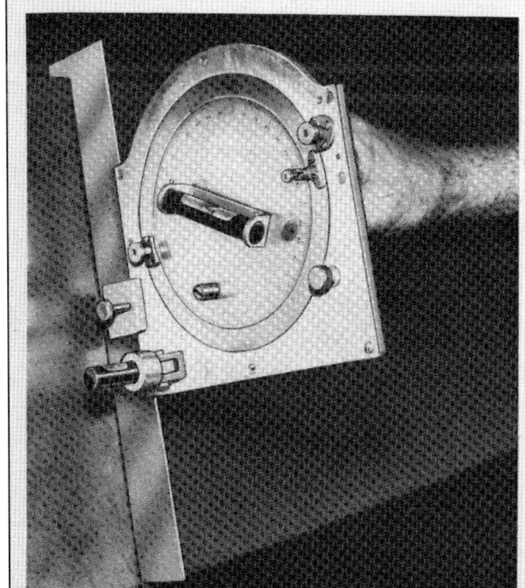

Figure 154—Determining Blade Angle with Protractor

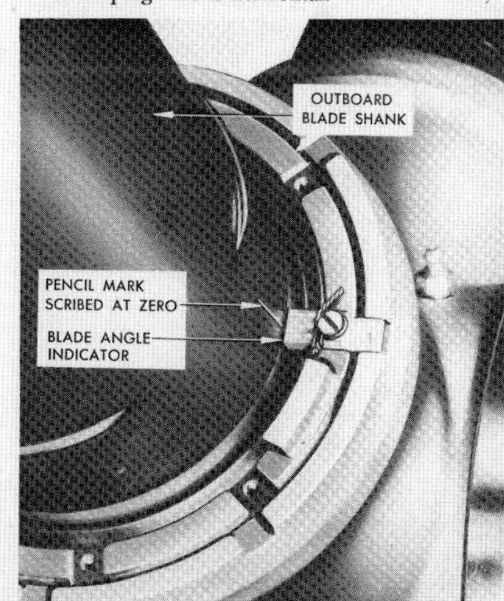

Figure 155—Location of Scribed Pencil Mark

24. Remove the pump cap from the regulator filter well, then replace the external filter and safety.

25. Check the hydraulic fluid level in the outboard regulator as follows:

With the hand pump installed in the regulator filler hole, make certain the propeller is turned so that the pump is horizontal.

Remove with the hand pump, any hydraulic fluid which is above the level of the pump fitting when the pump is horizontal.

If no excess fluid is present, remove pump and add fluid to the regulator until it appears at the regulator filler hole.

Replace and safety the filler plug.

26. Install the blade cutout plates on the inboard spinner with a Phillips screwdriver.

27. Run the engine. Start at 2300 RPM with the propeller control in the "Increase RPM" position. Pull the propeller control back and allow the engine to drop to 1800 RPM or less. Move the propeller control forward to the full "Increase RPM" position. Repeat this process three times and after 2300 RPM is reached for the last time shut off the engine. This purges air from the propeller hydraulic system.

28. Re-check the position of the scribed pencil mark made on the shank of the blade. If the mark indicates that the blade angle differential is not within the specified tolerance, remove the cap from the transfer shaft, loosen the nut and turn the shaft the necessary number of notches to make the correction. (One notch represents five-tenths of a degree.) It is not necessary to use the hand oil pump to change the blade angle after adjustment is made. If an adjustment is made, run the engine and again shut it off with the propeller control in the "Increase RPM" position and recheck the angle differential.

29. Check the fluid level in both regulators. Use the procedure described in step 19, under Installation of Inboard Propeller Component.

30. Install the spinner on the outboard component as follows:

Take outboard spinner shell assembly and slip over the hub so dowel holes in shell bulkhead slide over the six dowels on the outside diameter of the regulator. Make sure the chafing ring on the front bulkhead of shell slides onto pilot diameter of outboard hub before securing spinner.

Insert the six retaining screws that hold the shell on the hub and tighten them.

Install blade cutout plates. Make sure that each one is mounted over the proper opening. Each plate is stamped with a number and a corresponding number can be found near each opening.

31. The maximum governing RPM can be changed by adjusting the load on the governor spring. To make the adjustment, remove the filler plug from the inboard regulator. A slotted screw, just inside regulator, has a bearing face in contact with the governor spring. This screw has 14 equally spaced serrations or notches on its bearing face that engage 14 like notches on the fixed portion of the governor. The force of the spring on the screw keeps it locked at all times. It is possible to turn the adjustment or slotted screw by inserting a screw driver in the filler hole and engaging the slot. Turn the screw clockwise to increase in RPM. Each 1/14 turn (one notch) changes the maximum control speed about 14 engine RPM.

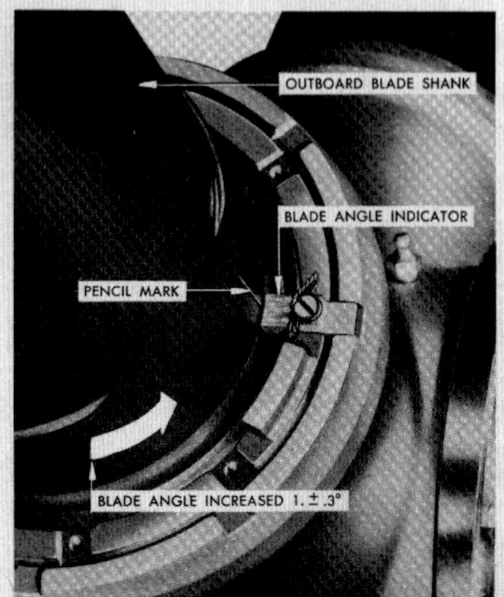

Figure 156—Location of Scribed Pencil Mark After Adjustment

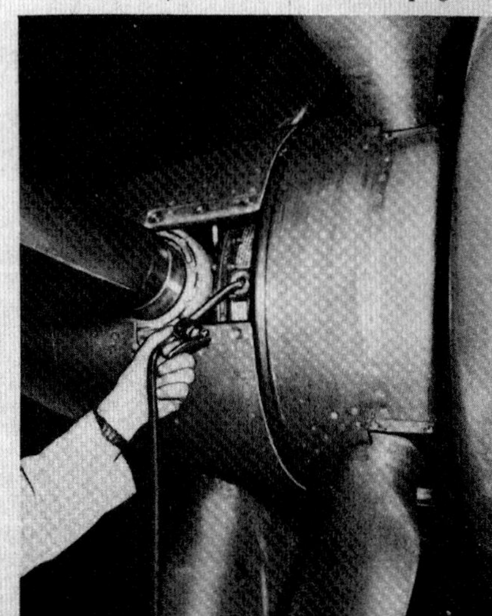

Figure 157—Adding Fluid to Regulator

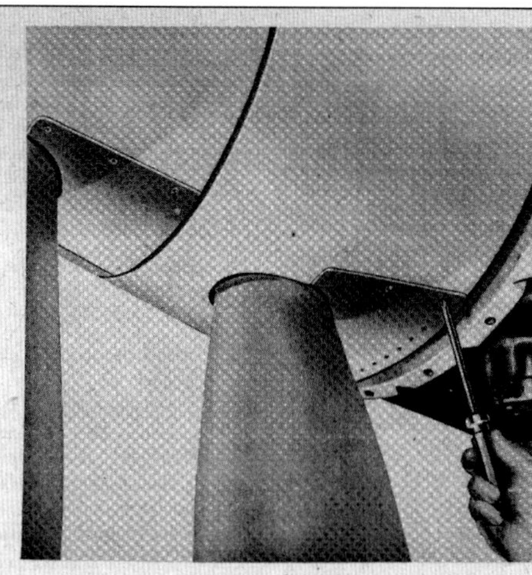

Figure 158—Removing Blade Cutout Plates

Removal of Inboard Propeller Component

1. Check the ignition switch for "OFF" position.
2. Turn the number one blade of each component down.
3. Remove the spinner blade cutout plates with a screwdriver. *(See figure 158.)*
4. Reach through blade plate holes of the outboard spinner and remove the six spinner retaining bolts.
5. Remove the outboard spinner shell.
6. Remove outboard component shaft nut lock ring with the fingers. *(See figure 159.)*

Figure 159—Removing Outboard Component Shaft Nut Lock Ring

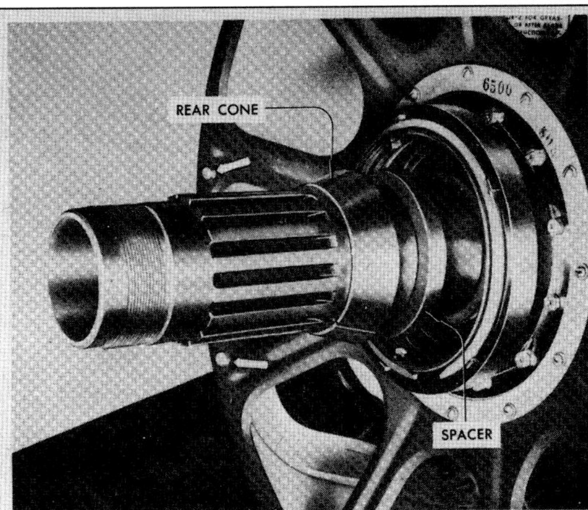

Figure 160—Installing Outboard Component Rear Cone and Spacer

7. Place the hoist slings about the two upper blades of the outboard component as near the hub as possible.
8. Use the hoist to relieve the propeller shaft of the weight of the outboard component.
9. Loosen the outboard shaft nut by turning counter-clockwise with the shaft nut wrench and adapter and a 4-foot bar. Turn until it is free of the threads and gradually raise the hoist to relieve the shaft of the propeller weight.
10. Manipulate the hoist carefully to prevent the propeller weight from damaging the shaft or hub. Exercise special care to prevent nicking the rear cone seat in the hub. Pull the propeller slowly off the shaft and place it on a dolly so that the regulator is not supporting any of the weight.
11. Remove the outboard rear cone and spacer ring. *(See figure 160.)*
12. Screw the inter-shaft bearing puller completely onto the number 50 shaft. Attach the puller to the bearing and remove the inter-shaft bearing. *(See figure 161.)*
13. Install the outboard shaft thread protector.

Figure 161—Installing the Inter Shaft Bearing

Figure 162—Installing Inboard Spinner

Removal of Outboard Propeller Component

1. Remove the six inboard spinner mounting bolts with a one-half inch universal socket and speed handle. *(See figure 162.)*
2. Remove the inboard spinner with the hands only.
3. Disconnect the propeller control linkage from the control lever.
4. Remove the inboard shaft nut lock ring with the fingers only.
5. Attach hoist slings to the two upper blades of the inboard component. (Number one blade must be down.) Use the hoist to relieve the shaft of the propeller weight.
6. Loosen the inboard shaft nut, with the shaft nut wrench and adapter, and a 4-foot bar, until it is free of the threads; gradually hoist the propeller to relieve the shaft of the propeller weight.
7. Manipulate the hoist carefully to prevent the propeller weight from damaging the shaft or hub. Exercise special care to prevent nicking the rear cone seat in the hub. Pull the propeller slowly off the shaft and place it on a dolly so that the regulator is not supporting any of the weight.
8. Remove the inboard rear cone.
9. Apply a light coat of oil to the shafts and see that thread protectors are installed on both.

Lubrication of Propeller Hub Assemblies

At 60 hour intervals lubricate blade bearings and gears. A power or hand grease gun may be used, filled with grease Specification No. Y-3581 or equivalent.

Rotate propeller until pressure relief grease fitting is at the top. Place the grease gun on one of the bottom fittings and apply grease until it appears at the pressure relief fitting. Then apply more grease at remaining fitting until the grease forced through the pressure relief fitting is clear. The reason for this procedure is to exclude air by forcing grease into the hub sockets around the blade bearings.

Lubrication of Propeller Regulator Assemblies

1. At 30 hour intervals or after a week or more of standing idle, check oil level in regulators. Check inboard regulator any time the maximum governing RPM of the engine decreases. Rotate propeller until the filler plug is on the horizontal centerline of propeller. Remove the filler plug and, if the oil is below this level, fill with oil Specification No. Y-3587. Replace the filler plug and safety wire. Complete this operation for both regulators.
2. At 60 hour intervals and five hours after new oil has been added to the regulator, remove and clean the filters on the outside of the regulators. Turn the propellers so that the filter will be at the bottom of the regulator. This positioning prevents any oil from running down on the hub assembly and permits easier wiping of oil from parts after filter is removed. Take snap ring and cartridge out of filter cap. Clean thoroughly by washing in unleaded gasoline or equivalent. Reassemble and install in regulators. Take particular care to see that "0" ring seals are replaced correctly. Tighten in place and safety wire.

STARTING SYSTEM

The engine has a combination inertia and direct-cranking Jack and Heintz, JH-4P, starter mounted on the right side of the accessory drive housing. The starter is designed for either manual or electric cranking. The hand cranking equipment consists of a support assembly with a hand crank gear box receptacle, and a manual meshing handle on the right side of the power pack. (See Manual Starting illustration.)

Removal of Starter — Disconnect the electrical plug and flexible drive shaft from the starter. Disconnect the lower end of the manual meshing rod from the crank on the starter. Remove the castle nuts and washers and pull the starter carefully away from the engine with special tool No. F12115. Install a cover plate over the starter jaw. Put the old gasket and a cover plate on the engine mounting pad.

Inspection of Starter — After the starter has been completely dismantled, thoroughly clean all parts with clean unleaded fuel or benzol solvent and compressed air. Examine and check all parts for wear. In addition, the following outline is provided as an aid in overhauling the starter.

1. Brushes—Replace worn brushes before their maximum wear limit is reached to insure proper operation between inspection periods. Worn-out brushes cause burned commutators and insulation. Replace if less than 3/32 inch of brush projects behind the holder. Install new brushes at each overhaul. When replacing a worn brush, seat the brush properly by inserting a strip of No. 000 sandpaper between the brush and commutator with sanded side next to the brush and pull in the direction of rotation until the brush is 75% seated. Do not use emery cloth or coarse sandpaper. Wipe binding brushes and their brush boxes clean with a gasoline moistened cloth. Remove sand or metal particles with compressed air. Use caution when installing brushes. Be sure the insulation around brush leads protects leads from motor housing.
2. Ball and Roller Bearings—Clean and inspect all ball and roller bearings. If ball bearings are too loose or turn roughly, or if the roller bearings are cracked, replace them. Lubricate all bearings (not of the grease seal type) with a light film of grease, grade 375, Specification No. 3560. Do not wash new bearings received in sealed boxes from the factory; lubricate only.
3. Clutch Mechanism—Thoroughly clean all parts and inspect clutch discs for scoring or wear. If worn or scored discs are found, replace in sets only. The discs and clutch pack shall be coated with No. 32 Gredag Grease on assembly.
4. Oil Seal—If Duprene oil seal is worn or torn, replace it.
5. Bearing Spacers—If bearing seizure has occurred, inspect adjacent spacers for scoring and replace if scored or worn.
6. Roller Bearing Rings and Races—Replace rings and races if too pitted or scored.
7. Gears—Replace gears in pairs if the teeth show serious wear or if cracks have developed at the roots of the teeth.

Installation of Starter — Remove the cover from over the starter jaw.

CAUTION—*Do not rest the starter on jaw end without using the shipping cover. Failure to observe this will cause burns or scratches on the jaw teeth, which impair the disengagement of starter and engine jaws.*

Remove the cover and gasket from the engine mounting pad. (If you have exchanged starters, check the size of the engine mounting pad, number and direction of engine jaw teeth against the starter to make certain you have the right model.)

Wipe the mounting pad and starter mounting flange clean. Use a new gasket and mount the starter in position so that meshing linkage, flexible shaft coupling, and electric plug assume their correct locations. Put on the washers and castle nuts and lock with cotter pins. Connect the manual meshing rod to the starter. Connect the flexible shafting and plug the electrical connection into the receptable on the starter.

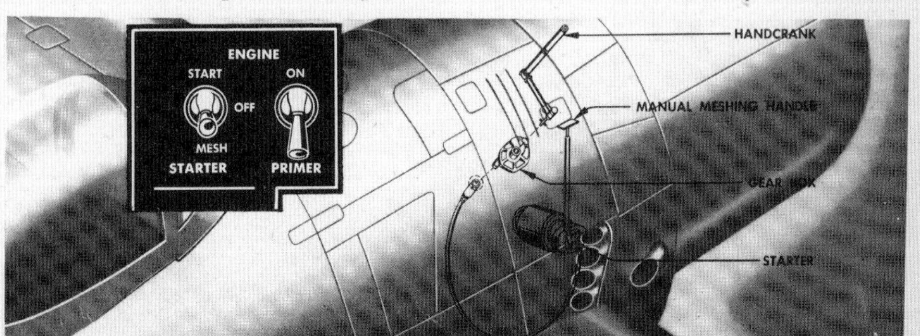

Figure 163—Manual Starting

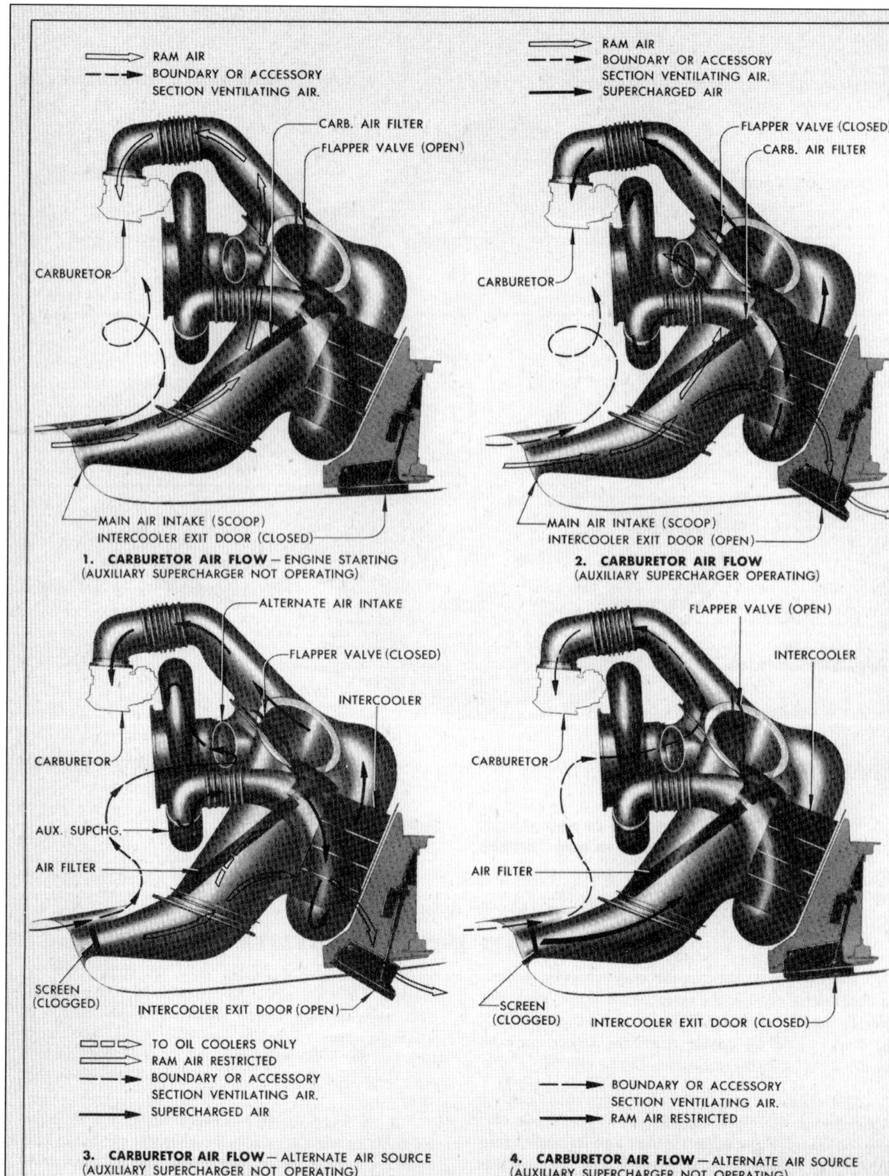

Figure 166—Air Induction Schematic

Manual Scan: National Archives, RG 287

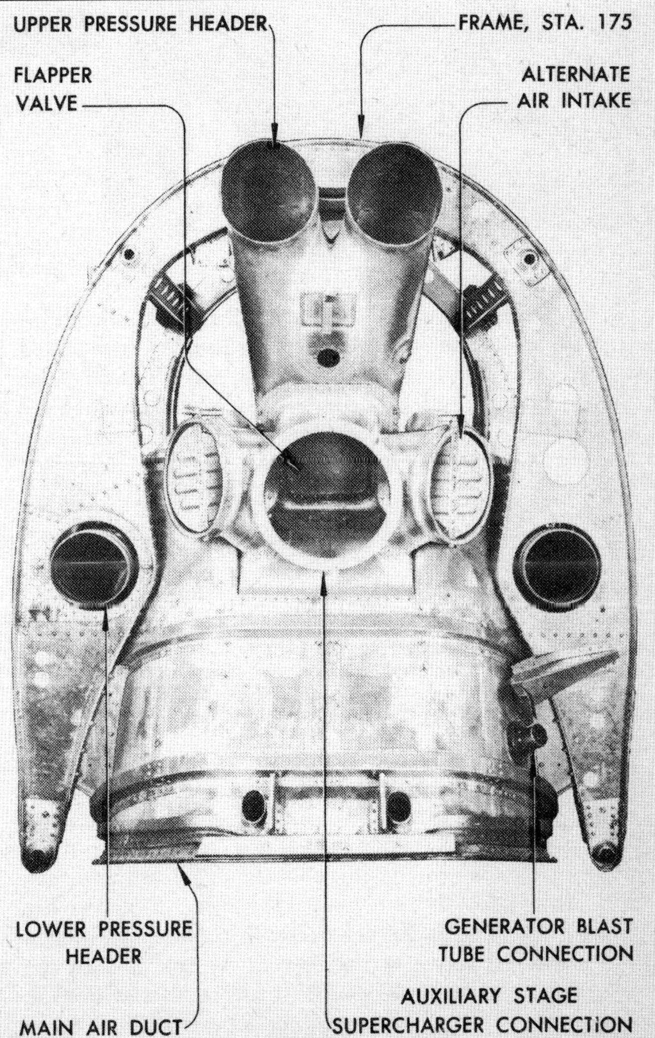

Figure 167—Air Induction System, Front View

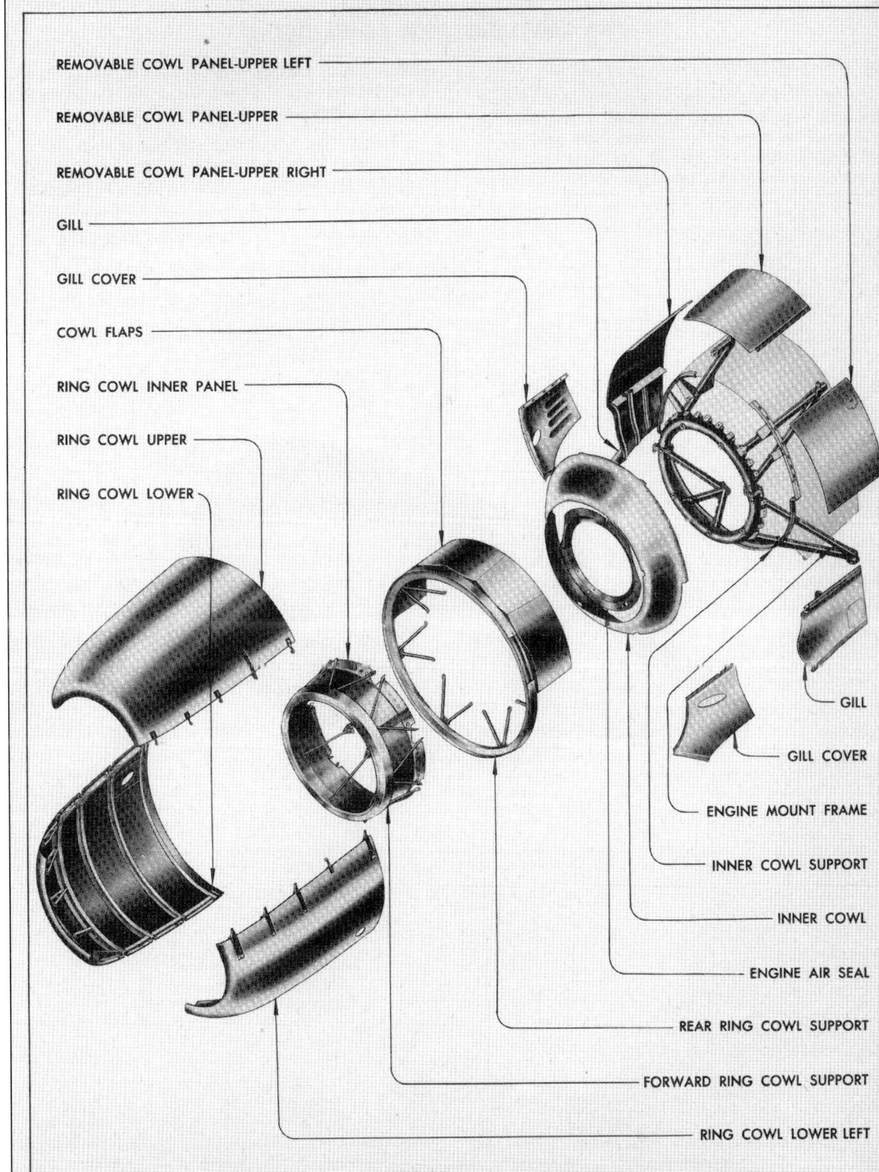

Figure 175—Engine Cowling

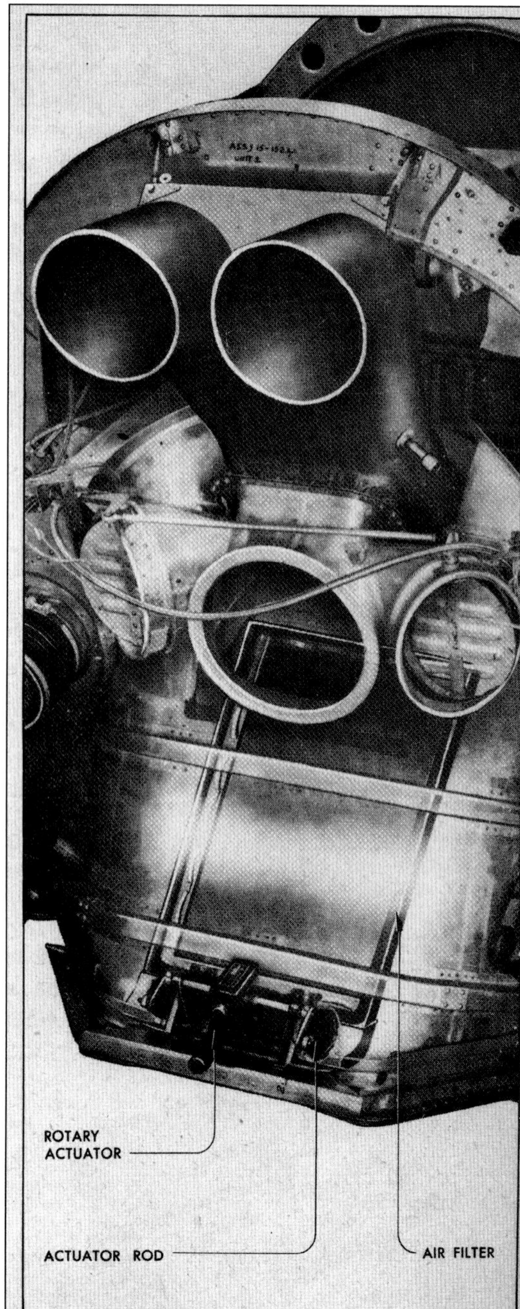

Figure 169—Carburetor Air Filter

stacks where they protrude from the body. The left hand gill has an access door in the lower rear corner for access to the Y-drain cock.

Gill covers hide the forward portion of each gill, and cover the exhaust stacks.

Removal of Gill Cover and Gill:

1. Remove lower removable cowl.
2. Loosen the screws and fasteners holding the gill cover and remove cover.
3. Remove screws holding the gill and slide it aft so the holes on the forward edge clear the pins on the inner cowl support.

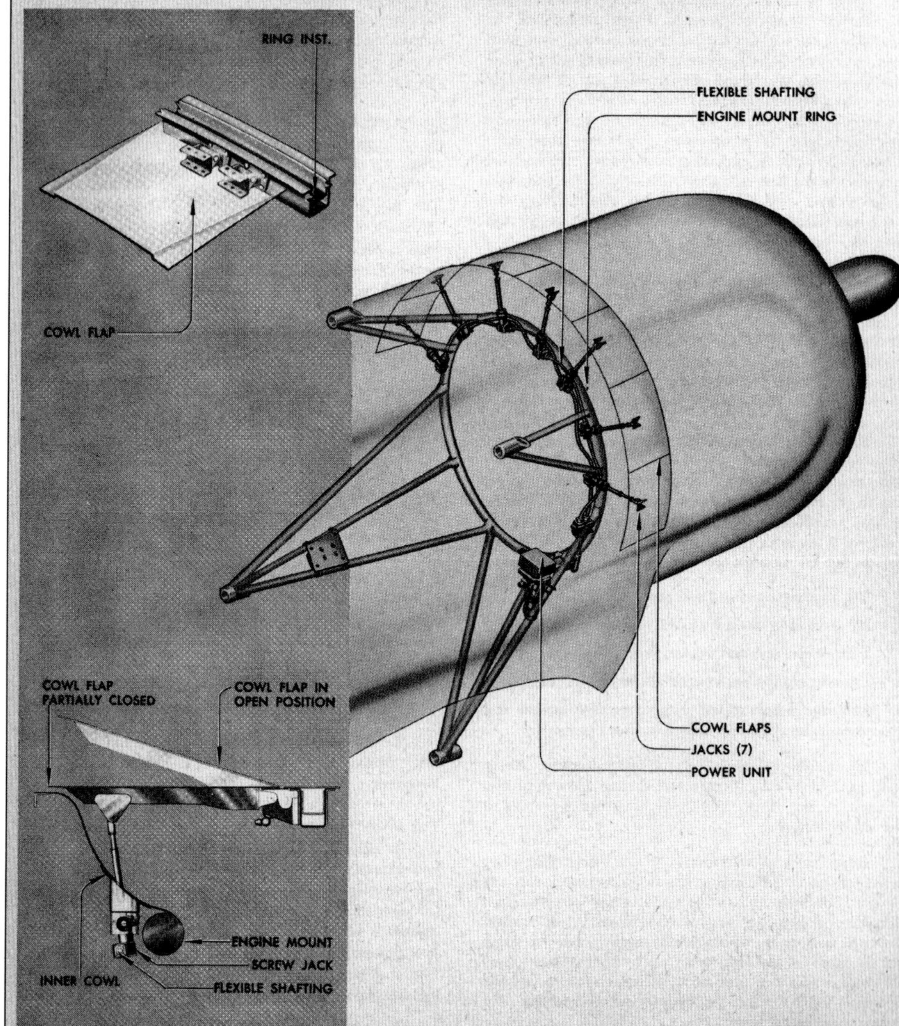

Figure 177—Cowl Flap Drive

Removal of Engine Exhaust Stacks—

1. Remove the ring cowls.
2. Open the cowl flaps wide.
3. Lower the air scoop.
4. Remove bolts at ports, clamps from engine mount and ring-cowl supports.
5. Remove the stacks.
6. Seal ports and both ends of each stack.

Lubrication of Engine Exhaust Stacks — Lubricate the universal ball joints and support clamps with motor oil or glycerine. Do not use lubricants containing powdered zinc. For example, thread anti-seize containing powdered zinc and petrolatum, at the high temperatures encountered in an exhaust system, cause the metal to become brittle and crack.

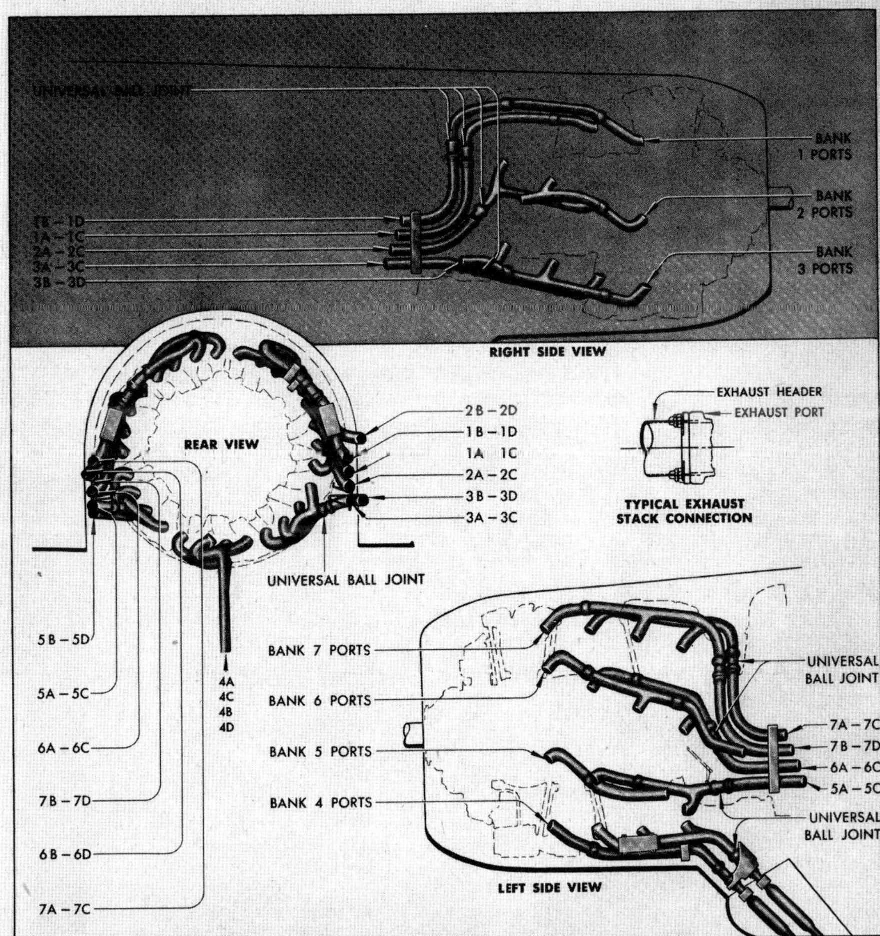

Figure 179—Engine Exhaust Stacks

Figure 180—Exhaust Stack Removal

Manual Scan: National Archives, RG 287

ENGINE MOUNTING

The engine mounting units are: The welded steel-tube engine mount, two wing drag struts, seven flexible mounts each made up of a bracket, a pedestal which houses a rubber shock absorber, and a mounting bolt. The engine mount is a ring supported by ten tubular struts bolted to station 175 frame at four places. The mounting ring is made of two semi-circular tubes bolted together. This construction is necessary for removal and installation of the mount, because the ring has a smaller diameter than the auxiliary stage supercharger housing.

The seven flexible mount brackets, fastened to the mounting ring by internal wrenching bolts, connect the engine to the ring. The bracket of each flexible mount is bolted to the engine crackcase and the pedestal is bolted to the blower case at the shock absorber housing. The two drag struts bolt to the under side of the mounting ring and to fittings on the inboard wing ribs. (For details of engine mounting see Engine Mounting illustration.)

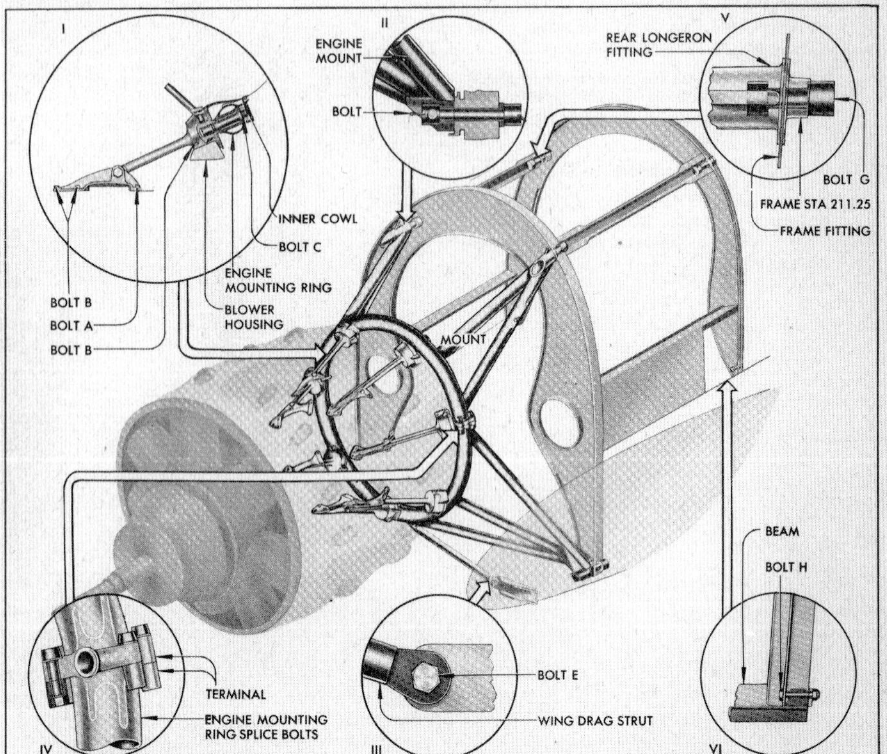

DETAIL	BOLT	SIZE	TYPE	TORQUE WRENCH SETTING	DETAIL	BOLT	SIZE	TYPE	TORQUE WRENCH SETTING
I	A	5/8″	STANDARD	100-800 INCH POUNDS	III	E	1″	STANDARD	3700-5500 INCH POUNDS
I	B	7/16″	STANDARD	500-550 INCH POUNDS	IV	F	5/8″	INTERNAL WRENCHING	1400-1700 INCH POUNDS
II	C	3/4″	INTERNAL WRENCHING	2500-3000 INCH POUNDS	V	G	7/8″	INTERNAL WRENCHING	3700-4900 INCH POUNDS
II	D	1″	INTERNAL WRENCHING	5100-7900 INCH POUNDS	VI	H	5/16″	INTERNAL WRENCHING	100-140 INCH POUNDS

Figure 181—Engine Mounting

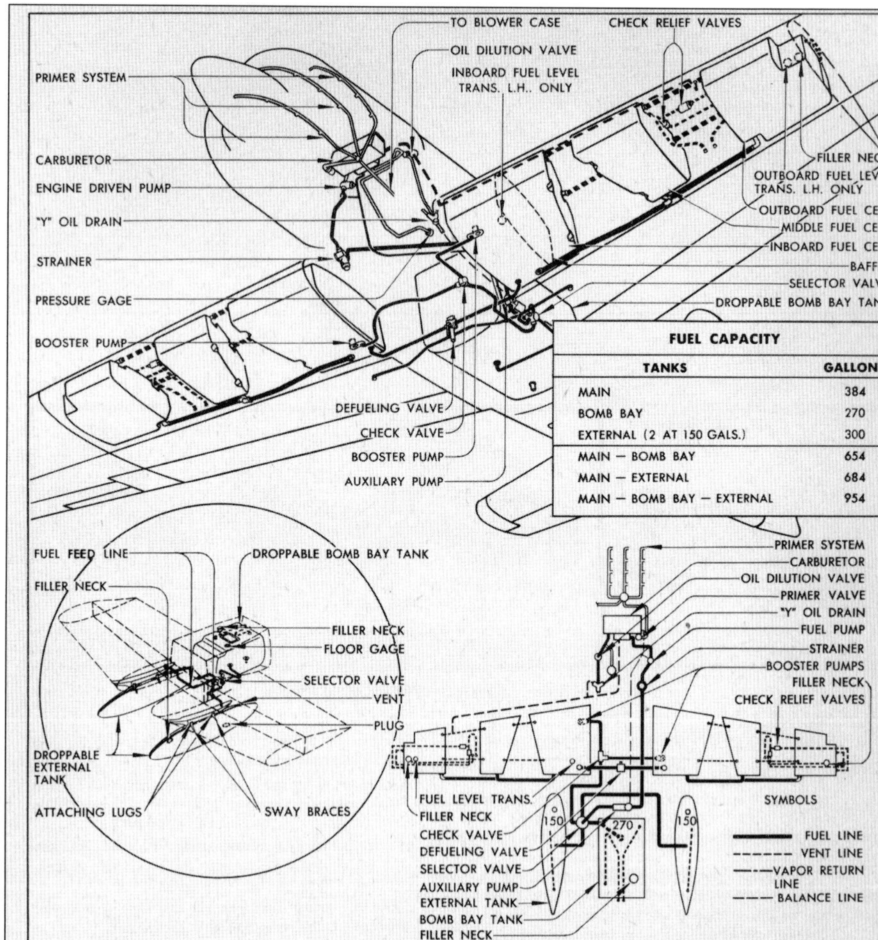

FUEL CAPACITY

TANKS	GALLONS
MAIN	384
BOMB BAY	270
EXTERNAL (2 AT 150 GALS.)	300
MAIN — BOMB BAY	654
MAIN — EXTERNAL	684
MAIN — BOMB BAY — EXTERNAL	954

Figure 182—Fuel System

FUEL SYSTEM

The main fuel tank has six inter-connected self-sealing fuel cells (three in each inboard section of the wing forward of the spar). The fuel system schematic diagram shows the fuel path from tank to carburetor. The double check valve prevents the fuel from flowing back to the main tank cells from the selector valve.

A line from the carburetor inlet chamber to the vent line between the two left outboard fuel cells handles vapor return (8-15 GPH) for all fuel tanks. The fuel quantity gage on the instrument panel shows main tank quantities only. The quantity transmitters are in the inboard and outboard cells of the left wing. The system includes the necessary equipment for oil dilution and engine priming.

For long missions auxiliary droppable fuel tanks, consisting of a bomb bay tank and two external tanks, may be added to the system.

The main tank holds 384 gallons and the total capacity with auxiliary tanks is 954 gallons.

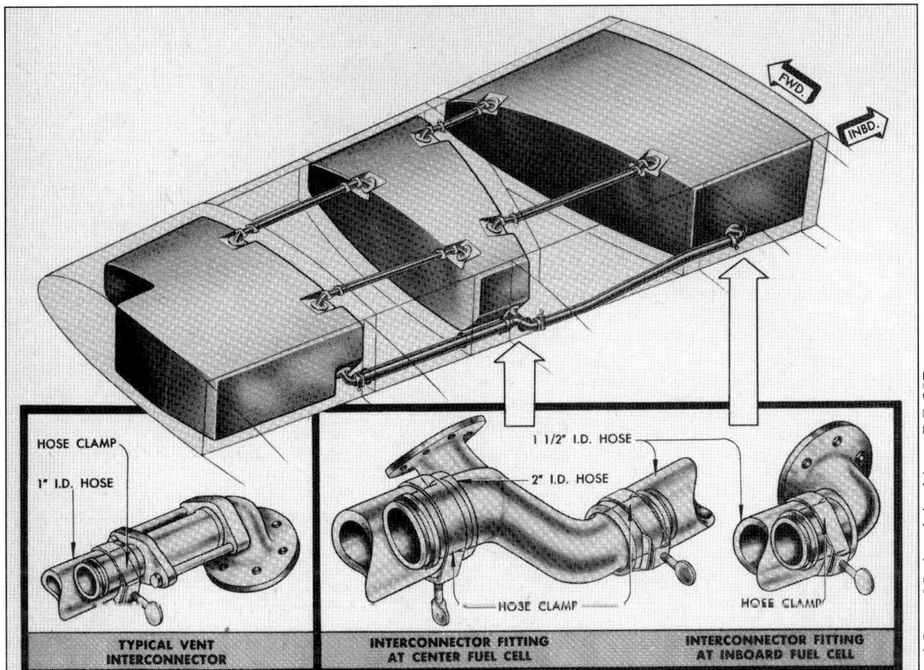

Figure 183—Fuel Cell Interconnector Fitting Details

Figure 184—Bomb Bay Fuel Tank

BOMB BAY FUEL TANK

The bomb bay fuel tank is self sealing, and internally strengthened by four fiber columns. The inspection door, filler neck, two vent connections, a fuel quantity gage, and a grounding plug are on the upper surface. The fuel outlet (center) and a drain are on the bottom of the tank. The tank is supported by a beam and strap assembly equipped with fittings for the bomb shackle eye bolts and hold-down turnbuckles. A removable pin on each side of the tank support serves as a cable attachment for the two MK-7 bomb hoists used to lift the tank into place.

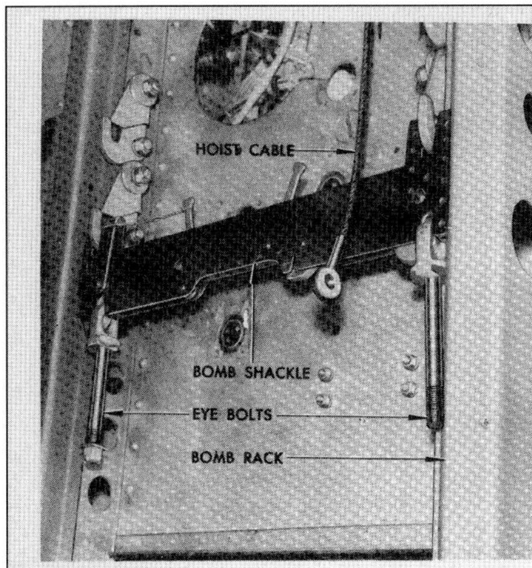

Figure 185—Bomb Shackle and Eyebolts Installed

Installation of Bomb Bay Fuel Tank—

1. Inspect condition of tank; check presence of bomb racks and releases in bomb bay; see that bomb shackles and eye bolts are fastened to each rack.
2. Install the turnbuckle fittings (BAC 3-32629) on the left and right hand bomb bay longerons. Attach the turnbuckle guards (BAC 3-32642) to the fittings.
3. Install the turnbuckles.
4. Install the breakaway fitting bracket (BAC 6-20825) and place the fitting in the bracket.

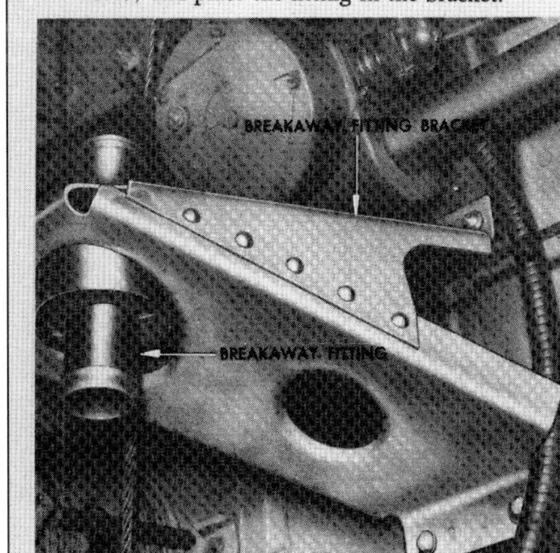

Figure 186—Bomb Bay Tank Breakaway Bracket and Fitting

5. Clamp the 3 inch hose (AN 878-20-12) to the upper end of the breakaway fitting.
6. Connect the combination tube (BAC 15-17386-11) hose (BAC 15-17386-5) line between the breakaway fitting and the rear upper intake on the fuel selector valve. (See Bomb Bay Fuel Tank Fuel Line Connections illustration.)
7. Open the bomb bay doors and move the tank under the bomb bay.
8. Slide the canopy back and either move the seat up or remove it.
9. Install an AN-MK-7 Model I portable bomb hoist in each of the fittings in the seat well, as to form an "X." Each cable runs over a pulley and down to the fuel tank hoisting beams. Pull the pins, insert the cable fittings and replace the pins.

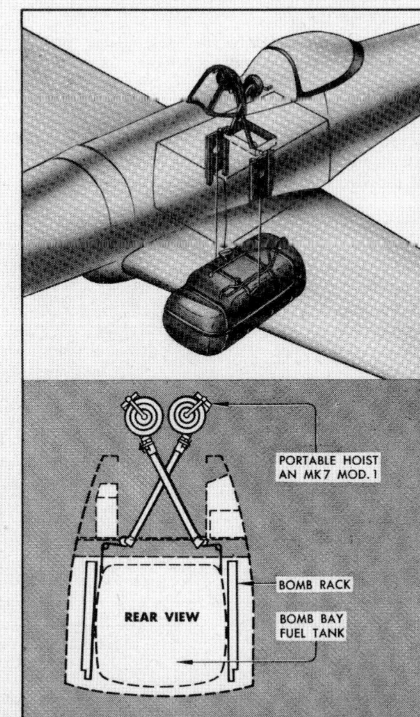

Figure 187—Hoisting Bomb Bay Fuel Tank

Manual Scan: National Archives, RG 287
Manual Scan: National Archives, RG 287

Figure 188—Bomb Bay Fuel Tank Installed

10. With one man standing in the steps on each side of the cockpit, wind up both hoists at the same speed. Place one man in the aft end of the bomb bay to guide the tank and give signals.

CAUTION—*Raise the tank very carefully to prevent damage to tank or equipment.*

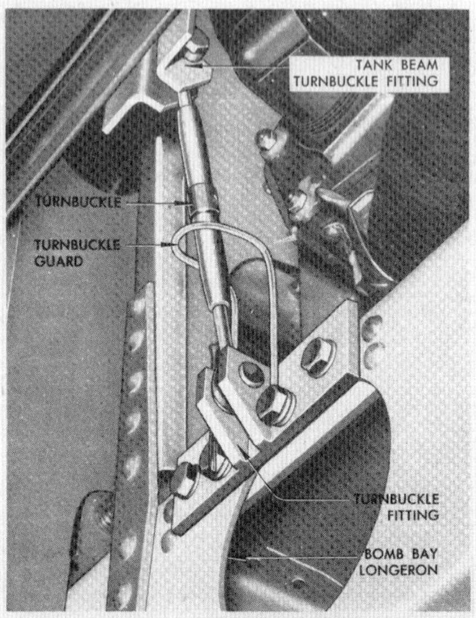

Figure 189—Bomb Bay Fuel Tank Tie-down Turnbuckle Connection

11. When the tank is in place, swing the eye bolts on the bomb shackles into the fittings on the tank support beams. Install washers, nuts and cotters.

12. Put the upper end of the four tiedown turnbuckles in the fittings on the tank support beams and tighten enough to hold down the tank securely. Connect the tank fuel line to the lower end of the breakaway fitting.

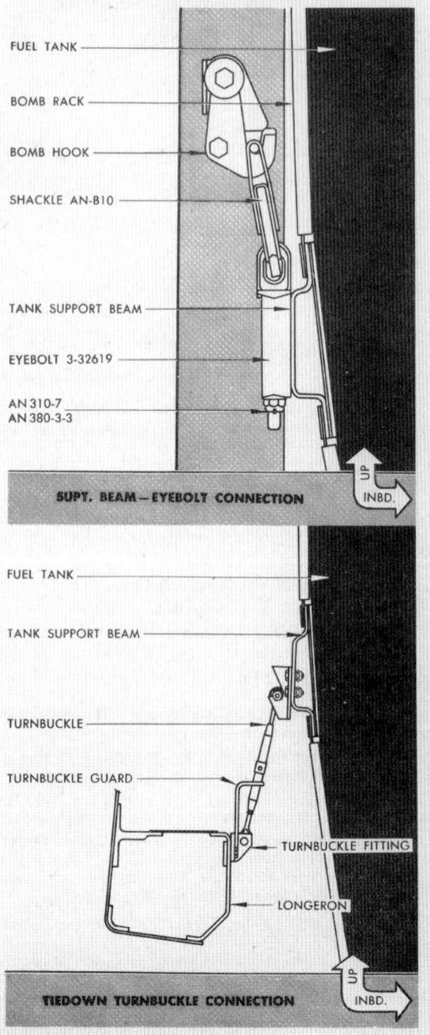

Figure 190—Bomb Bay Fuel Tank Connections

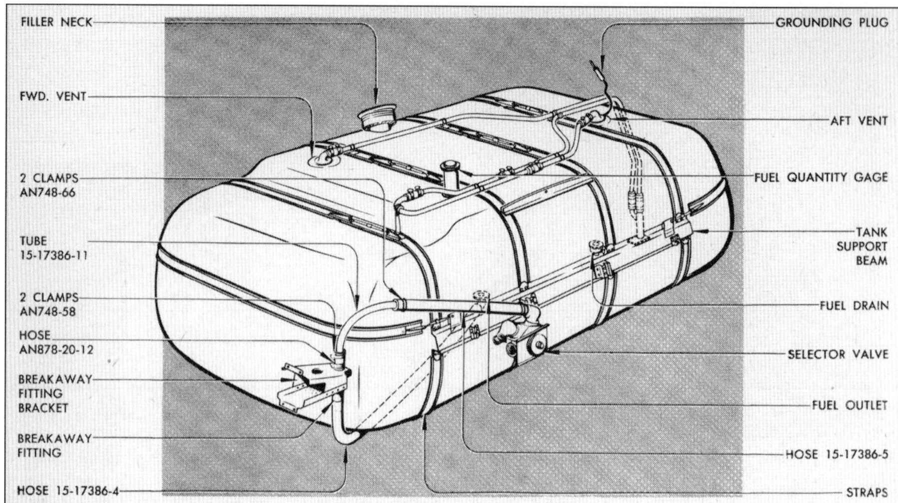

Figure 191—Bomb Bay Fuel Tank Fuel Line Connections

tighten enough to hold down the tank securely. Connect the tank fuel line to the lower end of the breakaway fitting.

Plug in the bonding cable from the tank to its receptacle under the cockpit floor. The bonding plug must be connected before any fuel is put into the tank and remain in place until the tank is empty.

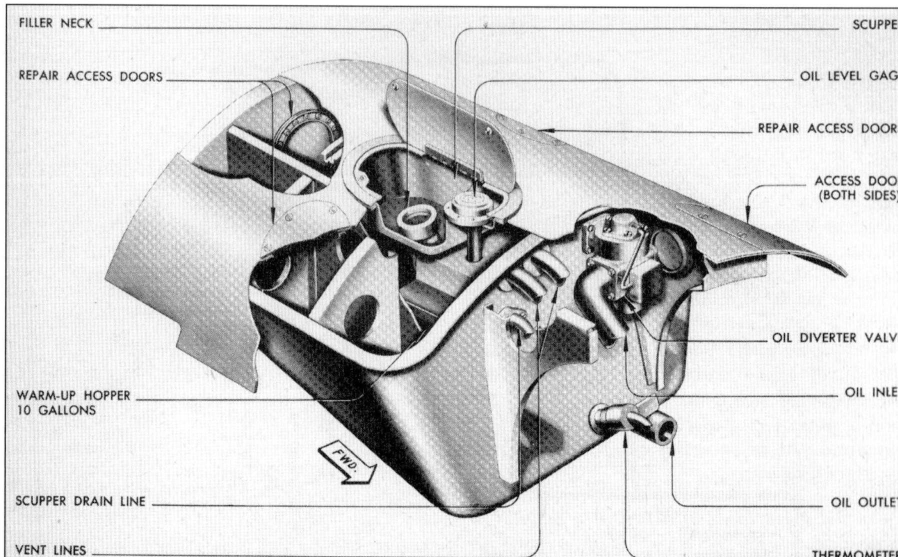

Figure 204—Oil Tank

OIL SYSTEM

THE OIL SYSTEM CONSISTS OF AN OIL TANK, A DIVERTER VALVE, TWO OIL COOLER UNITS, TWO FLOATING CONTROL THERMOSTATS AND A "Y"-OIL DRAIN. THE SYSTEM LUBRICATES AND HELPS TO CONTROL THE TEMPERATURE OF THE ENGINE AND ITS ACCESSORIES. THE TWO OIL COOLER UNITS, THE FLOATING CONTROL THERMOSTAT, AND THE OIL COOLER FLAPS ARE USED TO ACCOMPLISH THIS LATTER FUNCTION. THE SYSTEM OIL SUPPLY TANK IS PART OF THE AIRPLANE STRUCTURE. THE SYSTEM OPERATES UNDER A NORMAL PRESSURE OF 80-85 PSI AT THE ENGINE RATE OF 350 POUNDS (47 GALLONS) PER MINUTE.

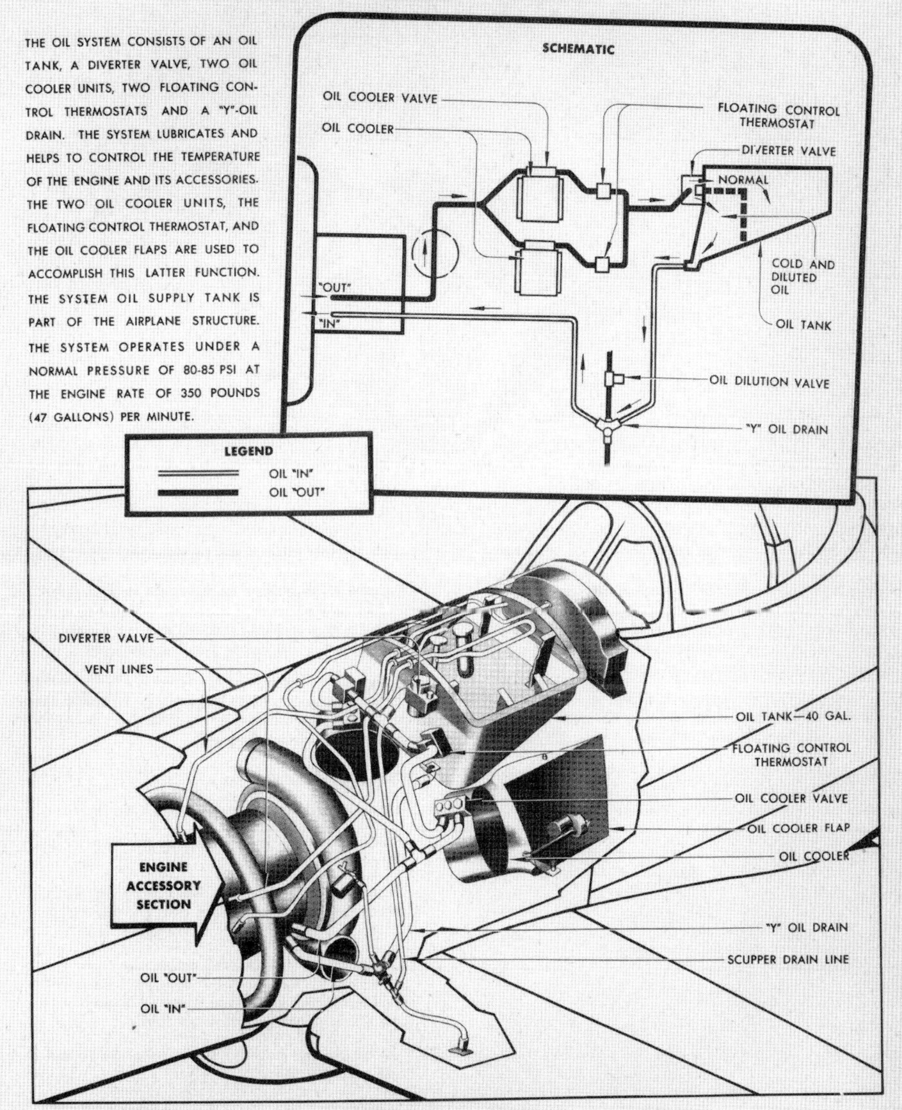

Figure 203 — Oil System

Figure 205—Oil Tank Quantity Gage

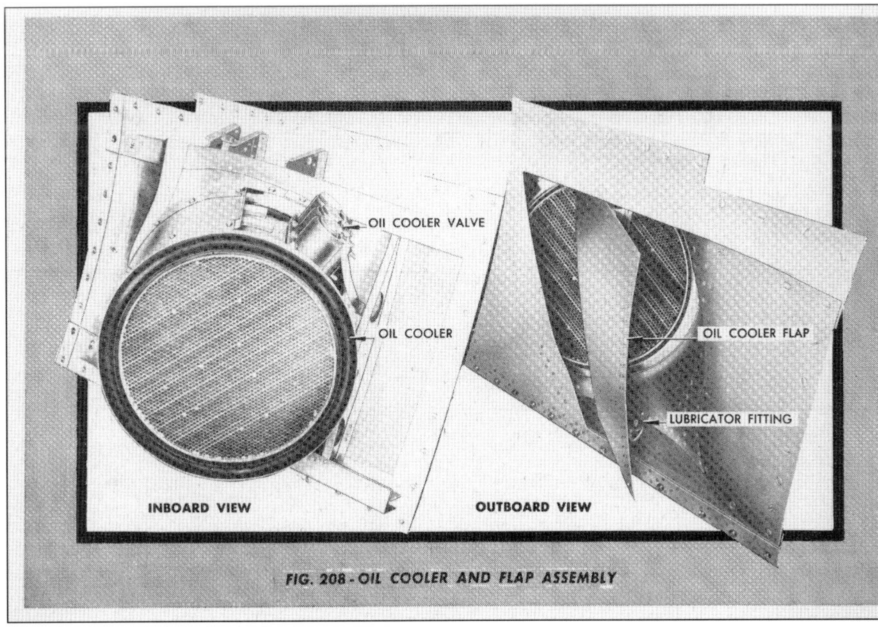

FIG. 208 - OIL COOLER AND FLAP ASSEMBLY

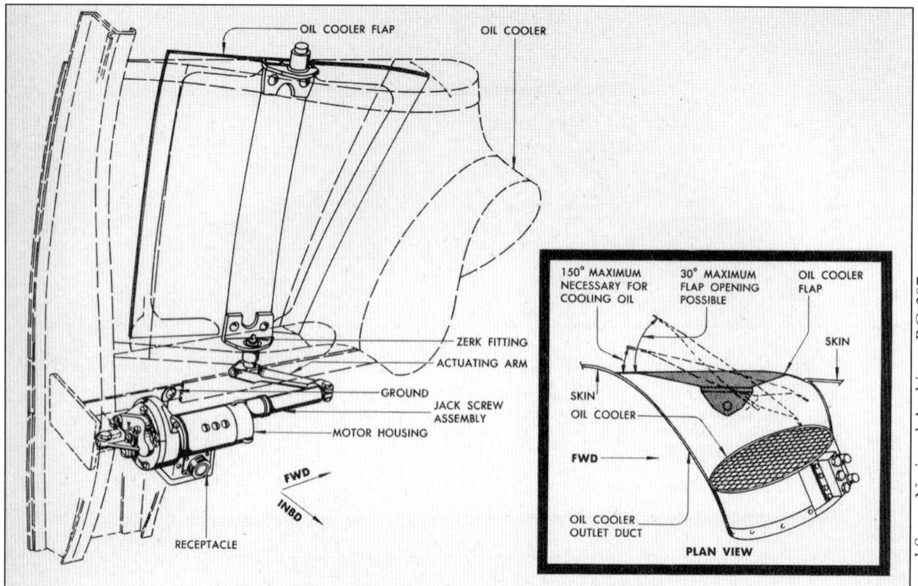

Figure 210 — Oil Cooler Flap and Actuator Installation

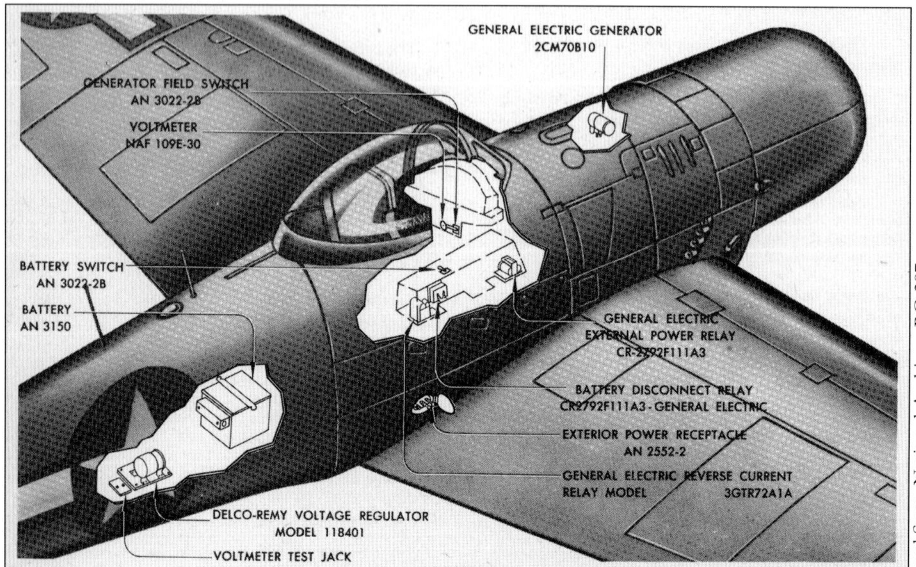

Figure 214. (Sheet 1 of 2 Sheets) Electrical Power Circuit

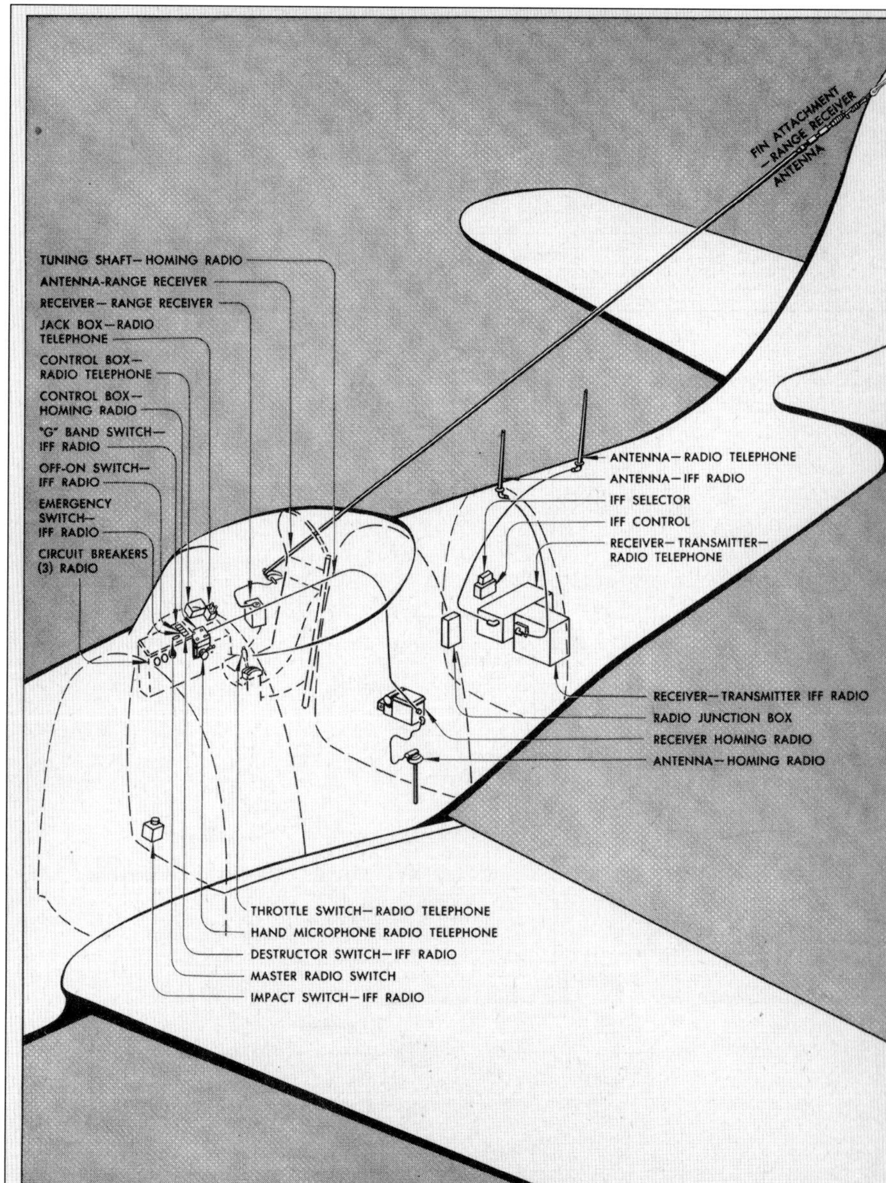

Figure 222 — Radio Equipment

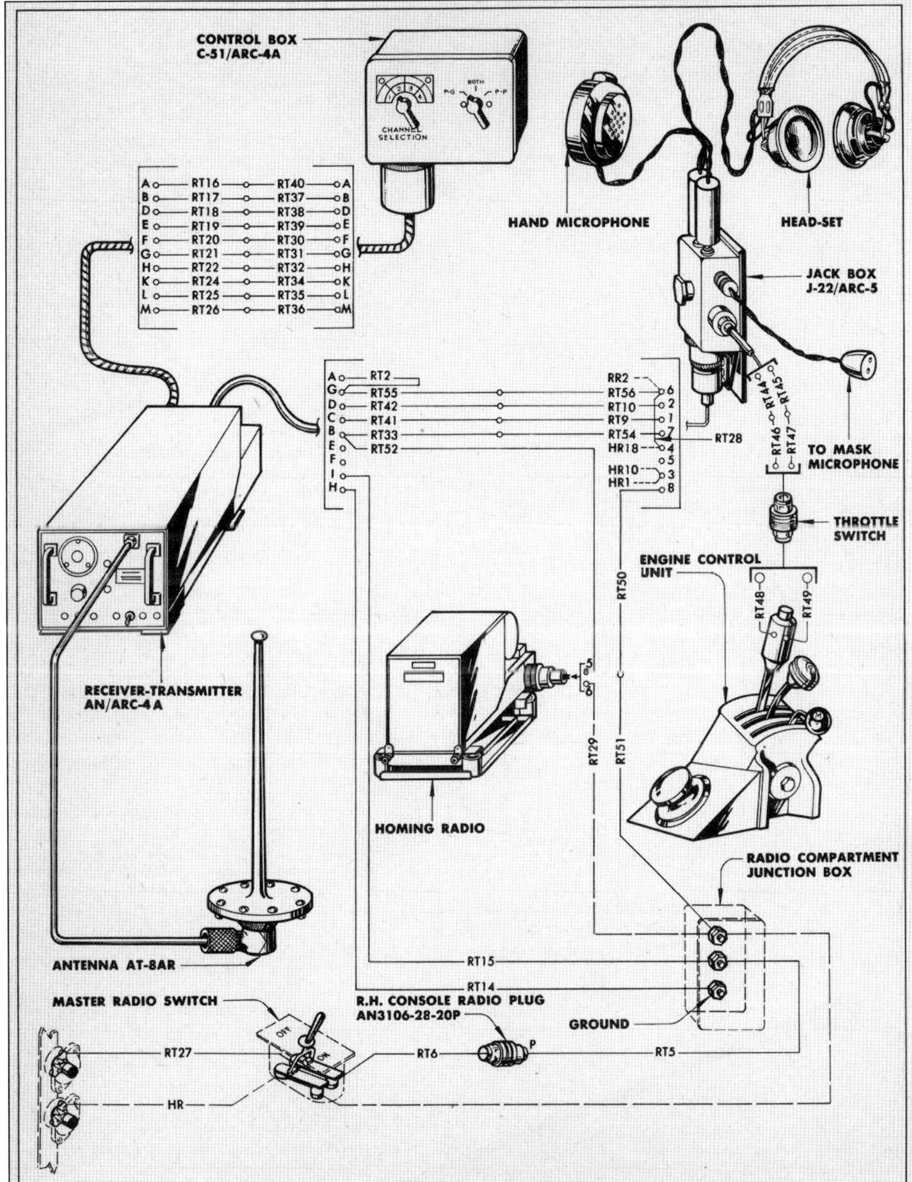

Figure 223 — Radio Telephone Circuit

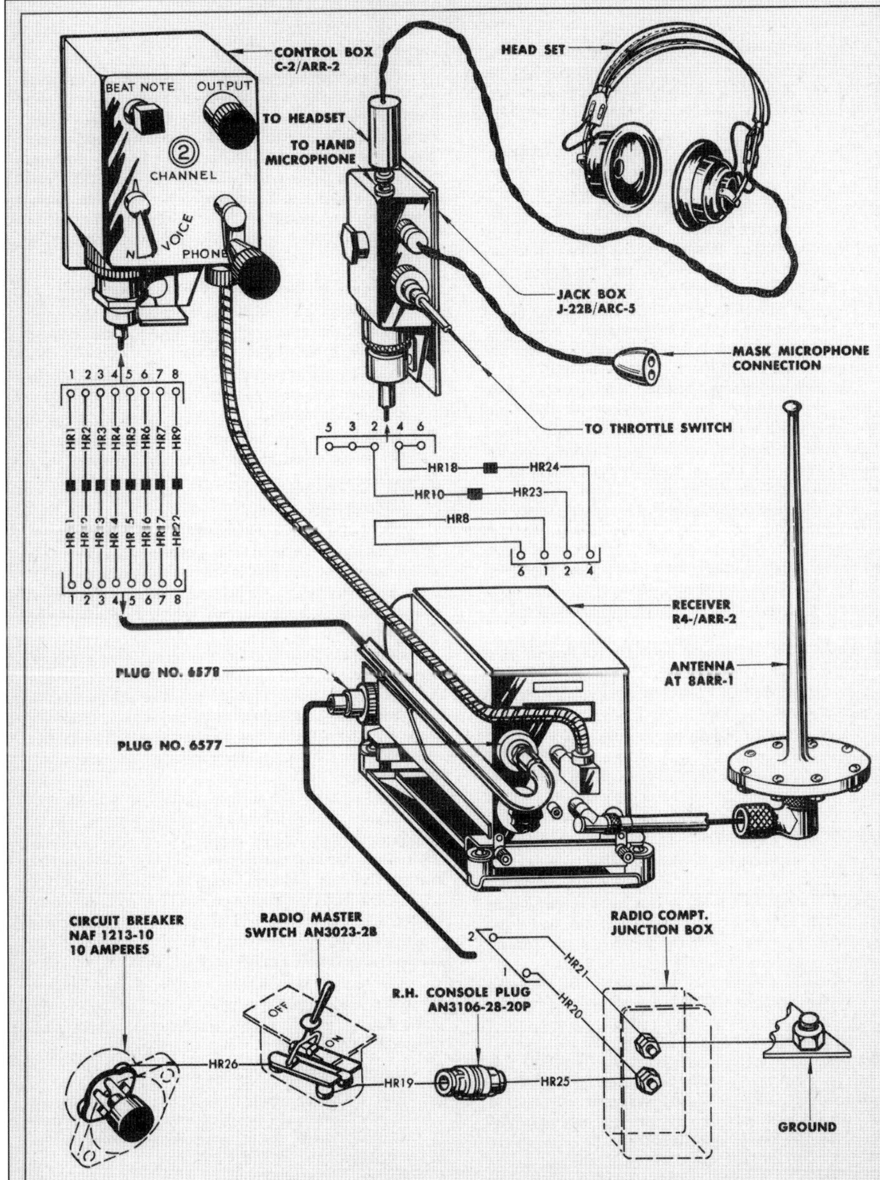

Figure 224—Homing Radio Circuit

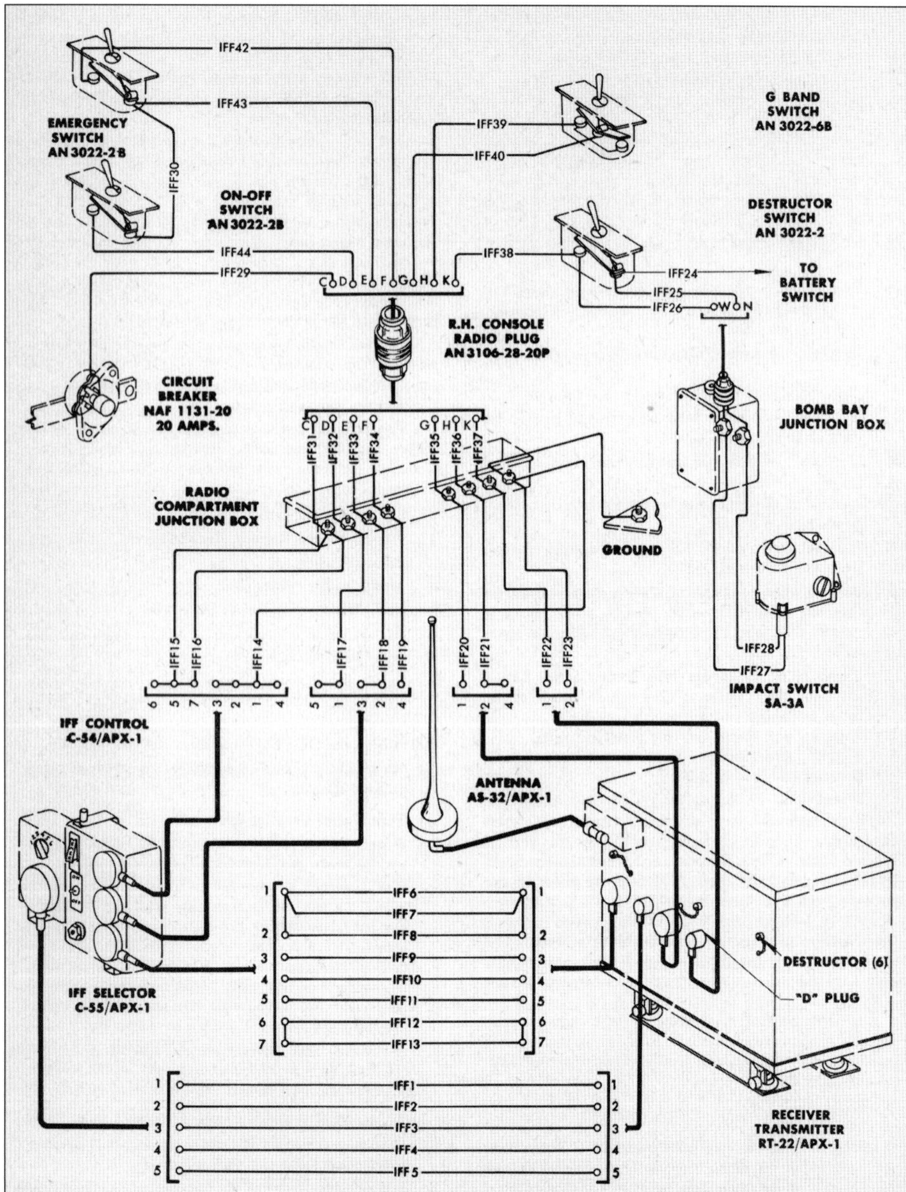

Figure 225—IFF Radio Circuit

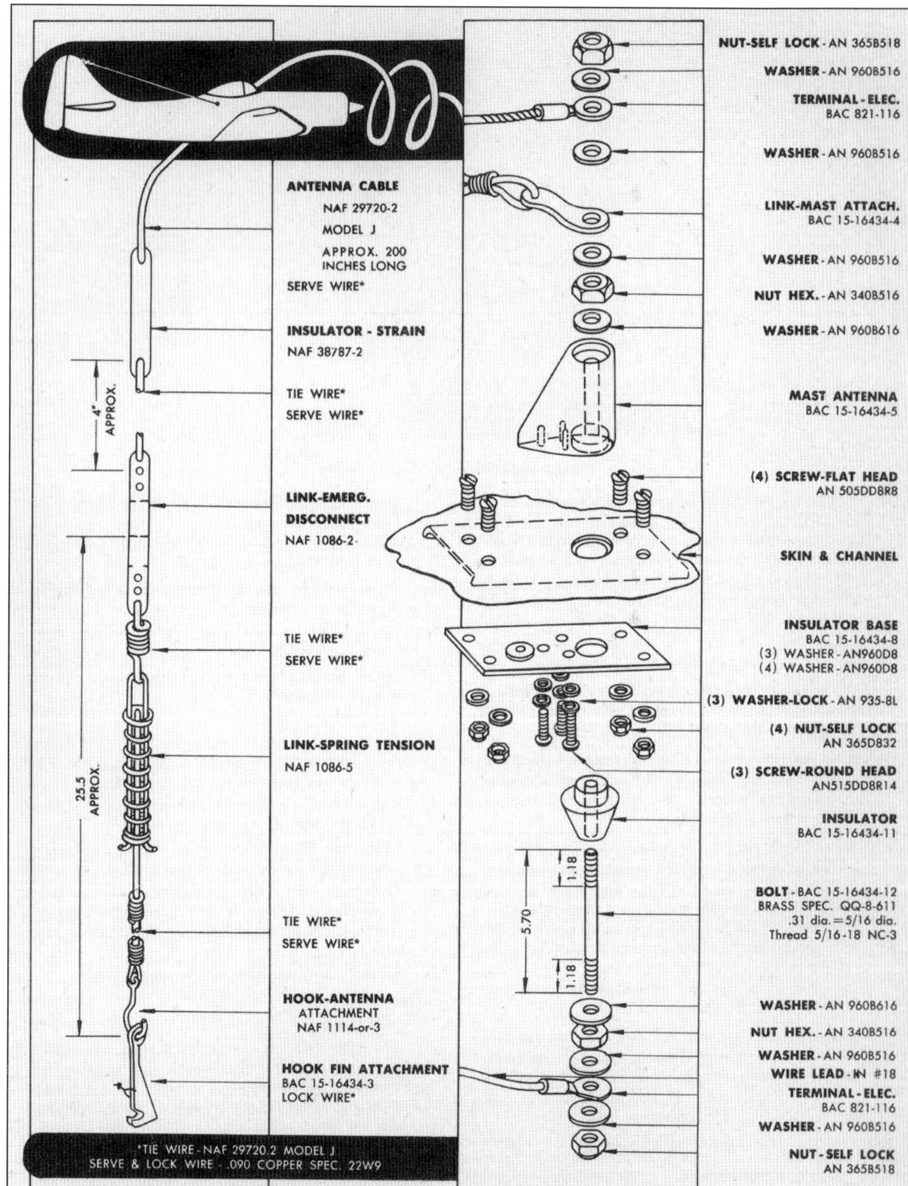

Figure 227—Range Receiver Antenna Installation

LIGHTS

INTERIOR LIGHTS

The following types of interior lights are used: Cockpit lights to illuminate the side panels, Chartboard lights, to illuminate the chartboard, and Instrument lights, to illuminate the instrument and inclined panels. The Cockpit lights are red so as not to impair the pilot's night vision.

Cockpit Lights—The five 28 volt cockpit lights (three on the right and two on the left side of the cockpit) receive power through a five ampere circuit breaker in the circuit breaker panel. A 50 ohm dimming rheostat on the right hand control stand switches the lights ON and OFF and varies the voltage to the lights from 0 to 28 volts. The middle cockpit light on the pilot's right can be unsnapped and used as an extension light.

Chartboard Lights—The two 28 volt chartboard lights (just below the gunsight) receive power through the same five ampere circuit breakers as the cockpit lights. Each light is turned ON and OFF by a switch in its base.

Instrument Lights—Twenty-four instrument panel lights are controlled by a 100 ohm rheostat on the right hand control stand. This rheostat turns the lights ON and OFF and varies their voltage from zero to 28 volts for the required intensity. A 50 ohm resistor is added in series with the lights on the inclined panel to obtain uniform lighting on the main instrument panel. A snap cover over the rear of the light allows replacement.

Spare Bulbs—Spare bulbs for about 50% replacement are stowed in the aft end of the right hand control stand.

EXTERIOR LIGHTS

The XF8B-1 has the following external lights: A section light, two formation lights, three position or running lights, three recognition lights, and an approach light. The MASTER EXT. LTS. switch must be on before the section, formation or position lights can be turned on with their individual switches. The master switch is on the right hand control stand.

A BOTH-ON-FLASH toggle switch adjacent to the formation light switches on the right hand console allows the momentary flashing of section and formation lights in combat areas.

Formation Lights—Two circular formation light assemblies indicate the position of the airplane during formation flying. They are mounted, one in each outboard wing slightly inboard of the wing tip joint, with their lunar white lenses flush with the upper wing surface.

Both light assemblies are controlled by a BRIGHT-DIM toggle switch on the right hand control stand. A 75 ohm resistor connected in series with the DIM side of the switch is used to cut the intensity of the lights. This resistor is under the junction box on the right hand side of the bomb bay.

Section Light—The lunar-white section light is on the top surface of the fuselage aft of the cockpit between the IFF and radio telephone antennae. This light has both ON-OFF-FLASH (this same switch also controls formation lights) and BRIGHT and DIM switches. A 150 ohm resistor is wired in series with the DIM side of this switch, to permit reduction of light intensity. The resistor is near the radio compartment junction box.

Position Lights—The three position lights are installed as follows: one white diffusing (frosted) tail light on the aftmost part of the tail section, one light with a red lens in a plexiglass housing in the left hand wing tip, and one light with a green lens in a plexiglass housing on the right hand wing tip. A spare set of red, green and white non-diffusing tail light resin lenses comes with the airplane. The spare lenses are used for signal and recognition purposes during tactical operations.

Two switches, marked BRIGHT-OFF-DIM on the right hand control stand, control the operation of the lights. One switch controls the tail light while the other controls the wing lights. Resistors are connected in series with the DIM side of the switches to dim the lights. The 15 ohm wing light resistor is under the junction box on the right hand side of the bomb bay and the 150 ohm tail light resistor is near the radio compartment junction box.

Recognition Lights—The three recognition lights (red, amber and green) are used for steady or flashing signals between the plane and ground. The lights are in the radio compartment access door on the bottom of the fuselage in a triangular pattern with the red light forward, the amber aft left, and the green aft right.

The lights receive power directly from the battery (independent of the battery switch), and are protected by a 10 ampere circuit breaker on the right hand control stand.

Each of the three lights is controlled by a toggle switch on the right hand console marked with STEADY, OFF and KEY positions. Any one or more of the three lights may be used for signaling by moving its switch to the position marked KEY. Code signals can then be transmitted by working the keying switch next to the individual recognition switches.

Approach Light—The approach light is in the leading edge of the left hand outboard wing just outboard of the skin break. The light operates on 28 volts and is automatically turned on when the arresting hook is fully extended for a carrier landing. Thus the light warns of arresting hook failure. An ON-OFF toggle switch on the right hand side of the radio compartment junction box allows the lights to be turned on manually for test purposes or when the airplane is practicing carrier landings.

Figure 231—Location of Exterior Lights

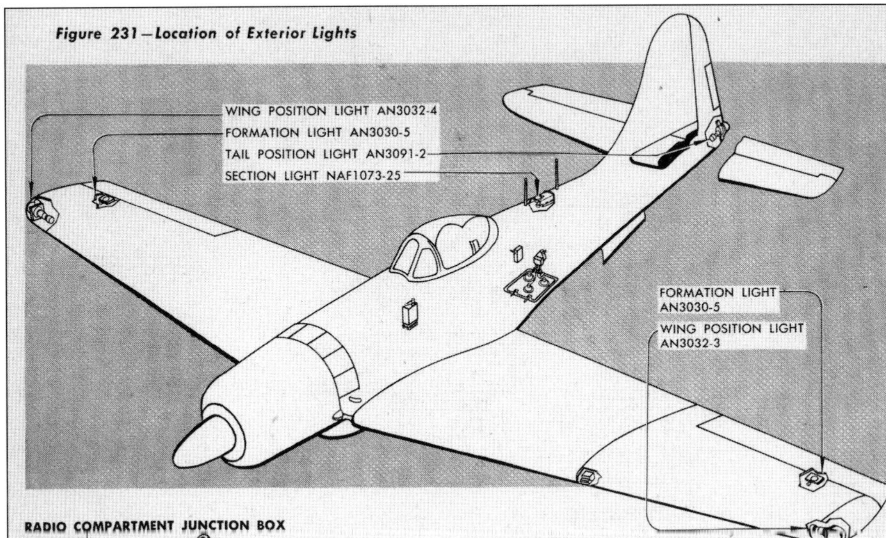

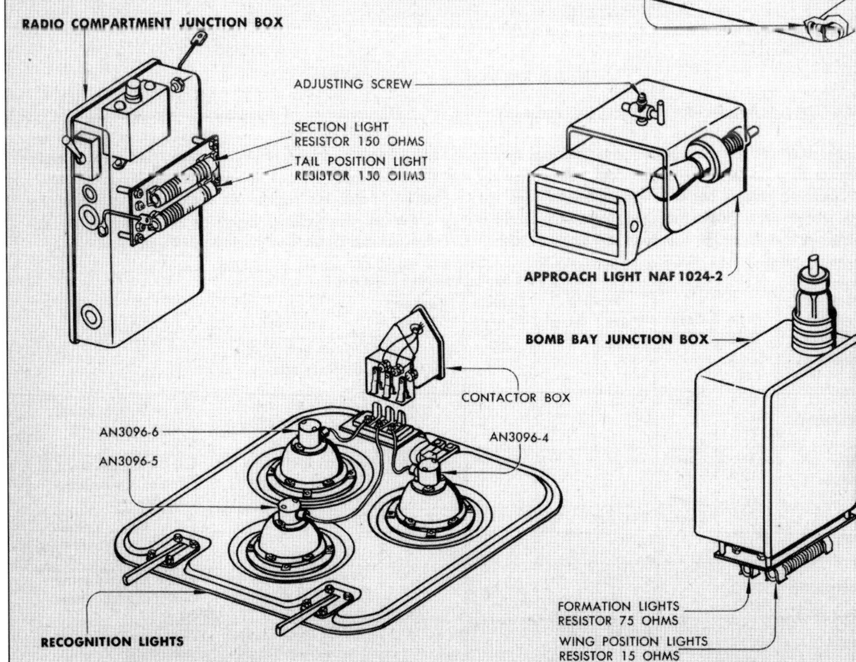

Figure 232—Details of Exterior Lights

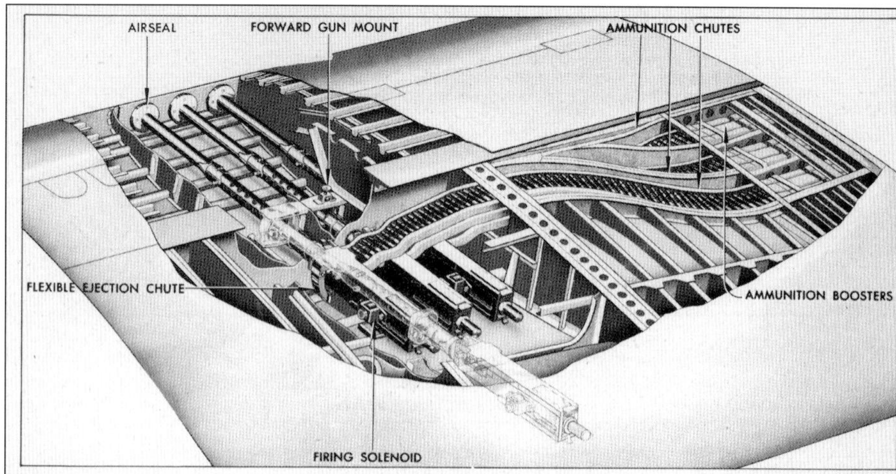

Figure 233—.50 Caliber Gun Installation

ARMAMENT

GUNNERY

The airplane has six caliber .50 machine guns or six 20 MM cannons or a combination of both. In the case of the combination, the 20 MM guns are outboard of the caliber .50 guns because of the chute clearance with the 20 MM overhead feeder. The gunnery equipment also includes feed chutes, ejection chutes, ammunition boxes, gun mounts, blast protection tubes, and manual gun-charging tools.

The trigger is on the control column hand grip and the guns are fed from ammunition boxes by booster motors through fixed chutes. The armament master switch, a camera switch and three gun selection switches are on the panel to the left of the gun sight. The armament master switch must be ON before any of the guns will fire. Each selection switch controls a gun in each wing for symmetrical fire. When the trigger is pressed the gun relays operate the guns and the booster motors. The trigger solenoid and ammunition booster motors are protected by a 25 ampere circuit breaker.

An auxiliary ammunition booster control panel is installed in each gun bay mounted on the outboard rib. The panels each contain three toggle switches and a circuit breaker. The purpose of the panel is to give the men loading the guns a convenient means of operating each ammunition booster without danger of firing the guns. The switches can be used for loading either .50's or 20's.

The ammunition boxes and chutes hold about 400 rounds per gun or 200 rounds per cannon.

Caliber .50 Guns—The caliber .50 gun is an air cooled M-2 machine gun capable of firing between 750 and 850 rounds per minute. A blast tube on the forward end of the gun barrel jacket extends to the leading edge of the wing. The gun feeds from the side and ejects shells and links out the bottom of the wing. An MK5 firing solenoid on the side of the gun operates the gun trigger.

The forward gun mount is a fixed trunnion ahead of the wing spar. The rear mount is adjustable and is beneath the gun aft of the wing spar.

The gun is manually charged with a handle that is inserted in the side of the breech. Access is through either the flap opening or the lower gun bay access door. A pull of about 20 pounds is required. The charging handle is clipped to the lower gun access door in the left hand wing by a spring clip.

Adjustment of Caliber .50 Guns—Each gun is adjusted vertically and horizontally at the rear gun mount. Access is through the hinged door aft of the three ejection chutes on the underside of the wing. Use special tool F12114 to make the adjustments.

1. To adjust the guns vertically remove the lock wire between the adjusting nut and the lower checknut. Loosen both the large lower checknut and the small upper checknut. Turn the large adjusting nut. Tighten the checknuts and lock wire.
2. To adjust the guns horizontally, loosen the set screw on the rear of the mount, and loosen the nut on the horizontal mounting bolt. This bolt turns the screw assembly for right or left movement of the guns. The guns can be adjusted for either parallel or converging fire.

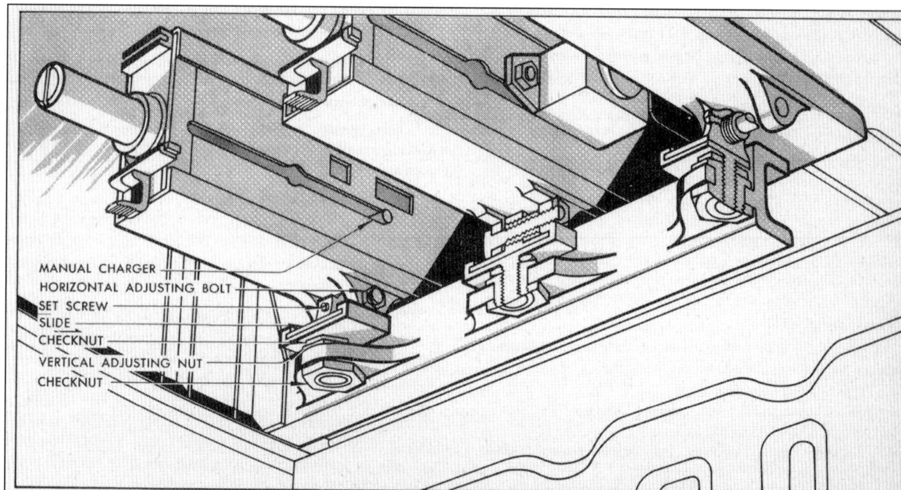

Figure 236—.50 Caliber Gun Rear Mount

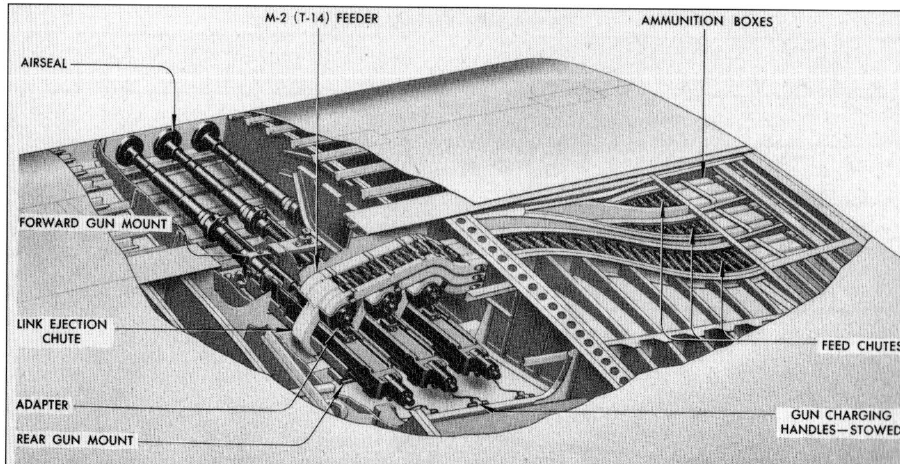

Figure 238—20 MM Cannon Installation

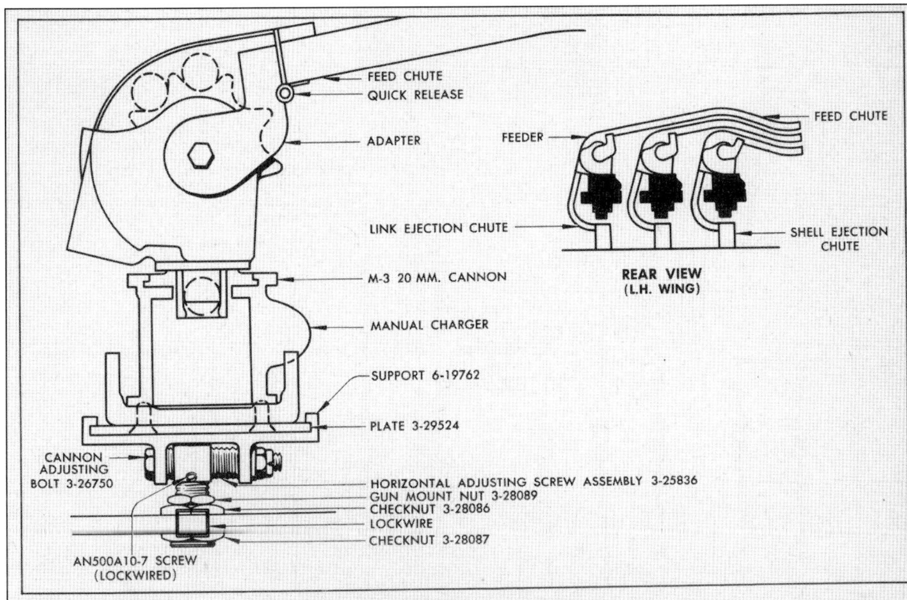

Figure 240—20 MM Cannon Rear Mount

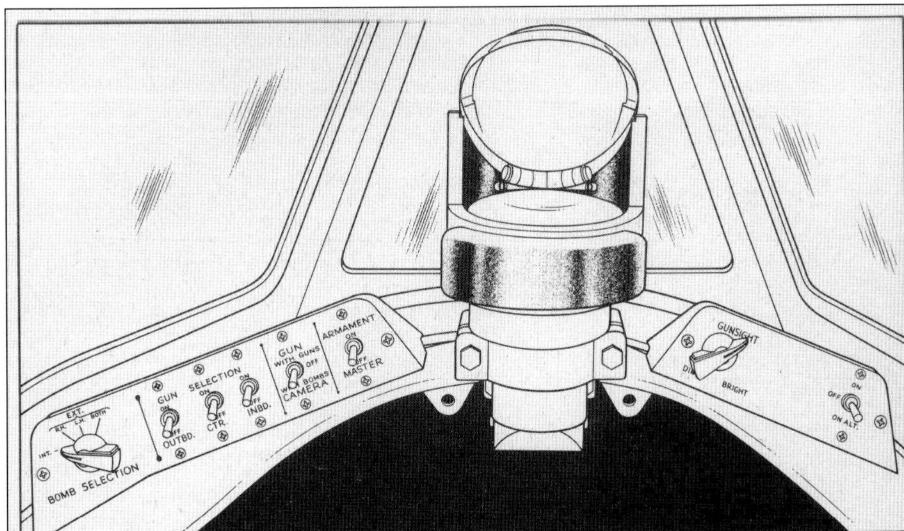

Figure 242—Mark 8 Gunsight Installation

Figure 243—Mark 23 Gunsight Installation

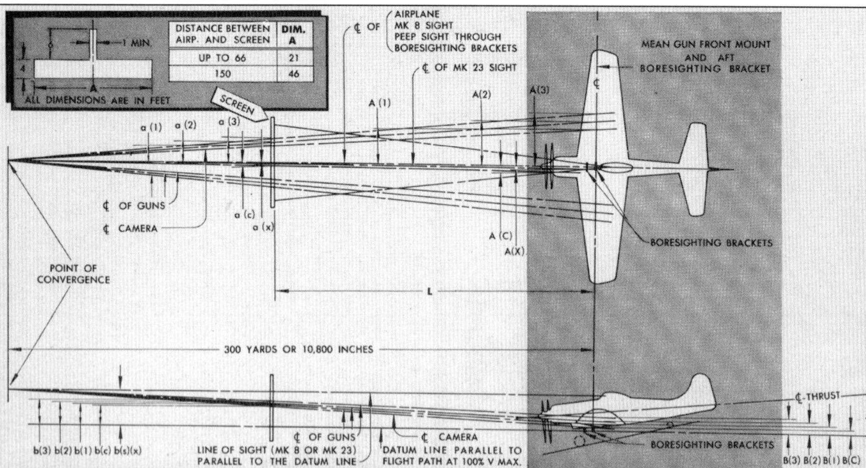

BORESIGHTING DIMENSIONS FOR HORIZONTALLY AND VERTICALLLY CONVERGING FIRE AT 300 YARDS RANGE.

"L" FEET	OBJECT	"A" INCHES		"a" INCHES		"B" INCHES		"b" INCHES	
50	INBD. GUN	$A_{(1)}$	116.520	$a_{(1)}$	110.048	$B_{(1)}$	28.466	$b_{(1)}$	32.154
	CENTER GUN	$A_{(2)}$	124.463	$a_{(2)}$	117.545	$B_{(2)}$	29.472	$b_{(2)}$	33.105
	OUTBD. GUN	$A_{(3)}$	132.402	$a_{(3)}$	125.042	$B_{(3)}$	30.481	$b_{(3)}$	34.058
	MK 8 SIGHT	$A_{(S)}$	0.			$B_{(S)}$	*95.370		
	CAMERA	$A_{(C)}$	7.06	$a_{(C)}$	6.668	$B_{(C)}$	4.543	$b_{(C)}$	9.561
	MK 23 SIGHT	$A_{(X)}$	1.125	$a_{(X)}$	1.063	$B_{(X)}$	*95.410		
150	INBD. GUN	$A_{(1)}$	116.520	$a_{(1)}$	97.101	$B_{(1)}$	28.466	$b_{(1)}$	39.532
	CENTER GUN	$A_{(2)}$	124.463	$a_{(2)}$	103.716	$B_{(2)}$	29.472	$b_{(2)}$	40.371
	OUTBD. GUN	$A_{(3)}$	132.402	$a_{(3)}$	110.331	$B_{(3)}$	30.481	$b_{(3)}$	41.212
	MK 8 SIGHT	$A_{(S)}$	0.			$B_{(S)}$	*95.370		
	CAMERA	$A_{(C)}$	7.06	$a_{(C)}$	5.8833	$B_{(C)}$	4.543	$b_{(C)}$	19.597
	MK 23 SIGHT	$A_{(X)}$	1.125	$a_{(X)}$	.938	$B_{(X)}$	*95.410		

*WITHOUT SUNFILTER

"L" IS THE DISTANCE, IN FEET, TO THE BORESIGHTING SCREEN, MEASURED FROM THE ℄ OF THE AFT BORESIGHTING BRACKET, PARALLEL TO AND IN THE DIRECTION OF THE LINE OF FLIGHT.

"A" IS THE ACTUAL HORIZONTAL OFFSET IN INCHES, MEASURED PERPENDICULAR TO THE VERTICAL ℄ OF THE AIRPLANE.

"B" IS THE ACTUAL VERTICAL OFFSET, IN INCHES, MEASURED PERPENDICULAR TO THE DATUM PLANE.

"a" IS THE HORIZONTAL OFFSET, IN INCHES, TO THE BORESIGHTING POINT ON THE SCREEN. THE OFFSET IS MEASURED FROM A LINE ERECTED PERPENDICULAR TO THE DATUM LINE AT THE POINT ESTABLISHED BY THE PEEP SIGHT OF THE BORESIGHTING BRACKETS.

"b" IS THE VERTICAL OFFSET, IN INCHES, MEASURED PERPENDICULAR TO THE DATUM LINE, TO THE BORESIGHTING POINT ON THE SCREEN.

THE DATUM PLANE IS PARALLEL TO THE LINE OF FLIGHT AT MAXIMUM SPEED AT AIRPLANE CRITICAL ALTITUDE, WITH MILITARY LOAD FOR PRIMARY COMBAT CONDITION, MINUS 1/2 FUEL LOAD. IE. THE THRUST ℄ OF THE AIRPLANE IS 5° DOWN FROM THE LINE OF FLIGHT.

Figure 248—Boresighting Procedure

Manual Scan: National Archives, RG 287

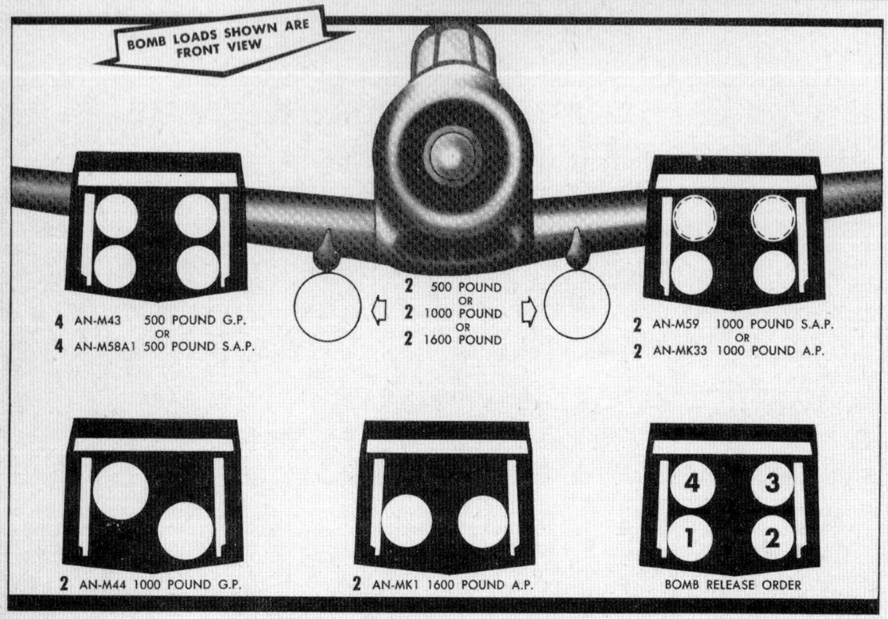

Figure 249—Basic Bomb Loads

Manual Scan: National Archives, RG 287

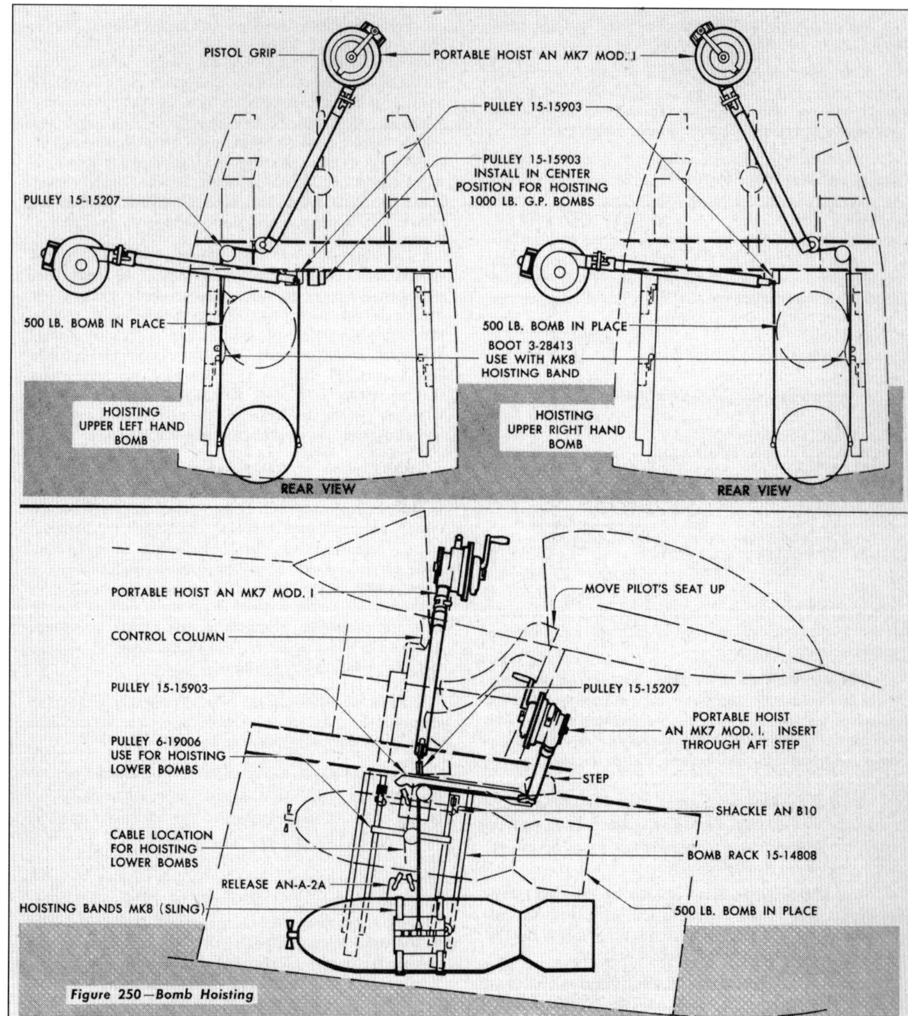

Figure 250—Bomb Hoisting

Manual Scan: National Archives, RG 287

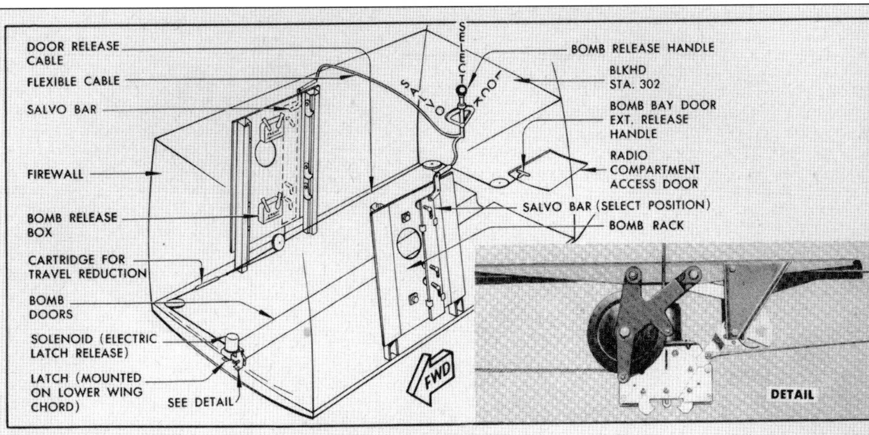

Figure 252—Bomb and Bomb Door Release Mechanism

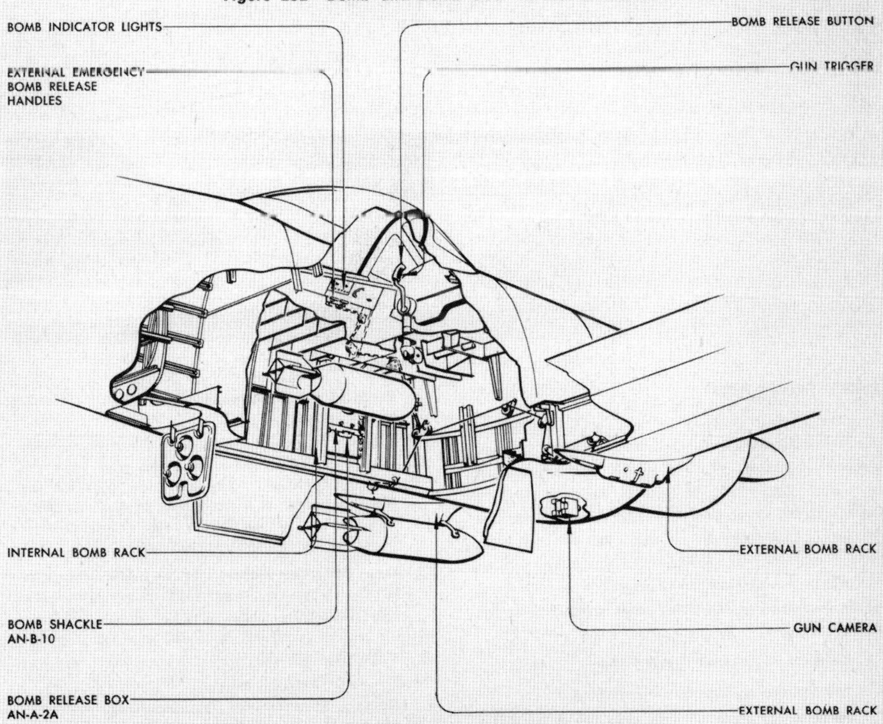

Figure 253—External Bomb Release System

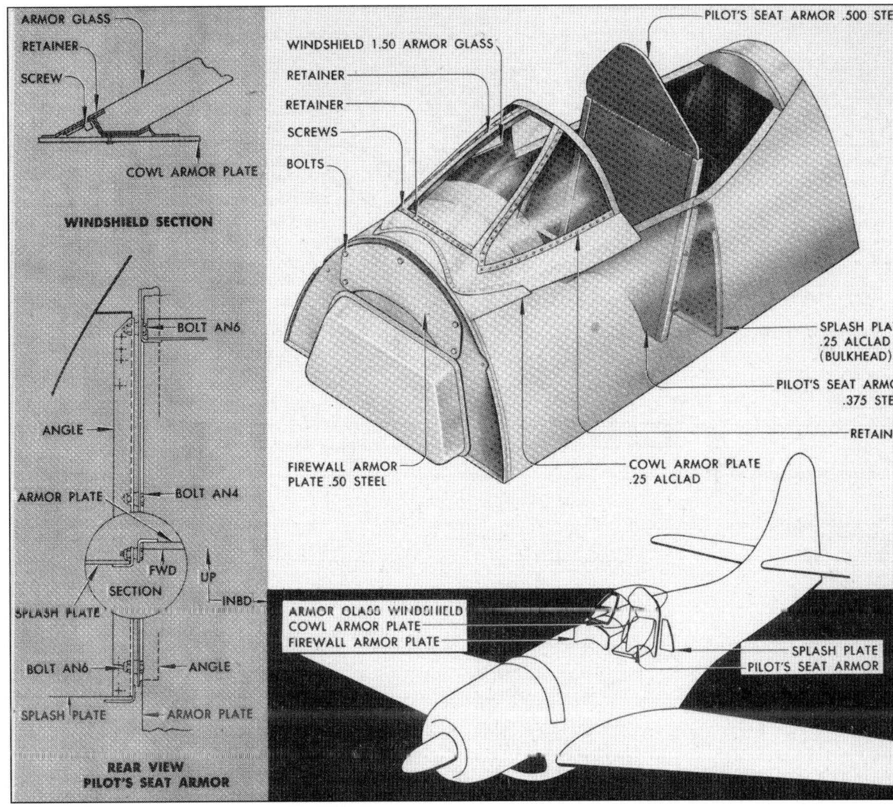

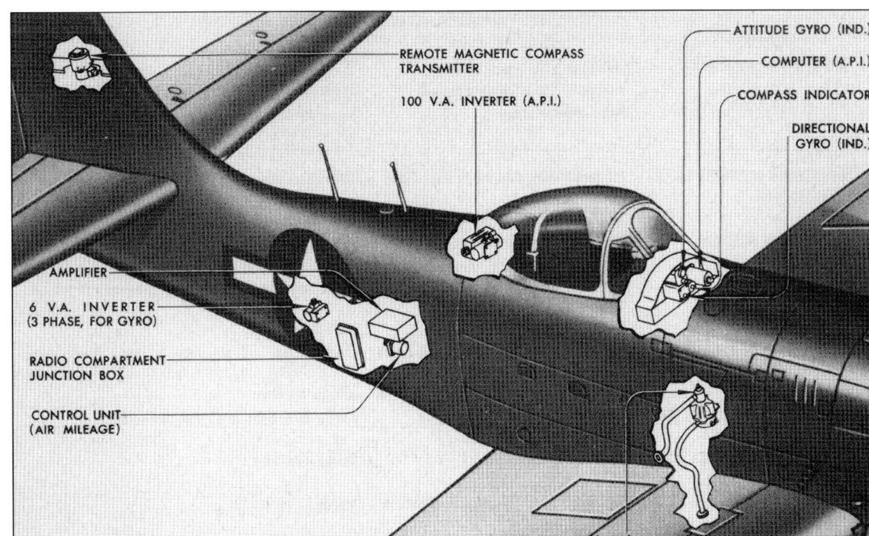

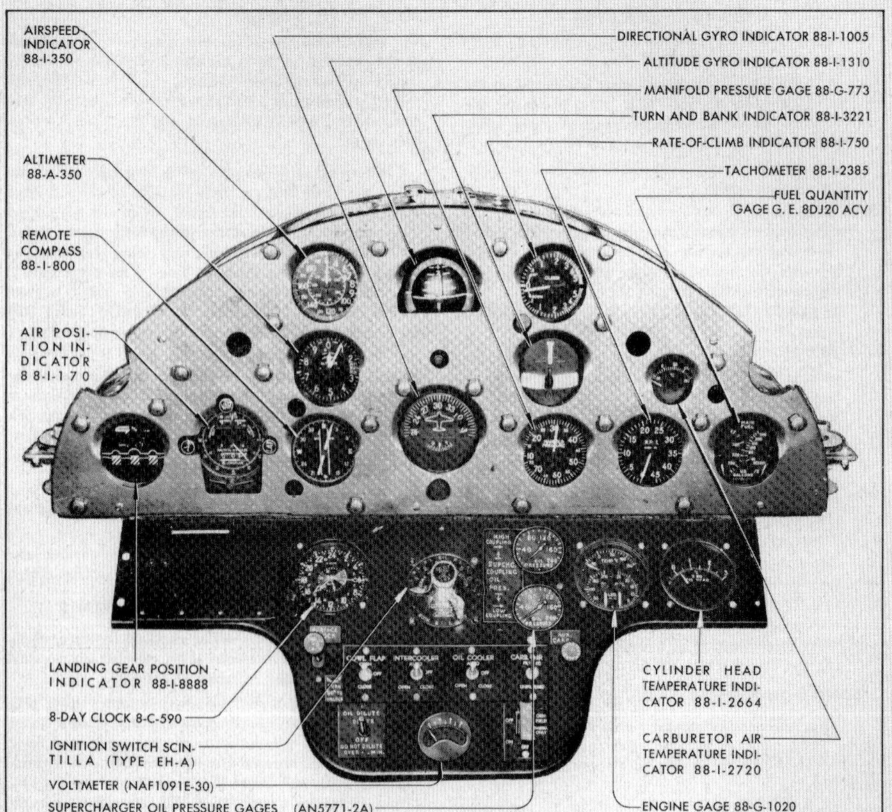

Figure 255—Instrument Panel

INSTRUMENTS

MAIN INSTRUMENT PANEL

The following instruments are on the main instrument panel directly forward of the pilot's seat. The panel has a false front or reflector panel which contains the 24 instrument lights for illuminating the instruments on both the main instrument panel and the inclined panel.

1. Landing Gear Position Indicator .... FSSC No. 88-I-1888
2. Air Position Indicator .... FSSC No. 88-I-170
3. Remote Compass Indicator .... FSSC No. 88-I-800
4. Remote Compass Correction Card .... FSSC No. 88-C-200
5. Directional Gyro .... FSSC No. 88-I-1005
6. Manifold Pressure Gage .... FSSC No. 88-G-773
7. Tachometer Indicator .... FSSC No. 88-I-2385
8. Fuel Level Indicator .. General Electric 8DJ20ACV
9. Carburetor Air Temperature Indicator .... FSSC No. 88-I-2720
10. Turn and Bank Indicator .... FSSC No. 88-I-3221
11. Altimeter .... FSSC No. 88-A-350
12. Altimeter Correction Card .... FSSC No. 88-C-175
13. Airspeed Indicator .... FSSC No. 88-I-350
14. Airspeed Correction Card .... FSSC No. 88-C-150
15. Attitude Gyro .... FSSC No. 88-I-1310
16. Rate of Climb Indicator .... FSSC No. 88-I-750
17. Card Holder .... FSSC No. 88-H-500
18. Card Holder .... FSSC No. 88-H-570

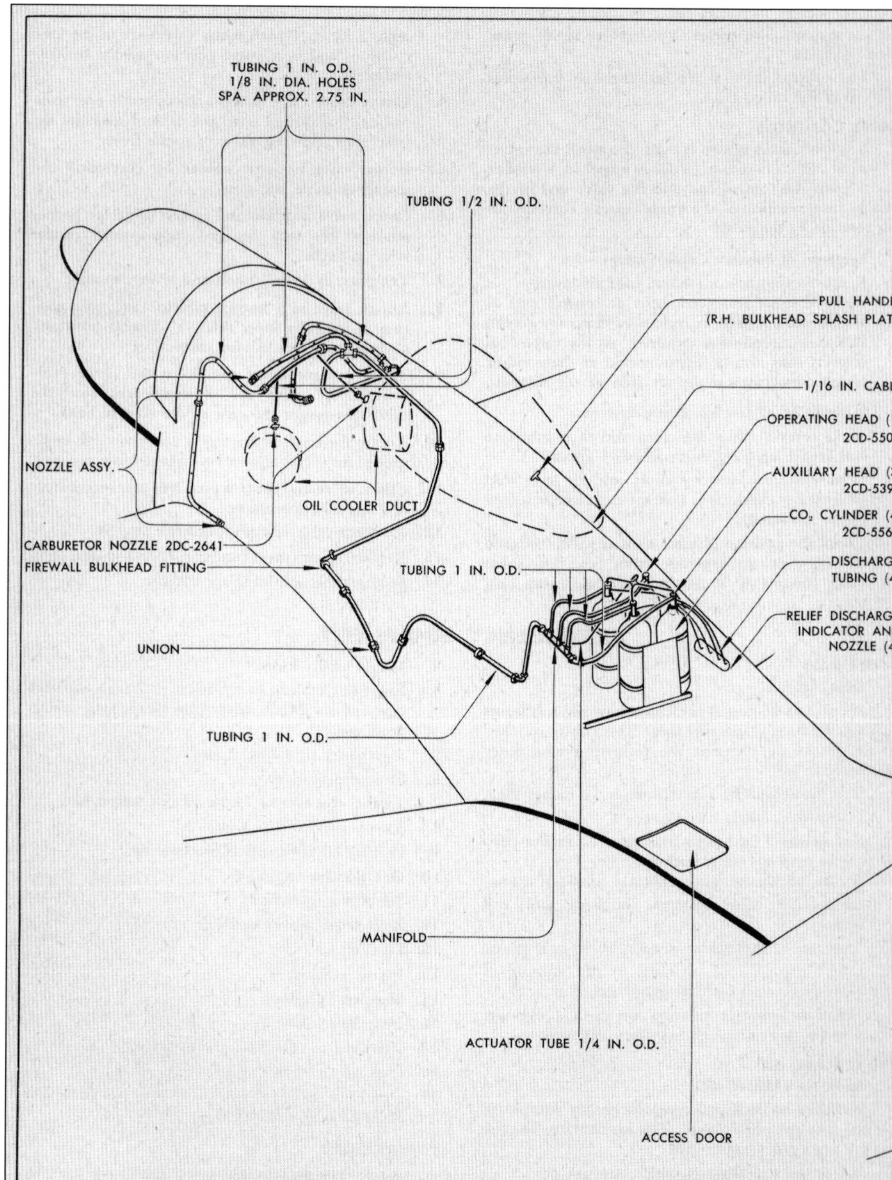

Figure 269—Fire Extinguisher System

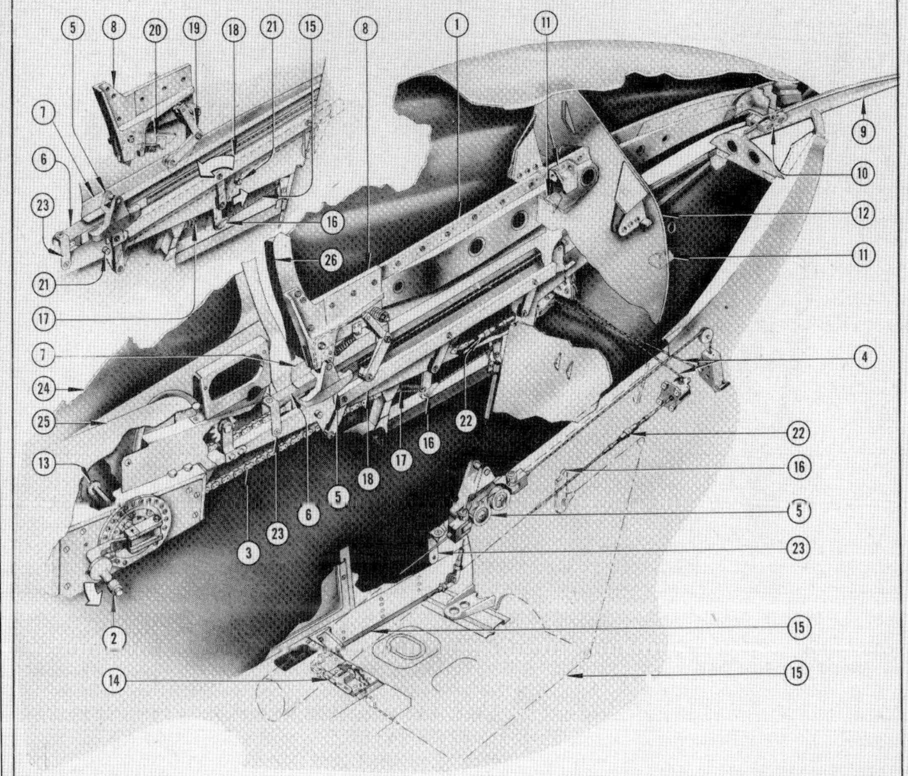

ENCLOSURE (CANOPY) REMOVAL

1. ENCLOSURE (CANOPY)
2. ENCLOSURE HAND CRANK
3. CHAIN—GEAR DRIVEN BY ENCLOSURE HAND CRANK
4. CABLE—COUPLED TO CHAIN
5. TRUCKS—RUN ON TRACKS
6. TRACKS—
7. SILL—
8. JETTISON TRIGGER ASSY—LOCKS ENCLOSURE TO TRUCK
9. REAR TRACK
10. REAR ENCLOSURE TRUCK—SECURES AFT END OF ENCLOSURE
11. ENCLOSURE SUPPORT FITTINGS—GIVE ADDITIONAL SUPPORT WHEN ENCLOSURE IS CLOSED
12. SEAT ARMOR PLATE—
13. EXTERNAL RELEASE PLUNGER—LOCATED UNDER RUBBER PAD ON R.H. SIDE BELOW WINDSHIELD
14. JETTISON "TEE" HANDLE—ON COCKPIT FLOOR TO RIGHT OF CONTROL COLUMN
15. R. & L.H. JETTISON CABLES—
16. R. & L.H. JETTISON CRANK—
17. TENSION SPRING—RETAINS LOCKING TENSION ON JETTISON BAR
18. JETTISON BARS—ROTATE FORWARD AND UP TO DEPRESS TRIGGER
19. TRIGGER—DEPRESSED TRIGGER RELEASES HOOKS
20. HOOKS—UNLOCKED HOOKS RELEASE TRUCKS
21. JETTISON BAR LIMIT STOPS—
22. TURNBUCKLES—EVENLY ADJUST CABLE AND CHAIN SYSTEMS
23. TRACK TIE STRAP—REMOVAL OF STRAPS ALLOW REMOVAL OF TRUCKS FOR SERVICING
24. WINDSHIELD—
25. COWL—
26. RUBBER SEAL—

Figure 272—Canopy Removal

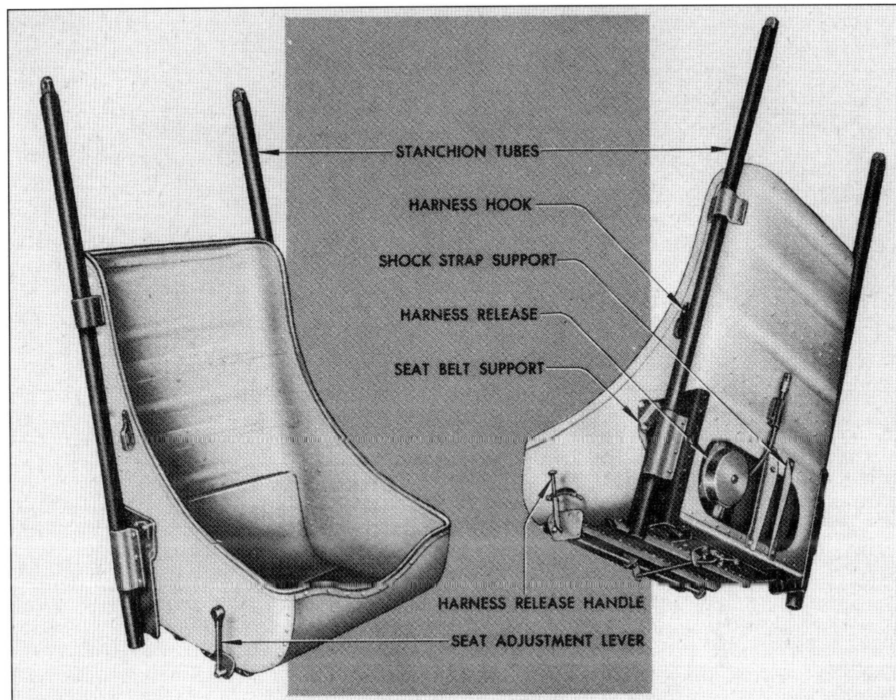

Figure 271—Pilot's Seat

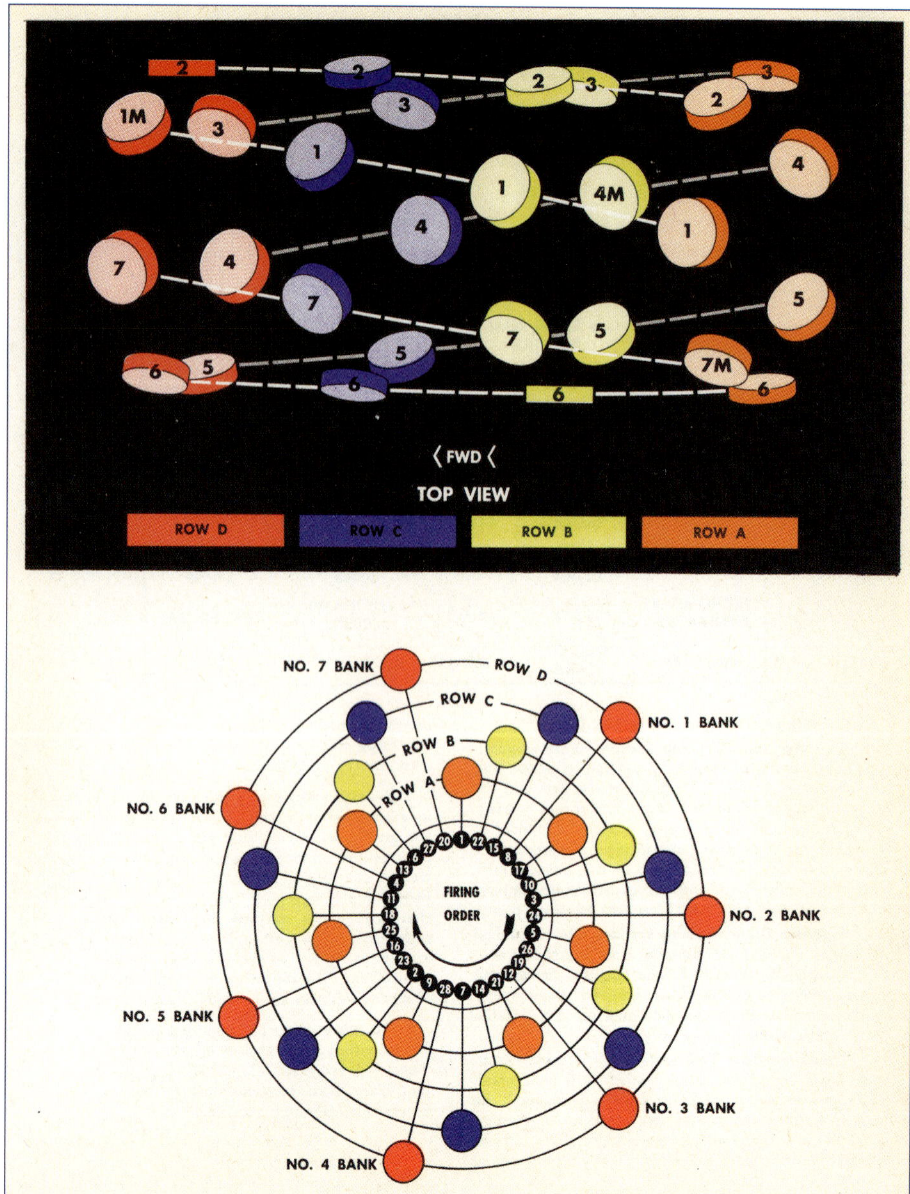

Figure 100—Cylinder Arrangement

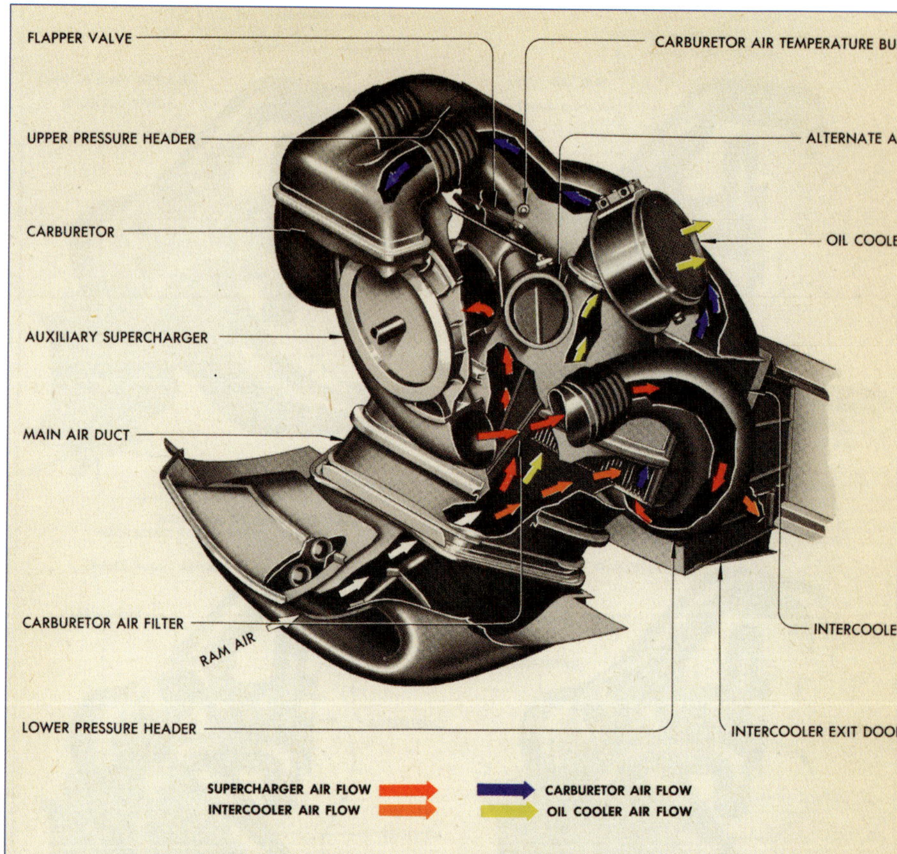

Figure 165—Air Induction System

CARBURETOR AIR INDUCTION SYSTEM

This system, housed in the rear accessory section, includes the air scoop, the main air duct, the two lower pressure header ducts, the intercooler and air exit flap, oil coolers and oil cooler flaps, the upper pressure header duct, and the carburetor intake elbow.

When ram air enters the air scoop a small amount is directed to the heat exchanger, but the major part goes up through the main air duct and is divided four ways. The forward center portion goes through the air filter to the carburetor either by way of the intercooler and auxiliary stage supercharger, if operating, or directly through the flapper valve and upper pressure header. The two oil coolers receive the side portions. The rear portion, when auxiliary supercharger is working, goes through the intercooler and exits through the intercooler exit door. (Air Induction and Air Induction Schematic illustrations show this clearly.)

If the scoop screen becomes blocked, the alternate air ports provide a source of carburetor air, or, in case of a carburetor icing, they allow the pilot to draw warm air into the carburetor from the engine accessory compartment.

Appendix 9

Pilot's Manual

This appendix reproduces the original three-color XF8B-1 Pilot's Manual in its entirety. A remarkably well-preserved copy was found by the author in the National Archives in a collection of Navy aircraft manuals, most of which were for production aircraft. It presents a relatively comprehensive guide to piloting this huge, powerful fighter from a carrier and employing it both as a fighter and bomber in combat. The quality of the illustrations and overall presentation is quite high, a sign that it was perhaps produced when Boeing still had reasonable hope of the Navy procuring its "five-in-one" fighter in considerable quantity. The author has examined manuals from other experimental Navy aircraft of the period and found that few were as elaborate as this one. It is to be enjoyed both for the information it imparts about operating the XF8B-1 and as a rare example of fine graphical design from the World War II era.

Manual Scan: National Archives, RG 287

Front cover of the Boeing XF8B-1 Pilot's Manual, a hardback with an ersatz leather exterior and a spiral binding. The manual is reproduced on the following 61 pages at slightly less than life size to fit the format of this book.

PILOT'S MANUAL

BOEING

XF8B-1

NAVY FIGHTER

D-5850

R E S T R I C T E D

This document contains information affecting the National Defence of the United States within the meaning of the Espionage Act, 50 U.S.C., 31 and 32 as amended. Its transmission or the revelation of its contents in any manner to an unauthorized person is prohibited by law.

Manual Scan: National Archives, RG 287

RESTRICTED

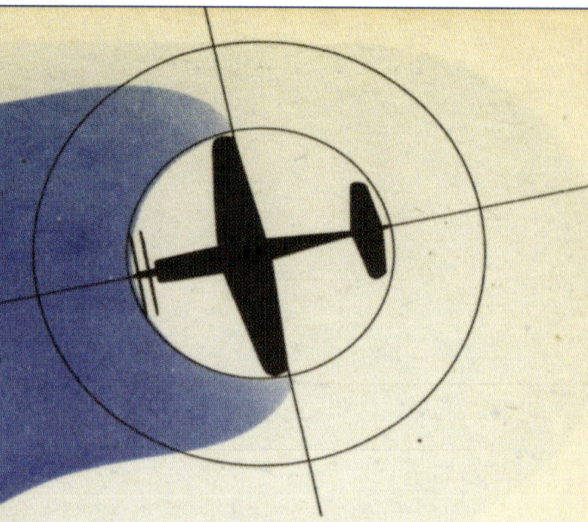

XF8B-1 Navy Fighter

This airplane is a single place, low wing, Navy fighter. Its features are range, speed, maneuverability, and striking power. In addition to six .50 caliber machine guns or six 20 MM cannons or a combination of the two, the airplane is designed to carry bombs. It uses a 3000 HP Pratt & Whitney R4360-10 engine. The following chart gives some interesting statistics.

EMPTY WEIGHT	13,693 POUNDS
GROSS WEIGHT, FIGHTER	17,752 POUNDS
FUEL—WING TANK	395 GALLONS
FUEL—BOMB BAY TANK	270 GALLONS
FUEL—WING EXTERNAL TANKS	300 GALLONS
BOMBS—INTERNAL AND EXTERNAL—MAX. EACH	2000 POUNDS
TORPEDO—BELOW BODY	2000 POUNDS
HORSEPOWER—MAXIMUM CONTINUOUS	2500 H P
HORSEPOWER—TAKE-OFF AND MILITARY	3000 H P
WING AREA	490 SQ FT
WING LOADING—17,752/490	36.3 LB/SQ FT
POWER LOADING—17,752/3000	5.9 LB/HP

1

Manual Scan: National Archives, RG 287

TABLE OF CONTENTS

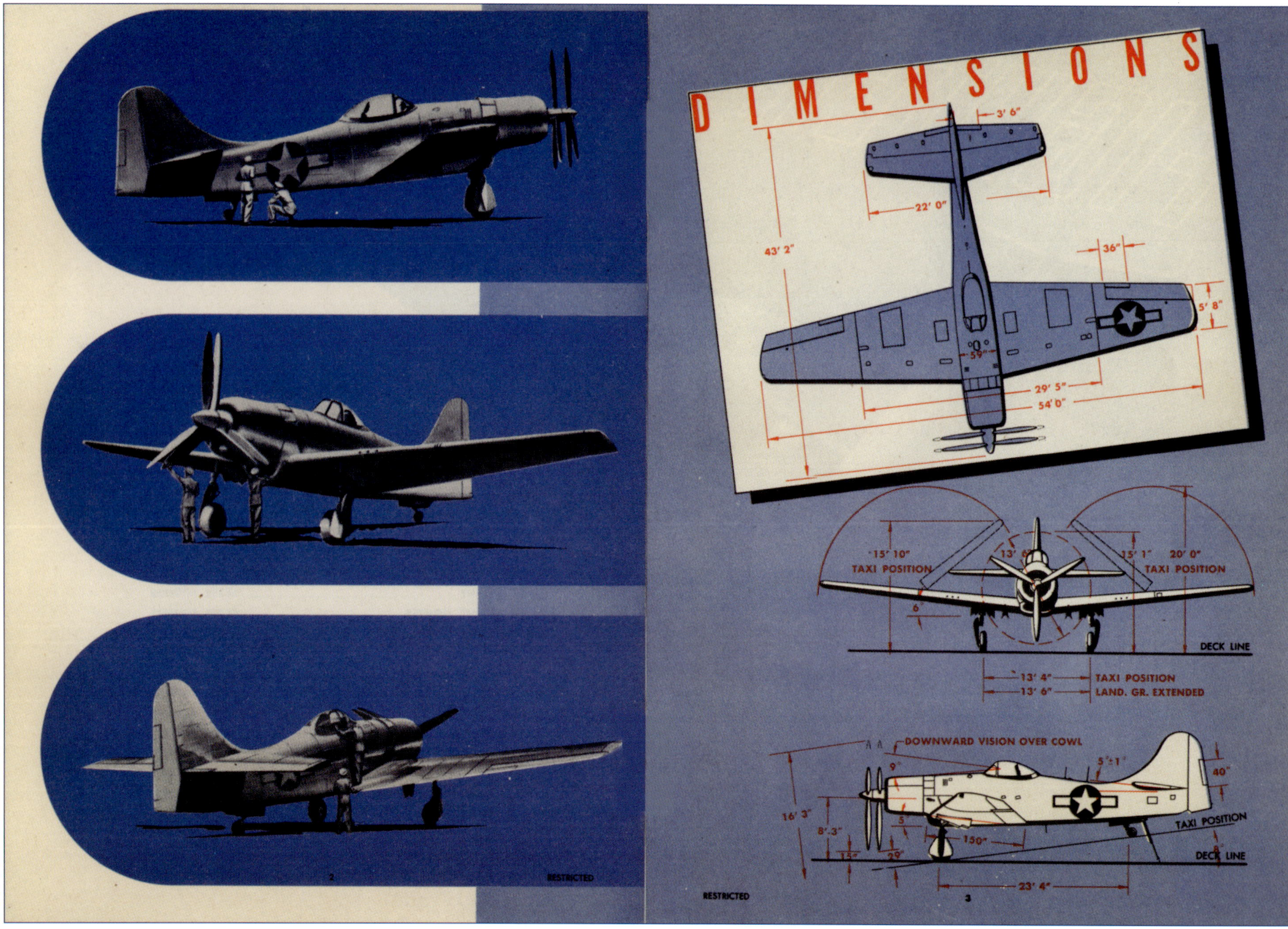
DIMENSIONS
3' 6"
22' 0"
43' 2"
36"
5' 8"
29' 5"
54' 0"
15' 10"
TAXI POSITION
15' 1"
20' 0"
TAXI POSITION
DECK LINE
13' 4"
13' 6"
TAXI POSITION
LAND. GR. EXTENDED
DOWNWARD VISION OVER COWL
16' 3"
40"
TAXI POSITION
DECK LINE
150"
23' 4"
2
RESTRICTED
RESTRICTED
3

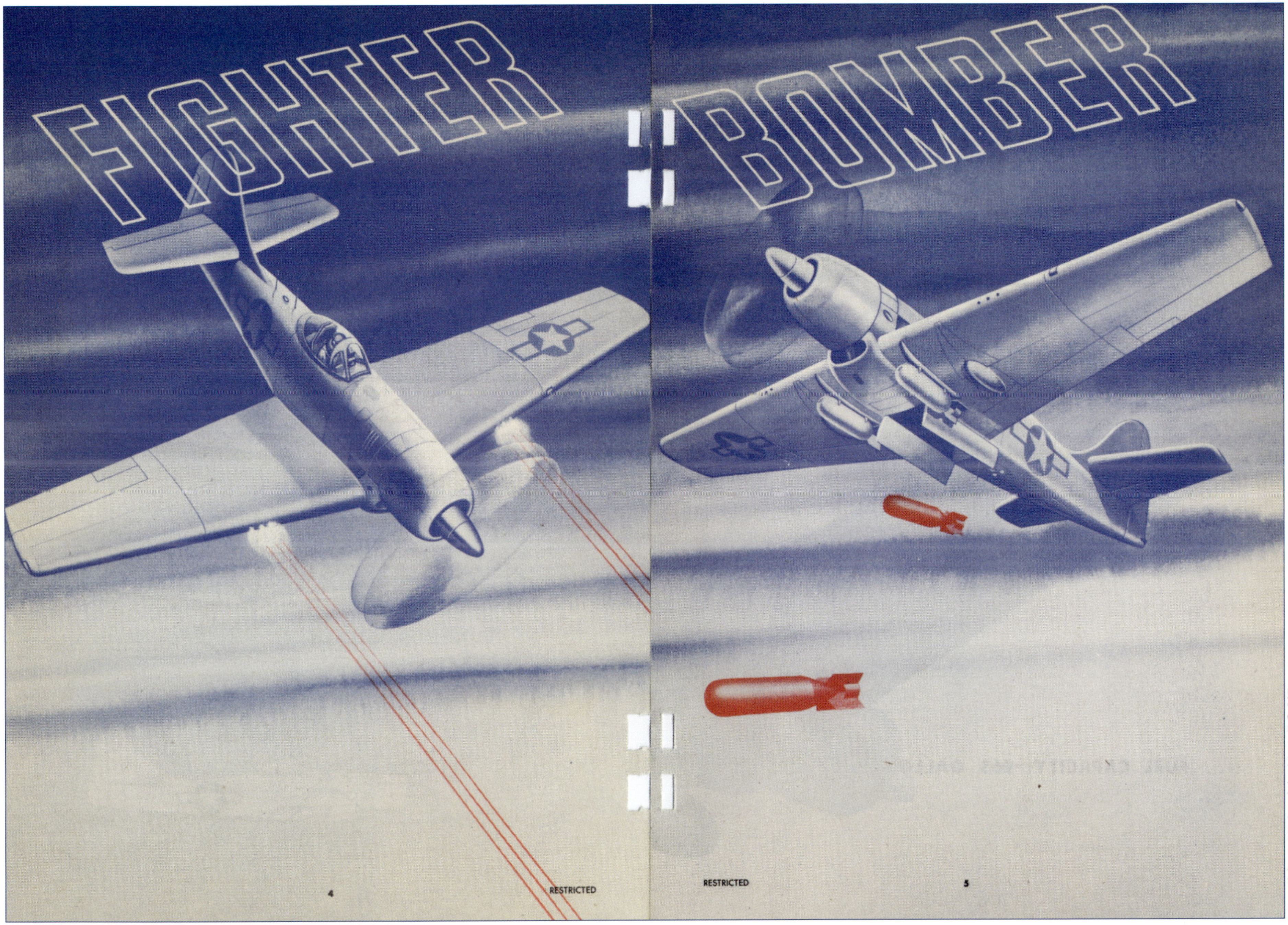

Manual Scan: National Archives, RG 287

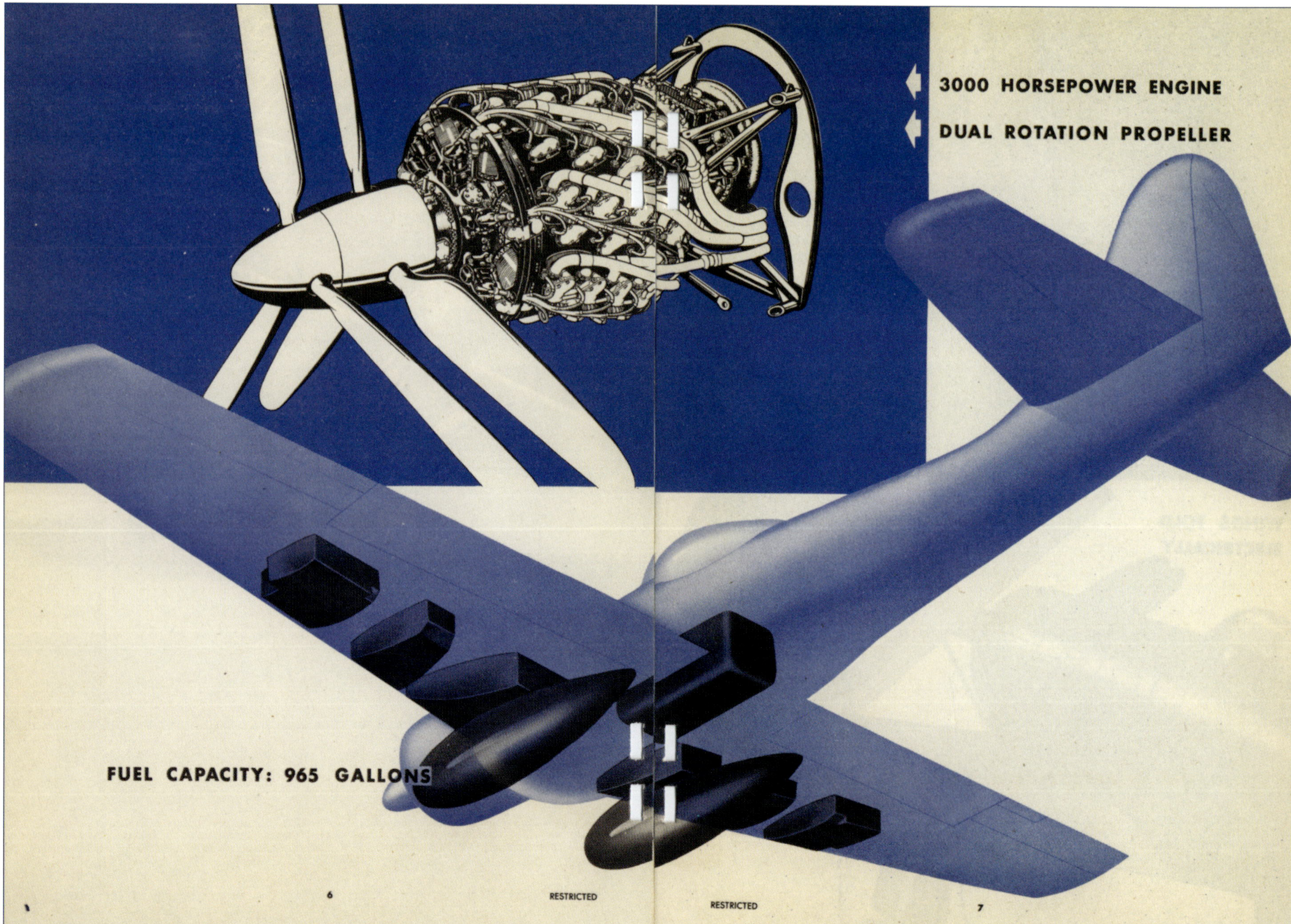

Manual Scan: National Archives, RG 287

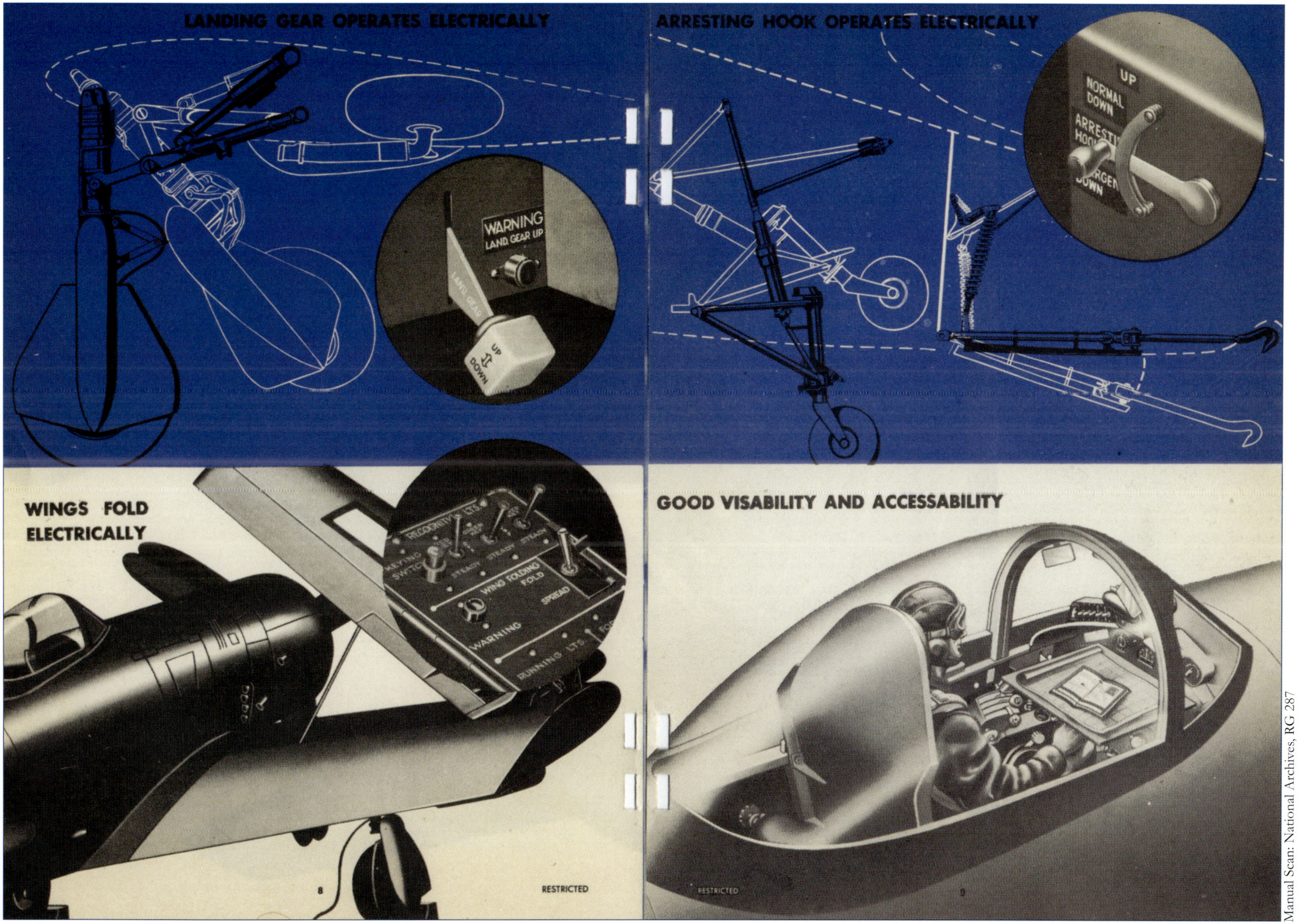

Manual Scan: National Archives, RG 287

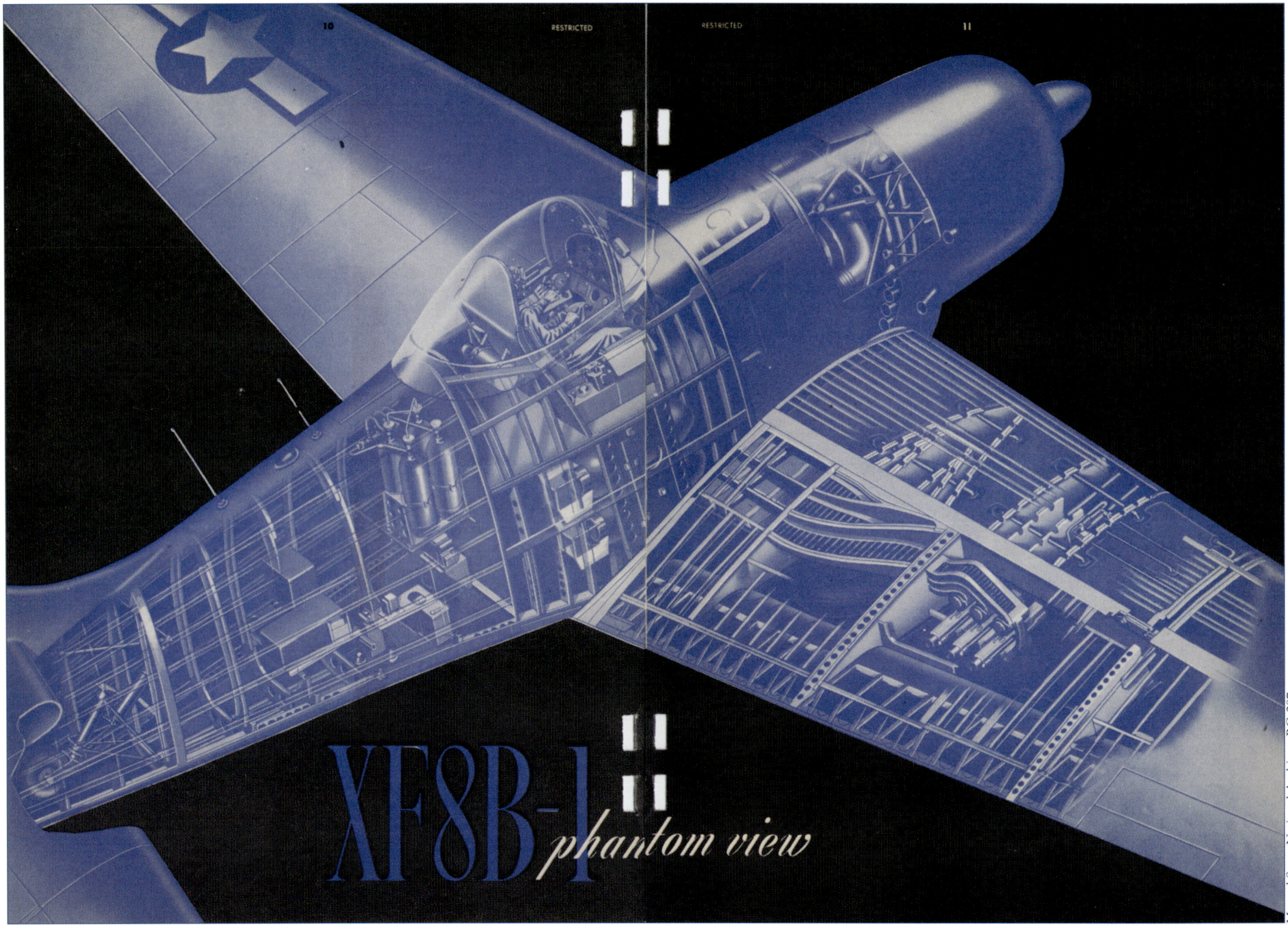

Manual Scan: National Archives, RG 287

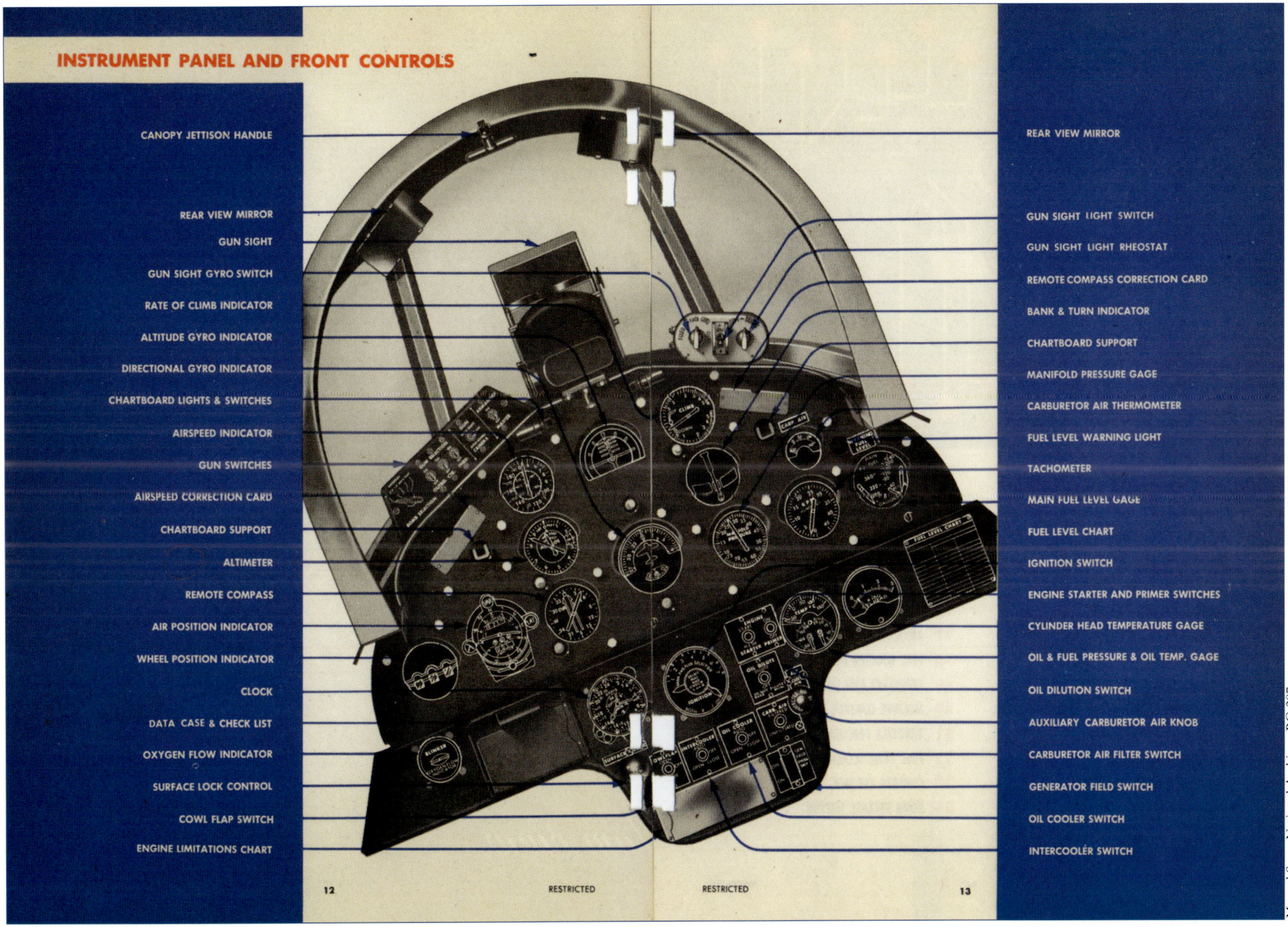

Manual Scan: National Archives, RG 287

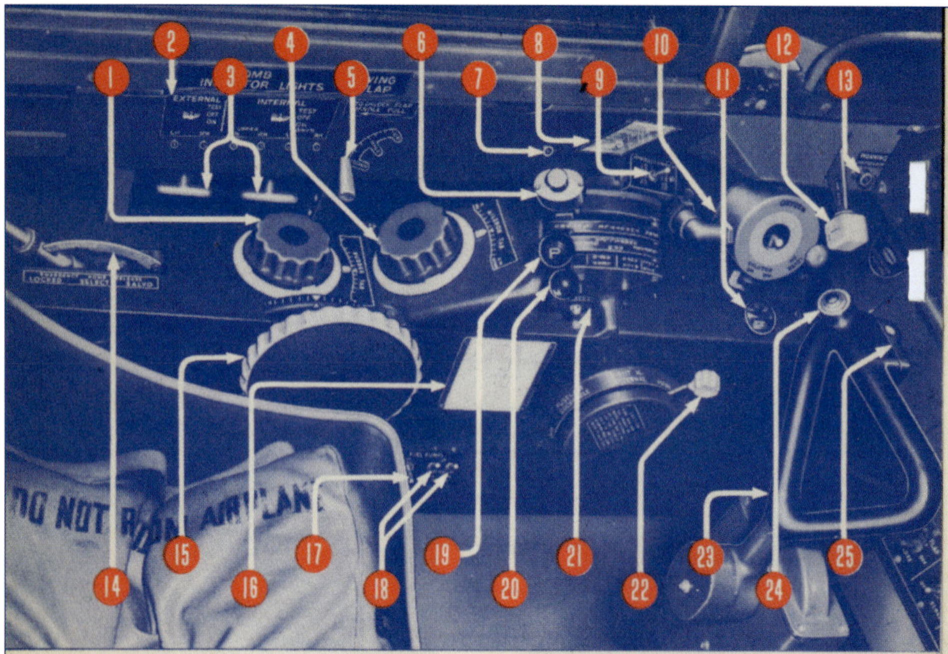

LEFT SIDEWALL CONTROLS

1 RUDDER TRIM TAB KNOB
2 BOMB INDICATOR LIGHT PANEL
3 EXTERNAL BOMB RELEASE HANDLES
4 AILERON TRIM TAB KNOB
5 WING FLAP TOGGLE
6 THROTTLE
7 SUPERCHARGER INDICATOR LIGHT
8 ALTIMETER CORRECTION CARD
9 SUPERCHARGER SWITCH
10 OXYGEN REGULATOR
11 OXYGEN PRESSURE GAGE
12 LANDING GEAR TOGGLE
13 LANDING GEAR WARNING LIGHT
14 BOMB RELEASE HANDLE
15 ELEVATOR TRIM TAB WHEEL
16 FUEL SYSTEM DIAGRAM
17 AUXILIARY FUEL PUMP SWITCH
18 FUEL BOOSTER PUMP SWITCHES
19 PROPELLER RPM HANDLE
20 MIXTURE CONTROL HANDLE
21 THROTTLE FRICTION KNOB
22 FUEL TANK SELECTOR HANDLE
23 CONTROL COLUMN
24 BOMB RELEASE BUTTON

14 RESTRICTED

RESTRICTED 15

RIGHT SIDEWALL CONTROLS

1 RECOGNITION LIGHT SWITCHES
2 WING FOLDING SWITCH
3 CANOPY CRANK
4 FORMATION AND SECTION LIGHT SWITCHES
5 VOLTMETER
6 INSTRUMENT LIGHTS RHEOSTAT
7 BATTERY SWITCH
8 COCKPIT LIGHTS RHEOSTAT
9 IFF RADIO SWITCHES
10 IFF EMERGENCY SWITCH
11 HAND MICROPHONE
12 RADIO TELEPHONE CONTROL BOX
13 WING FOLDING WARNING LIGHT
14 RUNNING LIGHTS SWITCHES
15 CHARTBOARD STOWAGE
16 MASTER EXTERIOR LIGHTS SWITCHES
17 PITOT HEATER SWITCH
18 MASTER RADIO SWITCH
19 CIRCUIT BREAKER PANEL
20 IFF DESTRUCTOR SWITCH
21 COCKPIT COLD AIR HANDLE
22 HOMING RECEIVER CONTROL BOX
23 COCKPIT AND WINDSHIELD HOT AIR KNOB
24 RANGE RECEIVER

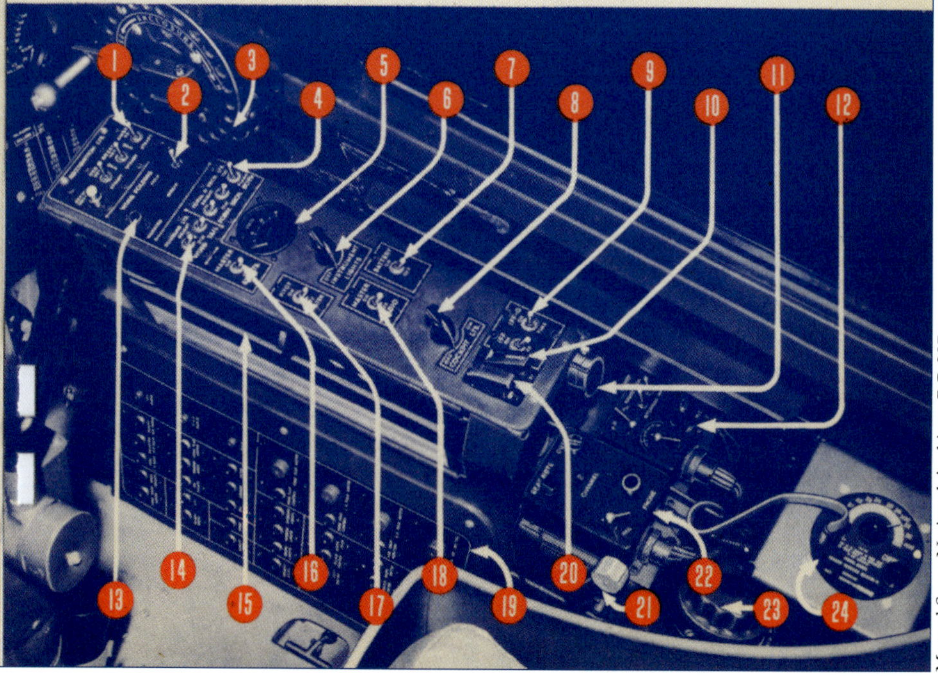

Manual Scan: National Archives, RG 287

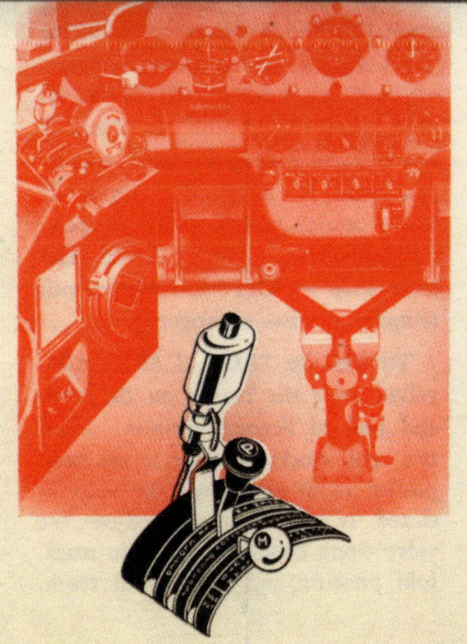

POWER PLANT

Engine—A 3000 HP (military rating), 28 cylinder, Pratt & Whitney Wasp Major R-4360-10 engine powers the XF8B-1.

Propeller—The six bladed dual rotation Aeroproducts propeller has one control, the "PROPELLER RPM" handle on the left control stand. Propeller torque is neutralized by opposite rotation of the blades and RPM hunting is eliminated by the high pressure hydraulic system. The propeller clears the deck by 15 inches during the take-off runs.

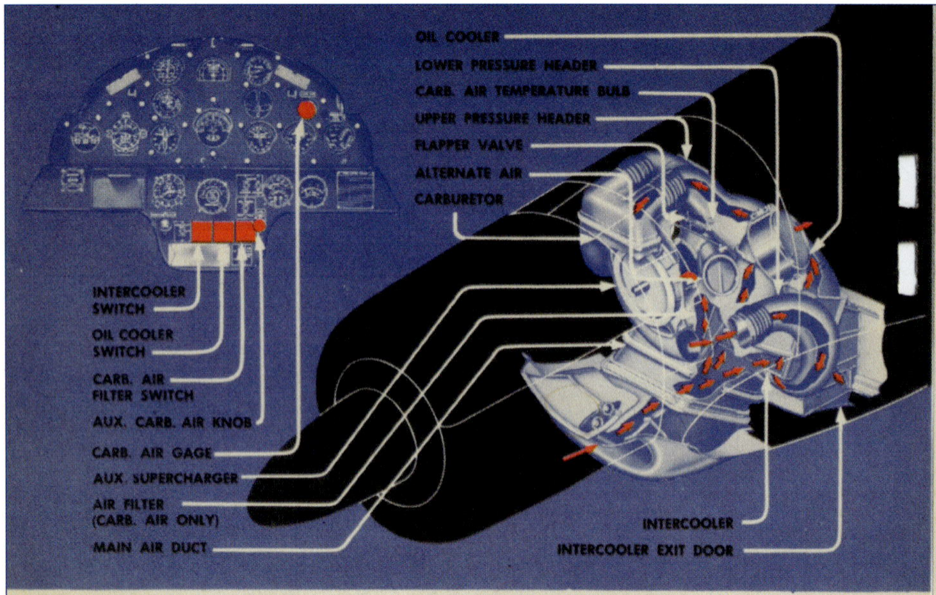

AIR INDUCTION SYSTEM

The air scoop supplies air (ram or supercharged) to the carburetor, to the intercooler (for cooling carburetor air) and to the oil coolers.

The supercharger is used to increase manifold pressure only when the throttle is wide open. To increase power, hold the "SUPERCHARGER" switch at "INCREASE MAN PR" until the desired pressure is obtained. To decrease the pressure the switch is pushed to "DECREASE MAN PR" and held until the desired pressure is reached or until the amber light goes out. After that manifold pressure is decreased by closing the throttle.

The intercooler switch, on the instrument panel has "AUTO," "OPEN," "CLOSE" and "OFF" position. During normal operation the switch is in the "AUTO" position. If the air temperature with the switch in "AUTO" is too high, turn to "OPEN" momentarily and then let it snap to "OFF" and repeat until the temperature levels off at the desired point. If the temperature is too low, turn to "CLOSE," then let it snap to "OFF" and repeat until temperature rises to proper level.

To use the "AUX. CARB. AIR" valves press the button on the knob and pull to desired position. Turn the knob clockwise after it has been pushed in to make sure the valve is closed. If it has been screwed out, the valve won't close, and a loss in manifold pressure and power will result.

18 RESTRICTED

FUEL SYSTEM

The XF8B-1 uses fuel, Spec. AN-F-28, Grade 100/130, which is carried in a main tank (6 wing cells), a droppable body tank, and two droppable external tanks.

A red light shows on the instrument panel when the main tank fuel supply is below 40 gallons. This is enough for 30 minutes flight at 40% power.

The tank selector handle on the left console can be set to "OFF," "FUSELAGE DROPPABLE," "RIGHT H. EXTERNAL," "LEFT H. EXTERNAL, or "MAIN." To change from one tank to another move this handle. The tank selector handles also turns on the booster pumps when set at "MAIN" or the auxiliary fuel pump if any other tank is selected.

Unless the engine is running, the handle must always be at "OFF" or fuel will be pumped into the blower case and the propeller will have to be pulled through by hand before the engine can be started.

If your mission requires the auxiliary tanks, always use the "MAIN" tank for warm-up, take-off, and climb because the vapor return line from the carburetor connects to the main tank.

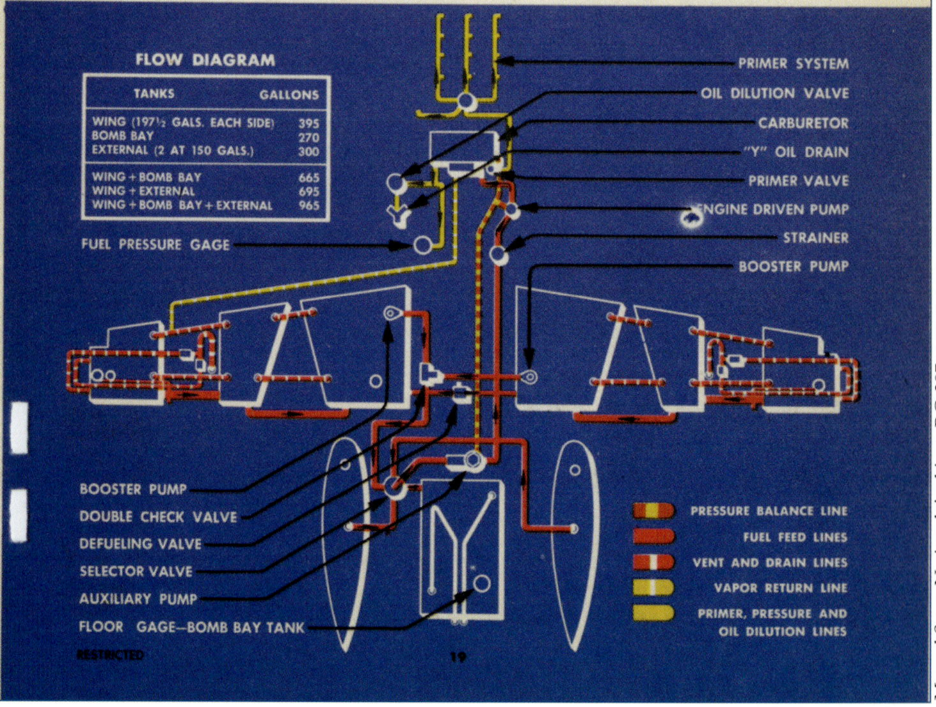

Manual Scan: National Archives, RG 287

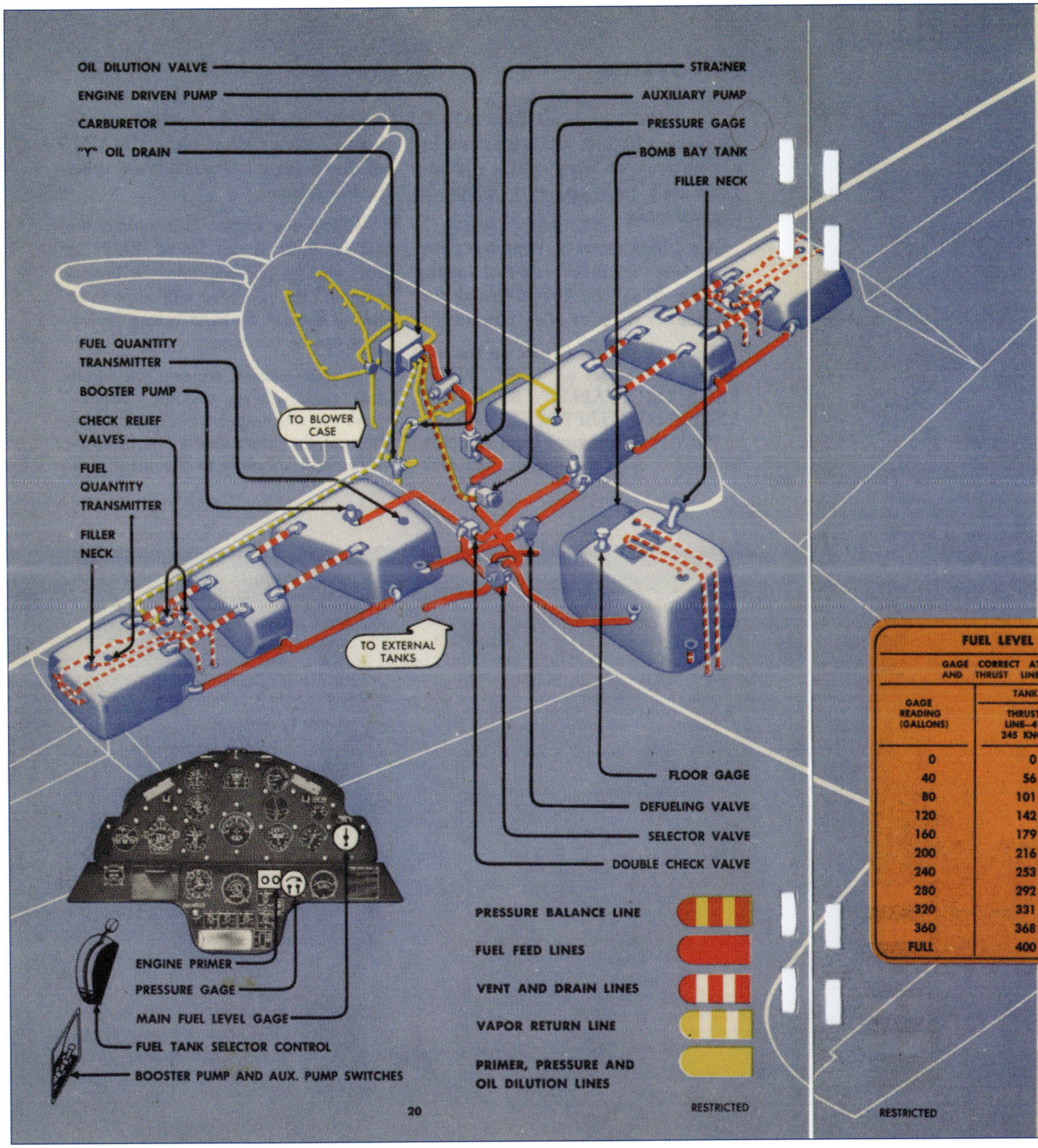

FUEL LEVEL CHART

GAGE CORRECT AT 140 KNOTS AND THRUST LINE LEVEL (0°)

GAGE READING (GALLONS)	TANK CONTAINS GALLONS	
	THRUST LINE–4½° 245 KNOTS	THRUST LINE +8° 3 PT. POS.
0	0	0
40	56	28
80	101	56
120	142	87
160	179	124
200	216	164
240	253	209
280	292	241
320	331	293
360	368	346
FULL	400	406

FUEL SYSTEM Continued

The return flow is from 8 to 15 GPH and so if the "MAIN" tank fuel gage reads "FULL" the returning fuel will run overboard.

The "OFF"—"ON" booster pump switches, just aft of the tank selector handle, are spring loaded to the "ON" position (must be held "OFF" to save battery power in an emergency.)

The auxiliary fuel pump "OFF"—"ON" switch is next to the booster pump switches. It is unnecessary to turn this switch "ON" unless the fuel pressure drops below 16 PSI when the selector handle is set to "MAIN."

Priming—To prime the engine, move the tank selector handle to "MAIN" and press the primer switch on the instrument panel. It is well to remember when priming that most of the difficulties encountered in starting this engine are the result of giving it too much fuel.

Oil Dilution—Push the dilution switch on the instrument panel:

1. To dilute the oil before stopping the engine to prepare for an anticipated cold weather start.

2. To dilute the oil for an emergency take-off without warm-up only if the oil has been diluted at shut-down.

Mixture Control—There are "IDLE CUTOFF," "AUTO LEAN," "AUTO RICH," and "FULL RICH" settings. Intermediate settings are not effective and should not be attempted.

21

22 RESTRICTED

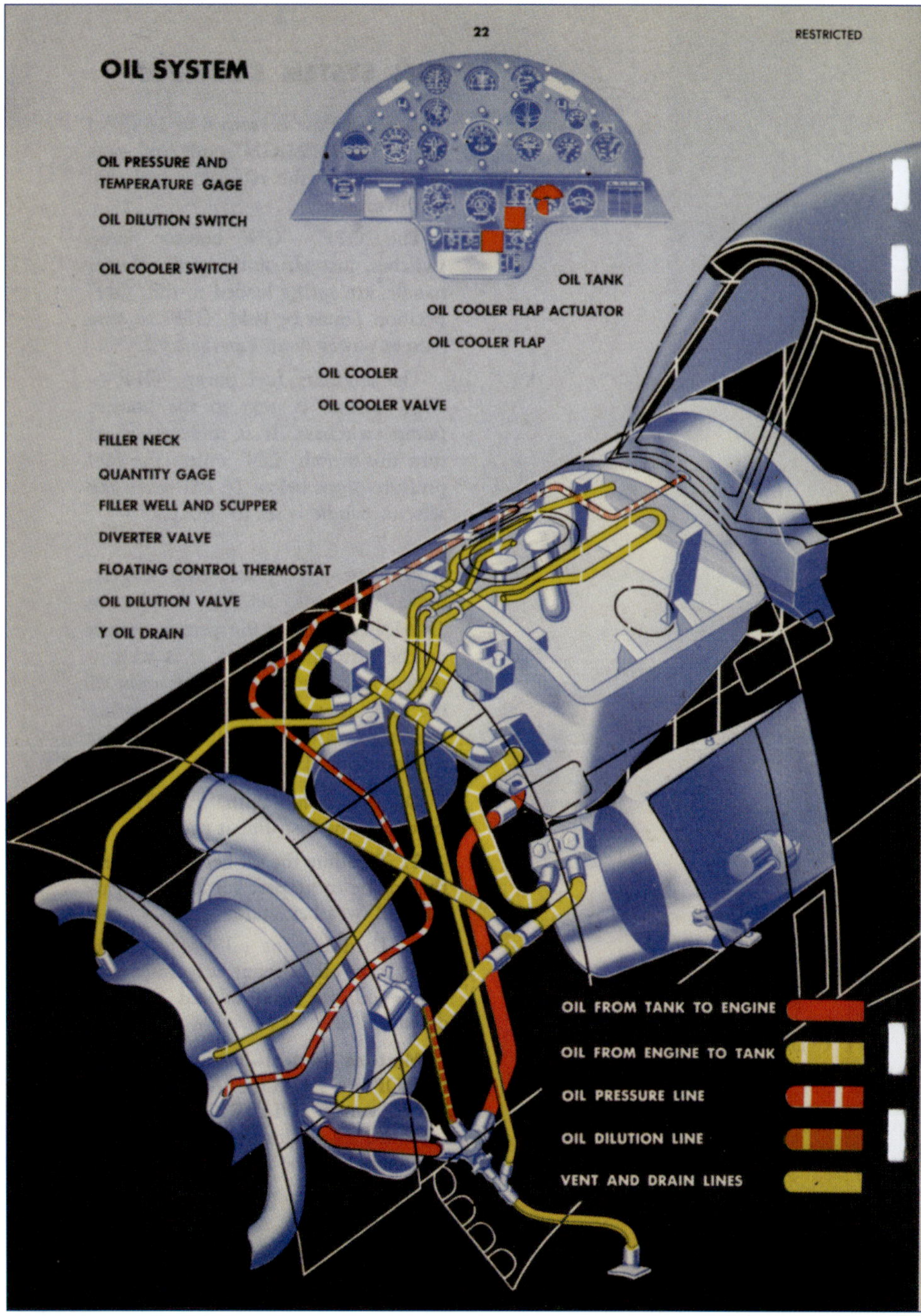

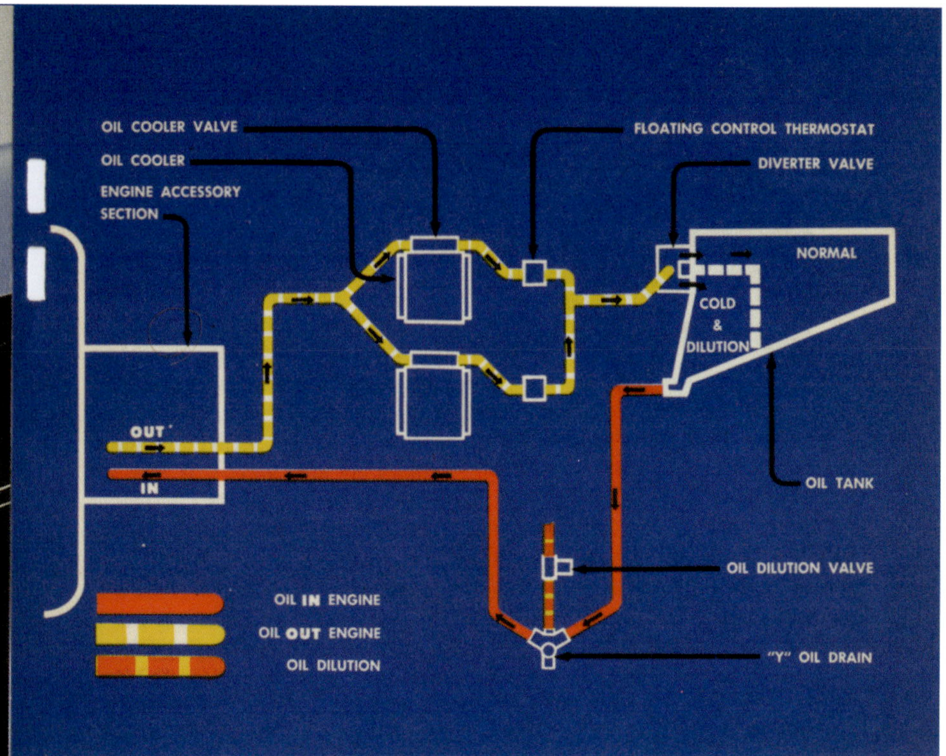

Oil System—The oil tank forms the top section of the cowling just in front of the windshield and has a capacity of 40 gallons. The oil cooler switch, on the instrument panel, has four positions: "AUTO," "OPEN," "CLOSE," and "OFF." When the switch is in the "AUTO" position a thermostat opens and closes the oil cooler doors to maintain a normal operating temperature. If, with the switch at "AUTO," the temperature exceeds the safe operating range, push the oil cooler switch to the "OPEN" position, hold the switch in that position for a moment, then let it snap to "OFF." Let the temperature level off and repeat if necessary until the temperature is in the proper range. If the temperature is below the safe operating range push the switch to "CLOSE" and use the same procedure as above until the temperature comes up to the proper level.

A single gage on the instrument panel shows both the oil pressure and oil temperature. The oil quantity gage is in the filler well under the cowling and cannot be seen from the cockpit.

RESTRICTED 23

STARTING SYSTEM

Ignition—The seven dual magnetos are controlled by a four position ("OFF"—"L"—"R"—"BOTH") master lever switch, and a knob switch used for testing. Set the nob switch to each magneto number, pull it out, and turn it to "R" or "L" to test the plugs in that bank of cylinders. For normal operation return the knob switch to "O" and the lever switch to the "BOTH" position.

Starting System—The XF8B-1 has an electric and handcranking, inertia and direct cranking starter with both electric and manual meshing. It connects to the airplane circuit, but external power should be used if available. The starter switch has "OFF," "START," and "MESH" positions. In "START" the motor turns on; in "MESH" the starter and engine jaws engage, the motor keeps cranking, and ignition boost is sent to the three top cylinder banks. In "MESH" the starter brushes are also lowered if they had previously been lifted off the commutator by manual meshing.

If electric power is not available, a hand crank and a gear box (not stowed in the airplane) can be plugged into the right side of the engine. The hand crank must be accelerated to 96 RPM before meshing. Pushing the meshing handle engages the jaws, lifts the motor brushes to make hand cranking easier, but does not give ignition boost.

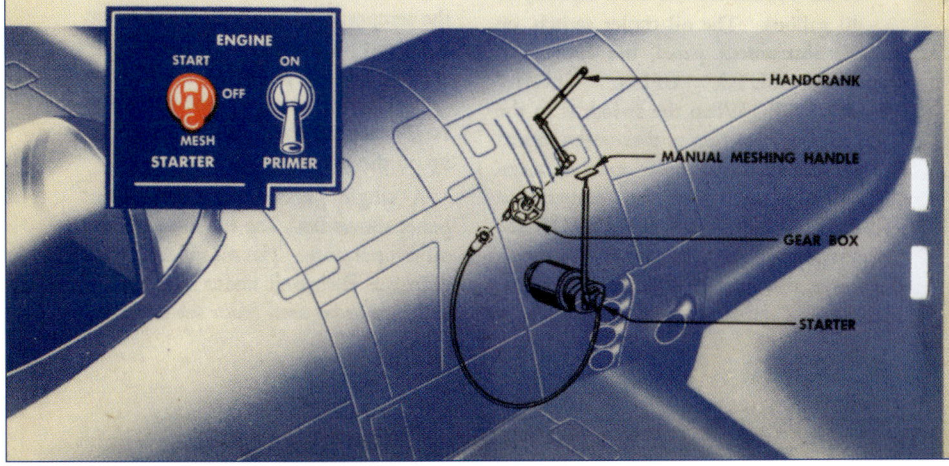

FLIGHT CONTROLS

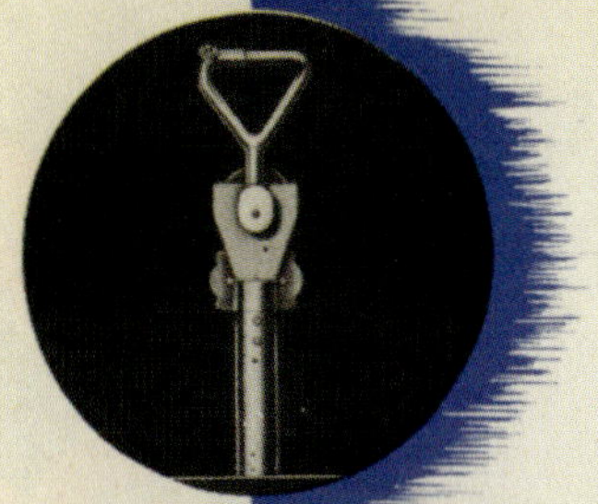

Ailerons—The pivoted spade grip at the top of the stick controls aileron movement. Only the grip (not the control column) moves in aileron control.

Elevators—The control column and grip move together for elevator control.

Rudder—The rudder pedals are adjustable both for leg length and for the amount of toe in and toe out. Toe pressure on the pedals applies the brakes.

Surface Lock—The ailerons, elevators, and rudder, are locked by pulling out and turning the "SURFACE LOCK" knob on the instrument panel, and moving the controls to neutral. The ailerons, though locked, will move because of spring action in the tab torque tubes. The knob also moves the throttle back and locks it in the closed position.

Tabs—The aileron, elevator, and rudder trim tab control wheels are on the left console in the cockpit. These tabs can be preset to balance the airplane for varying load conditions.

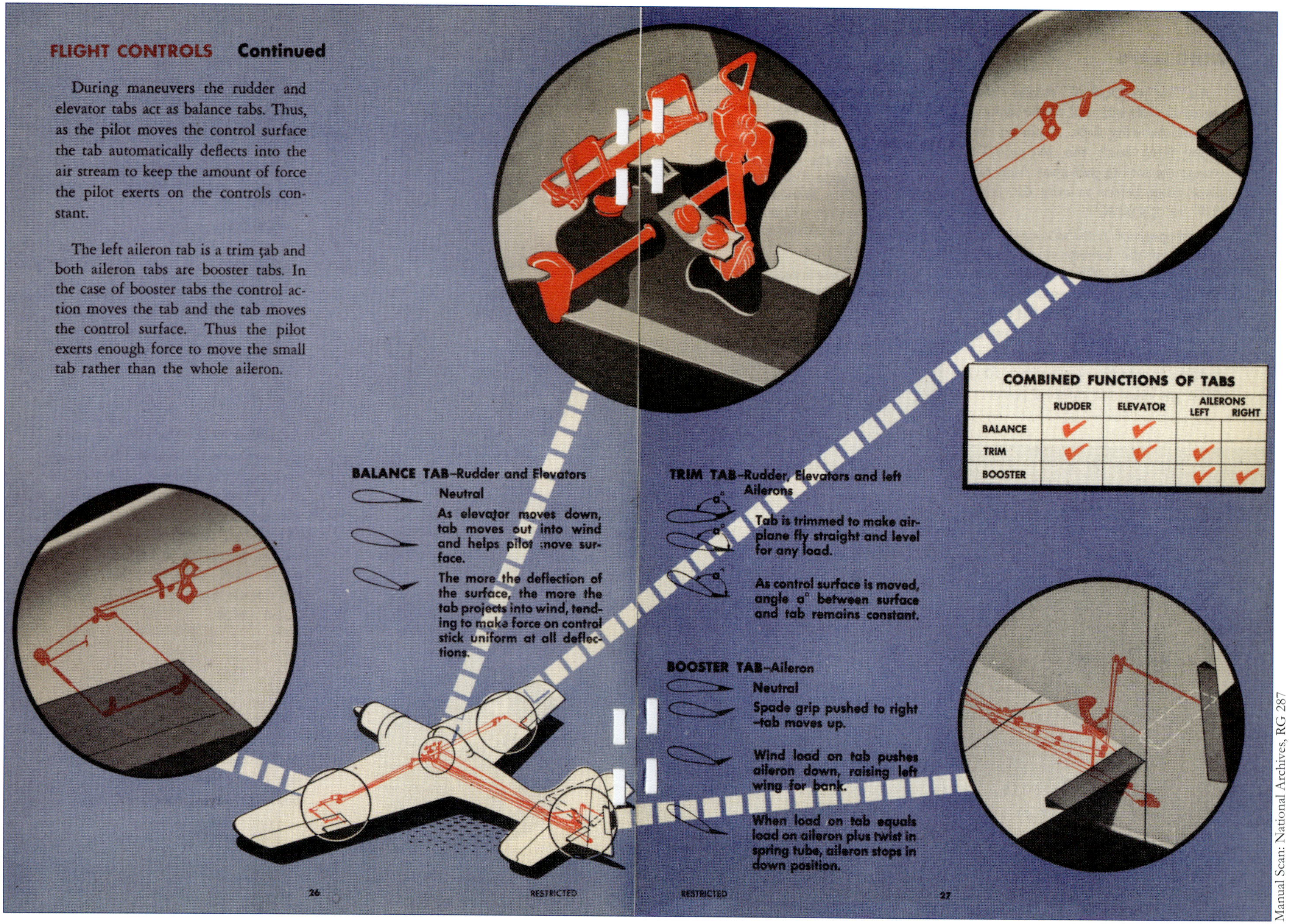

FLIGHT CONTROLS Continued

During maneuvers the rudder and elevator tabs act as balance tabs. Thus, as the pilot moves the control surface the tab automatically deflects into the air stream to keep the amount of force the pilot exerts on the controls constant.

The left aileron tab is a trim tab and both aileron tabs are booster tabs. In the case of booster tabs the control action moves the tab and the tab moves the control surface. Thus the pilot exerts enough force to move the small tab rather than the whole aileron.

BALANCE TAB–Rudder and Elevators

Neutral

As elevator moves down, tab moves out into wind and helps pilot move surface.

The more the deflection of the surface, the more the tab projects into wind, tending to make force on control stick uniform at all deflections.

TRIM TAB–Rudder, Elevators and left Ailerons

Tab is trimmed to make airplane fly straight and level for any load.

As control surface is moved, angle a° between surface and tab remains constant.

BOOSTER TAB–Aileron

Neutral

Spade grip pushed to right –tab moves up.

Wind load on tab pushes aileron down, raising left wing for bank.

When load on tab equals load on aileron plus twist in spring tube, aileron stops in down position.

COMBINED FUNCTIONS OF TABS

	RUDDER	ELEVATOR	AILERONS LEFT	AILERONS RIGHT
BALANCE	✓	✓		
TRIM	✓	✓	✓	
BOOSTER			✓	✓

26 RESTRICTED RESTRICTED 27

Manual Scan: National Archives, RG 287

WING FLAPS

An "UP"—"DOWN" toggle rheostat on the left side wall of the cockpit controls the wing flaps. A pin on the toggle lever holds the setting. To change the setting pull away from the pivot point before moving the lever "UP" or "DOWN."

Flap operation requires considerable power and the battery alone cannot handle the load. The generator does not deliver sufficient power until the engine is turning up 1000 RPM or better, so if it is necessary to raise or lower the flaps when the engine is not running or turning over less than 1000 RPM you must use external power.

There is a switch in the right wing fold which automatically prevents the wing flaps from operating until after the wings are completely spread. If, during the time the wings are folded, the rheostat toggle is set for positioning the flaps, then, as soon as the wings are spread, the flaps will assume the set position without further action by the pilot.

A pressure switch connected to the pitot pressure system will raise the flaps

TOGGLE HAND CRANK

whenever the air speed exceeds 130 knots (150 MPH). If the speed later drops below 120 knots (138 MPH) the flaps will return to whatever position is set on the toggle rheostat.

A hand crank attachment on the right console allows hand operation of the flaps in case of electrical failure. When the crank is in the attachment (crank is stowed in the right console) a safety switch prevents electrical operation. It takes about five minutes (360 turns of the crank) to lower the flaps by hand.

A twenty inch section of the flaps extends over the wing fold. This must be folded back by hand when the airplane is stowed and extended by hand before take-off is made.

Wing Flap Motor Failure—Check the circuit breaker (must be in) if the flaps don't work when you move the control toggle. In emergency it may be possible to keep the motor running by holding the circuit breaker in even though it is trying to pop out from overload. If the flaps don't move (always check flap position and movement by looking over the side of the cockpit) release the circuit breaker to keep from discharging the battery.

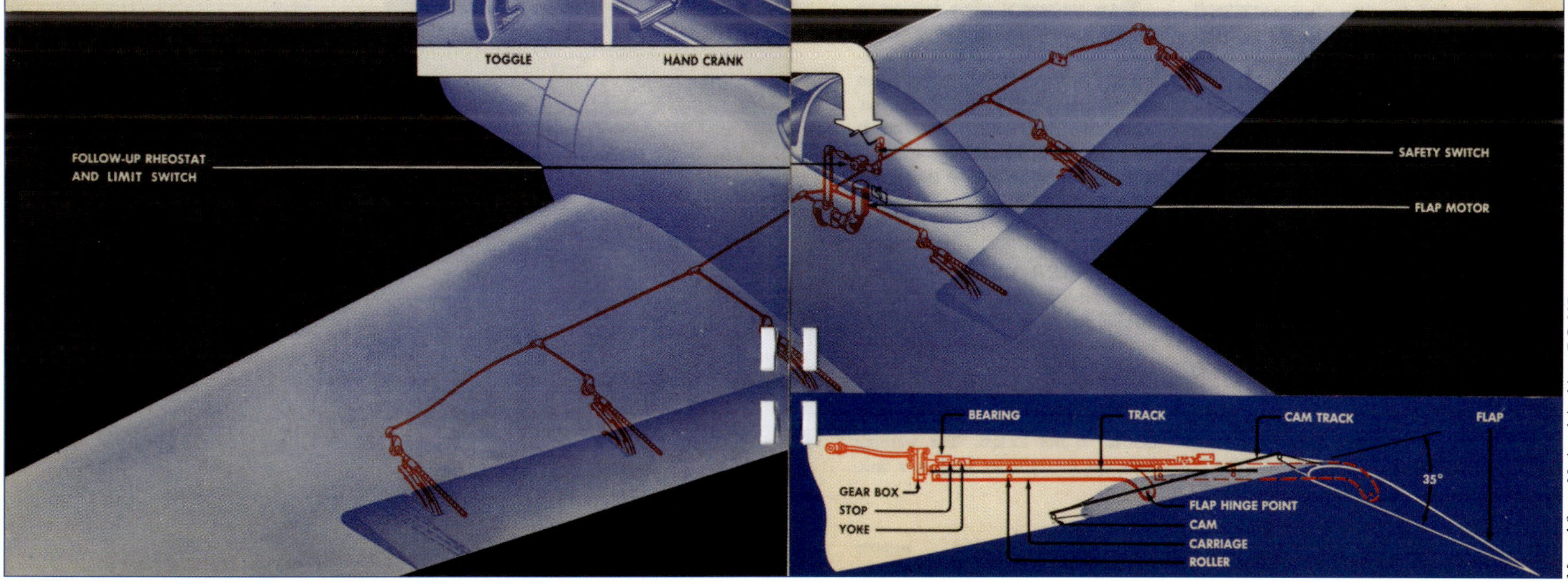

WING FOLDING

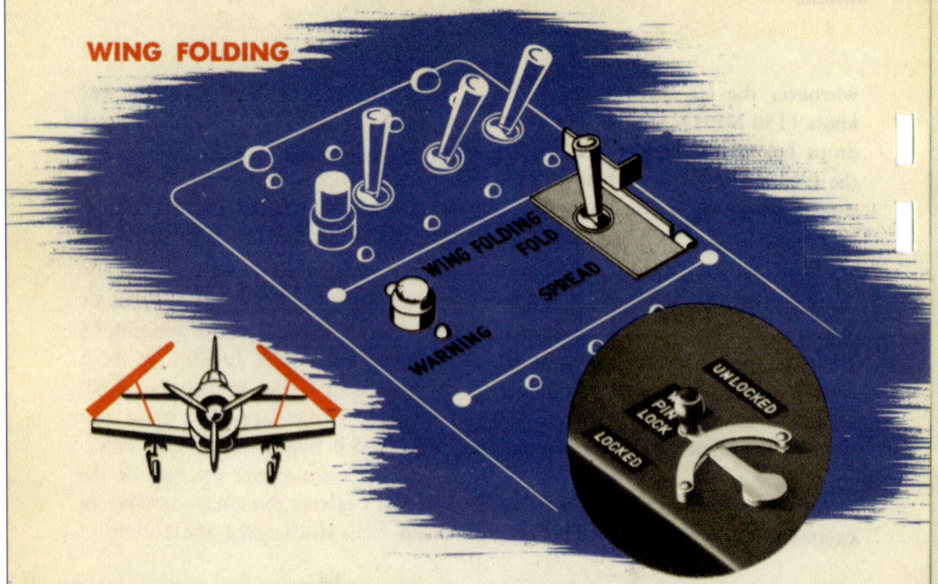

To fold the wings, place the "WING PIN LOCK" control handle at "UNLOCKED," raise hinged guard from the "WING FOLDING" toggle switch, check throttle position with power source (see following paragraph), and flip the "WING FOLD" toggle switch to "FOLD."

The XF8B-1 wings are electrically folded. External power or generator power must be used because the battery can't handle wing folding. If the engine is running, the throttle setting must be above 1000 RPM to use generator power and below 1000 RPM to use external power. If the engine is stopped the external power will not cut in to fold or unfold the wings when the throttle is set above 1000 RPM.

There are several safety features to prevent accidental wing folding during flight. First, a squat switch on the landing gear prevents folding except when the airplane is on the deck or ground. Second, the "WING FOLD" switch is protected by a hinged guard which must be moved before the switch can be pushed to "FOLD." Third, the "WING PIN LOCK" control handle at the rear of the right console must be moved to "UNLOCK" or the pin will not come out even if the "WING FOLD" switch is pushed to "FOLD." Fourth, a red cylinder extends from the top of the wing and a red warning light on the right console in the cockpit remains on if the "WING PIN LOCK" is not locked. The warning light and the cylinder work as a unit.

LANDING GEAR

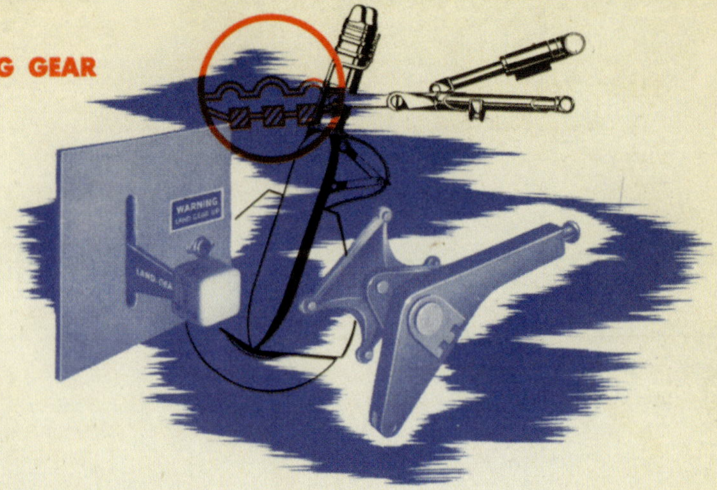

The XF8B-1 landing gear is electrically operated. A control handle at the upper left corner of the instrument panel operates up-locks which prevent the wheels from vibrating down, and the switch which turns on the retracting motor. Limit switches shut off the landing gear motor when the gear is fully retracted or extended. The landing gear position indicator, on the instrument panel, shows whether the wheels are up or down. If the throttle is closed below about 1000 RPM before all the wheels are down, a red warning light next to the control handle lights up.

Don't attempt to raise or lower the gear above 152 knots (175 MPH).

A squat switch on the right wheel prevents retraction of the landing gear when the airplane is on the deck.

Landing Gear Emergency Operation—If the landing gear doesn't come down when the lever is pushed to "DOWN," check the circuit breaker. If it is popped out and if it is necessary to get the wheels down in a hurry, push it in and hold it there. The motor may still work even though the circuit breaker is trying to pop out from the overload. If, however, the wheels still don't come down, release the circuit breaker at once to keep from discharging the battery.

If the landing gear motor or the electric power fails, the wheels can't be extended or retracted by a hand crank. The crank is stowed on the right control stand and is inserted for use in the side of the stand in a socket connected to the retracting screws through a torque tube system. It takes 230 turns of the crank (about 3½ minutes) to raise or lower the landing gear. A safety switch prevents electrical operation when the crank is in the socket.

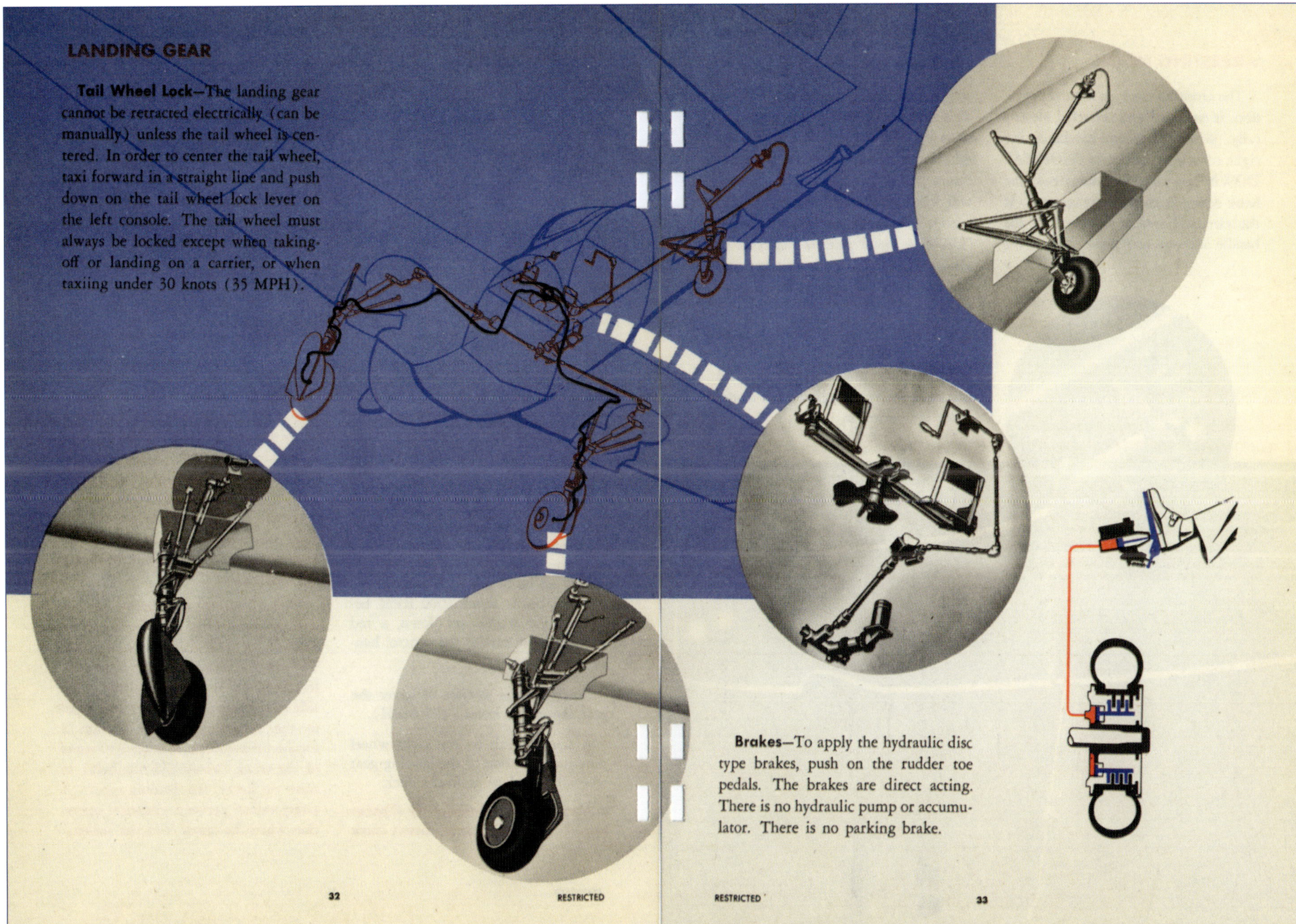

LANDING GEAR

Tail Wheel Lock—The landing gear cannot be retracted electrically (can be manually) unless the tail wheel is centered. In order to center the tail wheel, taxi forward in a straight line and push down on the tail wheel lock lever on the left console. The tail wheel must always be locked except when taking-off or landing on a carrier, or when taxiing under 30 knots (35 MPH).

Brakes—To apply the hydraulic disc type brakes, push on the rudder toe pedals. The brakes are direct acting. There is no hydraulic pump or accumulator. There is no parking brake.

32 RESTRICTED

RESTRICTED 33

Manual Scan: National Archives, RG 287

ARRESTING HOOK

The arresting hook, in normal operation, is extended and retracted electrically. When the control handle on the right console is moved to "NORMAL DOWN" position, the motor runs the hook down in about eight seconds. If the electrical system fails, spring the handle inboard and move it past the stop lug to "EMERGENCY DOWN." This unlatches the hook and allows it to swing free, but it cannot be retracted. If the electrical system again becomes operative, the retracting screw will follow the hook down and relatch with it. When the handle is returned to "UP," the motor retracts the hook in about 11 seconds. Limit switches stop the motor in the up and down positions.

Lowering the arresting hook turns on the approach light. The light may be turned on for practice landings with the hook up by a toggle switch in the radio compartment.

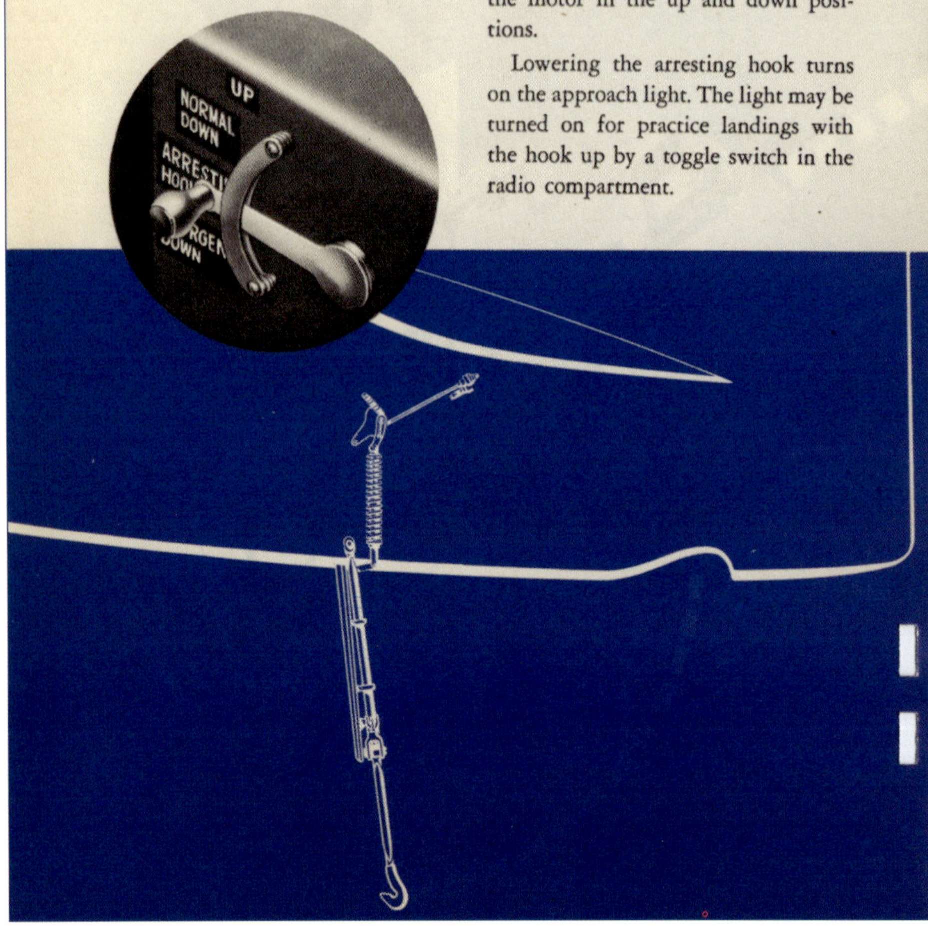

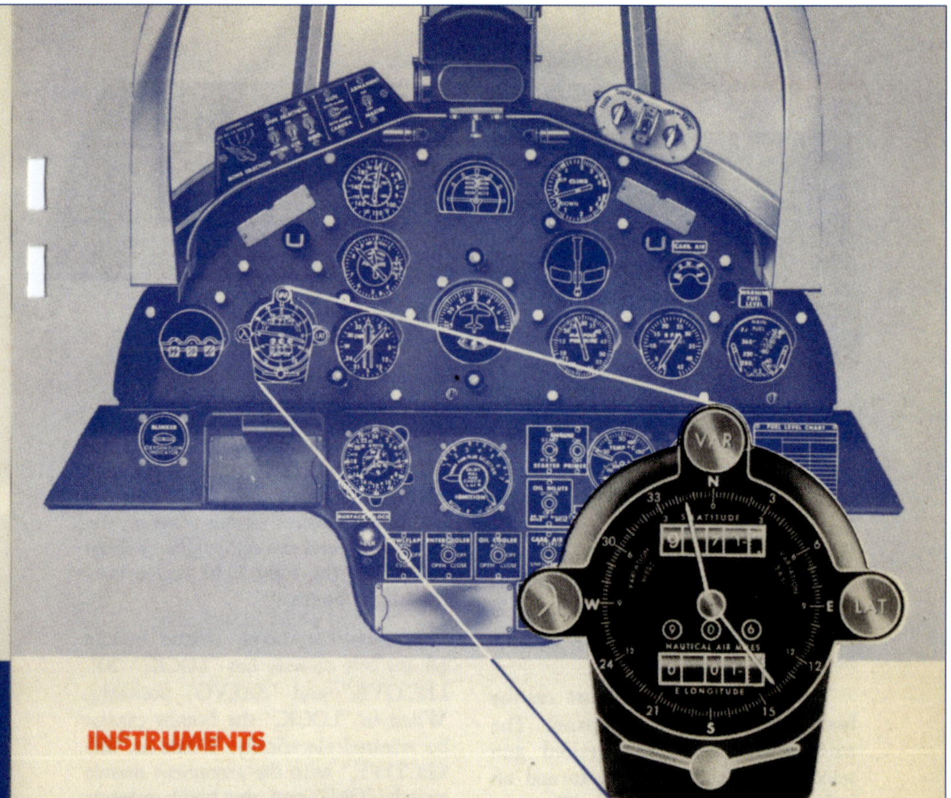

INSTRUMENTS

The instrument panel and right and left consoles have the usual primary and secondary flight and engine instruments. They are conventional and the arrangement is shown by the photographs in the front of the book.

The A.P.I. (Air Position Indicator), when set for longitude, latitude, and magnetic variation at the point of take-off, will show the airplane's air position at all times during the mission and show the air miles covered. Three knobs on the face of the dial are used to make the original settings, and two levers at the bottom are used to set for north or south latitude and east or west longitude. AN 05-35-34 describes the instrument and its use.

The fuel quantity gage indicates the fuel in the main tank only. The bomb bay tank gage is visible through a hole in the floor. The external tanks do not have fuel quantity gages.

The oil quantity gage is not visible from the cockpit.

Manual Scan: National Archives, RG 287

ARMAMENT

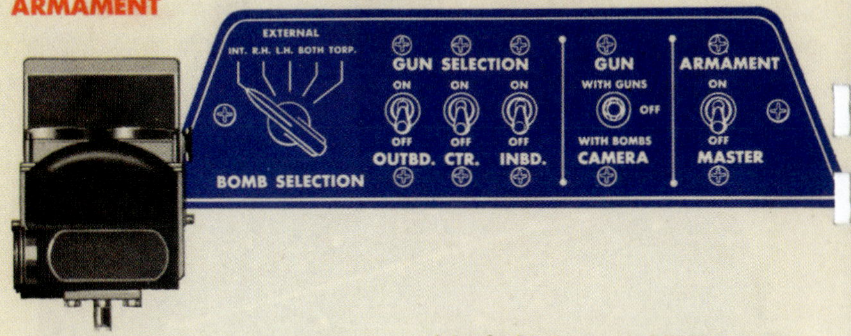

Guns and Cannon—The XF8B-1 has, mounted in the wings, six .50 caliber machine guns, or six 20 MM cannon or a combination of both. The ammunition boxes hold approximately 400 rounds for each machine gun or 200 rounds for each cannon.

The armament switches are on the hood over the instrument panel. The master switch and the desired gun selection switches must be turned on before the guns can be fired. The guns are charged by running down the wing flaps, inserting a charging rod through the flap opening, and pulling back on the charging lug.

The Mark 23 gun sight computes lead and elevation when range and wingspread are set up. A pointer above the crashpad sets up wingspread. Range is set by twisting the throttle handle. A handle on the right side of the sight masks all the fixed reticle image except the center cross. The image selector switch, to the right, has "FIXED" (for rocket sighting bore-sighted with the guns), "GYRO" (center dot and six-diamond circle), and "FIXED & GYRO" (both images) positions. An "OFF"—"ON" switch beside the selector switch turns on the gyro motor and the sight light. A rheostat beside the sight light switch controls light intensity.

Bombs—The bomb release handle on the left console has "LOCK," "SELECTIVE," and "SALVO" positions. When in "LOCK," the bombs cannot be released electrically. When in "SELECTIVE," with the armament master switch "ON," and the bomb selector switch set to any rack, the bombs can be released from that rack one at a time by pressing the button on the left top of the spade grip.

When pushed to "SALVO," all internal bombs are released unarmed. Two red pull handles above the bomb release handle drop the external bombs unarmed.

The gun camera in the air scoop is operated by setting the gun camera switch to "WITH GUNS" or "WITH BOMBS" and pressing the trigger or bomb release button respectively.

36 RESTRICTED

BOMB LOADS

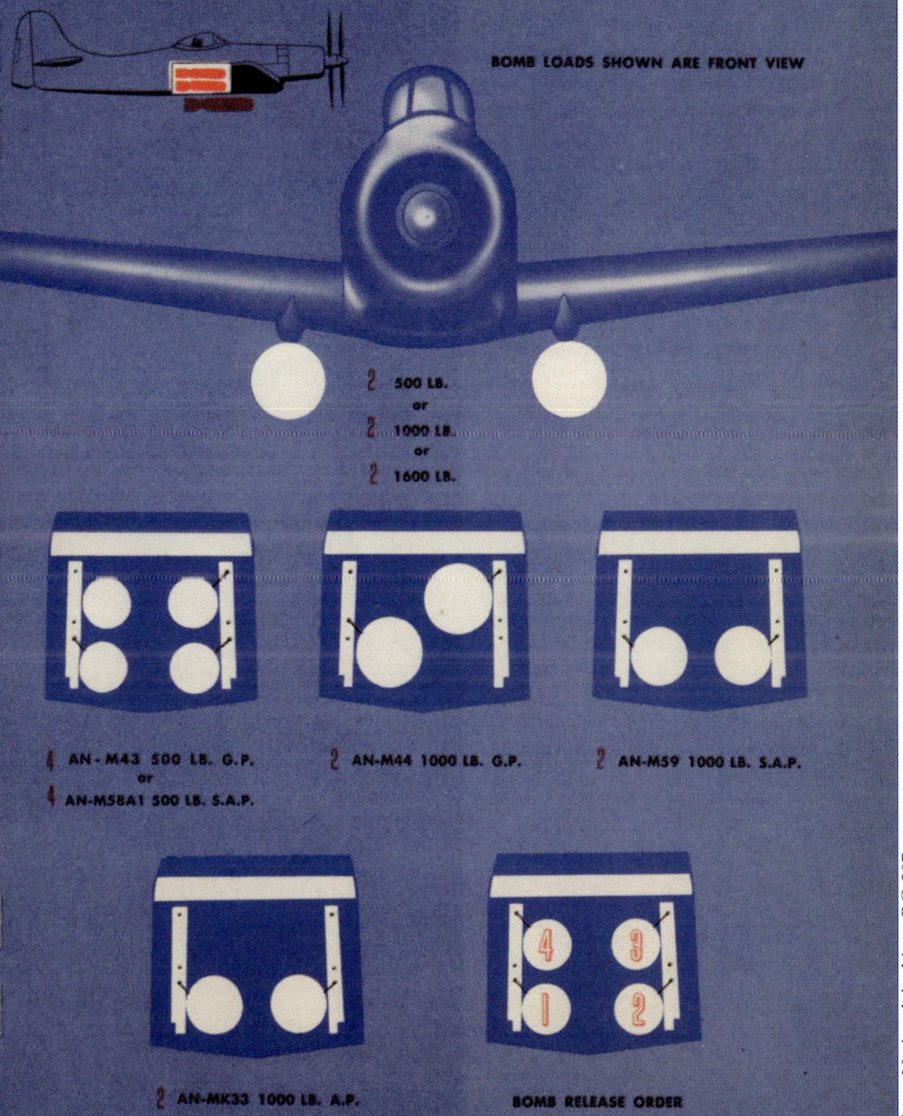

RESTRICTED 37

PILOT'S ARMOR PROTECTION

The airplane's armor plate protects the pilot from enemy gun fire (up to .50 caliber) originating in a 30 degree cone from the rear and a 15 degree cone from the front. Half inch steel plate protects the pilot's head and 3/8 inch plate protects his back below the structure line. Three-eighths inch plate and 1.50 inch armor glass protects him from the front. Quarter inch duralumi-num at the sides of the seat and over the instrument panel, as well as the engine, oil tank, structure, and other equipment provide supplementary pro-tection.

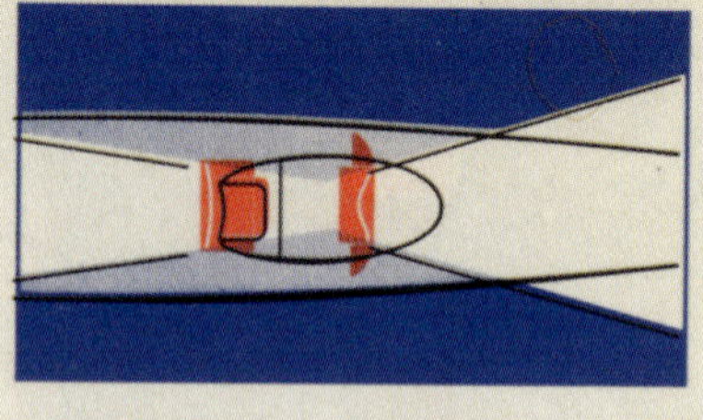

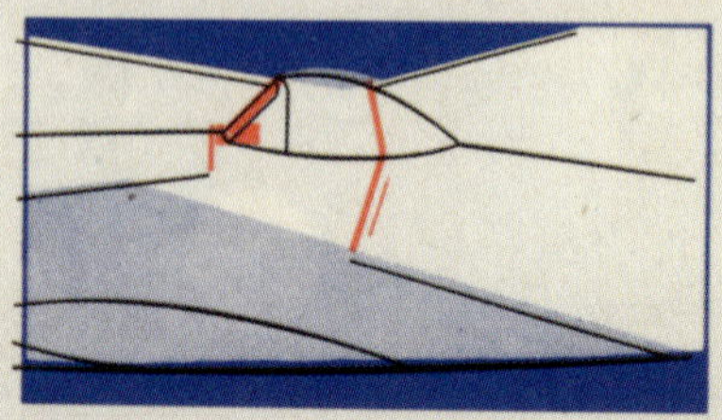

ELECTRICAL POWER

Battery—The XF8B-1 has a 17 ampere-hour 24 volt battery. It is designed to carry light loads when the generator is not running or when external power is not available, and to aid the generator during peak load periods. It should be used alone only for such light loads as instruments, lights, priming, opening the cowl flaps, etc. Do not use the battery alone to operate the radios, shut the bomb doors, retract or extend the landing gear or wing flaps, fold or spread the wings, or to fire more than two guns at a time.

The battery "OFF"—"ON" switch on the right console cuts the battery in and out of the electrical system. The recognition lights, IFF radio destructor, and the cockpit receptacle are connected directly to the battery and not the power bus so are not affected by the position of the switch.

Battery Failure — The battery discharges rapidly during peak electrical loads such as occur during taxiing, combat, or landing, but recovers during take-off, climb, level flight, etc. If, however, the discharge was too rapid, part of the electrolyte may have boiled away. This prevents complete recharging.

If the battery is discharged before starting the engine and when external power is not available, it may be impossible to get the necessary power for fuel and ignition boost, and engine priming.

Use the voltmeter to check the battery charge during flight. If the engine is above 1000 RPM and the system is carrying a heavy load, a voltmeter reading below 20 for more than 5 seconds indicates a low battery charge.

Generator—A 200 ampere 28 volt direct current engine driven generator carries the electrical load and recharges the battery. It is driven at three times engine speed and is cut into the electrical system automatically when the engine speed passes 700 RPM. Turn the switch on the instrument panel under the red guard to "OFF" to cut out the generator if attempting a crash landing.

The voltmeter, on the right console, shows when the generator is operating.

Manual Scan: National Archives, RG 287

ELECTRICAL POWER Continued

Generator Failure—If the engine RPM is above 700 and the voltmeter reads "0," some part of the generator circuit has failed.

Battery Use After Generator Fails

1. Turn off all but essential equipment. To get the greatest possible service out of the battery charge, turn the battery switch to "OFF," except for necessary instrument or radio use.

2. If the battery switch only is "ON" (instruments and electric fuel pumps using power) the battery lasts about 15 minutes.

3. With continuous use of above equipment plus one radio, the battery lasts 12 or 13 minutes. If all radios are used with above equipment it will last 9 minutes.

4. If the instruments only are used (booster pumps may be held "OFF" if the engine fuel pump maintains 16 PSI) the battery lasts about 30 minutes.

5. If operating on auxiliary tanks, the auxiliary fuel pump can only be turned off with the battery switch. If on Main tank, turn "OFF" the auxiliary fuel pump switch.

Note: The above figures are based on a battery with full charge (17 ampere hour).

External Power—The external power receptacle is on the right side of the fuselage above the trailing edge of the wing. The external source must provide 24 volt direct current (battery cart, auxiliary power plant, or ships generator). Use external power if the engine is not running or is turning up less than 700 RPM. (Generator doesn't cut in unless the engine is turning over 700 RPM or better.)

External power should be used for electrical starting except in emergency, since the starter motor will drain the battery rapidly. Use external power for wing folding unless the engine is turning over at more than 1000 RPM.

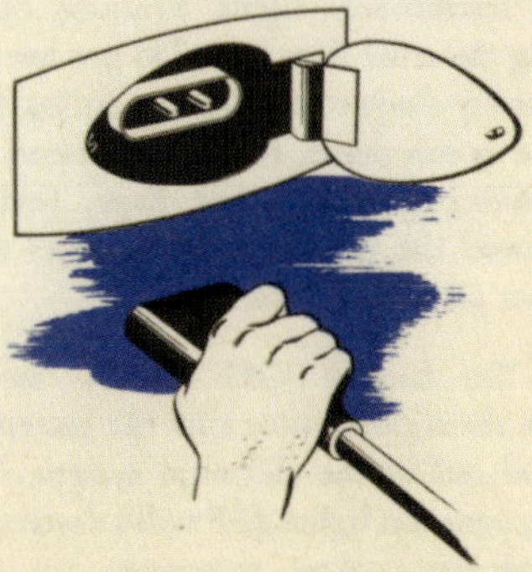

CIRCUIT BREAKERS

All XF8B-1 circuits except the IFF radio destructor, starter motor, battery, generator, tachometer, and thermocouple circuits are protected by thermal pushbutton type circuit breakers. The circuit breaker panel, pictured above, is on the right console. A luminous wing and a red area around the circuit breaker (except for the seven in the top row) shows if the circuit breaker pops out. The radio circuit breakers (in the top row) must cool before they can be reset but all others may be held in to operate the equipment in these circuits during an emergency.

The homing receiver has, in addition to the circuit breaker protecting its wiring, a 10 ampere fuse on its mounting rack which protects the equipment. This, by the way, is the only fuse in the XF8B-1.

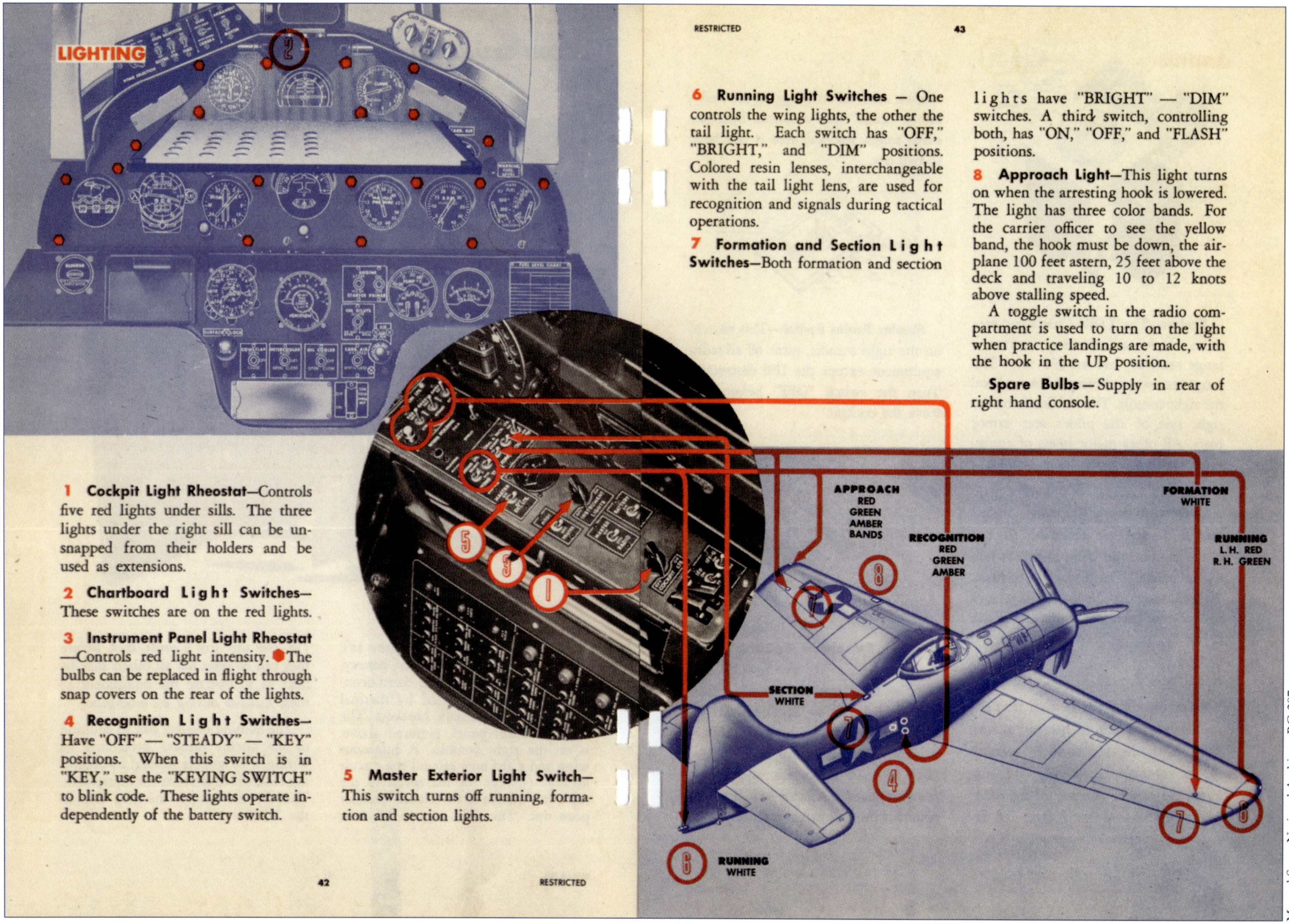

1 Cockpit Light Rheostat—Controls five red lights under sills. The three lights under the right sill can be unsnapped from their holders and be used as extensions.

2 Chartboard Light Switches—These switches are on the red lights.

3 Instrument Panel Light Rheostat—Controls red light intensity. ● The bulbs can be replaced in flight through snap covers on the rear of the lights.

4 Recognition Light Switches—Have "OFF"—"STEADY"—"KEY" positions. When this switch is in "KEY," use the "KEYING SWITCH" to blink code. These lights operate independently of the battery switch.

5 Master Exterior Light Switch—This switch turns off running, formation and section lights.

42 RESTRICTED

RESTRICTED 43

6 Running Light Switches — One controls the wing lights, the other the tail light. Each switch has "OFF," "BRIGHT," and "DIM" positions. Colored resin lenses, interchangeable with the tail light lens, are used for recognition and signals during tactical operations.

7 Formation and Section Light Switches—Both formation and section lights have "BRIGHT" — "DIM" switches. A third switch, controlling both, has "ON," "OFF," and "FLASH" positions.

8 Approach Light—This light turns on when the arresting hook is lowered. The light has three color bands. For the carrier officer to see the yellow band, the hook must be down, the airplane 100 feet astern, 25 feet above the deck and traveling 10 to 12 knots above stalling speed.

A toggle switch in the radio compartment is used to turn on the light when practice landings are made, with the hook in the UP position.

Spare Bulbs—Supply in rear of right hand console.

Manual Scan: National Archives, RG 287

RADIOS

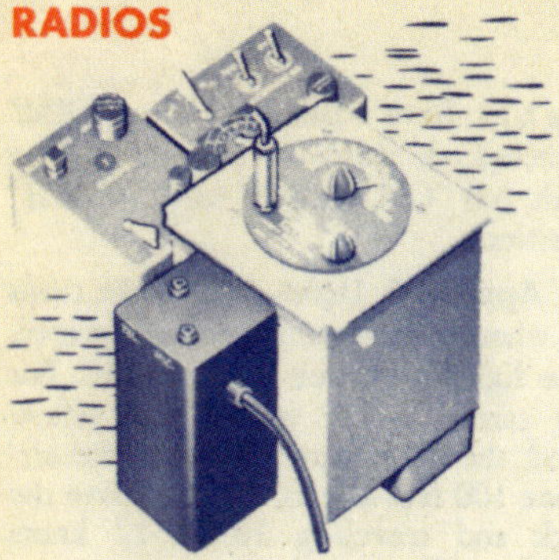

Radios—The XF8B-1 has a two way radio telephone, a homing receiver, a range receiver, and an IFF set. The range receiver and control boxes are on the right console. The jackbox is on the right side of the pilot's seat armor plate. All other major items of equipment are in the radio compartment.

Microphones — The hand "mike" stays in the airplane, plugs into the top of the jackbox, and is cut in by a switch on the "mike." The throat, lip, or mask "mike" issued to the pilot plugs into the jackbox extension cord, and is cut in by the microphone button on the throttle.

Headset—Plug the headset into the top of the jackbox to hear all radios. Tune in the desired radio by turning up its volume control and turning down the volume controls of the other radios. Always use the jackbox and extension cord, never plugging the headset or "mike" into a control box; the cords might not pull free if you have to bail out.

Master Radio Switch—This switch, on the right console, turns off all radio equipment except the IFF destructor. Turn the switch "OFF" before you leave the cockpit.

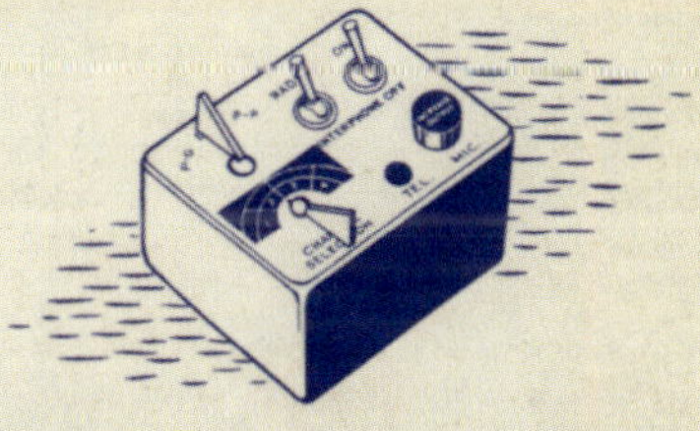

Radio Telephone Controls — The radio telephone has five controls: an "ON"—"OFF" switch, a volume control, a "RADIO"—"INTERPHONE" switch which must be left on "RADIO" to receive and transmit, a "P-G" — "BOTH" — "P-P" switch, and a four position channel selector switch which provides the following connections:

SWITCH POS.	TRANS. CHANNEL	RECEIVER CHANNEL
1	P-P	P-P & P-G No. 1
2	P-G No. 1	P-P & P-G No. 1
3	P-G No. 2	P-P & P-G No. 2
4	P-G No. 3	P-P & P-G No. 3

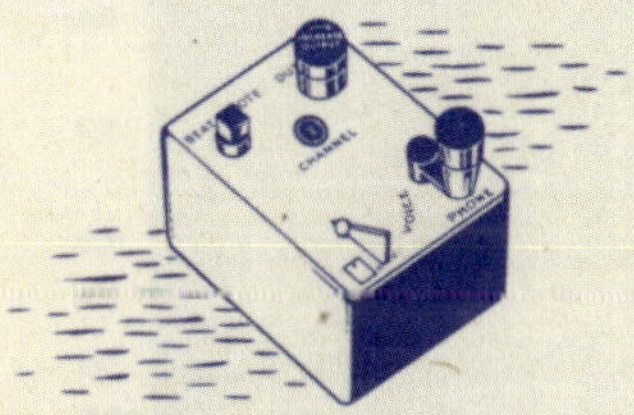

Homing Receiver Controls — The homing receiver control box has four controls: a channel selector crank (the channel number appears in a cutout on the face of the control box) to tune in any one of six transmitters, a volume control, a switch labeled "OFF"—"NAV" — "VOICE" to separate the voice and CW signals. (The "OFF" position is blocked and covered by a metal tab and the set can be turned on and off only by the master radio switch), and a "BEAT NOTE" knob for varying the pitch of CW signals.

Don't use the "PHONE" jack in the homing receiver control box as the cord may not pull free if you have to bail out.

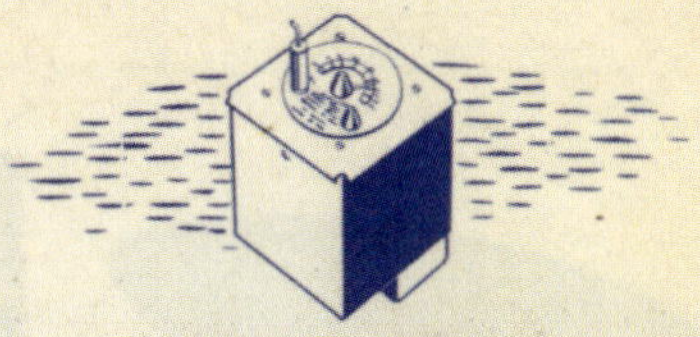

Range Receiver Controls — The range receiver has two controls: an "OFF"—"ON" — "VOLUME" control knob, and a tuning knob and dial.

There is a phone jack connected to the jackbox on the seat armor.

IFF Radio Controls—Four switches on the right console control the IFF radio: an "ON"—"OFF" switch, an "IFF—G" band switch (in accordance with the orders of the commanding officer it will be turned on or held at the "TIME" position. At all other times it will be off), an "EMERGENCY" switch (under green guard) to be used

if the pilot is in trouble, requires assistance or the airplane is damaged, and a "DESTRUCTOR" switch (under red guard) to destroy the set if a forced landing is to be made in enemy territory. A hard shock parallel to the thrust line of the airplane also will set off the destructors.

OXYGEN

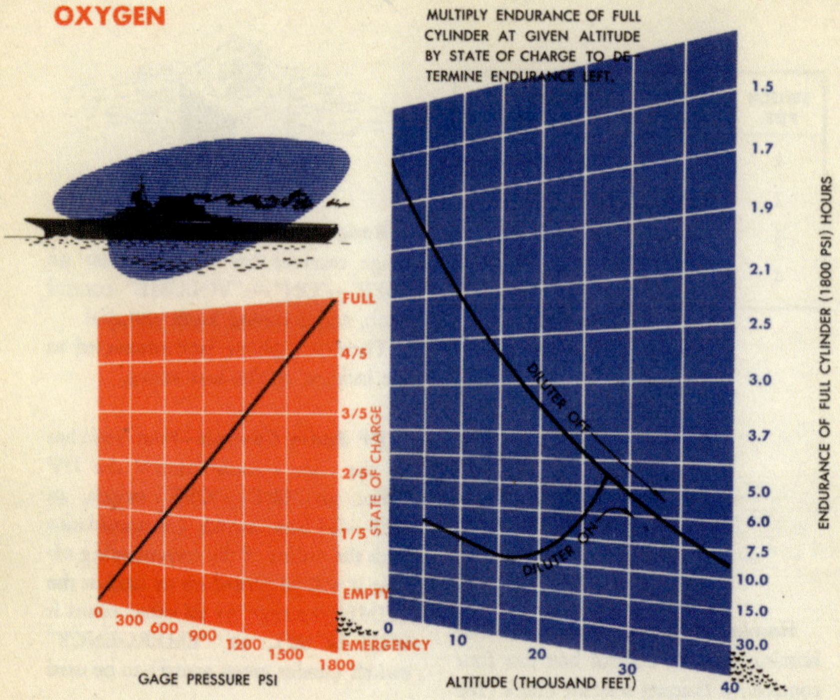

Oxygen Bottle — The high pressure (1800 PSI) oxygen bottle is behind the seat armor. The shut-off valve is reached through a hole to the left of the seat. The filler valve is on the left console near the bottle.

Mask—When not in use, the oxygen mask is stowed in a pocket on the left console. The mask is connected to the oxygen regulator by a flexible hose, with a disconnect joint near the mask.

Regulator — The diluter demand regulator at the forward end of the left console automatically regulates the proportion of air and oxygen sent to the mask at all altitudes. Oxygen is admitted only when the wearer inhales. If pure oxygen is needed, turn off the diluter lever. If a steady flow is needed, turn on the red "EMERG." knob.

Pressure Gage—The pressure gage, just below the regulator, indicates the amount of oxygen left in the bottle.

Flow Indicator—The blinker type flow indicator shows that the demand valve is working properly and that oxygen is flowing to the mask.

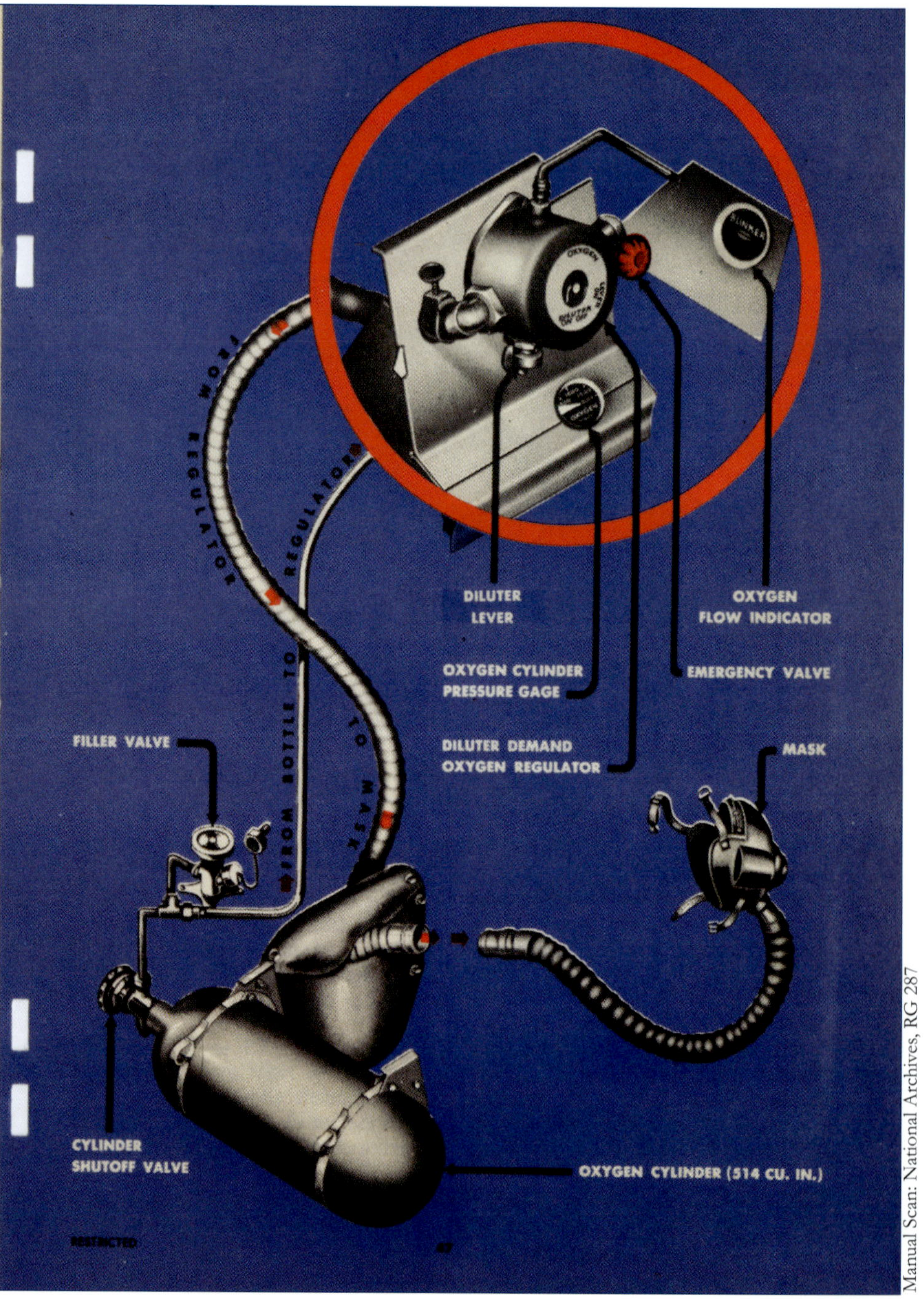

HEATING & VENTILATING

The heating and ventilating controls on top of the right console consist of a knob and pointer set on a calibrated dial having three stated conditions "OFF"—"CABIN HEAT MAX."—"DEFROST MAX." In the "OFF" position the warm air is spilled overboard through the engine accessory section. In the CABIN HEAT MAX.' position the hot air is directed into the cockpit, and in the "DEFROST MAX." position it is directed against the inside of the windshield. When the pointer is moved between the positions the air is split between the cockpit and windshield or overboard.

A cold air "ON"—"OFF" control lever on the right console below the radio controls allows mixing cold air with the hot air entering the cockpit or the use of cold air alone if it is too hot.

EMERGENCY EQUIPMENT

Emergency Canopy Release—In emergency, jettison by pulling T handle above the windshield.

Normal Canopy Release—If inside, crank at forward right corner. If outside, press rubber patch below windshield on the right side, and push canopy back.

Backpad Kit—Forms seat pad, has separate harness and contains:

Rations (3 Cans)	Sunburn Ointment
Water (2 Cans)	Compass & Matches
First Aid Kit	Jungle Machete
Salt Tablets	Pocket Knife
Safety Pins	Sharpening Stone
Fishing Kit	Corrosive Preventive
Whistle	Cotton Line (25 Ft.)
Magnifying Glass	Canvas Gloves
Signaling Mirror	Poncho
Adhesive Tape	Mosquito Headnet

Very Pistol and Six Red Cartridges

Parachute Life Raft—Attach to chute—holds:

Bullet Hole Plugs	Bailing Cup
Co_2 Inflation Bottle	Sea Anchor
Can of Water	Oral Inflation Tube
First Aid Kit	Sea Marker Dye
Hand Paddles (2)	Repair Kit

Seat Parachute—A standard issue seat parachute will be worn by the pilot.

Engine Fire Extinguisher—To operate the engine CO_2 fire extinguisher system pull the release handle at the rear of the right hand console. Flames blowing out of the cowl flaps indicate fire around the cylinders. Open the cowl flaps wide to limit trapped heat damage and pull extinguisher handle. If the fire is in the accessory section the flames will come out of the ventilating slots on the sides of the nacelle.

Manual Scan: National Archives, RG 287

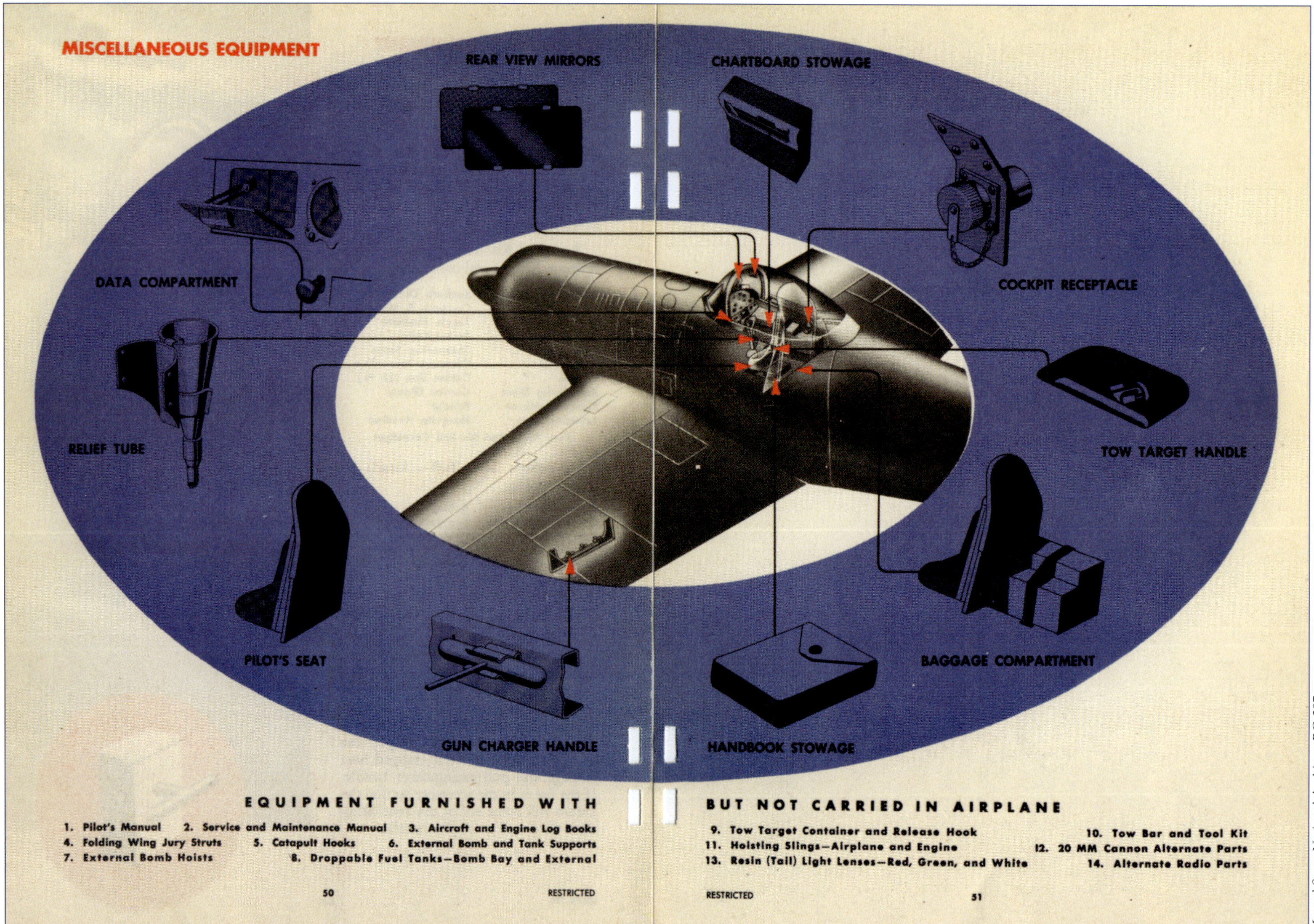

Manual Scan: National Archives, RG 287

SEC-2

The XF8B-1 Navy fighter is designed for high speed and maneuverability at low and medium altitudes. The comments of two test pilots are summarized in the following paragraphs.

The airplane has very good ground handling characteristics. The rudder is very light and is effective above 25 knots (29 MPH). The brakes hold the airplane at military power, but there is some tendency for the tail to rise.

Shortest take-off is made with full flaps from a 3-point attitude. The dual rotation propeller eliminates fighting the rudder.

In the air, the airplane has good stability about all axes down to very low speeds. Longitudinal trim is moderately affected by changes in speed. and only slightly by power changes, landing gear position, or flap position. Changes in directional trim with speed and power changes are negligible, due to the dual rotation propeller.

The airplane has good stall characteristics with power on and off. Warning occurs several knots prior to stall with buffeting and increased elevator forces. *Both* the rudder and the ailerons are effective in checking rolling tendencies.

In a wave-off there is no tendency to roll, and only slight stick force is required to correct longitudinal trim.

For a flaps up landing, the best trim speed is 105 knots (121 MPH). Elevator control is ample and the forces are moderate. For a partial or full flaps landing, best trim speed is 85 to 95 knots (98 to 109 MPH). Full up elevator should be used for landing flare.

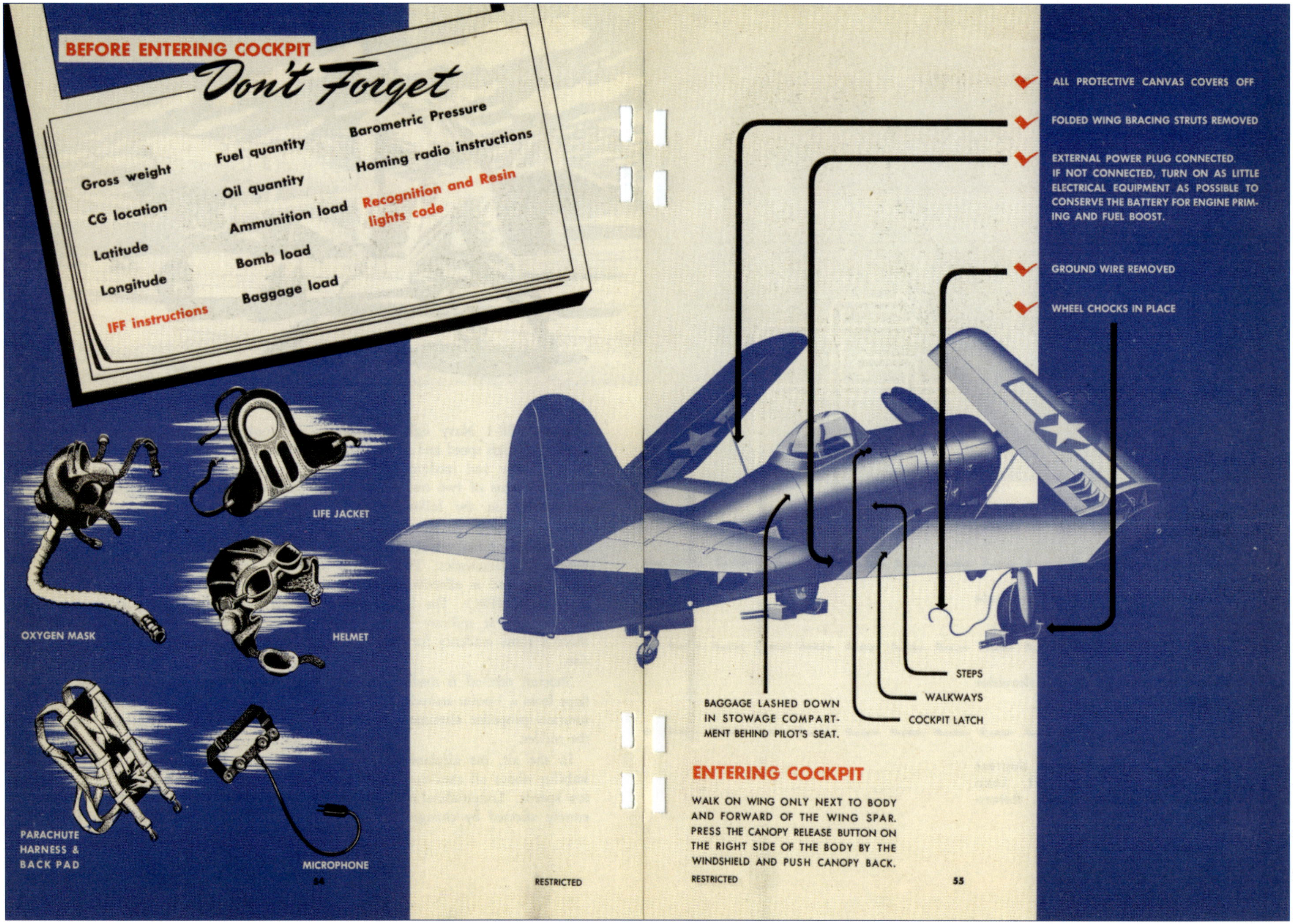

Manual Scan: National Archives, RG 287

BEFORE STARTING ENGINE

HARNESS AND SEAT ADJUSTMENT

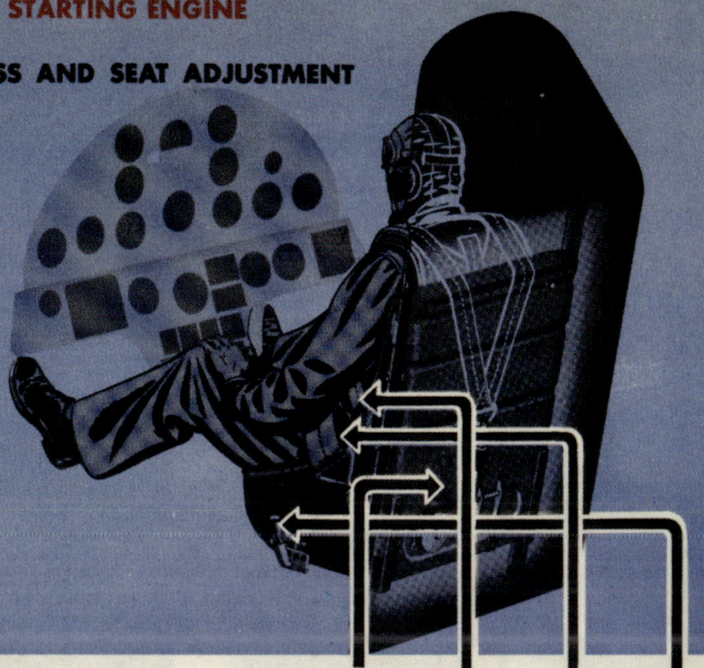

1. Adjust the seat height with the handle on the right side.

2. Attach the life raft and parachute to the harness.

3. Fasten the safety belt and shoulder harness.

4. To adjust shoulder harness, depress and move left handle aft. Lean forward to unwind cable. Return handle forward.

LEFT SIDEWALL CONTROLS

If oxygen will be used, open the oxygen bottle (knob counterclockwise).

See that the oxygen filler is closed.

Put on the oxygen mask. Be sure the flexible tube quick disconnect fitting is fully engaged.

With the red EMERGENCY knob on the regulator "OFF" (clockwise). pinch the mask tube and inhale lightly. If the mask leaks, tighten the suspension straps. Adjust the nose wire.

Turn the diluter "OFF", inhale, and check the flow indicator. It should "blink". Turn diluter "ON" again. If oxygen will not be used, remove the mask and turn the bottle "OFF".

See that the . . .

1. Bomb release lever is at "LOCK".
2. Wing tank release handles seat.
3. Tail wheel handle is at "LOCKED".
4. Bomb bay fuel tank gage is visible if tank is installed.
5. Elevator, rudder and aileron tab wheels are centered.
6. Wing flap control handle is "DOWN" (visually check the flap position).
7. Supercharger amber light is "OFF", supercharger not running.
8. Throttle microphone switch does not stick and handle turns sight range dial.
9. Propeller pitch handle is at full "INCREASE" RPM for 2700 RPM.
10. Mixture handle is at "IDLE CUT-OFF".
11. Fuel tank selector handle is "OFF" at all times when the engine is not running. *This is mandatory.*
12. Fuel pump switches are: Auxiliary—"OFF", L. H. booster—"ON", R. H. booster—"ON".
13. Oxygen pressure is 1800±PSI.
14. Landing gear handle is "DOWN".
15. Put the bomb indicator light switches momentarily on "TEST". All bulbs must light. Switch to "ON". Indicates bombs loaded.

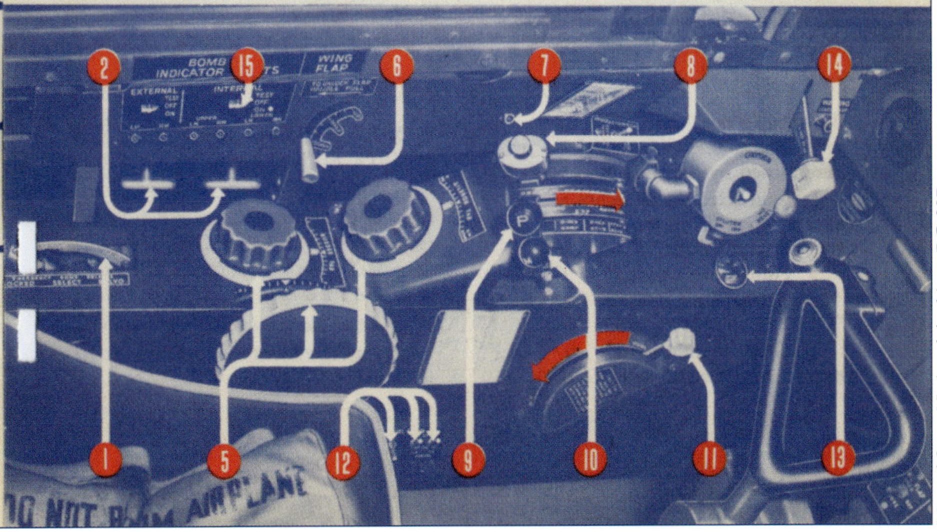

Manual Scan: National Archives, RG 287

BEFORE STARTING ENGINE Continued

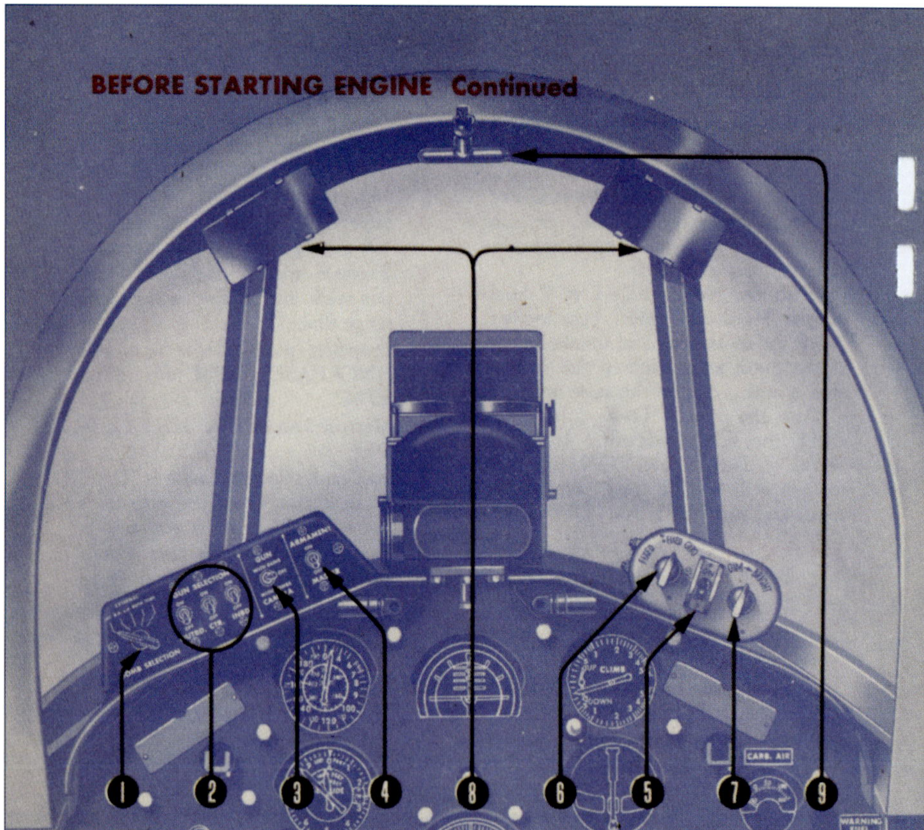

See that the . . .

1. Bomb selection switch is set as determined by the mission.
2. Gun selection switches are "ON" except when firing on battery alone or for special missions.
3. Gun camera switch is "OFF".
4. Armament master switch is "OFF".
5. Gun sight switch is "OFF" except for selector switch check.

Selector switch is turned to "FIXED", "FIXED & GYRO", and "GYRO" to check sight lights and motor (turn sight switch "OFF").

7. Gun sight light rheostat is between "DIM" and "BRIGHT". To prevent confusion do not turn the light off with the rheostat.
8. Rear view mirrors are adjusted.
9. Emergency canopy release handle is seated.

INSTRUMENT PANEL CONTROLS

See that the . . .

1. Chartboard light switches are "OFF".
2. Attitude gyro knob is "OFF".
3. Rate-of-climb pointer is "ZERO".
4. Altimeter is set to field altitude or barometric pressure.
5. Landing gear position indicator shows all wheels down.
6. Air position*indicator is set for latitude, longitude, and magnetic variation of starting point.
7. Remote compass course marker is set.
8. Directional gyro course is set, gyro is caged.
9. Fuel gage is showing fuel quantity in taxi position. Check calibration card for quantity in flight position.
10. Clock is wound and set(pull out knob to set). Set civil date by pushing in red dimple with pencil point.
11. Ignition switch lever is "OFF"; knob at "ZERO".

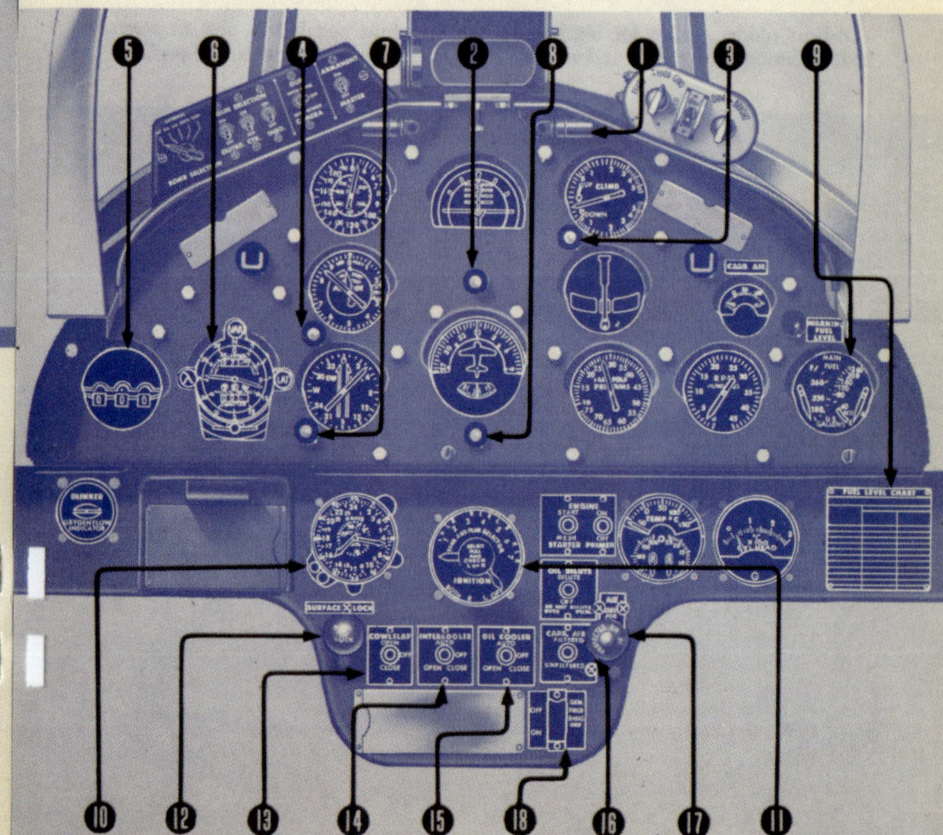

Manual Scan: National Archives, RG 287

BEFORE STARTING ENGINE Continued

12. Surface lock knob is pushed in Push throttle handle forward and return to 1/8 to 1/4 open for 1000 RPM. Operate control column and rudder pedal. Visually check elevator, rudder and aileron movement.

13. Cowl flaps operate by flipping switch to "CLOSE" till flaps are fully closed, and then back to "OPEN".

14. Intercooler switch is "AUTO".

15. Oil cooler door operates when switch is moved to "CLOSE", "OPEN" and "AUTO".

16. Carburetor air filter switch is at "UNFILTERED" except when filter is installed and dust or icing conditions are present.

17. Auxiliary air knob is pushed in except in icing conditions.

18. Generator field emergency switch is "ON" (guard closed).

RUDDER PEDAL ADJUSTMENT

Adjust rudder pedals for leg length and the amount of toe in and toe out. To adjust pedals fore and aft turn the knurled wheel between the pedals.

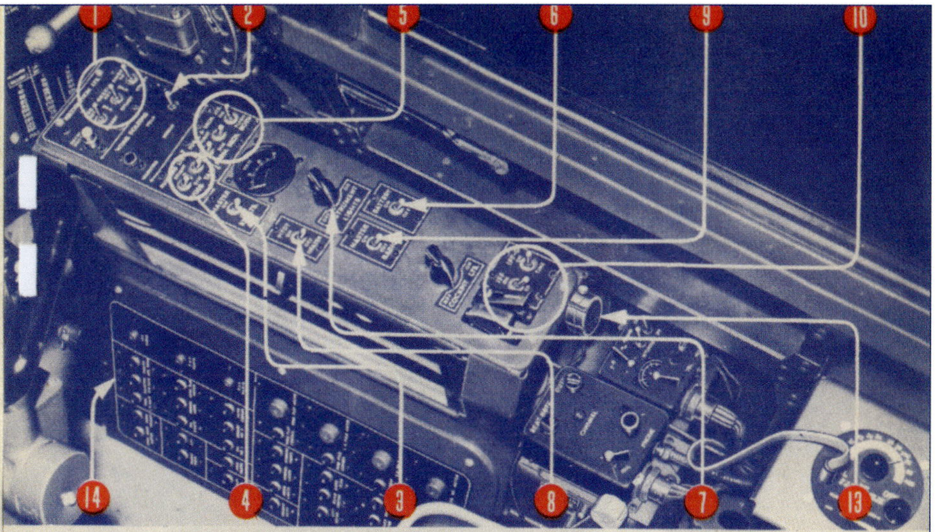

RIGHT SIDEWALL CONTROLS

See that the . . .

1. Recognition light switches are "OFF".

2. Wing "FOLD-SPREAD" switch is "OFF".

3. Master exterior lights switch is "OFF" unless running, formation, or section lights are to be turned on.

4. Wing and tail running lights switches are "OFF" unless night flight or for check of "BRIGHT" and "DIM" setting (lights visible from cockpit when wings folded and rudder swung either way).

5. Formation and section light switches are "OFF" unless checking formation and section lights.

6. Battery switch is "ON".

7. Instrument lights rheostat "OFF" during daytime unless checking bulbs; turn "OFF" or "DIM" if three or more lights are out. (Spares in console.)

8. Pitot heater switch is "OFF" unless icing is expected.

9. Master radio switch is "ON". (For radio operation see page 96.)

10. IFF radio destructor, emergency, "ON"-"OFF", and "G"-band switches "OFF" unless C.O. says otherwise.

11. Screw cap is on the cockpit receptacle unless electrical equipment is attached.

12. Tow target handle is recessed.

13. Microphones are plugged in. (Hand mike" on top of jackbox; lip, throat or mask "mike" to extension cord from side of jackbox.)

14. Circuit breakers are pushed in.

15. Fire extinguisher handle beside seat is in the clips.

16. Fireman with extinguisher is standing by.

STARTING ENGINE

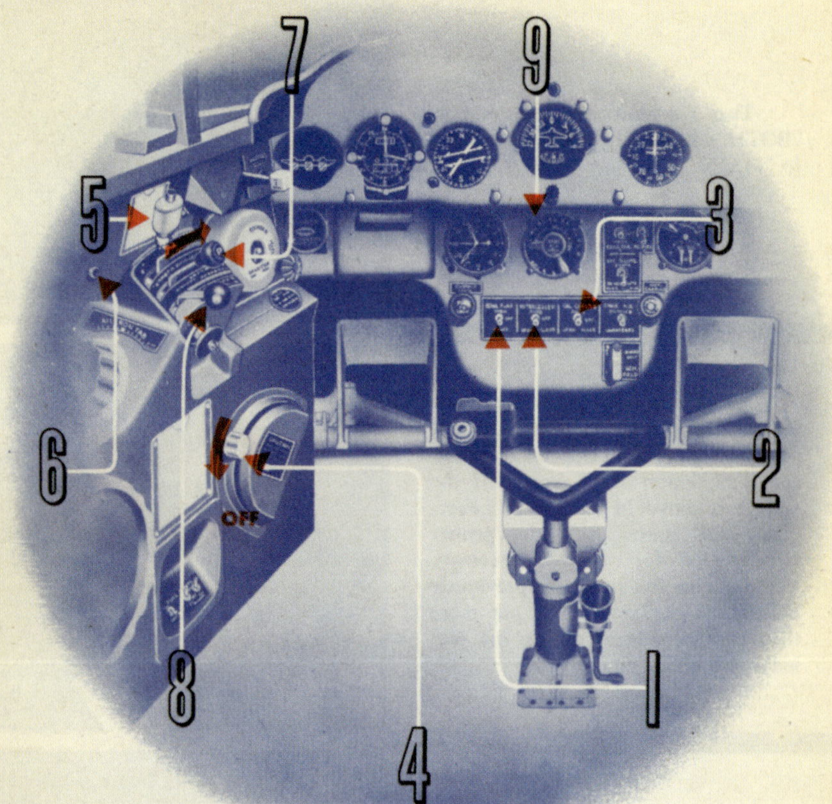

1. Cowl flaps full "OPEN".
2. Intercooler switch "AUTO".
3. Oil cooler switch "AUTO".
4. Tank selector "OFF" (mandatory).
5. Throttle 1/8 to 1/4 open for 1000 RPM.
6. Supercharger amber light off.
7. Propeller handle full "INCREASE RPM" for 2700 RPM.
8. Mixture handle "IDLE CUTOFF" (mandatory).
9. With ignition switch "OFF", have propeller pulled through by hand, nine or ten blades to clear the cylinders if the engine has not been run for one or more hours.

RESTRICTED 63

Manual Scan: National Archives, RG 287

ENGINE STARTING Continued

1. Turn the ignition switch lever to "BOTH." Turn the fuel tank selector to "MAIN."

2. Hold the starter switch to "START" for no longer than 20 seconds as there is no overspeed governor, and a maximum of 10 seconds if the voltage is above 24 volts. While energizing the starter hold the primer switch "ON" for two to six seconds. If the engine has been run previously during the day, prime for not more than two seconds; if during the previous two hours, do not prime.

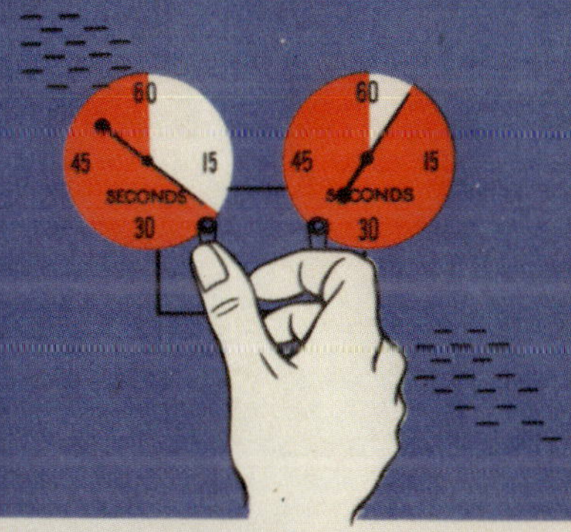

3. Push the starter switch to "MESH" and hold until the engine is running or until the starter slows down to its constant slow speed. Allow one or two minutes cooling time before a new start.

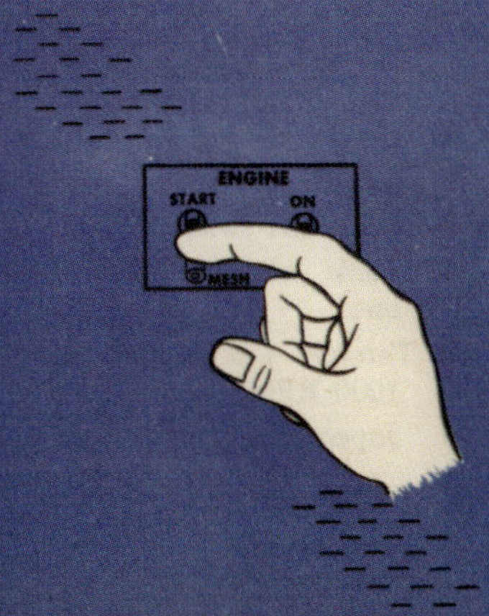

4. If the engine does not start in 10 to 15 seconds after meshing, make another attempt. Be sure to return the tank selector handle to "OFF" and the mixture handle to "IDLE CUTOFF."

5. After the first few pops when the engine starts, move the mixture handle steadily and evenly to "AUTO RICH."

IMPORTANT

Do not move tank selector to "MAIN" until ready to energize starter, nor move mixture handle to "AUTO RICH" too rapidly, or engine will flood and must be pulled through.

If propeller kicks when starter switch is flipped to "START," propeller must be pulled forward by hand a half turn to disengage starter and engine jaws.

If starter does not run when switch is flipped to "START," flip it to "MESH" momentarily to lower brushes in starter.

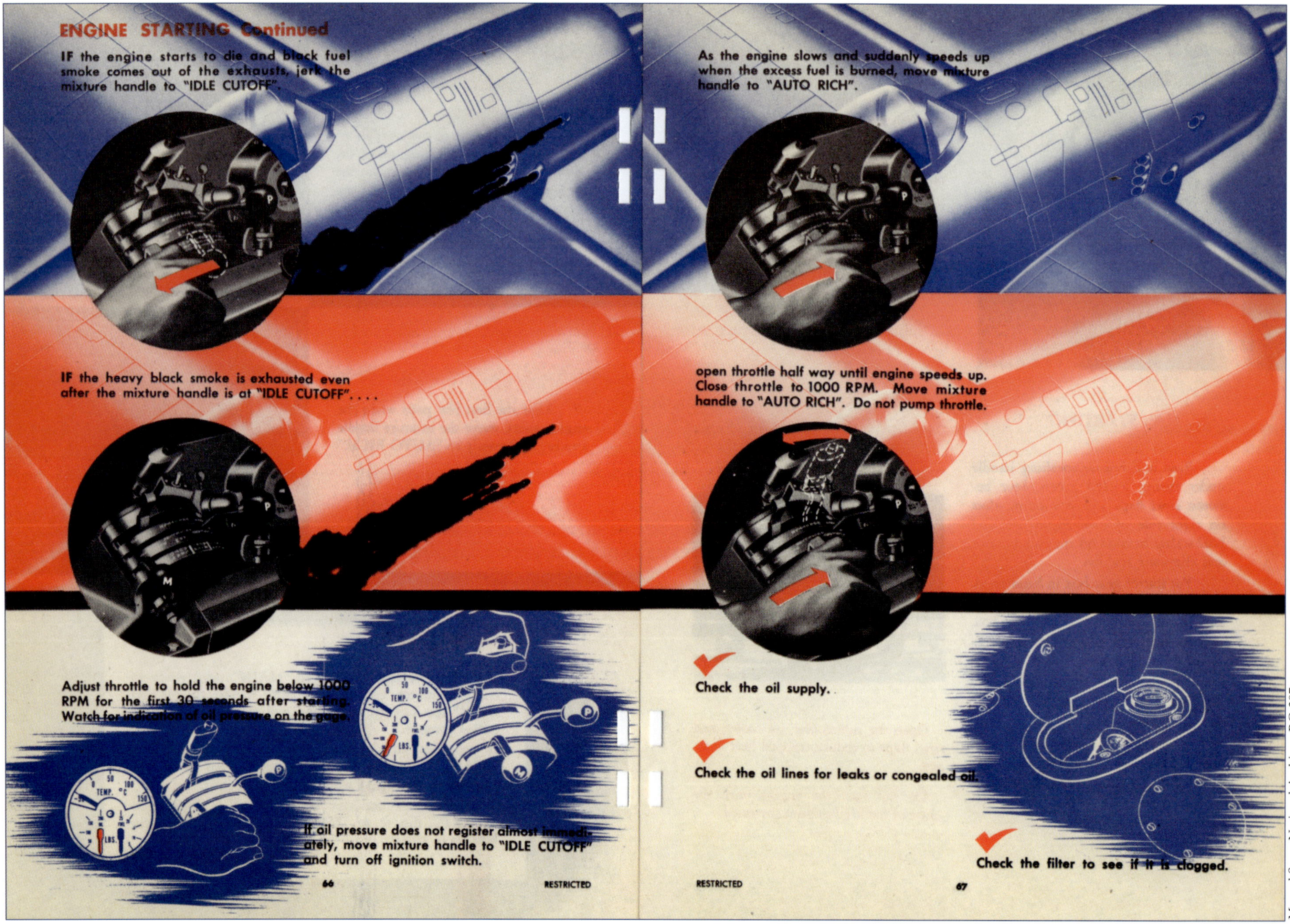

ENGINE STARTING Continued

IF the engine starts to die and black fuel smoke comes out of the exhausts, jerk the mixture handle to "IDLE CUTOFF".

IF the heavy black smoke is exhausted even after the mixture handle is at "IDLE CUTOFF"....

Adjust throttle to hold the engine below 1000 RPM for the first 30 seconds after starting. Watch for indication of oil pressure on the gage.

If oil pressure does not register almost immediately, move mixture handle to "IDLE CUTOFF" and turn off ignition switch.

66 RESTRICTED

As the engine slows and suddenly speeds up when the excess fuel is burned, move mixture handle to "AUTO RICH".

open throttle half way until engine speeds up. Close throttle to 1000 RPM. Move mixture handle to "AUTO RICH". Do not pump throttle.

Check the oil supply.

Check the oil lines for leaks or congealed oil.

Check the filter to see if it is clogged.

RESTRICTED 67

Manual Scan: National Archives, RG 287

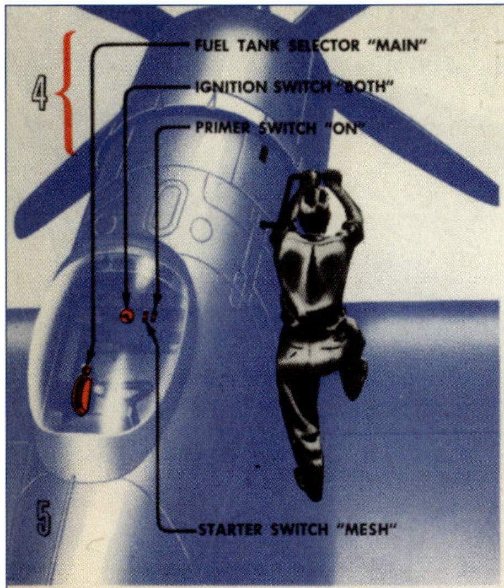

MANUAL STARTING

1. Push and release meshing handle under spring loaded access door between cowl flaps and ventilating slots on right side of cowling, to lift and hold starter brushes off the commutator and eliminate friction.

2. Put starter gear box in hand crank socket just aft of meshing handle access door and insert crank in gear box.

3. Turn crank slowly counterclockwise and accelerate to 96 RPM.

4. Not more than 20 seconds before meshing, switch ignition to "BOTH," set fuel tank selector to "MAIN," and prime.

5. Push meshing handle till engine starts, then release. If you need ignition boost, turn starter switch to "MESH" instead of using handle.

ENGINE FIRE

Fire in the engine will come out the cowl flaps. Fire in the accessory section will come out the ventilating slots on the side. Fire in the air ducts will come out the oil cooler and intercooler doors.

If fire breaks out while starting the engine hold the starter switch on "MESH" until you have the mixture at "IDLE CUTOFF," the tank selector at "OFF," and the ignition switch "OFF." Pull the fire extinguisher handle and, if on the ground, have the portable extinguishers directed at the cowling, air scoop, or exhaust stacks.

Open the intercooler, oil cooler, and cowl flaps to reduce trapped heat damage.

Do not start the engine until the cause of the fire has been corrected.

WARM UP

1

Adjust throttle to about 1000 RPM (after 30 seconds run) with propeller control at full "INCREASE RPM." The engine should be held on or below 1000 RPM until oil temperature reaches 40°C (104°F). Normal oil pressure is 80 to 90 PSI. The initial oil pressure may exceed 400 PSI.

2

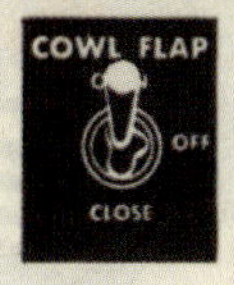

Open cowl flaps wide even in cold weather to prevent burning the ignition wire insulation.

3

Engine is factory set for 450 RPM minimum idling speed. Run below 700 RPM as little as possible, and run up occasionally to clean the plugs if idling below 800 RPM.

4

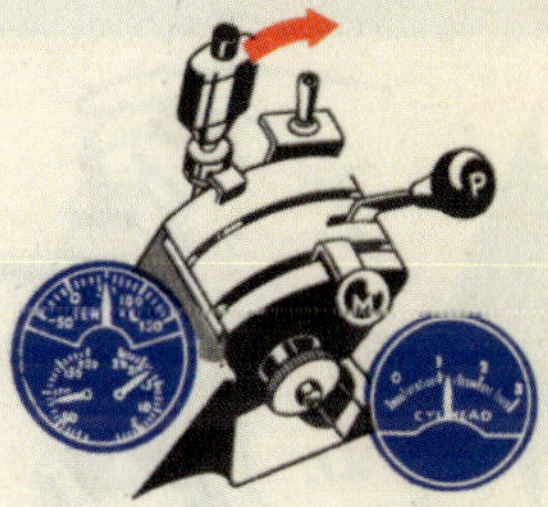

With oil-in temperature above 40°C (104°F), cylinder temperature at 120°C (248°F), and PROPELLER RPM handle at full INCREASE RPM, advance throttle to the power needed for ground test, emergency take-off, or taxiing.

5

Disconnect external power after starting; the generator cuts in at about 700 RPM. Increase the RPM before applying any heavy electrical loads such as folding wing, operating flaps, bomb doors, or radios.

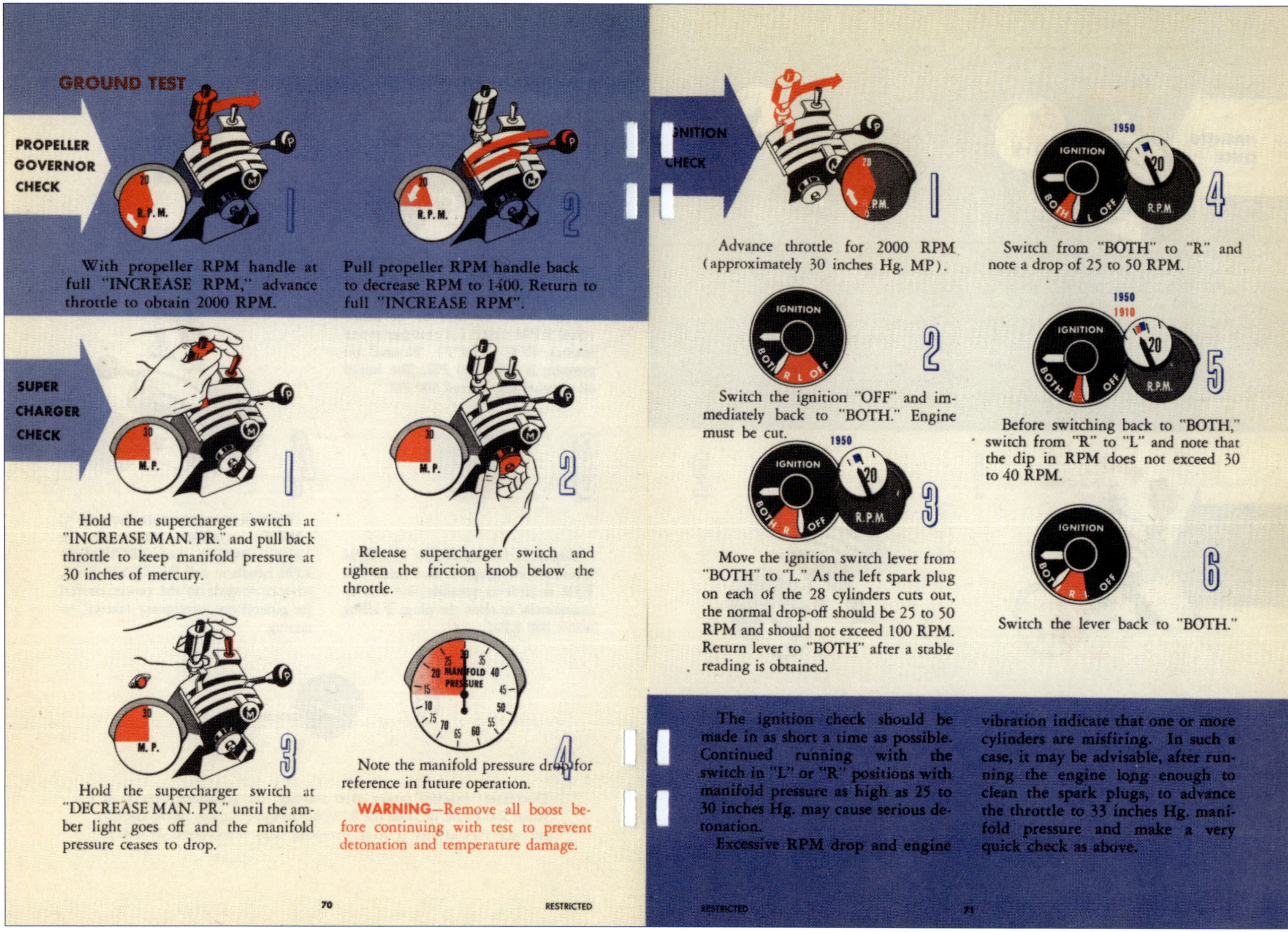

GROUND TEST

PROPELLER GOVERNOR CHECK

1. With propeller RPM handle at full "INCREASE RPM," advance throttle to obtain 2000 RPM.

2. Pull propeller RPM handle back to decrease RPM to 1400. Return to full "INCREASE RPM".

SUPER CHARGER CHECK

1. Hold the supercharger switch at "INCREASE MAN. PR." and pull back throttle to keep manifold pressure at 30 inches of mercury.

2. Release supercharger switch and tighten the friction knob below the throttle.

3. Hold the supercharger switch at "DECREASE MAN. PR." until the amber light goes off and the manifold pressure ceases to drop.

4. Note the manifold pressure drop for reference in future operation.

WARNING—Remove all boost before continuing with test to prevent detonation and temperature damage.

70 RESTRICTED

IGNITION CHECK

1. Advance throttle for 2000 RPM (approximately 30 inches Hg. MP).

2. Switch the ignition "OFF" and immediately back to "BOTH." Engine must be cut.

3. Move the ignition switch lever from "BOTH" to "L." As the left spark plug on each of the 28 cylinders cuts out, the normal drop-off should be 25 to 50 RPM and should not exceed 100 RPM. Return lever to "BOTH" after a stable reading is obtained.

4. Switch from "BOTH" to "R" and note a drop of 25 to 50 RPM.

5. Before switching back to "BOTH," switch from "R" to "L" and note that the dip in RPM does not exceed 30 to 40 RPM.

6. Switch the lever back to "BOTH."

The ignition check should be made in as short a time as possible. Continued running with the switch in "L" or "R" positions with manifold pressure as high as 25 to 30 inches Hg. may cause serious detonation.

Excessive RPM drop and engine vibration indicate that one or more cylinders are misfiring. In such a case, it may be advisable, after running the engine long enough to clean the spark plugs, to advance the throttle to 33 inches Hg. manifold pressure and make a very quick check as above.

RESTRICTED 71

Manual Scan: National Archives, RG 287

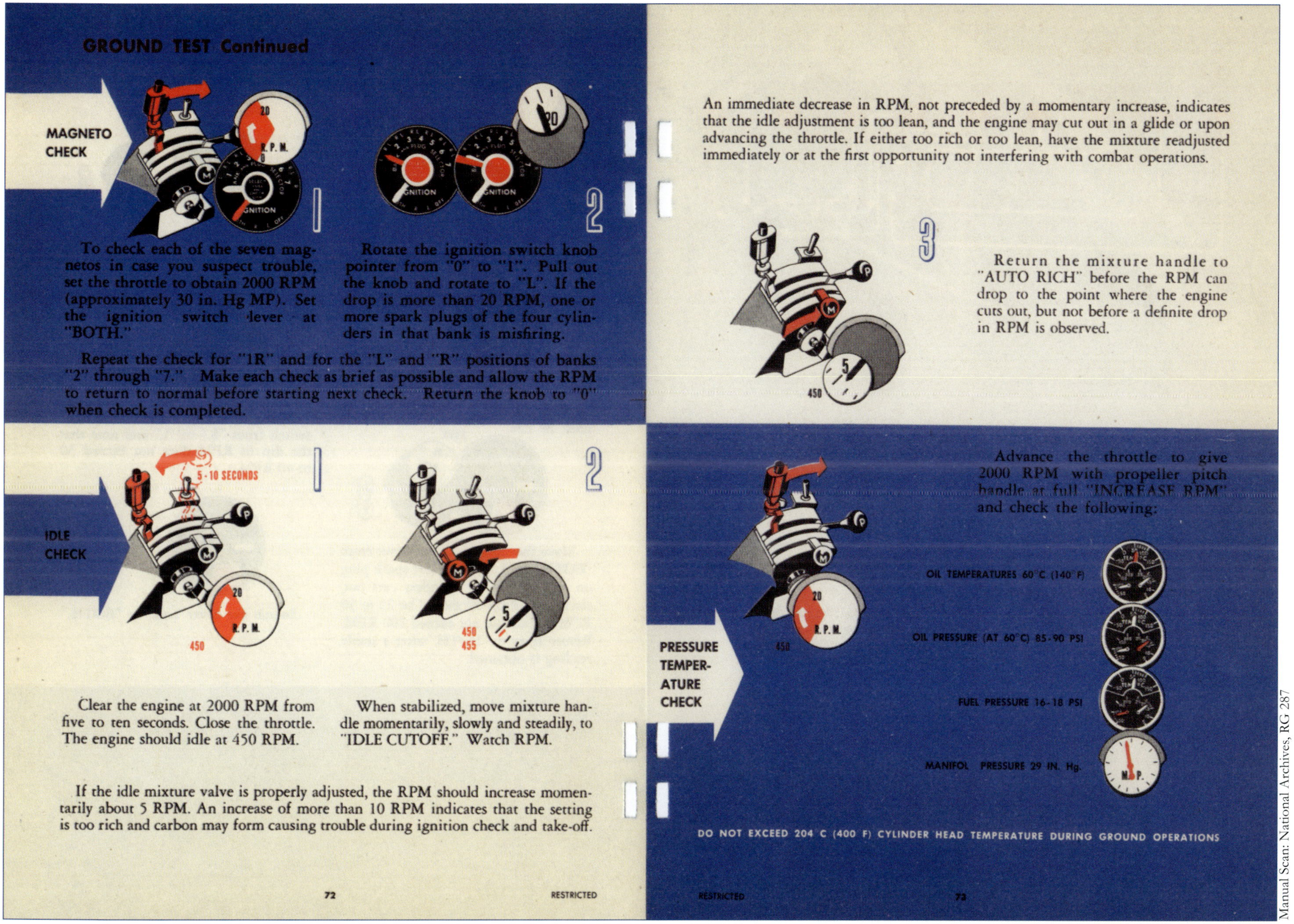

GROUND TEST Continued

MAGNETO CHECK

1

To check each of the seven magnetos in case you suspect trouble, set the throttle to obtain 2000 RPM (approximately 30 in. Hg MP). Set the ignition switch lever at "BOTH."

2

Rotate the ignition switch knob pointer from "0" to "1". Pull out the knob and rotate to "L". If the drop is more than 20 RPM, one or more spark plugs of the four cylinders in that bank is misfiring.

Repeat the check for "1R" and for the "L" and "R" positions of banks "2" through "7." Make each check as brief as possible and allow the RPM to return to normal before starting next check. Return the knob to "0" when check is completed.

IDLE CHECK

1

Clear the engine at 2000 RPM from five to ten seconds. Close the throttle. The engine should idle at 450 RPM.

2

When stabilized, move mixture handle momentarily, slowly and steadily, to "IDLE CUTOFF." Watch RPM.

If the idle mixture valve is properly adjusted, the RPM should increase momentarily about 5 RPM. An increase of more than 10 RPM indicates that the setting is too rich and carbon may form causing trouble during ignition check and take-off.

72 RESTRICTED

An immediate decrease in RPM, not preceded by a momentary increase, indicates that the idle adjustment is too lean, and the engine may cut out in a glide or upon advancing the throttle. If either too rich or too lean, have the mixture readjusted immediately or at the first opportunity not interfering with combat operations.

3

Return the mixture handle to "AUTO RICH" before the RPM can drop to the point where the engine cuts out, but not before a definite drop in RPM is observed.

PRESSURE TEMPERATURE CHECK

Advance the throttle to give 2000 RPM with propeller pitch handle at full "INCREASE RPM" and check the following:

DO NOT EXCEED 204°C (400°F) CYLINDER HEAD TEMPERATURE DURING GROUND OPERATIONS

RESTRICTED 73

Manual Scan: National Archives, RG 287

TAXI

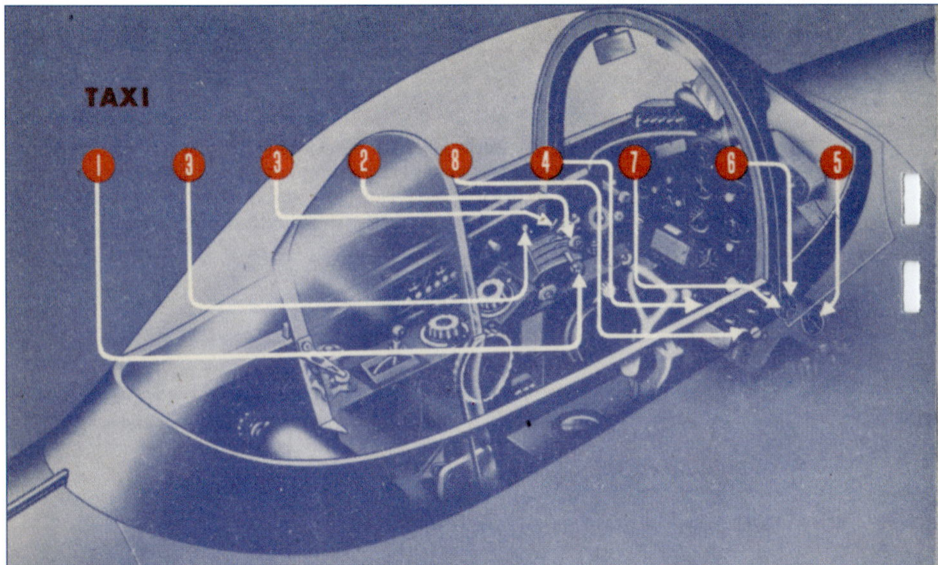

1. Mixture handle "AUTO RICH."
2. Propeller pitch handle "INCREASE RPM."
3. Auxiliary supercharger not running (warning light off). To check, hold switch at "DECREASE MAN. PR." Manifold pressure indication must not drop.
4. Cowl flaps full "OPEN."
5. Cylinder temperature max. 204°C (400°F).
6. Oil temperature at least 40°C (104°F) preferably 60°C (140°F).
7. Oil pressure 80 to 100 PSI.
8. If icing conditions are present, hold air filter switch to "FILTER" for five seconds and pull "AUXILIARY AIR" knob during taxi to prevent icing. *Push knob in before take-off.*

1. Use throttle to regulate power.
2. With tail wheel locked, taxi "off the spot" until tail surfaces clear other airplanes. Unlock tail wheel by raising tail wheel lock handle.
3. Steer with rudder and brakes.

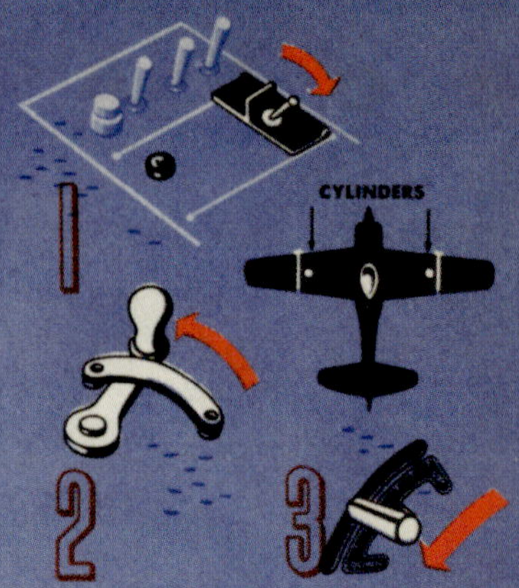

1. Spread wings while taxiing to employ full generator power, by holding wing folding switch to "SPREAD."
2. At the same time pull the wing pin lock handle toward "LOCK." Handle will not go to "LOCK" until wing pin is fully inserted. Red warning light goes off and red cylinders at wing folds disappear into wings when the pins are locked.
3. The wing flaps will automatically move to the position set on the control rheostat when wings are fully spread.

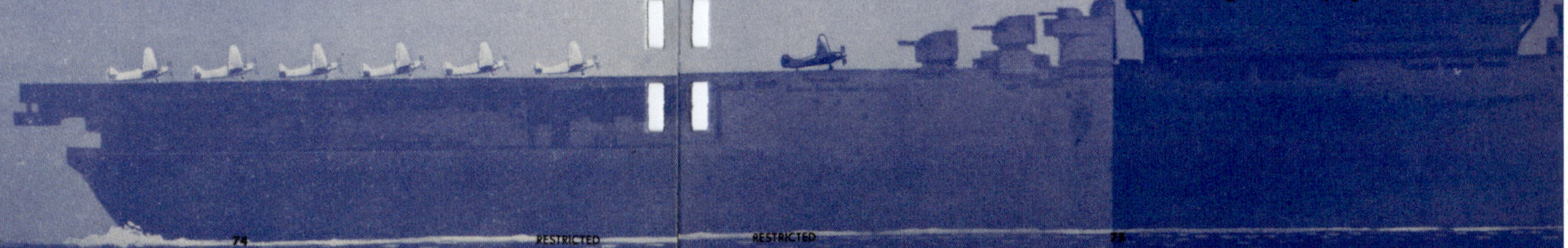

74 RESTRICTED RESTRICTED 75

Manual Scan: National Archives, RG 287

TAKEOFF

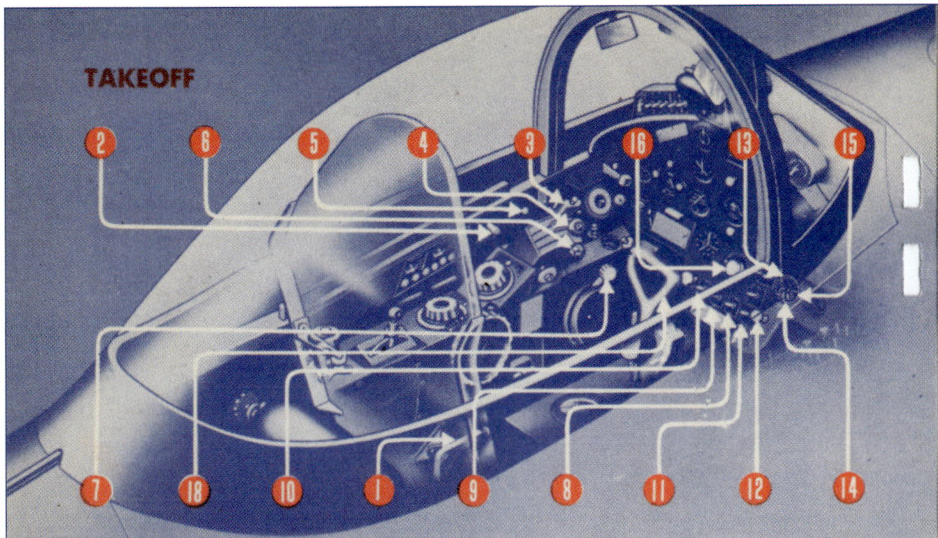

1. Tail wheel handle unlocked (carrier), locked (land).
2. Wing flap switch "DOWN" Visually check positioning marks on flaps aft of wing trailing edge.
3. Throttle set for 2000 RPM ignition check.
4. Propeller pitch handle at "INCREASE RPM."
5. Supercharger amber light off.
6. Mixture handle "AUTO RICH."
7. Fuel tank selector handle on "MAIN."
8. Oil cooler switch "AUTO."
9. Intercooler switch "AUTO."
10. Cowl flaps as required to maintain take-off cylinder temperature between 120°C (250°F) and 232°C (450°F).
11. Carburetor air filter switch "UNFILTERED" unless dusty or icing. (Hold five seconds for full travel).
12. Alternate air knob pushed in unless icing conditions are present.
13. Oil temperature at least 40°C (104°F), preferably 60°C (140°F).
14. Oil pressure 80 to 90 PSI.
15. Fuel pressure 16 to 18 PSI.
16. Check ignition. Switch lever "BOTH" to "R," "BOTH" to "L" (drop 25 to 50 RPM, Max. 100 RPM), "L" to "R" (drop 30 to 40 RPM).
17. Obtain radio or visual clearance for take-off.
18. Controls free.
19. Safety belt fastened and shoulder harness latched against forward pull.

76 RESTRICTED

1. Advance throttle to 52 in. mercury manifold pressure and take off at 2700 RPM (five minutes maximum).
2. Touch the brakes to stop the wheel rotation.
3. Landing gear switch "UP." Tail wheel must be centered before wheels will retract.

1. Wing flap switch "UP" after clearing all obstacles.
2. Before five minutes operation at take-off power, first throttle back to 43.5 in. Hg. manifold pressure and then set propeller pitch handle for 2550 RPM. For further reduction of power, reduce the manifold pressure two inches to four inches mercury, then reduce approximately 200 RPM in alternate steps until the desired engine speed is obtained, and finally, adjust the manifold pressure as desired.

RESTRICTED 77

Manual Scan: National Archives, RG 287

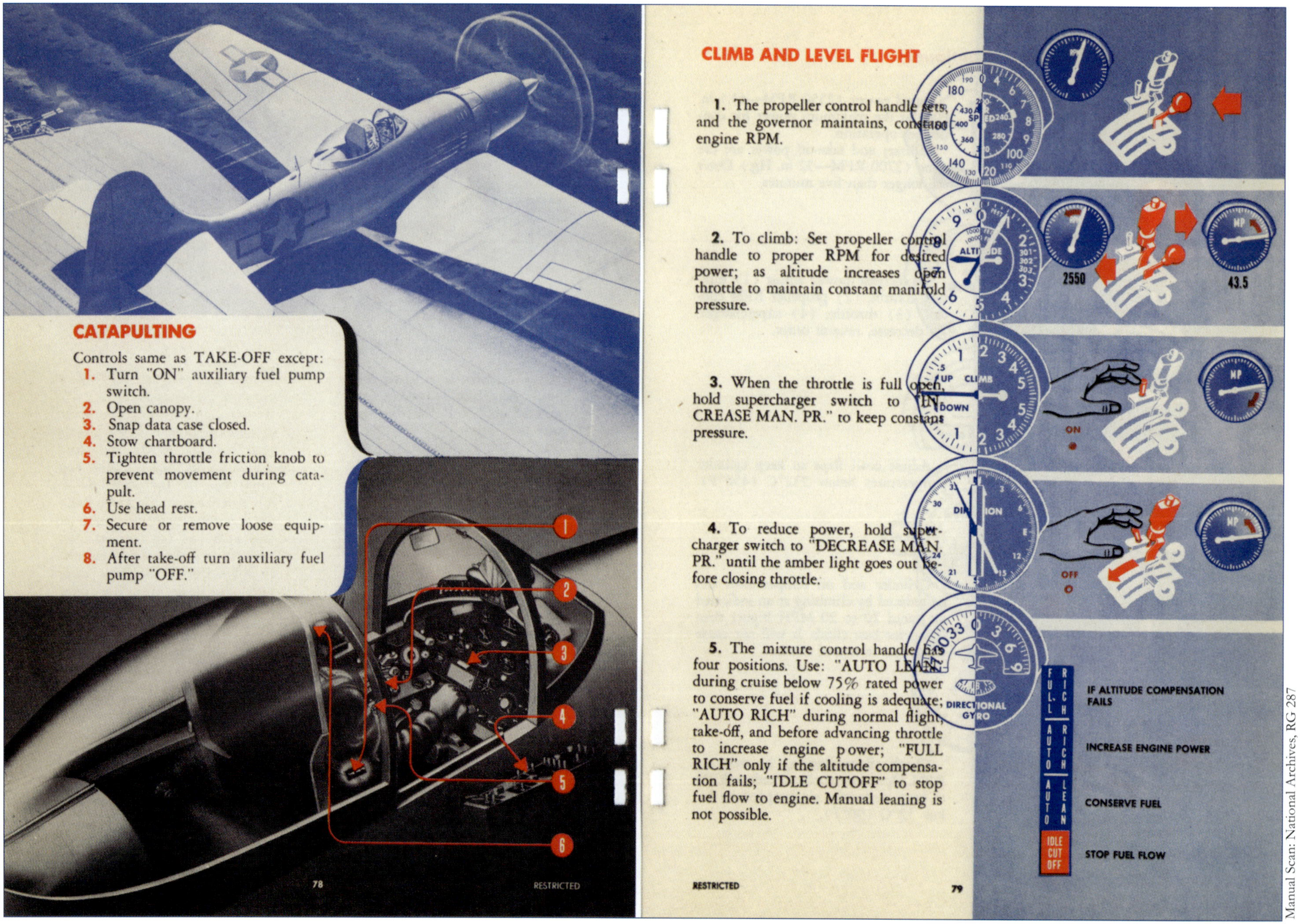

CATAPULTING

Controls same as TAKE-OFF except:

1. Turn "ON" auxiliary fuel pump switch.
2. Open canopy.
3. Snap data case closed.
4. Stow chartboard.
5. Tighten throttle friction knob to prevent movement during catapult.
6. Use head rest.
7. Secure or remove loose equipment.
8. After take-off turn auxiliary fuel pump "OFF."

78 RESTRICTED

CLIMB AND LEVEL FLIGHT

1. The propeller control handle sets, and the governor maintains, constant engine RPM.

2. To climb: Set propeller control handle to proper RPM for desired power; as altitude increases open throttle to maintain constant manifold pressure.

3. When the throttle is full open, hold supercharger switch to "INCREASE MAN. PR." to keep constant pressure.

4. To reduce power, hold supercharger switch to "DECREASE MAN. PR." until the amber light goes out before closing throttle.

5. The mixture control handle has four positions. Use: "AUTO LEAN" during cruise below 75% rated power to conserve fuel if cooling is adequate; "AUTO RICH" during normal flight, take-off, and before advancing throttle to increase engine power; "FULL RICH" only if the altitude compensation fails; "IDLE CUTOFF" to stop fuel flow to engine. Manual leaning is not possible.

RESTRICTED 79

Manual Scan: National Archives, RG 287

CLIMB AND LEVEL FLIGHT Continued

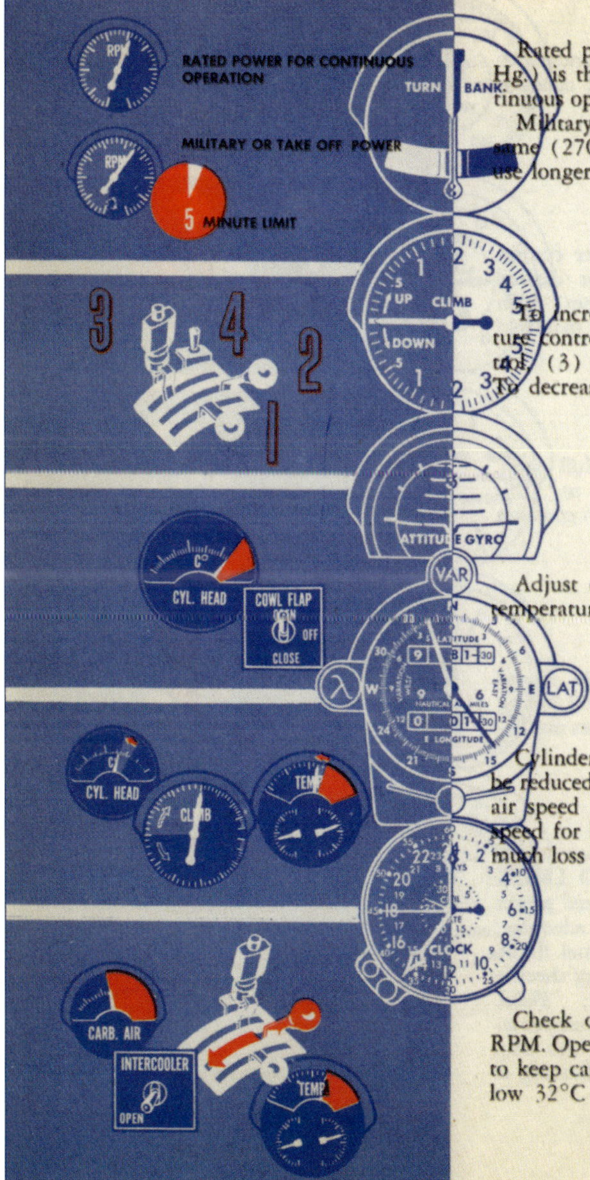

Rated power (2550 RPM—43.5 in. Hg.) is the maximum power for continuous operation.

Military and take-off power are the same (2700 RPM—52 in. Hg.) Don't use longer than five minutes.

To increase power adjust (1) mixture control, (2) propeller RPM control, (3) throttle, (4) supercharger. To decrease, reverse order.

Adjust cowl flaps to keep cylinder temperatures below 232°C (450°F).

Cylinder and oil temperatures can be reduced by climbing at an indicated air speed 10 to 20 MPH higher than speed for best climb. It will not cause much loss in rate of climb.

Check oil overheating by reducing RPM. Open intercooler or reduce RPM to keep carburetor air temperature below 32°C (90°F).

DIVING

Keep the manifold pressure above 15 in. Hg. and the RPM between 2130 and 2330 during steep prolonged dives. Any manifold pressure above 15 inches within the engine limits for the RPM, mixture, and altitude can be used except that higher manifold pressures increase diving speed. Pressures below 15 inches cool and foul up the engine.

Do not exceed the maximum safe overspeed of 3060 RPM for 30 seconds. If, however, the maximum is exceeded: close the throttle immediately; move propeller RPM control to "DECREASE RPM" to increase propeller pitch, and reduce air speed to the minimum for safe glide.

During a dive from high altitude always remember manifold pressure will build up rapidly at a constant throttle setting.

Open the throttle slowly at the end of a dive so the partly cooled engine won't cut out.

The mixture handle must always be at "AUTO RICH."

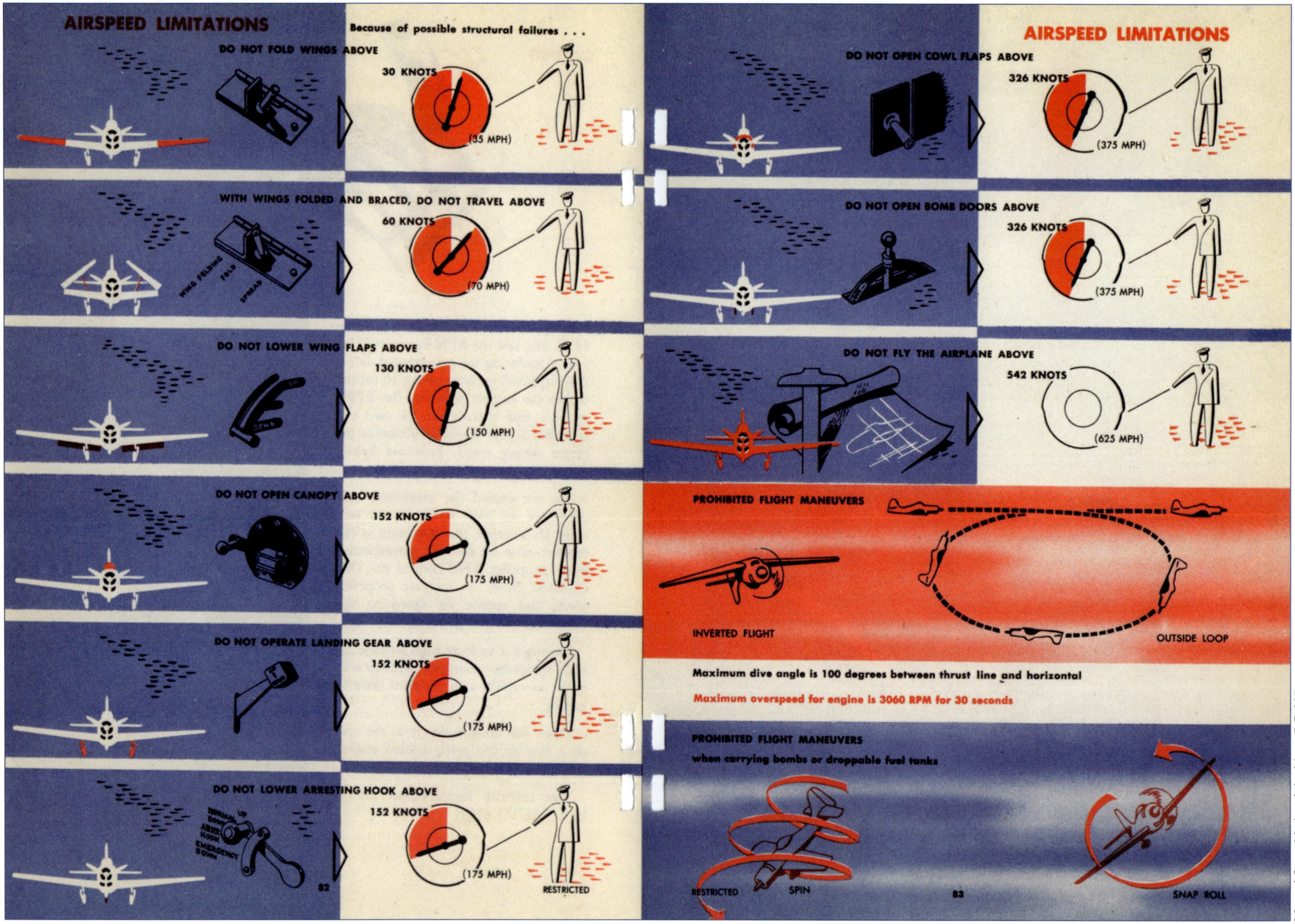

Manual Scan: National Archives, RG 287

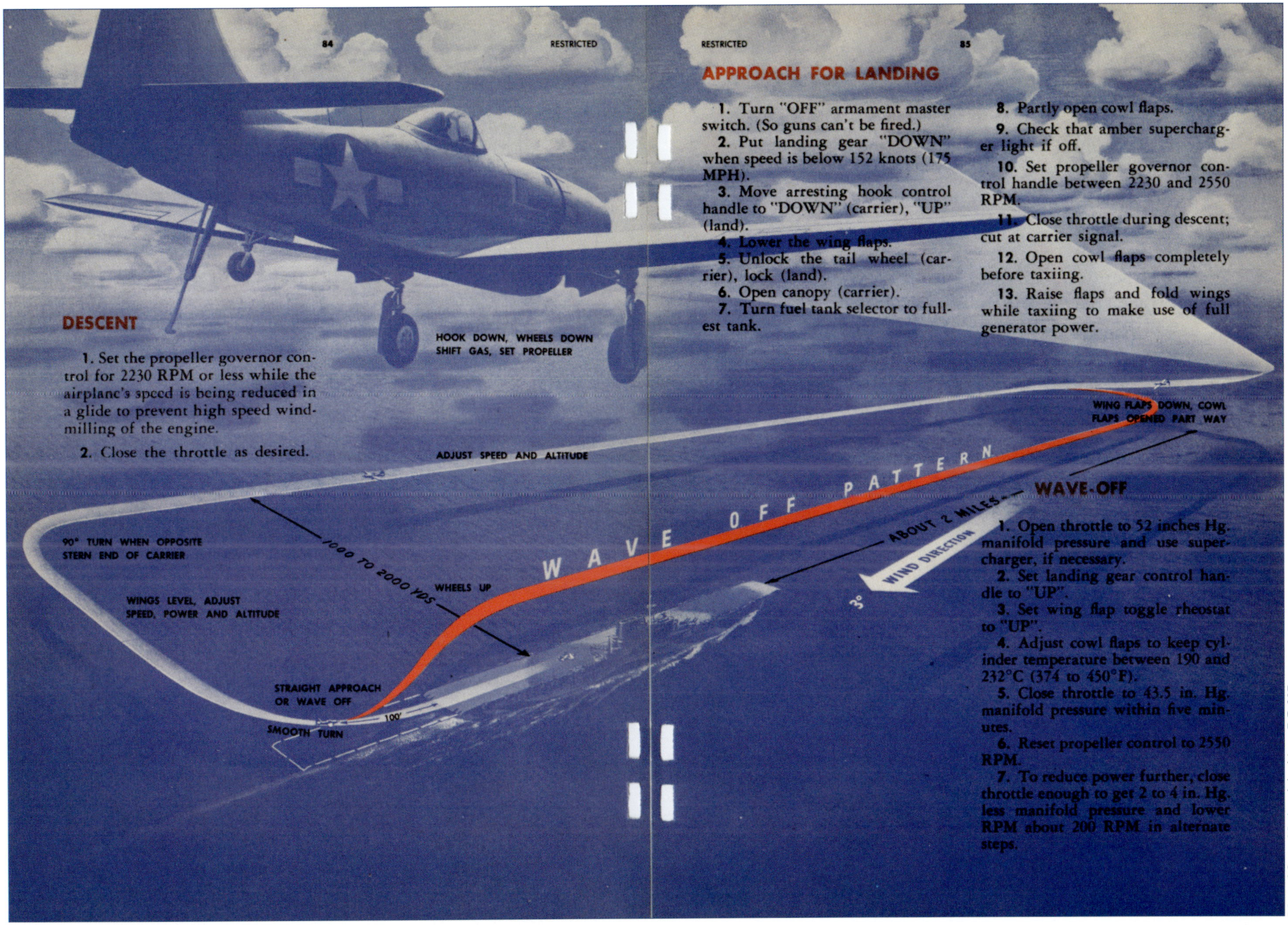

84 RESTRICTED

RESTRICTED 85

APPROACH FOR LANDING

1. Turn "OFF" armament master switch. (So guns can't be fired.)
2. Put landing gear "DOWN" when speed is below 152 knots (175 MPH).
3. Move arresting hook control handle to "DOWN" (carrier), "UP" (land).
4. Lower the wing flaps.
5. Unlock the tail wheel (carrier), lock (land).
6. Open canopy (carrier).
7. Turn fuel tank selector to fullest tank.
8. Partly open cowl flaps.
9. Check that amber supercharger light is off.
10. Set propeller governor control handle between 2230 and 2550 RPM.
11. Close throttle during descent; cut at carrier signal.
12. Open cowl flaps completely before taxiing.
13. Raise flaps and fold wings while taxiing to make use of full generator power.

DESCENT

1. Set the propeller governor control for 2230 RPM or less while the airplane's speed is being reduced in a glide to prevent high speed windmilling of the engine.

2. Close the throttle as desired.

WAVE-OFF

1. Open throttle to 52 inches Hg. manifold pressure and use supercharger, if necessary.
2. Set landing gear control handle to "UP".
3. Set wing flap toggle rheostat to "UP".
4. Adjust cowl flaps to keep cylinder temperature between 190 and 232°C (374 to 450°F).
5. Close throttle to 43.5 in. Hg. manifold pressure within five minutes.
6. Reset propeller control to 2550 RPM.
7. To reduce power further, close throttle enough to get 2 to 4 in. Hg. less manifold pressure and lower RPM about 200 RPM in alternate steps.

Manual Scan: National Archives, RG 287

STOPPING ENGINE

If circumstances permit, check idle mixture adjustment as in GROUND TEST.

1. Idle engine until cylinder temperature is below 204°C (400°F).
2. Propeller control at full "INCREASE RPM".
3. Cowl flaps full open.
4. Open throttle to 1200 RPM for 30 seconds.
5. Mixture handle to "IDLE CUT-OFF" and open throttle.
6. When engine stops, turn ignition "OFF".
7. If engine doesn't stop, close throttle, turn ignition "OFF", and slowly open throttle wide. Have idle cutoff valve adjusted.
8. Turn fuel tank selector "OFF".
9. Leave cowl flaps open.
10. Mixture at IDLE CUTOFF".

86 RESTRICTED

OIL DILUTION

When you anticipate a cold start with outside air temperature below 0°C (32°F), dilute oil with fuel as follows:

Idle or stop the engine to allow the cylinder temperature to fall below 148°C (300°F) and the oil temperature below 50°C (120°F). If the engine is stopped the oil tank should be refilled after cooling to dilute all of the starting oil. Restart the engine and run at 800 RPM.

Watch the oil pressure gage.

Press the oil dilution switch

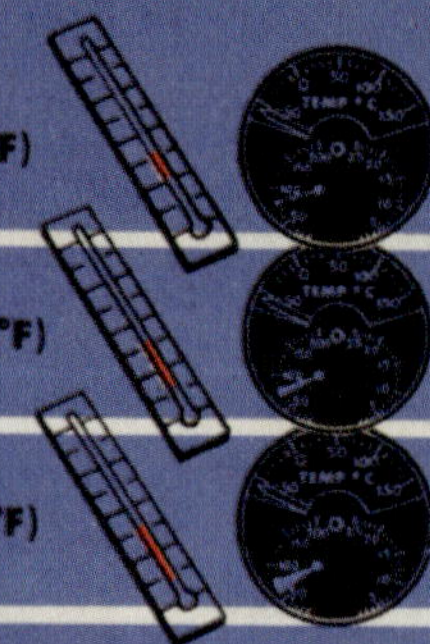

IF THE OUTSIDE TEMPERATURE IS . . .	DILUTE UNTIL PRESSURE DROPS . . .
0° to -12°C, (32° to 10°F)	10 PSI
-10° to -18°C, (15° to 0°F)	15 PSI
-18° to -23°C, (0° to -10°F)	20 PSI

When the oil pressure drop is complete, advance the throttle to 1200 RPM for 30 seconds, move mixture to "IDLE CUTOFF", open throttle, turn ignition switch "OFF" and turn fuel tank selector switch to "OFF".

If the engine is run again after dilution before the cold start, redilute as above to the final oil pressure obtained during the first dilution.

If the oil has not been diluted before a cold start, do not dilute before the start. It will not aid in starting and may cause trouble.

When the dilution valve is opened, the indicated fuel pressure will drop sharply, and should return to normal immediately after releasing the switch. If it does not, stop the engine immediately and check for a leaking valve.

Allow adequate warm up.

Guard against fire and over dilution.

RESTRICTED 87

Manual Scan: National Archives, RG 287

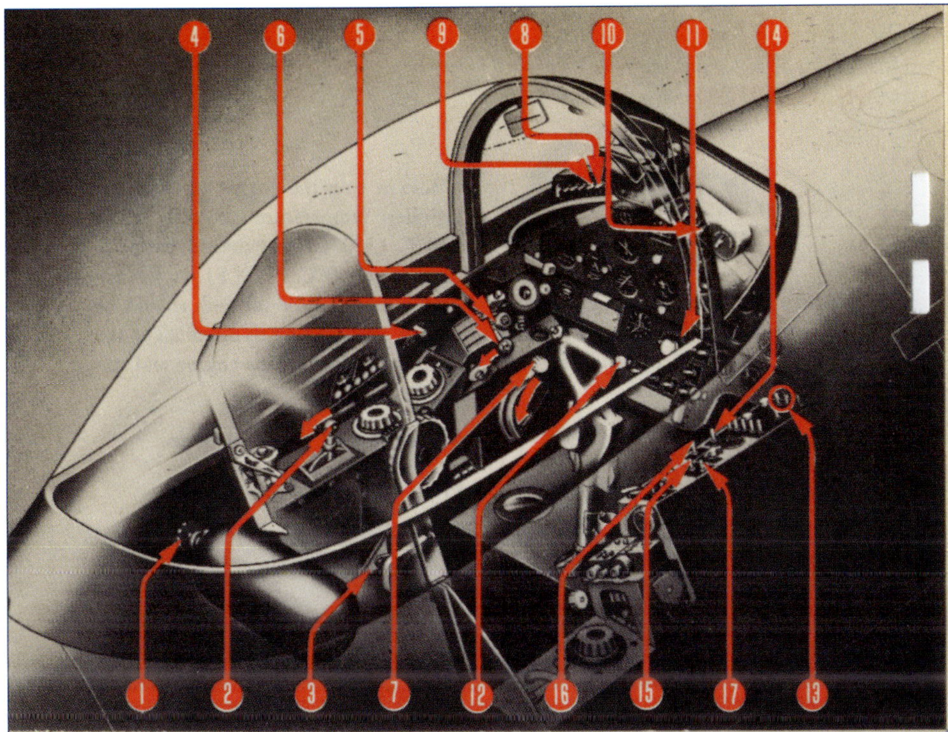

BEFORE LEAVING AIRPLANE

See that the . . .

1. Oxygen bottle is off (knob clockwise).
2. Bomb release handle is at "LOCK".
3. Tail wheel is "UNLOCKED".
4. Wing flap toggle is "UP".
5. Propeller RPM control is at full "INCREASE RPM".
6. Mixture control is at "IDLE CUTOFF".
7. Fuel tank selector handle is "OFF".
8. Armament master switch is "OFF".
9. Gun camera switch is "OFF".
10. Guns sight switch is "OFF".
11. Ignition is "OFF", knob at zero.
12. Surface lock knob is pulled out. Move surface controls to neutral to engage locks. Throttle automatically closed.
13. Recognition light switches are "OFF".
14. Master exterior light switch is "OFF".
15. Master radio switch is "OFF".
16. Pitot heater switch is "OFF".
17. Battery switch is "OFF".
18. Wheel chocks are in place before releasing brake. There is no parking brake.

TOWING

Always keep a man in the cockpit during towing to unlock the tail wheel, and apply the brakes. Unlock the tail wheel by raising the lever on the side of the left console. If the tail wheel is not unlocked, a shear bolt in the tail wheel treadle will fail when the airplane turns, and must be replaced.

If using tow cables, do not try to turn the airplane by the cables alone. As the tractor starts to turn, apply the brake in the direction of the turn. Always keep *both* cables taut.

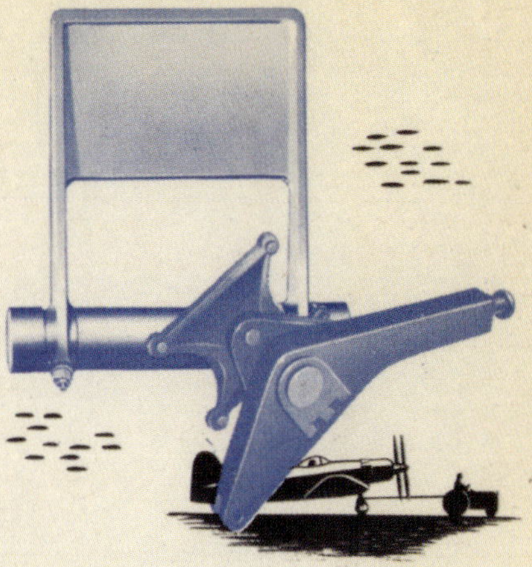

TIEDOWN

Tie down rings are located in the nose of each wing inboard of the fold. The catapult ring on the tail wheel can be used for the tail tie down. Other tie down points are the wheel axles and struts.

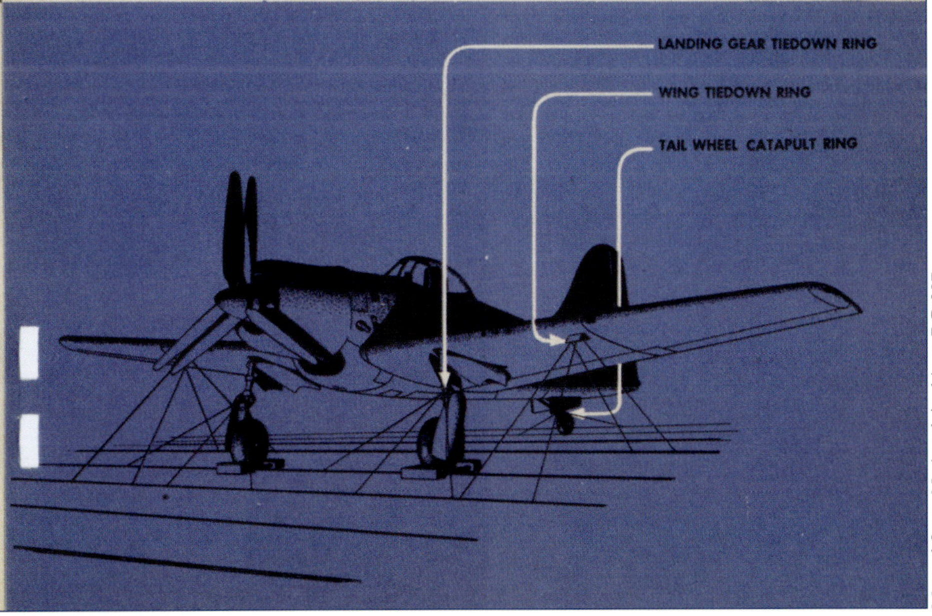

SEC-3

FIRING GUNS

1. Before entering cockpit, check ammunition and gun charging.

2. After take-off, turn on desired gun selector switches. Circuit breakers should be in. Turn on armament master switch.

3. Turn on gun sight switch. Adjust "BRIGHT"—"DIM" rheostat for desired brilliance of reticle image. Set selector switch for "FIXED", "GYRO", or "FIXED & GYRO". Lever on left side of sight masks all of fixed reticle image except center cross. Set wing span of target by pointer above crash-pad on sight. Get range by twisting throttle handle to keep circle of diamonds on wing tips of target.

4. To fire guns, press trigger on control column grip. Jammed guns cannot be cleared in flight.

5. To shut down guns, turn off armament master switch.

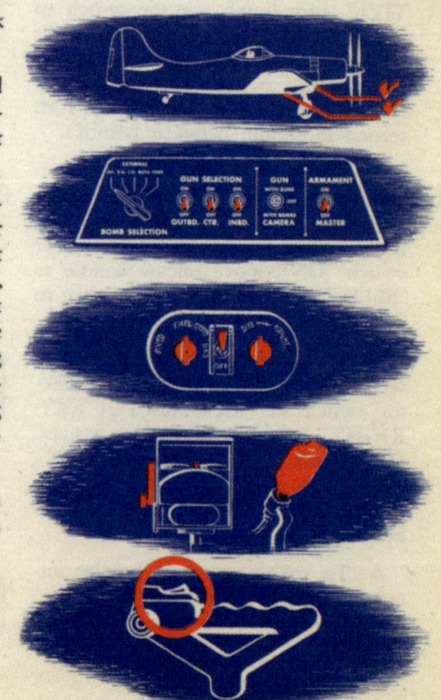

RESTRICTED 91

BOMBING

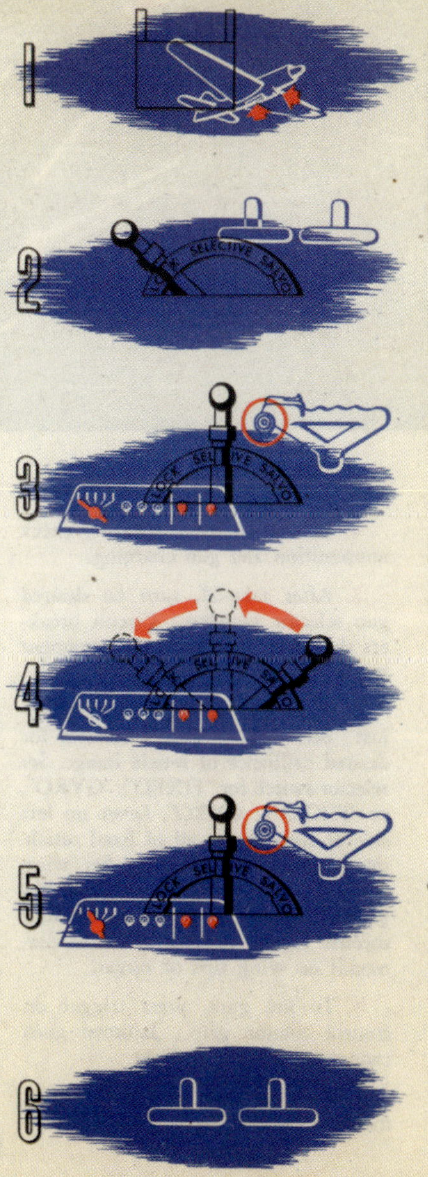

1. Before entering cockpit, obtain bomb loading, see that bomb doors are closed and check camera installation.

2. Before starting engine, see that the bomb release lever is on "LOCK" and that the external bomb emergency release handles are seated. Test bomb indicator light bulbs and turn lights off. You cannot release bombs from both internal and external racks at one time even in unarmed salvo. Internal bombs must be dropped armed one at a time. External bombs can be dropped armed either separately or together, but must be separately jettisoned unarmed.

3. To release internal bombs armed, move bomb release handle to "SELECTIVE", turn bomb selector switch to "INTERNAL", set camera switch to "BOMBS" if desired, turn on armament master switch, and press bomb release button for each bomb (3/10th second minimum between bombs).

4. To release internal bombs unarmed at any time, move bomb release handle to "SALVO". To close doors again, turn armament master switch "ON", move release handle to "SELECTIVE" for ten seconds; then to "LOCK".

5. To release external bombs armed, separately or together, set bomb selector switch to "EXT. LEFT", "EXT. RIGHT" or "EXT. BOTH" as desired. Move bomb release handle to "SELECTIVE", set camera switch if desired, turn on armament master switch. Press bomb release button.

6. To release external bombs unarmed, pull the red T-handles.

USE OF GUN CAMERA

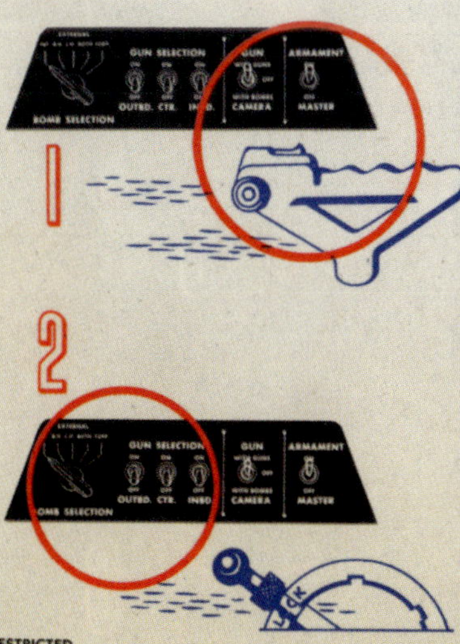

1. To operate the gun camera, turn on the armament master switch, set the camera switch to "WITH BOMBS" or "WITH GUNS" and press the bomb release button or the gun trigger. The camera alone may be operated in practise but the gun selection switches must be "OFF" and the bomb release handle at "LOCK" to prevent firing the guns or dropping bombs accidentally.

2. The camera is parallel to the gun sight. To record the results of a bombing, return the bomb release handle to "LOCK", swing the airplane around to sight the target through the gun sight, and press the bomb release button as long as you desire.

USE OF OXYGEN

Preflight Check

1. Red "EMERGENCY" valve closed.
2. Filler valve closed (clockwise).
3. Bottle open (knob counterclockwise).
4. Pressure 1800±50 PSI.
5. Mask on. Be sure flexible tube quick disconnect coupling is secure.
6. Pinch mask tube and inhale lightly. If mask leaks, tighten or adjust suspension straps and nose wire.
7. Turn diluter lever "OFF", inhale and check flow (indicator blinks).
8. Turn the diluter lever "ON".

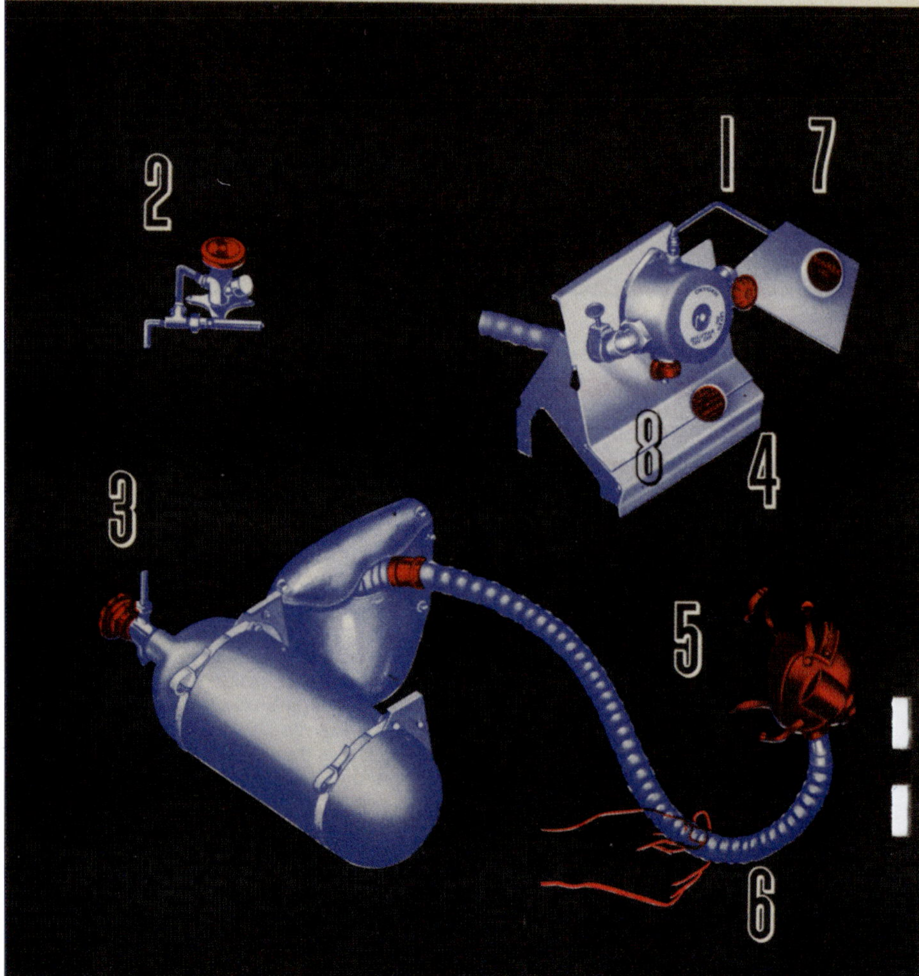

OPERATING INSTRUCTIONS

Always use oxygen above 10,000 feet and above 5000 feet for combat or tactical night flights.

Keep diluter lever "ON" except when:

1. On long flight above 30,000 feet.
2. Flight Surgeon orders pure oxygen or it is needed to treat injury or shock.
3. Poison gas in cockpit is suspected. If carbon monoxide is suspected in the cockpit reduce throttle to normal cruise, and set mixture to "AUTO LEAN" if possible.

Keep regulator red "EMERGENCY" knob "OFF" except:

1. To revive pilot if fainting.
2. To give positive oxygen flow if mask leaks excessively.
3. If pilot has to remove mask temporarily (loosen on one side and hold as near nose as possible).
4. When flow indicator doesn't blink.

Turn off emergency valve as soon as possible or descend to a safe altitude. Watch blinker to check oxygen flow. Check pressure gage for endurance.

For endurance of a bottle that is not full, see diagram on page 46.

ALTITUDE (Feet)	DILUTER ON (Hours)	DILUTER OFF (Hours)
5,000	7.3	1.8
10,000	8.7	2.1
15,000	11.0	2.6
20,000	9.3	3.3
25,000	6.3	4.1
30,000	5.2	5.2
35,000	6.5	6.5
40,000	8.3	8.3

Manual Scan: National Archives, RG 287

RADIO OPERATION

Headset and Microphones—Plug headset and hand "mike" into jacks on top of jack box on seat armor. Plug throat, lip, or mask "mike" into extension cord.

Master Radio Switch—Turn on the switch 30 seconds before using the radio. Do not run the radios on the battery only (with no generator or external power), or limit the number of radios operating. Turn off after parking airplane.

Voice Communication—Master radio switch "ON". Radio telephone "ON-OFF" switch "ON". "RADIO-INTERPHONE" switch on "RADIO". "P-G", "BOTH", "P-P" as desired. Channel selector switch set to desired channel as follows:

SW. POS.	TRANS. CHANNEL	REC. CHANNEL
1	P-P	P-P & P-G No. 1
2	P-G No. 1	P-P & P-G No. 1
3	P-G No. 2	P-P & P-G No. 2
4	P-G No. 3	P-P & P-G No. 3

"INCREASE OUTPUT" knob set for desired volume. Depress "mike" button on throttle or switch on hand "mike" to talk over radio telephone, and release to receive.

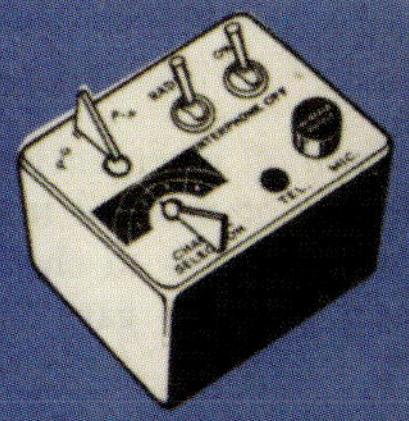

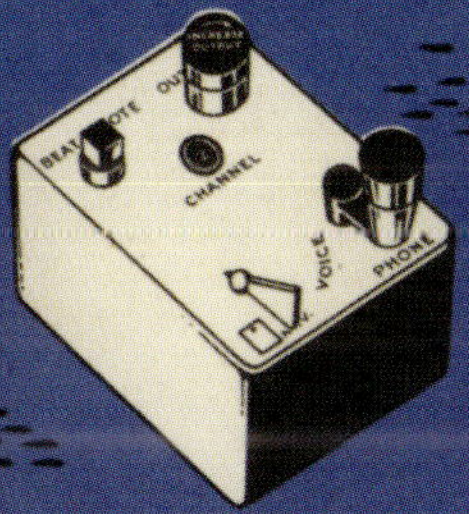

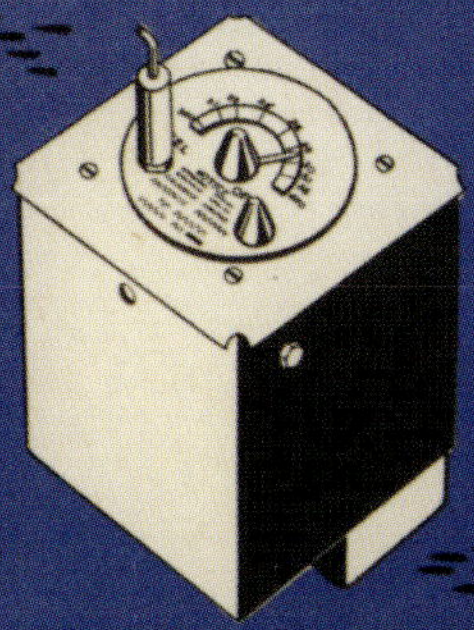

Identification—Master radio switch "ON". IFF "ON-OFF" switch "ON" before take-off. IFF-"G" switch at "OFF" unless commanding officer instructs otherwise. Do not use the "EMERGENCY" switch under the green guard unless you are in trouble or need assistance. "DESTRUCTOR" switch "OFF" unless a forced landing in enemy territory is to be made.

Homing—Turn master radio switch "ON". Turn the "OFF"-"NAV"-"VOICE" switch to "NAV" for code signals. Turn channel selector crank until correct number appears in dial window. Adjust "OUTPUT" knob for volume control. Set "BEAT NOTE" knob for the desired pitch of code signals.

Range Signal Reception—Turn master switch "ON". Turn "OFF"-"ON"-"VOLUME" knob "ON." Use knob and dial to tune in desired range station. Adjust the volume.

SEC-4 EMERGENCY OPERATIONS

EMERGENCY OPERATIONS Section 4

EMERGENCY TAKE-OFF

In an emergency, you can take off without an engine warm up or ground test providing that the oil temperature has shown a definite increase (at least 10°C—18°F) since starting and that the oil pressure is steady below 100 PSI. Use the oil dilution system, carefully, to reduce the oil pressure if necessary, but only if the oil has been diluted when the engine was last shut down.

Manual Scan: National Archives, RG 287

ENGINE FAILURE DURING TAKEOFF

1

If the engine fails and it appears possible to stop on the deck, close the throttle and apply the brakes.

2

If you cannot stop, release the brakes, apply full right rudder to go off the side of the carrier, and flip the landing gear handle to "UP". On land, apply the brakes and if the airport runs out, retract the landing gear and slide straight ahead.

3

If the engine fails immediately after take-off from a carrier, maintain airspeed by nosing down, flip the landing gear handle to "UP", wing flap control handle to full "DOWN", turn to the right and land in the water.

In take-off from an airport, land straight ahead. Only change directions sufficiently to miss obstructions. If there is time, switch ignition "OFF" and set fuel tank selector handle to "OFF" to prevent fire. In any case, do it after landing.

ENGINE FAILURE DURING FLIGHT

1

If you are within gliding distance of a landing area, immediately move the prop-pitch handle to "DECREASE RPM". Close cowl flaps, oil cooler and intercooler doors.

2

Switch off all electrical equipment possible (radios, electric fuel pumps, pitot heater, lights) to conserve battery charge. Flip wing flap control switch to full "DOWN", and if the flaps do not reach limit of travel before battery fails, crank them down with the hand crank. It takes about 25 seconds to lower the flaps electrically, and about 5 minutes with the crank (360 turns).

3

If it is possible to land on a deck or an airport, lower the landing gear electrically (8 seconds) if battery power is available, or with the hand crank (3 1/2 minutes—230 turns).

4

If you have to land on water or rough ground, leave the landing gear retracted. Jettison all bombs and extra fuel tanks.

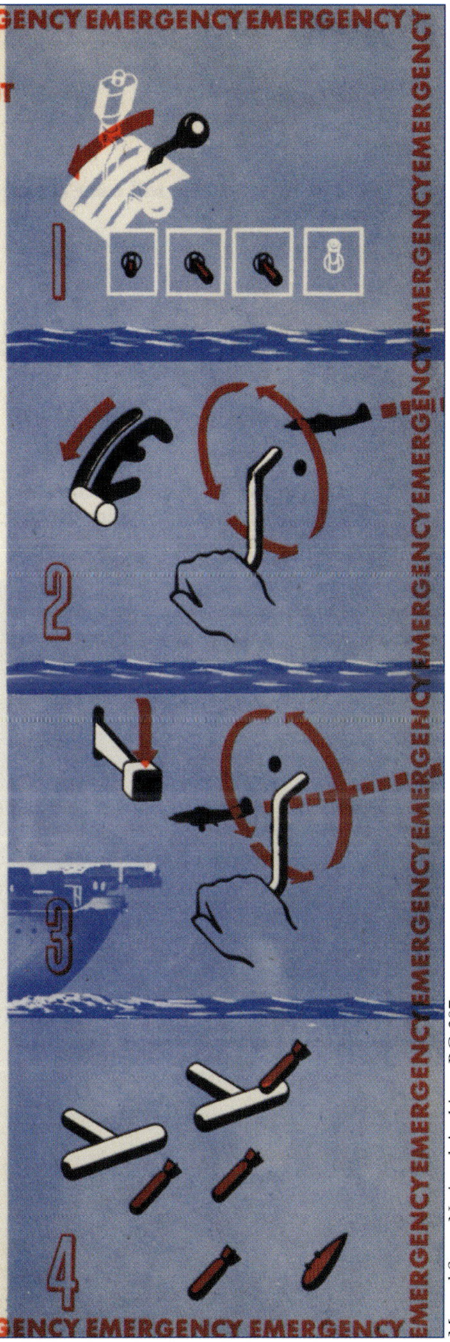

Manual Scan: National Archives, RG 287

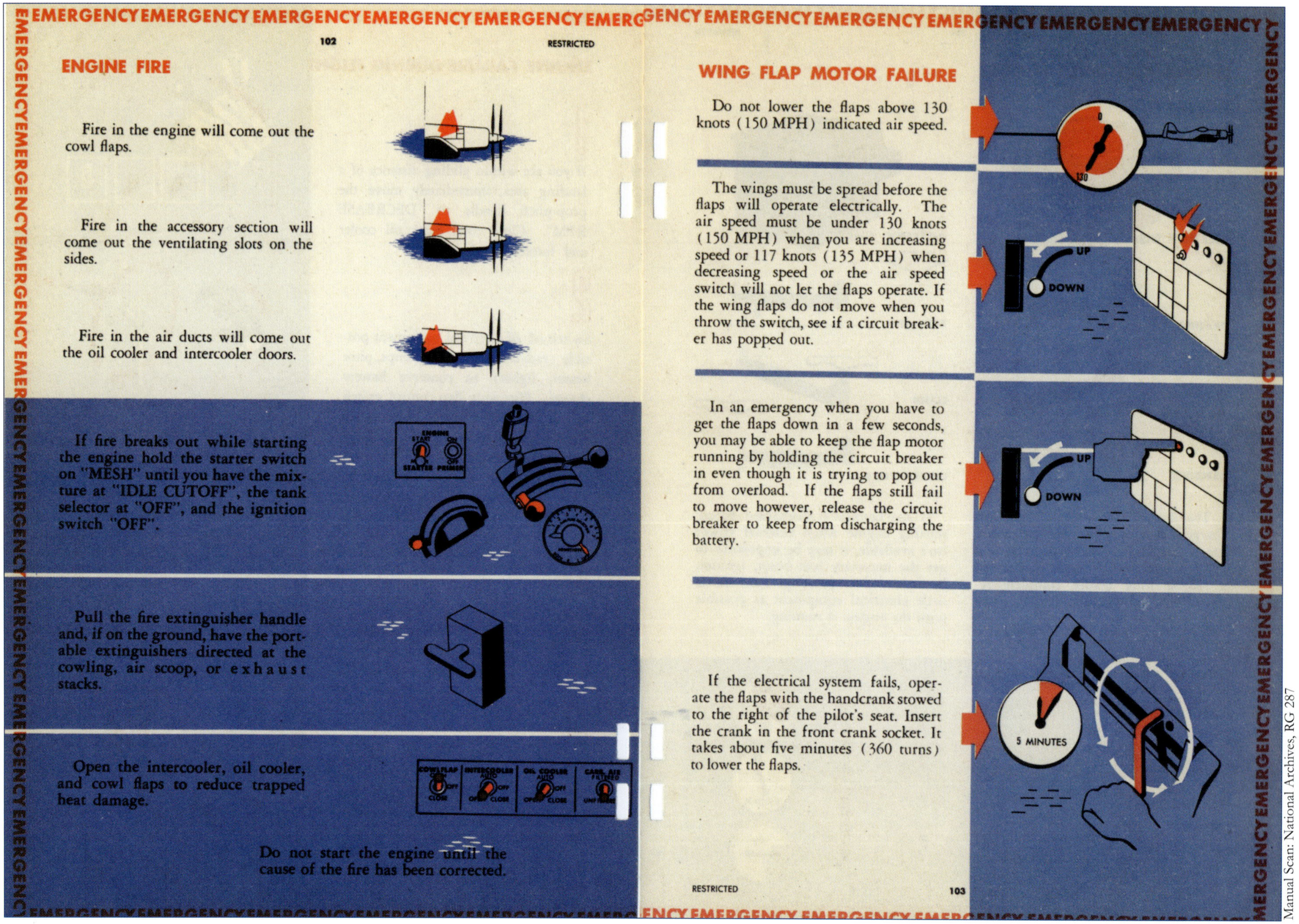

102 RESTRICTED

ENGINE FIRE

Fire in the engine will come out the cowl flaps.

Fire in the accessory section will come out the ventilating slots on the sides.

Fire in the air ducts will come out the oil cooler and intercooler doors.

If fire breaks out while starting the engine hold the starter switch on "MESH" until you have the mixture at "IDLE CUTOFF", the tank selector at "OFF", and the ignition switch "OFF".

Pull the fire extinguisher handle and, if on the ground, have the portable extinguishers directed at the cowling, air scoop, or exhaust stacks.

Open the intercooler, oil cooler, and cowl flaps to reduce trapped heat damage.

Do not start the engine until the cause of the fire has been corrected.

WING FLAP MOTOR FAILURE

Do not lower the flaps above 130 knots (150 MPH) indicated air speed.

The wings must be spread before the flaps will operate electrically. The air speed must be under 130 knots (150 MPH) when you are increasing speed or 117 knots (135 MPH) when decreasing speed or the air speed switch will not let the flaps operate. If the wing flaps do not move when you throw the switch, see if a circuit breaker has popped out.

In an emergency when you have to get the flaps down in a few seconds, you may be able to keep the flap motor running by holding the circuit breaker in even though it is trying to pop out from overload. If the flaps still fail to move however, release the circuit breaker to keep from discharging the battery.

If the electrical system fails, operate the flaps with the handcrank stowed to the right of the pilot's seat. Insert the crank in the front crank socket. It takes about five minutes (360 turns) to lower the flaps.

RESTRICTED 103

Manual Scan: National Archives, RG 287

EMERGENCY EMERGENCY EMERGENCY EMERGENCY EMERGENCY EMERGENCY

104 RESTRICTED

ELECTRICAL POWER FAILURE

BATTERY

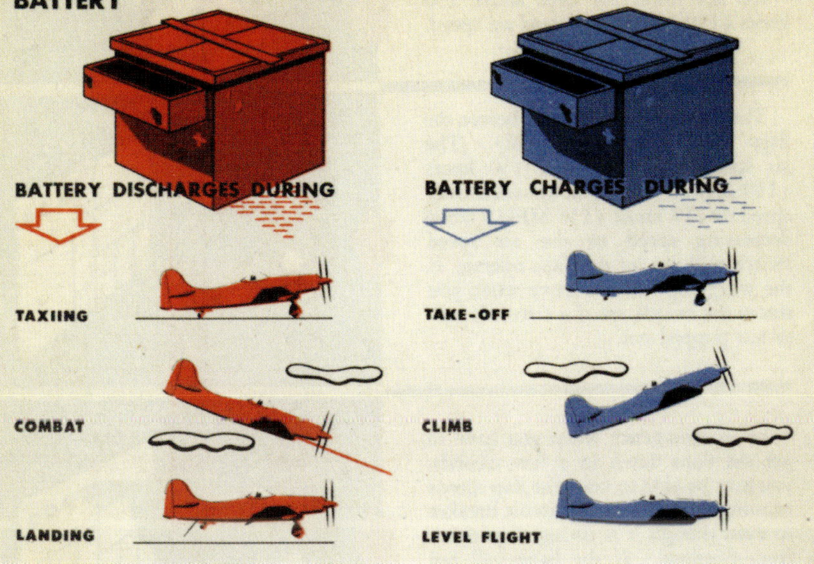

The battery may have been discharged so rapidly that the electrolyte has boiled away, thereby preventing a full recharge. It may also be discharged a second time before complete recharge, and make the recharging time even longer.

If the battery is discharged before starting engine when external power isn't available, it may be impossible to get the necessary fuel boost, ignition boost, and fuel priming. Turn on as little electrical equipment as possible until the engine is running.

LOW BATTERY

The battery is low when the voltage is below 20 for more than five seconds when the engine is run above 1000 RPM and a heavy system load is applied.

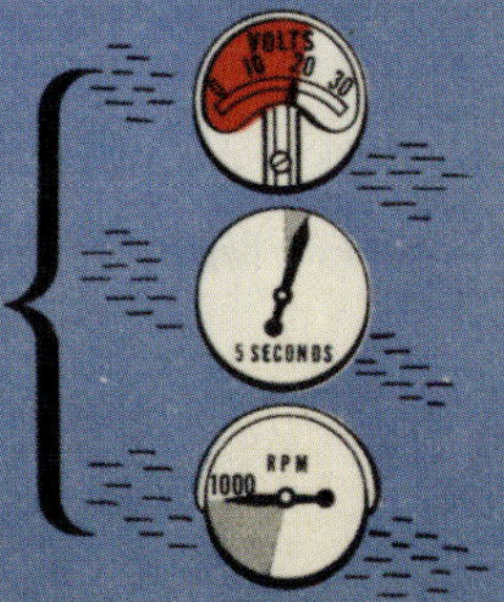

RESTRICTED 105

BATTERY USE AFTER GENERATOR FAILS

Turn off all but essential equipment. To get the greatest possible service out of the battery charge, turn the battery switch to "OFF," except for necessary instrument or radio use.

If the battery switch only is "ON" (instruments and electric fuel pumps using power) the battery lasts about 15 minutes.

With continuous use of above equipment plus one radio the battery lasts 12 or 13 minutes. If all radios are used with above equipment it will last 9 minutes.

If operating on auxiliary tanks, the auxiliary fuel pump can only be turned off with the battery switch. If on main tank, turn "OFF" the auxiliary fuel pump switch.

If the instruments only are used (booster pumps may be held "OFF" if the engine fuel pump maintains 16 PSI) the battery lasts about 30 minutes.

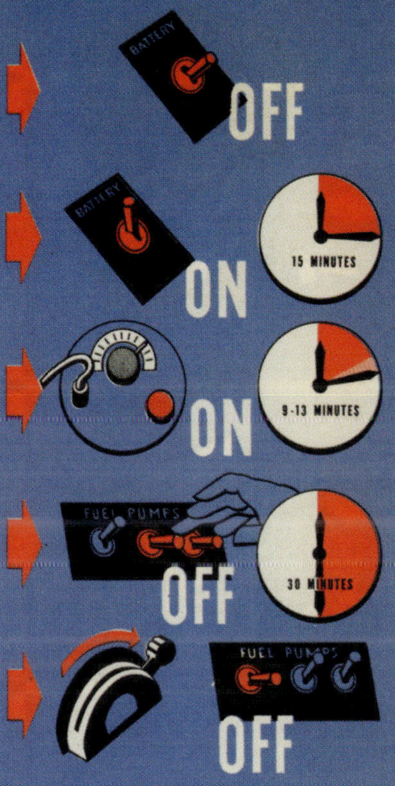

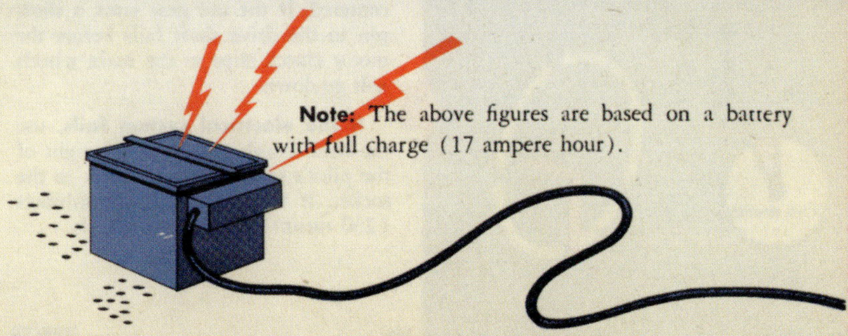

Note: The above figures are based on a battery with full charge (17 ampere hour).

EMERGENCY EMERGENCY EMERGENCY EMERGENCY EMERGENCY EMERGENCY

Manual Scan: National Archives, RG 287

LANDING GEAR FAILURE

Do not raise or lower the landing gear over 152 knots (175 MPH) indicated air speed.

If the landing gear doesn't operate when you move the handle, see if the circuit breaker has popped out.

In an emergency when you have to get the wheels down quickly, try to keep the retracting motor running by holding the circuit breaker in even though it is trying to pop out from overload. If the landing gear still doesn't move however, release circuit breaker to keep from discharging the battery.

The landing gear cannot be retracted if the weight of the airplane is on the wheels or if the tail wheel is not centered. If the tail gear jams, a shear pin in the drive shaft fails before the motor clutch slips so the main wheels will go down.

If the electrical system fails, use the hank crank stowed to the right of the pilot's seat. Insert the crank in the socket. It takes about 3 1 2 minutes (230 turns) to lower the wheels.

106 RESTRICTED

EMERGENCY LANDING WITH WHEELS RETRACTED

Jettison Bombs and Fuel Tanks—Set the bomb release handle to "SALVO" and pull the two external tank release handles.

Close the Bomb Doors—Return the bomb release handle to "SELECTIVE" and turn the armament master switch "ON." Allow 10 seconds for the doors to close, then turn the armament master switch "OFF."

Tighten Shoulder Straps—Move adjustment lever aft, lean back, and return handle forward.

Open the Canopy—Use canopy crank on the right side.

Lower Wing Flaps to Retard Speed.

Make a Carrier Type Landing at as Low an Altitude as Possible.

RESTRICTED 107

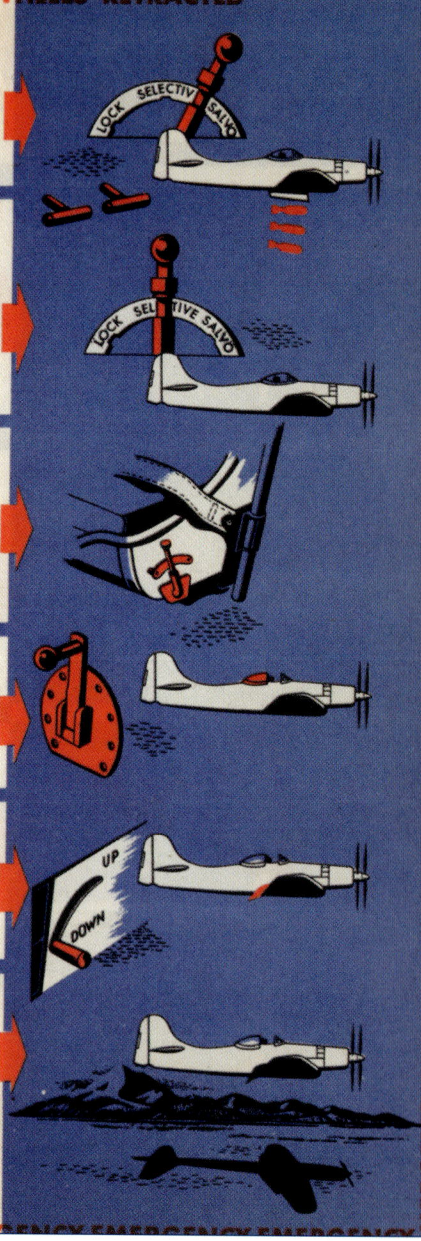

Manual Scan: National Archives, RG 287

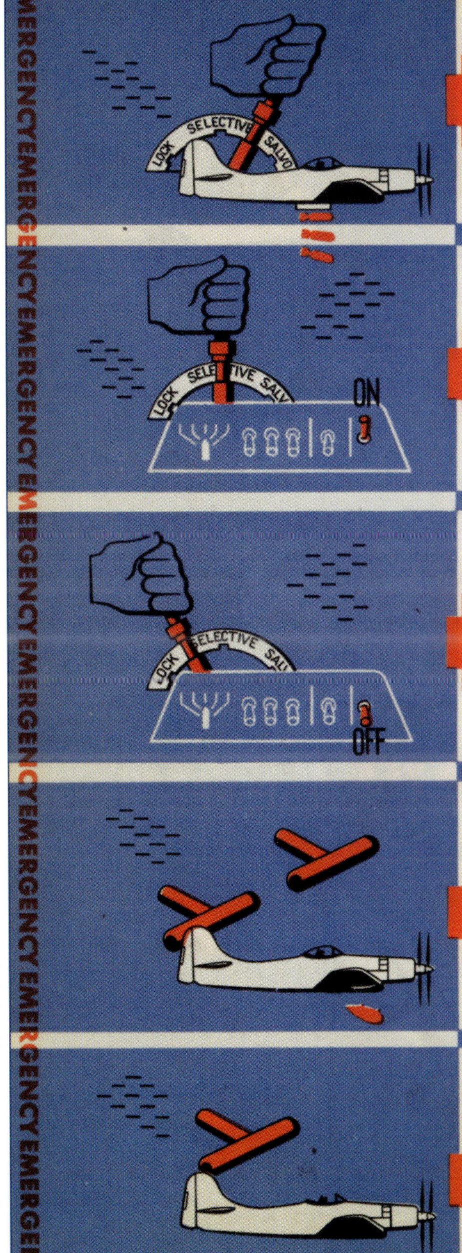

JETTISONING

Internal Bombs or Fuel Tank
Move bomb release handle to "SALVO."

When bomb bay is empty, return handle to "SELECTIVE" and turn armament master switch "ON" to close doors.

Allow 10 seconds for the bomb doors to close, return handle to "LOCK," and turn armament master switch to "OFF."

External Bombs or Fuel Tank
Pull red T-handles on the left sidewall.

Canopy
Pull red T-handle at the top of the windshield.

DESTRUCTION

IFF Radio Destruction—If forced to land in enemy territory, raise the red "DESTRUCTOR" guard on the right console and turn the switch "ON" to destroy the radio.

If the explosion is not heard or felt, the destructor may be faulty. When on the ground, open the radio compartment hatch and destroy the radio. Tear out wiring, destroy circuit diagrams, nameplates and coding discs.

If the radio hatch is jammed, locate a point six inches to the rear of the hatch and 24 inches up from the bottom of the airplane on the left side. Shoot through the skin at this point.

Burn all documents relating to the radio or its operation.

Homing Receiver Destruction—To destroy, enter radio compartment hatch and smash receiver. The receiver is just forward of the hatch about 20 inches above the bottom of the fuselage. Destroy all nameplates and circuit diagrams and tear out as much wiring as possible.

If you can't get in the radio compartment, but can enter the bomb bay, shoot straight aft along the centerline of the airplane about 20 inches above the bottom.

If you can't get in either compartment locate a point six inches aft of the bomb bay and 20 inches above the bottom and shoot straight through the fuselage.

Burn all documents relating to the receiver or its operation.

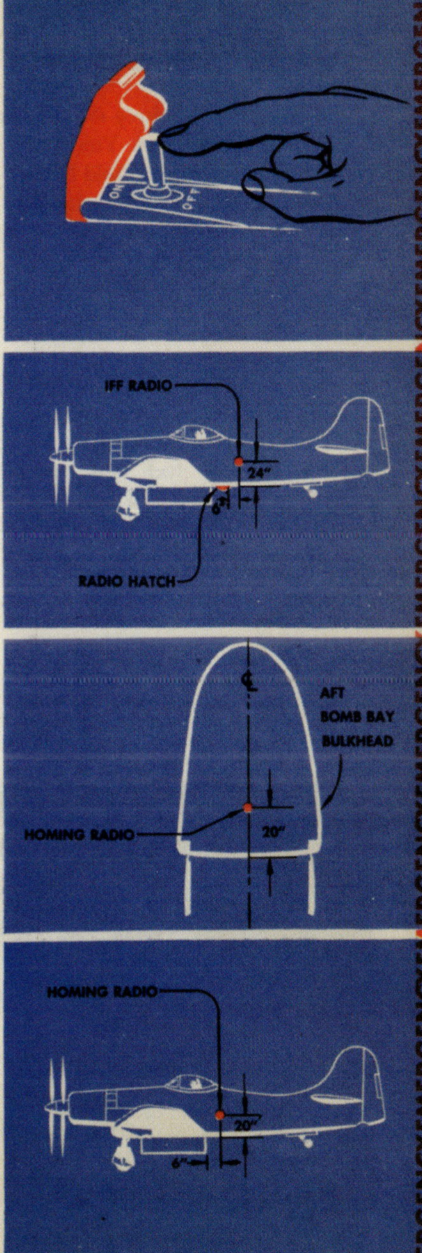

AIRPLANE DESTRUCTION

The best way to destroy the airplane is by burning gasoline. You can release fuel from the main tanks by opening the defueling valve in the intercooler air exit door just forward of the bomb bay doors.

If you can part the fuel lines in the nacelle, set the fuel tank selector handle to a full tank and turn the battery switch "ON." Fuel will spray into the nacelle.

EMERGENCY EXIT

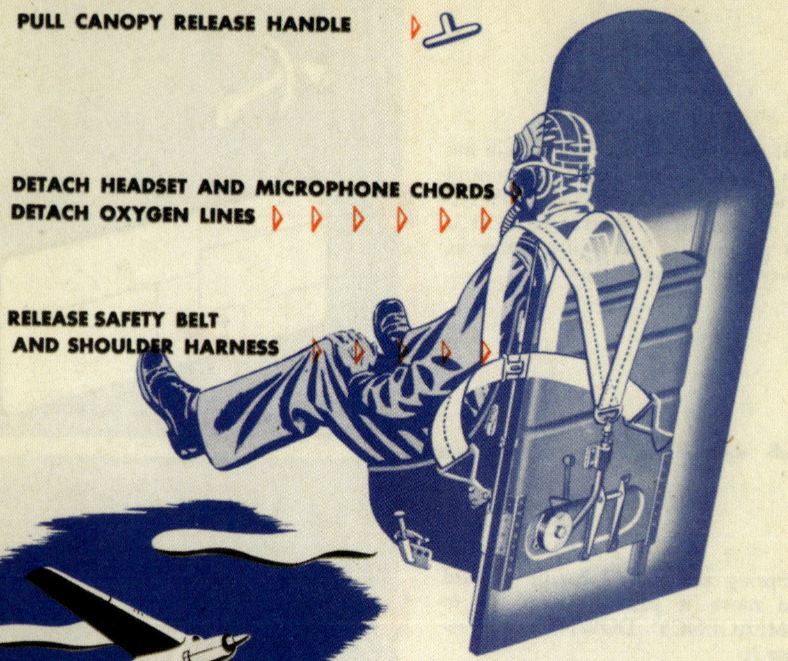

1. Detach oxygen lines, headset and microphone chords.

2. See that parachute, backpad and life raft are properly attached. Check life jacket.

3. Release safety belt and shoulder straps and keep them free from catching on your clothing.

4. Pull emergency canopy release handle.

5. If possible, roll the airplane up side down and fall out.

6. If you bail out in level flight, lower the landing gear and the wing flaps to slow down the airplane. Trim the airplane for stability if necessary. Go over the left side head first to clear the range antenna and slide off the wing. The high elevator stabilizers aid in clearing the tail.

Manual Scan: National Archives, RG 287

EMERGENCY EMERGENCY EMERGENCY EMERGENCY EMERGENCY EMERGENCY

ARRESTING HOOK FAILURE

If the arresting hook motor will not run the hook down when the control handle is set to "NORMAL DOWN," see if the circuit breaker is in. If it has popped out and will not stay in, lower the hook as follows:

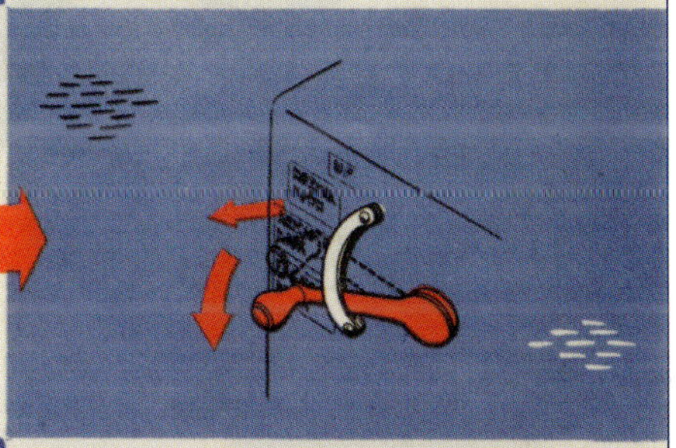

Spring the control handle inboard and move it past the stop lug to "EMERGENCY DOWN," then release it.

If the hook still will not come down, it may be possible to lower it by holding the circuit breaker in even though it is trying to pop out. However, if the hook does not come down within 10 to 15 seconds, release the circuit breaker to prevent discharging the battery.

The hook may be raised the same way if the circuit breaker pops out when the handle is returned to up.

EMERGENCY EMERGENCY EMERGENCY EMERGENCY EMERGENCY EMERGENCY

Manual Scan: National Archives, RG 287

POWER PLANT CHART

AIRCRAFT MODEL
BOEING XF8B-1

PROPELLER
AEROPRODUCTS
6 BLADED, DUAL ROTATION

ENGINE MODEL
PRATT & WHITNEY
R-4360-10

GAGE READING	FUEL PRESS.	OIL PRESS.	OIL TEMP.	CARB. AIR TEMP.	OIL CONS. (1)
DESIRED	17	80-90	70° C	30° C	40
MAXIMUM	18	90	85° C	38° C	QT./HR.
MINIMUM	16	50	40° C		
IDLING	8	25			

MAX. PERMISSABLE DIVING RPM: 3060 (30 SECONDS)
MIN. RECOMMENDED CRUISE RPM: 1400
OIL GRADE: (S) 1120 (W) 1120
FUEL GRADE: 100/130 SPEC. AN-F-28

WAR EMERGENCY (COMBAT EMERGENCY)			MILITARY POWER (NON-COMBAT EMERG.)			OPERATING CONDITION			MAX. CONTINUOUS (NORMAL RATED)			MAX. CRUISE (NORMAL OPERATION)		
			5 MINUTES 232° C			TIME LIMIT MAX. CYL. HEAD TEMP.			UNLIMITED 232° C			UNLIMITED 204° C		
			AUTO RICH 2700			MIXTURE RPM			AUTO RICH 2550			AUTO LEAN 2150		
MANIF. PRESS.	SUPER CHARGER	FUEL GAL./MIN. (2)	MANIF. PRESS.	SUPER CHARGER	FUEL GAL./MIN. (2)	STD. TEMP. °C.	PRESSURE ALTITUDE	STD. TEMP. °F.	MANIF. PRESS.	SUPER CHARGER	FUEL G.P.H. (3)	MANIF. PRESS.	SUPER CHARGER	FUEL G.P.H. (3)
						-55.0	40,000 Ft.	-67.0						
						-55.0	38,000 Ft.	-67.0						
						-55.0	36,000 Ft.	-67.0						
	TO BE FURNISHED BY NAVY DEPARTMENT BUREAU OF AERONAUTICS					-52.4	34,000 Ft.	-62.3						
						-48.4	32,000 Ft.	-55.1						
						-44.4	30,000 Ft.	-48.0						
			46.0	ON*	6	-40.5	28,000 Ft.	-40.9	39	ON*	282	28	ON*	—
			50.0	ON*	6	-36.5	26,000 Ft.	-33.7	44	ON*	282	31	ON*	—
			53.0	ON*	6	-32.5	24,000 Ft.	-26.5	47	ON*	282	33	ON*	124
			53.5	ON*	6	-28.6	22,000 Ft.	-19.4	47	ON*	282	35	ON*	124
			53.5	ON*	6	-24.6	20,000 Ft.	-12.3	47	ON*	282	35	ON*	124
			53.5	ON*	6	-20.7	18,000 Ft.	-5.2	47	ON*	282	35	ON*	124
			53.5	ON*	6	16.7	16,000 Ft.	2.0	47	ON*	282	35	ON*	124
			53.5	ON*	6	-12.7	14,000 Ft.	9.1	47	ON*	282	35	ON*	124
			53.5	ON*	6	-8.8	12,000 Ft.	16.2	47	ON*	282	35	ON*	124
			53.5	ON*	6	-4.8	10,000 Ft.	23.4	47	ON*	282	35	ON*	124
			53.5	ON*	6	-0.8	8,000 Ft.	30.5	47	ON*	282	33	OFF	124
			53.5	ON*	6	3.1	6,000 Ft.	37.6	41	OFF	282	33	OFF	124
			48.0	OFF	6	7.1	4,000 Ft.	44.7	41	OFF	282	33	OFF	124
			48.0	OFF	6	11.0	2,000 Ft.	51.8	41	OFF	282	33	OFF	124
			48.0	OFF	6	15.0	SEA LEVEL	59.0	41	OFF	282	33	OFF	124

NOTES

(1) OIL CONSUMPTION: MAX. U.S. QUART PER HR. PER ENGINE.
(2) GAL./MIN. APPROX. U.S. GAL. PER **MINUTE** PER ENGINE.
(3) GHP: APPROX. U.S. GALLON PER HOUR PER ENGINE.
VALUES ARE FOR LEVEL FLIGHT WITHOUT RAM.

TO DETERMINE CONSUMPTION IN BRITISH IMPERIAL UNITS MULTIPLY BY 10, THEN DIVIDE BY 12.
RED FIGURES ARE PRELIMINARY SUBJECT TO REVISION AFTER FLIGHT CHECK.

Fuel Flows in Red are Estimated Maximum

*After Throttle is Full Open, use Supercharger to obtain desired Man. Press.

TAKEOFF CONDITIONS
NORMAL: 2700 RPM, 52 MP, AUTO RICH, CYL. 232° C MAX.
EMERGENCY: 2700 RPM, 52 MP, AUTO RICH, OIL BELOW 100 PSI, 10°-18° C RISE

CONDITIONS TO AVOID
INVERTED FLIGHT
OUTSIDE LOOPS

DATA AS OF 11-20-44, BASED ON PRATT AND WHITNEY CURVES, NO. 1731 -5, -6, AND -16.

Manual Scan: National Archives, RG 287

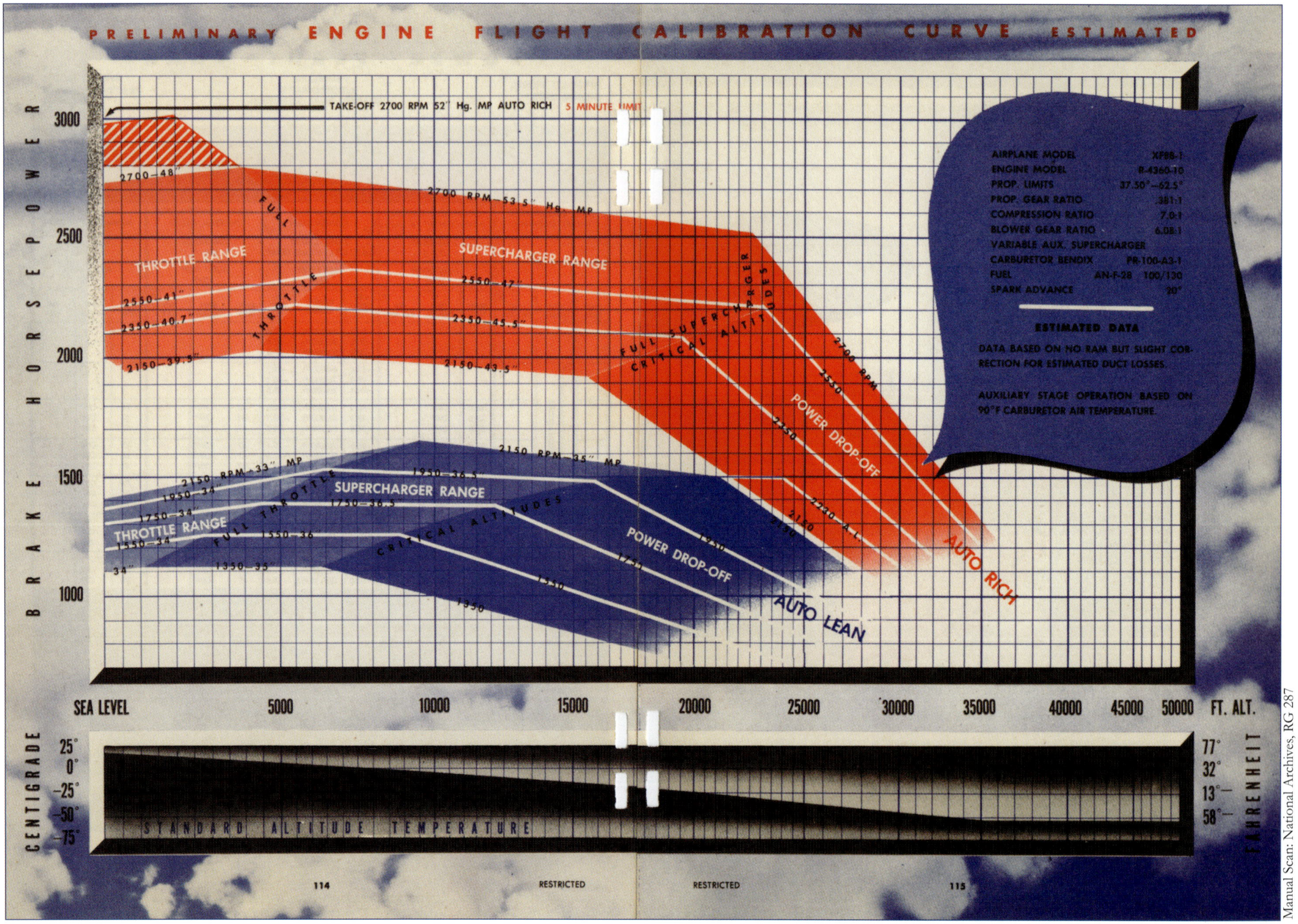

Manual Scan: National Archives, RG 287

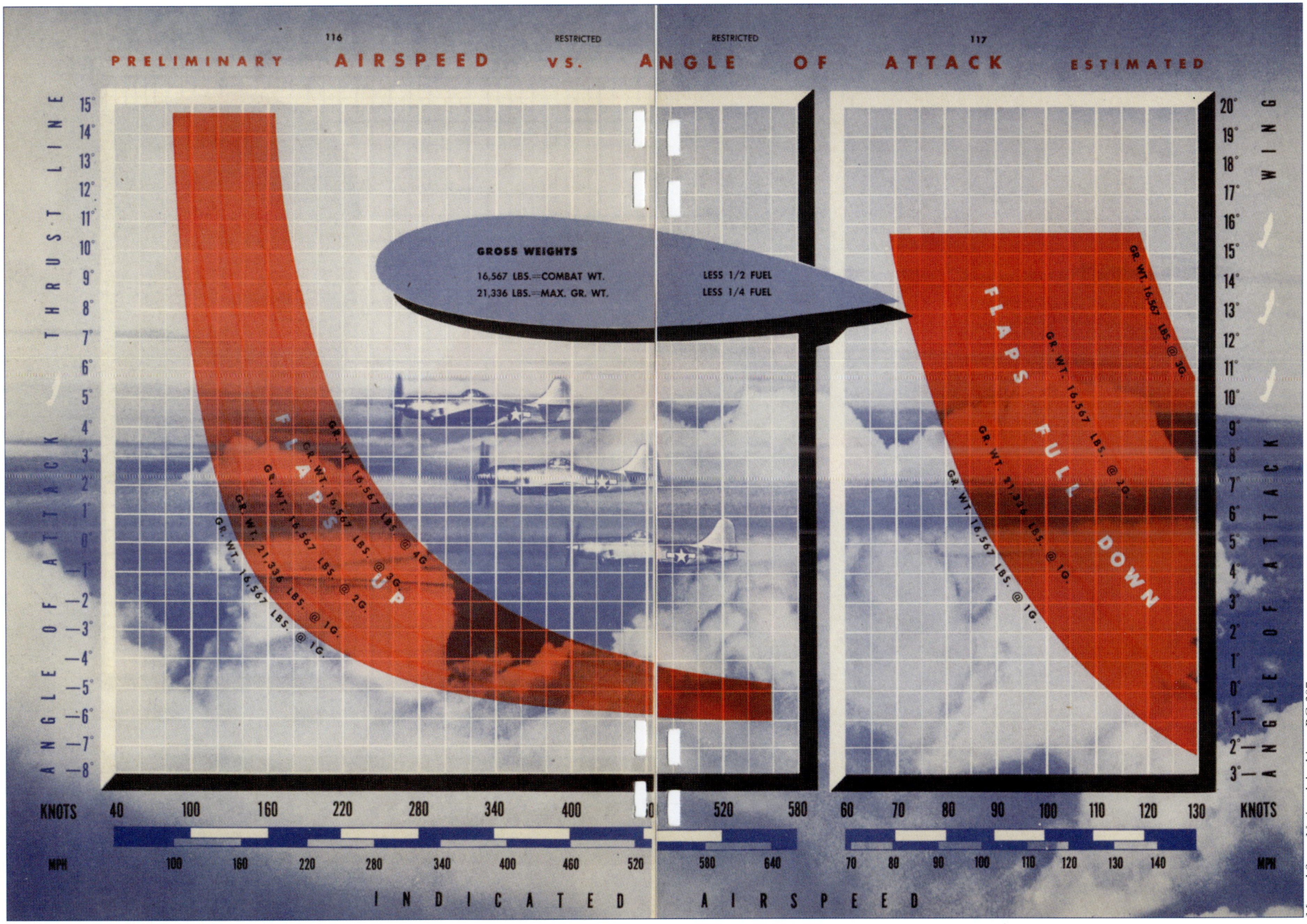

Manual Scan: National Archives, RG 287

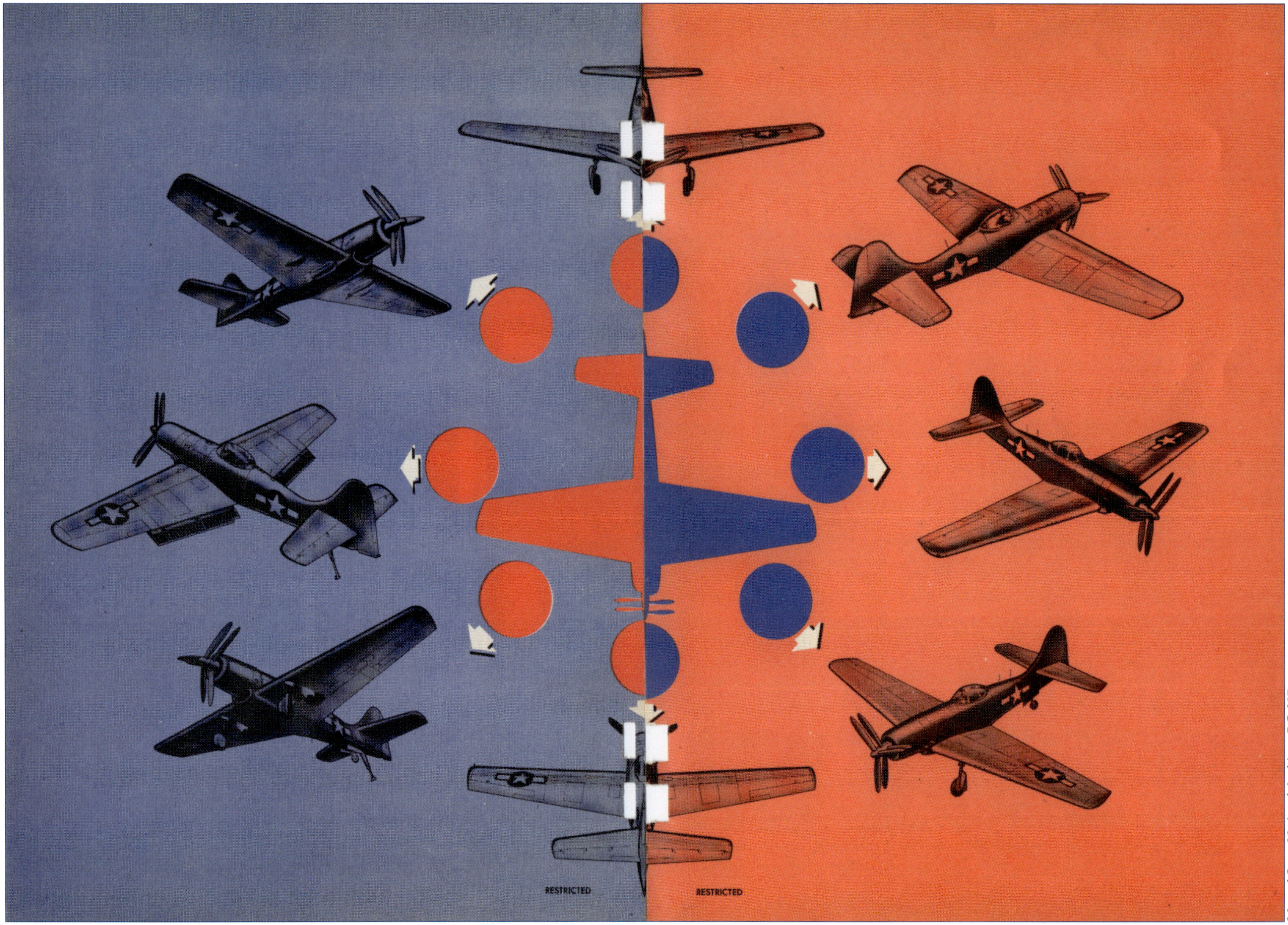

Manual Scan: National Archives, RG 287

Appendix 10

Color Gallery

The first XF8B-1 prototype was initially flown in an overall natural metal finish. Markings were the typical stars and bars in use towards the latter half of WW II, with extensive black stenciling applied over all of the XF8B-1's main surfaces. Wheel wells and other internal surfaces that were routinely exposed to the elements were finished in zinc chromate green. The cockpit interior was finished primarily in the standard interior green used by the Navy at that time; instrument boards were finished in Instrument Panel Brown lacquer. Other colors were used for various details in the cockpit, but research has not yielded the detailed description found for the other prototypes.

The second and third prototypes were painted overall in Semi-Gloss Sea Blue with national insignia and stenciling in white. In early 1946, the first XF8B-1 was extensively modified and brought up to the standards of its stable mates, receiving an identical scheme. A prominent white "Boeing" logo was carried on the cowling of these aircraft while under flight test at the company; this was removed or painted over upon transfer to the Navy. The wheel wells, welded steel tubular engine mounts, bomb bay, and other internal surfaces that were routinely exposed to the elements were finished in zinc chromate primer.

The cockpit for these planes was finished in several colors. The left-hand and right-hand control panels and the control column were finished with one coat of Cockpit Blue lacquer on the exposed surfaces only. The pilot's seat, lower surfaces of the cowling forward, and floor were finished with one coat of Cockpit Gray lacquer on the exposed surfaces only. The reflector and exposed surfaces of the instrument boards were finished with one coat of Instrument Panel Brown lacquer. The exposed surfaces of the rudder pedals were finished with one coat of sand color lacquer. The knobs were finished in a coat of lacquer conforming to Tenite II Color No. 15935, which consisted of "Preservative" White Lacquer No. 1533, Shorn's Carmine Red Lacquer, Mattson Automotive Lacquer – Black, and "Preservative" Raw Sienna Lacquer No. 1521; the color used depended on the function of the knob. The interior exposed metal surfaces of the canopy stripping, upper surfaces of the cowling forward, and armament indicator panels were finished with one coat of Non-Specular Sea Blue enamel or lacquer. The pilot's seat armor was finished with one coat of Semi-Gloss Sea Blue lacquer.

When the second and third prototypes were taken over by the Navy for testing, they received additional markings in white as well as red stripes on the insignia. The color profiles on the following pages and back cover show all of the known color schemes for the aircraft at various points in their brief careers. These are for general reference only; modelers and artists who would like more precise information on US Navy aircraft colors from this period should consult the *Official Monogram U.S. Navy and Marine Corps Aircraft Color Guide, Volume 2: 1940 to 1949* or the equivalent reference.

Photo: National Archives, RG 72-AC

A rare vintage color photo of the XF8B-1 interchangeable power unit scale model, which still survives at the Boeing Historical Archives in Seattle, Washington.

Front view and profile of Boeing XF8B-1 no. 57984, as it appeared during early flight tests.

Top view of XF8B-1 no. 57984 as it appeared during early flight tests.

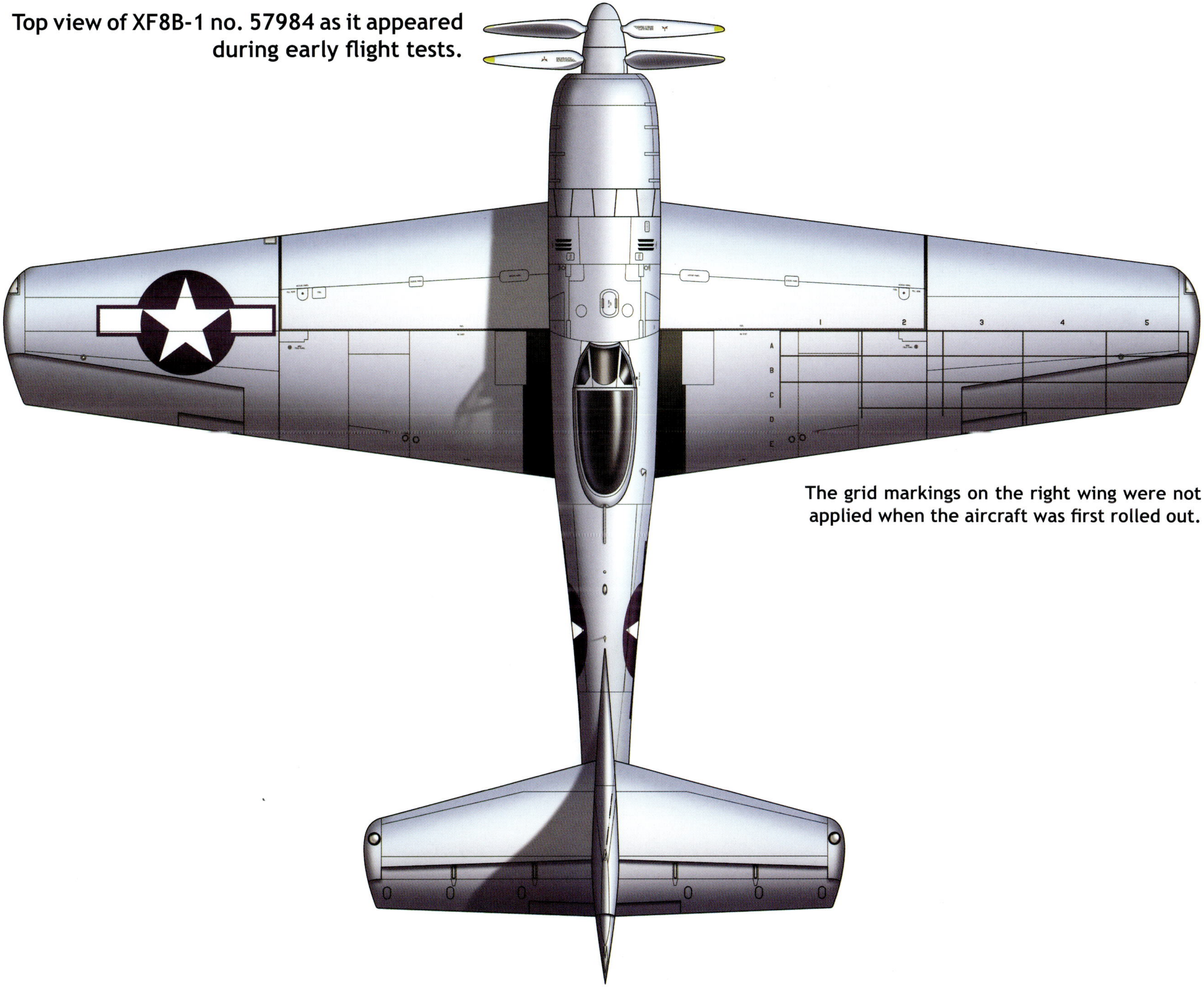

The grid markings on the right wing were not applied when the aircraft was first rolled out.

Profile of XF8B-1 no. 57984 midway through its career. Note the olive green anti-glare paint on the nose, Insignia Blue stripe along the right side of the fuselage, and the revised exhaust stacks.

Close-up of Pratt & Whitney logo applied to cowling.

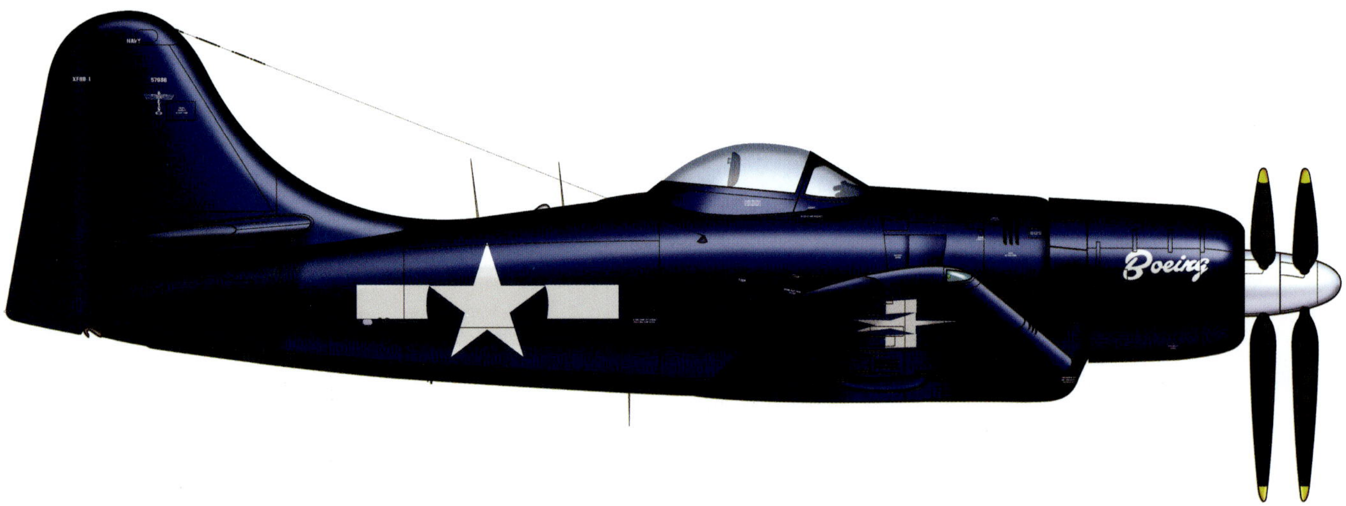

No. 57984, late in its career, painted in an overall Semi-Gloss Sea Blue with a natural metal spinner. The aircraft received numerous modifications to bring it up to the standard of the second and third prototypes, the most obvious being a new, more aerodynamic canopy.

Front view and profile of XF8B-1 no. 57985 under test at NATC in 1946. The overall color was Semi-Gloss Sea Blue.

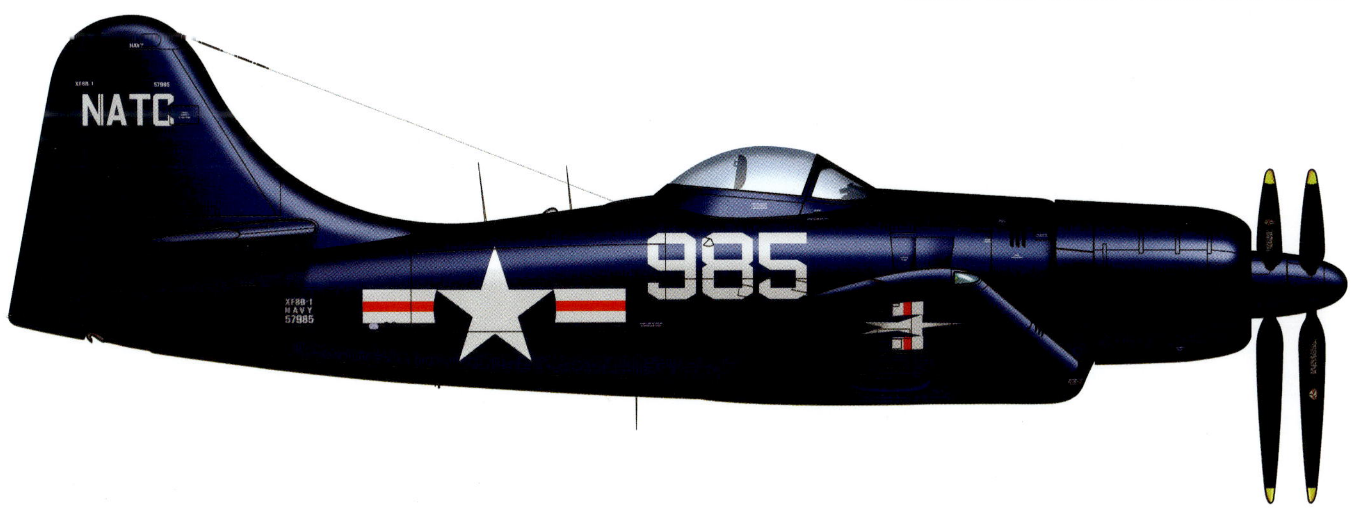

Top view of XF8B-1, BuAer No. 57985, under test at NATC in 1946.

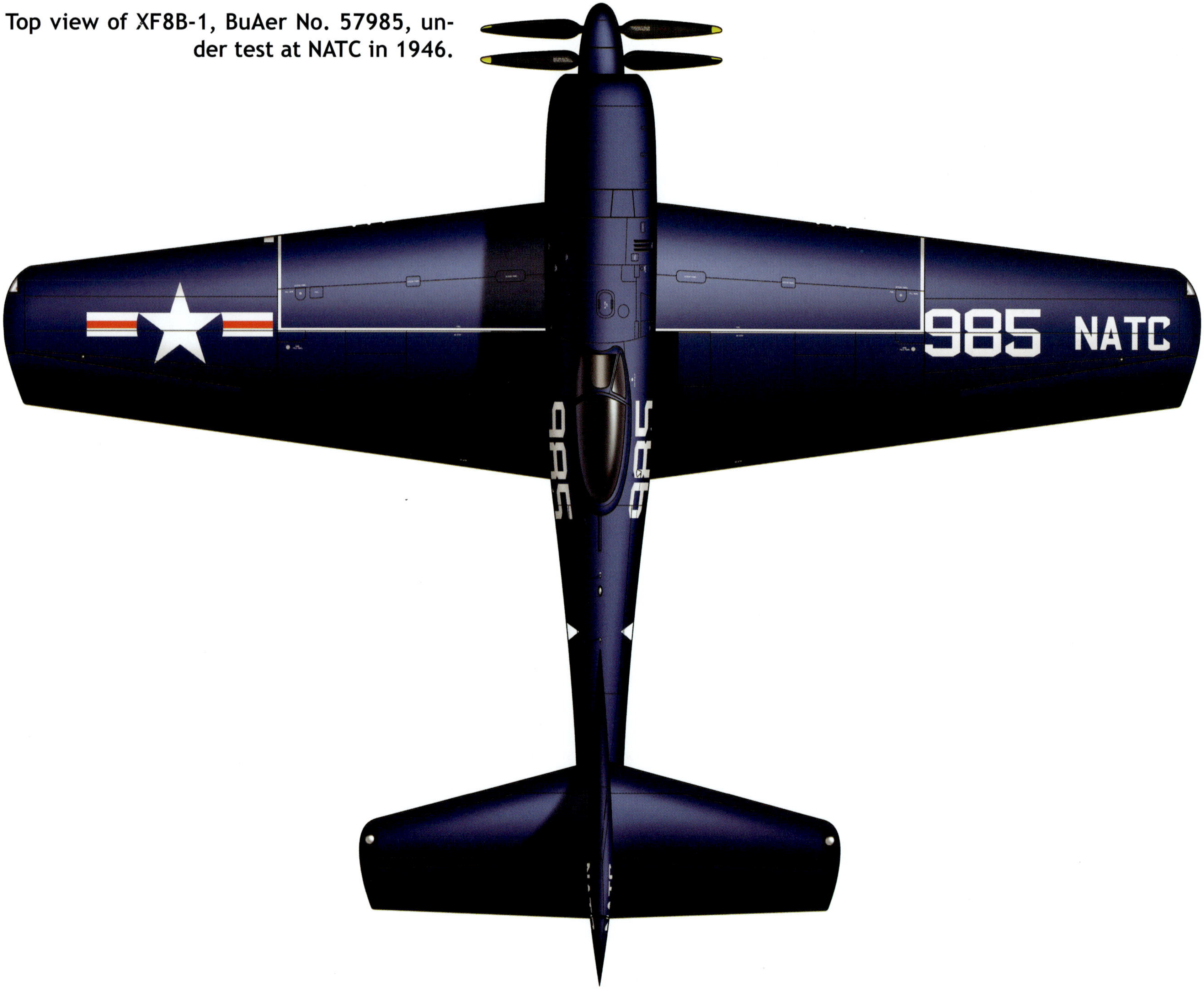

An early general arrangement drawing of the XF8B-1 featured drop tanks mounted higher than those later fitted to the actual aircraft. This drawing, which is reproduced in Appendix 2, appears to show the top surface of the tank intersecting with the bottom wing, resulting in a conformal type tank. Also conspicuous in the drawing is the spinner, which was of small diameter than the one fitted to the actual aircraft. This artist's impression shows how the resulting aircraft could have looked had the design been frozen at this earlier stage.

Artist's impressions of the first XF8B-1 carrying a Mk. 13 Mod. 9 torpedo mounted on a centerline rack. Proposed in 1944, the illustrations are based on a Boeing blueprint found in official BuAer files. It appears to be an early study and probably does not represent the final configuration. The feasibility of adapting the XF8B-1 to the VTB role was the subject of extensive study in BuAer from June 1944 through 1945; the relative superiority of existing VTB types, such as the Martin Mauler, ultimately killed development of this XF8B-1 variant.

These illustrations depict the first XF8B-1 prototype equipped with eight 4" rockets mounted on Mk. 9, Mod. 1 launchers on the outer wing panels. BuAer initially requested the study on June 15, 1944. Boeing did not respond until May 12, 1945, but by then the contract was in jeopardy, with BuAer cancelling the rocket installation study entirely on July 18.

Artist's impressions of XF8B-1 no. 57985 equipped with two Mk. 13 Mod. 9 torpedoes on its inboard hardpoints. The possibility of carrying two torpedoes externally was first mentioned on June 1, 1944 in BuAer contract correspondence; scattered references to this configuration were made several times thereafter until 1945, when it was realized that no production contract for the XF8B-1 was forthcoming. Unfortunately, no general arrangement drawing of this variant could be found, so the exact mounting details of the torpedoes remain speculative.

It was also proposed to fit the XF8B-1 with two 300 gallon wingtip drop tanks along with the standard 150 gallon drop tanks mounted on the inboard hardpoints, creating an ultra long range variant. These renderings are based on a front view drawing found in a piece of Boeing promotional literature; no side view drawing of the wingtip tank installation has been located. I assumed Boeing would have utilized the type of 300 gallon tanks used on the P-82 Twin Mustang and other aircraft of the period, though it is conceivable the company could have designed and fitted its own. While the endurance of this variant would have undoubtedly been impressive, such long missions would have been grueling and pushed pilots to their physical limits.

To supplement the XF8B-1's internal bomb capacity, Boeing proposed carrying additional ordnance externally. In this notional illustration, the second prototype is shown carrying two 500 lb. practice bombs. These renderings are based on the same drawing that served as the basis for the long range variant above. Exact mounting details of the bombs are speculative.

Two 1,000 lb. bombs mounted on the inboard hardpoints were also considered. Such a heavy bombload would have undoubtedly hurt the aircraft's overall performance.

The final known type of ordnance considered for external carriage was the 1,600 lb. armor piercing bomb. In this configuration, the XF8B-1 was more of a low altitude attacker than the high altitude fighter it was initially conceived to be. With modifications, Boeing's big fighter could have admirably filled the role, but this variant never left the drawing board.

As early as September 1944, the Navy displayed interest in developing a two seat version of the XF8B-1 for low altitude "scant" attack, nightfighting, and torpedo bombing. Correspondence concerning a two seater persisted into 1945. The artist's impressions shown here are based on a plan in Appendix 2 which probably represents an early configuration study; note the high drag canopy, which appears to be based on that of the first prototype. Several combinations of ordnance, drop tanks, and radar were to have been carried externally. The configuration shown here could represent a long range torpedo bomber, for instance. It features one AN/APS-4 transmitter-receiver on the outer most right pylon; four 150 gallon drop tanks; and one MK. 13 torpedo mounted on the centerline.

Another configuration conceived of for the two seat XF8B-1 comprised one AN/APS-4 transmitter-receiver; two 11.75" diameter "Tiny Tim" rockets; two 150 gallon drop tanks; and one massive 300 gallon centerline drop tank. These artist's impressions underscore the fact that the XF8B-1 had the potential to be a formidable "truck" with tremendous load-carrying capabilities. Unfortunately, it never had the chance to demonstrate these in service.

Bibliography

Archival Holdings

Boeing Historical Archives, Seattle, Washington

National Archives and Records Administration, College Park, Maryland; Record Groups consulted: RG 72, 287, 342, 428

Books

Elliott, John M., Maj. USMC (Ret.), *Official Monogram U.S. Navy and Marine Corps Aircraft Color Guide, Volume 2: 1940 to 1949*, Monogram Aviation Publications, 1998

Reynolds, Clark G., *Admiral John H. Towers : The Struggle for Naval Air Supremacy*, Naval Institute Press, 1991

Magazines

Koehnen, Richard, "Boeings Five in One Fighter," Airpower, July 1975